A HISTORY OF THE GREAT WAR

A HISTORY OF THE GREAT WAR

World War One and the International Crisis of the Early Twentieth Century

Eric Dorn Brose
Drexel University

New York Oxford
OXFORD UNIVERSITY PRESS
2010

Oxford University Press, Inc., publishes works that further Oxford University's objective of excellence in research, scholarship, and education.

Oxford New York
Auckland Cape Town Dar es Salaam Hong Kong Karachi
Kuala Lumpur Madrid Melbourne Mexico City Nairobi
New Delhi Shanghai Taipei Toronto

With offices in
Argentina Austria Brazil Chile Czech Republic France Greece
Guatemala Hungary Italy Japan Poland Portugal Singapore
South Korea Switzerland Thailand Turkey Ukraine Vietnam

Published by Oxford University Press, Inc.
198 Madison Avenue, New York, New York 10016

http://www.oup.com

Library of Congress Cataloging-in-Publication Data

Brose, Eric Dorn, 1948–
A history of the Great War : World War One and the international crisis of the early twentieth century / Eric Dorn Brose.
p. cm.
Includes bibliographical references and index.
ISBN 978-0-19-518194-4—ISBN 978-0-19-518193-7
1. World War, 1914–1918. 2. World War, 1914–1918—Causes.
3. World War, 1914–1918—Campaigns. 4. World politics—19th century.
5. World politics—1900–1918. 6. World politics—1919–1932.
7. International relations—History—20th century. I. Title.
D521.B73 2010
940.3—dc22 2008046829

CONTENTS

PART THREE
SLOWLY OUT OF THE ABYSS • 1918–1926

MAPS

PREFACE

THE CHRONOLOGICAL SCOPE

In the autumn of 1911, war broke out between Italy and the Ottoman Empire of Turkey. In earlier years modern wars had been fought involving many of the industrializing nations—Japan and China (1894–1895), the United States and Spain (1898), Britain and the Boer Republics (1899–1902), and Japan and Russia (1904–1905)—but there had been no fighting on European soil since Turkey's punitive expedition against Greece in 1897, and no major combat since the Russo-Turkish War of 1877. More importantly, there had been none between any of Europe's Great Powers—Britain, France, Germany, Austria-Hungary, and Russia—in the forty years since 1871, although tensions had been ratcheting up for several decades.

The Italo-Turkish War, in turn, sparked the First Balkan War in 1912, unleashing more intense combat and civilian atrocities on European soil. This was followed in 1913 by the Second Balkan War. In the summer of 1914 Balkan troubles finally sparked what came to be known as the "Great War" or "World War," later called World War One, which eventually dragged most of Europe and the world into its bloody quagmire, inflicting over four years of suffering, misery, maiming, and death on the belligerent nations. More than 37 million soldiers were killed, wounded, or never found again. Nor did Armistice Day, November 11, 1918, end the killing, for war continued in what had been the Austro-Hungarian Empire until 1919, in what had been the Russian Empire until 1920, in the Middle East until 1922, and North Africa until 1926. The war-ending treaty process took nearly as long to complete.

A History of the Great War has a global scope in many different respects, the first being to widen the chronological focus of most World War One studies to include (1) an analysis of the international and technological forces that generated international tension and made wars more prevalent already before 1914, (2) the causes and course of the inextricably related Great War to 1918, and (3) the violent and problematic aftermath of the struggle to 1926. Most of the early twentieth century, in other words, was a protracted international crisis. This study's three parts analyze the international phenomenon of the Great War in its chronological entirety.

THE GEOGRAPHICAL SCOPE

For much of the time since 1918 histories of the Great War remained extremely Eurocentric, covering mainly the critical western front in France and Flanders; paying less attention to the eastern front in Poland, Galicia, and the Balkans; and treating the war in the Middle East, Africa, Asia, and at sea as a sideshow. One could find many specialized studies of the extra-European theaters, of course, but almost never a one-volume history of the Great War in its global complexity and significance. This began to change in recent years, most notably with Hew Strachan's companion volume to the BBC's documentary *The First World War*, but there remains room for improvement, especially in this crucial area.[1]

Indeed, emphasis on the global combat of the Great War goes beyond mere coverage preference. Huge tracts of territory were fought over and changed hands, and many hundreds of thousands died as a result. Furthermore, the outcome of the war in Europe hinged not only on the highly significant campaigns there—campaigns that receive extensive coverage in the present study—but also to a great degree on the worldwide struggle, especially in the strategically important arc spanning Northeast Africa, Palestine, Mesopotamia, Central Asia, and India. Turkey and Germany unleashed a holy war against Britain and Russia here in the main hope of enervating Britannia's imperial power and tipping the balance in Europe. The failure of this effort was just one measure of the vastness of that imperial power. Similarly, the war at sea enabled Britain and France to draw on the human and material resources of the world while blockading Germany and cutting it off from vital imports. The contribution to victory of the maritime and imperial power of Britain, and the importance of this "imperial surplus" of resources, is one of the main themes of this volume. After its Jihad failed, in fact, Germany risked a submarine campaign to drain this imperial surplus, but the gamble backfired when the United States declared war and lent its considerable power to Germany's enemies.

THE SCOPE OF SOURCES

Certainly any new history of the Great War must incorporate both the classic works as well as the latest research—it must be comprehensive and current in scope. With regard to the latter, this study benefits from the veritable spate of new books that have appeared on the Great War in the last ten to twenty years. One that I have moved front and center is the historical theorizing by Williamson Murray and MacGregor Knox on the concept of "revolutions in military affairs" (RMA). Much like the situation military establishments find themselves in today, when facing rapid changes, especially rapid *technological* changes, generals and admirals must make timely and effective strategic, operational, and tactical adjustments—RMA—or lose wars.[2]

But so much more has been published. Monographs on German Chief of the General Staff Alfred von Schlieffen and the "Schlieffen Plan"; on his successors Helmuth von Moltke and Erich von Falkenhayn; on British Secretary for War

Horatio Herbert Kitchener; on technological decision making in the German army; on the strategic and operational thinking of the French army; on the crucial battles of Tannenberg, Gallipoli, Verdun, the Somme, and Passchendaele; on the war at sea, including new research on the *Lusitania* sinking; on politico-religious personalities like Gregory Rasputin; on home front politics; on both the civilians' war and the soldiers' war; and on the dynamic relationship between men and women have taken their places alongside magnum opus studies by Great War doyens John Keegan, Holger Herwig, Hew Strachan, and David Stevenson.[3] Historians have finally sorted out the myriad causes of the Great War furthermore, reaching a reasonable consensus after debating this issue for nearly a century. Similarly, the dust has also settled since the fall of the Soviet Union, enabling historians to shake off the influence of Communist historiography and reassess the fall of the Romanovs, the rise of the Bolsheviks, and the Russian Civil War. It is high time for a work that synthesizes all of this in reasonable length for use in college classrooms.

Rather than citing this literature in typical "suggested reading" sections, I adopt the traditional approach of the notes. This is a superior aid for students pursuing research projects as well as historians scrutinizing my research, for each passage of a chapter is thereby anchored in the sources. Anyone interested in the desperate and complex thinking behind Germany's decision to wage unlimited submarine warfare, for example, or the near collapse of Russia during the Great Retreat of 1915, or the remarkable career of Lawrence of Arabia, can consult the notes on that section.

THE SCOPE OF INTERPRETATION

The Scholarly Division of Oxford University Press targets upper-class undergraduates, graduate students, and professors. Its authors have free reign to break the mold of the "facts only, please" textbooks designed largely for freshmen. Accordingly, this study has interpretive scope. In offering greater than usual coverage of the worldwide side of the Great War, for example, I am arguing that the wider war played an important part in the war's outcome. It is also my choice to depart from usual practice and devote a third group of chapters to postwar violence. Because the dynamic forces that triggered the war and made it last so long were also at work for years after 1918, it seems appropriate to treat the entire period as an integral whole—and to do this globally, for the war had a major postwar impact not only on Europe but also on Russia, the Middle East, and other parts of the world. In later chapters I hint that the postwar world, stretching well into the twentieth century, while certainly not idyllic, would probably have been less troubled and chaotic had belligerents parlayed the real possibilities for peace in 1917 into reality. Even a brief cautious consideration of such a hypothetical alternative—the details of which I leave to the reader's imagination—measures the significance of what actually happened, namely, the failure of German parliamentarians to wrest control of the war effort from High Command and initiate peace talks on the basis of the *status quo ante*.

The argument that the Great War and the treaties that ended it "shaped" the rest of the twentieth century, however, needs to be carefully qualified.[4] Clearly the war set extremely problematic forces in motion. One, the rabid militarism of Adolf Hitler's Nazis and Benito Mussolini's Fascists, reveled in the camaraderie of arms, worshipped violence of all sorts, and regarded the First World War as a rehearsal for the Second. Equally troublesome, the Communist regime of the Soviet Union saw class warfare and struggle against the capitalist nations of the world as inevitable. But the war also mobilized pacifist forces embodied in the veterans who felt fortunate to have survived; the soldiers, parents, siblings, and relatives who deeply mourned the loss of those millions who did not return; and the politicians and advocates of peace who were sickened by the prospect of more violence. By the time Europe and the world had resolved most of the issues of the Great War around 1926, pacifist forces were ascendant, but with the Great Depression, an economic catastrophe induced in so many ways by the disruption of the Great War itself, this relationship inverted, creating a favorable climate for war, not peace. The pacifist worldview asserted itself in the decades after the second great world conflagration, however, eventually emerging in the democratic and pacified European Union of today.[5] In these ways the Great War did indeed shape the twentieth century.

THE SCOPE OF INDEBTEDNESS

It is an honor to be publishing my third book with Oxford University Press. As before, I have benefited from the inspiration and support of a top-notch, first-rate team. Shortly after 9/11 the editor of the Scholarly Division at that time, Peter Coveney, encouraged me to write a history of World War One that put the "world" back into it, which, considering the impact of the Great War on the Middle East, was a great idea. Halfway through the writing Peter yielded to Brian Wheel, a sensitive, talented, proactive editor whose comments on the first draft proved just as useful as each of the six outside readers, including Stephanie Cousineau of the University of Calgary, Graydon Tunstall of the University of South Florida, and Kris Alexanderson of Rutgers University. Without their insightful critiques, of course, most of which I agreed with, *A History of the Great War* would be far inferior to the final product. As I have said before, however, books are not written by committee, which leaves full responsibility for remaining weaknesses at my doorstep alone. Finally, I am indebted to Brian's able and tactful assistant, Laura Lancaster, who saved me weeks of labor by expediting the whole publication process, and to production editor, Miriam Sicilia, who likewise kept the wheels turning with no squeaks.

Many thanks also go to the History Department at West Point and its expert cartographer, Frank Martini. Although their primary mission is educating the Corps of Cadets, the officers and professors of the United States Military Academy are also highly committed to educating the public. With this latter goal in mind, they allowed us to use their excellent collection of Great War maps as templates for Oxford's cartographer, Bill Nelson, who reduced the number of site names and other terrain details to those actually mentioned in the text while retaining all military details. Sixteen of these are in a color insert, while thirteen black and white maps appear in the text. The reader will benefit tremendously from their accuracy and attention to operational detail. Moreover, Oxford allowed me to use an additional three maps from my *History of Europe in the Twentieth Century* (2005). The Audio-Visual Department of Drexel University, and especially its graphics tsar, Peter Groesbeck, deserve special thanks, too. Peter created six maps and scanned and enhanced half of the book's photographs that were taken from two remarkable illustrated histories of the Great War that appeared in its immediate aftermath.[6]

Many others at Drexel and closer to home helped me over the last four years. I have taught my Great War course once or twice a year while writing the book, which resulted in many useful discussions and questions from scores of good students. My department head, Donald Stevens, not only permitted me to teach the course more often than he required, but also provided a flexible teaching schedule conducive to writing. Similar support came from Donna Murasko, dean of the College of Arts and Sciences. My friends Peter Napoli, Jack Brumbaugh, Larry Sawatski, and George McCarron, and my father, Robert Brose, all ex-servicemen, asked excellent questions and gave me insights to the realities of war that helped tremendously. George also allowed me to use some rare photographs in the possession of his wife, Mary Anne, whose grandfather, Joseph Dugan, fought with the American Expeditionary Force. Finally, I thank my wife, Faith Sumner. She has a wealth of those qualities so necessary to support a writer: the tolerance to let me work when I need to and the tact to tell me when enough is enough. In flying the troops around the globe with World Airways, moreover, she has gained a store of knowledge and sympathy for the anxieties of men going into harm's way—and the exuberant relief of those coming out of it—realities her father, Virgil Sumner, a veteran of the Korean War, braced her for early in life. This book is dedicated to Faith.

THE SCOPE OF STYLE

It is time to turn back the clock to 1914, setting the scene in early August in the ministerial office of British Foreign Secretary Edward Grey. This scene, like all sixteen vignettes in the book, is carefully chosen to relate to the subject matter of the chapter. Some of the longer chapters have a second scene midway. The goal is to enhance readability by introducing chapter content in a more engaging way.

NOTES

1. Hew Strachan, *The First World War* (New York, 2003). Also see John R. Morrow, Jr., *The Great War: An Imperial History* (London, 2004). An early exception to the rule was Cyril Falls, *The Great War 1914–1918* (New York, 1959).
2. MacGregor Knox and Williamson Murray, *The Dynamics of Military Revolution: 1300–2050* (Cambridge, UK, 2001). An earlier study in the RMA mold is Allan R. Millett and Williamson Murray, eds., *Military Effectiveness* (Boston, 1988), 3 vols. See especially Vol. 1, *The First World War*. The concept of RMA grew out of the work of scholars and officers in the historical division of the Pentagon, the so-called Office of Net Assessment.

3. John Keegan, *The First World War* (New York, 1999); Holger H. Herwig, *The First World War: Germany and Austria-Hungary 1914–1918* (London, 1997); Hew Strachan, *The First World War*, Vol. 1, *To Arms* (Oxford, 2001); and David Stevenson, *Cataclysm: The First World War as Political Tragedy* (New York, 2004).
4. There is a tendency in some of the literature to draw too facile a shaping, causative connection between the First World War and the rest of a war- and genocide-ridden century. See above all Jay Winter and Blaine Baggett, *The Great War and the Shaping of the 20th Century* (New York, 1996); and Stéphane Audoin-Rouzeau and Annette Becker, *1914–1918: Understanding the Great War*, trans. Catherine Temerson (New York, 2002).
5. For Europe's remarkable transformation, see Eric Dorn Brose, *A History of Europe in the Twentieth Century* (New York, 2005); and James J. Sheehan, *Where Have All the Soldiers Gone? The Transformation of Modern Europe* (Boston, 2008).
6. Harry S. Canfield, *The World War: A Pictorial History* (New York, 1919); and *Harper's Pictorial Library of the World War* (New York, 1920), 12 vols.

PART ONE

INTO THE ABYSS
1871–1914

CHAPTER 1

The Long Descent

The long gentle face and fine, delicate features of Sir Edward Grey lacked luster on this midsummer day. Haggard and almost gaunt, they betrayed the unmistakable stress of the crisis that was dragging Europe and the world into a war of frightful proportions. Since the previous evening, Britain's foreign secretary of eight years had been organizing notes and documents for the most important speech of his career. The clock on the mantel of his huge, ornate workroom in the Foreign Ministry struck two o'clock in the afternoon as he returned from the latest of a series of critical cabinet meetings. It was Monday, August 3, 1914, and Grey had only one hour to gather the most important materials spread all over his desk and conference table, rush to eat at Queen Ann's Gate, and somehow get to the House of Commons.[1]

Moving frenetically from table to table, the foreign secretary's thoughts raced through the tragic escalation of events of the past five weeks: the assassination by Serbian terrorists of the heir to the Austro-Hungarian throne in Sarajevo; Germany's seeming desire to rush to war in support of Austria-Hungary; Vienna's harsh, merciless ultimatum to Serbia; Russia mobilizing its army to back outgunned Serbia; Germany's declarations of war against Russia and then France; and just today news of Germany's intention to march through neutral Belgium to attack France. Many members of the British cabinet had favored British noninvolvement in the conflagration unfolding on the continent with this ineluctable march of events, but Grey had managed to convince them that British obligations, honor, and imperial interests would not allow her to stand aside. Only days earlier his assistant, Sir Eyre

Crowe, sat before Grey's desk and painted a dire scenario for the British Empire: "If Germany and Austria win, crush France and humiliate Russia, with the French fleet gone, Germany in occupation of the Channel, with the willing or unwilling cooperation of Holland and Belgium, what will be the position of a friendless England?" Or, if France and Russia win, "what would then be their attitude towards England?" Would we not be threatened in "India and the Mediterranean by resentful former allies?"[2] Of the two scenarios, the first unnerved Grey and Crowe more, for in their view Germany seemed bent on imperial dominance, convinced "that there was not room in the world for both the British and German Empires."[3]

A secretary entered to announce that Prince Karl Max Lichnowsky waited anxiously in the antechamber. Grey met the German ambassador at the door. There was nothing new to report from Berlin, but what could Grey say about Britain's disposition in the crisis? Would the foreign secretary ask Commons for a declaration of war? "It is not a declaration of war, but a statement of conditions." "Is the neutrality of Belgium one of the conditions?" Grey was not at liberty to say anything to Lichnowsky before going before Parliament. "In an hour's time the whole world will know."[4] The German emissary had done as much as Grey over the past week to keep Europe from blowing itself up. He left the room a broken man.

Within the hour Grey stood before the benches and gallery of a packed House of Commons. After reviewing the relentless buildup of the crisis and expressing his opinion that Britain remained honor-bound (if not technically treaty-bound) to aid France, and duty-*and*-treaty-bound to protect neutral Belgium, he made the case *for British interests*:

> If France is beaten in a struggle of life and death, beaten to her knees, loses her position as a great power, becomes subordinate to the will and power of one greater than herself... and if Belgium fell under the same dominating influence, and then Holland, and then Denmark... I do not believe, for a moment, that at the end of this war, even if we stood aside and remained aside, we should be in a position, a material position, to use our force decisively to undo what happened in the course of the war, to prevent the whole of the west of Europe opposite to us... falling under the domination of a single power.... If we were to say that all those things mattered nothing, were as nothing, and to say we would stand aside, we should, I believe, sacrifice our respect and good name and reputation before the world, and should not escape the most serious and grave economic consequences.[5]

He did not ask the House to vote that day, but the vast majority of deputies from all parties knew that Grey was right—if the British Empire were threatened, then war was near.

Later that evening the foreign secretary and a friend stood at the window of the room where he had prepared the speech. They looked at the gas streetlamps being lit below. Seeing this, Grey remarked ominously, "The lamps are going out all over Europe; we shall not see them lit again in our lifetime."[6]

On August 4, 1914, the British ultimatum to Germany regarding violation of Belgian neutrality expired and Britain entered the war on the side of France, Russia, and Serbia. Thus, with the declaration of belligerency by Britain, whose power extended throughout the world, Europe's war became the world's war.

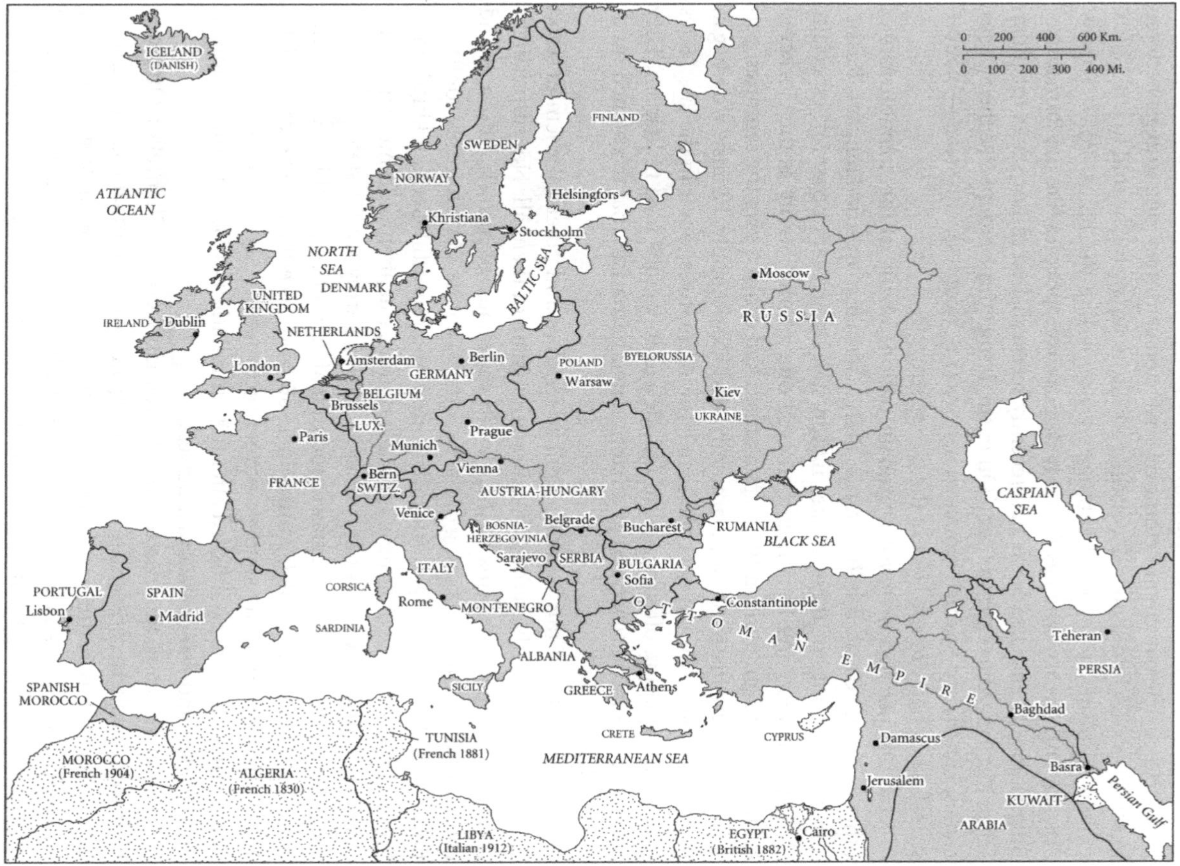

Europe in 1914

THE GREAT POWERS OF EUROPE 1871–1899

Laurence Lafore aptly entitled his classic analysis of the coming of war in 1914: "the long fuse."[7] Indeed the underlying causes of the conflict lay far back in European history. The continent's ethnic diversity and centuries-long struggle between feuding peoples had spawned a distinct ethnic hierarchy by the mid to late 1800s. On the bottom lay resentful subjugated groups like the Finns, Poles, Czechs, Slovaks, and Croats, whereas formerly dispossessed peoples like the Rumanians, Bulgarians, Greeks, and Serbs had recently reestablished minor states for themselves but longed to expand them. Other surviving ethnic groups like the Swedes, Danes, Dutch, and Spanish remained nations (i.e., peoples) with states—"nation-states"—but had dropped out of the power struggle.

On top perched the great dominant nations, many of them conquerors of other peoples: Great Britain, France, Italy, Germany, Austria-Hungary, Russia, and Turkey. Some of these greater nation-states were very powerful, especially Germany, France, and Britain, but all eyed one another warily as they jockeyed for position. Frightening military apparatuses had evolved over the centuries, permeating society institutionally, culturally, and ideologically. Pacifists who began to organize peace movements and search for alternatives to war in the late 1800s feared this squaring-off process and Europe's deeply embedded militarism. They condemned what struck them as an antiquated barbarism that threatened modern civilization.[8]

At the center of this Europe so full of enemies and potential enemies stood Germany, arguably the most powerful nation-state of them all. Not surprisingly, therefore, Germany remains to this day in the center of historical debates and controversies about the coming of the twentieth century's first horrible conflagration.[9] Already in the early nineteenth century the powerful German kingdom of Prussia ranked as one of Europe's greatest powers, but after midcentury this militaristic country—it was said that Prussia was "an army with a state"—gathered the other thirty-odd German states around it after a series of brilliant campaigns, defeating Denmark in 1864; Austria in 1866; and once mighty France in 1870–1871, seizing from it the strategic border provinces of Alsace and Lorraine. The new German Empire established after the humiliation of France won the immediate respect and fear of the other powers.

The architect of this rise to power, Prussian/German Chancellor Otto von Bismarck, sought to consolidate the empire's gains with diplomatic savvy and skill. By the late 1880s Berlin had formed a defensive alliance with Austria-Hungary and Italy; fashioned an ingenious agreement with Russia that guaranteed mutual neutrality in certain wartime scenarios; and brokered an agreement whereby Italy, Austria-Hungary, and Great Britain guaranteed the status quo in the Eastern Mediterranean, thereby checking Russia's ambition to push aside the failing Turkish Empire of the Ottomans and gain control of the Bosporus and the Dardanelles, the straits linking the Black Sea to the Aegean. Thus Berlin could claim with good reason to be the hub of Europe. In 1890, however, Emperor William II, the unstable, mercurial, capricious grandson of the first kaiser, dismissed Bismarck and allowed the treaty with Russia to expire. Almost immediately St. Petersburg began negotiations with France, heretofore successfully isolated by Bismarck, and these talks culminated by 1892 in a Franco-Russian defensive alliance directed against Germany that went into effect in 1894.[10]

Prussian/German military planners, headed by an operational genius, Chief of the Prussian General Staff Alfred von Schlieffen, cursed the kaiser privately for placing Germany in the predicament of facing a two-front war but gradually over the course of the 1890s formulated a bold operational plan that called for the bulk of Germany's divisions to first move west. Because test firing in the mid-1890s had proven that existing heavy artillery technology did not seem to allow for German armies to break through France's formidable line of fortresses stretching between the Swiss and Belgian borders, Schlieffen opted to send powerful forces through less heavily fortified Belgium despite the fact that since 1839 it was internationally recognized as a neutral state (i.e., that could not be legally violated). This outflanking maneuver would produce quick victory in battles along the Franco-German frontier. After crippling the French army, numerous German army corps would be entrained and sent east to deal with the slow-moving Russians while remaining troops mopped up in France.[11] The underlying assumption that Austria-Hungary and Italy would provide assistance on other fronts added additional risks to Schlieffen's scheme, for, fearing leaks, he did not coordinate operational thinking with either of his allies.

As the turn of the century drew near Great Britain faced the likelihood of a Franco-Russian, German-Austro-Hungarian-Italian showdown for hegemony on the continent and thus felt compelled to give more serious consideration to choosing sides.[12] She had fought alongside France against Russia in the Crimean War (1853–1856) but afterward adopted a policy of "splendid isolation" founded on the confidence of possessing the largest navy in the world and of enjoying unrivalled industrial prowess—with good reason in 1850 England claimed to be "the workshop of the world."

Technological change occurred rapidly during the second half of the century, however, and much of this scientific-engineering dynamism emanated from Germany, not Britain, thereby calling the wisdom of isolation into question. Indeed, industrial latecomer Germany was making rapid strides in the late 1800s to close the gap with Britain. German industries were growing at twice the rate of Britain's and the Central European juggernaut had also forged ahead qualitatively by pioneering or widely adopting many of the newest technologies of the second industrial revolution. Thus Germany's steel, machine tool, chemical, and electrical industries had no equal in Europe—or even a close second.

Imperial competition with France and Russia also caused brows to furrow in the offices of the colonial and foreign ministries. In the Middle East, Central Asia, and Far East Britain eyed Russian expansion warily. In 1898, moreover, French and British expeditions squared off against one another at Fashoda in the Sudan, nearly triggering war. International reaction to the Boer War, which broke out in 1899 between Britain and the ethnically Dutch Transvaal and Orange Free State in southern Africa, further heightened anxieties about remaining isolated, not so splendidly, without an ally. Indeed vitriolic pro-Boer press attacks in Germany, France, and Russia reinforced Britain's sense of national vulnerability during this hard-fought, difficult victory, especially with half a million soldiers deployed in Africa to defeat the Boers. It came as little surprise, therefore, when Colonial Secretary Joseph Chamberlain approached the powerful Germans about negotiating an alliance, for it made good sense to consider standing with them against long-standing imperial nemeses France and Russia.

THE MILITARY REVOLUTION IN TECHNOLOGY AND THE REVOLUTION IN MILITARY AFFAIRS (RMA)

As noted, the pace of technological change factored into these diplomatic considerations. The forces of production evolved so quickly after 1850, in fact, that historians are correct to speak of a so-called second industrial revolution.[13] The first industrial revolution of the late 1700s and early 1800s had been stamped with "Made in Britain." Three key, interlocking, mutually reinforcing technologies stood behind this almost exclusively British transformation: coke-fired iron manufacture; reciprocating steam engines; and sulfuric acid mass-produced in lead vats or chambers. Although critical for domestic or civilian production processes, all three technologies also found quick military applications in the form of wrought and cast iron cannon, ironclad steam-powered warships, and increased gunpowder output—sulfuric acid was a key ingredient in making black powder. Already by the mid-1800s it had become clear, however, that other nations would also benefit militarily as the technologies spread abroad. Steam locomotives transported troops in Prussian army maneuvers as early as 1839, for instance, and army units moved by rail in the War of Italian Unification (1859–1860), the American Civil War (1861–1865), and the Wars of German Unification (1864–1871).[14]

The obvious connection between industrial and military prowess in the first industrial revolution helps to explain the nervousness in European capitals as a second wave of technologies swept through Europe in the late 1800s, followed by successive waves that hit the continent after 1900. Inexpensive, flexible, strong steel replaced iron for many uses; powerful steam turbines supplanted the increasingly inefficient reciprocating engines; and the highly scientific "contact" process resulted in larger quantities of more highly concentrated sulfuric acid. But engineers and scientists went beyond merely solving problems related to the breakdown of the technology of the first industrial revolution: they also spawned devices and processes that created new material possibilities: electrical power and equipment, wireless telegraphs, telephones, synthetic chemicals for manufacturing and medicinal uses, nitrogen-based high explosives, and ingenious machine tools to shape all kinds of items requiring precise tooling.

These scientific and technological breakthroughs had the potential to revolutionize the art of warfare, for they resulted in killing machines like magazine repeating rifles shooting thirty to forty bullets a minute; machine guns capable of spewing out six hundred bullets a minute; semirecoilless rapid-firing field artillery firing hundreds of shells per hour; and artillery shells packed with extremely powerful nitrogen explosives that were also "smokeless," thus helping artillerymen conceal their batteries.[15] It was not as obvious as one might think, however, that armies would adopt everything from the cornucopia of new weapons produced by the quickly evolving second industrial revolution.

In recent decades historians have adopted a new conceptual framework for understanding the process of technological change and military response.[16] They identify different categories of far-reaching, multifarious change that have the potential to fundamentally alter the nature of warfare. These transformations need not be technological: thus the French Revolution radically altered the scale and intensity of the wars that ravaged Europe after 1792 without changing to any great degree the weapons used by warring nations. As explained earlier, however, already in its early stages the second industrial revolution spawned a range of new or potential weapons. As it gathered momentum after 1900, this building wave of technological change brought forth automobiles, airplanes, steam-turbine-powered ships, and submarines, all of which challenged army and navy establishments—just as iron ships, railroads, magazine rifles, machine guns, and semirecoilless artillery had done earlier—either to adopt the weaponry and determine the best tactical and operational adjustments or to reject the new devices altogether.

Responses to ongoing "military revolutions" like the technological one that unfolded in the late 1800s and early 1900s are obviously spread out over decades. There are no guarantees, moreover, that the resulting adjustments will be made intelligently, rationally, objectively, or even at all. Thus Germany first shunned its own rapid-firing artillery designs, only adopting them after France took the lead. All field artillery establishments tended to favor lighter, 75–77 mm guns for their mobility, furthermore, over the allegedly less mobile but, as the Great War would prove, much deadlier and more destructive 150–155 mm pieces. This halting process of adoption and adjustment has been dubbed a "revolution in military affairs," or RMA, a label that has entered and become fairly well ensconced in military literature. However, this process is clearly just as spread out and ongoing over decades—"evolutionary" in other words—as the technological "military revolution" to which it reacts. It is advisable to describe the RMA process of the early 1900s, therefore, as a generally embryonic one.[17]

The machine guns of Hiram Maxim are perhaps the best example of hesitation to adopt new weaponry. Although first invented in 1884, they were not used in combat until the British deployed them against African Matabele warriors in 1893. The lethal devices saw only limited use, furthermore, in the Boer War nearly a decade later. By this time Germany and the other powers experimented with machine guns during their annual maneuvers, but working these machines into tactical and operational practice proved slow due mainly to the cumbersome nature of the early guns as well as understandable (albeit contradictory) concerns over resulting rates of killed and wounded and what this could mean for the survival of the warrior's honorable profession. Indeed the new technology conjured up frightening images even in Germany, the nation with the greatest military reputation. Thus one general of the early 1890s, contemplating the horrendous

Granddaughter of Dreadnought: Fifteen-Inch Guns of HMS *Queen Elizabeth* in 1914
Harper's Pictorial Library

casualties that machine guns would inflict, complained that after battles there would not be enough troops left to bury the dead. And there were tactical dilemmas too. Should machine guns find adoption as offensive or defensive weapons, or both? If attacking machine gun positions, should cavalry be used at all? Should the infantry disperse to avoid slaughter? What was the proper tactical adjustment to the new weapon?

Naval technology represented one RMA plane of change and response, however, that was already fairly well advanced at this time, for decades earlier navies had overcome their prejudices against ironclad steam-driven warships; retired the old beloved sailing vessels; and then feverishly experimented with steel ship design, weaponry, and propulsion, churning out a series of "one-off samples [of ships] incorporating the latest untested devices in the hope that some of them would work."[18] As explained later, with the design of HMS *Dreadnought* in 1904 this process finally spawned a new generation of steel battleships firing big-gun shells packed with the latest nitrogen explosives.

Significantly, the naval dimension of RMA also impacted international relations in 1898 when Germany began to parlay its technological advantages into world-threatening, anxiety-generating military superiority with passage of a naval bill designed to expand and modernize the empire's third-rate fleet.[19] In 1900 a second, even more ambitious bill followed that envisioned an eventual force of fifty-eight heavy cruisers and battleships, so-called capital ships with eight- to twelve-inch gun calibers, and a 2:3 capital ship ratio with Britain. The world's naval leader now had to take notice, for her long-standing policy—now clearly in jeopardy—had been to maintain superiority over the combined ships of the next two naval powers.

It was no coincidence, therefore, that alliance negotiations actually took place, first in 1898, and then again in 1901.[20] Germany bargained for British help or, minimally, neutrality in the event of a continental war, while Britain sought German aid against Russia in East Asia. Both rounds of negotiations broke down when each side decided it had no reason to trade. Germany presented no threat in 1900, for its fleet construction was at least a decade from completion, and Berlin sensed that it could strike a better deal years later when Britain, still presumably worried about France and Russia, would need the help of German ships launched in the interim.

Historians agree, however, that Germany had let slip a brilliant diplomatic opportunity, for in 1902 Britain, already beginning to regard Germany more as foe than friend, signed a defensive pact with Japan. Although London wanted it mainly to counter Russian expansion in Asia, the alliance would also free up naval squadrons for use against other enemies, possibly including Germany, which the British Admiralty reckoned would become the world's second naval power within four years. In 1903, moreover, the Admiralty decided to establish a new North Sea fleet based at Scapa Flow and a second newly constructed station at Rosyth on the east coast of Scotland.

In 1904, finally, Britain drew up plans for a new class of superships. The "dreadnought" battleships first launched in 1906 scrapped reciprocating steam engines for faster turbines, used more efficient oil rather than coal fuel, discarded smaller guns useless at long range, and boosted the usual complement of heavy armament from four to ten 12-inch guns. Germany responded in kind. The naval race was on, and soon *Dreadnought* herself was obsolete as ever bigger ships were launched. The growth of the German fleet is therefore an instructive example of how general technological change, manifesting itself quickly as killer armaments technology, could generate anxieties and exacerbate relations between the Great Powers.

IMPERIALISM AND THE INTERNATIONAL ECONOMY

Already by the early 1800s European colonies, or former colonies like the United States of America, occupied 35 percent of the earth's surface.[21] Outside of its conquests close to home like Ireland, Britain had imperial holdings in the Caribbean, South Africa, India, and Indonesia, while also possessing the English-speaking "white dominions" of Canada, Australia, and New Zealand, which would progress toward autonomy and self-governing home rule as the century unfolded. Holland was also entrenched in Indonesia—the so-called Dutch East Indies—while Russia had pushed east beyond the Ural Mountains and south toward Central Asia. Furthermore, although France and Spain had been forced out of many of their Caribbean colonies by independence movements or by the British, both still had possessions there. Spain also held the Philippines.

The improved weaponry of the first industrial revolution, however, followed several decades later by the awesome firepower of the second, greatly added to Europe's military advantage, for preindustrial lands and peoples had no defense against steam-powered warships armed with huge modern guns and army battalions equipped with repeating rifles and machine guns. By 1914 Europeans controlled over 84 percent of the globe. In the relatively brief span of the 1880s and 1890s, for example, British, French, and German expeditions subjugated almost the entire continent of Africa. By 1899 the United States had extended Yankee civilization into the Pacific by taking the Philippines and Guam from Spain and also annexing Hawaii, Eastern Samoa, and Wake Island (see map, p. 89). Russia, similarly, had reached Vladivostok—which means literally "rule over the east." Simultaneously, Britain was expanding east from India into Burma (Myanmar) and Malaysia and north from India into Persia (Iran) and Afghanistan. Russia extended southward from the Caucasus and Kazakhstan into Persia on a collision course with Britain. In the Far East Chinese sovereignty eroded as Britain, France, Russia, and the United States bullied the once proud Asian hegemon. Having successfully modernized and westernized, furthermore, Japan joined the Europeans in undermining Chinese independence after winning a brief war in 1894–1895. Anti-imperial Chinese revolutionaries attempted to oust the hated foreigners in 1900, but the so-called Boxer Rebellion failed to break the tremendous power of the unwanted outsiders.

Accelerating industrialization provided Europeans not only with the armaments they needed to control most of the world but also with a much greater incentive to do so. Indeed Europe's investing businessmen now searched for oil, rubber, copper, nitrates, and other natural resources and precious metals needed to fuel growing industry and commerce back home. They sought colonies and the penetration of weak states as markets to increase sales and amortize domestic investments on a quicker schedule; as farm or plantation sites to produce tea, coffee, fruit, and sugar craved by consumers of all classes with money to spend; and as a high-risk, high-return investment alternative to low-yield government bonds in the homeland. And when revolution or expropriation threatened nitrate mines, railroad investments, and banana, coffee bean, and sugar cane plantations throughout Latin America, oil wells in Mexico and Persia, and the Suez Canal and coastal stretches along the sea route around Arabia to India, and, when native debt cancellation terminated lucrative loans to the Bey of Tunisia, the Khedive of Egypt, the Sultan of Turkey, the Shah of Persia, and the Empress of China, Europe answered with political intimidation or the establishment of military protectorates. The extent of European investment was truly impressive: by 1914 Britain had sunk ten billion dollars abroad, France five billion, and Germany four billion—an amount roughly equal to the combined annual national income of these three powerhouse states in 1913. One historian has aptly dubbed prewar Europe "the world's banker."[22]

The spreading worldwide pattern of European colonies and protectorates combined with the vast, intricate, rapidly expanding network of European commerce and investment in the decades before 1914 to create an interconnected, interdependent world economy.[23] Relatively free travel and trade were the lubricants of this "globalization" process. Although nations had erected tariffs walls, they were very low in comparison to later decades, and, reinforcing free trade was the fact that business travelers and emigrants could move about Europe and the world without passports. Travel and trade, in other words, were largely unimpeded by government restrictions. As one scholar recalled after the war, a man of business

> could order by telephone, sipping his morning tea in bed, the various products of the whole earth, in such quantity as he might see fit, and reasonably expect their early delivery upon his doorstep; he could at the same moment and by the same means adventure his wealth in the natural resources and new enterprises of any quarter of the world, and share, without exertion or even trouble, in their prospective fruits and advantages.... He could secure forthwith, if he wished it, cheap and comfortable means of transit to any country or climate without passport or other formality, could dispatch his servant to the neighborhood office of a bank for such supply of the precious metals as might seem convenient, and could proceed abroad to foreign quarters... and would consider himself greatly aggrieved and much surprised at the least interference.[24]

The governments of the industrialized nations further contributed to this free global economy by adhering to a "gold standard" whereby all major currencies were freely exchangeable for gold at fixed exchange rates. Theoretically a nation with a large surplus of imports over exports could reach the point where importers who had been paid, say, in dollars, and had accumulated too many of them, lost confidence in the dollar and exchanged their dollar holdings for American gold. To a great extent the gold standard worked, however, because it did not have to work, and this was because the British pound sterling, not gold, usually functioned as the lynchpin of the global economy. The nature of world trade imbalances should have sent the currencies and later the gold of the United States, Latin America, and Asia to Britain, British pounds and gold to continental Europe, and European currencies and gold to the world outside Europe—each of these regions had a mix of trade deficits and surpluses with the others. However, because the pound was so ubiquitous in this system, nations found it easier to exchange pounds, not gold. Not surprisingly, the pound was the world's strongest and most valuable currency, worth almost five dollars or nineteen German marks. Given the importance of the British Empire and Britain's currency, investment, trade, and merchant marine—70 percent of commercial shipping in the world was owned by British firms—it should be easy to appreciate that London, "the city," grew into the business hub of this world trading system. British clearinghouses handled and settled international accounts for companies from all over the world; British investment houses, insurance brokers, and shipping agents had no equal either in the volume of business transacted, expertise, or the cheapness of services rendered.

THE RUSSO-JAPANESE WAR AND THE TACTICAL MILITARY CHALLENGE 1904–1905

In February 1904 war broke out in the Far East between Russia and Japan. Russia had continued its expansion into East Asia by stationing forces in Manchuria, which Japan perceived as a threat. Emboldened by its alliance with Great Britain and frustrated by failed negotiations with Russia, Japan decided on a preemptive strike against the Russian fleet at Port Arthur. With one bold stroke the modernizing island nation destroyed or incapacitated one of the tsar's three fleets. Port Arthur eventually surrendered after a lengthy siege. The Japanese army also forced battered Russian army units out of Korea and southern Manchuria. A desperate bid to reverse Russian fortunes by steaming the Baltic Fleet around the world ended disastrously in May 1905 when a powerful Japanese flotilla concentrated its full fire on successive Russian ships as they steamed in line formation through the Tsushima Straits—a brilliant maneuver known as "crossing the T." Tsar Nicholas finally sued for peace that summer.

Now Russian "Rule over the East" receded as Tokyo forced St. Petersburg to recognize Japanese spheres of influence in Korea and Manchuria. The exhilarating, emboldening victory of an Asian power over a great European state produced a "demonstration effect" in many parts of the world as China introduced Japanese-style political reforms and nationalistic, independence-minded movements seized power in Persia in 1906 and Turkey in 1908.

The Russo-Japanese War was significant in other respects, for much more than the Sino-Japanese War, the Spanish-American War, and the Boer War it opened a vista to the nature of warfare in the machine age. The rapid fire of rifles and artillery pointed to the wisdom of mastering dispersed-order tactics and digging trenches to protect soldiers—and both sides quickly recognized this wisdom. Field artillery began to fire from hidden "defiladed" positions, unleashing a deadly steel rain on hapless thousands caught unawares in the open field. For their part the Japanese grew more reliant on higher-caliber artillery pieces to crush entrenched or fortified defenders, while the Russian army became the first to deploy large numbers of machine guns, which the Japanese immediately copied. One foreign military observer commented upon the "uncontestable value" of these "soulless devices without nerves [that] literally mow down the attackers."[25] The two-week Battle of Mukden in early 1905 starkly illustrated the lethality of a full range of killing machines that scythed through 160,000 men on both sides. Before the war ended half a million had fallen.

Within a few years of the Russo-Japanese War British, German, French, and many other military establishments had studied and debated the conflict adequately enough to make appropriate adjustments. Navies already building or considering dreadnoughts were confirmed in their thinking by the clear lesson of Tsushima Straits, namely, that only bigger guns firing at long range mattered in modern sea battles. Armies learned too, experimenting more energetically now with offensive and defensive uses of machine guns. Soon detachments began appearing in every regiment. The Germans increased the number of heavy 150 mm field artillery units, moreover, eventually forcing the reluctant French to play catch-up. Most nations also shed the brightly colored uniforms of former days for drabber gray, brown, or khaki colors—only the French refused to abandon the red and blue of Napoleonic glory days—while annual maneuvers and war games often witnessed the practice of more practical dispersed-order infantry and dismounted cavalry tactics. The latter transitions were far from complete, however, because many commanders refused to recognize the folly of the mad, "cost what it may" dash forward in densely packed ranks. Furthermore, one especially unfortunate conclusion drawn rather consistently from the Russo-Japanese War by European armies, regardless of whether individual corps commanders favored massed or dispersed tactics, was that infantry attacks could succeed in the age of modern technology. The Japanese seemed to have demonstrated this at Mukden. That such assaults had carried the day against the inefficient and poorly led Russian army—and might fail against better-prepared and better-equipped west European armies—had been widely overlooked. Nevertheless, Europe's RMA, only inching ahead before 1904, had now leapt forward.

DIPLOMATIC REALIGNMENTS IN EUROPE 1905–1907

In stark contrast to military-scientific studies prompted by the Russo-Japanese War, many politicians, businessmen, and intellectuals of liberal persuasion had become convinced by this time that globalization and the interdependent, inextricably entwined economies of the great powers of the world had made war irrational if not impossible. The best-known statement of this viewpoint appeared in 1910 with the first edition of British writer Norman Angell's *The Great Illusion*. War, he hinted, had become passé. "The day for progress by force has passed; it will be progress by ideas or not at all." And because these principles "of free human cooperation between communities are, in a special sense, an English development, it is upon England that falls the responsibility of giving a lead." He was taking a jab here at Germany, and it seems clear that the underlying purpose of the book was, in fact, to influence German progressive opinion in such a way as to ward off an economically counterproductive clash between the two great commercial/industrial nations. Hence he argued that "it is the elaborate interdependence which, not only in the economic sense, but in every sense, makes an unwarrantable aggression of one state upon another react [negatively] upon the interests of the aggressor."[26] These ideas resonated widely in both German and British shipping, trading, and banking circles. Thus German shipping magnate Albert Ballin stood at the forefront of efforts to reconcile German-British differences, and when war threatened in 1914 the bankers and traders of "the city" spoke out most vociferously against the impending insanity of war.

That Angell felt the need to make a statement against the economic irrationality of warfare in modern industrial times reflected the underlying weakness of his argument, however, for reality staked out a different position. We have already seen that imperial expansion driven above all else by the economic imperatives of the second industrial revolution exacerbated already existing tensions between the Great Powers of Europe—witness the Franco-British crisis over Fashoda, the so-called Great Game that pitted Russia against Britain as both pushed deeper into Central Asia, and especially Germany's construction of a world-class fleet to protect its embryonic empire and advance the cause of German influence and power in Europe and the world—Germans wanted their "place in the sun." The

Germany's Imperial War Lord: William II
Herbert Bayard Swope, *Inside the German Empire: 1916* (New York, 1917)

latter threat had begun to enter British thinking when they signed an alliance with Japan in 1902, constructed a North Sea harbor at Rosyth in 1903, and laid keels for the first dreadnoughts. However, the argument that imperialism was the *primary* force driving Europe to war in 1914 overlooks the underlying significance of the power struggle *within Europe itself*—Angell's major concern. And nothing better demonstrates this point than the crisis that broke out over Morocco in 1905–1906, an international incident that nearly triggered the Great War.[27]

In 1904 Britain and France decided that their common interest in curbing German ambition dictated a settlement of imperial differences in Africa. The compromise negotiated that year saw France recognize Egypt and the Sudan as Britain's sphere of influence while Britain agreed to French predominance in Morocco, Algeria, and Tunisia. This so-called cordial understanding, or Entente Cordiale, contradicted a long-standing assumption in German diplomatic circles, namely, that the Franco-British conflict would perpetuate itself to the point of driving Britain into an agreement with Germany on terms more favorable to Germany than were possible in 1898 and 1901. In order to break up this seemingly unnatural Franco-British Entente, therefore, Kaiser William II bluntly declared in 1905 that Germany also claimed interests in Morocco. Behind the scenes in Berlin diplomats and generals assumed that France would humiliatingly bow before this pressure, for the year before France's ally, Russia, had been attacked by Japan in the Far East, precipitating a bloody war that tied down the bulk of the Russian army in Manchuria. With Russia unable to provide reliable military assistance in a prospective European war, France would submit to German demands in Morocco, and Britain, observing the undeniable weakness of its newfound diplomatic partner, would abandon Paris and initiate another round of alliance talks with mighty Germany.

Germany's maneuver backfired terribly. Although wavering at first, French backbone stiffened when Britain opposed German demands. After this most recent example of the kaiser's bullying behavior and tactlessness, in fact, London grew even more alarmed that German militarism threatened British interests. Events now ran an embarrassing and humiliating course for Germany when an international conference at Algerciras in 1906 upheld the French hold on Morocco. Although the treaty also guaranteed German commercial interests in Morocco, it was evident that bluff and bluster had only solidified the Franco-British Entente Cordiale. The meager, largely face-saving gains in the Moroccan Crisis shocked a German public anxious about the threat posed by an increasing number of enemies in Europe. Indeed Germans questioned for the first time whether the nation's leadership could deal competently with foreign challenges in the hostile, warlike atmosphere of Europe.

Britain's reaction to the Moroccan Crisis is critical to understanding the eventual outbreak of war in 1914; for the world's premier empire accelerated the process of maneuvering itself into a favorable position should a European war break out. Already in September 1905, for instance, the British General Staff conducted war games to probe the operational feasibility of shipping an expeditionary force to France and Belgium to defend against German aggression. Simultaneously, the Royal Navy accelerated construction of the dreadnought battleships, a truly frightening new class of capital ships. But the diplomatic, potentially military readjustment did not stop there. London also gave tacit approval to President Theodore Roosevelt's 1904 policy of policing all foreign investments in Latin America—the so-called Roosevelt Corollary to the Monroe Doctrine of 1823—by withdrawing Britain's Caribbean Fleet and concentrating these ships in waters closer to home to confront the German threat.

Coming in January 1906 in the midst of the Moroccan Crisis, the change of government in London from the Conservative Party to the Liberal Party also affected the shifting diplomatic-military realignment in Europe. That the Liberals would continue and even strengthen Britain's anti-German policy was far from obvious to contemporaries. Indeed many Conservatives expressed alarm that the new government would move in the opposite direction. From backbench members of parliament well into the cabinet, antiwar sentiments like those of Angell ran strong, especially among radicals who abhorred the notion of increased military spending and opposed entangling commitments like those that appeared to be resulting from the Moroccan Crisis. In the new Foreign Minister Sir Edward Grey, however, the Tories found an ally. As early as 1903, for instance, he had "come to think that Germany is our worst enemy and our greatest danger."[28] He believed, very correctly, "the policy of Germany to be that of using us without helping us; keeping us isolated, that she may have us to fall back on." And in 1905, shortly before the Liberal victory at the polls, he spoke out against the widespread rumor "that a Liberal Government would unsettle the understanding with France in order to make up to Germany—I want to do what I can to combat this."

It was Grey, in fact, who now worked hard to deepen the commitment to France. As the crisis over Morocco escalated in early 1906 he encouraged the War Office "to be ready to answer the question, what could they do if we had to take part against Germany. . . . The more I review the situation the more it appears to me that we cannot [keep out of a war] without losing our good name and our friends and wrecking our policy and position in the world." Meeting finally in June 1906 the Committee of Imperial Defense (CID) opted for a British Expeditionary

Force of up to six divisions to help blunt a German invasion. "We must join the French," said Henry Wilson, director of Military Operations at a subsequent CID meeting. Britain signed no formal treaty with France as France had with Russia, and hence there was no parliamentary debate or approval, but nevertheless a commitment had been made.

Grey's efforts did not stop with the ongoing Entente and slide into military alliance with France. In August 1907 Britain negotiated a colonial agreement similar to the Entente Cordiale of 1904, this time with tsarist Russia—much to the dismay of radical backbenchers, who were unhappy that liberal England had eased so close to an authoritarian state. The largely autonomous foreign minister ignored them. Britain and Russia agreed to spheres of influence and buffer zones to simmer down the Great Game in Persia, Afghanistan, and Tibet. Like the earlier deal with France, Britain designed this pact specifically to "sacrifice" outstanding imperial problems that could cause further "quarrels" and undermine the now much-needed assistance of Russia "as a counterpoise to Germany on land."[29] Thus, far from rushing into war because of imperial conflicts, three of Europe's Great Powers defused those conflicts to better brace themselves for war in Europe.

The so-called Triple Entente of France, Russia, and Britain had come into alarming, frightening focus. It did not mean war, but it stood to reason that countries standing together diplomatically could also stand together militarily. This was not a good sign for the maintenance of peace in Europe.

NOTES

1. See Edward Grey (Viscount Grey of Fallodon), *Twenty-Five Years 1892–1916* (New York, 1925), 2:1–30.
2. See Crowe's minutes of 24 July 1914 printed in G. P. Gooch et al., eds., *British Documents on the Origins of the War 1898–1914* (London, 1926), 11:81–82.
3. Grey, *Twenty-Five Years,* 2:29–30.
4. For the conversation, see ibid., 2:13–14.
5. The speech is printed in ibid., 2:308–326.
6. Ibid., 2:20.
7. Laurence Lafore, *The Long Fuse: An Interpretation of the Origins of World War I* (Philadelphia, 1965).
8. For an insightful analysis of the far-reaching influence of military establishments and the emergence of pacifism, see James J. Sheehan, *Where Have All the Soldiers Gone? The Transformation of Modern Europe* (Boston, 2008), 3–41.
9. For an excellent general survey of the long-term origins of the war, see the latest edition of James Joll, now with co-author Gordon Martel, *The Origins of the First World War* (Harlow and London, 2007). Also see Lafore, *The Long Fuse;* Volker R. Berghahn, *Germany and the Approach of War in 1914* (New York, 1993); Hew Strachan, *The First World War,* Vol. 1, *To Arms* (Oxford, 2001), 1–102; David Fromkin, *Europe's Last Summer: Who Started the Great War in 1914?* (New York, 2004), 17–117; and David Stevenson, *Cataclysm: The First World War as Political Tragedy* (New York, 2004), 3–35.
10. For a good introduction to the system of alliances in Europe, see Joachim Remak, *The Origins of World War I 1871–1914* (Fort Worth, TX, 1967).
11. For these developments, see Eric Dorn Brose, *The Kaiser's Army: The Politics of Military Technology in the Machine Age, 1870–1918* (New York, 2001), 69–84, 183–216; Annika

Mombauer, *Helmuth von Moltke and the Origins of the First World War* (Cambridge, UK, 2001), 42–105; and Terence Zuber, *Inventing the Schlieffen Plan: German War Planning 1871–1914* (Oxford, 2002). For the raging debate over Zuber's work, see below, chap. 3.

12. For discussions of British diplomacy, see Zara Steiner, *Britain and the Origins of the First World War* (London, 1977); and Niall Ferguson, *The Pity of War: Explaining World War I* (New York, 1999), 31–55.

13. See David S. Landes, *The Unbound Prometheus: Technological Change and Industrial Development in Western Europe from 1750 to the Present* (Cambridge, UK, 1969; Joel Mokyr, *The Lever of Riches: Technological Creativity and Economic Progress* (New York, 1990); and Eric Dorn Brose, *Technology and Science in the Industrializing Nations 1500–1914*, 2nd ed. (Amherst, NY, 2005).

14. See Dennis E. Showalter, *Railroads and Rifles: Soldiers, Technology, and the Unification of Germany* (Hamden, CT, 1975); Daniel R. Headrick, *The Tools of Empire: Technology and European Imperialism in the Nineteenth Century* (Oxford, 1981); and Eric Dorn Brose, *The Politics of Technological Change in Prussia: Out of the Shadow of Antiquity, 1809–1848* (Princeton, NJ, 1993), 164–189.

15. See William H. McNeill, *The Pursuit of Power: Technology, Armed Force, and Society since A.D. 1000* (Chicago, 1982), 185–306; David Stevenson, *Armaments and the Coming of War: Europe, 1904–1914* (Oxford, 1996),15–63; David G. Hermann, *The Arming of Europe and the Making of the First World War* (Princeton, NJ, 1996), 7–21; and Brose, *Kaiser's Army*, 7–182.

16. See MacGregor Knox and Williamson Murray, "Thinking about Revolutions in Warfare," in their edited collection, *The Dynamics of Military Revolution 1300–2050* (Cambridge, UK, 2001), especially 11–14.

17. For studies on the reaction of specific armies to these challenges, see Tim Travers, *The Killing Ground: the British Army, the Western Front and Emergence of Modern Warfare 1900–1918* (London, 1987); Douglas Porch, *The March to the Marne: The French Army 1871–1914* (Cambridge, UK, 1981); Brose, *Kaiser's Army;* David R. Jones, "Imperial Russia's Forces at War," in Allan R. Millett and Williamson Murray, (eds., *Military Effectiveness*, Vol. 1, *The First World War* (Boston, 1988), 249–328; and Bruce W. Menning, *Bayonets before Bullets: the Imperial Russian Army 1861–1914* (Bloomington, IN, 1992).

18. Dennis E. Showalter, "Mass Warfare and the Impact of Technology," in Roger Chickering and Stig Förster, eds., *Great War, Total War: Combat and Mobilization on the Western Front, 1914–1918* (Cambridge, UK, 2000), 75.

19. For the rise of the German navy and the naval competition with Britain, see Jonathan Steinberg, *Yesterday's Deterrent: Tirpitz and the Birth of the German Battlefleet* (London, 1965); Holger H. Herwig, *'Luxury' Fleet: The Imperial German Navy 1888–1918* (London, 1980); Paul M. Kennedy, *The Rise of the Anglo-German Antagonism 1860–1914* (London, 1980); and Robert K. Massie, *Dreadnought: Britain, Germany, and the Coming of the Great War* (New York, 1991).

20. For the following, see Ferguson, *Pity of War*, 45–55.

21. See Bernard Porter, *The Lion's Share: A Short History of British Imperialism, 1850–1914* (New York, 1975); and Eric Hobsbawm, *The Age of Empire, 1875–1914* (New York, 1989).

22. Herbert Feis, *Europe The World's Banker 1870–1914: An Account of European Foreign Investment and the Connection of world Finance with Diplomacy before World War I* (New York, 1965).

23. D. K. Fieldhouse, *Economics and Empire 1830–1914* (London, 1973).

24. John Maynard Keynes, *The Economic Consequences of the Peace* (New York, 1920), 12.

25. David G. Herrmann, *The Arming of Europe and the Making of the First World War* (Princeton, NJ, 1996), 68. For European reactions to the Russo-Japanese War, see 67–74, 87–95. For the German army, also see Brose, *Kaiser's Army*, 138–182.

26. Norman Angell, *The Great Illusion: A Study of the Relation of Military Power to National Advantage* (London, 1913), 361, 295. Also see the discussion in Ferguson, *Pity of War*, 21–23.

27. For the crisis, see Eugene N. Anderson, *The First Moroccan Crisis 1904–1906* (Hamden, CT, 1966); and Joll, *Origins*, 62–66. For a discussion centering on the kaiser's role and shifting positions throughout 1905–1906 as well as background on this problematic ruler, see Brose, *Kaiser's Army,* 112–137. For an argument in contrast to the argument above that imperialism was, in fact, the driving force behind European rivalries, see John H. Morrow, Jr., *The Great War: An Imperial History* (London, 2004).
28. Citations here and below in Ferguson, *Pity of War,* 58, 64, 66.
29. Citations in ibid., 60, 61. Also see Beryl Williams, "Great Britain and Russia 1905–1907," in F. H. Hinsley, ed., *British Foreign Policy under Sir Edward Grey* (Cambridge, UK, 1977), 133–147.

CHAPTER II

From Peace to War

It was the last springtime of the old century. The Hague radiated with resplendent, spirit-lifting color. Coaches carrying representatives from twenty European and six non-European states streamed in grand succession past the fountains, flower gardens, and marble nymphs surrounding wooded Huis ten Bosch, site of the world's first peace conference. A military honor guard took position in front of this exquisite "House in the Woods," whose black enameled gate, red bricks, and white window frames reflected the sunlight of early afternoon as if beaming its confidence in mankind to the heavens. The beautiful scene seemed to presage the opening of a pacific new era.[1]

The guard received each coach of dignitaries, announced the parties with great pomp, and ushered them inside. Green-baize desks for scores of delegates were set up in a great ballroom, the Oranje Zaal. On walls rising three stories to the ceiling hung golden damask and frescoes by the Great Masters, most depicting—fittingly or unfittingly—martial triumphs of past Dutch princes on horseback. Accompanying Cupid and Venus on high, leering eerily and insidiously at the throng below, hovered Death in the form of a skeleton. Optimists shuddered but soon found a more appropriate omen in a mural allegorically representing the Treaty of Westphalia that had ended a vicious, thirty-year round of fighting in 1648. Peace enters the Oranje Zaal to close the doors of the Temple of Janus, whence issue, according to an old Roman legend, the "dogs of war." A brief opening address by Dutch Foreign Minister Maurice de Beaufort reinforced the spirits of all champions of a new, nonviolent world order. He pointed out that they, like allegorical Peace, had

Princess of Peace: Bertha von Suttner
Courtesy of the Library of Congress

the same higher purpose "of preventing calamities which threaten the whole world."[2]

One lone woman listened with the others, Bertha von Suttner, the Austrian antiwar activist. Ten years earlier she had written her highly controversial novel, *Lay Down Your Arms,* and for a decade champions of "the ancient ideal of war," as a diary entry described them, had ridiculed her followers as "utopians," or less charitably as "wrong-headed idiots." She knew that her enemies had stacked their delegations with militarists: Germany sent Baron von Stengel, an advocate for war, and America included Alfred Mahan, a well-known proponent of sea power. A seasoned crusader, Suttner knew a movement was afoot to "civilize" warfare with more rules about treatment of prisoners and thereby scuttle the most ambitious goals of the peace movement—arbitration and disarmament.

Still, she could not help but feel the power of the moment. For the first time in history pacifists had convened a conference to root out the still potent "remnants of the old barbarism" and secure a just and lasting peace. Since time immemorial the Dutch had built their dykes to control the fury of the sea. Was it really so utopian to construct institutions to dam up "the rage of one people against another"? After the twentieth century had passed, would peace advocates make pilgrimages to The Hague as the site of the first permanent court of international justice? Bertha von Suttner was determined to make it happen.[3]

THE PEACE MOVEMENT 1889–1907

The worldwide peace movement drew opposite conclusions from the second industrial revolution than either the soldiers, who sought to harness it for their own purposes, or liberals like Norman Angell, who believed that war had become an economic anachronism. Since the late 1880s pacifists like Suttner, Swedish explosives manufacturer Alfred Nobel, and Russian writer Ivan Bloch had led a movement to reverse the frightening drift into high-tech warfare, a trend they feared had momentum on its side. They wanted to establish alternatives to the old ways of settling disputes, like disarmament favored by Suttner or arbitration preferred by Nobel.[4]

The latter solution seemed more pragmatic, in fact, given the escalating arms race in Europe. Accordingly, advocates of this novel method, many of whom were lawyers naturally favoring extension of the rule of law into the international arena, began to hold conferences to formulate detailed and elaborate arbitration mechanisms. Their work proceeded against the backdrop of disturbing developments on the world scene, for in 1894 Japan went to war against China and in 1898 the United States and Spain clashed. The rapidly industrializing powers, America and Japan, won easily, unsheathing their technology in frightening fashion.

Hoping to reverse the apparent trend of established states warring against one another, peace advocates convened a meeting at The Hague in May 1899. They succeeded in getting international backing for a purely optional arbitration procedure decided by judges assembled ad hoc—one crisis at a time. Significantly, both parties to a dispute had to agree to arbitrate in order for this "World Court" to convene and then render a decision. The near uselessness of the new arrangement became evident later that same year when the Boers opted for arbitration; the British, confident of victory, did not; and war threatened. As the crisis mounted, pacifists courageously demonstrated in London's Trafalgar Square. "A war of aggression and annexation will excite in South Africa such fierce racial hatred," they warned, "as will create a second Ireland."[5] But war, not peace, prevailed. "Our time civilized? Ridiculous!" lamented Suttner. "There are a few thousand civilized people, no more than that."[6] She had exaggerated, and soon her underlying optimism revived, but the statement reflected well her depressed mood at the turn of the twentieth century.

After the shocking casualties of the Russo-Japanese War—the fourth war in a decade waged by developing industrial states—the peace movement redoubled its efforts. A second conference at The Hague in June 1907 attended by delegates from forty-four nations put forward an ambitious proposal whereby many different types of minor disputes would automatically be adjudicated by the existing World Court. The proponents of this approach, many coming from the judicial community of the United States, assumed that nation-states, once accustomed to the sacrifice of sovereignty on less-threatening issues like health and labor; fishing and navigation; debts and finance; and trade, commerce, and communications would very gradually learn to appreciate the need for binding arbitration in times of more serious international crisis.

Great Britain and France supported America's motion; Germany and Austria-Hungary opposed it, and Russia, still lamed from the Far Eastern conflict with Japan, offered only tenuous, lukewarm backing and then finally voted against. Without unanimous consensus, the motion failed. Nevertheless, the fact that thirty-three of forty-four nations had approved seemed to affirm Bertha von Suttner's bold statement of 1905, reflecting her old bright outlook, that "two philosophies, two eras of civilization are wrestling with one another" and that "a vigorous new spirit is supplanting and threatening the old." Could the "instinct for self-preservation in human society" prevail over the centuries-old approval of "might is right"?[7]

SOCIALIST ANTIWAR EFFORTS 1889–1907

The socialist parties of Europe viewed upper-class efforts at The Hague warily and skeptically. Mostly Marxist in persuasion, they assumed that nothing would come of the conferences because upper-class business interests dictated that wars would be fought and territory seized in Europe and the world. Despite their eloquence, the Suttners, Nobels, and Blochs of the world had no power to overturn or alter these capitalist imperatives and dynamics. Only the socialists, the advocates of the downtrodden masses, could end wars that served capitalist (but not working-class) interests.

Already in 1889 ten social democratic parties had assembled in Paris to form a Socialist International, an umbrella organization dedicated to advancing the workers' cause, terminating capitalism, and, by so doing, also waging "war against war."[8] Indeed from the Marxist perspective workers should never fight fellow proletarians—"Workers of the world unite," German revolutionary Karl Marx had said, "you have nothing to lose but your chains." Once social, economic, and political institutions dominated by greedy, profit-seeking private property owners had been swept away, the fundamental cause of military conflagrations would be rooted out.

For nearly two decades after the founding of the International, European social democrats did nothing to implement their ideas, preferring to wait for the final, inevitable victory of the proletariat and the downfall of the capitalist system that allegedly caused war. This triumph offered the only way out—the panacea. However, four wars in the world within a span of only eleven years transformed socialist antiwar rhetoric into an actual agenda item at the International's tri-annual congresses. Meeting in Stuttgart, Germany, in August 1907, the seventh congress brought proposals from the French and Russian delegations for a general strike, a massive work stoppage in the midst of a war-threatening crisis that would grind the wheels of the war machines to a halt and topple warmongering regimes.

Unfortunately the host German delegation could not accept these resolutions. Worried that direct action of this sort would mobilize the mighty German army against a movement that had made tremendous progress in terms of recruiting members as well as accumulating strike funds, health insurance funds, printing houses, buildings, land, and other real property, leaders of the Social Democratic Party of Germany (SPD) balked. A compromise resolution in Stuttgart saved international working-class face by renouncing war as unacceptable and obliging every member organization to use the antimilitarist means it deemed most practical to stop wars from breaking out. The backers of the resolution had kowtowed to the hosts and omitted any mention of a general strike. The socialists of the International mocked efforts being made simultaneously at The Hague but in reality had put up no dyke to the bloody flood that threatened to inundate

Europe and the world. Would the next congress at Amsterdam in 1910 succeed in erecting a more effective bulwark to war?

THE AUTHORITARIAN STATES

After the Great War, American President Woodrow Wilson pointed a finger of blame at the militaristic nondemocratic states of Europe that he saw as the root cause of the conflagration. Both the pacifist and socialist movements contributed to the coming tragedy with their own internal weaknesses and divisions, to be sure, but there is certainly a measure of truth to Wilson's accusation. At Stuttgart in 1907, for example, German socialists blocked the idea of a massive strike to stop European war machines from rolling largely for fear of the likely punishment that Germany's military regime would mete out. That same year at The Hague, moreover, failure to make more progress toward peace-maintaining institutions hinged largely on the stance of Europe's three great authoritarian powers: Germany, Austria-Hungary, and Russia.

Thus the German spokesman at The Hague, Alfred Marshall von Bieberstein, paid lip service to the idea of arbitration publicly but privately railed against it as a "kind of leveling scheme" that would allow smaller, weaker states to check the ambitions of more powerful nations. "A kind of spider web would be created in which even the smaller states would feel like spiders—and perhaps here and there the great powers will become the flies in the web."[9]

Even worse was the likelihood that the democratic spider principle could contaminate domestic politics in states still largely controlled by monarchs, generals, and conservative bureaucrats rather than elected representatives. Already in 1906, for instance, Austro-Hungarian officials who, like their German counterparts, had successfully restrained parliamentary institutions, reacted with disdain and alarm to the "strongly socialistic"[10] precedent of their parliamentary deputies attending a pacifist conference in London to formulate arbitration procedures for their government. The establishment of arbitration practices would strengthen the position of advocates of parliamentarism at home, in other words, by enabling them to intervene during times of international crisis in foreign policy decisions reserved for the elite.

Russia abandoned the cause of arbitration at The Hague, furthermore, as soon as a majority of nations appeared willing to approve it. Indeed the tsar could not afford to tolerate leftist tendencies on the international level while struggling against leftists at home. The Russo-Japanese war had triggered a revolution in Russia and forced Tsar Nicholas II (1894–1917) to establish a parliament, the Duma, but it too had limited powers. The Russian monarchy remained nearly absolute and he wanted to keep it that way.

Germany, Austria-Hungary, and Russia were not democratic, in other words, and their authoritarian leanings contributed to blocking not only the socialist scheme for a general strike but also the rudimentary beginning to arbitration desired by bourgeois pacifists—and the absence of both made war more likely. This was not the only way, however, that East-Central European authoritarianism

Germany's Ruling Men March to the Traditional Drummer
Kaiser William with Marshall's Baton, Crown Prince William, and Five Hohenzollern Princes
Canfield, *World War*

contributed to the approaching storm.[11] Many conservatives in these countries were probably "retreating by attacking," that is, fleeing from mounting domestic pressures and unruly elements at home by attempting to deflect and distract them with war—to rechannel the raw emotion of their grievances against foreign foes.

It is not that these states were totally averse to all reform. Thus Germany and Austria had made significant concessions to bourgeois liberals in the 1860s. Both states established imperial diets with power of the purse that became entrenched in the legislative process. However, Emperor Francis Joseph of Austria-Hungary (1848–1916) and his German counterparts, Kaisers William I (1871–1888) and William II (1888–1918) retained far-reaching executive powers such as exclusive control of military affairs and foreign policy, including the decision to go to war. These liberal compromises assured domestic political tranquility for a few decades, but with the growth of organized labor movements and the emergence of assertive socialist political parties in the late 1800s, the political equilibrium began to deteriorate. The socialists quickly established themselves on the left wing of their respective parliaments, demanding labor and social legislation and political reforms much more extensive than rulers were willing to accept—collective bargaining, unemployment insurance, the eight-hour day, and genuine democratic institutions.

Of the two states, Germany came under the greater leftist pressure, for it industrialized more rapidly and therefore its labor force also grew more rapidly. Already in the elections of 1890 the SPD captured a higher share—19.5 percent—of the votes cast than any of the other major parties, a figure that expanded to 31.7 percent in 1903 and 34.8 percent in 1912. German patriots looked severely askance at these developments, for it seemed to them that the socialists divided the nation against itself at a time when it needed domestic solidarity to face enemies abroad. Radicals in militantly nationalist organizations like the Pan German League and the German Defense League went so far as to argue that war in Europe, which seemed likely anyway given the standoff between alliances, would be beneficial for the domestic politics of the empire, for it might unleash a surge of patriotism, distract the workers from their radical demands, and thus heal German divisions. Many in the army and high places were tempted by the same thoughts. The desire to dam up democratic forces and shore up authoritarianism was therefore an additional factor—although probably a secondary one—making war in Europe a more distinct possibility in the years before 1914.[12]

A similar dynamic existed in Russia. The eastern colossus undertook industrial reforms in the 1890s designed to accelerate industrial growth and close the technological gap with Germany. Although tremendous progress was made, the rapid expansion of the labor force created even more political turbulence than in Germany, for Russia's Draconian regime banned labor unions, ignored the need for social reform, and allowed no release of pressure through elections, which remained out of the question in the absolutist state of Nicholas II. Consequently, radical revolutionary organizations came into being, like the Russian Social Democratic Labor Party and in 1903 the offshoot of this party, the Bolsheviks, the most revolutionary organization in Europe, led by a determined, resolute, subversive Marxist, Vladimir Ilyich Lenin.

In addition to these problems, however, Russia had not solved the older problem of peasant unrest over periodic famine, high taxes, indemnity payments to the nobility (dating from the time of serfdom's abolition in 1861), and above all, the peasants demand for more land—their "land hunger." Russia's failure to address these grievances led in 1900 to the formation of the Socialist Revolutionary Party, known commonly as the SRs, an organization dedicated to the cause of peasant revolution and determined to destabilize the regime through systematic assassination of its officials.

The joint pressures on the state emanating from industrial and peasant unrest encouraged some Russian leaders, notably Interior Minister Vyacheslav Plehve, to surreptitiously maintain a collision course with Japan before 1904, for he believed a "small victorious war" would defuse domestic explosiveness and "hold back revolution."[13] After an ignominious defeat sparked revolution in 1905 and the opening of a Duma in 1906, the error of such thinking became so evident that continued domestic instability began to function more as a force for peace. The tsar and his later advisers knew, in other words, that another disastrous war had the potential to ignite another revolution, and thus they had to place this consideration on the scales with others in any crisis, especially the imperative of maintaining, whatever the cost, Russian honor and strategic interests as well as Slavic solidarity with allies like Serbia. Which would prove the weightier force?

As we have already seen, however, the same need to protect tsarism from any further erosion of authority could cut in the other direction, as it did at The Hague, by undermining the growing consensus for at least making a start with arbitration. Indeed as the delegates gathered there Nicholas, who never intended to rule as a parliamentary monarch, so curtailed suffrage requirements for the unruly Duma that peasant and proletarian representation all but ended—an ominous sign for the future of the monarchy.

THE DOGS OF WAR RETURN TO EUROPE 1908–1913

Three wars broke out in the volatile Mediterranean/Balkan region from 1911 to 1913 before another Balkan crisis one year later, the assassination of Francis Ferdinand, heir to the Austro-Hungarian throne, finally sparked the Great War, the first general European conflagration in a century. In order to appreciate these escalating, earthshaking developments it is first important to discuss the fading great power position of Austria-Hungary and the rise of its upstart rival, Serbia, whose extremist sympathizers murdered the Austro-Hungarian archduke in June 1914.[14]

Once the dominant state in Europe, the realm of the Habsburgs had suffered a steady decline for centuries. Vienna could neither roll back the Protestant Reformation in the 1500s and 1600s nor prevent Prussia from seizing the rich province of Silesia in the1700s. Repeated defeats at the hands of France in the 1790s and early 1800s gave way to a brief revival of influence in the decades after 1815, but both Italy and Germany unified at Austria's expense in the 1860s. Defeated by Prussia in 1866, Austria in her weakened condition granted autonomy to the unruly Hungarians in 1867. For over four decades thereafter, however, the so-called Dual Monarchy of Austria-Hungary grew internally more fragile and unstable. The compromise of 1867 contributed to this dilemma by whetting the appetite of other ethnic minorities within the empire for Hungarian-style rights to govern their own domestic affairs in return for supporting unified financial, foreign, and military policies in Vienna. If Hungarians received concessions, why not Czechs, Slovaks, Ukrainians, Rumanians, Italians, Croats, and Serbs? The emergence of independent Serbian and Rumanian states in the late 1870s exacerbated these internal tensions by providing ethnic minority groups with a distinctly superior alternative to continued Austro-Hungarian suppression. A few of the most problematic minorities within Austria-Hungary were tempted to secede, in other words, in order to merge with a free Serbia or a free Rumania—a fiery agenda stoked by nationalist agitators in Bucharest and Belgrade eager to dismember the Dual Monarchy.

As the Serbian government in particular intensified its anti-Austrian rhetoric after 1903, Austro-Hungarian leaders gave more serious consideration to bold preventative measures. The basic fear that a greater Serbia would "tear the empire to pieces," as one Austrian official put it, finally prompted Vienna to annex the provinces of Bosnia and Herzegovina in October 1908. Although Vienna had administered these Turkish provinces since 1878, it thought formal acquisition would block Serbia from demanding (or perhaps just taking) territories inhabited by Slavic ethnic brethren. "We have reconquered again the place that belongs to us among the powers," boasted Foreign Minister Alois Lexa von Aehrenthal. The annexation would prevent a final "appeal to the sword" if it intimidated the Serbs, but if they opposed the move Austro-Hungarian generals were prepared to use force. Indeed the firebrand Austrian chief of staff, Franz Konrad von Hötzendorff, had counseled war for years as the best way to eradicate "the dangerous nest of vipers in Belgrade."[15] The strategic location of Bosnia and Herzegovina adjacent to Serbia would facilitate military operations if they became mandatory.

Tragic Habsburgs: Francis Ferdinand, Sophie, and Family
Canfield, *World War*

Serbian patriots reacted with fury to the annexation. Assuming that fellow Slav and fellow Orthodox Russia would react with the same rage to Austro-Hungarian rule over Slavs in Bosnia-Herzegovina, the government in Belgrade made preparations for war. For six months the crisis threatened to erupt into a European conflagration. Although unwilling to go to war over Balkan complications, Britain and France nevertheless protested the Austro-Hungarian move, claiming correctly that it violated the Treaty of Berlin of 1878, which had provided only for the administration of the provinces, not full sovereignty over them. Germany's reaction proved to be the real determinant of the outcome of the crisis. Knowing that Austria-Hungary was ill prepared for war and certainly not able to cope militarily if left to its own devices, Berlin issued a thinly veiled warning to Russia that war against Austria-Hungary meant war against Germany too. In no position to square off against technologically dangerous Germany after the crippling of the Russian army and navy in the Far Eastern debacle against Japan, Russia swallowed its pride and backed down in March 1909. The crisis was over.

Half a year of protesting, wrangling, and saber rattling, however, had deepened European divisions. As noted earlier, Britain and France acted in unison, thus solidifying their Entente. Although it is true that the two democracies denied Russia military backing in the hopes of defusing the escalating crisis, and also that Britain refused to accede to Russian demands for access to the Black Sea for Russian warships—outlawed since the Treaty of Berlin in 1878—London and Paris had nevertheless spoken out quickly and jointly in support of Russia's anti-Austrian stance. As for Serbia and Russia, many in both capitals, including those in high places, swore revenge against the Germanic powers after such a humiliating and allegedly unmanly backing away from the brink. Their anger was very public and evident. Thus Edward Grey observed the "strong Slav feeling that has arisen in Russia" and that "bloodshed between Austria and Serbia would certainly raise the feeling to a dangerous height."[16] Making the same kind of observations in Berlin, German Chief of the General Staff Helmuth von Moltke wrote Hötzendorff that Germany would honor its 1879 defensive alliance and declare war if Russia attacked Austria-Hungary. "The moment Russia mobilizes [its army], Germany will also mobilize,"[17] wrote the most important soldier in the German army. It is significant, however, that Moltke also pledged German aid in the event of a European war *provoked by an Austrian attack on Serbia.* "In effect," writes Annika Mombauer, "Moltke [had] changed the alliance from a defensive to an offensive one."[18]

A series of international incidents in North Africa now ratcheted national anxieties in Europe to higher levels. France sent troops to Morocco in April 1911 to squash rioting there. Perceiving this as a violation of the Algeciras Treaty of 1906 that had sanctioned a French protectorate in Morocco for all intents and purposes but had not stated this formally and literally, Germany dispatched a gunboat to reinforce demands that Germany receive some form of compensation. Officials in the Foreign Ministry also hoped to mollify nationalist agitators who insisted that Germany erase the perceived humiliation of the First Moroccan Crisis. Both France and Britain bristled at Germany's bullying behavior. "It is a trial of strength," barked Sir Eyre Crowe of the Foreign Office. David Lloyd George of the Exchequer trumpeted that "national honor" was at stake. The crisis eventually blew over when French Chief of Staff Joseph Joffre informed an alarmed and disappointed cabinet that he could not guarantee victory in the field against the powerful German army. Berlin received part of the French Congo as compensation and then stood down in its turn.

Even more than the crisis of 1905–1906, however, the Second Moroccan Crisis widened cleavages in Europe. This nerve-wracking confrontation accelerated the transformation of a cordial diplomatic understanding between Britain and France into a military alliance, for instance, because in the aftermath Britain finalized plans for a British Expeditionary Force to confront Germany's anticipated move through Belgium. Britain and France also undertook naval talks to divide fleet deployments. Britain withdrew most of its Mediterranean Fleet to home waters, while France left protection of the Channel to Britain and reassigned these ships to the Mediterranean. Moreover, France took steps after 1911 to enhance the military worth of its alliance with Russia by lending vast sums of money to St. Petersburg for construction of railways in White Russia (Belarus) and Poland to speed Russian troops on their way to battles in eastern Germany when war broke out. The French army also revamped its previous defensive strategy in favor of an offensive one, in large part to assure Russia of Paris's firm commitment to the alliance and to encourage Russia to follow suit. These efforts paid off two years later when the Russian war minister pledged to attack Germany with 800,000 men fifteen days into mobilization. "One can affirm," wrote Joffre later, "that the

Russian General Staff's certainty about our offensive plans and our commitment to the clauses of the military agreement, a certainty reinforced at every contact with our General Staff, strongly contributed to leading the Russian General Staff to intensify its effort."[19] Put differently, France had encouraged Russia to overcome any reservations it might have—domestic, military, or otherwise—about going to war.

The French transition to offensive thinking reflected more, however, than the need to embolden the Russians. Indeed many influential thinkers in this western democracy had yielded to the urge for violence and a radical sorting out of Europe's deep-seated problems. In philosopher Henri Bergson, for instance, France found a tribune of "vitalistic" action. His immensely influential *Creative Evolution* refuted the dominant rationalism of science and shifted focus to the nonrational drives of man and a "real self" embedded in the subconscious. It was here, buried deep, that one tapped into élan vital, the vital urge that made man—and nations of men—great, enabling them to rise above seemingly overwhelming forces of resistance. One attendee of Bergson's lectures, Georges Sorel, wrote *Reflections on Violence*, a dark portrait of Europe that predicted war and anarchy on a continent that worshipped armed cataclysm. The French turn to offensive operational thinking cannot be separated from this intellectual groundswell, for the soldiers also drank deeply of Bergson and Sorel.

In Germany, too, advocates of solving international problems the old-fashioned way were stepping to the fore. Thus Chief of the General Staff Helmuth von Moltke, eyeing Russia's rapid recovery with French assistance, urged the kaiser in 1912 to strike sooner rather than later despite gloomy premonitions that the resulting war would be a long, brutal slugfest. Cavalry General Friedrich von Bernhardi's paean to the inevitability and desirability of combat, *Germany and the Next War*, also called for preemptive strikes. His message resonated in the aggressive nationalistic circles of the Pan German League and the German Defense League.

The 1911 crisis over Morocco touched off the first of three localized shooting wars, this time over Turkish Tripoli. Sensing that France wanted to extend its holdings in North Africa, Italy seized the province in order to block French expansion as well as to preempt the "Young Turk" regime that had seized power three years earlier from realizing its goal of revitalizing Ottoman power. To Italy's surprise, however, the Turks decided to fight for their territory, thus forcing Rome to wage an unexpectedly difficult campaign requiring the mobilization of 100,000 soldiers. For a brief time in the autumn of 1911 the fighting actually spread as far as Constantinople (Istanbul), causing the first casualties on European soil in over thirty years. In November Turkey was finally forced to sue for peace and cede Tripoli to Italy.

In 1912 international crisis and war spread to the Balkans, where ethnic relations simmered explosively in Ottoman-controlled territories. The Young Turks came to power in 1908 determined to strengthen their authority in the region. In Macedonia and Albania this resolve translated into suppression of religious and community rights and the disbanding of all clubs harboring dreams of national independence. Worse still, in Macedonia the Turks expropriated land from

Bulgarians, Serbs, and Greeks and then settled Muslims on these properties. Constantinople responded to the retaliation of ethnic terrorist bands in 1910 and 1911 with ruthless crackdowns on entire villages—thousands of people were arrested and dozens killed. A rising of Albanian nationalists in Kosovo in 1911 met the same ironfisted fate. When a second revolt in 1912 gained the upper hand, however, the Turks yielded to Albanian demands for an autonomous greater Albania that extended Muslim rule, ominously, into Christian Macedonia.

The alarming concession to the Albanians—one that unleashed a wave of fearful rumors about the impending "extermination" of Christians by Muslims—galvanized Serbia, Montenegro, Greece, and Bulgaria into action. They formed a "Balkan League" in the late summer of 1912, ready to eliminate the perceived Muslim threat, seize territory from the Turks, and prevent Austria-Hungary from expanding its foothold out of Bosnia. The four small nations put a half million soldiers into the field and attacked in October 1912. As the Turks fell back toward Constantinople casualties quickly rose to a shocking 100,000. With Turkish authority crumbling, Christian soldiers and civilians lashed out at Muslims, hanging "spies" and murdering, raping, and burning in one village after another as a vindictive payback for the long, brutal rule of the Ottomans. The "liberation" of the Balkans "unleashed the accumulated hatreds, the inherited revenges of centuries,"[20] wrote one team of international investigators (also see chap. 6). Although peace finally came in May 1913, war broke out again that summer when Bulgaria attacked Serbia in a bid for even more territory. Greek, Serbian, and Rumanian troops easily defeated the Bulgarians, once again perpetrating combatant deaths and terrible atrocities against civilians.

Either Balkan War could have touched off a greater European explosion by pulling Austria-Hungary into the conflict, followed in all probability by Russia, Germany, France, and perhaps Britain too. Indeed many officials and soldiers in the multinational Dual Monarchy advocated war as a solution to the empire's internal ethnic discord. Vienna watched with mounting alarm during the First Balkan War, for instance, as Serbia expanded southward across Albania to the Adriatic. Belgrade's insistence on an outlet to the sea triggered an Austro-Hungarian ultimatum that forced Serbia to withdraw its soldiers from Albania. Vienna grew even more upset over Russia's meddlesome behavior in the Balkans. The Russian minister in Belgrade referred openly to Austria-Hungary as "the next sick man of Europe," a derisive reference to long-standing Turkish and now Austrian weakness. In early 1914 the Russian military press inflamed Balkan relations even more by tauntingly writing about the coming "partition of Austria-Hungary." In a hostile reply, Vienna reminded St. Petersburg of the precarious state of its own multinational empire.

Successive nerve-fraying crises militarized Habsburg diplomacy after 1912–1913, leaving its leaders committed to a subsequent policy of force. In Russia, too, Pan Slav zealots argued that national honor could not allow it to stand aside if ever again the German race threatened Slavic peoples. It helped to keep the peace during these Balkan Wars that France offered no encouragement to Russia and Germany sought to restrain Austria-Hungary. However, the resentful reactions in Vienna and St. Petersburg—leaders there raised angry questions about the worth of allies who did not stand shoulder to shoulder in a tense situation—caused worries and second thoughts in Paris and Berlin. For the sake of alliance solidarity, in other words, neither France nor Germany felt it could afford to disappoint its ally again. Could the wider peace of Europe and the world survive another crisis or localized war? Since 1904, alarmingly enough, there had been four wars involving at least one European country and three major war-threatening crises involving all of the Great European Powers.

The foundering of the peace movements added to the mounting sense of despair. For its part the Socialist International gathered representatives from twenty-six nations at a special congress in Basel, Switzerland, in 1912 as reports of casualties and atrocities streamed in from the Balkans during the first war. The noble antiwar rhetoric of so towering a figure as French socialist Jean Jaures could not conceal the unfortunate truth, however, that the international labor movement still could not agree on a strategy to halt the outbreak of war. Two years before Basel at Copenhagen, German moderates had again refused their support for a resolution to declare a general strike if war neared. The 1910 congress could only agree to postpone further discussion to August 1914 at another special gathering scheduled to coincide with the twenty-fifth anniversary of the founding of the International. Victor Adler, leader of the Austrian socialists, saw through the emotional sentiments expressed so eloquently in Switzerland to the hard, unpleasant realities: "It unfortunately does not depend on us Social Democrats whether there is a war or not."[21]

Bourgeois pacifists could offer nothing more concrete. Plans for a third peace conference at The Hague in 1913 crumbled as a second war ravaged the Balkans. The champions of peace were unprepared in any event, for six years of lobbying and negotiations with leaders of the Great Powers had produced no breakthrough agreement to accept mandatory arbitration procedures. "We thought there was a far more widespread sense of justice," complained Bertha von Suttner in one of her last statements. "The peace movement is not yet powerful enough," she admitted, "to overthrow the deep-seated forces of ancient despotism."[22]

THE JULY CRISIS OF 1914

The incident that finally touched off Europe's powder keg occurred on June 28, 1914, when assassins killed Archduke Francis Ferdinand and his wife Sophie in Sarajevo, Bosnia.[23] Gavrilo Princip, a Bosnian Serb who had entered into a convoluted and still shadowy plot with five ethnic brethren, committed the murders. He and fellow assassins of Young Bosnia, an organization committed to uniting all South Slavs by violence, had completed paramilitary training in Belgrade with the aid of sympathetic officers in the Serbian army and intelligence service, themselves organized for pro-Slavic terrorism in the Order of the Black Hand, and then crossed into Austrian Bosnia with the help of compatriot border guards. Although Black Hand leaders initially tried to cancel the mission, the six young men, mistakenly believing that the archduke's presence in Bosnia presaged a preemptive military strike against Serbia, insisted on carrying out the shootings.

This was the height of tragedy and irony, for Francis Ferdinand had been the most consistent and articulate voice for peace and calm in Vienna. In 1913, for example, he had "categorically rejected" Hötzendorff's urgings for war against Serbia.

> Let us assume that no one else will contest us, [that we] can settle accounts with Serbia in peace and quiet. [But what can Vienna gain thereby?] Only a pack of thieves and a few more murderers and rascals and a few plum trees.... [However], that most favorable case, that no one contests us, is more than unlikely....If we take the field against Serbia, Russia will stand behind her, and we will have war with Russia. Should the Austrian emperor and the Russian tsar topple one another from the throne and clear the way for revolution?

"War with Russia," he concluded, "means the end of us."[24] Within four years of his death these dire predictions would come true.

After the violent deed, Bosnian Muslims and Croats destroyed the shops and businesses of resident Serbs, sensing correctly who had armed and assisted the assassins and wanting to demonstrate their dissociation from the act to angry Austro-Hungarian officials. Hundreds of Serbs were beaten to death or lynched. Jumping to the same conclusions, Francis Joseph and his ministers decided to use the killings as a convenient pretext for war. Diplomats set immediately to work on an ultimatum to Serbia that they intended to be so harsh as "to make a refusal almost certain, so that the road [be opened] to a radical solution by means of a military action."[25] The goal: partition of the victim among Austria-Hungary, Bulgaria, Greece, and Albania. Vienna's demands were presented on Thursday, July 23, with a forty-eight-hour time limit. When Belgrade refused the most objectionable demand for a sovereign power, that Austro-Hungarian officials participate in an investigation of the Serbian roots of the plot, Serbia's response was rejected on the twenty-fifth. Historians have been correct, therefore, in assigning a portion of the responsibility for the outbreak of the Great War to the Austro-Hungarian leadership that rashly went to the brink of war—and of course to the terrorists and their helpers who perpetrated the deadly act in Sarajevo.[26]

While writing the ultimatum in early July, Austria-Hungary also asked Germany if it would honor commitments to the Dual Monarchy should the long-desired punitive expedition against Belgrade spark a wider war. Kaiser William II and his civilian and military advisers agreed to this "blank check" of military assistance, gambling that Serbia would be quickly crushed and the declining power of Germany's only reliable ally revitalized.[27] It is significant that German Chancellor Theobald von Bethmann Hollweg, nerves frayed after successive crises, opted to cast the die with Vienna in the desperate hope that a war which seemed inevitable could be contained in the Balkans—he did not want the Great War. On the military side of this "army with a state," Helmuth von Moltke and War Minister Erich von Falkenhayn at first took no serious notice—crises had come and gone before, and perhaps this one would not let the tocsin sound either. As the critical month of July unfolded, however, they both argued for war. The sooner the better, for France and Russia had introduced army expansion programs that lessened the odds of victory in a few years when these plans reached fruition. Besides, how great was the risk? Russia seemed too beset by internal discord to gamble on military conflict and a probable revolution with the lesson of the Russo-Japanese War still fresh in official minds. However, if St. Petersburg opted to uphold its honor abroad whatever the cost at home—that is, if she chose to mobilize and fight—German generals liked their chances of defeating both Russia and her ally France. In fact, Moltke had also accepted the distinct possibility of British intervention, which did not greatly concern him: the western campaign offered a tempting opportunity to squash all of the best forces of the anti-German Entente. Moltke harbored anxieties, to be sure, but was quite ready "to roll the iron dice." Confident of German backing, Austria submitted its ultimatum to Serbia, and a few days after its rejection, in the night of July 28–29, bombarded Belgrade. Thus Germany sealed its much larger share of the historical responsibility for the outbreak of the Great War with its troubled mixture of arrogance and anxiety—the former, significantly enough, outweighing and canceling out the latter.

How would France and Russia respond to Serbia's fate? Since the 1920s historians have debated this problematic reaction, focusing on Russian confidence in French backing as well as the encouragement France may have given its ally during this tragic, peace-ending crisis. The main accusation of Franco-Russian culpability came from Harry Elmer Barnes, who argued that Paris and St. Petersburg conspired after 1912 to exploit Balkan turbulence and bring on a European war that would enable France to retake Alsace and Lorraine, lost to Germany in 1871, and Russia to push the Turks aside and gain control of the Bosporus and Dardanelles.[28] In his recent biography of French President Raymond Poincaré, John Keiger called many of Barnes's strident views into question by utilizing Poincaré's private papers to demonstrate that the native of Alsace and Lorraine did not advocate war and was actually much less anti-German than once assumed.[29] More recently, historians have emphasized important facts on both sides. Swinging the debate back somewhat toward Barnes, Eugenia Kiesling showed that during his state visit to Russia in mid-July 1914 Poincaré, although not at all desirous of war, nevertheless pledged alliance solidarity. "If France's willingness to back Russia's play against Austria increased the risks of embroilment in a war [France] did not want, at least she would not have to fight alone."[30] It is also true, on the other hand, that the allies did not coordinate specific military plans during these talks and that on July 30 Paris cabled Moscow not to resort "to any measure which might offer Germany a pretext for a total or partial mobilization of her forces."[31]

France's moderating message might have served the cause of peace far more if it had come earlier. Indeed since receiving a copy of the harsh text of the Austro-Hungarian ultimatum to Serbia, Russian officials had waxed belligerent. "It is European war," said Foreign Minister Sazonov. "[Austria-Hungary has] set fire to Europe." On July 24 came a Serbian plea for assistance to the tsar.

> We cannot defend ourselves. Therefore we pray Your Majesty to send help as soon as possible. Your Majesty has given so many proofs of your previous good will and we confidently hope that this appeal will find an echo in your generous Slav heart.

Nicholas knew that he could not ignore this entreaty, for if he showed weakness and acted dishonorably, "Russia will never forgive the sovereign."[32] Thus, despite the anxiety and frustration French vacillation caused in Russia so far into the crisis, St. Petersburg decided anyway on full mobilization knowing full well, as it had realized ever since signing the French alliance in 1892, "that a European war was *on* as soon as the mobilization order [went] out of the telegraph office."[33] Nicholas and his advisers decided that the prestige and honor of the nation demanded mobilization on behalf of fellow Slavic/Orthodox Serbia—matters of honor outweighed real concerns about the danger of another revolution in the midst of war.

And war it would be, for Russia's mobilization schedules and timetables for millions of troops were so complicated, and had taken so long to prepare, that the army possessed only one mobilization plan. These fateful orders, moreover, sent troops in motion on Friday, July 31, to bivouacs not just on the southwestern frontier near Serbia but all along the entire western border, including, alarmingly, the frontier with Germany. It is difficult to avoid the conclusion, therefore, that Russia shared with Germany the lion's share of the responsibility for the coming of a European-wide war.

For once Russia's grandiose call-up began, Germany, possessing only one mobilization plan itself, grew nervous as the limited time available for its long-planned march through Belgium to outflank the French began to tick away. Early on August 1, therefore, Berlin warned Russia to stand down within twelve hours or face war with Germany. Having received no favorable reply to its ultimatum, Germany declared war on Russia late on August 1, occupied neutral Luxembourg on August 2, declared war on France August 3, and invaded Belgium early on Tuesday, August 4, 1914. The violation of Belgian neutrality precipitated the final decision for war in London later that day.

Upper-class pacifists and working-class antimilitarists could not prevent the worst from happening. The former held private meetings and sent telegrams to foreign offices but for the most part watched passively in horror. Having accomplished nothing since the second peace conference at The Hague in 1907 except make preparations for a third meeting in 1915 and, having little or no influence with politicians in London, Paris, Berlin, Vienna, and St. Petersburg, the hands of the pacifists remained tied. The antiwar sentiments of the Socialist International also changed nothing. Nationalist impulses undermined good intentions. The general strike debate at Copenhagen in 1910, for instance, had quickly deteriorated into finger-pointing and squabbling between German, French, and English delegates. Four years later, in late July 1914, they were no closer to agreement on direct action to stop war. A special congress meeting in Brussels produced no consensus on the urgent need to proclaim a massive antiwar general strike. In the final week of the crisis every labor movement in Europe held (or planned to hold) antiwar street demonstrations, but the wheels of war began to turn anyway.

Now, as alarms sounded repeatedly in newspapers, parliaments, and the streets, widespread beliefs about the legitimacy of defending one's country against invaders, spies, and assassins assumed much greater prominence. With crowds in Vienna clamoring for punishing the murdering Serbs, with the usually staid German bourgeoisie making citizens' arrests of alleged enemy agents and workers peering anxiously eastward for the coming of the dreaded Cossacks, with Russian patriots calling for a defense of Slavic peoples against Germanic aggressors, with French laborers listening to reports of enemy troops violating the eastern frontier, with British citizens watching angrily as German soldiers seized Luxembourg and parts of Belgium and peering frighteningly through North Sea mists for the appearance offshore of Germany's powerful fleet, most people in Europe responded patriotically to mobilization orders, joined their army units, and marched to the front.

THE POPULAR REACTION: UNRAVELING THE RIDDLE OF WAR ENTHUSIASM

For almost a century historians have pondered why Europeans reacted with such apparent enthusiasm to the tocsin that sounded war in August 1914. The cheering tens of thousands who surrounded the royal palaces of George V, William II, Francis Joseph, and Nicholas II, jubilant scenes later to be the center of focus in every Great War documentary shown in twentieth-century history classes, already captured the attention of contemporary movie-house audiences. Within months of war's outbreak, in fact, patriots in every belligerent nation pointed with pride to their *union sacrée* or *Burgfrieden*—to the "spirit of 1914."

By the 1920s social scientists jaded by the fate of those 10 million who had died for their country condemned the alleged "mental contagion" and "immense crowd infection"[34] that seemed to have swept up the masses and rushed them over the cliff like lemmings. A second, even costlier, world war—caused, some would argue, by the first—prompted even more pessimistic assessments like Barbara Tuchman's best seller, *The Proud Power*. "The working class went to war willingly, even eagerly, like the middle class, like the upper class, like the species." Eschewing the traditional focus on prewar diplomacy and the timing of declarations of war that, like "the fever chart of the patient," said nothing about "what caused the fever,"[35] she devoted five hundred pages to describing the bellicose sickness that caused Europe's pandemic of war after 1914.

Tuchman's 1962 work probably had more influence than academic historians would like to admit, for in succeeding decades they too turned away from narrower diplomatic and economic explanations of the origins of the Great War to analyses of "the mood of 1914."[36] They investigated underlying values and assumptions in Europe about the costs and benefits of peace and war, nonviolence and combat, material prosperity and the all-cleansing martial cataclysm.[37] For the lead-up antebellum decade they focused more than ever before on the mind-set of the artistic and intellectual community and its impact on the high school, university, and twenty-something youth who flocked to the colors. From their works we learned more about the Peter Pan-like yearning of young Britons for an adventuresome break with the boring bourgeois world of adults; the convoluted preaching and troubling violence-worship of Bergson and Sorel; the psychotic longing of Italian Futurists for breaking away from the pacifistic clutches of women and flinging men into combat; the Pan Slav mania of Russian painters and the preoccupation of compatriot composers and choreographers for humanity's sacrificial rites of spring; the new psychology of Sigmund Freud with its illumination of irrational impulses and urges; the German Expressionist images on canvas and in poetry of an apocalyptic end and rebirth of the world; and the widespread, all-pervasive influence of Friedrich Nietzsche and his message of a new breed of larger-than-life men who would seize the day and, sparing no human expense, forge a more heroic order. The shallow materialism of industrialism, the ugliness of cities, and the depressing mediocrity of a leveling democracy revolted Nietzsche. As an atheist, he turned his back on the regenerative potential of Christianity. Rather, the new superior man, a "Roman Caesar with the soul of Christ," needed to "wage wars for the sake of thoughts and their consequences." In *Thus Spake Zarathustra,* Nietzsche asked, "O my brothers, am I cruel?" The answer—that only destruction was creative—broke from traditional philosophy's rationalism and idealism. "For creators are hard.... This new commandment, O my brothers, I give unto you: become hard!"[38] Even Gavrilo Princip and his fellow conspirators discussed Nietzsche in the cafes and back rooms of Zagreb and Belgrade in the months before doing their bloody deed.

Surely this research provides insights to the phenomenon of war enthusiasm in 1914, especially the spontaneous prowar parades of German university students in Berlin and other large cities; the wave of voluntary enlistments in conscript countries like Germany and France; and most notably the situation in nonconscript Britain, where before the end of the year a million men volunteered. Although the bellicose ideas and proactive mentality of 1914 have definite explanatory value, they certainly do not suffice, on the other hand, to explain the phenomenon of popular support for the war in all its variegated complexity.[39] Some who stoically went to war, for instance, masked their anxiety and tried to deal with the nagging suspicion that panicky cowardice, not heroic bravery, lurked inside them. Would they prove themselves or not? Nor was every soldier or recruit naïve about the nature of combat in the industrial age. Newspapers had covered the nasty Balkan Wars, Russian veterans had not forgotten Mukden; nor had the Boer War faded from the memory of survivors and victims' families.

> War's bloody hell [blurted one British mother as the last days of peace lapsed]. Ah'm tellin' you God's truth. Two o' my lads went i' South Africa. Bloody hell, that's wha' 'tis."[40]

It is facile to assume, furthermore, that the fervent desire for peace of the socialist rank and file who demonstrated in Germany on July 28, the many followers of Jean Jaures who wept after his assassination on July 31, and the British laborites who packed Trafalgar Square while the cabinet met on August 2, that their peaceful inclinations somehow disappeared or were transformed into aggressive war fever as the ambassadors presented their declarations of belligerency.

Indeed, while many people streamed in celebratory mood to the royal castles, others—perhaps the majority—resigned themselves to the unavoidable need to defend the nation and do one's duty whatever it might cost. "No cries of hurrah," wrote the leading SPD newspaper in Germany. People sensed "the power of events" leading to war and knew they were "standing at the door to the terrible, the bloody, the terror-bringing." Similarly, liberal journalist Theodor Wolff recalled the "heavy hearts" of the German people. "The determination with which we went to war sprang not from joy, but from duty."[41] There is ample evidence of like sobriety and concern in Britain, where the brutally frank mother quoted above was echoed by more than one British pastor sermonizing about approaching Armageddon, and in France, where rural districts were reportedly shocked, upset, and desolate but still quite ready to defend the soil of the motherland.

Doing Their Duty: General Sir John French among British Volunteers in 1914

Used with the permission of *The Trustees of the Imperial War Museum, London*. Photo Number: Q 70032

In Austria-Hungary, however, the cheering crowds of Vienna contrasted sharply with a subdued mood in Prague that soon manifested itself in strikes, demonstrations, and desertions from an army fighting for the interests of Austrians and Hungarians, not Czechs. And in Russia nearly half of all provinces suffered anticonscription riots and police crackdowns that killed five hundred people well before the army approached the German and Austro-Hungarian borders—with Jaures and the hapless residents of Belgrade the Great War's first casualties. Four percent of Russian draftees did not report for duty, and many of those who did lacked "thinking patriotism, the intelligent knowledge of the objects they were fighting for," said a British observer. A Russian general agreed, noting that "the drafts arriving from the interior of Russia had not the slightest notion what the war had to do with them."[42] For Austria-Hungary and Russia these were early ominous signs.

It is important for purposes of historical accuracy to gauge the complexity of popular reactions during the critical days between Austria's rejection of Serbia's ultimatum reply on Saturday, July 25, and the German invasion of Belgium on Tuesday, August 4—the need to describe "how it really was," or as Germans say, *"wie es eigentlich gewesen."* Getting a good measure of the range of popular sentiment in 1914 is also critical for properly understanding domestic politics in the belligerent nations as the war unfolded, for the longer it lasted the more the one side that had favored peace but supported war with sober defensive resolve began

What Does the War Have to Do With Us? Russian Conscripts in 1914
Used with the permission of *The Trustees of the Imperial War Museum, London*. Photo Number: Q 81558

to question the need for more killing, while the other camp that had welcomed war with more aggressive or imperialistic emotions and agendas not only saw no need to end the war but also condemned as cowards or traitors those who disagreed. Some nations would split apart entirely along these lines of fissure.

THE GREAT WAR: WHY DID IT HAPPEN?

The culture of war lay deeply embedded in a European continent whose peoples had conquered or been conquered over many centuries, indeed many millennia. As the greatest nation-states began to maneuver themselves into the most favorable position to fight a war after 1900, therefore, some Europeans high and low viewed this without surprise, for going to war seemed to be a natural and unavoidable fact of life. Some even welcomed it as a steeling process for a people and the only honorable arbiter of national disputes that had always been resolved when one state took another's territory and held it by right of conquest.[43]

Existing tensions worsened as the second industrial revolution and its attendant technological change generated novel weapons that heightened the fears and anxieties of nations like Britain and France, former industrial leaders surpassed by Germany in many critical, military-related sectors; Russia, a former great power that struggled to pass the threshold of its own industrial takeoff; and Turkey, whose Young Turk regime dreamed of reviving Ottoman greatness and, like Russia, tried to accelerate industrialization.[44] Simultaneously, imperialism offered up new colonies for the Europeans, potential markets, and arenas of struggle in the wider world.

As the leading nations of Europe realized that they could not afford to stand alone in such a hostile atmosphere, they signed alliance treaties that divided the continent (and colonial regions) into two armed camps—Germany and Austria-Hungary on one side; France, Russia, and Britain on the other; and Italy, officially linked to Berlin and Vienna but unofficially leaning the other way as militant nationalists longed to expand across the Adriatic into Austrian-held territory and pragmatists recoiled from the nightmare of pitting Italy's navy against the powerful fleets of Britain and France. These entangling alliances endangered the peace by threatening to drag allied powers into a local conflict that one ally (like Austria-Hungary) or patron lesser power (like Serbia) had provoked. The likelihood of such a scenario increased with the resurgence of ethnic nationalism, particularly in the Balkans, the powder keg of Europe.

It was even more unfortunate for Europe and the world that domestic political crises in certain countries exacerbated and complicated international affairs. Thus Austria-Hungary's problem with disgruntled Serbians, Croatians, Rumanians, and other ethnic minorities menaced relations with neighboring countries in the Balkans and eventually triggered war. In Germany, too, socialist pressure on an unstable government to cater to workers' reform needs, democratize the political system, and temper its dangerous militarism influenced the outcome of the July Crisis. Although little military action was anticipated in the east during the first month or so of war, German political leaders considered an immediate declaration of war against Russia necessary to rally the notoriously antiwar Social Democrats to a seemingly just cause against the most reactionary regime in Europe.

Aligned against the forces pushing Europe into the abyss were the opponents of war. The pacifist and antimilitarist causes attracted millions of people to their banners, certainly enough to justify Bertha von Suttner's claim that "a vigorous new spirit" had arisen to challenge the old belligerent attitudes. Indeed, the growing alternative mind-set of pacifism explains the intensifying paeans of militarism, for "in societies where war is taken for granted," observes James Sheehan, "there is no need to demonstrate that war itself [has] a moral purpose or a social function."[45] Although far from a tiny minority, however, the antiwar activists had little or no influence where it counted. Suttner was feted in small countries like Switzerland, for example, or across the ocean in America, but reviled at home in Central Europe. And the socialists, for all their influence among workers and ability, right into the July Crisis, to mobilize greater numbers in the streets than their prowar opponents, could do little in schools and universities, the opinion-making bourgeois press, or the chancelleries of power. When war finally came, furthermore, it became hard to distinguish between the "vigorous new spirit" and the old, for no one denied the right and the need to defend one's country, and people of all nations believed that enemies had provoked the conflict.

NOTES

1. Bertha von Suttner, *Memorien* (Bremen, 1965), 410. Although these memoirs are not available in translation, readers should see Brigitte Hamann, *Bertha von Suttner: A Life for Peace,* trans. Ann Dubsky (Syracuse, NY, 1996), 134–164.
2. Cited in William I. Hull, *The Two Hague Conferences and Their Contributions to International Law* (New York, 1970), 36, 7.
3. Citations in Suttner, *Memorien,* 407–408, 409–410, 426; and Hamann, *Life for Peace,* 140.
4. For the peace movement, see Barbara Tuchman, *The Proud Tower: A Portrait of the World Before the War 1890–1914* (New York, 1962); Roger Chickering, *Imperial Germany and a World Without War: The Peace Movement and German Society 1892–1914* (Princeton, NJ, 1975); Sandi E. Cooper, *Patriotic Pacifism: Waging War on War in Europe 1815–1914* (New York, 1991), 91–115; Hamann, *Life for Peace*; and James J. Sheehan, *Where Have All the Soldiers Gone? The Transformation of Modern Europe* (Boston, 2008), 22–41.
5. Cited in Cooper, *Patriotic Pacifism,* 104.
6. Cited in Hamann, *Life for Peace,* 155.
7. Cited in Cooper, *Patriotic Pacifism,* 87.
8. See James Joll, *The Second International 1889–1914* (London, 1955); and Geoff Eley, *Forging Democracy: The History of the Left in Europe, 1850–2000* (New York, 2002).
9. Cited in Chickering, *Imperial Germany and a World Without War,* 221–222.
10. Citations in Cooper, *Patriotic Pacifism,* 107.
11. For an introduction to politics in these countries, see Eric Dorn Brose, *A History of Europe in the Twentieth Century* (New York, 2005), 30–33, 55–58, 62–63.
12. For an excellent discussion of this thesis, the so-called "primacy of domestic politics," in Germany and throughout Europe, see James Joll and Gordon Martel, *The Origins of the First World War* (Harlow, 2007), 138–184. For Germany in particular, see Wolfgang Mommsen, "Domestic Factors in German Foreign Policy Before 1914," *Central European History* 6 (March 1973): 11–43.
13. Cited in Edvard Radzinsky, *The Last Tsar: The Life and Death of Nicholas II* (New York, 1992), 69.
14. For the following, see Laurence Lafore, *The Long Fuse: An Interpretation of the Origins of World War I* (Philadelphia, 1971), 151–224; Samuel R. Williamson, Jr., *Austria-Hungary and the Origins of the First World War* (New York, 1991), 58–163; Graydon A. Tunstall, Jr., "Austria-Hungary," in Richard F. Hamilton and Holger H. Herwig, eds., *The Origins of World War I* (Cambridge, UK, 2003), 112–149; and Joll and Martel, *Origins of the First World War,* 68–86.
15. Citations in Lafore, *The Long Fuse,* 148, 152; and Tunstall, "Austria-Hungary," in Hamilton and Herwig, *Origins,* 116.
16. Cited in Niall Ferguson, *The Pity of War: Explaining World War I* (New York, 1999), 61.
17. Cited in Joll and Martel, *Origins of the First World War,* 69.
18. Annika Mombauer, *Helmuth von Moltke and the Origins of the First World War* (Cambridge, UK, 2001), 111.
19. Cited in Eugenia C. Kiesling, "France," in Hamilton and Herwig, *Origins,* 242. Also see David Allan Rich, "Russia," 212.
20. Citations in the Report of the International Commission for International Peace, 1913, printed in *The Other Balkan Wars: A 1913 Carnegie Endowment Inquiry in Retrospect* (Washington, DC, 1993), 47, 71.
21. Cited in Joll, *Second International,* 154.
22. Cited in Cooper, *Patriotic Pacifism,* 184.
23. The latest discussion of this crisis and summary of recent research is Joll and Martel, *Origins of the First World War,* 12–48, but also see David Stevenson, *Cataclysm: The First*

World War as Political Tragedy (New York, 2004), 9–35; and David Fromkin, *Europe's Last Summer: Who Started the Great War in 1914?* (New York, 2004), 113–253.
24. Cited in Tunstall, "Austria-Hungary," in Hamilton and Herwig, *Origins*, 124.
25. Cited in Stevenson, *Cataclysm*, 10–11.
26. For historians who emphasize Austro-Hungarian culpability, see Lafore, *The Long Fuse*; Williamson, *Austria-Hungary*; and Tunstall, "Austria-Hungary," in Hamilton and Herwig, *Origins*, 112–149.
27. For the German reaction, see Volker R. Berghahn, *Germany and the Approach of War* (New York, 1973), 186–214; Mombauer, *Helmuth von Moltke*, 186–206; and Fromkin, *Europe's Last Summer*, 153–251.
28. Harry Elmer Barnes, *The Genesis of the World War: An Introduction to the Problem of the War Guilt* (New York, 1926).
29. John F. V. Keiger, *Raymond Poincaré* (Cambridge, UK, 1997).
30. Eugenia C. Kiesling, "France," in Hamilton and Herwig, *Origins*, 247–248. Also see David Alan Rich, "Russia," in *Origins*, 216–225.
31. Cited in Fromkin, *Europe's Last Summer*, 233.
32. Citations in Joll and Martel, *Origins of the First World War*, 18–19, 163.
33. Barnes, *Genesis*, 660.
34. Caroline Playne, *The Pre-War Mind in Britain* (London, 1928), 329–330.
35. Tuchman, *Proud Tower*, xiv.
36. "The Mood of 1914" chapter appeared in James Joll's original 1984 edition as well as the 2007, Joll and Martel, *Origins of the First World War*, 254–298. Although revised to reflect the most recent research, the qualified argument of this third edition chapter still leans heavily toward the view that war was greeted enthusiastically.
37. See the discussions of this literature in Hew Strachan, *The First World War* (Oxford, 2001), 1:133–141; and Brose, *History of Europe in the Twentieth Century*, 132–148.
38. Citations in Hans Kohn, *The Mind of Germany* (New York, 1960), 218; and Hajo Halborn, *A History of Modern Germany 1840–1945* (New York, 1969), 398.
39. For the best general discussions and references to additional sources on specific countries, see Ferguson, *Pity of War*, 174–211; and Strachan, *First World War*, 1:103–133, 141–162.
40. Cited in Martin Gilbert, *The First World War: A Complete History* (New York, 1994), 22.
41. Citations in Jeffrey Verhey, *The Spirit of 1914: Militarism, Myth, and Mobilization in Germany* (Cambridge, UK, 2000), 75, 7.
42. Alfred W. F. Knox, *With the Russian Army 1914–1917* (London, 1921), xxxii; and Alexei Brusilov, *A Soldier's Notebook 1914–1918* (London, 1930), 37.
43. See Sharon Korman, *The Right of Conquest: The Acquisition of Territory by Force in International Law and Practice* (Oxford, 1996). Also see the excellent discussion of "the mood of 1914" in Joll and Martel, *Origins of the First World War*, 254–298.
44. See, in particular, David S. Landes, *The Unbound Prometheus: Technological Change and Industrial Development in Western Europe from 1750 to the Present* (Cambridge, UK, 1969), 248. Landes sees war's outbreak as the end result of economic and technological dynamism and accompanying national rivalry, in contrast to the Marxist view, which stresses the crisis and contradictions of a dying capitalism.
45. Sheehan, *Soldiers Gone*, 40.

PART TWO

THE ABYSS
1914–1918

CHAPTER III

The Opening Campaigns

1914

The lights burnt late into the evening inside the building of the Great General Staff on the Königsplatz in Berlin. In November 1905 the chief of this elite unit of the German army, Count Alfred von Schlieffen, opened the last and most elaborate war game of his thirteen-year career. Now, six weeks later, he stood in the main conference room before the participating officers. Their bold blue uniforms with distinctive red trouser stripes, signifying membership in Germany's military brain trust, lent an air of martial sobriety to the assemblage. All eyes locked on Schlieffen, whose receding hair, elongated ears, and chiseled features marked him as an old and frighteningly serious soldier. His intensity was legendary—sometimes Christmas Eve and Christmas Day turned into normal work times for his subordinates. Tonight's task was less onerous, for the men of the corps assembled to listen to the master's synopsis of the lessons of the recently concluded forty-two-day simulation.

1905's game posited simultaneous campaigns against the Russians, the French, and—for the first time in such games—a British Expeditionary Force (BEF). The ground rules divided the German army roughly evenly between defensive positions in east and west—in East Prussia 19 corps (38 divisions of 12,000 infantry each); along the western frontier 16 corps (32 divisions). The eastern campaign went smoothly, resulting in the annihilation of Russian forces in five weeks and the transfer of 3 corps to Antwerp. Only days earlier the French and British had extended their strong left (northern) wing eastward through most of Belgium along a line stretching from Antwerp to the fortress zone of Liége. Farther south a French assault into Alsace and Lorraine had already been beaten back, allowing the transfer of 3 additional corps by rail to Antwerp. In the sixth week of mobilization German forces, having already defeated the Russians, struck the Franco-British left flank south of Antwerp and rolled southward down their line, while other army groups, having already won in Alsace and Lorraine, attacked from Metz to entrap the allies. By Day 42 of the exercise Germany had surrounded the French and British in southern Belgium and Luxembourg.

Having summed up the results, Schlieffen commented on the game's contribution to general operational thinking. Even if Germany opted initially to assume a defensive posture, war could never be allowed to bog down into siege or "positional" warfare. Opportunities for attack or counterattack had to be seized regardless of the risks. In such maneuvers it was always better to envelop the enemy's flank in force in order to achieve decisive victory, for the alternative was one or two years of attrition, exhaustion, and economic chaos. "It is not true that he considered *only* a short war possible," recalled one of his General Staffers. "The truth is that his goal was *as short a war as possible.*"[1] With the end discussion finally terminated, the lights were allowed to dim on the Königsplatz.

THE PLANS OF SCHLIEFFEN AND MOLTKE

Since 1894, when the Franco-Russian alliance went into effect, German army leaders faced the unenviable task of simultaneously waging war against enemies that outflanked the empire on opposite fronts. Berlin's strategic options were limited to three: defeat France and then turn against Russia; defeat Russia and then turn against France; or, as in the 1905 simulation described in the opening vignette, divide the army to defend both east and west, and then counterattack. Clearly, with British participation in a continental war increasingly likely after 1906, whichever strategy Germany chose had to settle matters as quickly as possible in Europe lest the mighty Central European juggernaut face an enervating long-term war of attrition exacerbated by a blockade of the superior British fleet.

Much was at stake—the destiny of empires, the future of homelands, all, in short, that leaders and followers fought for. Important enough at the time, Germany's strategic decisions in 1914 became over subsequent decades a subject of intense historical scrutiny and more recently a topic of raging historical debate. For most of the twentieth century one interpretation dominated Great War monographs and textbooks concerning what Schlieffen planned in the event of a two-front war—namely, that he adhered rigidly, almost monomaniacally, to a massive offensive sweep through Belgium from the first moment of mobilization with the bulk of the German army marching toward Paris, swinging around the city, and then trapping the French somewhere southeast of the capital in a Hannibal-like battle of annihilation. The victory had to be total and quick—inside of forty days—for a mobilizing Russia would soon threaten in the east. This thesis ruled so thoroughly, and for so many years, that it became a seemingly unshakeable historiographical orthodoxy.[2]

The scene opening our current chapter, however, shows a different side of Schlieffen's mind-set. The vignette is grounded in a document describing Schlieffen's last war game that was found in German archives a decade ago by Terence Zuber, author of a remarkable and highly controversial article on the operational plans of the long-time chief of the German General Staff. In this revisionist work, Zuber argues that Schlieffen was much more flexible concerning wartime options. In the case of the aforementioned simulation, which came just months before his retirement, he considered a division of forces, defensive dispositions at war's onset, and counterattack in the first weeks of combat. It is also instructive that even after counterattacking Franco-British forces on the western front, German armies never strayed far from their own border in a quest for crippling battle victories. This latter point is central to Zuber's overall argument.[3]

Others have been quick to point out that Schlieffen designed simulations like this one to educate future generals, not to practice an actual mobilization plan, and that he clearly preferred attacking first, not defending, and then counterattacking later.[4] Furthermore, they have shown that other war games that very same year actually played out the "sweep around Paris" scenario. Nevertheless, a consensus seems to be building that Germany's great operational genius kept his mind open. Like generals before and after him, Schlieffen would exploit the situation he faced in the field to find the most effective route to victory.

Zuber also found other documents dealing with German war planning from 1892 to 1906, the years when Schlieffen headed the General Staff. Three of the most interesting deal with the so-called staff rides (*Stabsreisen*) of 1904 and early 1905, simulations or war games played out in the field by Schlieffen and his underlings. In all three exercises the chief preferred to send most of his forces west, not east, with two or three army groups invading Belgium with operational orders to swing as far north as Lille before pivoting southward to envelop the French. In all of these cases, however—even when Schlieffen commanded German armies personally during the third ride in 1905—the right-wing armies wheeled southward almost immediately out of eastern Belgium in order to outflank French armies attacking into Lorraine. This response had the added advantage of keeping German armies near railroad hubs in western Germany for transfer to the eastern front where a Russian invasion threatened. "The decisive battle in the west had to be fought and won close to the German railheads," writes Zuber. "If the Germans had fought the battle further west, say between Verdun and Rheims ... then these German forces, no matter how victorious, would have been unavailable for immediate rail movement east."[5]

The document usually used by historians to prove that Schlieffen and his successors adhered to a grandiose operational plan to encircle French armies near Paris is the master's final position paper (*Denkschrift*) before leaving office in early 1906. But even here, argues Zuber, Schlieffen remained preoccupied with winning the decisive battles in Belgium or along the Franco-Belgian frontier and presented only a worst-case scenario wherein the French army might fall back to defensive positions between Verdun and Paris, in which case the German right-wing armies would be forced to envelop this line by swinging around Paris. Maps prepared by the General Staff five years after Schlieffen's retirement in order to gauge the total elapsed time that would have been required for such a victory estimated thirty-one days just to reach the Somme River far to the north of Paris. Clearly any final victory around the capital would take far longer than the thirty-nine-day campaign described in most standard works as "the plan." Underscoring the nightmarish nature of this contingency, Zuber observes that "even if the campaign ended at [around fifty days] . . . in a two-front war it would take nearly as long again to march the troops back to German railheads for transfer east."[6]

As readers can readily imagine, Zuber's challenge to Schlieffen Plan historical orthodoxy was guaranteed to ruffle feathers and provoke criticism. In one informative rejoinder, for instance, Terence M. Holmes argues that certain conditions prevailing in the winter of 1905–1906 made the march on Paris a more distinct albeit disturbing possibility to Schlieffen.[7] First, with Russia lamed by war and revolution, France might opt not to attack but rather to defend along its fortress line, thereby making it easier for them to establish a firm northern front between Paris and Verdun. It should also be noted that Schlieffen now had to reckon with the BEF on the French left flank, reinforcing the need to swing on a more northerly and westerly arc around the enemy.[8] In one of the most recent contributions to this heated debate, moreover, Gerhard P. Gross, digging even deeper in the archives than Zuber, unearthed two war-games documents from 1905 demonstrating that Schlieffen actually played out scenarios whereby his divisions swung through Belgium and penetrated far into France in search of a smashing victory. Like Holmes, however, Gross believes these were very specific to 1905's unique opportunity to fight in the west without worrying about Russia in the east and that even so they probably represented worst-case scenarios—one of these games did not produce victory until the fifty-sixth day of mobilization, clearly too long in a two-front war.

Although the master does not seem to have held out much hope for winning a quick battle of annihilation deep inside France, his successor in early 1906, Helmuth von Moltke, waxed far more pessimistic. A gloomy, brooding man with a predilection to envision dire scenarios, he predicted a "general European war of murder," a "massacre whose horror can only make one shudder to think." It would be "a people's war that cannot be won in one decisive battle but will turn into a long, difficult, painful struggle."[9] The unnerving possibility of a long war weighed even more heavily on him after a General Staff study of 1910 concluded that a war against France could not be won in a single campaign. Because Schlieffen's final paper had looked into such a single-campaign victory, however, Moltke decided to test the relevancy and feasibility of winning near Paris—hence the preparation of maps in 1911 mentioned earlier. The conclusion was a very unfavorable one. The German army did not possess the necessary regular and reserve corps to conduct such an extensive maneuver, for one thing, nor did it seem wise to weaken defending forces in Lorraine in order to beef up the right-wing enveloping armies that might have to drive all the way to the enemy capital and beyond.

Related to this latter point, Moltke expected the French to attack, not defend. And when they attacked, Moltke, like Schlieffen in earlier war games, preferred to decide the opening campaign in Belgium, the Ardennes Forest, eastern France, and Lorraine. His own staff rides of 1906 and 1908 unfolded much as his predecessor's of 1904 and 1905 had done. Once the French committed themselves to an offensive, the Germans counterattacked along the Franco-German border while right-wing armies wheeled due south out of Belgium to envelop the French fortress line. The maneuver in Belgium, wrote Moltke in 1906, was not "an end in itself" but rather "a means to an end."[10] As Holmes explains, "the whole purpose of the advance through Belgium was to engage the French army in the open, but once the French emerged from their fortified positions that object was achieved and there was no need for the detour [toward Paris]."[11] Thus both men sought minimally a rapid crippling of the French army—one that would eliminate perhaps nine enemy corps and permit the transfer of an equal number of German corps to East Prussia while remaining German divisions mopped up in a second campaign that would eventually force France to surrender well into the autumn or early winter.

Contingency Planner: Alfred von Schlieffen
Walter Goerlitz, *The German General Staff: 1657–1945* (New York, 1953)

As Germany mobilized its huge army in late July 1914, Moltke's operational orders remained consistent with prewar General Staff thinking. Anticipating a main French thrust into Lorraine and possibly a secondary strike into Belgium, he deployed his forces accordingly. Of eighty-one regular and reserve divisions available, Moltke distributed sixty-eight into seven armies for the initial fighting in the west. Two divisions would stand guard in Schleswig-Holstein against a possible British landing in northern Germany, while two more divisions were held in reserve, bringing maximum possible strength on this front to 1.7 million men (including a handful of *Ersatz* or replacement divisions available after mobilization). Only nine regular and reserve divisions, one lone army, were left to defend East Prussia.

The First, Second, and Third Armies, consisting of thirty-two divisions or almost 40 percent of total army strength—far less than what Schlieffen recommended in his last paper—would invade Belgium along a front from Liège to Bastogne. A coup de main at the Fortress of Liège would clear the path for First and Second Armies.[12] The object here, recalled Moltke, was to engage Franco-British-Belgian forces and "drive them southeastwards and away from

Contingency Planner: Helmuth von Moltke
Walter Goerlitz, *The German General Staff: 1657–1945* (New York, 1953)

Paris."[13] Fourth and Fifth Armies, with a combined strength of twenty divisions, would advance out of Lorraine to meet the main French drive head-on, while Sixth and Seventh Armies, sixteen divisions strong, stood at the ready in southern Lorraine and Alsace to defend, counterattack if the opportunity presented itself, and then roll up the French fortress line from the south. Two of Germany's heaviest siege guns, the huge 420 mm "Gamma" howitzers, were positioned here for this explicit purpose. The ideal scenario, therefore, was a crippling double envelopment along the frontier—and if the iron dice rolled luckily enough, perhaps that elusive, unlikely campaign of annihilation.[14]

FROM THE FRONTIERS TO THE MARNE

French General Headquarters (GQG), headed by General Joseph Joffre, went into action with Plan 17 but intended, like German High Command (OHL), to be flexible and watch closely how events unfolded on the frontiers.[15] The aim was to recapture the lost provinces of Alsace and Lorraine and then proceed from there. The plan's main offensive thrusts would pierce southern Lorraine around Sarrebourg (Saarburg) and through the Ardennes Forest into northern Lorraine. Joffre deployed 23 divisions with his First and Second Armies for the southern operation, with 20 divisions allotted to Third and Fourth Armies for the Ardennes strike—later reduced to 18 by an overconfident Joffre. Fifth Army's 13 divisions were echeloned on the left rear flank of Fourth Army, ready to attack eastward with Third and Fourth Armies or move into southern Belgium if the enemy threatened there. A significant number of reserve and territorial divisions were also available. With the British and the Belgians, Paris would have about 2.2 million men in the field.

Although there was still no definitive coordination with the British, Joffre assumed that the four- (later six) division BEF, commanded by Sir John French, would take up positions on the left flank of General Charles Lanrezac's Fifth Army. The Belgian army's badly trained and poorly equipped six divisions brought total allied strength in the north to twenty-three divisions, and to their left, spread thinly along the Belgian border, three territorial divisions (Group D'Amade). No one at GQG or in the BEF had any idea, however, whether the Belgians would

Monster Gun: Stationary 420 mm Gamma Howitzer
Karl Justrow, *Die Dicke Berta und der Krieg* (Berlin, 1935)

defend Liège, fall back to Antwerp, or move south to link up with the British and the French—in fact, the Belgians did not yet know themselves. It should be clear from all of this that French planning could not have been more favorable to the Germans if they had themselves drawn up enemy operations. The allies' Achilles heel lay on the left flank where Germany's initial thirty-two divisions (plus two in Schleswig-Holstein) possessed a smashing quantitative preponderance and the added advantage of a comparatively well-planned and coordinated attack.

With declarations of war being made in the first days of August, King Albert of Belgium decided to send one division to reinforce the Liège garrison, one division to the Fortress of Namur at the confluence of the Sambre and Meuse Rivers, and the rest to defend eastern Belgium on the Gette River below Diest. Not anticipating any extra troops at Liège, the German coup de main suffered heavy losses on August 5–7 and failed to take most of the forts surrounding the city. This setback forced OHL to order forward all available heavy siege guns. Commencing fire on August 12, four batteries of Skoda 305 mm howitzers on loan from the Austrians and one battery of gargantuan 420 mm "M-Guns"—a more mobile variant of the Gamma devices—destroyed enough of the forts in two days to allow the German First Army under Alexander von Kluck to cross the border. Behind it marched Karl von Bülow's Second Army. Moving parallel to them on the southern side of the Meuse, Max Klemens von Hansen's Third Army streamed into southern Belgium toward Dinant. By August 20 he was approaching the town, while Bülow surrounded Namur and Kluck entered Brussels.

Lanrezac, meanwhile, had moved north into the salient formed by the Sambre and the Meuse. Having landed in France and proceeded to the country surrounding the Fortress of Maubeuge, the BEF now moved forward to Mons, fifteen kilometers to the west of Fifth Army's left flank. Joined by the defending division at Liège, five

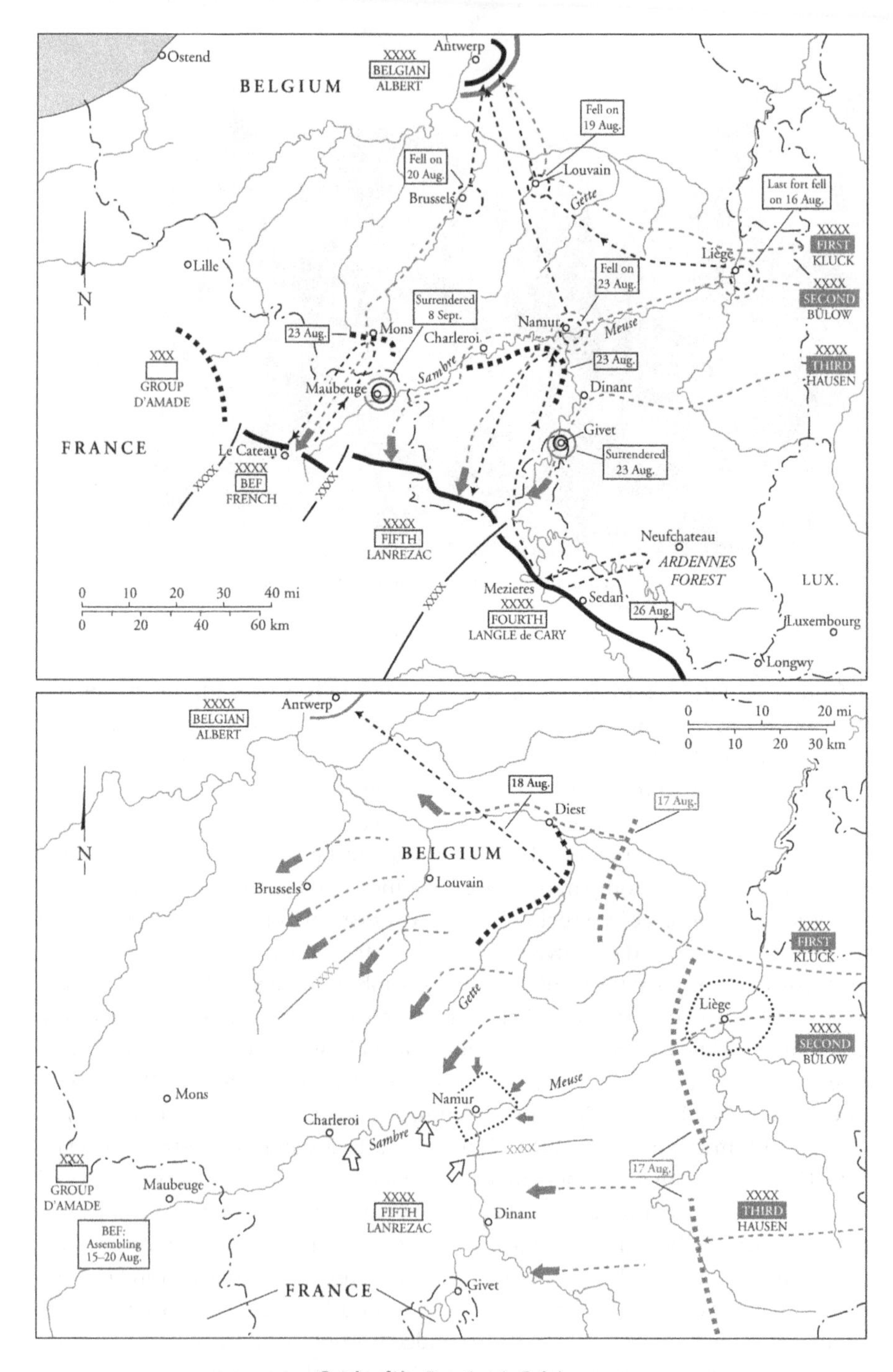

Battle of the Frontiers in Belgium

Maps Courtesy of the Department of History, United States Military Academy

divisions of the Belgian army retreated inside the walls of Antwerp. GQG received reports in mid-August that the Germans were advancing in strength into Belgium, but Joffre actually welcomed this, for he assumed it meant OHL would concentrate fewer divisions in the center, where his Third and Fourth Armies could smash through the enemy's "most sensitive point"[16] and unhinge the door swinging through Belgium.

The major combat of what came to be known as the Battle of the Frontiers took place on August 20–23. The first furious fighting occurred in southern Lorraine where the French Second Army, having progressed thirty-five kilometers, was hit at Morhange by the German Sixth Army that counterattacked with superior artillery fire from 105 mm and 150 mm howitzers. The barrage crushed Second Army formations that were assembling in tight ranks for the days' march, forcing it to flee and thereby compelling an exposed First Army to retreat as well. Both French armies managed to extricate themselves from the region they had invaded because the Germans, badly mauled themselves, took two days to regroup before giving chase. As would happen frequently (although not universally) on the western front in 1914, both sides had paid too little attention to available infantry tactics that, by spreading units out as opposed to packing them together, would have limited casualties. The French Third and Fourth Armies attacking into the Ardennes met the same fate on August 22. In terrible clashes that took a heavy toll on both sides, neither army could gain an advantage. Finally, a fateful assault at Neufchateau by French Fourth Army's 17,000-man strong Colonial Corps triggered collapse along the whole line. Charging with bayonets repeatedly against entrenched German regulars backed by machine guns and heavy artillery fire, the colonials suffered unsustainable losses—11,000 men went down. "They were trying to beat down a hail of artillery, machine gun, and rifle fire with bare steel,"[17] writes one historian. Their rout caused the rest of Fourth Army to retreat, making withdrawal mandatory for Third Army as well. Once again, however, the bloodied German Fourth and Fifth Armies could not immediately follow up their victory.

Matters were decided on the Sambre-Meuse during the days of August 21–23. Having spotted Lanrezac's army through short-range aerial reconnaissance, Bülow wheeled Second Army south, crossed the Sambre, and attacked the French with eight divisions on August 21–22 even though he was outnumbered. However, he ordered Hausen's Third Army to mount an assault on Lanrezac's right flank at Dinant on August 23 and Kluck's First Army simultaneously to sweep west and south around the French left.[18] This operational scheme was therefore quite consistent with pre-1914 war games and staff rides, which typically featured such a southerly turn in Belgium to find and destroy the enemy in the field. The headstrong commander of First Army balked at this command, for, although he had not located the BEF there were some indications that it was to the northwest, and if this were true Bülow's orders would expose First Army to a flanking attack. Kluck therefore countermanded both Bülow and Moltke, who had supported Bülow, and moved only three of his five corps south to Mons, where they ran headlong into the BEF's two corps in strong defensive positions behind a canal. Kluck's costly attacks failed repeatedly until the British finally disengaged and fled to the southwest. Second and Third Army also met stiff resistance on August

Waiting for the Onslaught: General Joseph Joffre
Canfield, *World War*

23, then could not prevent Lanrezac from escaping on the following day. Kluck forged ahead in hot pursuit of the BEF, inflicting heavy losses at Landrecies and Le Cateau on August 25–26. He could not entrap the retreating BEF, but these battles, coming after British disappointment over not winning at Mons, severely undermined the morale of an army whose regulars were accustomed to fighting overmatched natives in the empire, not German regulars, and whose reservists were untested and often unfit—both subsequently deserted in high numbers, the highest percentages of the British army, in fact, of the entire Great War.[19]

Even with these misfortunes the Germans could still have trapped the allies in the Sambre/Meuse salient. On August 22 OHL ordered four divisions from Fourth Army to disengage and march northwest over the Meuse to strike Lanrezac's right rear flank. Prince Albrecht, commanding Fourth Army, countermanded the order, however, due to worries over the ferocious bayonet charges of the French Colonial Corps. Its thousands of mangled corpses may have been more, therefore, than a gory symbol of the futility of modern combat, for they had probably saved the French Fifth Army. Joffre, however, would have none of this. In one of the most outrageous statements of the Great War, the French commander in chief did not blame himself for failing to sense that Third and Fourth Armies had hardly attacked OHL's "most sensitive point"—in fact they flew into forces greater by two divisions—and instead laid failure at the doorstep of his officers and men, who despite allegedly superior numbers against a supposedly weak point in the enemy line had committed "many individual failures." The most recent historian of French operations accurately labels this "pure balderdash."[20]

Having failed to crush the allies near the border to facilitate rapid reinforcements by train to the east where the Russians were threatening, all seven German armies now gave chase. In the south Sixth and Seventh Armies, bolstered by all reserve and *Ersatz* divisions as well as a large contingent of 210 mm, 305 mm, and 420 mm heavy artillery, drove toward the Fortress of Epinal. A successful French counterattack on August 25 halted the attackers for two days, and then Moltke ordered the assault to shift north to the Fortress of Nancy. If they could reduce the forts they should proceed west to strike the rear of French armies defending against the onrushing German armies. The attack on Nancy commenced September 3.

In the center the German Fourth and Fifth Armies crossed the Meuse with great loss of life as France's rapid-firing 75 mm field gun pounded the enemy from long-range hidden positions. Once across the river, however, the attackers attempted to slip around the fortress zone at Verdun. They were reinforced by Hausen's Third Army, which raced south out of Belgium—almost exactly as practiced in prewar games. By September 2 the German front here extended from the region around Verdun to Rheims. Their mission was to close with Sixth and Seventh Armies in a pincer movement that would trap four French armies to the west of the fortress line. The operation would include an assault on five of Verdun's forts on the Meuse south of the main fortress complex.

In the north First and Second Armies' 17.5 divisions pursued Lanrezac's Fifth Army, the BEF, and other divisions that Joffre hastily tried to assemble.[21] Kluck routed everything sent against him in a series of battles from August 26 to August 29. Bülow fought a bloody battle with Lanrezac at Guise-St. Quentin on August 29–30 and then paused to regroup. By early September both advancing armies had crossed the Marne River east of Paris.

At this point Moltke ordered First and Second Armies to face west to shield the flank of Third, Fourth, and Fifth Armies as they closed their trap. OHL had learned from aerial reconnaissance that Joffre, gambling that the fortress line could hold off the Germans with fewer field divisions, had shifted soldiers from his First and Second Armies to the region around Paris, where they joined garrison forces, divisions that had retreated from the north, colonial troops, and a patchwork of other units. Thus Kluck and Bülow should parry the blow of this impending counterattack.

Joffre's assembled forces struck on September 5–6 just as Moltke's final offensive was commencing in the east. What has come to be known as the Battle of the Marne should really be thought of as the Battle of France, for altogether 56 allied and 43.5 German divisions engaged one another in a titanic struggle along a line stretching from Paris to the eastern frontier. To the surprise of the Germans, GQG had cobbled together two new armies: one, the Sixth, that sortied from Paris; and another, the Ninth, that moved into line on Fifth Army's right flank south of the Petit Morin River. The BEF manned Fifth army's left flank southeast of Paris. Kluck and Bülow were outnumbered two-to-one by enemy forces they incorrectly assumed were beaten and demoralized. "That men will let themselves be killed where they stand is a well-known thing and counted on in every plan of battle," recalled a dumbfounded Kluck. "But that men who have retreated for ten days, sleeping on the ground and half dead with fatigue, should be able to

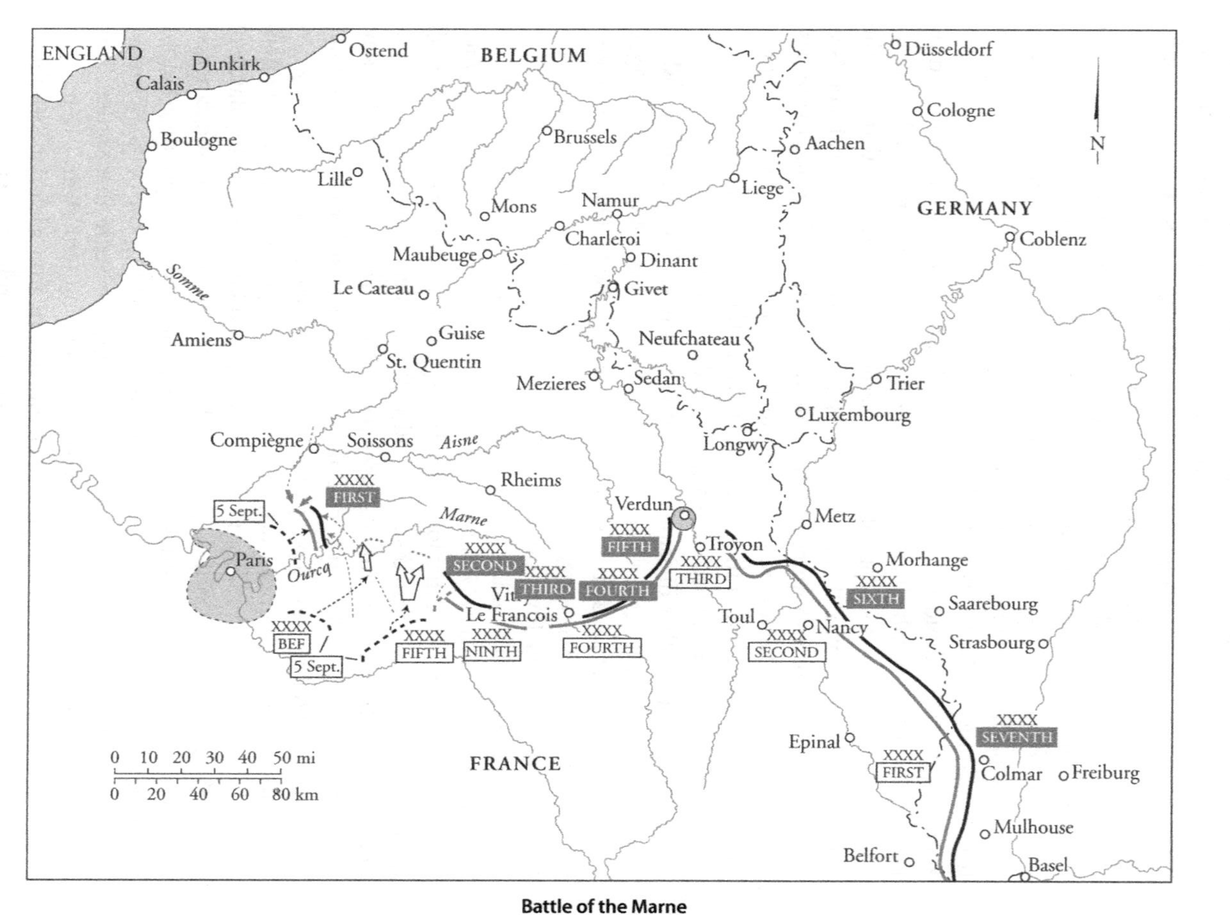

Battle of the Marne

Maps Courtesy of the Department of History, United States Military Academy

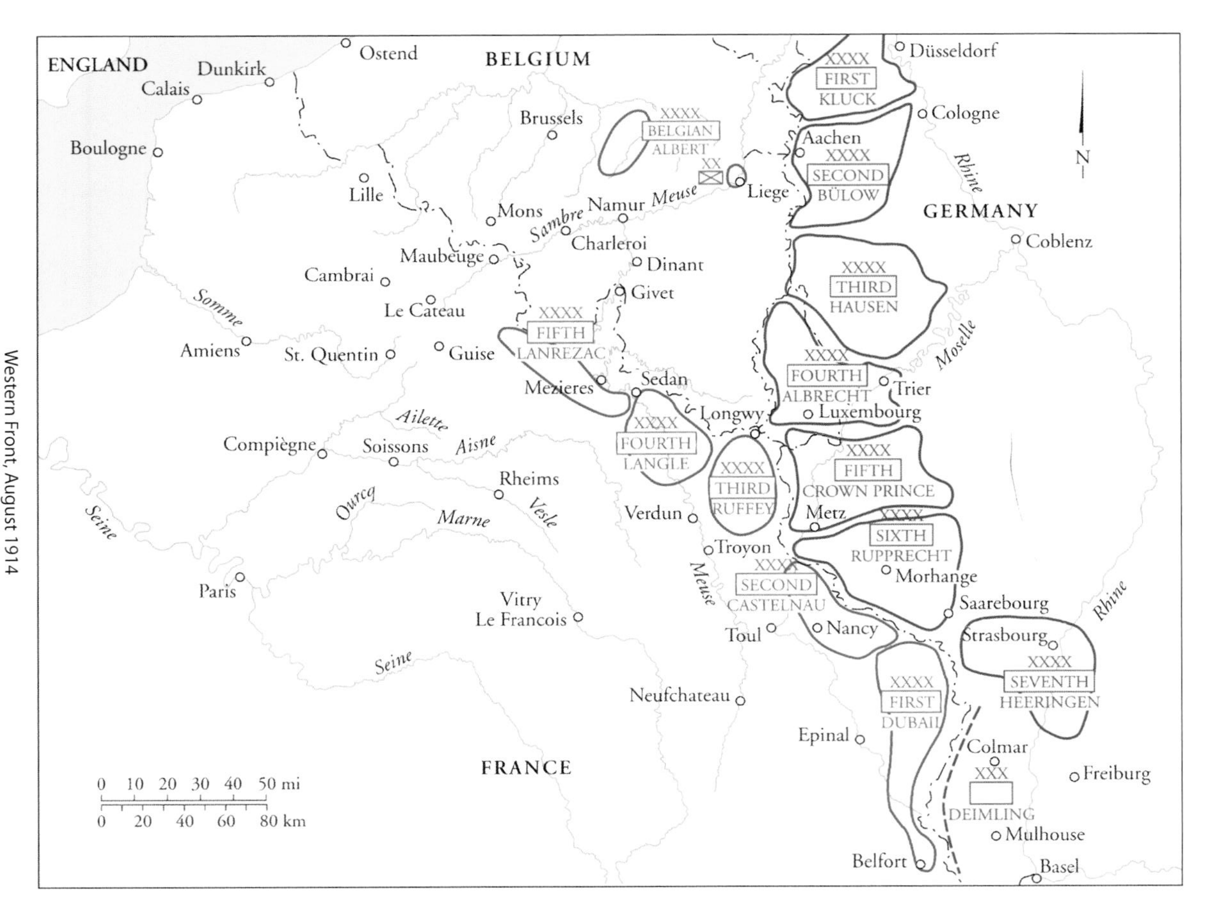

Western Front, August 1914
Maps Courtesy of the Department of History, United States Military Academy

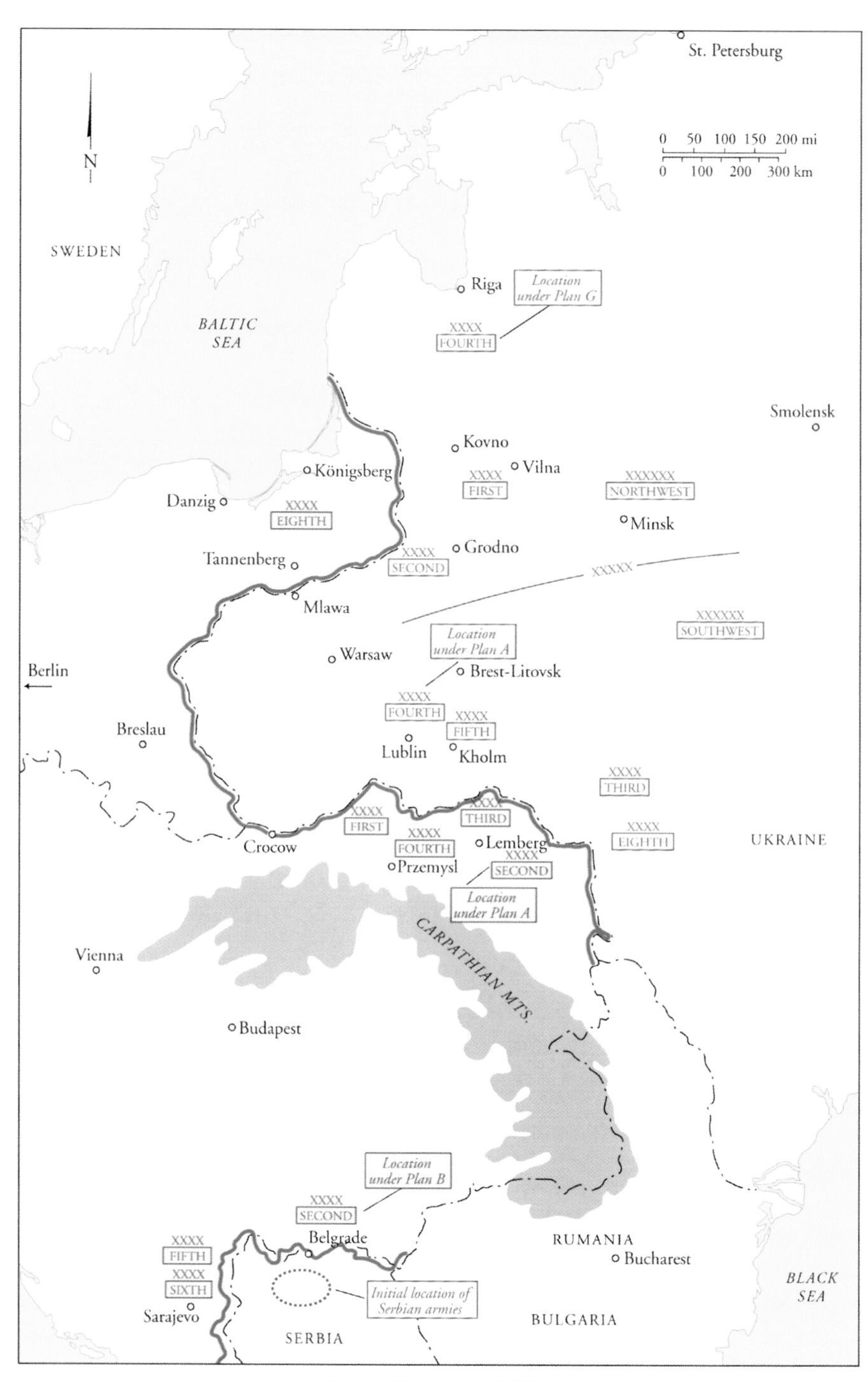

Eastern Front, August 1914
Maps Courtesy of the Department of History, United States Military Academy

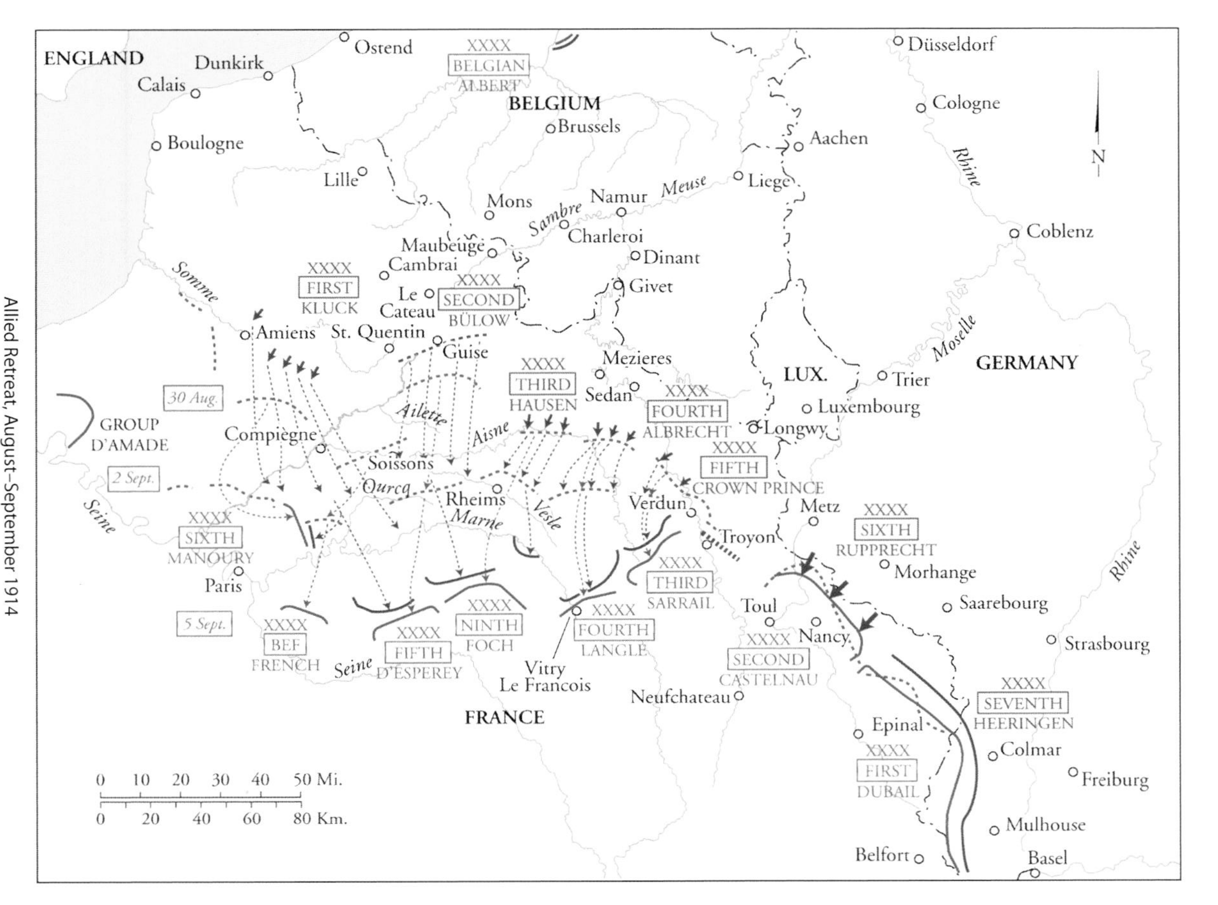

Allied Retreat, August–September 1914
Maps Courtesy of the Department of History, United States Military Academy

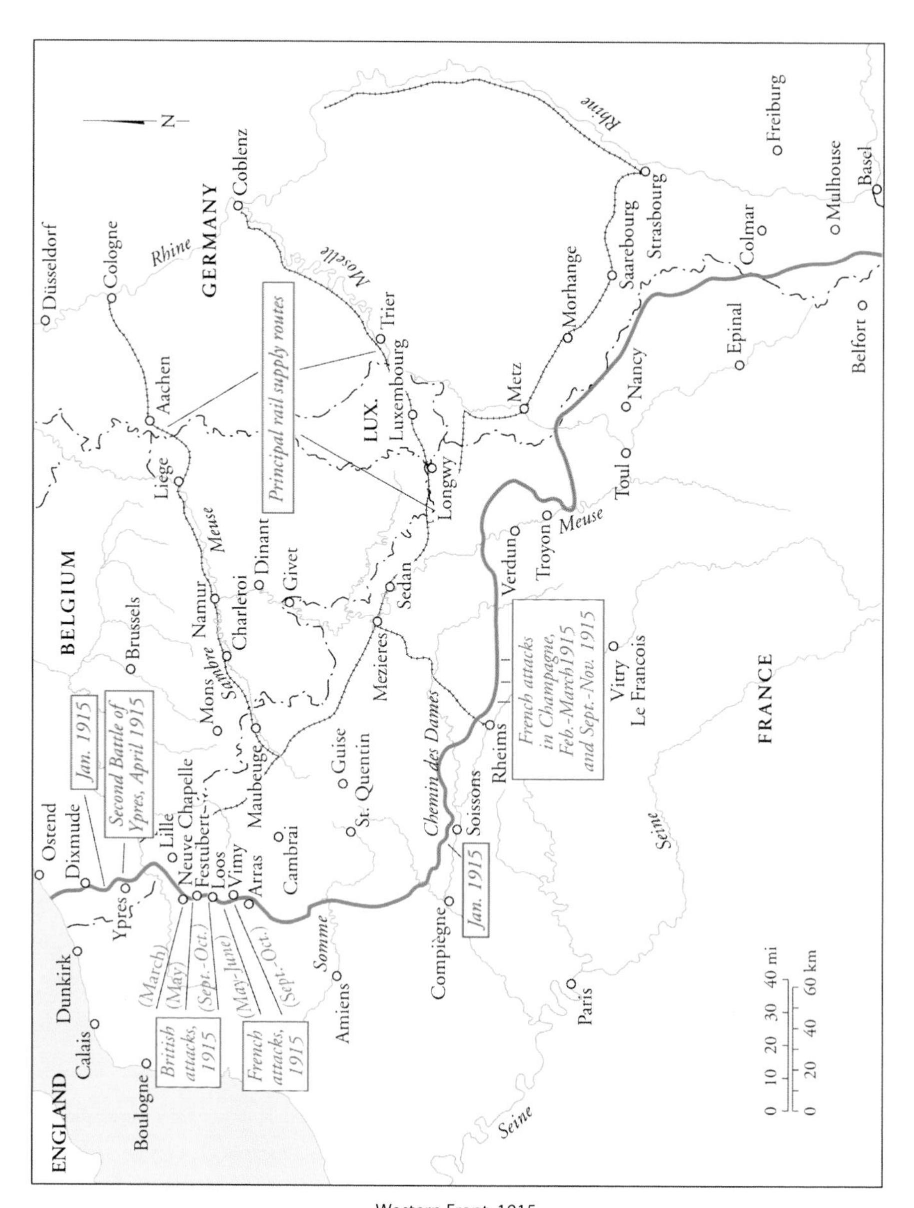

Western Front, 1915
Maps Courtesy of the Department of History, United States Military Academy

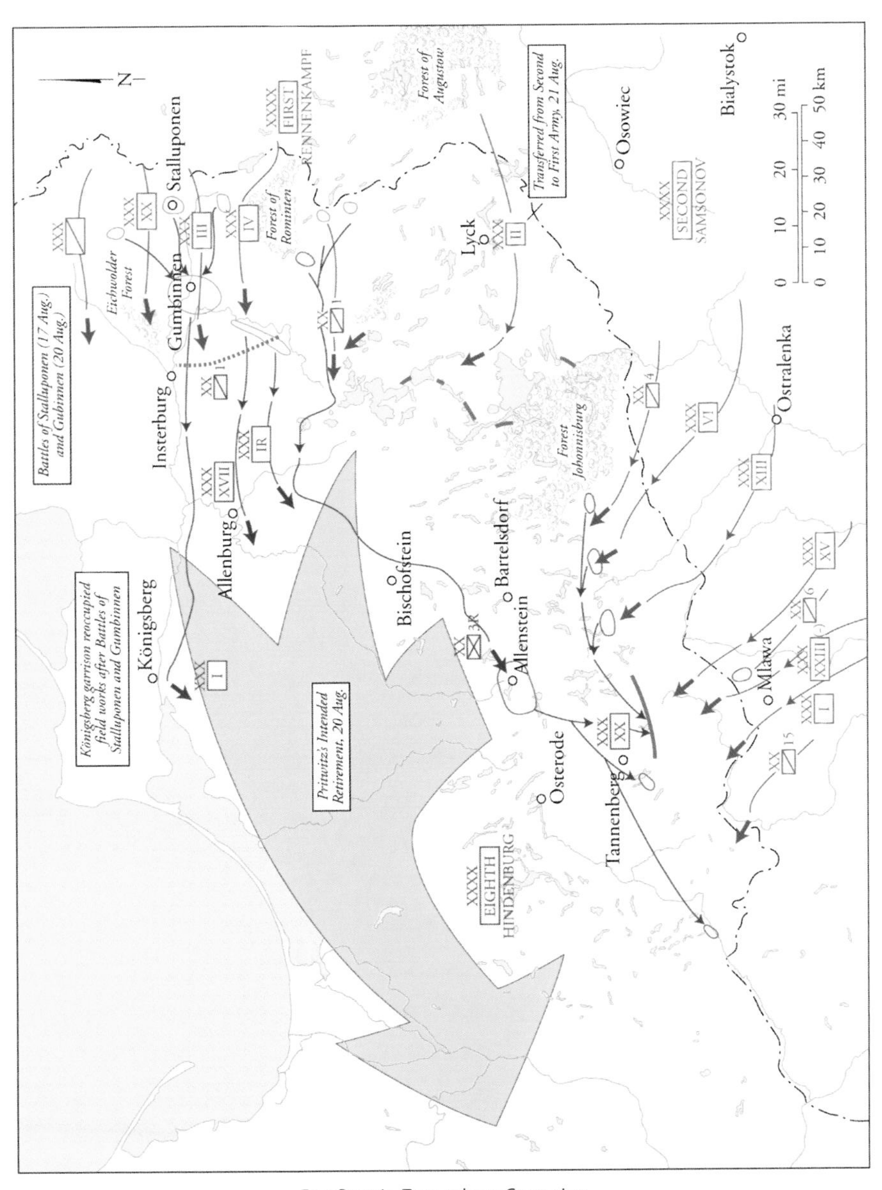

East Prussia, Tannenberg Campaign

Maps Courtesy of the Department of History, United States Military Academy

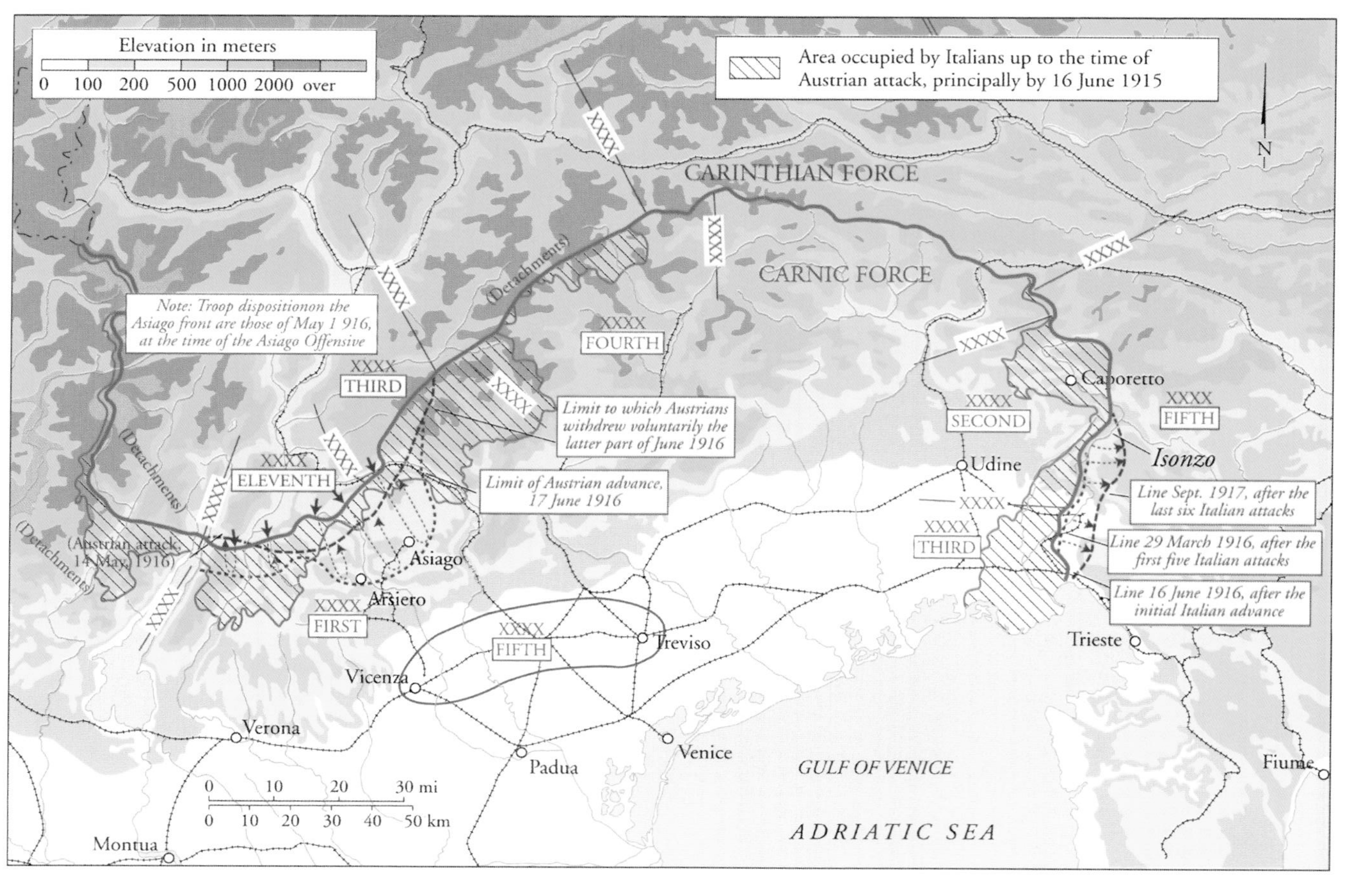

Isonzo and Trentino Campaigns, 1915–1916
Maps Courtesy of the Department of History, United States Military Academy

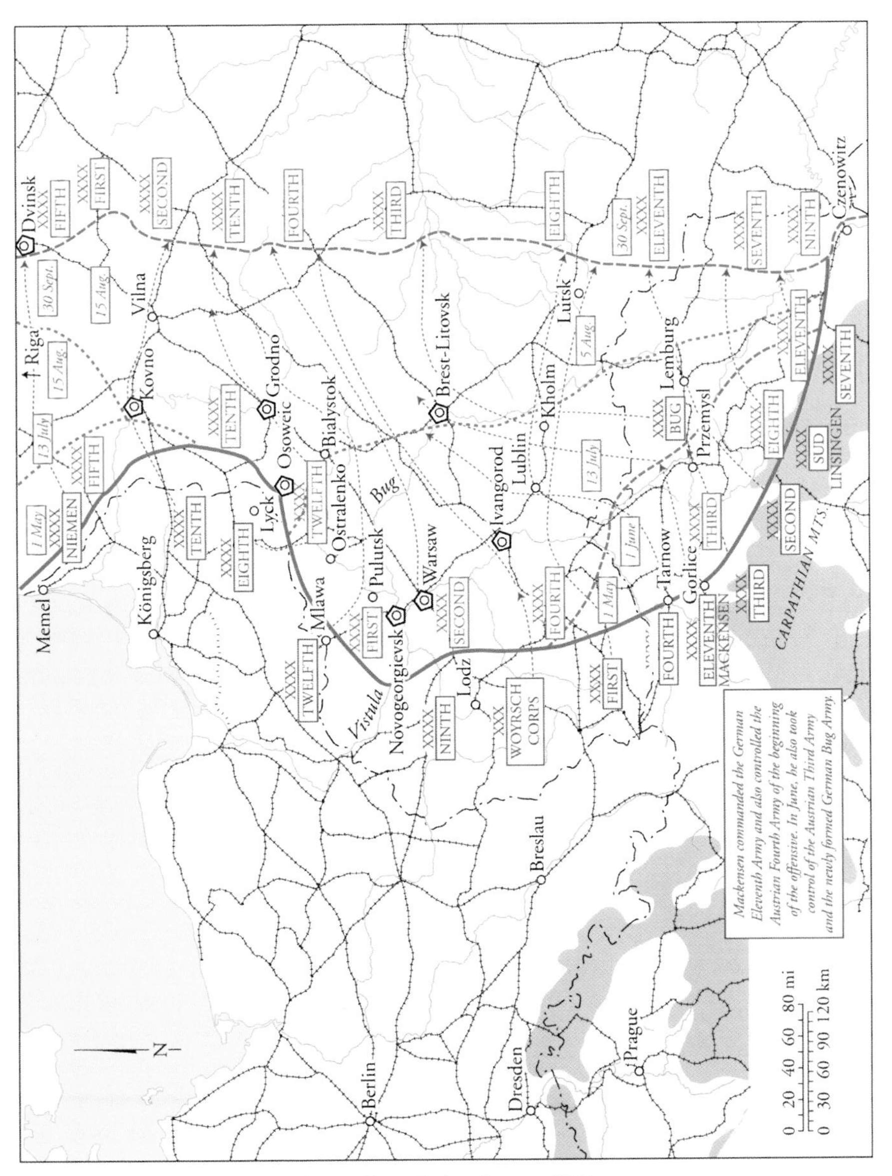

Eastern Front, Spring–Summer 1915

Maps Courtesy of the Department of History, United States Military Academy

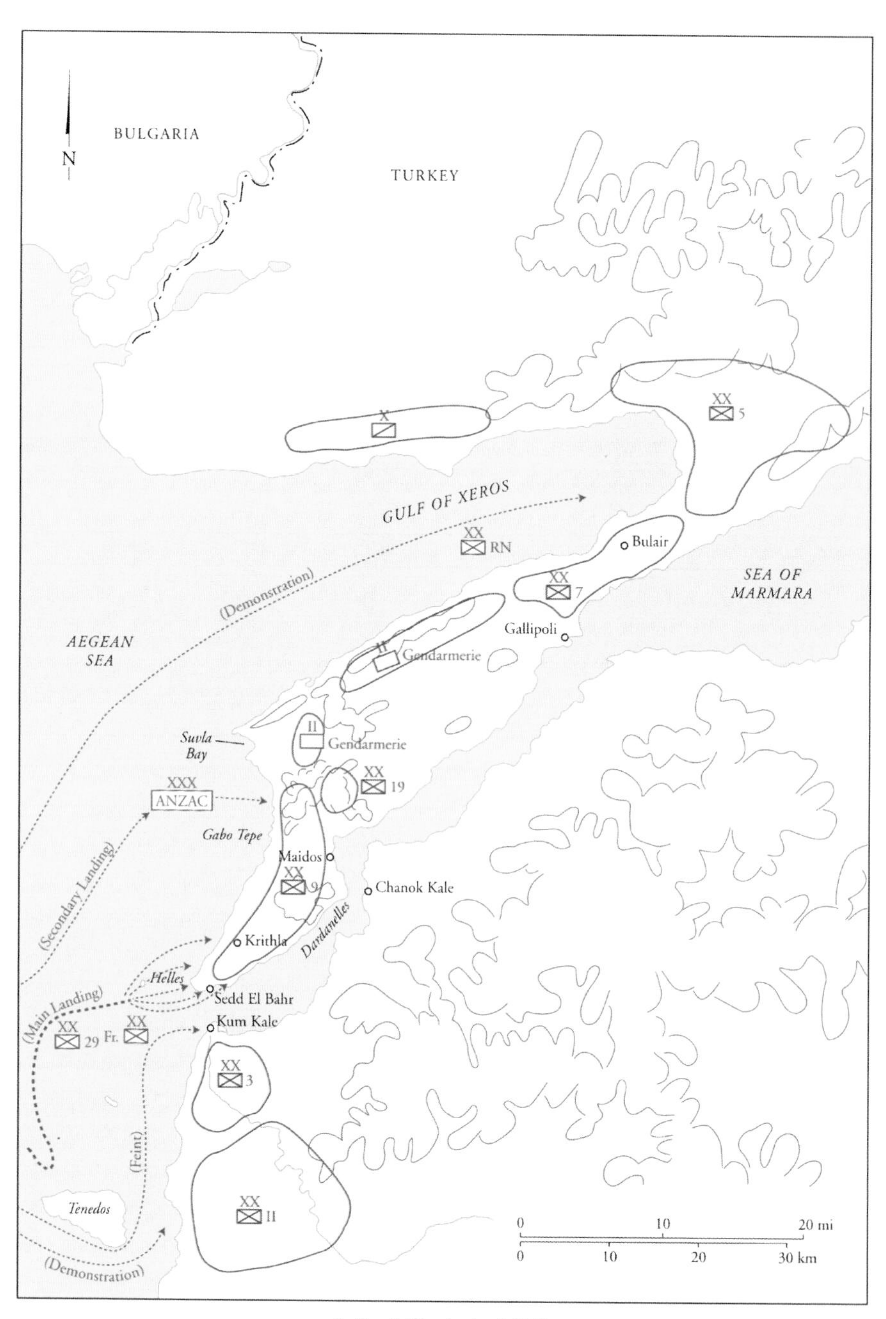

Gallipoli, March–April 1915
Maps Courtesy of the Department of History, United States Military Academy

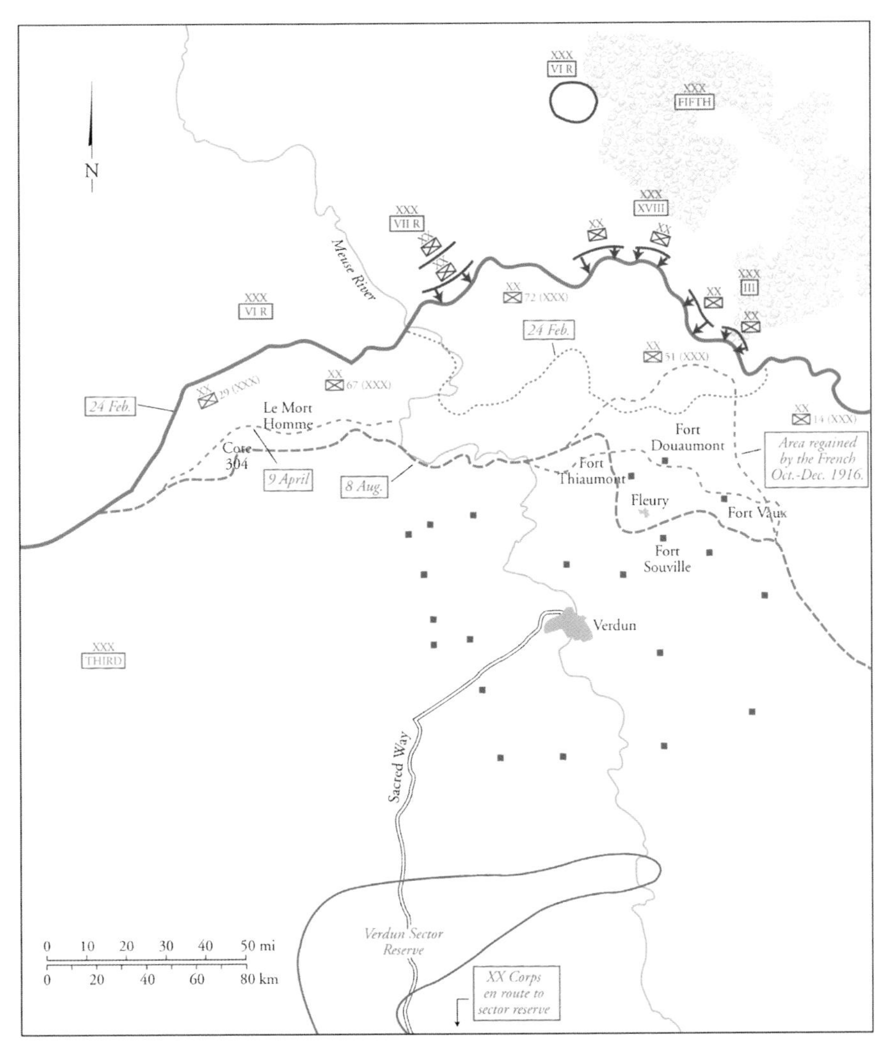

Battle of Verdun, 1916
Maps Courtesy of the Department of History, United States Military Academy

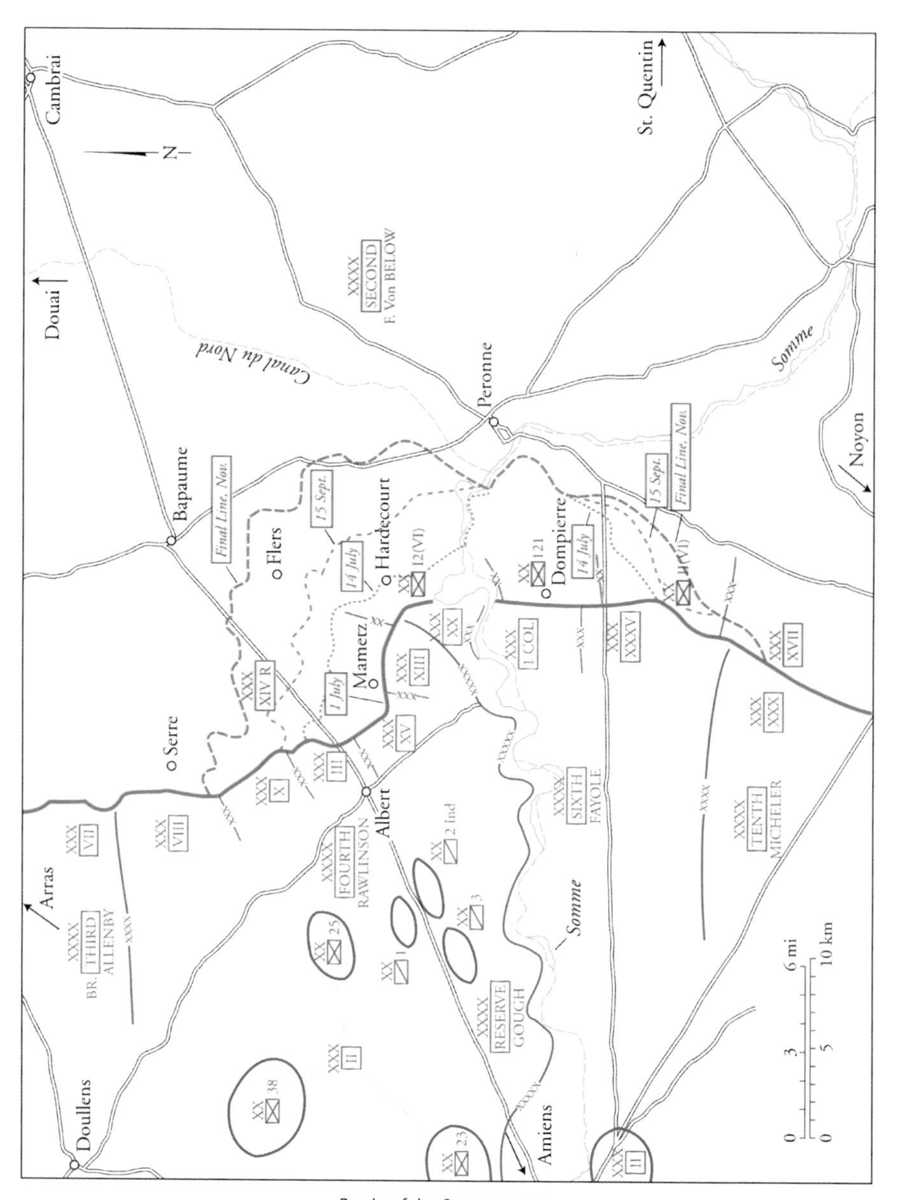

Battle of the Somme, 1916
Maps Courtesy of the Department of History, United States Military Academy

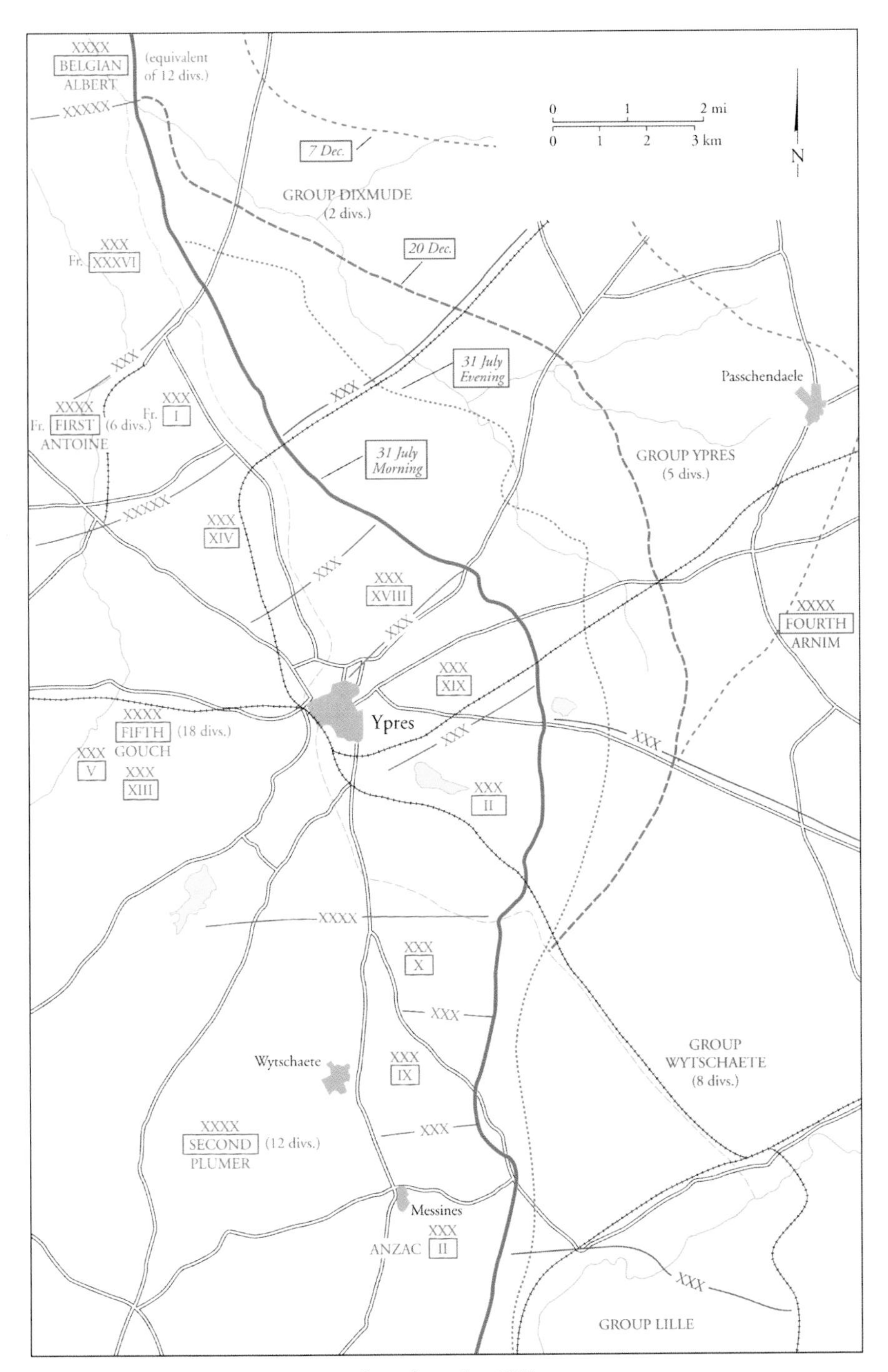

Ypres Campaign, 1917
Maps Courtesy of the Department of History, United States Military Academy

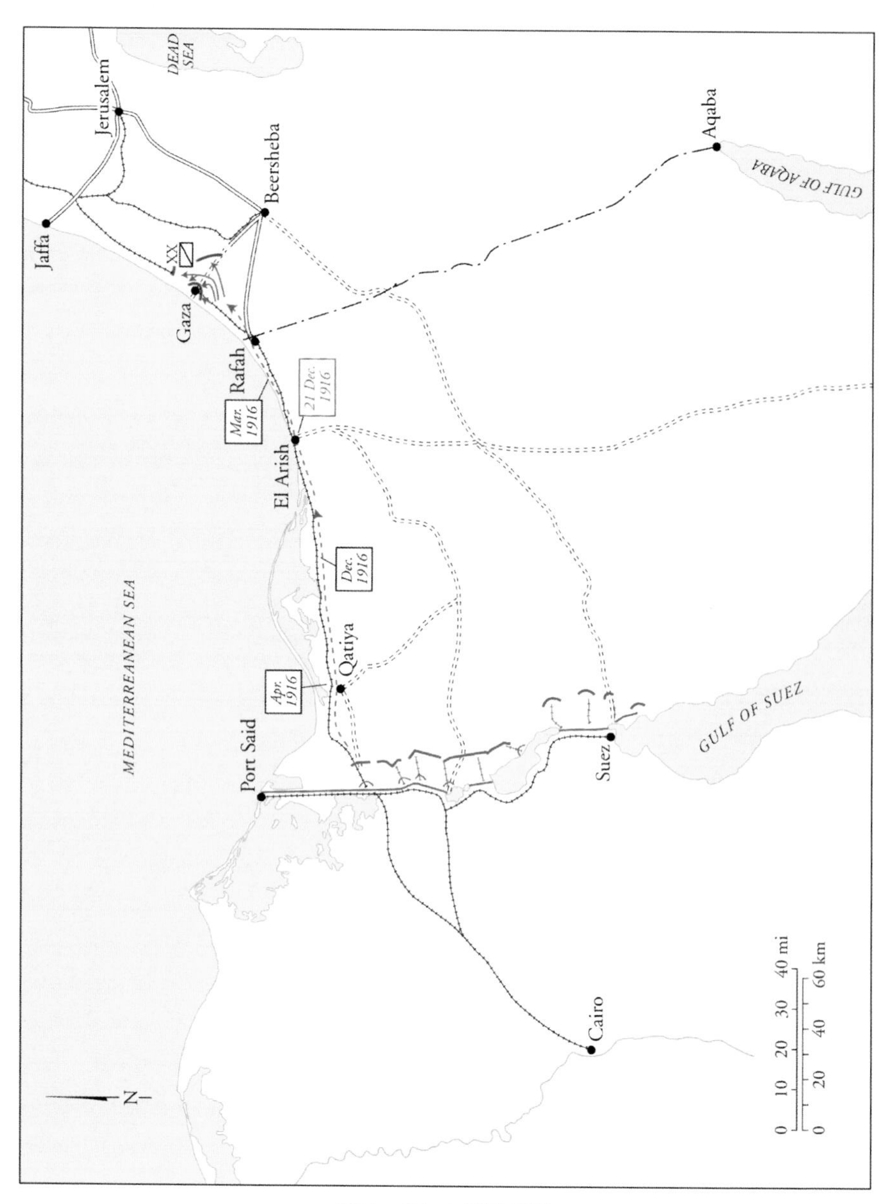

Sinai and Gaza, 1916–1917
Maps Courtesy of the Department of History, United States Military Academy

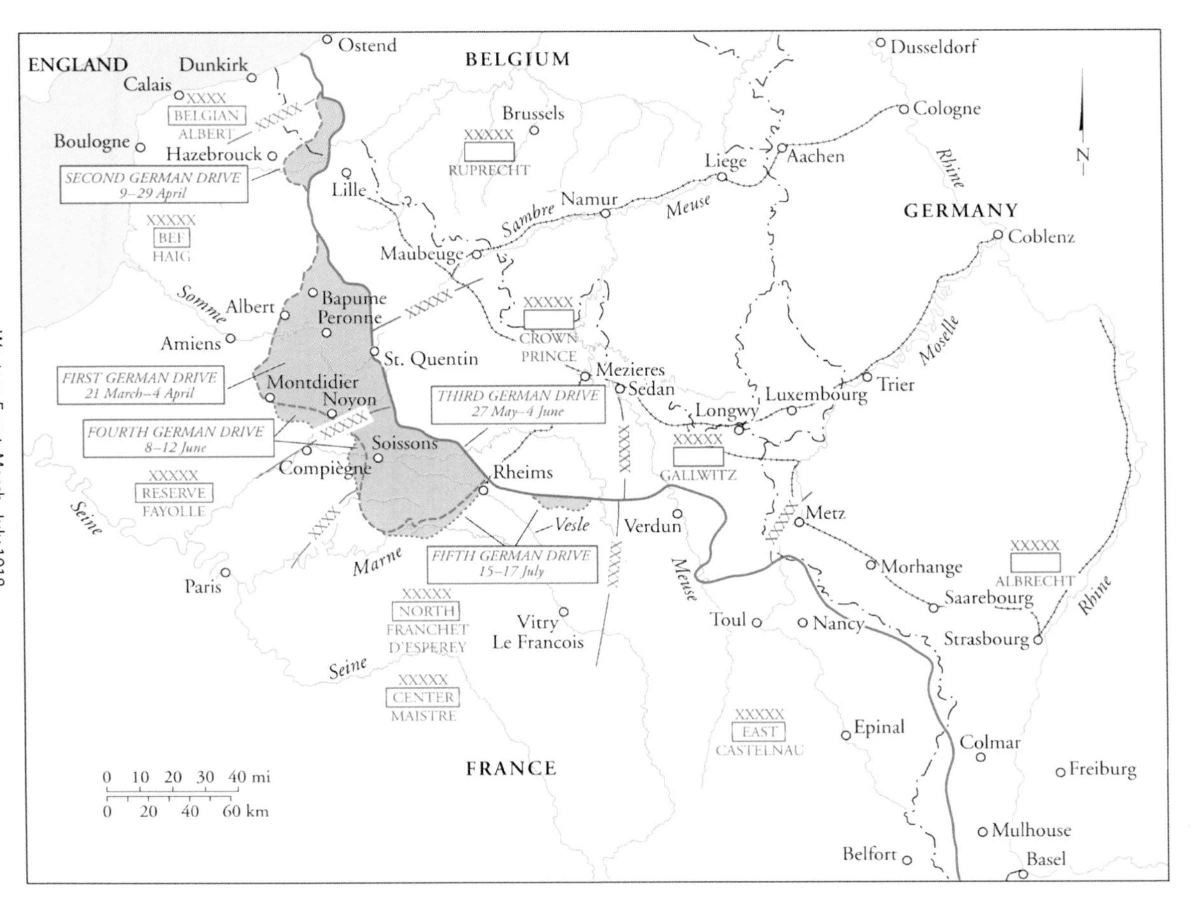

Western Front, March–July 1918

Maps Courtesy of the Department of History, United States Military Academy

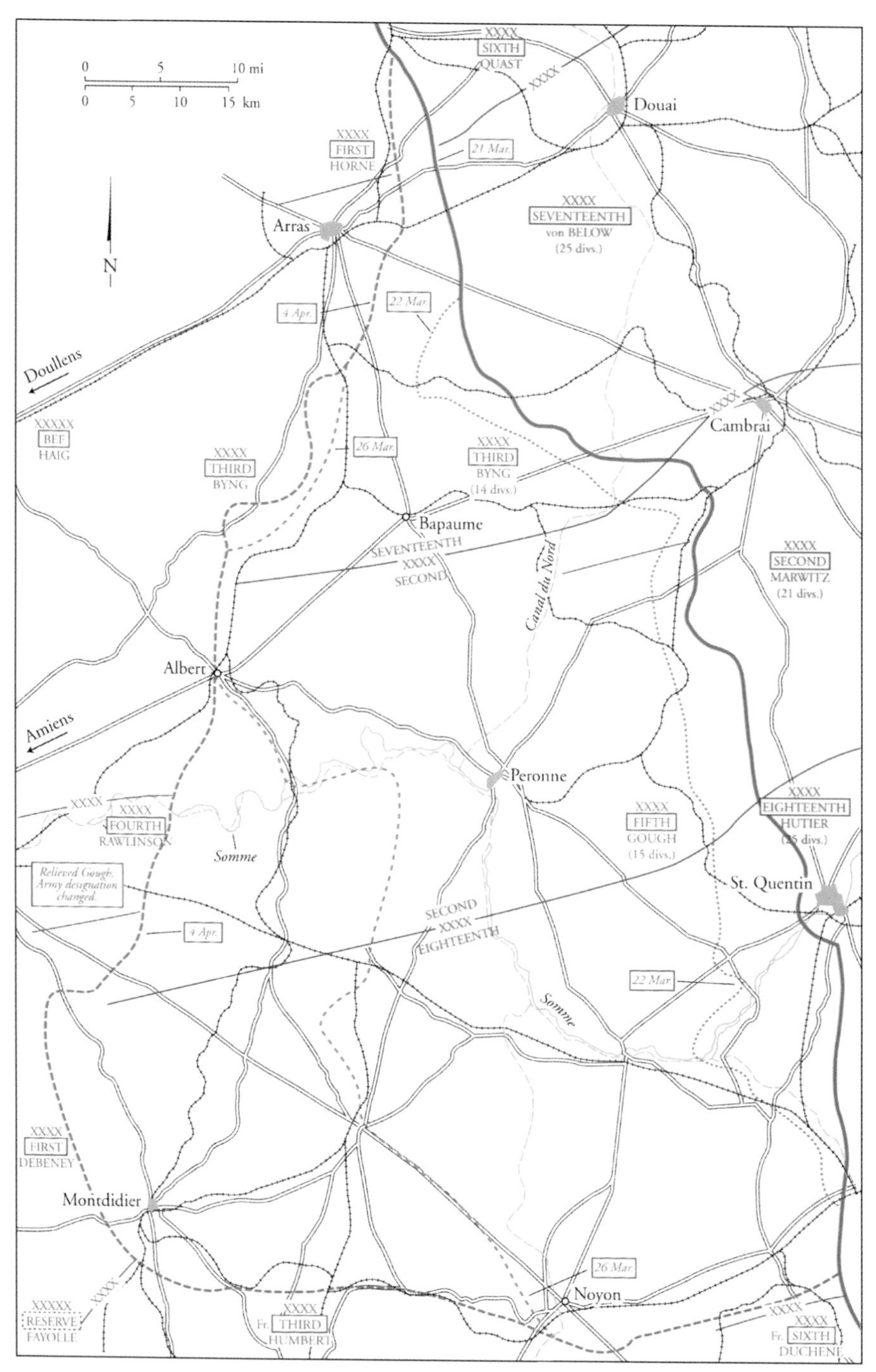

Operation *St. Michael*, March–April 1918
Maps Courtesy of the Department of History, United States Military Academy

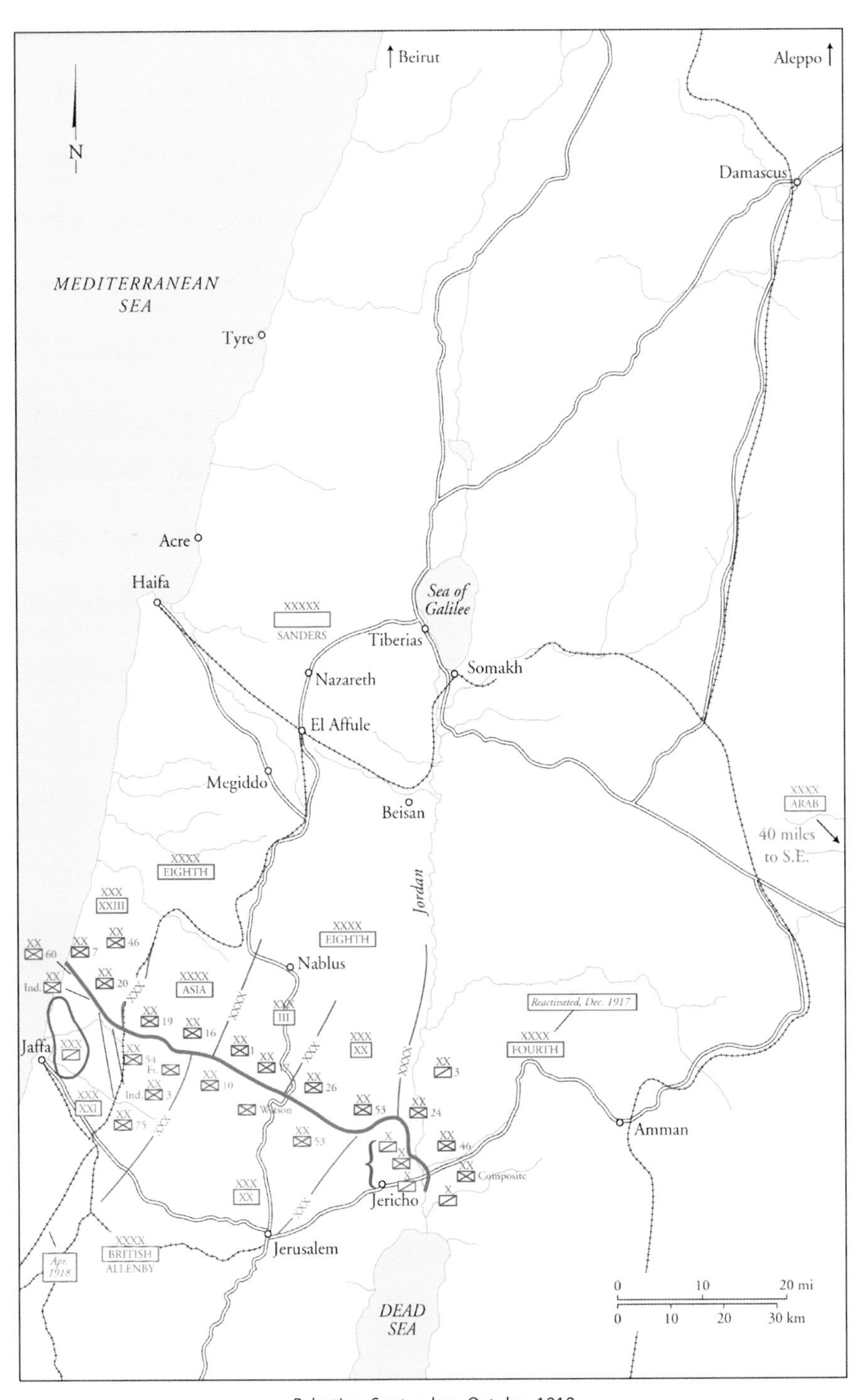

Palestine, September–October 1918
Maps Courtesy of the Department of History, United States Military Academy

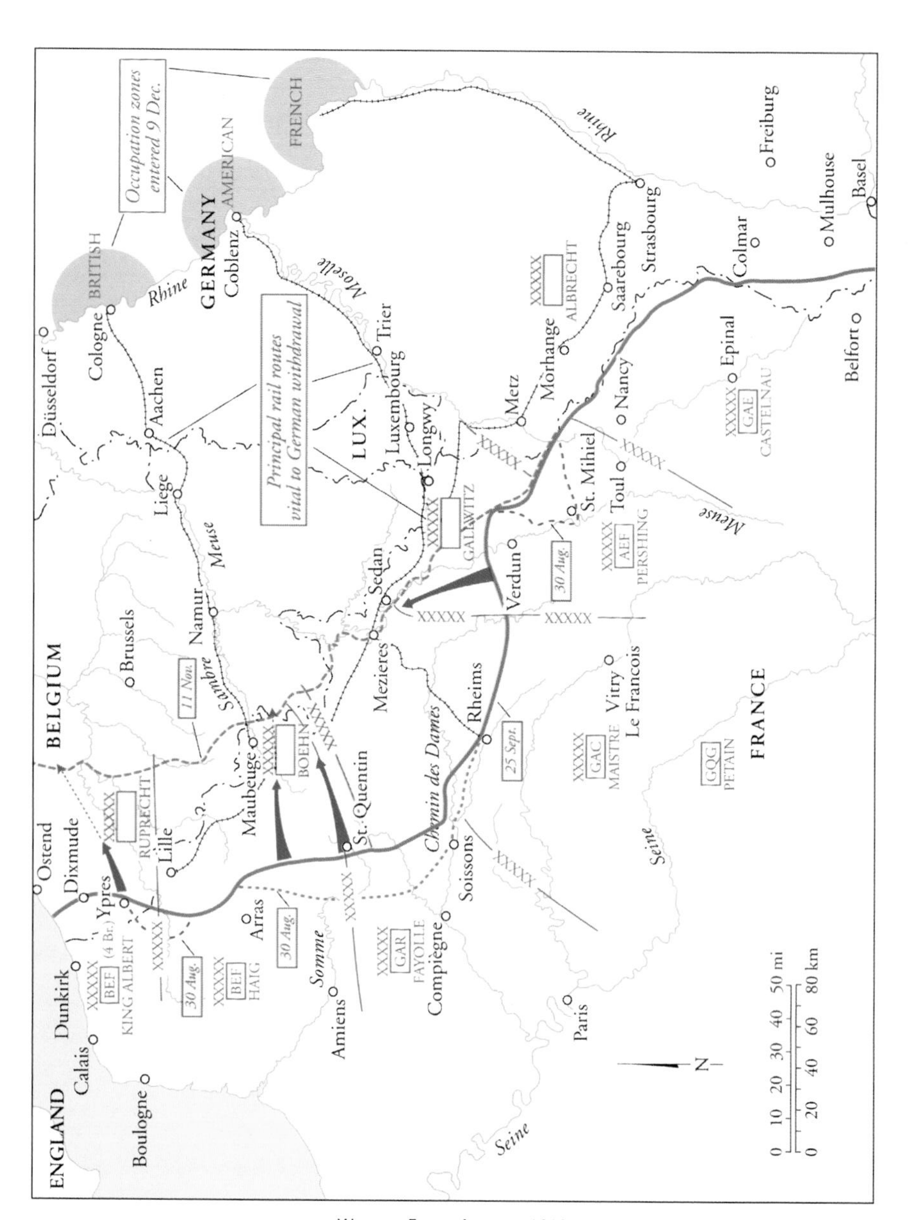

Western Front, Autumn 1918
Maps Courtesy of the Department of History, United States Military Academy

take up their rifles and attack when the bugle sounds, it is a thing upon which we never counted—it was a possibility not studied in our war academy."[22] That the decimated BEF, the battered French Fifth, and war-weary elements of the French Sixth took part in the battle was indeed a remarkable feat.

Allied Left Meets the German Right: Sir John French
Canfield, *World War*

For four days the firing and shelling and killing escalated in intensity. With his right rear flank threatened by the sudden appearance of the French Sixth Army, Kluck undertook a complex maneuver, turning his whole army back across the Ourcq River. At first the tide seemed to turn in Kluck's favor, but the steady buildup of French divisions—some rushed to the Ourcq in taxicabs—eventually imperiled First Army. Worse still was the position of Second Army, for by shifting to the rear Kluck left a huge fifty-kilometer gap open on Bülow's unguarded right flank. Second Army, and to its left, Hausen's Third Army, fought tenaciously and aggressively, actually pushing back the French Ninth Army and elements of the Fifth. However, Fifth Army pounded away at Bülow's weak right, and then the BEF began to move into the fifty-kilometer gap. Finally on September 9 a representative from OHL, Lieutenant Colonel Richard Hentsch, visited the headquarters of First and Second Armies. With shells nearly depleted and both armies falling below 50 percent of their initial strength, Hentsch ordered a retreat to the Aisne-Vesle River line.

Meanwhile, the battle along the fortress line reached its climax. As the German Sixth and Seventh Armies pushed west they ran up against the so-called Position de Nancy, a heavily fortified zone fifteen kilometers long and two kilometers deep, replete with outforts, barbed wire-shielded infantry trenches, and hidden artillery batteries near rail lines that could transport the cannon to new positions once the Germans got the range. Short of shells and depleted in the ranks, the advance bogged down. The assault on Verdun was much more dramatic. With elements of the German Fifth Army assaulting forts on the Meuse from the east and units of Fourth Army sweeping around from the west, GQG actually ordered the evacuation of the entire Verdun complex. The commandant ignored the order, which proved to be the correct decision because the German divisions threatening to break through at Fort Troyon ran out of heavy artillery shells after four days of fighting. Moltke ordered Third, Fourth, and Fifth Armies to retreat and take up positions next to Kluck and Bülow on September 11.

Monster Gun: Mobile 420 mm Howitzer Used at Liège
Karl Justrow, *Die Dicke Berta und der Krieg* (Berlin, 1935)

Looking for Battle: The German First Army in Brussels, August 20, 1914
Used with the permission of *The Trustees of the Imperial War Museum, London*. Photo Number: Q 88431

Germany had rolled the iron dice, hoping first for crushing victories along the frontier, and when these eluded them, crippling victories farther west. Germany had gambled—and had lost. So had the families of four nations. German casualties to mid-September 1914—dead, wounded, missing—probably exceeded a third of a million. French figures were higher, around four hundred thousand, with the heaviest per diem losses coming on the frontiers.[23] To these we must add tens of thousands of British and Belgian men who paid the ultimate price. Soldiers and civilians believed in the causes they fought for; they were not lambs led to slaughter, but this was human tragedy writ large—in three weeks of combat on the western front more had fallen than in the entire eighteen months of the Russo-Japanese War only eight years earlier.

CRISIS AND CONFUSION IN MILITARY AFFAIRS

The concept (introduced in chap. 1) of a revolution in military affairs (RMA), a long-term adjustment inside military establishments to weapons possibilities created by rapidly evolving industrial technology and the need, consequently, for accompanying tactical and operational changes, provides an informative prism through which to view the opening campaigns of the Great War on the western front.[24] Beginning in the 1880s and 1890s with new nitrogen-based explosives, magazine rifles, machine guns, and semirecoilless rapid-firing artillery of both light and heavy caliber, and continuing after 1900 with the advent of airships, airplanes, automobiles, wireless telegraphy, radios, and telephones, the armies of the Great Powers debated what all of this would mean in actual combat. The Boer War, the Russo-Japanese War, the Italo-Turkish War, and the Balkan Wars did not adequately prepare military leaders, however, for what happened on European ground in 1914. No one can read the future, of course, but so much of the prewar debate on weaponry, tactics, and operations was unrealistically off the mark that it seems more like crisis and confusion in military affairs than a rational adjustment process. However, of the two main combatants, Germany and France, the French were probably further along in the RMA process than the Germans. Furthermore, campaign circumstances, the fact that the Germans were attacking and advancing as opposed to defending and retreating, magnified the significance of technological choices made in the German army, especially during the battles on the frontiers so central to its operational goals.[25]

The airplane, for example, had appeared on the military scene in 1909–1910 when the French began to purchase greater numbers of aircraft and experiment with them on maneuvers. Although somewhat more cautious about the new device, Germany reacted by developing its own airplane squadrons. The airship had entered the tactical/operational equation a few years earlier with the Germans gaining the early lead over the French. Although both army establishments had only begun to appreciate the usefulness of airplanes and airships, preferring for reconnaissance to rely mainly on cavalry that served neither side well in 1914, the Western allies made more significant intelligence breakthroughs from the air during the early campaigning. The French fliers who spotted and confirmed

Looking for the BEF: The Taube
Julius Hoppenstedt, *Das Volk in Waffen*, Vol. 1, *Das Heer* (Dachau, Germany 1913)

Kluck's line of march east of Paris, thereby emboldening Joffre to counterattack, represent the most famous example, but the BEF's flying corps also reported six German divisions bearing down on Mons a day before the battle—unfortunately, Sir John French chose to ignore the report. French nonrigid airships based at Maubeuge also contributed to knowledge of the German move through Belgium. Their flexible canvas structure enabled them to get aloft despite the eerily stormy and windy weather of August 1914.

All of this contrasts sharply with German conservatism. Indeed the Germans lost their best opportunity for victory along the frontiers at the Battle of the Sambre-Meuse—and faulty reconnaissance contributed to this outcome. Both the "Taube" scouting plane and the zeppelins assigned to the right-wing armies could have spotted the BEF as it advanced from Le Havre and Boulogne to Mons, where Kluck certainly would have enveloped it as ordered. However, the German army had not developed a deep enough appreciation for the airplane's capabilities, sending pilots out on short cavalry-like, fifty-kilometer missions when three times that distance was quite feasible. The General Staff had also ignored prewar arguments from army technicians about the liabilities of zeppelins on windy days. The idea of maintaining a mixed fleet of rigid and nonrigid airships had essentially been scotched before the war. Summer storms prevented the rigid aluminum-frame zeppelins from making any long-range missions, in fact, until well after the battle ended.

Germany's hesitant response to newly evolving communication technologies, coupled with their inherent limitations at an early stage of technological development, put another strange stamp on outcomes along the frontiers. The German army reacted cautiously and professionally, aware of the need to improve operational communications during the leap in the dark to mass

Looking for Battle: The BEF in Le Havre, August 16, 1914
Used with the permission of *The Trustees of the Imperial War Museum, London*. Photo Number: Q 51472

army campaigns—annual maneuvers involved no more than 4–6 corps, not 35–40—but remained unconvinced after maneuvers and special tests with wireless, radio, and telephones that commanders could dispense with dispatch riders and automobiles for sending and receiving intelligence and orders. In this early phase of RMA, therefore, the German army adopted the newer but relied more on the older technology, whose slower transmission of information reinforced the already existing tradition of army autonomy from central command and within armies of autonomous corps command, both of which in their turn strengthened Moltke's self-effacing predilection for deferring to the judgment of subordinate generals. The odd result was that OHL, despite having to sift through the mass of radio messages, telephone calls, and dispatched communiqués, and usually having to react to stale information, nevertheless sensed brilliant opportunities—that First Army and part of Fourth should close the trap on Lanrezac and the BEF—but did not insist that directives be executed. There is no evidence that the French army was better equipped to communicate, but its task proved easier as the front receded in friendly territory replete with civilian telegraph and telephone services and interior lines of road and rail transportation.

Infantry tactics offer another glimpse of RMA in a very early stage. Most (but not all) generals failed to appreciate the tactical changes required when hurling infantry or cavalry against rapid-firing weapons, despite the fact that both German and French regulations emphasized the need to disperse, seek cover, and prosecute attacks cautiously and cleverly. Instead, all too often commanders ordered the tight-ranked shock formations of former days in frontal as opposed to flanking attacks. This phenomenon was more complex than tactical conservatism or backwardness, to be sure, for often the rapid pace of the advance dictated attacking directly from the line of march rather than waiting to deploy according to regulations, but frequently these kinds of assaults went forward before the artillery was in position to support them, and when the infantry got too far forward fire from their own batteries took a heavy toll. In the French case tactical mistakes also resulted from the incomplete training of recruits called into service in the immediate prewar period. Similarly, German officers and soldiers in reserve units tended to resort to older ways learned in earlier years' training. Judging from France's higher casualty rate on the frontiers, where 140,000 men were lost to Germany's 80,000–90,000, French tactics may have been more lacking.

What strikes one during the early going, however, is that Germany could afford these casualty levels only if it won on the frontiers, for afterward OHL, which had all available troops in the field and was outnumbered from the outset, had to shift four divisions to East Prussia, peel off eight divisions (including two from Schleswig-Holstein) to besiege Belgian and French fortresses, plus other units to protect lengthening supply lines and guard prisoners. The allies, in marked contrast, more than made up for their fallen with two BEF reinforcement divisions, one hundred thousand French soldiers from reserve depots (i.e., infantry for eight divisions), two divisions from Algeria, and six divisions from the border with Italy, which had decided for neutrality. OHL clearly faced longer odds after it failed to deliver a crippling blow along the borders—a cold fact that magnifies the historiographical importance of the Zuber debate.

If we shift the RMA focus to artillery, this conclusion seems even more justified, for Germany possessed its greatest firepower advantage during the Battle of the Frontiers. France's response to the possibilities freed up by modern technology came in 1898 with the 75 mm field gun, the first semirecoilless rapid-firing piece. Springing from a German design, interestingly enough, it shot twenty shells per minute. Even when operating at half speed it could saturate a field with ten thousand shrapnel balls per minute, making it more effective against infantry than either magazine rifles or machine guns. Shields were added in 1900. Until the early 1900s the German artillery establishment had adhered stubbornly to improved versions of the lighter, more mobile, but slower-firing guns that had carried them to victory over France in 1870, a conservatism that also impeded the advent of higher-caliber, arced-trajectory howitzers, which worked so well against entrenched defenders. The French challenge, and later the Russo-Japanese War, moved the General Staff to intervene, however, and by 1914 Germany had refitted its field batteries with a shielded rapid-firing gun, the C-96nA, and added 105 mm and 150 mm howitzers to all corps. GQG sent its divisions into battle trusting mainly the 75, but Germany not only had more C-96nAs in line but also a two-to-one advantage in light and heavy field howitzers versus France's heavy guns. The high trajectory of the howitzers proved very effective in the rugged hilly terrain of Alsace, Lorraine, and the Ardennes, whereas the French 75s with their flatter trajectory provided less support. German gunnery aided tremendously in OHL's victories at Morhange and Neufchateau.

Allegedly Too Slow: German 150 mm Howitzers on the Move
Max Köhler, *Der Aufstieg der Artillerie bis zum Grossen Krieg* (Munich, Germany 1938)

During OHL's pursuit of the French and British to the Marne, on the other hand, logistics and technological factors associated with the artillery swung the advantage away from the pursuers. For one thing, the quick fire capability, mobility, and long range of the 75s—a longer barrel sent shells one thousand meters farther than the C-96nA—proved ideal for the "hit and run" of GQG's aggressive retreat. German casualties began to mount rapidly as the French field artillery ambushed advancing infantry columns from concealed flanking positions at maximum range and often hit the German artillery, too, as it raced forward attempting to get into range to fire back. Burned too often in this effort, C-96nA crews increasingly hung back for their own protection—to the dismay of the infantry.

The farther into France Moltke's armies drove, moreover, the longer supply lines stretched. Exacerbating the situation, allied demolition crews had quickly and efficiently destroyed tracks and tunnels, thereby depriving the invaders of almost all use of the railroads. The allies, on the other hand, had ever shorter routes to shell depots and full use of railroads behind the lines. The French had entered the war, furthermore, with about 20 percent more ammunition for their 75s, a product of their somewhat longer experience with rapid fire. Therefore the German artillery drew dangerously close to the end of its shells as the critical final battles approached. "I watched the disappearance of our munitions trains in 1914 with great worry,"[26] recalled the quartermaster general of artillery at OHL.

The only real edge the attackers possessed during the chase were their 105 mm and 150 mm howitzers, which were excellent for dislodging dug-in defenders at long range, but stubborn opposition to this weapon from field artillerists in the prewar period—the 150 mm "elephants" were too slow, they argued, and would only impede the advance into enemy territory—held production numbers well below heavy artillery demands; nor had Germany produced howitzer shells in adequate quantities. Assuming there were still abundant shells and that a German battalion or regiment commander under enemy shell fire could get word back to corps headquarters, the four 150 mm and six 105 mm batteries controlled there were not capable of providing support for all twenty-four thousand infantrymen in the corps. That OHL fielded more heavy guns than the French was therefore small consolation, for too often the infantry had no howitzer support. Thus the German advance grew increasingly difficult and casualties rose higher than Moltke could afford on the eve of the decisive clash.

In sum, neither army on the western front, and certainly not the German army, was adequately prepared to fight a modern war. The price of this incomplete or insufficient RMA—the carnage of the opening campaigns—was high. It could be argued, in fact, that the shocking experience of failed tactics and operations gone so terribly and tragically awry constituted another "military revolution"—a radical change, a shocking reality that cried out for accelerating and completing RMA in the midst of the worst war in history to date. In the late summer of 1914, well before the onset of trench warfare in 1915, military leaders who before the war had placed a greater emphasis on manufacturing rifles and low-caliber, flat-trajectory field guns noticed the deadliness of machine guns and high-caliber howitzers and demanded that industry produce them in far greater quantities. Once the trenches dominated operations, heavy high-explosive artillery, tanks, airplanes, and new infantry tactics would eventually combine on the battlefield to help offenses overcome defenses. The RMA of the early twentieth century would not run its full course, however, until the opening stage of another terrible war in 1939–1940.

THE "RACE TO THE SEA"

After ordering his horde to retreat after the Battle of the Marne, Chief of the General Staff Helmuth von Moltke yielded office to former Minister of War Erich von Falkenhayn. His first order of business was to halt the allies as they moved north from the Marne to the Aisne.[27] To bolster his lines and fill the problematic gap between First and Second Armies, Falkenhayn transferred the bulk of Seventh Army from Alsace. The river line and steep ridges behind it also proved too great an obstacle for the British and French. After failing to flank the German positions, they broke off their attacks toward the end of September.

However, neither Falkenhayn nor Joffre had abandoned the notion of regaining movement and outflanking the enemy. Joffre cobbled sixteen divisions together into a new Tenth Army and ordered elements of it north of the Somme to sweep around Arras and then southward into the German rear. From October 1 to October 6 Tenth Army collided with an army of eleven divisions OHL had shifted from southern Lorraine and reconstituted, the Sixth, which had orders to retake the territory above the Somme, push south to Paris, and envelop the allies. Falkenhayn placed eight cavalry divisions on Sixth Army's right flank to sweep through the coastal areas of Flanders. During the bloody weeklong battle Tenth Army shifted to the defensive and stopped the Germans. Nevertheless, each army had nullified the plans of the other. Both sides now turned their eyes farther north to the stretch between Arras and the sea, for this region offered the only remaining outflanking opportunities.

Moltke's Successor: General Erich von Falkenhayn
Walter Goerlitz, *The German General Staff: 1657–1945* (New York, 1953)

By the middle of October the allies had moved nineteen divisions into the area from La Bassée to the Channel—the Belgian field army, which had extricated itself from Antwerp, in the north; the BEF in the center; and the French farther south.[28] Facing them were twenty-four German divisions that mounted assaults at Dixmude on October 16 and Ypres on October 19. The fighting raged along this line until November 22 with the fiercest struggles taking place in front of Ypres, which would therefore give its name to the entire battle. In one of the best-known actions of the campaign on November 10 at Langemarck, northeast of Ypres, German high school and university students who had volunteered in August and received hasty training attacked hardened British riflemen and were cut to pieces. The valiant assault would later be dubbed the *Kindermord* (Massacre of the Innocents).

Casualties on both sides at Ypres totaled a quarter of a million. By this time German casualties on the western front since early August had passed three-quarters of a million. French losses probably exceeded a million.[29] With neither side able to outflank or dislodge the other—they had never undertaken a race to the sea, nevertheless it has been so labeled—both armies began to burrow into the earth. By Christmas 1914 the trench works that would put their indelible stamp on the modern memory of the Great War stretched over 650 kilometers from the Swiss border to the English Channel. Meanwhile, significant campaigns even more costly in blood had taken place in the east.

THE EASTERN FRONT

East Prussia

Having deployed seven armies in the west, OHL reserved its last army, twelve infantry divisions (with one cavalry division), for the defense of East Prussia. Of these, however, only six were regular line divisions with the full complement of seventy-two cannon and twenty-four machine guns (plus howitzer support from corps command), while three were reserve divisions with half the light artillery and no machine guns. The final three were even less effective territorial guard (*Landwehr*) divisions that had only their rifles to bolster the esprit de corps of the middle-aged men who proudly served units whose origins dated back to the Napoleonic Wars. Together with garrison troops from Königsberg and the Vistula River fortresses, these forces constituted the German Eighth Army under the command of Maximilian von Prittwitz.

In this northern theater Russia readied First and Second Armies, altogether thirty divisions, each with sixteen battalions versus Germany's twelve, plus nine cavalry divisions and superior numbers of guns. If these forces concentrated in East Prussia, Eighth Army would be outnumbered, outgunned, and probably overrun, leaving the road to the Vistula River—and three hundred kilometers beyond it, Berlin—wide open. Unfortunately for Russia its forces went forward piecemeal. In a costly administrative and operational foul-up, over a third of total infantry strength of First and Second Armies stayed behind to garrison fortresses, needlessly shore up the rear, or prepare for later border crossings. Already badly outgunned per corps in artillery, the Russians compounded the problem by leaving two-fifths of their guns behind, many of them in fortresses that could play no role in East Prussia (also see chap. 5). Russian headquarters (*Stavka*) was also forming Ninth Army near Warsaw and Tenth Army in southern Lithuania to reinforce the first wave after it had cleared East Prussia. In hurrying two partial armies of four forward, the less-than-clear-thinking rush of honor to aid France is discernible.[30]

The German commander positioned six divisions (plus cavalry and *Landwehr*) behind the Angerapp River west of Gumbinnen, leaving one two-division regular corps (20th) south of Tannenberg and one reserve division (3rd) near Allenstein to protect the southern flank against the slowly advancing twelve divisions of the Russian Second Army of Alexander Samsonov. After the more rapidly advancing six divisions of the Russian First Army of Paul Rennenkampf crossed the northeastern frontier, advance elements clashed at Stallupönen on August 17, and then Pritwitz attacked with his three main corps (1st, 17th, and 1st Reserve) at Gumbinnen three days later—simultaneously with the first major battle on the western front. His losses heavy, the Russian commander decided to halt, regroup, and resupply, while Prittwitz also reacted cautiously, intending to retreat to the Vistula River. His center corps (17th) had lost eight thousand men—over 25 percent—by rushing from the line of march into battle without waiting for artillery preparation.

The Heroes of Tannenberg: Generals Paul von Hindenburg and Erich Ludendorff
Harper's Pictorial Library

Exacerbating matters for the two Russian armies, however, Samsonov badly executed the overall operational plan. Rennenkampf was to cross the border a few days before him, engage Eighth Army, and hold it while Second Army cut off the German line of retreat. In theory, even with these limited forces, it could have worked, but in practice, because Samsonov's advance was delayed two days, the smaller German forces could face first Rennenkampf and then Samsonov, possessing rough numerical equality in both battles. The Battle of Gumbinnen allowed this potential to become reality, for when Pritwitz's chief of operations, Max Hoffmann, pointed out that Samsonov could reach the Vistula first, Prittwitz agreed to a daring proposal for taking advantage of Rennenkampf's halt by exploiting German train lines to dispatch three corps south to meet Samsonov, leaving only cavalry and *Landwehr* to screen west of Gumbinnen and around the lakes farther south.

Second Army, meanwhile, crossed the border along a broad one-hundred-kilometer front, not counting his far right corps (2nd), which, unable to negotiate the lake region, meandered north and was reassigned to Rennenkampf. Second Army's remaining five corps (1st, 23rd, 15th, 13th, and 6th) had inadequate supply lines back to Poland, a deficient store of wire for telephone lines, and thus virtually nonexistent communication with one another or with Samsonov. Ten artillery-poor divisions groped their way blindly into unfamiliar terrain—and disaster.

By the time German troops were in position, two new commanders headed Eighth Army: Paul von Hindenburg, a retired general with good connections to the kaiser, and Erich Ludendorff, his aggressive, high-strung chief of staff. OHL had tired of Prittwitz's apparent caution, for his orders had been as follows: "When the Russians come, not defense only, but offensive, offensive, offensive."[31]

What was later dubbed by Hoffmann the Battle of Tannenberg began in the center on August 24 between the German 20th and Russian 15th corps and seesawed indecisively for a few days while the three German corps descended on the unsuspecting Russians. By August 27–28, however, Eighth Army's far better generalship, ground communications, intelligence gathering from both airplanes and airships, and superiority in artillery, shells, and machine guns multiplied the effect of the element of surprise. As Samsonov's three center corps thrust disjointedly forward, gaps opened with 1st on the left and 6th on the right. The Germans hit these corps, sending them reeling backward in disarray. The assault from Hindenburg's right against the Russian 1st corps and elements of 23rd was especially devastating. The attackers waited this time for the artillery to get into place and the barrage of thirty well-aimed six-gun batteries decimated the defenders. On the German left 17th and 1st Reserve Corps smashed the Russian 6th. Now, as Samsonov's flanking units crumbled, Eighth Army surrounded five divisions of the Russian center. What might have happened in Belgium happened in East Prussia: Second Army lost 50,000 men dead or wounded, and by the end of the month the Germans had rounded up 92,000 prisoners. Overwhelmed by defeat and disgrace, the Russian commander walked off into the woods and apparently shot himself.

The shattered remnants of Second Army fell back over the border to Mlawa, where Stavka began the rebuilding process, partly from forces that had been left behind—a feat accomplished quickly enough to take the edge off Germany's victory celebration. But a huge victory it was. As long as the war lasted, Russian soldiers and generals never quite overcame the feeling of inferiority when fighting Germans that germinated in their minds with the annihilation of Second Army at Tannenberg. Hoffmann and Ludendorff added an extra dose of salt to Russia's wounds by naming the battle after the nearby village where Slavs had defeated Teutons in 1410, thus neatly reversing for propagandistic purposes history's verdict on which was the dominant race. The most important effect of the battle, however, was that East Prussia had been saved for now. The dreaded specter of Cossacks sacking and pillaging all the way to Berlin vanished. Hindenburg and Ludendorff became national heroes overnight.

Having received four divisions from the western front (11th and Guard Reserve Corps), Hindenburg and Ludendorff now turned back to deal with the Russian First Army. In the meantime, Rennenkampf, out of touch because of poor communications, had resumed a slow, steady, 80–100 kilometer advance but made no move to extricate Samsonov. *Stavka* had considerably beefed up his forces, enabling a First Army buildup behind the Deime River to shield against a German thrust from Königsberg and prepare to take the critical fortress complex. Seven divisions were deployed to their left south of the River Pregel. *Stavka* ordered Rennenkampf to attack all along the line on September 14.

Hindenburg and Ludendorff preempted him with their own assault, however, on September 7 (see map, p. 76). Four corps attacked frontally to fix the Russians between Heilsburg and Bischofsburg, while 1st and 17th corps swung around the enemy's southern flank. By September 10 Eighth Army's envelopment reached Lyck, thereby threatening another Tannenberg. Accordingly, Rennenkampf pulled all of his divisions out of East Prussia and retreated across the border along with Tenth Army, which had been moving into place from Lithuania. With these extra forces he was strong enough to counterattack two weeks later, however, driving the pursuing Germans back to their own territory. Russian forces moved into the vacuum and occupied a narrow strip of East Prussia.

Better Communication Than the Russians: German Field Telephone in East Prussia
Harper's Pictorial Library

Unlike the fighting in France, Eighth Army achieved brilliant victories in East Prussia, inflicting 310,000 casualties on First and Second Armies while itself losing only a fraction of this. Much like the western campaign, on the other hand, Germany had not only not delivered a decisive knockout blow to the enemy but also continued to face large and threatening—indeed growing—numbers of enemy soldiers. Farther south in Galicia, moreover, the situation was far worse.

Galicia

As developments unfolded in East Prussia an even larger clash occurred in Galicia.[32] The Austro-Hungarian forces under the command of Chief of Staff Franz Conrad von Hötzendorff comprised three armies when operations began on August 22. Conrad's plans called for First Army to enter Russian Poland and drive toward Lublin. On its right Fourth army would cross the frontier and advance on Kholm. Each army had nine divisions. Third Army's eleven divisions, Conrad's largest concentration, were positioned east of Lemberg to attack north or east or guard against Russian attacks across the river Bug. The chief of staff did not anticipate a large Russian concentration in this sector, however, despite intelligence reports to the contrary, which the headstrong general ignored. Besides, he anticipated the arrival of two corps from Second Army in transit from Serbia to reinforce Third Army on August 28 and a third corps shortly thereafter. Once concentrated, Austria-Hungary would have thirty-seven infantry divisions and ten cavalry divisions. Conrad's operational goal had far-reaching strategic implications: to destroy Russian forces, "liberate" the Polish people, and then arc southeastward toward Kiev to free Ukrainians from Moscow's yoke. The war in the east would be brought to a rapid and victorious end. "We would be far better off," said the emperor after these plans failed, "with a man who doesn't want to bridge oceans."[33]

Indeed Conrad would have been better advised to remain on the defensive. His grandiose designs were originally bolstered by assumptions that Germany would join the attack in northern Poland, facilitating a joint envelopment of Warsaw, and further that Rumania would enter the alliance, aiding both campaigns against Russia and Serbia, thus freeing up all of Second Army for Galicia—so-called War Plan R. But Moltke informed him on August 3 that Germany would defend East Prussia instead, and Rumania did not budge from its neutrality.

Furthermore, unknown to Conrad, whose cavalry reconnoitered unsuccessfully, *Stavka* mustered 53.5 large infantry divisions and 18 cavalry divisions. It also possessed a preponderant advantage in field artillery, heavy artillery, and machine guns. Moscow planned a two-pronged assault. The Russian Fourth and Fifth Armies were ordered to descend on the fortress zone of Przemysl from Poland. Still forming, Ninth Army stood in reserve. Third and Eighth Armies would cross the frontier from the east and strike the fortress town of Lemberg (Lvov). Double envelopment victory in Galicia would be followed by the invasion of Hungary. Once again overeager to help France, however, Russian armies went forward without having assembled all of their strength in men and guns.

On August 23 Conrad's First Army collided with the Russian Fourth at Krasnik and on August 26 the Austro-Hungarian Fourth ran into the Russian Fifth at Komarov (see map, p. 78). Tactical judgment failed on each side as both armies flung infantry, cavalry, and field artillery into the open for frontal assaults against strong defenses. The Austrian had chosen many of his elite formations for the offensive, however, and by August 29–30 many of the Russian units had retreated, offering Conrad the possibility of enveloping those left exposed. Unwisely, he moved his best three divisions from Third Army north to finish the job of encirclement, but by the end of the month the appearance of the Russian Ninth Army on the Russian right flank stabilized the northern line.

In the meantime disaster unfolded east of Lemberg. Unaware of what he faced, the commander of Conrad's now-weakened Third Army left the river defenses of the Gnita Lipa behind and assaulted the Russians on the Zlota Lipa and at Zloczov on August 26. Even though the Russians had not finished concentrating, the attackers were still outnumbered two-to-one and fell back in panic toward the Gnita Lipa, some over it to Lemberg. When the Russians hesitated to exploit their gains, Conrad gathered reinforcements and ordered an attack between the Lipas. Having built up to full strength, the Russian Third and Eighth Armies counterattacked and drove all before them, including six divisions from Second Army recently detrained from Serbia. On September 2 Lemberg, Conrad's supply center, was abandoned without a fight. Left behind were vast quantities of locomotives, wagons, munitions, and cannon. Alarmed that his rear was crumbling, Conrad ordered Fourth Army to reverse direction and halt the Russians, but even though now slightly outnumbered themselves, Third and Eighth Armies continued to press forward.

On the Defensive Again: German Machine Gun Crews Entrenched in East Prussia
Harper's Pictorial Library

On September 11, with his First Army now isolated in the north, the Austro-Hungarian chief of staff executed a retreat to the San River and then fell back to a line stretching from the vital rail junction at Cracow in the north to the Carpathian Mountains farther south. The Russians surrounded and besieged Przemysl—the Verdun of the East—on September 21. They also pressed their advance to the Carpathians and began to probe the passes. On the other side lay the Hungarian plains and largely undefended gateway to Budapest, four hundred kilometers away.

Conrad's armies remained in position north of the Carpathians, foiling for now the grand strategic designs of the Russians. But his own lofty plans of conquest and liberation were but an embarrassing memory. Austria-Hungary had at least avoided annihilation, but its forces were in a precarious position. They had suffered over a third of a million casualties—fully a third of fighting strength—including one hundred thousand prisoners. As in France and East Prussia, both sides girded for a longer war than either had anticipated.

Poland and Galicia

A week after Przemysl came under siege, a second major campaign got under way in Poland and Galicia.[34] Suspecting correctly that Russia intended to push its armies over the German border into Silesia, OHL, now under Chief of Staff Erich von Falkenhayn, transferred 11 of 13 divisions from the German Eighth Army to Silesia and ordered this newly constituted Ninth Army to disrupt Stavka's plans with a drive on Warsaw. Eighth Army received the newly raised 25th Reserve Corps to buttress its defense of East Prussia. Conrad agreed to strike from Cracow in the south with three armies totaling 31 divisions. In what was largely a return

Bridging Oceans: Franz Conrad von Hötzendorff
Canfield, *World War*

to prewar plans of joint enveloping action in Poland, the Germans jumped off on September 28; the Austro-Hungarians on October 4. Ninth Army reached the Vistula River south of Warsaw by October 9—the same day Conrad lifted the siege of Przemysl and pushed his First Army over the Vistula in the direction of Sandomierz.

These operations could not possibly continue to succeed given the strength *Stavka* mustered to counter them. Russia now stationed five armies from north of Warsaw to Sandomierz with two more behind the San—easily three times as many troops as the advancing enemy. These forces counterattacked on October 21 and pushed the Germans and Austro-Hungarians back to their original positions by the end of the month. Przemysl was once again besieged. Ninth Army had withdrawn in good order, punishing the Russians as they pursued, but Conrad's armies were now dangerously close to a spent force.

The Russian high command now formulated bold plans for a drive out of Poland to Berlin and in the south a crushing blow at Conrad and an advance through the Carpathians to Budapest. The northern thrust was ordered for November 14, but Hindenburg and Ludendorff delegated Ninth Army to August von Mackensen and once again struck preemptively, this time near Kutno at the weak junction of the Russian First and Second Armies. The effect of this concentrated attack, backed as it was by an awesome five-to-one superiority of field and heavy artillery, smashed and nearly annihilated Rennenkamp's First Army while inflicting heavy losses on Second Army as well. Mackensen got as far as Lodz but had thrust too far into the mass of concentrated Russian armies to press farther, even with reinforcements from East Prussia and the western front that bulged his army to 16.5 divisions. Nearly enveloped itself, Ninth Army fell back to the southwest and entrenched in early December.

Conrad, meanwhile, faced determined Russian assaults around Cracow and on the mountain passes of the Carpathians. Austro-Hungarian General Headquarters (AOK) had bolstered its front north of Cracow by shifting its southernmost

Second Army into line on Mackensen's right rear flank. Counterattacking with the Austro-Hungarian First and Fourth Armies on November 16, Conrad's weary troops stopped the Russians at Cracow and actually advanced in the north to capture Chenstokhov (Czestochowa), holy city of the Polish people. But, like Mackensen, he had thrust into superior numbers of Russian divisions, which pushed the attackers back to their jump-off points and beyond by November 26.

Death's Head Hussar: General August von Mackensen
Canfield, *World War*

Having weakened their Carpathian front by transferring Second Army north, the Austro-Hungarians now had only Third Army to defend five Carpathian passes leading to the Hungarian plain. One of them, at Lupkow, fell on November 20. With disaster near on December 3, Conrad redeemed himself somewhat from earlier ineptitude with a brilliant counterattack into a gap that had opened between the Russian Third and Eighth Armies. One German division had been dispatched to reinforce the attack. The Russians fell back and the danger of Cossacks flooding into Hungary subsided.

The human costs of the autumn campaigns in Poland and Galicia, however, were staggeringly high. Austria-Hungary had bled the most, sacrificing 750,000 dead, wounded, and missing men, pushing their total since August over a million. Russia admitted to losses of well over 500,000, but the true figure was certainly higher, placing their total war losses on the eastern front well over a million too. Better led, better trained, and better equipped, Germany lost a "mere" 100,000 since Tannenberg and the Masurian Lakes. Thus far, moreover, the killing and dying and maiming had not reversed the building momentum of stalemate. Each side awaited the next round of this bloody slugging match, the one that would bring victory and ensure that previous sacrifices had not been in vain.

Serbia

The first shots of the Great War were fired in the early morning of July 29 when the artillery of the Austro-Hungarian Second Army opened fire on Belgrade.[35] The Dual Monarchy's bid to eradicate the Serbian "viper's nest" began in earnest on August 12 when Fifth Army crossed the river Drina (see map, p. 79) and engaged

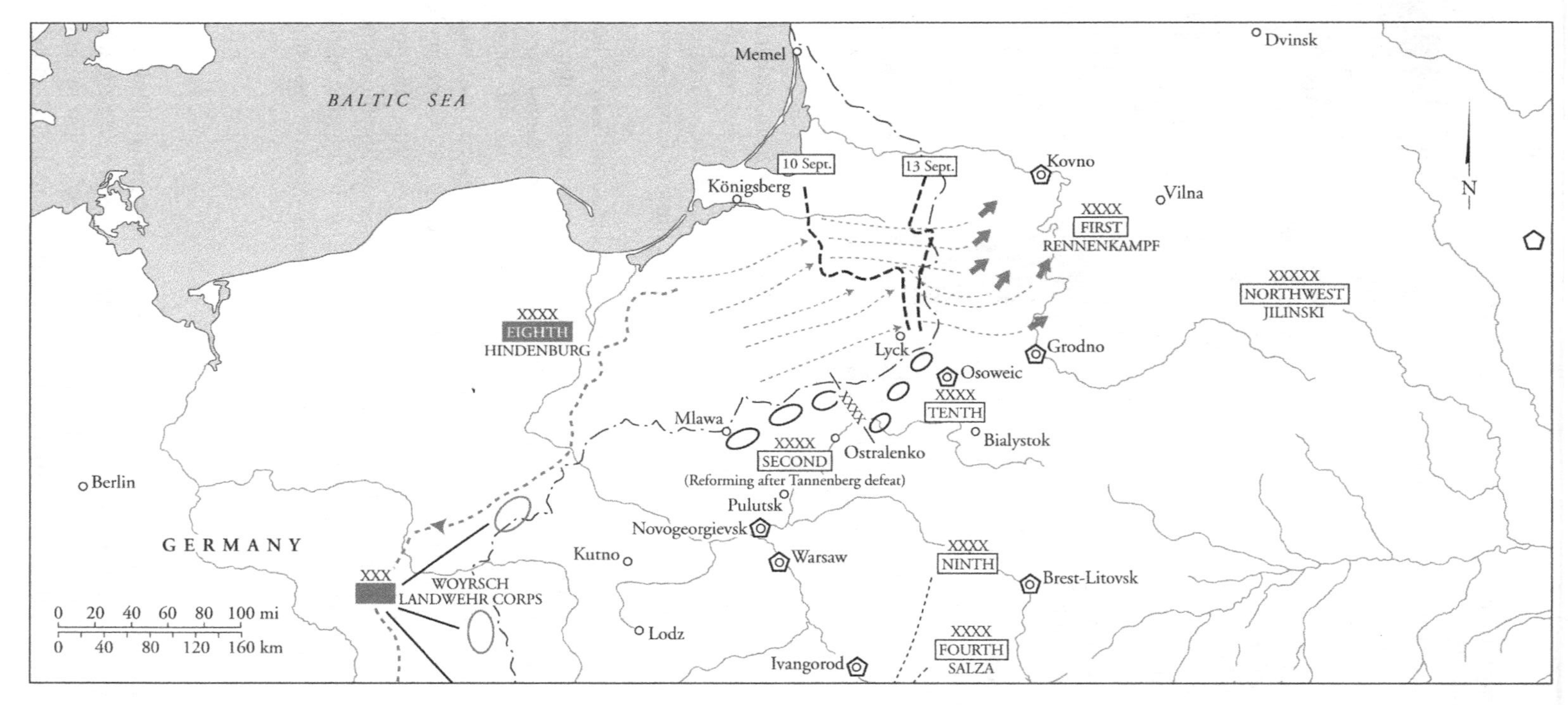

Battle of the Masurian Lakes

Maps Courtesy of the Department of History, United States Military Academy

the Serbian Second and Third Armies. Their wily commander, Radomir Putnik, a veteran of the Balkan Wars, refused to be drawn onto the Cer plains southeast of the Drina but rather entrenched on high ground farther back overlooking the flat ground over which the enemy had to advance.

The Austro-Hungarian commander, Oskar Potiorek, severely underestimated the numbers and resilience of his enemy and the difficulty of dislodging him from formidable defenses. Consequently an attack that also displayed no tactical innovation bogged down. Casualties soared as the Serbs' 75 mm. rapid-firing field guns tore huge holes in tightly drawn-up ranks. Making matters worse, Potiorek's operational plan called for Sixth Army to attack farther south at Visegrad, but it was poorly coordinated with Fifth Army's advance and did not begin until August 20, eight days after Fifth Army began to cross the Drina. Potiorek was further hampered by Conrad's decision to withdraw Second Army and transfer it to Galicia. Only one corps was temporarily detached to help dislodge Putnik, and this proved insufficient for the task. Serb counterattacks hammered the invaders and actually liberated the homeland by August 24.

On September 6 Putnik swung over to the offensive, pushing two armies over the Save River, Serbia's northern border where the lone remaining corps of the Austrian Second Army defended. Potiorek now seized the opportunity to attack again across the Drina with both Fifth and Sixth Armies to threaten Putnik's rear. Although the Serbs had to pull back over the Save, intense fighting in mountainous terrain proved once more that Austria-Hungary had no tactical answer and had not left adequate forces in this sector to defeat the tenacious, well-equipped Serbs. By September 22 Potiorek's troops had withdrawn for a second time across the Drina and Serb troops pushed up to the river.

The following day Putnik struck into Bosnia in an attempt to reach Sarajevo. After a campaign that lasted until the end of October, the Austro-Hungarian Sixth Army and hastily mobilized fortress troops finally managed to rid Bosnia of the Serbs. Just as in the other theaters of action in the summer and early fall of 1914, stalemate ensued as each army stared warily at the other across river entrenchments.

AOK reinforced Potiorek in October 1914 for a third invasion of Serbia. If crowned by success, perhaps Bulgaria would be moved to enter the war on the side of Vienna and Berlin, thereby also facilitating Turkish belligerency. Rumania, moreover, would be given good reason at least to remain neutral. Fifth Army crossed the Save on November 6 while Sixth Army moved over the Drina and into the Jagodjna hills on the other side. Backed by more heavy artillery this time, the two armies drove the Serbs back to the Kolubara River and then back to the Morava. On December 2 Potiorek vaingloriously announced to Francis Joseph that he was laying "town and fortress Belgrade" at "His Majesty's feet."[36]

Pride had once again come before a fall, for Potiorek's troops were running out of food and ammunition and had struggled through the snowy campaign in their summer uniforms. Only one day after the conqueror's overconfident missive

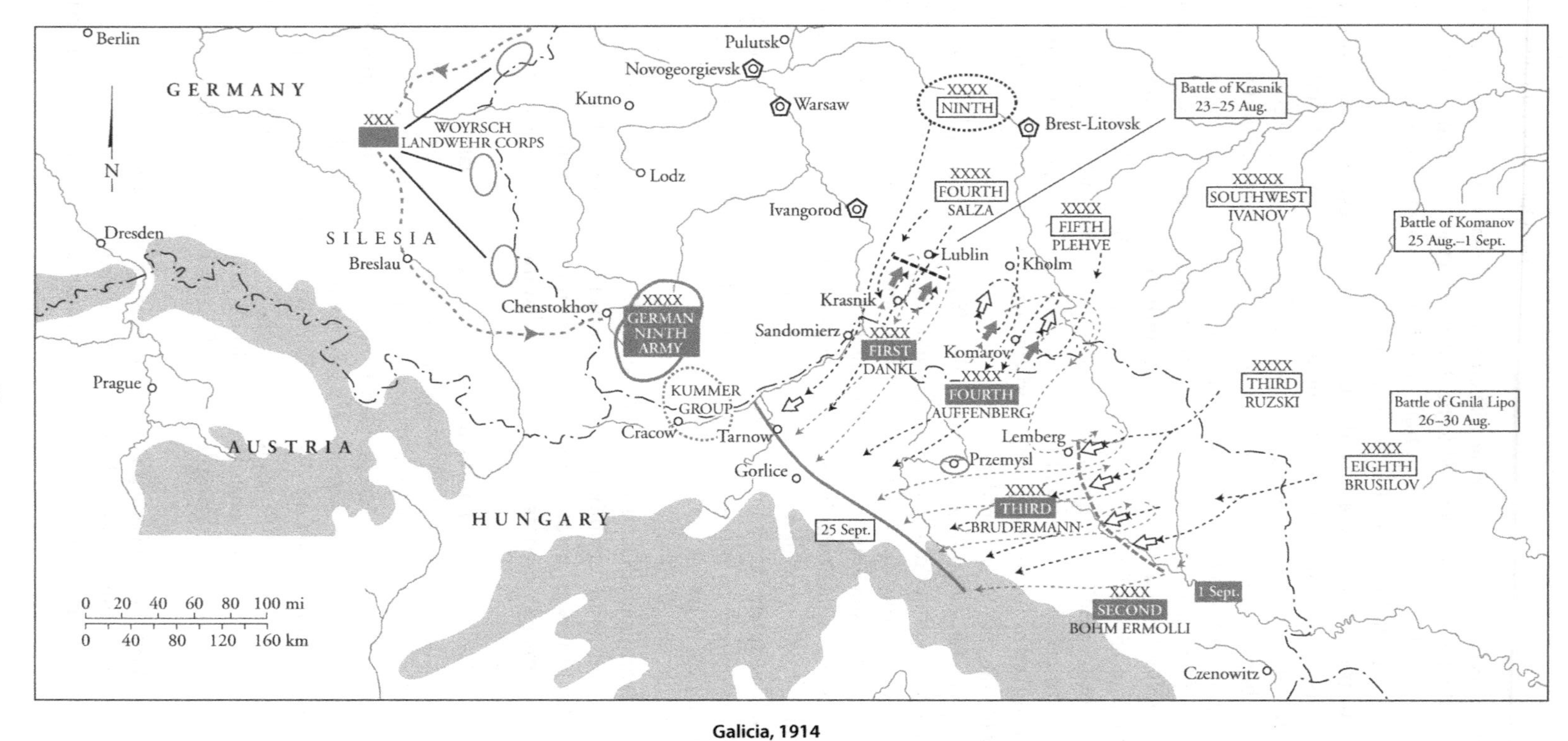

Galicia, 1914

Maps Courtesy of the Department of History, United States Military Academy

Balkans

to his sovereign, Putnik unleashed a massive counterattack that pushed Austro-Hungarian forces all the way out of Serbia by December 15.

Both sides had suffered unsustainable losses since August. Potiorek left behind over 200,000 dead, wounded, and missing. Serbia, which was to sacrifice by far the highest percentage of population of any warring nation of the Great War—5.7 percent—had lost over 130,000. It had won the early battles—but the war still continued as AOK contemplated its next move. "The war," wrote an Austrian officer, "is adopting in its present course ever more the character of a stubborn wrestling match, in which in the end success will be awarded to the side—given similar personal and moral qualities—whose material resources endure longer."[37]

THE EXEGENCIES OF A LONGER WAR

Not everyone had expected the European war to be over in a matter of weeks or months, but such naïve expectations were widespread enough that when bloody stalemate ensued there was at first surprise and in some cases borderline panic. Consternation soon gave way to quiet resolve, however, as the belligerent nations improvised solutions to the problems of a war that was lasting much longer than they had anticipated.

One reaction of this sort occurred in the financial world.[38] As the nations went to war that summer, common people refused cash for coin and took money out of bank accounts to stuff it under mattresses, politicians suspended gold standards, bankers declared bank holidays, and economists predicted financial disaster. Thus John Maynard Keynes (of later macroeconomic theory fame) stated with certainty that Europe's wealth could not be easily converted to war purposes and that when liquidity dried up within a year the powers would have to make peace. Sir John French's chief of staff also asserted confidently that the financial strain of feeding huge populations and mass armies would make war impossible to wage past eight months. Secretary for War Horatio Herbert Kitchener disagreed. "No financial pressure has ever stopped a war in progress,"[39] he told startled cabinet colleagues. The war would rage for at least two or three years, necessitating an immediate call for five hundred thousand volunteers to man twenty-five new divisions.

Kitchener was right, as it turned out, and the others wrong. Although business experienced difficulties in transition and some nations proved much better at making the transition than others, capital wealth could be retooled; economies could bear the burden of producing both butter and guns; and people, especially in the war's early flush of patriotism, could tolerate paying more taxes and lending more money to the state. Taxes covered roughly a quarter of the war's massive $45.3 billion cost in Britain and about a sixth of Germany's $32.4 billion outlays, but the so-called hidden tax of inflation reduced the difference between the two rival states. Thus Germany allowed its money supply to rise rapidly, inducing a tripling of the cost of living even with controls, while Britain restrained the growth of circulating currency and saw only a doubling of prices. Russia and Austria-Hungary ran the printing presses even faster and rising money supply pushed up the cost of living, respectively, fivefold and elevenfold. Taxes and inflation aside, however, most warring nations mainly borrowed at home and abroad to cover the bulk of their expenditures. The national debt of Russia rose during the war by a factor of four, France's by five, Germany's by eight, and Britain's by eleven. Neither during the opening campaigns nor during the four-year war of attrition that followed, however, did "financial pressure stop a war in progress."

The dawning reality of a longer war also produced a flurry of activity in foreign offices and chancelleries. If battlefield results demonstrated how evenly balanced power was in the two warring camps—something historians would later quantify and confirm[40]—then the nations fighting one another had to seek out new allies to tip the balance. Japan declared war against Germany in late August

1914 for its own reasons; no one pressured Tokyo. But the quest for friends with armies in Europe got under way that autumn with intense lobbying in the most important neutral capitals: Rome, Athens, Bucharest, Sofia, and Constantinople. Germany and Austria-Hungary achieved the first coup in November when Turkey joined their alliance and invaded the Russian Caucasus late the following month. Already hard-pressed on other fronts and critically short of shells and munitions, Russia pleaded for both military and economic assistance from Britain and France.

Russia provides a classic example, in fact, of economic unpreparedness for a long war. Its huge army, although already giving Vienna and Berlin fits on the eastern front, did not possess anything approaching an adequate military-industrial infrastructure. Russia's stock of rifles nearly sufficed for the units that took the field in August 1914, for example, but combat losses and the raising of new armies that summer and fall meant that monthly production capacity of about 60,000 fell shockingly below the 200,000 required. Soon many recruits trained without weapons and, much worse, went into combat unarmed with orders to pick up the rifles of fallen comrades. Furthermore, the nation's partial dependency on German chemical imports for powder production—now cut off—and comparatively low output of steel—Germany produced many times more—led very quickly to an explosives/munitions crisis in the artillery. *Stavka* entered the war confident that Russia's daily output of 3,500 fully armed shells would more than meet the army's field gun needs but already during the first battles in East Prussia and Galicia called frantically for 5,000, and then 15,000 in November after Mackensen shook First and Second Armies at Kutno.[41] Not until May 1915 could industry deliver this amount, however, which by then was considered woefully inadequate. Alas, Russia had to go it largely alone, for enemy fleets blockaded the Baltic and Black Seas, ice shut Murmansk and Archangel throughout much of the year, and only a trickle of allied aid or foreign arms purchases came over the badly overcrowded single track of the Trans-Siberian Railroad.

As summer turned to autumn 1914, Britain, France, and Germany also scrambled to increase shell output. Although it was one of the world's industrial leaders, Britain had devoted little of its capacity to the six-division BEF, producing 3,400 shells per day at war's outbreak. By March 1915 output had nearly quadrupled, and with huge American purchases swelling stocks in artillery depots, 2 million shells had reached the rapidly expanding British army. France, turning out fewer than 5,000 shells a day for its 75s in early August, reached 10,000 by the Battle of the Marne and over 62,000 daily in March. By this point production of shells far outpaced domestic production of nitrogen explosive to fill them, but France made up the shortfall with powder imports from America. Germany had the greatest output of field gun shells at the outset: 5,700 per day. This rose sevenfold to 40,000 in December 1914 with even faster growth achieved for light and heavy howitzer shells, but by Christmas OHL had shot up more than twice what it produced and shell stocks had run down to a dangerously low level. As shell production doubled in 1915 and tripled again in 1916, the crisis passed.

The prospect of a long war presented Germany with a dilemma much greater than production of artillery shells, nevertheless, as worried bureaucrats, industrialists, and consumers peered anxiously into the North Sea for German merchant ships that were not making port. Altogether 639 vessels, 44 percent of the German merchant marine, were trapped in neutral harbors or else sunk or confiscated by the British blockade. Agriculturally only 75 percent self-sufficient, Germany could find some consolation in its large 1914 harvest and the brisk trade in food it conducted that autumn with neutral countries like Holland and Denmark. Imports from the former country doubled by December and imports from the latter nearly quintupled despite British efforts to interfere with foreign goods shipped over neutrals to Germany. That first Christmas, nevertheless, Germany's caloric intake had fallen more than 25 percent.[42] And what would 1915 bring?

Although almost fully self-sufficient agriculturally when the war broke out, Austria-Hungary fared much worse during the opening campaigns. The blockade, of course, affected the Dual Monarchy too, but Russian capture of Galicia, responsible for an eighth of the empire's agricultural output, combined with the blockade to create urban food shortages and queuing at grocery stores as early as October 1914, a dire circumstance exacerbated in Vienna by the two hundred thousand refugees who flocked into the capital from the war zone. Officials attempted cleverly in January 1915 to turn popular ire against the enemy for trying to "starve us out." What the Entente's "mass armies" could not do "they want to achieve by cutting off our imports of foodstuffs and placing our population in danger of starvation." But insiders knew it was more complicated and controversial than that, for Hungary, responsible for five-eighths of the empire's cereal crops, had exacerbated matters that month by selfishly banning food shipments to Austria. Dilution of wheat bread with barley, rye, corn, and potato meal became necessary, and in April even this "heavy unappetizing bread"[43] was rationed, triggering the first food riots in May as women plundered stores. The situation deteriorated further when Italy joined the Entente, somewhat neutralizing Turkey's entry on the other side, and tightened the blockade of Central Europe.

In one very critical respect the blockade harmed not only Germany's and Austria-Hungary's long-term ability to feed themselves but also their ability to wage war: imports of nitrate ores were cut off.[44] In peacetime, for example, Germany consumed 40,000 tons of nitrogen annually for all industrial purposes (including explosives manufacture) and 200,000 tons for fertilizer. This peacetime consumption level was entirely inadequate in wartime, of course, and even that proved impossible to maintain, for over 95 percent of the raw nitrates required to support German nitrogen production of 120,000 tons—half of national consumption—had been imported, as had finished fertilizer and industrial nitrogen products that constituted the other half of nitrogen consumption. Deprived of these imports in early August, the German army had to rely on nitrate stockpiles, which were exhausted by late October 1914. After that the war effort depended on what the nation could turn out domestically (i.e., without relying in any way on imported materials), which had amounted to a mere 11,000 tons of nitrogen annually, produced from coke by-products and, ingeniously enough, the air.

Fortunately for Germany, its scientists, engineers, and businessmen came to the rescue. The main contributions were made by Fritz Haber of the Kaiser Wilhelm Institute for Physical Chemistry and Carl Bosch of the Badenese Aniline and Soda Factory. Before the war Haber had devised a way to extract ammonia from air (which is over 79 percent nitrogen gas) by catalyzing it under intense heat and pressure, but Bosch's firm engineered this so-called synthetic fixation of nitrogen process, thereby creating the potential for a spectacular increase in German nitrogen production to 200,000 tons a year. Coke by-product processes yielded another 70,000. Finally, Walther Rathenau, head of the German General Electric Company, presided over a reorganization of the largest chemical, armaments, and other war-related firms that enabled a new bureaucratic structure controlled by these companies, the War Raw Materials Office, to secure available inputs at low cost with no limits to the prices they charged the state for finished explosives and munitions. Consequently, Germany was able to more than triple explosives production from 1,200 tons per month in August 1914 to 4,000 tons by late 1915. This was well below what the army wanted—6,000 tons—but enough to continue the war. Agriculture would suffer, on the other hand, receiving only 70 percent of its needs. Without adequate fertilizer, harvests shriveled as the war dragged on, falling from 4,343,000 tons of wheat in 1914 to 2,484,000 three years later—a 42.8 percent decline. The Austrian half of the Dual Monarchy suffered an even greater 88 percent drop.

Great Britain and France did not face these problems—just the opposite, in fact, as imports of food streamed into their ports from all over the world. So did nitrates and other raw materials required for the manufacture of explosives, such that French output doubled in 1915 to 3,000 tons a month and Britain's rose meteorically over 6,000—altogether more than twice what Germany could produce in late 1915, which it then had to distribute to two fronts, not just one. Furthermore, the allied production figure did not include significant purchases from the United States, Canada, India, and Australia. Producing 3,000 tons a month in October 1915, for example, France consumed 4,500 thanks to its U.S. purchases. Similarly, Britain could afford to concentrate on powder production, construction of warships, and other war-related items in 1915 while buying 3.5 million artillery shells and 178 million rounds of small-arms ammunition on the American market largely with loans from American banks. The following year America sold Britain a phenomenal 20.9 million shells and 554 million pistol and rifle rounds.[45] These figures illustrate well the "zero-sum" nature of Britain's naval power, which provided access to world manufacturing and financial markets and also enabled it to blockade Central Europe. One side benefited in proportion to the other side's losses, in other words, just as game theory would have it. The economic numbers discussed above also make it easy to appreciate, on the other side of the equation, Berlin's intense desire for victories at sea and war-reversing battles on land elsewhere in the world. Accordingly, our focus now widens to cover this side of the Great War's early phase.

NOTES

1. My Italics. Cited in Annika Mombauer, *Helmuth von Moltke and the Origins of the First World War* (Cambridge, UK, 2001), 95.
2. The standard work is Gerhard Ritter, *The Schlieffen Plan: Critique of a Myth,* trans, B. H. Liddell Hart (London, 1958). The notion of a Schlieffen "Plan" was later popularized by Barbara Tuchman, *The Guns of August* (New York, 1962). For the orthodoxy at its height, see Holger H. Herwig, *The First World War: Germany and Austria-Hungary 1914–1918* (London, 1997); and John Keegan, *The First World War* (New York, 1999).
3. Terence Zuber, "The Schlieffen Plan Reconsidered," *War in History* 6 (1999): 262–305. The entire document is printed (with war game maps) in Zuber's *German War Planning, 1891–1914: Sources and Interpretations* (Woodbridge, NJ, 2004), 167–185. Also see the rejoinder article by Terence M. Holmes, "The Reluctant March on Paris: A Reply to Terence Zuber's 'The Schlieffen Plan Reconsidered,'" *War in History* 8 (2001): 208–232. It is noteworthy, however, that Holmes accepts the basic argument of Zuber, namely, that Schlieffen considered the drive on Paris a worst-case scenario, not the main goal of the offensive. As the polemic with Holmes proceeded, Zuber buttressed his case with *Inventing the Schlieffen Plan: German War Planning, 1871–1914* (Oxford, 2002). Many works appearing since the Zuber-Holmes exchange accept all or most of his original thesis. See Eric Dorn Brose, *The Kaiser's Army: The Politics of Military Technology in Germany during the Machine Age 1870–1918* (New York, 2001), 69–84, 165–172, 183 ff; Hew Strachan, *The First World War* (London, 2003), 44–45; and David Stevenson, *Cataclysm: The First World War as Political Tragedy* (New York, 2004), 38–39. One that does not is Mombauer, *Helmuth von Moltke.* Remaining most adamantly opposed is Holger H. Herwig. See his "Germany," in Richard F. Hamilton and Holger H. Herwig, *The Origins of World War I* (Cambridge, UK, 2003). For more recent critiques of Zuber researchers must read German. See Hans Ehlert, Michael Epkenhans, and Gerhard P. Gross, eds., *Der Schlieffenplan: Analysen und Dokumente* (Paderborn, 2006), especially the piece by Gross, "There was a Schlieffen Plan: Neue Quellen," 117–160.
4. For these points, see Holmes, "Reluctant March," 222; and Robert T. Foley, "Der Schlieffen Plan: Ein Aufmarschplan für den Krieg," in Ehlert et al., *Der Schlieffenplan,* 101–116. Holmes cites Schlieffen's comment that the forty-two-day scenario was unlikely but that contemplating it would prevent boredom. That the game was so extensive and elaborate seems to indicate, however, that more was afoot than preventing boredom.
5. Zuber, "Schlieffen Plan," 282.
6. Ibid., 298.
7. Holmes, "Reluctant March," 208–232.
8. For this, see Brose, *Kaiser's Army,* 82–84.
9. Cited in ibid., 169.
10. Cited in ibid., 276, n. 131.
11. Holmes, "Reluctant March," 223.
12. The attack, probably the work of Erich Ludendorff of the General Staff, had been conceived around 1908–1909. See Mombauer, *Helmuth von Moltke,* 96–98. The plan became the only available option in 1913 when it became clear that budgetary constraints would limit the number of heavy siege howitzers required to destroy the forts. See Brose, *Kaiser's Army,* 167–171.
13. Moltke's memoirs are cited in Holmes, "Reluctant March," 227.
14. See Brose, *Kaiser's Army,* 167–172, 212.
15. For recent accounts of the western front in 1914, see Hew Strachan, *The First World War* Vol. 1, *To Arms* (Oxford, 2001), 163–280; Brose, *Kaiser's Army,* 183–225; and Robert A. Doughty, *Pyrrhic Victory: French Strategy and Operations in the Great War* (Cambridge, MA, 2005), 46–104.

16. Cited in Doughty, *Pyrrhic Victory*, 63.
17. John Keegan, *Opening Moves: August 1914* (New York, 1971), 81.
18. Moltke had placed Bülow overall command of the three armies to ensure better coordination.
19. See Alexander Watson, Enduring the Great War: Combat, Morale and Collapse in the German and British Armies, 1914–1918 (Cambridge, UK, 2008), 142–148.
20. Doughty, *Pyrrhic Victory*, 75.
21. Four German divisions had been transferred to the eastern front and six divisions besieged Antwerp and other fortresses. Moltke also deployed the two divisions from Schleswig-Holstein to Antwerp.
22. Cited in Tuchman, *Guns of August*, 485.
23. For casualty estimates inclusive of the Marne, as well as through the race to the sea, see Michael Howard, "Men against Fire: The Doctrine of the Offensive in 1914," in Peter Paret, ed., *Makers of Modern Strategy from Machiavelli to the Nuclear Age* (Princeton, NJ, 1986), 523; Keegan, *First World War*, 135–136; Strachan, *First World War*, 230, 241; and Doughty, *Pyrrhic Victory*, 104.
John Mosier (*The Myth of the Great War: How the Germans Won the Battles and How the Americans Saved the Allies* [New York, 2001], 120–121) lists 329,000 French soldiers dead or missing through September. With wounded included the total casualty figure would have exceeded a million, but he exaggerates French losses and underestimates German—only 200,000 dead and missing through November, or about 500,000 total losses, which seems far too low. His unquestioning reliance on German medical corps data that was undoubtedly incomplete or even falsified cannot be trusted. Thus the German government admitted to 467,500 total casualties on both fronts in November, also obviously unreliable (see Robert B. Asprey, *The German High Command at War: Hindenburg and Ludendorff Conduct World War I* [New York, 1991], 136).
24. See MacGregor Knox and Williamson Murray, "Thinking about Revolutions in Warfare," in their edited collection, *The Dynamics of Military Revolution 1300–2050* (Cambridge, UK, 2001), especially 11–14. Still invaluable detailed discussions of the various armies of the Great War in the RMA context are found in Allan R. Millett and Williamson Murray, eds., *Military Effectiveness*, Vol. 1, *The First World War* (Boston, 1988).
25. For the following passage, see Brose, *Kaiser's Army*, 98–101,165–167, 182–184, 191–192, 194–215; and Strachan, *First World War*, 1:220, 224–242.
26. Cited in Brose, *Kaiser's Army*, 211.
27. For the western campaigns in the autumn of 1914, see Keegan, *First World War*, 123–137; Strachan, *First World War*, 1:262–280; and Doughty, *Pyrrhic Victory*, 97–104.
28. Antwerp finally fell to the Germans on October 10, but the Belgian field army of fifty thousand soldiers managed to escape to the west. See Doughty, *Pyrrhic Victory*, 102–103.
29. See n. 23.
30. For the battles of Tannenberg and the Masurian Lakes, see Norman Stone, *The Eastern Front 1914–1917* (London, 1975), 44–69; W. Bruce Lincoln, *Passage Through Armageddon: The Russians in War and Revolution 1914–1918* (New York, 1986), 60–78; Dennis E. Showalter, *Tannenberg: Clash of Empires* (Hamden, CT, 1991); and Strachan, *First World War*, 1:281–335.
31. Cited in Strachan, *First World War*, 1:319.
32. For the fighting in Galicia, see Stone, *Eastern Front*, 70–91; Holger H. Herwig, *The First World War: Germany and Austria-Hungary 1914–1918* (London, 1997), 89–94; John Keegan, *The First World War* (New York, 1999), 155–161; and Strachan, *First World War*, 1:347–357.
33. For Conrad, see Herwig, *First World War*, 90, and for the quote, Strachan, *First World War*, 1:347.

34. For Galicia and Poland in the autumn of 1914, see Stone, *Eastern Front,* 92–107; Herwig, *First World War,* 106–110, 119–120; Keegan, *First World War,* 163–170; and Strachan, *First World War,* 357–373.
35. For the Serbian campaigns in 1914, see Herwig, *First World War,* 87–89, 111–112; Keegan, *First World War,* 151–155; and Strachan, *First World War,* 1:335–347.
36. Cited in Herwig, *First World War,* 111.
37. Cited in Hew Strachan, *The First World War* (New York, 2003), 27.
38. See Niall Ferguson, *The Pity of War: Explaining World War I* (New York, 1999), 318–338; and Hew Strachan, *Financing the First World War* (Oxford, 2004).
39. Cited in Ferguson, *Pity of War,* 319.
40. See L. L. Farrar, Jr., *Arrogance and Anxiety: The Ambivalence of German Power, 1848–1914* (Iowa City, 1981), 17–18, 37–39, who estimates that the Triple Entente had 55.6 percent of the power in Europe in 1910, Germany and Austria-Hungary 44.4 percent, but that Berlin and Vienna, growing faster, would have had 48.7 percent in 1920 to their enemies' 51.3 percent.
41. For figures on Russia as well as the other nations discussed below, see Strachan, *First World War,* 1:1037, 1055, 1067–1068, 1100–1108.
42. Thierry Bonzon and Belinda Davis, "Feeding the Cities," in Jay Winter and Jean-Louis Robert, *Capital Cities at War: Paris, London, Berlin 1914–1919* (Cambridge, UK, 1997), 310–311.
43. For the empire's food problems (and citations), see Herwig, *First World War,* 272–277; and Maureen Healy, *Vienna and the Fall of the Habsburg Empire: Total War and Everyday Life in World War I* (Cambridge, UK, 2004), 36–40.
44. For this crisis and its resolution, see Gerald D. *Feldman, Army Industry and Labor in Germany 1914–1918* (Princeton, NJ, 1966), 45–64, 152; L. F. Haber, *The Chemical Industry 1900–1930* (Oxford, 1971), 198–200; and Strachan, *First World War,* 1:1025–1027.
45. For this paragraph, see Strachan, *First World War,* 1:1057, 1084, 1106, 1108.

CHAPTER IV

The Wider War

1914–1915

Valparaiso glistened in a November Chilean sunrise. For the jubilant sailors of Germany's East Asia Squadron the sight of the shiny town stretching around the bay with so many merchant ships flying the homeland's black and white imperial colors; the green hills nearby; and more distantly, the gray and white of soaring, snowcapped mountains seemed like a visual reward for the smashing victory over British ships two days earlier. Into the roadstead of the harbor steamed the light cruiser *Nürnberg* flanked by heavy cruisers *Gneisenau* and the flagship, *Scharnhorst*. Respecting the laws of neutrality, two warships, light cruisers *Leipzig* and *Dresden*, remained offshore.[1]

Once the ships docked the German ambassador to Chile and his staff boarded *Scharnhorst* to welcome Admiral Maximilian Graf von Spee. No longer sharing his men's optimism, the mood of this aristocratic seaman was already turning morose as a premonition of his own death, the death of two sons serving with him, and the destruction of the entire squadron—mass death at sea—weighed down heavily upon his soul. To be sure, the day before he had written a friend about "the joy which reigns among us" but quickly added that the sinking of two British cruisers "might not mean much on the whole in view of the enormous number of English ships."[2]

On shore Spee resisted the clicking cameras and the hurrahs of so many resident Germans as he walked with a visiting delegation of Chilean admirals and German dignitaries to Valparaiso's German Club. Inside he mounted the grand staircase and strode past portraits of Kaiser William I, Chancellor Otto von Bismarck, Field

Marshall Helmuth von Moltke the Elder, and a large bust of Kaiser William II. For thirty minutes Spee tolerated toasts to his victory in the grand reception hall, until one mindlessly inebriated German raised his glass and called for all to drink to the "damnation of the British Navy." Spee refused for himself and his officers, replying nobly that he would only toast "the memory of a gallant and honorable foe."[3]

Presently he and his men left the building. As they did a woman moved out from the crowd and offered him a bouquet of flowers. "They will do nicely for my grave,"[4] he commented depressingly. Later that evening on board *Scharnhorst* Spee talked to a retired colleague living in Valparaiso about what was so troubling. "I am quite homeless. I cannot reach Germany; we possess no other secure harbor; I must plough the seas of the world doing as much mischief as I can until my ammunition is exhausted or a foe far superior in power succeeds in catching me."[5]

THE FLIGHT OF GERMANY'S EAST ASIA SQUADRON

When news of war pulsed into wireless stations across the globe in early August 1914, Graf Spee was caught off guard with no preconceived plan of operations.[6] In stark contrast to Helmuth von Moltke's "sooner-the-better" approach to war in Europe, the commander of Germany's East Asia Squadron realized that "later" was preferable for a navy unready to challenge Britain's economic and military power on the world's seas. Germany had commissioned thirty-three light cruisers since the late 1890s, all with enough 20–28-knot speed to overtake enemy merchant vessels, all with 4.1-inch guns adequate to sink commercial prizes. Six more of the fastest 4.1-inch light cruisers were scheduled to join the German fleet in 1915. Unable to slug it out in sea battles with capital ships (i.e., battleships, battle cruisers,[7] and heavy cruisers), these smaller vessels had been designed either to protect destroyers on coastal patrol or rove the seas as predators. In 1914, however, German naval leaders could mostly only dream about scores of light cruisers raiding enemy commerce, driving up freight rates and insurance premiums, bombarding enemy bases and colonies, drawing out the Royal Navy, and then repairing to German sea havens spread throughout the world, for Germany possessed only two good overseas naval stations: at Dar-es-Salaam in East Africa and Tsingtao in China. Not surprisingly—and most unfortunately for Berlin—when the European shooting of 1911–1913 suddenly widened into a worldwide conflagration in 1914, the German navy had twenty-six of its light cruisers in home waters bottled up like the rest of the German High Seas Fleet by the Grand Fleet of Britain. Of the ten modern ships overseas—seven light cruisers, two heavy cruisers, and one battle cruiser—six came under Spee's control within days of war's outbreak: the heavy cruisers *Scharnhorst* and *Gneisenau* and light cruisers *Emden, Leipzig, Dresden,* and *Nürnberg*. The squadron also had the *Prinz Eitel Friedrich*, an armed merchantman capable of raiding unarmed commerce.

Built by Germany on land seized from China in 1898, the harbor town of Tsingtao at the base of the Shantung peninsula was home to the East Asia Squadron. Its peacetime mission was to show the flag, demonstrate German power and prestige in the Far East, and police Germany's far-flung Pacific holdings—the

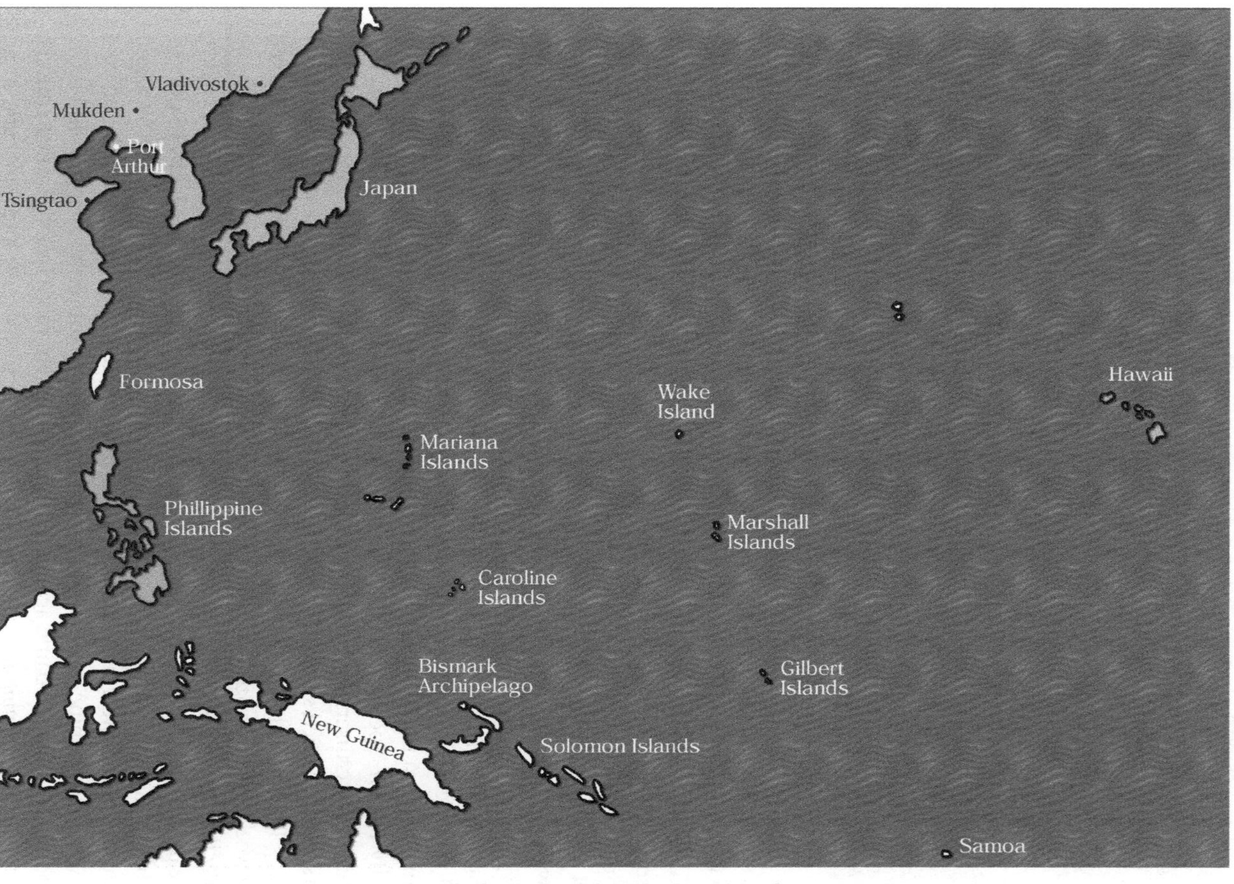

The Far East and the West-Central Pacific

One of Graf Spee's Raiders: Light Cruiser *Emden*
Harper's Pictorial Library

Mariana, Caroline, Marshall, and Gilbert Islands in the north; German New Guinea, the Solomon Islands, the Bismarck Archipelago, and West Samoa in the south. The squadron's wartime mission would depend on the enemies it faced. Spee could acquit himself well against Chinese forces on land near Tsingtao; the 4 Russian and French ships in the region; and perhaps also, although chances were slimmer, against Britain's pared-down Far Eastern Fleet with its 1 battleship, 2 heavy cruisers, and 2 modern light cruisers—definitely not, however, against Japan and its powerful fleet of 14 battleships (including 4 modern dreadnoughts), 1 battle cruiser, 15 heavy cruisers, 18 light cruisers, 51 destroyers, and 13 submarines. Given the likelihood of Japan entering the war on the side of its longtime ally Britain, Spee opted in early August to move *Emden*, *Prinz Eitel Friedrich*, and his heavy cruisers to Pagan Island in the northernmost Marianas, for defense of Tsingtao seemed suicidal against the combined might of Britain and Japan.

The admiral caucused with his ship captains on August 13. *Nürnberg* had arrived a week earlier; *Leipzig* and *Dresden* were still steaming west toward him through the Pacific. Although it was very tempting, only one captain, Karl von Müller of *Emden*, leaned toward taking the entire squadron west into the Indian Ocean to destroy British merchantmen and Australian and Indian troopships headed for Suez and Europe. There were no friendly coaling stations, and Spee needed to take on coal every eight or nine days, an especially important factor for his heavy cruisers. The possibility of a sea battle against Britain's faster and more heavily armed cruisers, *Minotaur* and *Hampshire*, her bigger light cruisers, *Newcastle* and *Yarmouth*, or an encounter with the twelve-inch guns of Australia's new battle cruiser, *Australia*, also argued against going west or south. Spee concluded, therefore, that the wisest move was to dispatch one lone ship, *Emden*, for commerce raiding in the west. One ship operating alone could refuel from the holds of captured merchantmen, but a whole squadron could not. With the rest of his flotilla Spee wanted to dash for the coast of South America, joining *Leipzig* and *Dresden* under way. Coal and provisions were available in Valparaiso, and from there his ships could round the Horn, disrupt Britain's critical South American trade in nitrates and foodstuffs, and perhaps break through the Atlantic to join the German High Seas Fleet. Even if he encountered a more powerful squadron of British warships, this would weaken Britain in the North Sea, increase the chances of a German North Sea victory, and most important of all, break Britain's threatening blockade of Germany.

The remarkable voyage of the *Emden* presents historians with an opportunity to speculate about alternative strategies. For three months after leaving Spee on August 14, Müller's light cruiser ravaged allied shipping in the Indian Ocean and Bay of Bengal. By erecting a fourth funnel made of canvas he succeeded in disguising *Emden* as a British four-funneled light cruiser, a ploy that consistently allowed him to gain the element of surprise. Müller intercepted thirteen neutral merchant ships and sank sixteen British merchantmen, a Russian cruiser, and a French destroyer. He also bombarded the Burma Company's oil tanks at Madras, destroying half a million gallons of kerosene. The effect of his raids was compounded by the sorties of another light cruiser, *Königsberg*, from German East Africa into surrounding waters. The British and Australians were eventually forced to keep merchantmen in port and provide heavy escorts for troop convoys headed for Europe. One of the forty allied warships hunting for *Königsberg* and *Emden*, the Australian light cruiser *Sydney*, finally caught up with Müller on November 9, forcing his ship to run aground and surrender.

Could Spee have done more harm to the allied war effort if he had divided his squadron to engage in solo surface raiding? For instance, *Emden*, *Königsberg*, and *Karlsruhe*, a German light cruiser wrecking havoc in the Caribbean until an internal explosion sank it in Barbados on November 4, destroyed 2 percent of the British merchant marine and forced the Admiralty to commit scores of ships to hunt the seas. Five more raiders might have caused much more serious disruption, especially if the presence of *Gneisenau* and *Scharnhorst* in the Indian Ocean had forced Britain to commit six or seven of its battle cruisers to protect shipping and troop convoys and destroy the East Asia Squadron.

As *Emden* headed west from Pagan Island on August 14, 1914, Spee steamed east, reaching Christmas Island on September 7, where he learned that New Zealand had seized Samoa a week earlier. Hoping to destroy enemy supply ships at Apia, capital of Samoa, or perhaps even surprise *Australia* at anchor, Spee backtracked, suddenly appearing in the harbor a week later. The Germans found no prizes, however, and left without firing a shell. Spee went west until resuming his eastward trek under cover of darkness—an ancient ruse that at least succeeded in confusing the British into thinking that he intended to challenge them in the western Pacific. But Spee's real course took his ships over Bora-Bora, Papeete, Tahiti, and Easter Island, where *Leipzig* and *Dresden* joined the flotilla, and finally to Más Afuera, about five hundred miles from Chile, on October 26. Four days later Valparaiso and the magnificent gleaming white of the Andes came into view.

The British Admiralty were ignorant of the East Asia Squadron's position until October 4 as Spee neared Easter Island, but even then they remained uncertain about how many light cruisers accompanied him. London dispatched Rear Admiral Sir Christopher Cradock to meet the threat. His woefully inadequate force consisted of two obsolete cruisers, *Good Hope* and *Monmouth,* one modern light cruiser, *Glasgow,* and a converted liner with only six guns, *Ortanto.* Cradock steamed through the Straits of Magellan and moved up the coast of Chile, where disaster and death awaited him. Aware of his weaknesses, Cradock hoped to engage only a portion of Spee's squadron, or perhaps an isolated cruiser. As he moved south from Más Afuera, the German commander encouraged this faulty thinking by ordering all ships to signal with the call sign of *Leipzig,* which, consequently, Cradock thought he could trap near Coronel. Spee did not know of Cradock's presence either, assuming only that he had a chance to bring his combined strength to bear against *Glasgow,* which had also been sighted near Coronel. When the two fleets finally sighted one another late on the afternoon of November 1, Spee withdrew while the western sun blinded his gunners but then closed at dusk when Cradock's ships became silhouetted sitting ducks. *Good Hope* and *Monmouth* were sunk; *Glasgow* and *Ortanto* fled, fortunate to have survived a severe beating in the humiliating Battle of Coronel. The news of this debacle—two cruisers lost and the deaths of sixteen hundred sailors in only one hour—jolted the world's leading sea power.

The Admiralty immediately scanned the seas for ships to amass against Spee, who might soon round the Horn or slip through the Panama Canal, join *Karlsruhe,* and enter the Atlantic.

THE GAME OF POWER IN THE PACIFIC

As Spee fled on August 23, 1914, Japan declared war against Germany. Under the terms of her alliance with Great Britain she was not obligated to do so: only if Germany attacked British possessions in Asia would the alliance come into effect.[8] London originally asked Tokyo to maintain neutrality, but then on August 6, worried about Spee's intentions, Foreign Minister Edward Grey requested help in hunting down Germany's armed merchantmen without Japan actually becoming a belligerent. The Japanese government, however, had another agenda. Entering the fray against Germany offered Japan a brilliant opportunity to extend its interests in China and the Pacific by seizing German holdings, Tsingtao foremost among them. Tokyo justified its ultimatum and subsequent declaration of belligerency by claiming, dubiously, that Germany threatened the peace in Asia and that therefore the alliance terms had been met.

Forces of the Imperial Japanese Army and Navy converged on Tsingtao in early September. The first landings occurred far to the north at Lungkow, thereby cutting Tsingtao off from the mainland. The navy blockaded and bombarded from the sea. The main force went ashore at Laoshan Bay and succeeded in closing the ring by September 25. Facing 60,000 Japanese, 2,000 British and Indian troops, and over one hundred heavy siege guns with ample shells, German commander Clemens Meyer-Waldeck and his roughly 5,000 defenders had little chance of holding out, especially after the departure of Spee's firepower. Learning from their experience in the Russo-Japanese War, furthermore, the Japanese avoided suicidal

Looting the German Empire: Japanese Artillery Advances on Tsingtao
Harper's Pictorial Library

frontal assaults, methodically pushing their trenches closer to Tsingtao during the nighttime. They also frustrated German gunners by not registering shots and giving away their positions or the time of attacks, rather relying for accurate fire on the innovative tactic of forward observation from the air. As we shall see in later chapters, these were techniques it would take the European armies facing, admittedly, a more difficult challenge on the western front three years to master. Running low on ammunition, Meyer-Waldeck surrendered Tsingtao on November 7.

During this campaign other countries in the Pacific joined the anti-German landgrab. Escorted by Australian ships, an expeditionary force from New Zealand took Western Samoa without firing a shot on August 30. The Australians landed in German New Guinea and the Bismarck Archipelago on September 11, and within a week these colonies as well as the Solomon Islands had changed hands. In early to mid-October Japan completed the seizure of the German Pacific by occupying the Mariana, Caroline, Marshall, and Gilbert Islands. That Germany had nowhere near adequate naval strength in the Pacific to defend its holdings is less an indication of shortsighted naval policy than a measure of Berlin's sorely overstretched means of achieving the end of worldwide strength and status. The same process of imperial German collapse was playing itself out simultaneously in Africa.

Now the remaining Pacific powers eyed one another warily. Ensconced in the East Indies, Holland looked askance at the rapid buildup of the Japanese navy as well as Tokyo's thinly veiled expansionism. Great Britain, too, felt uneasy about its ally's ultimate intentions, for when Lord Grey suggested in November that the transfer of German islands be considered temporary in order to bargain at the peace table with Germany should it emerge victorious in Europe, Japan nodded approval in principle, then exposed its true agenda by asserting that "the Japanese nation would naturally insist on the permanent retention of all German islands north of the equator."[9] Australia and New Zealand also felt threatened, and worse, cheated out of further acquisitions. Having captured German New Guinea, the administrative headquarters of the German Pacific, they laid claim to the whole, which Japan, pointing to ancient rights of conquest, of course ignored. Overshadowing all of these potential conflicts were worsening relations between Japan and the United States. Already in possession of Hawaii, Wake Island, Eastern Samoa, Guam, and the Philippines, America had preferred at war's outbreak that all nations agree to maintain neutrality in the Pacific. This possibility was quickly swept aside, but Japan's policy in particular upset Washington. For its part, Tokyo, which had long considered the United States its major potential adversary at sea, intensified contingency planning for a naval confrontation with its racial enemy in the east—a tragedy that would await a second world war.

Japan's designs in China proved even more controversial. In August 1914 the rising Asian power already controlled Korea, Taiwan (Formosa), and Kwantung, adding Tsingtao three months later. In January 1915, however, Tokyo presented its far-reaching "twenty-one demands" to the president of China, Yuan Shih-Kai. They broke down into five groups. First, China should accept Japan's lease rights to the Shantung Peninsula. The second sought to solidify Japan's position in southern Manchuria and eastern Inner Mongolia, in particular its lease rights in Kwantung. Third, China should admit Japan to joint ownership of the Hanyehping Iron and Coal Company. Fourth, with an eye on America's desire to lease the harbor at Fukien, on the mainland across from Japanese-controlled Taiwan, China should pledge not to lease any harbors to foreign powers. The fifth group Tokyo labeled "wishes," not "demands." China should accept Japanese political and military advisers, a form of indirect control that would move Japan a step closer to the outright colonization of this once proud Asian giant. China refused to accept this status, Yuan himself traveling to Japan to negotiate milder terms. Mindful of its own position in China, Britain also protested, asserting that the fifth group represented an egregious violation of the alliance treaty between Britain and Japan. Not wishing to further disrupt Anglo-Japanese relations, Tokyo finally dropped group five, and London, eager to prosecute the war in Europe without Asian worries, found this acceptable. Yuan eventually yielded to these terms too. The ire of Washington increased, however, for American leaders of progressive stripe hoped for democracy and economic advancement in China, not Japanese encroachment.

SPEE'S TRAGIC DEMISE

First Lord of the Admiralty Winston Churchill and First Sea Lord Jacky Fisher desperately wanted to avenge the Battle of Coronel, Britain's worst defeat at sea in modern times.[10] Available strength, however, did not encourage the two top navy men in London. In the river Platte, Argentina, lay three old armored cruisers and the battered *Glasgow*. Another modern light cruiser, *Bristol*, could be brought from the West Indies and a fourth obsolete cruiser from the coast of Africa. In a daylight engagement these ships could perhaps have a fighting chance, but it was unlikely, for Spee's ships were state of the art and manned by the most accurate gunners in the German navy. Determined to avoid another Coronel, Churchill and Fisher ordered Admiral John Jellicoe to sacrifice two battle cruisers, *Invincible* and *Inflexible*, and steam them south without delay. A third battle cruiser, *Princess Royal*, was dispatched to the Caribbean in case Spee tried to pass through the Panama Canal. With their twelve-inch guns and twenty-five-knot speed, the battle cruisers would have a significant advantage when confronting Spee's East Asia Squadron. The hastily assembled flotilla, minus one of the old cruisers sent to Cape Town, united at the Abrolhos Rocks coaling station under the command of Admiral Frederick Sturdee. They left for the Falkland Islands on November 26, arriving at Port Stanley on December 7. After Coronel, *Glasgow* had wired home that "further operations against the same enemy are the unanimous wish of us all." "As it happened," recalled Churchill, "they were not to be denied this."[11]

In the five weeks that had elapsed since his triumphant albeit bittersweet entry to Valparaiso, Spee delayed his gamble on cruising undetected through the Atlantic. For its part, German naval command in Berlin eagerly anticipated the attempt, wiring him after Coronel to leave the Pacific "as soon as you think it advisable" and head for home. Because it would probably be necessary "to secure the cooperation of the High Seas Fleet in breaking through the enemy blockade in the North Sea," his intentions "should be communicated early."[12]

The prospect of coordinating an elaborate fleet engagement against a portion of the Grand Fleet, wedging it between Spee, who might slip through the Channel at night, and Germany's larger ships emerging in the North Sea at first light, watered the mouths of German naval commanders who desperately wanted to get into a war they had played little part in thus far.[13] German inactivity at the outset stemmed from the fact that its naval leaders expected the British to establish a blockade just off the coast and then strike the High Seas Fleet in port. However, when the enemy opted for a distant blockade in the Western Approaches to the English Channel and the far North Sea between Scotland and Norway, the German Admiralty was caught off guard with no prearranged plan to attack Britain's formidable fleet. Furthermore, the German General Staff had showed so little concern for intercepting the troop convoys of the British Expeditionary Force (BEF), assuming that this small force would be swept away by the army's massive invasion of Belgium, that no help was asked for at sea—or had been in the years before 1914. The navy briefly considered taking action on its own to block the BEF's crossing but hesitated to improvise highly risky and potentially costly operations.

The only actions that had occurred, moreover, had gone badly. On August 28 the British lured eight of Germany's light cruisers into the Heligoland Bight, where five battle cruisers and six more-heavily-armed light cruisers awaited. Three German light cruisers, including the newer *Köln* and *Mainz*, went down. Two days earlier light cruiser *Magdeburg* had run aground and scuttled in the Baltic. These four losses proved highly significant, for afterward Kaiser William II, shocked at the prospect of his beautiful, expensive ships going to the bottom, issued strict orders that the High Seas Fleet not risk major offensive battles. These directives would probably not apply, however, if Spee needed assistance getting home.

Indeed it seemed to be a propitious moment for action in the North Sea. After the departure of three battle cruisers to hunt down Spee that November, the British still possessed an approximate thirty-to-twenty advantage in state-of-the-art capital ships, but constant patrolling duty to maintain the blockade created breakdowns, such that five or six of the heavies were in port or dry dock for repairs on any given day. Thus *Scharnhorst* and *Gneisenau* would almost even the big-ship odds, while Spee's three light cruisers would actually give Germany an edge in this category if the German Baltic Fleet were thrown into the fray. On the other hand, many of Germany's light cruisers were old and slow, and none would be able to match Britain's six new *Southampton* cruisers with their six-inch guns, as Heligoland Bight had amply demonstrated.

Much was at stake, therefore, as Spee pondered his options. Depressed and preoccupied with the odds against him, however, he steamed away from home, *west* for Más Afuera, remaining there until November 15 before departing south for San Quintín, three hundred miles from the Horn. He stayed there a week and did not make it through the straits to Picton Island until December 2. Still there four days later, a now less hesitant Spee met with his captains and proposed an assault on the Falkland Islands as revenge for the allied seizure of Samoa. Few of his officers agreed with the plan, but on the basis of three-week-old information that there were no British ships in the Falklands, he overruled the opposition and decided on an attack for the morning of December 8—one day after Sturdee's powerful squadron steamed into Port Stanley.

Because of his gloomy indecision as well as what military historians refer to as "the fog of war"—the tragic dearth of adequate information in wartime—Spee and the East Asia Squadron had squandered an opportunity to slip into the Atlantic before Britain could block them. They were now doomed to suffer a disastrous defeat. The plan called for *Gneisenau* and *Nürnberg* to enter the harbor, destroy the wireless station and all coal stocks not needed by the squadron, and take the governor hostage. The rest of the ships would lie offshore. Had the whole squadron joined the attack, Spee could perhaps have inflicted considerable damage on Sturdee's ships, which were caught by surprise during coaling, but as it turned out, 12-inch shots from an obsolete British battleship grounded for harbor protection quickly convinced the two German ships to steam away. Knowing he had superior speed, Sturdee coolly finished coaling and gave chase, pulling within range of the German ships by early afternoon. Spee now divided his flotilla, sending the light cruisers to the southwest, hopefully to escape, while engaging *Invincible, Inflexible,* and an older heavy cruiser with *Scharnhorst* and *Gneisenau.* Twice Spee managed to come within the range of his 8.2-inch guns, but twice Sturdee pulled away to pound the Germans from a greater distance. Before sunset both of the big German ships had gone down. Spee, his son Heinrich, and fourteen hundred officers and men perished in the action. Meanwhile, *Glasgow* and two older cruisers went after the German light cruisers, sinking *Nürnberg* and *Leipzig* before dusk. Otto von Spee and nearly eight hundred sailors died horrifically. Spee's premonitions had come tragically true.

In one month (November 4–December 8, 1914) Germany lost *Karlsruhe* in the Caribbean, *Emden* in the Indian Ocean, and four of Spee's five ships in the

Falklands—*Dresden* had gotten away but was tracked down and sunk in early 1915. *Königsberg* was by this time trapped in East Africa and also soon destroyed. The loss of these eight ships was a debacle from which Berlin's overseas fleet could not recover, for now, except for two cruisers that had fled through the Dardanelles to Constantinople (Istanbul), the world's oceans were cleared of German surface ships.

This left the British free to exploit their colonies and dominions, both economically and militarily. In 1913 Britain drew about 25 percent of its imports from the empire, including much higher percentages for many critical foodstuffs and raw materials. During the war imperial imports doubled. Britain also enjoyed unimpeded access to world trade outside the empire, especially the crucial flow of oil from Persia and Mexico, nitrates from Chile, and foodstuffs and munitions from the United States. Before the conflict ended, furthermore, about 2 million allied soldiers shipped out of India, the British white dominions, and French Africa for battlefields in Europe and around the world. The sun did not set on the British Empire—or on its war effort.[14]

TURKEY ENTERS THE WAR

Dressed in a white summer suit appropriate for the Turkish heat of August, Henry Morgenthau, American ambassador to the Ottoman Empire, peered pensively out the window of the official Rolls Royce as it snaked along the shores of the Bosporus. A moment later the driver turned into a long promenade ground leading to the yellow limestone structure housing the German Embassy. The building's austere Baroque architecture and fierce-looking imperial eagles perched on rooftop corners loomed larger and larger as the car sped toward them. Leaving the backseat and striding quickly through the huge pillared front gate, Morgenthau put his final thoughts in order before meeting his German counterpart. Suspecting correctly that Turkey would not remain neutral for much longer, the American representative to the Sublime Porte wanted to discuss the implications of Turkish belligerency for the Middle East and Central Asia.[15]

Morgenthau was ushered up the main staircase and through a long corridor to the office of the German ambassador. A personal friend of the kaiser with great influence in German foreign policy circles, Baron Conrad von Wangenheim looked and acted the part of old Junker nobility. His short-cropped hair crowned a prominent forehead; imposing, deep-set eyes; thick, immaculately trimmed mustache; and strong, square chin. Morgenthau declined to smoke, but Wangenheim clipped the end of a large black cigar and lit it. Puffing away, he startled his guest with a series of shockingly bold predictions and assertions.

Enver Pasha knew what side his bread was buttered on, began the Junker, so yes, Turkey would certainly join Germany in the war. And why not, for the German Reich could not lose. The British might be powerful at sea, but the conflict would be decided on land, and on land the German army would prevail, especially if revolution removed Russia, Turkey's natural enemy, from the Entente.

Russia, Central Asia, and the Middle East

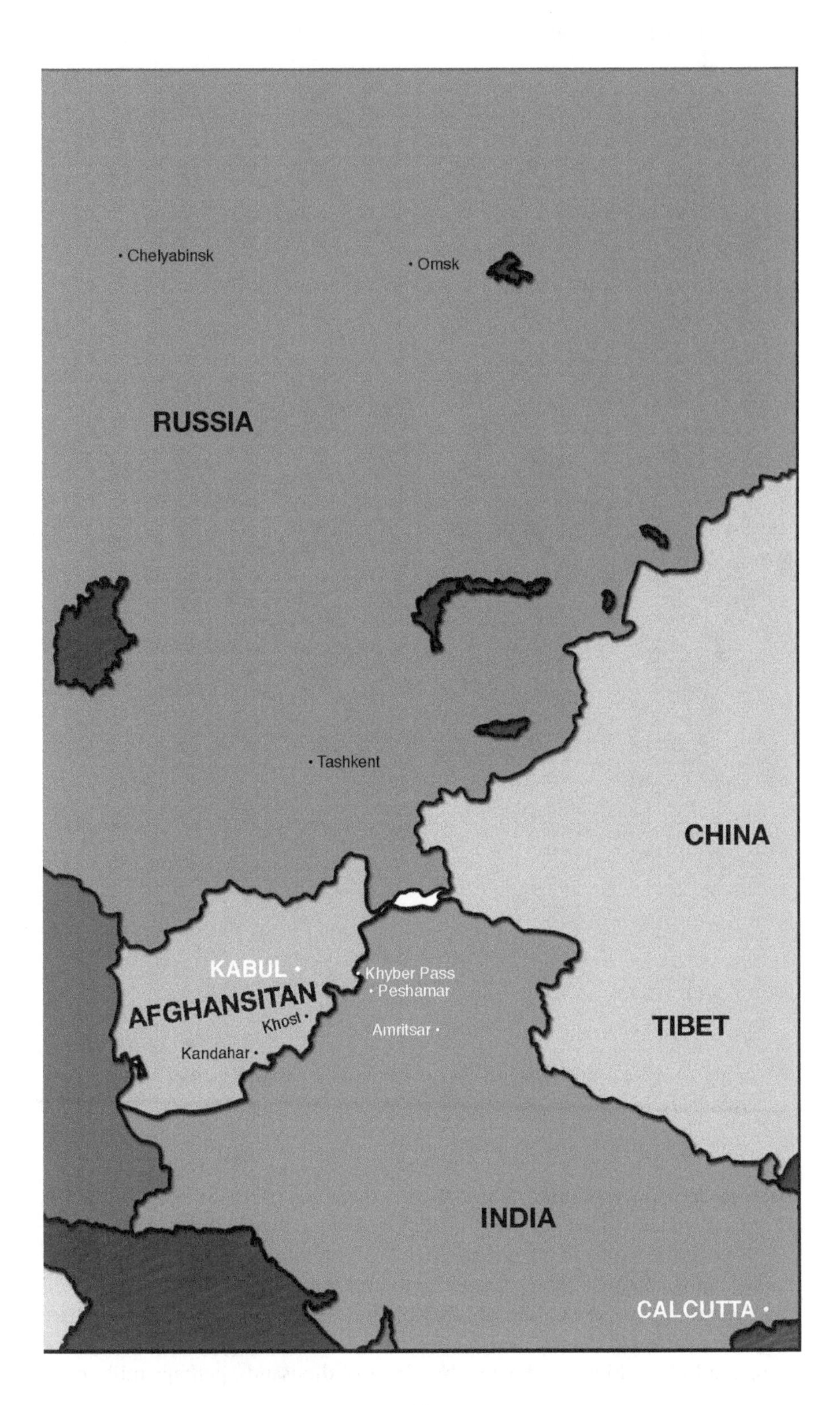

• Chelyabinsk
• Omsk
RUSSIA
• Tashkent
CHINA
KABUL •
• Khyber Pass
• Peshamar
AFGHANSITAN
Khost •
Kandahar •
Amritsar •
TIBET
INDIA
CALCUTTA •

Young Turks: Enver and Djemal Pasha on Jerusalem's Dome of the Rock
Courtesy of the Library of Congress

Backing Germany was Turkey's best chance, therefore, of regaining all of the territories taken away from her over the years by Britain, Russia, Italy, and Greece.

Now, however, came the real shocker. "The big thing is the Muslim world,"[16] barked Wangenheim, blowing smoke up toward the ceiling. Turkey's entry would put the authority of the Caliph of Islam behind German plans for an incendiary holy war that would destroy British interests in East Africa, Egypt, Persia, Afghanistan, and India, while also drawing hundreds of thousands, perhaps millions of soldiers away from the main European theaters of action. Let the British Empire burn up in Jihad, proclaimed the self-righteous Wangenheim to the horror of his American visitor: Great Britain had made a perfidious declaration of war against Germany and should thus suffer terrible consequences for its ill-considered action.

Wangenheim headed a list of highly influential figures in Germany who wanted to strike a serious blow at Britain's worldwide power. Scholars of Asia and Turkey like Max von Oppenheim and Ernst Jackh, industrialists like Prussia's steel baron August Thyssen, leading generals like Helmuth von Moltke, and also the kaiser himself dreamed of putting the torch of Jihad to British holdings and colonies from Africa to India. The significance of these designs magnified after German surface ships were swept from the high seas and German colonies seized by enemy countries within months of the outbreak of the war, for now, other than submarines (U-boats) or the High Seas Fleet, how else could Germany undermine Britain's position in the world?

Notwithstanding the persuasiveness of the German ambassador and his allies, however, Turkish belligerency was not a foregone conclusion.[17] At the time of the July Crisis, the Young Turks' Committee of Union and Progress (CUP), which had staged a coup against Sultan Abdul Hamid II in 1908, held power. Three individuals claimed the most influence in the badly factionalized CUP: Naval Minister Ahmed Djemal; Interior Minister Mehmed Talaat; and most dynamic of all, War Minister Enver Pasha, Wangenheim's most important contact. Although many Young Turks favored either a friendly neutrality or else joining the arguably more powerful Triple Entente, the Triumvirate of Djemal, Talaat, and Enver leaned the other way, insisting that the Triple Entente powers, not Germany and Austria-Hungary, stood the most to gain from any partition of the Ottoman Empire—and that Turkey's longtime foe, Russia, had for nearly a century pushed in this direction. Moreover, a German officer, Otto Liman von Sanders, had helped to reorganize and revitalize the Turkish army after its defeat in the First Balkan War in 1912. Most enticing of all, an alliance with Great Power Germany could perhaps lure Bulgaria and Rumania into a new Balkan League directed against Russia. In early August 1914 the Triumvirate signed an alliance with Germany and Austria-Hungary without informing other members of the CUP. No declaration of war against the Triple Entente came that month, however, because of the unreadiness of the Turkish army; the prudent desire to have a commitment from at least Bulgaria, if not also Rumania; and the opposition of the CUP majority.

Summertime developments soon undercut those Young Turks opposing the Triumvirate. First, in late July Britain seized two battleships built in England for delivery to the Turkish navy, provoking popular rage in Turkey against London. Second, in August two German warships, the battle cruiser *Goeben* and light cruiser *Breslau*, eluded pursuing British squadrons in the Mediterranean, slipped into the Dardanelles with Enver's permission, and joined the Turkish fleet. Enraged at this unfriendly and nonneutral act, Britain imposed a naval blockade on the Turkish coastline, thereby exacerbating a commercial crisis triggered initially by the outbreak of war in Europe and causing government coffers to empty.

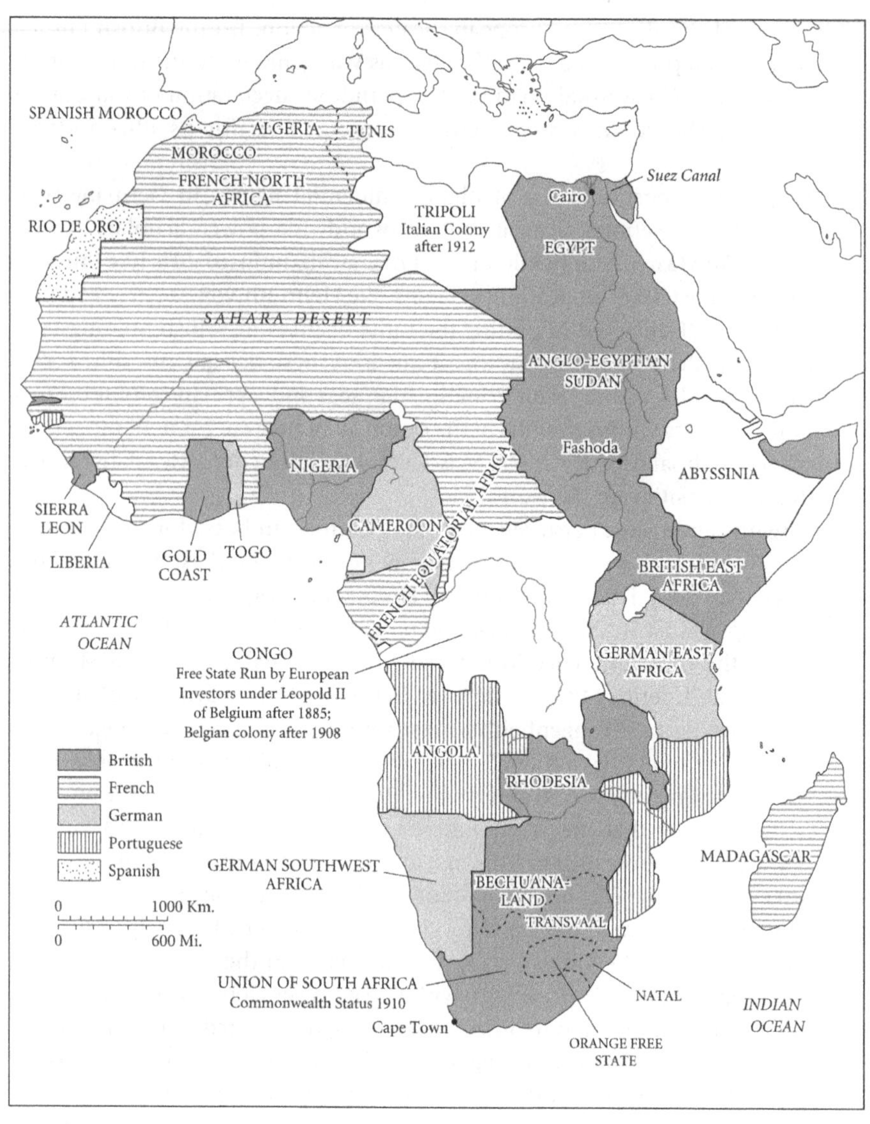

Africa

On October 11, therefore, the Triumvirate asked Germany for a large loan and Berlin agreed, depositing the first portion immediately but withholding the second larger installment until Turkey declared war. Enver now issued orders for a naval raid against Russia—again without informing the CUP—and on October 29, 1914, the Turkish fleet, with *Goeben* and *Breslau* in the vanguard, bombarded four ports on Russia's Black Sea coast. Presented with a fait accompli, the committee voted that day, seventeen to ten, for Enver's war policy.

On November 2, Russia declared war on Turkey. The next day four battleships, two British and two French, bombarded the mouth of the Dardanelles under Admiralty orders, thus presenting their own politicians with a similar fait accompli. On November 5 Britain and France declared war on Turkey; Constantinople followed suit on November 11. On November 14 the Shaikh-ul-Islam, the highest religious authority next to the Sultan-Caliph, declared a holy war against Russia, France, Britain, and Serbia, calling on Ottoman subjects and Muslims from northeastern Africa to India to rise up. Wangenheim, who had schemed hardest to set these events in motion, cheered actions that would aid Germany by deepening the worldwide nature of the Great War.

The Caucasus and Suez

Within days of declaring war on the Ottoman Empire an entire Russian corps, the 1st Caucasian, crossed the border into Turkish Armenia and proceeded toward Erzurum.[18] In its path lay the Third Turkish Army with paper strength of nearly 200,000 men but in reality able to field only a third that many fully trained and equipped combatants. Nevertheless, this proved sufficient to halt the Russians on November 11. The 1st Caucasian Corps fell back thirty kilometers in ten days but still held a forward position west of the main Caucasian army group still on Russian territory. Altogether the Russians numbered around 100,000 men.

The victory emboldened Enver Pasha to undertake grandiose plans: a thrust across the border with the object of destroying Russian forces drawn down in strength by the campaigning in Eastern Europe. By mid-December he could muster 120,000 soldiers. Such a drive might also ignite an uprising throughout the Caucasus of fellow Muslim peoples ethnically related to the Turks—Constantinople had proclaimed its Jihad only days earlier. But, as Liman von Sanders remembered his talk with Enver, the Turk had other thoughts. "At the conclusion of our conversation, he gave utterance to phantastic, yet noteworthy ideas—he told me that he contemplated marching through Afghanistan to India."[19] Clearly the Young Turks dreamed of a revitalized and all-conquering Ottoman Empire.

The operational scheme was no less bold. Mainly influenced by the German chief of staff of Third Army, Felix Guse, Enver intended to swing two corps through mountain roads and passes north of Russian positions to fall on their rear at Sarikamish. A third corps would fix the Russians frontally. The plan had potential, but not in winter. Almost immediately after the Turks pushed off on December 22, soldiers still ill clothed and ill equipped began to fall out and freeze in extremely harsh subzero temperatures—thirty thousand would die of the cold before the campaign ended. Both flanking corps had huge gaps in the ranks and had run low on ammunition and food by the time they struck Sarikamish on December 29. The Russians counterattacked two days later, forcing one Turkish corps to surrender on January 4, 1915, and the remnants of the other two to retreat. Enver's casualties amounted to three-quarters of Third Army. Only about eighteen thousand Turkish troops survived the battle. "The corpses of the rest littered the passes and the snowfields, where they were devoured by the packs of wolves which roam the mountains of eastern Turkey."[20] It was a debacle—and more than just militarily. As Hew Strachan observes, Sarikamish, trumpeted as the first act of Jihad, "might

Holy War: Reading the Jihad *Fatwa* to Turkish Soldiers in Jerusalem
Courtesy of the Library of Congress

well have provided the impetus to turn aspirations into reality [but] the conjunction of the declaration [of holy war] and of the catastrophe were too close." For the time being, at least, "Sarikamish confirmed the image of Ottoman decline."[21]

The dampening effects of the battle on Turkey's holy war were strengthened by the empire's nearly simultaneous debacle at Suez. Impressively crossing the Sinai Desert that winter with nineteen thousand men of the Turkish Fourth Army, Ahmed Djemal hoped to take the vital waterway and spark an Egyptian revolt against their British overlords. Some fifty thousand desert tribesmen rallied to the cause as he neared the canal. But the British had spotted his divisions from the air in time to entrench recently-arrived Indian regiments behind the canal when the attack came on February 3, 1915. Only a few pontoon bridges reached the other side, and they were soon destroyed. Djemal Pasha called off the attack and retreated back into the desert. The Bedouins who had accompanied him drifted back to peaceful pursuits.

Enver Pasha's defeat at Sarikamish was, however, the more significant of the two battles, and its significance stretched beyond the connection with Jihad. Thus Stavka, worried about Turkish troops pushing into the Caucasus, had pleaded with London and Paris to take action in the Dardanelle Straits—and the western allies soon complied. The Turkish defeat at Sarikamish would also have far-reaching and tragic consequences for Armenians and Greeks living in Turkey. Because the Russians had recruited an entire division of their own Armenian Christians to fight in the battle, Constantinople now implemented a long desired, premeditated, massive pogrom of Turkish Armenians. Simultaneously, the Young Turks escalated ongoing acts of revenge against Greeks under their rule living in Thrace and Asia Minor. They had been branded enemies of the state after the deaths of Turkish civilians in the Balkans during the war there in 1912. What followed were the worst atrocities against civilians in the Great War (see chap. 6).

THE WAR IN AFRICA

The last German surface ship to survive outside home waters, the light cruiser *Königsberg*, had put to sea from Dar es Salaam, capital of German East Africa, just days before the war broke out.[22] Her captain, Max Loof, abandoned his base, just as Spee had done at Tsingtao, to avoid a superior naval force: the British Cape Squadron. Three older and slower British cruisers trailed *Königsberg* until a squall afforded Loof the opportunity to steam away undetected at higher speed. He headed for the waters off Aden at the opening to the Red Sea astride the shipping lanes between Suez and India. On August 6 the first British merchant ship taken in the war, *The City of Winchester*, was captured by the German cruiser. Afterward Loof prowled the seas off East Africa, but word of his first prize, as well as the appearance of *Emden* in the Indian Ocean, kept allied merchantmen in the safety of their ports. In early September Loof vanished into the tree-shaded confines of the delta of the Rufiji River, some two hundred kilometers south of Dar es Salaam. He sallied forth on September 20, however, to raid the British harbor at

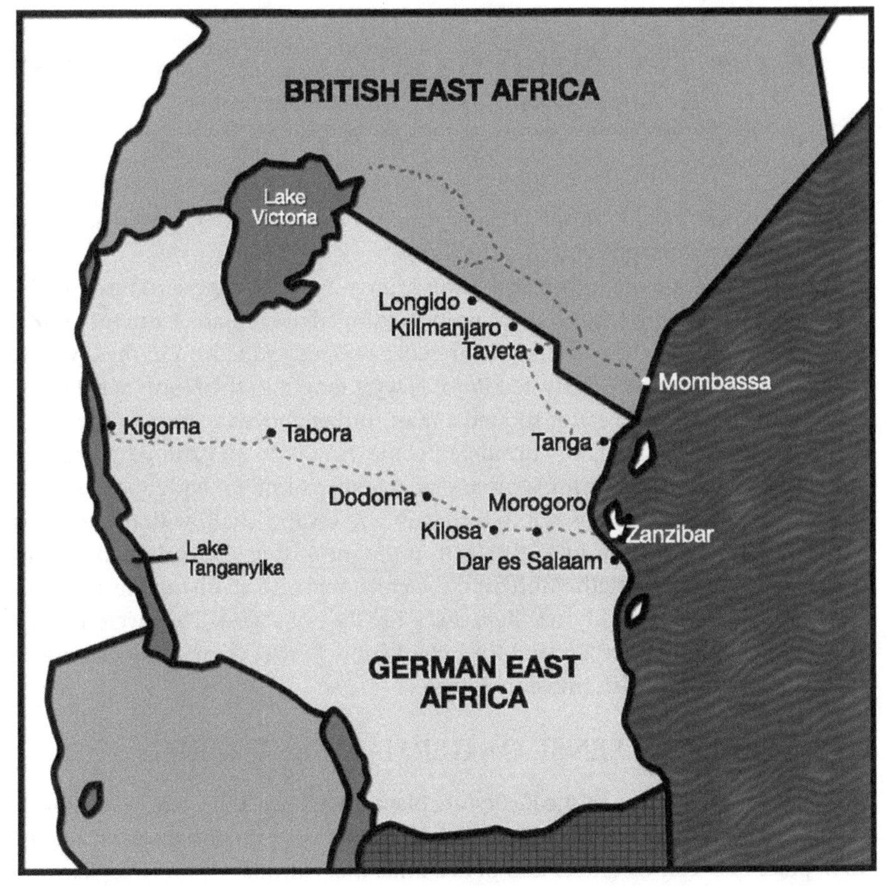

German East Africa

The Last Ship Outside Germany: Wreck of the *Königsberg*

Used with the permission of *The Trustees of the Imperial War Museum, London*. Photo Number: SP-989

Zanzibar, where a light cruiser, HMS *Pegasus*, was caught undergoing repairs and sunk. Loof again disappeared into the Rufiji.

By this time a score of British warships, including three modern heavy cruisers, searched for *Königsberg*. Similar numbers scanned the Indian Ocean for *Emden*, underscoring the likelihood that the presence of Spee's squadron in these waters would have significantly enervated Royal Navy strength in the North Sea. Finally on October 30 a British sailor spotted a mast jutting above the trees of the delta. Although trapped now, Loof considered complying with an Admiralty order to somehow slip away, make for Germany, and perhaps link up with Spee's squadron under way. But this was not to be. Unable to escape, shallow-draft monitors finally sunk *Königsberg* in July 1915, but in the meantime she had continued to drain British naval strength. Moreover, the crew managed to dismantle all of the ship's 4.1-inch guns and ferret them away to Dar es Salaam. They were refitted there as field artillery for General Paul von Lettow-Vorbeck's ongoing defense of the colony against British invasion forces.

THE DEFENSE OF GERMAN EAST AFRICA

While the dramatic saga of the *Königsberg* played itself out, the Great War came to East Africa.[23] During the late summer and early fall mostly inconsequential actions took place between volunteer and police units that skirmished on Lakes Victoria and Tanganyika or conducted raids across the frontiers of British East Africa, German East Africa, and Northern Rhodesia. Only one of these minor engagements was of any lasting significance. On August 15 one of Lettow-Vorbeck's best commanders, Tom von Prince, captured the strategic British town of Taveta, thus blocking a natural invasion route through the gap between the Kilimanjaro and Pare Mountains into German East Africa.

However, by early October London had delegated operational control to the British India Office, which decided to ignore self-serving German arguments that the war not extend to Africa lest the inter-European conflict undermine white colonial rule. Indeed Calcutta had overambitious plans to seize all of German East Africa, a prosperous colony that encompassed roughly twice the area of Germany itself. Major General Arthur Edward Aitken, a seasoned albeit arrogant and incompetent professional soldier, commanded about 8,000 men. It was a motley troop, consisting of one British battalion and the rest of Indians hastily thrown together from garrisons around the country. The Indian army in August 1914 boasted nine infantry and three cavalry divisions—140,000 Indian rank and file commanded by 15,000 British officers and NCOs and bolstered by 60,000 British regulars. By war's end there would be thirteen infantry divisions. However, because three-quarters of the British regular battalions along with many of the best Indian formations were shifted after war broke out to France, Egypt, Mesopotamia, and Persia, Aitken's rank and file were the dregs: poorly trained and equipped "Imperial Service Troops" usually held back by native provincial authorities for their own uses but now dragooned into the African fighting. These soldiers had little or no desire to fight.[24]

On October 16, 1914, Aitken sailed for Mombasa, landing there at the end of the month. He planned to capture the port of Tanga while another force of about fifteen hundred British, Indian, and East African volunteers moved south from British East Africa to seize Longido, the western terminus of the rail line to Tanga. After these victories he could take Dar es Salaam with its important wireless station and rail line to the interior and then move south to secure the rest of the colony. If successful he could establish the long-sought "Cairo to Cape Town" link—an uninterrupted string of British colonies running from Egypt to South Africa. Lettow-Vorbeck opposed Aitken with a small army of fourteen companies, only one of which guarded Tanga while three took up positions around Longido. His officers and NCOs were German whereas the rank and file were well-paid, well-equipped, disciplined Ascaris (i.e., African soldiers), but this did not phase Aitken: "The Indian Army will make short work of a lot of niggers,"[25] he boasted.

On November 3 Major Georg Kraut attacked the Anglo-Indian columns as they neared Longido. They were quickly routed and fled the battlefield. Lettow-Vorbeck, meanwhile, had moved all available units by rail to Tanga, managing to assemble over a thousand men by November 4 when Aitken, having wasted two days, finally assaulted the city. Although outnumbered eight to one,

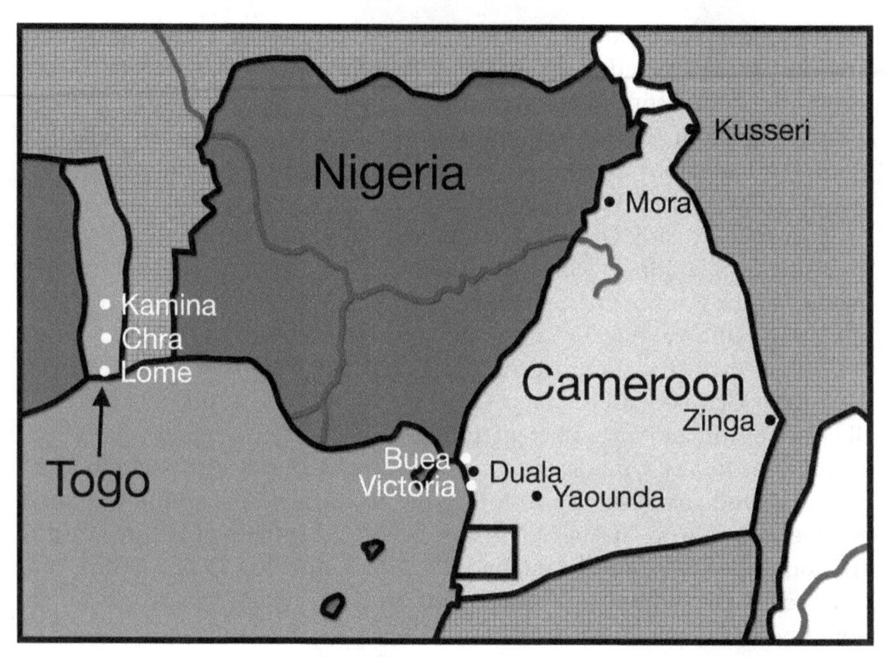

Togo and Cameroon

the defenders "made short work" of the invaders, inflicting over eight hundred casualties in seven hours. The German machine guns caused much of the carnage and demonstrated convincingly that the seasick sepoys Aitken deployed on his left flank were next to useless as they panicked and fled. "It was a ghastly sight,"[26] said one British officer. Aitken also abandoned his depot during a hasty reembarkation: 16 machine guns, 500 rifles, and 600,000 rounds of ammunition. The twin victories at Longido and Tanga ended the disastrous British campaign and gave Lettow-Vorbeck over a year to prepare for the next invasion. When it came (see chap. 6), his men were even better equipped, his numbers had grown, and, thanks to the *Königsberg*, they now possessed heavier artillery than the enemy.

Togoland

Togoland was the first German colony in Africa to fall.[27] Its capture meant a great deal to the British Admiralty, for the wireless station in Kamina ranged three thousand nautical miles, second only to the main wireless station at Nauen, Germany. From this inland town messages could be relayed to Germany's other African possessions—Cameroon, Southwest Africa, and East Africa—but also to ships off the coasts or at sea in the central and southern Atlantic. Already on August 12, therefore, two companies of the Gold Coast Regiment of the West Africa Defense Force under Captain F. C. Bryant landed at Lome, Togoland, and began to push inland to Kamina. A smaller French force moved west from Dahomey, joining Bryant at the Chra River six days later. The African and Senegalese regulars clashed with roughly the same number of their native counterparts on the German side on August 22, suffering heavy casualties but forcing the defenders to fall back on Kamina. With another column approaching from the north, the acting governor of Togoland, Major von Doering, destroyed the tall masts and precious equipment of the wireless station and surrendered on August 26.

Cameroon

The rapid conquest of German Cameroon appeared initially to be as foregone a conclusion as quick allied victory had been in Togoland. Even though it was a vast space—larger than either France or Germany—Germany could defend Cameroon with no more than fourteen companies of Ascari troops, which, with the German officers and NCOs, new Ascari recruits, the police force, and a few units of German settlers, meant at most 6,000 to 7,000 defenders. On the allied side Britain had at its disposal two cruisers, other smaller ships from the Royal Navy, and over 7,000 native infantrymen from the West Africa Defense Force, most of them from Nigeria, whereas France and Belgium could potentially commit an additional 20,000 native soldiers from the neighboring Belgian Congo, French Congo, and French Equatorial Africa. The allies would eventually build up their troop strength to about 13,000, thus securing a two- or three-to-one advantage.

Imperial Surplus: Ascari Battalion of the Nigerian Regiment Entrain for Cameroon

Used with the permission of *The Trustees of the Imperial War Museum, London*. Photo Number: Q-45771

Despite these imposing odds, Cameroon was not taken easily. Although the French won a few rapid victories in August and September, seizing first Zinga and then Kusseri just inside the eastern border, three British-led columns attacking across the northwest border were repulsed with heavy casualties. During the course of the autumn and winter, however, mounting allied strength proved insurmountable. The port of Douala capitulated to Brigadier General Charles Dobell's sailors and marines on September 27. With its surrender the British Admiralty had eliminated another important wireless station. Buea and its port of Victoria sent up the white flag seven weeks later.

As German forces fell back on the rugged interior of the colony, defending key outposts and giving ground begrudgingly, allied expeditions pushed inland from Douala, Zinga, and in April 1915, from Nigeria. By November the tenacious defense of the colony had all but ended—only isolated forts at Yaounda and Mora held out. Both surrendered in January 1916, but before they did the British and French death toll in Cameroon had risen above forty-two hundred, mostly from diseases.

SOUTHWEST AFRICA

In August 1914 London approached its former colony, the now autonomous Union of South Africa, with an important request. Four years earlier the South Africa Act had established a largely self-governing republic linked to the motherland by a governor-general who represented crown interests, including the defense of the territory by imperial troops. Thus South Africa joined Canada, Australia, and New Zealand as autonomous self-governing dominions of the British Empire. This measure had gone a long way toward reconciling bad feelings between English and Dutch settlers stemming from the vicious Boer War (1899–1902). Some measure of the act's success can be gleaned from the fact that both Prime Minister Louis Botha and the Defense Minister Jan Smuts had fought against Britain but were now loyal to the empire. When war broke out Botha wired London that imperial troops could be released for the fighting in Europe and that South Africa would raise an army to defend itself. Imperial military authorities responded gratefully and asked Botha if South Africa could contribute to the war effort by seizing the key ports of German Southwest Africa as well as the inland capital, Windhoek, with its vital wireless station. The task seemed feasible enough, for Berlin stationed only five thousand regular and reserve soldiers in a colony that was larger than the home empire.[28]

The first five thousand soldiers of South Africa's fledgling army advanced into Southwest Africa from three directions on September 19. One force under General Duncan McKenzie landed at Lüderitz on the Atlantic coast and started inland along the railroad. Because the Germans had destroyed the line east of the undefended harbor, his progress was extremely slow. Leaving the overcautious McKenzie alone, the defenders concentrated their efforts on a second South African column that had pushed two of its twelve companies across the Orange

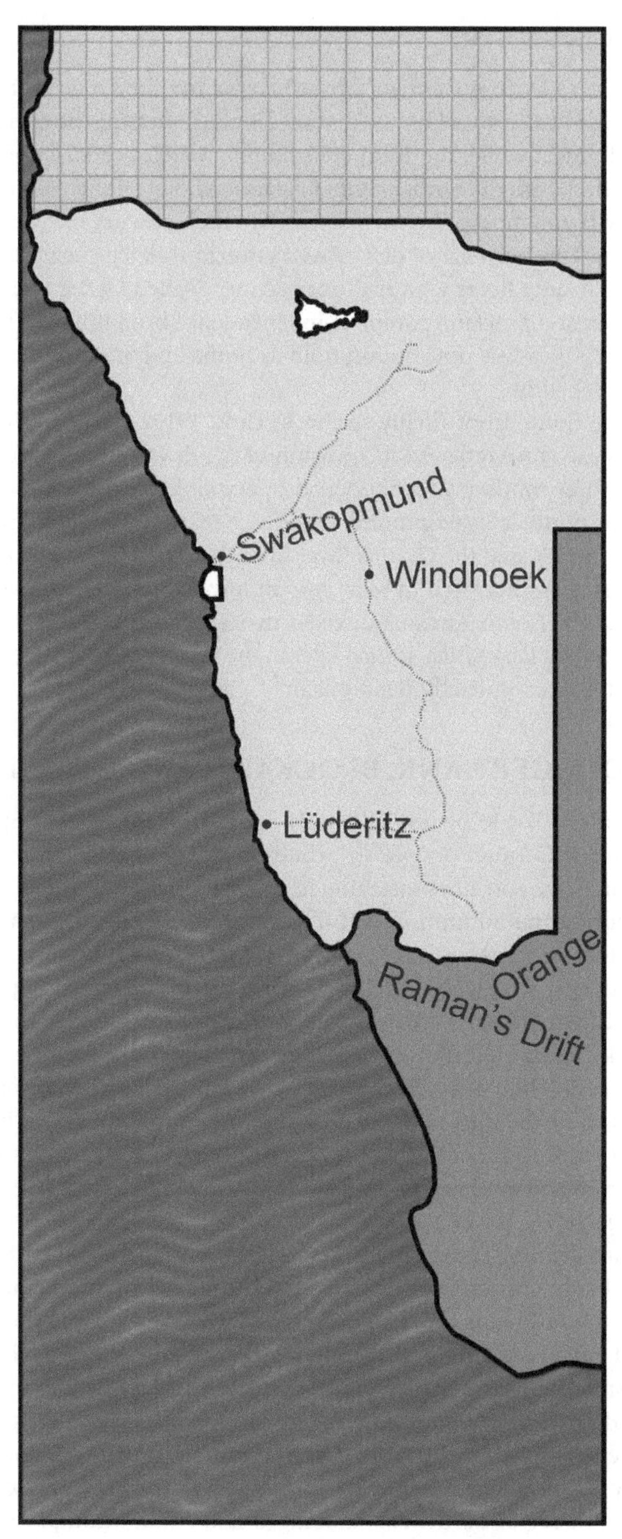

German Southwest Africa

River at Raman's Drift. A German force of twelve hundred men surrounded and captured this advance guard on September 26, thus blunting the entire operation in the south. Meanwhile, the third column under Colonel Salomon Marwitz, a Boer, refused to cross the border. Matters worsened on October 7 when the disaffected Marwitz and most of his men defected to the Germans and declared war on Great Britain. This overt act of defiance was not an isolated event but rather part of a plot by leading Boers who had not been reconciled by the South Africa Act to seize power and proclaim complete independence from Britain. The campaign in Southwest Africa was now put on hold as Botha and Smuts took two months to crush the rebellion.

With the home front finally secure in early 1915, a now beefed-up South African Defense Force renewed its invasion of Southwest Africa. Over half of the army, forty-three thousand men, opened operations in February. Botha himself landed in the north at Swakopmund, while McKenzie drove inland from Lüderitz and other corps crossed the Orange River from the south and the Kalahari Desert from the east. Windhoek fell in May, and on July 9 Germany's remaining troops surrendered. The South Africans directed their attention now to the pursuit of Lettow-Vorbeck in East Africa, joined later in the year by the West African Defense Force, which had completed operations in Cameroon.

DOGGER BANK, BLOCKADE, AND U-BOATS

The news of the Battle of the Falklands and the death of Graf Spee and his sons shocked a German people so proud of its fleet. Eager to avenge gallant comrades and give patriots something to cheer about, the German navy plotted revenge. During the autumn of 1914, however, the German naval communications system had been severely compromised. Between August and October three German naval codebooks fell into British hands, the most important from the scuttled light cruiser *Magdeburg,* and by early December decoding experts in "Room 40" of the Old Building of the Admiralty could decipher all wireless messages of the High Seas Fleet. Although warnings did not always come in time—thus German ships raided Hartlepool, Scarborough, and Whitby largely unopposed on December 16, killing eighty-six civilians and wounding hundreds more—when the High Seas Fleet put to sea on January 23, 1915, the British stood ready.[29]

German Admiral Franz von Hipper steamed into the North Sea that day with three battle cruisers, one heavy cruiser, four light cruisers, and nineteen destroyers. The following morning he reached the Dogger Bank, hoping to clear the area of British and neutral fishing ships that he suspected—incorrectly—were transmitting warnings of German naval sorties to the British Admiralty. Any destroyers or light cruisers patrolling the Dogger Bank would also be destroyed. To his considerable surprise and alarm, Hipper found himself engaged by Admiral David Beatty's four battle cruisers, nine light cruisers, and a superior number of destroyers—Room 40 had come through this time. The Germans turned and headed for home, but before they reached safer waters

The Civilians' War: Three Residents of Scarborough Did Not Survive This Hit
Harper's Pictorial Library

the British sunk the heavy cruiser *Blücher* and severely damaged battle cruisers *Seydlitz* and *Derfflinger* and the light cruiser *Kolberg*. No British ships were sunk, but Beatty's flagship, *Lion*, suffered so many direct hits that it had to withdraw from the action. The defeat strengthened the kaiser's resolve not to place his precious ships in further jeopardy—and for the next sixteen months he did not. The lack of a smashing naval victory against the Royal Navy during the war's first five months meant that the British blockade of Germany, and all that this meant for the critical importation of raw materials and food vital for the war effort, continued unabated.

Many in the German navy believed, therefore, that they now possessed only one weapon with which to undercut their enemies economically—the submarine. Already in early October 1914 German U-boat commodore Hermann Bauer had recommended attacking allied merchantmen, and his superior, Commander in Chief of the High Seas Fleet Friedrich von Ingenohl, agreed. "A campaign of submarines against commercial traffic on the British coasts will strike the enemy at his weakest point."[30] At first Ingenohl's superior, Chief of the Naval Staff Hugo von Pohl, balked, worried that accidental torpedoing of neutral ships would damage relations with these nations. He changed his mind in November, however, when Britain declared all of the North Sea a war zone, restricted the movement of merchant ships to specific channels, and then proceeded to search and seize neutral cargoes more aggressively, including food shipments not considered contraband under the norms of international law. Although incensed by this "hunger blockade," German Chancellor Theodald von Bethmann Hollweg still advised against using the U-boats for fear of provoking neutrals, especially the United States. Coming in the immediate aftermath of the near disaster at the Dogger Bank, Pohl's assurance that no neutral ships would be hit changed Bethmann's mind. The kaiser quickly consented, and on February 5, 1915, Germany declared the waters around Britain and Ireland a military area: "All enemy merchant ships in these waters will be destroyed, irrespective of the impossibility of avoiding in all cases danger to the passengers and crew." The German declaration added, ominously, that it might not "always be possible [under] the uncertainties of naval warfare...to avoid neutral vessels suffering from attacks intended for enemy ships."[31]

The fateful decision soon embroiled the German Empire in the kind of international problems that Bethmann had anticipated. U-boats had sunk 10 British merchantmen around the Isles in 1914 employing so-called prize rules, or cruiser rules, which required the submarine to surface and then enable crew and passengers to get to safety before destroying the ship. International law was jettisoned in 1915, however, for Churchill ordered merchant ships, armed at the outset of the war, to fire on or ram surfaced U-boats. Consequently, submarine captains opted increasingly to torpedo their prey from underwater without warning: 16 of 25 sinkings from mid-February to mid-March with the loss of 52 crew members. The British cried foul and tightened their blockade, while the United States protested both against Britain's restriction of American trade and Germany's "unrestricted" submarine warfare. But the sinkings continued—from February to September 1915 nearly 300 enemy ships, almost 800,000 tons of shipping, went down. Only in the month of August, however, did the number of ships destroyed exceed new ship production in Britain and the dominions; nor did these losses produce a major disruption to Britain's war economy. In any given month, for instance, 4,000 ships entered British harbors.

In the end Germany's campaign of unrestricted submarine warfare proved too great a diplomatic liability to continue. Real trouble started on May 7, 1915, when *U-20* sighted Britain's *Lusitania* off the southern coast of Ireland and fired a torpedo at the huge, 30,000-ton luxury liner. The forward starboard detonation near boiler room number one triggered a second explosion a moment later, caused most probably by damage to the steam lines that conveyed high-pressure superheated steam from the boilers to the turbines.[32] Water rushed into the gaping hole in *Lusitania*'s side so rapidly that she sank in eighteen minutes, taking 400 crew members and 800 terror-stricken passengers with her to the bottom of the Atlantic. Among the victims were 128 Americans.

Captain Walther Schwieger of *U-20* had committed one of the worst atrocities of the Great War. It could not be justified by the warning issued in New York City the morning of the ship's departure "that travelers sailing in the war zone on ships of Great Britain and her allies do so at their own risk."[33] Nor was it convincing, as Germany later claimed, that the *Lusitania* was a legitimate target because both *Jane's Fighting Ships* and *Brassey's Naval Annual* listed her as a "Royal Navy Reserved Merchant Cruiser." To be sure, the navy had reserved the right to use the big liner as an auxiliary cruiser or troop transport but had not done so—she had been released back to the Cunard Lines and was making her regular, preannounced transatlantic passenger run at the time of the attack. As speculated at the time and ever since, on the other hand, it is true that *Lusitania* carried contraband on her last voyage: small arms ammunition, shrapnel shells, and percussion fuses. To be lawful, however, Schwieger would have had to halt the ship, search it, allow passengers to get off, and then fire his torpedo. But, as explained previously, the Germans had largely opted to ignore prize rules three months earlier. The only justification for sinking a liner without warning under the international law of that day was when there were troops on board—but there were none.

Almost immediately British officials protested the "willful and wholesale murder"[34] of so many innocent civilians. Already at war with Britain, Germany watched with more concern for the American reaction. The British were incredulously angry, and the Germans somewhat relieved, however, when U.S. President Woodrow Wilson responded with what can only be described as a mild rebuke. During a speech in Philadelphia on May 10 he renounced the use of force, and the following day his government merely reminded Germany of "the practical impossibility of employing submarines in the destruction of commerce without disregarding those rules of fairness, reason, justice, and humanity."[35]

Realizing the gravity of the situation, Bethmann Hollweg and the kaiser nevertheless took quick steps to avoid a further deterioration of relations, and perhaps even war, with the United States. William issued orders to Admiral Gustav Bachmann, Pohl's successor as Chief of the Naval Staff, to avoid sinking neutral ships. After Bachmann deliberately suppressed the order and Danish, Norwegian, and Swedish steamers were torpedoed without warning, a second, stricter set of orders came from the imperial pen in early June: German submarines were not to fire on a merchantman unless absolutely certain of enemy status; furthermore, U-boats were ordered not to sink passenger liners.

Apparently not heeding these commands, U-boat captains sunk the White Star liner *Arabic* on August 19, 1915, and a smaller British cruise ship, *Hesperian*, on September 4. A rupture with the United States threatened, for three Americans had died on the *Arabic*. The German leadership responded immediately by sacking Bachmann and replacing him with the more compliant Admiral Henning von Holtzendorff. The kaiser refused to accept the resignation of naval secretary and father of the German fleet, Alfred von Tirpitz, who had sided with Bachmann. Holtzendorff proceeded to remove all U-boats from the English Channel and Western Approaches to Britain. Submarine warfare in the North Sea, moreover, would be conducted under prize regulations.

Refusing to subject his submarines to the danger of being fired on or rammed, Germany's U-boat commodore withdrew his boats from the North Sea. Germany's first major submarine campaign had come to a halt. Most American citizens refused to forget or forgive the shockingly infamous and tragic sinking of the *Lusitania*, but the crisis between Germany and the United States blew over.

The German navy had suffered a series of embarrassing and costly defeats at sea in 1914–1915 in the Battles of the Falklands, Heligoland Bight, and Dogger Bank. Worse still, German ships were swept from the world's oceans, the empire's Asian colonies captured, and all but one of its African holdings also taken. While Britain and France enjoyed unfettered access to their overseas possessions and world markets, Germany's giant industrial machine was starved of imports and could barely meet the army's munitions needs. Furthermore, submarine warfare had not only failed to accomplish its mission of cutting Britain off from imports of food and munitions but had nearly brought the most powerful neutral country in the world into the enemy camp.

As explained in following chapters, however, these maritime and imperial setbacks contrasted sharply with the remarkable victories of the German, Austro-Hungarian, Bulgarian, and Turkish armies in 1915. The so-called Central Powers clearly held the upper hand—on land—by the end of that year.

NOTES

1. For the setting, see Robert K. Massie, *Castles of Steel: Britain, Germany, and the Winning of the Great War at Sea* (New York, 2003), 236–237.
2. Cited in Barrie Pitt, *Coronel and Falkland* (London, 1960), 65.
3. Cited in ibid., 66–67.
4. Cited in ibid., 67.
5. Cited in Richard Hough, *The Pursuit of Admiral von Spee* (London, 1969), 116.
6. For this section, see Winston Churchill, *The World Crisis 1911–1918* (New York, 1931), 176–181, 226–250; Richard Hough, *The Great War at Sea 1914–1918* (Oxford, 1983), 87–98; Holger H. Herwig, *'Luxury' Fleet: The Imperial German Navy 1888–1918* (London, 1991), 28–68, 265–275; Paul G. Halpern, *A Naval History of World War I* (Annapolis, 1994), 70–84, 88–96; and Hew Strachan, *The First World War* (Oxford, 2001), 1:441–455, 466–480.
7. The British Admiralty introduced battle cruisers in the decade before 1914 and Germany followed suit. With the armament of a battleship but less heavily armored for purposes of

speed, the battle cruiser was designed to chase down and destroy light and heavy cruisers raiding commerce.

8. For this section, see Peter Lowe, *Great Britain and Japan 1911–1915: A Study of British Far Eastern Policy* (London, 1969); and Strachan, *First World War,* 1:481–494.

9. Cited in Strachan, *First World War,* 1:481.

10. For this section, see Hough, *Great War at Sea,* 99–120; Halpern, *Naval History,* 96–100; and Strachan, *First World War,* 1:466–480.

11. Churchill, *World Crisis,* 238.

12. Cited in Lloyd Hirst, *Coronel and After* (London, 1934), 156–158.

13. For the following, see Hough, *Great War at Sea,* 65–68; Herwig, *'Luxury' Fleet,* 143–167; and Halpern, *Naval History,* 7–9.

14. See Paul Kennedy, "Britain in the First World War," in Allan R. Millett and Williamson Murray, eds., *Military Effectiveness,* Vol. 1, *The First World War* (Boston, 1988), 31–79; D. K. Fieldhouse, "The Metropolitan Economics of Empire," and Robert Holland, "The British Empire and the Great War, 1914–1918," in Judith M. Brown and Wm. Roger Louis, eds., *The Oxford History of the British Empire* (Oxford, 1999), 4:98–99, 117, 136; and David Stevenson, *Cataclysm: The First World War as Political Tragedy* (New York, 2003), 200.

15. See Peter Hopkirk, *Like Hidden Fire: The Plot to Bring Down the British Empire* (New York, 1994), 54–65. Also consult Henry Morgenthau, *Secrets of the Bosphorus* (New York, 1918).

16. Cited in Hopkirk, *Like Hidden Fire,* 55.

17. For a well-written description of these events, see Hopkirk, *Life Hidden Fire,* 1–101. For scholarly details, see Ulrich Trumpener, *Germany and the Ottoman Empire 1914–1918* (Princeton, NJ, 1968), 21–61, 108–139; and Strachan, *First World War,* 1:644–680. Also see Mohammad Gholi Majd, *Iraq in World War I: From Ottoman Rule to British Conquest* (Lanham, MD, 2006), 45–81.

18. For the Caucasus and Suez, see Otto Liman von Sanders, *Five Years in Turkey,* trans. Carl Reichmann, (Annapolis, MD, 1927), 37–46; Hopkirk, *Like Hidden Fire,* 73–77; Keegan, *First World War,* 221–223; and especially Strachan, *First World War,* 1:712–742.

19. Sanders, *Five Years in Turkey,* 39.

20. Hopkirk, *Like Hidden Fire,* 76.

21. Strachan, *First World War,* 1:729.

22. For the saga of the *Königsberg,* see Byron Farwell, *The Great War in Africa* (New York, 1986), 127–160; and Keith Yates, *Graf Spee's Raiders: Challenge to the Royal Navy, 1914–1915* (Annapolis, MD,, 1995), 237–266.

23. For the following, see Farwell, Great War in Africa, 109–110, 161–189; and Strachan, *First World War,* 1:571–584. For the most recent discussion of the African campaigns, see Edward Paice, *Tip and Run: The Untold Tragedy of the Great War in Africa* (London, 2007).

24. See Judith M. Brown, "Britain, India, and the War of 1914–1918," and S. D. Pradhan, "The Indian Army and the First World War," in Dewitt C. Ellinwood and S. D. Pradhan, eds., *India and World War I* (Manohar, India, 1978), 24–27, 50–53.

25. Cited in Farwell, *Great War in Africa,* 163.

26. Cited in ibid., 170.

27. For the campaigns in Togoland, Cameroon, and German Southwest Africa, see Farwell, *Great War in Africa,* 21–104; and Strachan, *First World War,* 1:505–569.

28. After the brutal suppression of a native uprising in 1904 Germany stationed its own troops there rather than recruit Ascaris as it did elsewhere in Africa.

29. For the following, see Hough, *Great War at Sea,* 121–143, 169–176; Halpern, *Naval History,* 291–303; and Massie, *Castles of Steel,* 375–425, 503–552.

30. Cited in Massie, *Castles of Steel,* 515.

31. Cited in ibid., 519.
32. For a current and reliable explanation of the various possible causes, see Diana Preston, *Lusitania: An Epic Tragedy* (New York, 2002), 441–454.
33. Cited in ibid., 2. For a discussion of whether the attack was justified, see pp. 383–393.
34. Cited in ibid., 3.
35. Cited in Massie, *Castles of Steel*, 537.

CHAPTER V

The Stalemate in Europe

1915

April 22, 1915, brought mild and sunny weather to the trench lines of France. What made it a rather unusual day meteorologically was a change in the prevailing westerly winds. Beginning late in the afternoon they altered course and blew from northeast to southwest instead. A special artillery unit of the German Fourth Army a few miles northeast of Ypres had been waiting two weeks for such conditions. At five o'clock in the afternoon the "stink sappers" (*Stink-Pionere*), having received the code word along the line, "God punish England," scurried from their dugouts and removed the covers from nearly six thousand shallowly buried canisters and unscrewed the nozzles. Within minutes 160 tons of chlorine gas spewed from the ground. Innocently enough, nature took hold of man's insidious creation and sent it drifting toward French-Algerian and Canadian positions a few hundred meters away.[1]

Chief of the Prussian General Staff Erich von Falkenhayn hoped to overrun the allied salient near Ypres and perhaps push farther toward the coast, but mainly he aimed to distract the enemy's attention from a larger offensive set to unfold soon on the eastern front, one that was drawing away reserve divisions. Accordingly, there would be no extra troops to follow up any tactical surprise achieved with the new technology.

High military counsels in Germany were badly divided over the world's first major poison gas attack.[2] The Hague Peace Conference of 1899 had outlawed the use of "poison or poisoned weapons...arms, projectiles or material calculated to cause unnecessary suffering... and projectiles [designed for the] diffusion of asphyxiating or deleterious gases."[3] The same kind of murderously cold wartime mentality that would terminate twelve hundred civilians aboard the *Lusitania* two weeks later did not allow, however, for respect of international law. German legal experts advised Falkenhayn that the attack could be justified because the gas was released from containers—in fact, just to save artillery shells—and not from projectiles. On the other side of the debate, Duke Albrecht of Württemberg, commander of Sixth Army, argued that unleashing this new weapon would not only be immoral but also of dubious military value, for the allies, with the wind normally at their backs, would probably send ten times as much gas onto German positions. Karl von Einem of Third Army agreed and then expressed additional worries over the "tremendous scandal" that would compromise and disgrace Germany in the eyes of the world. "War has nothing to do with chivalry anymore," he wrote. "The higher civilization rises, the more vile man becomes."[4] Such sentiments did not carry the day, however, and "Operation Disinfection" went forward.

Stretching six thousand meters along opposing lines and bellowing high up into the air, a thick ghastly looking green-yellow cloud of gas moved eerily and threateningly with the breeze across "No Man's Land." The gaseous monstrosity took on a pinkish hue from certain angles as the descending western sun shone through it. To compound the shock and terror, German heavy artillery began to lay down a pounding barrage. Two French colonial divisions and a Canadian division were caught completely unawares. "Take a look at this, sir," said one Canadian artillery observer to his superior as he stared through binoculars at what was coming toward them. "There's something funny going on";[5] then he dove for cover from the incoming shells. But just then the wind shifted, compressing the gas cloud over the Algerians, whose forward units were engulfed. The soldiers grabbed their throats, choking and writhing in excruciating pain from the searing chlorine gas. In minutes many hundreds lay drowning in fluids given off by the lungs. Seeing this, others panicked, dropped their rifles, and ran, leaving a six-kilometer gap in the line.

Into the vacuum charged forty-two German battalions. Although they wore primitive gas masks, the advancing infantrymen were themselves wary of the gas at it rolled south toward Ypres. Having penetrated at places over three kilometers beyond the forward trench line of the French, the Germans dug in as darkness came—mercifully for the allies, for during the night the defenders managed to move up through roads clogged with retreating troops and civilian refugees to stop the tactical hemorrhage and prevent any further penetration.

When the fighting around Ypres ended in late May the German army had pushed the enemy back just over five kilometers. Although inconclusive—no breakthrough—the opening day of Second Ypres would nevertheless stand out as one of the quickest and greatest tactical victories on the western front in 1915, 1916, or 1917. Such was the nature of trench warfare; such was the nature of stalemate; such was the grisly, macabre nature of modern warfare in the early twentieth century.

TRENCH WARFARE ON THE WESTERN FRONT

During separate meetings in January 1915 of the respective General Headquarters of France (GQG) and Britain (GHQ), each agreed to step up offensive operations on the western front later that winter. The moment was critical. French commander Joseph Joffre was attacking in the Artois region around Vimy and in the Champagne area east of Rheims in a desperate attempt to drive the Germans out. GQG seemed to have learned little tactically since 1914, stressing massed "head-down attacks, one after the other."[6] Also lacking sufficient heavy artillery and as yet getting no help from the British Expeditionary Force (BEF), French armies experienced severe losses—casualties would mount to a quarter of a million by March. Joffre and British chief Sir John French agreed, therefore, that the BEF should take over some of the French line in the Artois, freeing the French for Champagne.

The joint operations agreed upon during these meetings were well conceived. If both offensives broke through, the German armies might be encircled. Or perhaps they would fall back toward rail lines bringing supplies from Metz northwest over Mézières, Hirson, the Douai Plain, and Lille. Should the allies seize this railroad, their enemy would lose the ability to supply his armies and have to withdraw. The main strategic goal—freeing French soil of the invaders—would be accomplished either way.[7]

The decision fell easier in Paris than in London. Earlier that month Field Marshall Lord Horatio Herbert Kitchener, secretary of state for war and the leading figure on Britain's war cabinet, had received an urgent request from Grand Duke Nicholas, chief of staff of the Russian armies, to attack Turkey and relieve pressure on the tsar's hard-pressed forces in the Caucasus. Although he was not sure where he would find the troops for such an expedition, Kitchener was tempted to comply. The size of the BEF was rapidly expanding—it would approach half a million men in March and two-thirds of a million in September—but the secretary had little faith in the ability of allied forces to penetrate German lines. Rather than squander troops on the western front, an assault through the Dardanelles Straits to Constantinople promised not only to knock Turkey from the war and entice Italy, Greece, Rumania, and Bulgaria to join the allies

The Empire Needs You: Horatio Herbert Kitchener
Canfield, *World War*

Trench Warfare: Germans at Dugout Entrance Ready to Fire Into the Barbed Wire
Harper's Pictorial Library

but also to open a sea lane for munitions exports to Russia. Producing 3,500 artillery shells a day in August 1914 and only 15,000 in May 1915, just a mere ninth of German-Austro-Hungarian output, Russia looked desperately to the West for help.[8] By March Kitchener had decided to limit reinforcements to France to build up forces for a landing at Gallipoli on the Dardanelles.

On March 10, 1915, as French attempts in Champagne ground to a costly halt, lead brigades of two British and two Indian divisions assaulted on a narrow two-kilometer front around Neuve Chapelle in the Artois. Sir John French was eager to prove the worth of the expanding BEF, both to Kitchener, whose eyes had strayed to Asia Minor, as well as to Joffre, who doubted the effectiveness of the British and felt somewhat betrayed that his ally had not taken over lines near Ypres as promised in January. This angered him so much, in fact, that he refused to participate in the offensive as planned. The battle plan drawn up by British First Army commander Sir Douglas Haig made operational sense. The attack was to overrun the town, capture the high ground at Aubers Ridge, and then as second-wave brigades were thrown into the gap, push ten kilometers to Lille and its important railheads. The assault would be preceded by a thirty-five-minute artillery barrage from five hundred guns (mainly light field pieces).

Despite this meticulous planning, however, the Battle of Neuve Chapelle proved a disappointment.[9] Although Haig caught the German front line regiments by complete surprise and the attackers quickly penetrated over one thousand meters and fanned out along a wider four kilometer front, communications breakdowns and delays between front and rear stalled the advance, kept reserves from moving into the gap, and prevented the artillery from providing additional support, giving the Germans all day to pour in reserves. When the British resumed their attack on March 11 they were quickly stopped. The German salient around

Neuve Chapelle had been flattened, but few on the war cabinet in London thought it worth 13,000 casualties and a large expenditure of shells. "He is not a really scientific soldier," Kitchener said of French, "without adequate... knowledge for the huge task of commanding 450,000 men."[10]

Before the British and French could launch a more coordinated attack, the Germans released their chlorine gas at Ypres. Having halted the enemy's advance during the night of April 22, the allies swung over to the offensive during the next four days, but lacking adequate artillery support in the region, were unable to dislodge the defenders. In the midst of this fighting the Germans made a second gas attack that failed because the allies improvised protective measures: handkerchiefs, towels, and bandages soaked in water or urine to absorb the deadly gas. Four more gas attacks in May brought a few additional gains as Canadian, British, and French troops fell back to within a few thousand meters of Ypres, but the town held. For a few kilometers of enemy territory the Germans had paid with 38,000 casualties. The allies, however, sacrificed 58,000 men to prevent a breakthrough.

While the battle for Ypres raged in early May the French, having stockpiled 200,000 shells and assembled nearly 1,100 guns, began a five-day artillery bombardment of the German trenches in front of Vimy Ridge. The shelling reflected a new awareness at GQG that infantry assaulting the ever more formidable German trench network required far more artillery support than hitherto provided—indeed 293 of the guns, or about 37 per frontline attack division, were heavier caliber and firing more high-explosive rounds. The ratio of heavies was at least triple the concentration of earlier that year.[11]

Simultaneously the BEF prepared to strike toward Aubers Ridge east of Neuve Chapelle. One British and one Indian division moved forward after a short artillery barrage on May 9, but the preponderance of small-caliber guns firing shrapnel failed to cut much barbed wire in front of the trenches or damage the deeply dug-in German regiments. Moreover, this time the forward defenders, safe in a strengthened trench network, were ready when the infantry attacked—machine gunners quickly inflicted eleven thousand casualties and Haig called off the attack.

On May 9, 1915, the French Tenth Army also went over the top at Vimy Ridge. Eight divisions in the first wave moved out into the hilly fifteen-kilometer front. As at Neuve Chapelle in March, the single system of German trench lines was overrun and units of one corps penetrated eight kilometers and beyond, finally managing to move up the slopes of the ridge. The critical rail lines of the Douai Plain lay directly below them. But the French had outrun their reserves, positioned ten kilometers back—a critical mistake—enabling German reinforcements to reach the top, push the French off, and plug the huge gap in the line.

The allies continued to attack throughout May and June. The BEF tried to pierce German trenches at Festubert, losing another 16,000 men and advancing a mere thirteen hundred meters despite a sixty-hour bombardment. To their south, the French Tenth Army fought a battle of attrition in the labyrinthlike trenches and strong points before Vimy Ridge. A Moroccan division managed again to

Trench Warfare: Aerial View of Dogleg Traverses

Used with the permission of *The Trustees of the Imperial War Museum, London*. Photo Number: Q-27637

attain the summit on June 16 but German counterattacks pushed them off. About 100,000 French soldiers had been killed or wounded for eight kilometers of precious native soil. The Germans paid dearly too—60,000 casualties.

The German Trenches

While the British and French floundered in costly tactical experimentation, the Germans had kept two tactical steps ahead. Gas represented one ghastly innovation that spring. Germany's new-look trenches represented another. Moltke gave the first orders to entrench in September 1914. Three months later over 650 kilometers of deeply dug entrenchments well positioned on high ground stretched from the English Channel to the Swiss border, but as GQG and GHQ met in January Falkenhayn issued new entrenchment guidelines to prepare for the onslaught he anticipated.[12] When the allies attacked in May 1915, the trenches were shielded by two belts of barbed wire, each five feet high and thirty meters deep. Behind the wire lay a trench network consisting of three lines a hundred meters apart. At regular intervals each trench had a zigzag "dog leg" traverse to shield defenders from shells landing nearby and prevent attackers from firing machine guns down the entire length of the trench. This network of trenches was supported one thousand meters back by concrete machine gun "pillboxes" to mow down enemy soldiers who pierced the forward positions.

After the near-breakthrough of the French at Vimy Ridge in May–June 1915, Falkenhayn ordered construction of a second trench system. During the summer

Trench Warfare: Deep German Dugout Under Construction
Harper's Pictorial Library

a second double belt of barbed wire went into place one thousand meters behind the rear pillboxes of the first trench system. Then came a second triple line of trenches also backed by machine gun emplacements. The defenders also burrowed ever more deeply into the ground. To make the system work optimally, monthly output of machine guns had increased nearly twelvefold. Both the first and second trench systems were linked by communication trenches for moving up reinforcements or retreating. Underground telephone cables connected the first line with the second as well as with artillery far to the rear. Falkenhayn's well-designed, kilometers-deep, double killing zones amounted to a massive engineering and construction project, but it was carried out before the allies attacked again in September.

Part of the reason Falkenhayn felt compelled to bolster defenses on the western front stemmed from escalating commitments on the eastern front. From August 1914 to July 1915 German strength in the east had risen from 11 to

Trench Warfare: Barracks Under a German Trench
Harper's Pictorial Library

40 percent of the army.[13] The number of regular and reserve infantry divisions facing the more numerous British and French remained the same, around 75 (plus 17 lightly armed *Ersatz* and *Landwehr*), but these 75 were quantitatively and qualitatively weaker. Some of the elite Prussian units had been transferred eastward, leaving a greater mix of less capable Saxon, Bavarian, and reserve divisions in the west. Reserve units had half the light artillery of a regular division, no heavy guns, and fewer or no machine guns, and most of the national guard-like *Landwehr* had no artillery, no machine guns, plus they had older men in the ranks. Furthermore, to spread the war effort over two main fronts, all western divisions had been downsized from 12 to 9 battalions. The scores of regiments freed up in this way, when a few thousand new recruits were mixed in, created many new divisions. By mid-1915 the same process had been carried out on the eastern front too, giving Germany around 50 regular and reserve infantry divisions there (plus 10–12 *Landwehr*). Falkenhayn had been forced to trade men (and quality in the ranks) for more elaborate field fortifications in France.

The logic of this decision was reinforced by the brutal reality of the blockade and what this meant for firepower on opposing sides of the line. The Haber-Bosch process produced invaluable results, but the conversion to mass production of nitrogen was gradual, not immediate. By the end of 1915 powder output remained a third below what the army demanded—and two to three times below the amount of explosives at the disposal of the British and French, who had the added advantage of concentrating on one front in Europe, not two. Shell production was also a major concern. To be sure, output had skyrocketed after the early campaigns of 1914. Led by the largest armaments manufacturer, the Krupp Works

Trench Warfare: Destroyed German Pillbox
Courtesy of the Library of Congress

in Essen, German industry cranked out about 65,000 artillery shells (of all calibers) a day by early 1915. Falkenhayn could not breathe easy, however, because he had to send some of these shells east, and second, because the western allies had redoubled their own productive efforts. Already by March 1915 France's daily shell output exceeded 60,000, and Britain, after a problematic retooling of ill-prepared state arsenals and private armaments firms, turned out or purchased on average about 16,500 daily.[14]

Thus Falkenhayn's bolstering of the trenches was a bid to stave off defeat on the western front. Poison gas should also be seen in this defensive context, for the idea behind Second Ypres was not so much to break through as to distract the allies from the ongoing shift of troops to the opposite front. Using the conceptional framework adopted in earlier chapters, both trenches and gas can be seen as major parts of an improvised "revolution in military affairs," wartime technological adjustments, in this case mainly of a defensive nature.[15] As explained later, however, Falkenhayn was not just defending. He had relented to the victors of Tannenberg, Paul von Hindenburg and Erich Ludendorff of the Eastern Command (*Ober-Ost*), who attacked in East Prussia/Lithuania in February 1915. The further deterioration of the Austro-Hungarian war effort—Przemysl surrendered in March—led to a major Central Power offensive in Galicia and Poland that spring and summer. If we widen focus on the German revolution in military affairs (RMA), therefore, its offensive side also comes into view.[16] Output of the war horse cannons of 1914, the 105 mm and 150 mm howitzers, rose meteorically in 1915, and the ineffective C-96nA field guns, whose output also increased quickly, were refitted with howitzer gun carriages to permit rapid fire at higher barrel elevation to rain steel on top of entrenched defenders. While reinforcing

Gas Warfare: British Troops Advance Through a Poison Cloud at Loos
Used with the permission of *The Trustees of the Imperial War Museum, London*. Photo Number: HU-63277B

the deadly killing zones on the western front, these guns and howitzers also punished the Russians horribly on the eastern front.

The Anglo-French Offensive of Autumn 1915

Joffre and French labored at the RMA drawing board too, of course. Despite their setbacks during the first half of 1915, in fact, both resolved to learn from their mistakes, hone their offensive techniques, and resume the attack, especially with bad news streaming into headquarters from battlefields in Poland, Asia Minor, and Italy, which had joined the Entente.[17] They believed that lengthier, heavier Vimy Ridge-style bombardments would finally inflict enough damage and confusion to let the infantry punch through German trenches. French's main reservation, fully supported by Haig, was that the BEF lacked sufficient heavy artillery for its part in the overall operation, but both gained confidence when promised large quantities of chlorine gas. Committing many more divisions, moreover, would permit attacking along broader fronts, thus increasing the likelihood of finding a weak spot or two, penetrating here and there, and destabilizing the whole German line. The longer the dam, the more explosive the dam break and thus the more destruction created downstream as military floodwaters swept away everything in their path. Joffre was especially insistent, finally, that positioning reserves closer to the front lines would better enable assailants to exploit breakthroughs. The operational goals of encircling the Germans or taking their lateral rail line, thereby liberating France, remained the same.

They would crack the dam at three points simultaneously: in the Artois at Loos and Vimy Ridge and farther east in Champagne. "The simultaneity of the attacks, their strength, their width, will prevent the enemy from massing infantry and artillery reserves on a point," said Joffre. He waxed especially sanguine about the assault in Champagne, unwisely waving off intelligence reports indicating enemy efforts to vastly deepen defenses there. "The Germans have only a very few reserves behind their thin line of entrenchments,"[18] he pontificated. Elite cavalry divisions, specially trained to cross trenches, move quickly through chewed-up terrain, and fight dismounted if necessary, should prepare to exploit the impending victory by advancing seventy-five kilometers through the breach as far as Mézières to cut the main east-west railway line available to German High Command (OHL).

Before their men went forward on September 25, 1915, guns pounded the German lines at these places for four days. At Champagne the French amassed over 2,100 tubes, including 683 "heavies" or 38 per first-wave division—almost the same proportion as at Vimy Ridge in May. This time, however, GQG ordered saturation fire to propel 18 divisions forward along a wide 25-kilometer front. This was to be the main attack, for the Germans held positions here with only 8 divisions and 600 artillery pieces. At Vimy Ridge Joffre assembled 1,900 guns, including 420 of heavy caliber, about 26 for each of 16 attack divisions fanning out along a 32-kilometer line, more than twice the frontage of May. Here too the bombardment would be vastly more intense. The two offensives were to expend an astonishing 5.2 million shells. At Loos the BEF moved out 8 kilometers wide, four times broader than Neuve Chapelle, this time deploying 6 divisions (with three in reserve). They would rely primarily on smaller field guns and poison gas.

Anglo-French morale was high that morning, but hopes once again proved illusory. In all three offensives the Germans had to fall back, but with a second system of trenches in place by autumn, allied attacks tended to lose momentum and dissolve at the second double belt of barbed wire between the first and second lines, which even the heavier bombardments, lacking sufficient high explosive rounds, had failed to break up. Thus although the massive French attack in Champagne obliterated and overran the first German trench system, generals and men alike were understandably dismayed—indeed in disbelief—that the heaviest bombardment in the history of warfare had done only half the job. The few strongholds in the second trench system that were secured proved too precarious to defend against counterattacks. Deployment of reserves was also problematic. At Vimy, for example, the French exposed their reserves nearer to the front line and suffered grievous losses to German artillery fire. They had to content themselves with capturing and holding one knoll on the northern end of the ridge.

Even greater controversy surrounded the British debacle at Loos, for it led to fifty thousand casualties and Kitchener's sacking of the BEF commander.[19] The battle lasted for almost three weeks, but the underlying mistakes and misfortunes had come early. The wind caught most of the poison gas and blew it back toward Haig's attackers. Nevertheless, within four hours they seized the entire 1,000–3,000 meters of the first trench system, including several formidable redoubts and the fortified village of Loos. When this was all but accomplished, Haig requested

Italian Soldiers Move Up Into Rugged Terrain
Canfield, *World War*

two raw reserve divisions (21st and 24th) under French's control, but they were 10 kilometers back, which neither French nor Haig had considered a major flaw in prebattle planning despite the springtime lessons of Neuve Chapelle and Vimy Ridge. Orders were transmitted slowly through the chain of command to the reserves, as earlier at Neuve Chapelle, and faulty staff work at Haig's headquarters caused further delays when both divisions lost time at railroad crossings. When the reserves finally caught up to the first wave it was too late in the afternoon to take on the second system of trenches.

Disaster awaited these two divisions the next morning when they assaulted a salient in the German second line that exposed the British to raking fire from three sides. As one German officer recalled, "Never have machine guns had such straightforward work to do with barrels becoming hot and swimming in oil they traversed to and fro along the enemy's ranks.... The effect was devastating." The final reserve division, the elite Guards, went forward too as the German artillery found the range, "more and more of them [advancing] through a real hell of explosion and flame—no halting, every gap filled immediately it was made,"[20] recalled one captain from the 21st. But the veterans met the same fate as the untested men from the newly raised "Kitchener" divisions. Machine guns and cannon do not discriminate.

"The Germans had shown that they had learnt much about the methods of defending an entrenched front," concludes John Keegan in summing up the autumn actions, "[and] the allies that they had learnt nothing about means of breaking through."[21] Having tried, however, they would try harder. Macgregor Knox and Williamson Murray have this kind of frustrating challenge in mind when they observe that "creating a revolution in military affairs in wartime is difficult enough, even when battle produces clear lessons paid for in blood."[22] But it had been "a close run thing" for Falkenhayn, too, as he shifted reserves frantically from one spot to the next. The allies' combined attacks in the Artois and Champagne convinced him of the necessity of a third trench system, which went into construction that fall and winter. He was determined to keep his RMA ahead.

The British and French faced horrendously long casualty lists for extremely limited gains when the fighting ended in late October: almost 250,000 casualties. German armies had again won defensive battles, but at a cost of about 140,000 men. Since December 1914 around a million soldiers had fallen on the western front. The gory stalemate continued.

ITALY JOINS THE ENTENTE

That neither side dealt a knockout blow in the first weeks of the war or succeeded in gaining much of an advantage into 1915 made the recruiting of new allies an extremely attractive means to break the deadlock. Japan declared its belligerency in August 1914 and seized Tsingtao and Germany's Pacific islands, but Turkey's joining the Central Powers in November was much more significant. Constantinople fielded a large army that quickly pressured Russia in the Caucasus and Britain at Suez, and its holy war, although not immediately successful, still represented a frightening potential threat to British interests from northeastern Africa to India. It is therefore easy to appreciate the worries in London, Paris, Belgrade, and St. Petersburg over the leanings of Rumania, Bulgaria, Greece, and Italy. But although the Balkans were collectively important, Italy remained the prize stakes, the only neutral country in the region capable by itself of counterbalancing the addition of Turkish power to the enemy coalition. Italy, however, was technically the ally of that opposing camp.

Fortunately for the Entente, Rome did not appear any more inclined in 1915 to honor the spirit of the Triple Alliance with Germany and Austria-Hungary than it had in August 1914. European diplomats had discounted the possibility of Italian participation on the German/Austro-Hungarian side, in fact, long before war broke out. Worsening Anglo-German relations after 1905 made it likely that Italy, the ally of Germany, would have to fight naval superpower Britain—a nightmare scenario that had not seemed possible when Rome joined the Triple Alliance in 1881. Irredentist outrage over Vienna's treatment of the Italian minority of Trentino/South Tyrol contributed to Italian unwillingness to wage a war to promote Austro-Hungarian interests. It came as little surprise, therefore, when Italy proclaimed its neutrality in the summer of 1914. But questions remained about whether that neutrality would last—about the prospect, in other words, that Italy would join the Entente. This possibility forced agents of the opposing belligerents to descend with their arguments, intrigues, and bribes into the catacombs of Italian domestic politics.

Important to our story, we follow them there.[23] Already by late 1914, Italian Prime Minister Antonio Salandra and Foreign Minister Sidney Sonnino wanted Italy to join the Entente, for 1915 could end the war and produce quick territorial gains for the victors. Moreover, both men thought the resulting nationalist fervor a powerful weapon to undermine the strong political position of their great democratic rival, former prime minister and master of Italian parliamentary politics Giovanni Giolitti. Social reforms to workers after 1900 and universal manhood suffrage in 1913 had produced only street riots in 1914 by their way of thinking, seeming proof that Giolitti had undermined the authority of the monarchy and state by making too many concessions to the people. King Victor Emmanuel agreed with the prowar policy of his top ministers. The possibility of Italian entry appeared so distinct, in fact, that Berlin sent former chancellor Bernard von Bülow to Rome in December, where he was joined in February 1915 by Matthias Erzberger, one of the most dynamic leaders of the influential German Catholic Center Party. Both men sought to exploit the reportedly widespread Italian sentiment for continued neutrality.

And this led them to Giolitti, who controlled the parliamentary majority after years of concessions to the leftist parties and more recently because he was the leading opponent of intervention. Giolitti correctly assumed that the war would be an extremely difficult undertaking for Italy, whose industry had not developed sufficiently and whose army had not yet fully recovered from the war against Turkey (1911). It seemed wiser, therefore, to remain neutral at least for the time being, build up the army and navy, and attempt to exact territorial concessions from Austria-Hungary as compensation for remaining neutral. These arguments

Deadly Moment of Impact: Three Fall Repelling the Russian Counterattack
Harper's Pictorial Library

deepened the loyalty of centrist liberal deputies closest to him as well as the largest socialist faction, the Social Democrats, who had adopted the orthodox Marxist position that workers of the world should unite, not fight one another. Through the labor movement and socialist-controlled municipal governments, the Social Democrats' antiwar influence extended deep into the masses. Pope Benedict XV also opposed intervention, both for religious pacifist reasons and also because he did not want to see the Vatican cut off from millions of Catholics in Germany and Austria-Hungary. The church's populist outreach strengthened support for neutrality among the people and widened Giolitti's following.

Thus Salandra, Sonnino, and Victor Emmanuel faced formidable opposition to their prowar agenda. Therefore they opted to weaken the neutralists by appearing to negotiate seriously with Vienna—a disingenuous and dissimulating effort they assumed would falter on Austro-Hungarian intransigence. This assumption proved correct throughout the winter as Italy demanded immediate cession of Trentino/South Tyrol, strategic border lands Austria-Hungary could not be expected to sacrifice in wartime. Sonnino's counterpart in Vienna, Count Stefan Burian, obliged by refusing to give them up. He also feared that such far-reaching concessions to the empire's Italian minority would accelerate the weakening of imperial authority as other subject minorities demanded autonomy, or worse, pushed for secession. Burian therefore refused to budge, a stance strengthened by his belief that Italy represented a negligible military threat. When Erzberger learned of this position in February he reacted with understandable anger and astonishment. Having received nothing from Vienna, Salandra and Sonnino opened negotiations with the Entente in March.

Erzberger had not been idle in the meantime. An extremely able and energetic politician, he proved his diplomatic worth by convincing Chancellor Bethmann Hollweg and the kaiser that only German pressure could force Austria-Hungary to make the kind of far-reaching sacrifices that would preserve Italian neutrality. By mid-May 1915 German intimidation had wrung from Burian and Kaiser Francis Joseph a rather amazing series of concessions, including immediate cession of Trentino/South Tyrol, the Isonzo River territory, and municipal autonomy for Trieste.

Vienna's offer came too late, however, for the Entente had already sealed a more attractive deal. Acting in great secrecy on April 26, 1915, Salandra and Sonnino signed the Treaty of London with Britain, France, and Russia. In return for a pledge to join the allies within one month, Italy, after the Central Powers were defeated, would receive the Austro-Hungarian territories of Trentino/South Tyrol (including the Brenner Pass), Istria (including the port of Trieste), most of Dalmatia, and several islands in the Adriatic Sea. Final victory would also produce Italian gains in Asia Minor and Africa.

The news of Austria's concessions heightened Italy's political crisis. Neutralist antiwar groups were already upset by rumors that the government had signed a treaty with the Entente, and for weeks the nationalist press had conducted a campaign of vilification not just against noninterventionist deputies in parliament but also against parliament itself, which they smeared as an institution of weaklings and traitors. These superpatriots glorified war for war's sake. They were flanked by various leftist factions of radicals, republicans, and renegade socialists—future Fascist dictator Benito Mussolini foremost among them—who railed against the authoritarian Central Powers and preached war as a means of establishing a revolutionary new order at home and abroad. Once Austria's concessions hit the newsstands, followed days later by press leaks of the terms of the Treaty of London, the nationalists and their strange-bedfellow leftist friends took to the streets, demonstrating for war and castigating the neutralists as weak-kneed, unmanly, and unworthy of Italy. Antiwar groups found it hard to counter these charges in such a heated atmosphere. They were also physically intimidated by police and prowar agitators. Even Giolitti refused to fight back politically and push Salandra from power largely out of concern for personal safety.

Meanwhile, Salandra submitted his resignation on May 13 in a bid to win public backing from the king. The ploy worked. Victor Emmanuel refused to accept the resignation and Salandra stayed in office, bolstered by the overt approval of the monarch for war. Succumbing reluctantly to the new political reality on May 20–21, both houses of parliament granted wartime emergency powers to the government. On May 24, 1915, two days before the expiration of the month Salandra and Sonnino had promised in the Treaty of London, Italy declared war on Austria-Hungary.

Italy was certainly not the only European country fighting for the advancement of power and national interests, but all of the others had carried their people with them in the knowledge or belief that they or another people (e.g., Serbia or Belgium) had been attacked. Even the opportunistic Young Turk troika could point to the ships of British and French crusaders off the Dardanelles. Because no nation had attacked Italy, however, and its people had entered the fray largely against their will, quick victory in the field became an absolute imperative if Rome were to avoid stiff antiwar opposition on the home front.

Waiting for the Onslaught: Grand Duke Nicholas
Alfred Knox, *With the Russian Army 1914–1917* (London, 1921)

Italy did not achieve this quick victory. On June 16 Italian commander Luigi Cadorna moved eighteen divisions over the border, advancing ten–fifteen kilometers unopposed to the Isonzo River. A week later he hurled his force across the river and up into the Bainsizza and Carso Plateaus, mercilessly rugged and rocky terrain that afforded the seven divisions that Austro-Hungarian High Command (AOK) desperately scraped together from other fronts a natural line of fortifications.[24] Cadorna's operational goals included capture of nearby Istria and then onward to the main strategic prize—Vienna. His choice of attacking on the Isonzo, although a superior alternative to the mountainous Trentino and Cisalpine Tyrol, made less sense than coming to the aid of Serbia or even reinforcing the allies at Gallipoli—and it proved a terrible mistake. Although numerically superior, Cadorna had only a few trained mountain units and little heavy artillery—6.5 big guns per division, about a sixth of what France used unsuccessfully at Vimy and Champagne against formidable but less imposing defenses. Furthermore, his adherence to frontal assaults, tactics that would supposedly force enemy soldiers into the open, made no sense given their ideal defensive positions. Not surprisingly, the attackers gained at most a thousand meters in two weeks. A second offensive got under way on July 18 with no better results. There would be a third fully stymied attempt that fall to break through.

By Christmas 1915 Italian casualties stood at nearly 250,000, while over 150,000 defenders had fallen, many of the wounded casualties on both sides victims of shell explosions that sent rock splinters into faces and eyes. One Austrian who did not survive wrote in his diary of "preparing myself to die as a brave Christian [amidst] a horrible bloodbath of unparalleled butchery."[25]

As usual in the Great War, however, parallels would be found—and surpassed—on the eastern front.

Galicia: Russian Bivouac in the Carpathians
Alfred Knox, *With the Russian Army 1914–1917* (London, 1921)

GERMAN/AUSTRO-HUNGARIAN VICTORIES IN GALICIA AND POLAND

1915 had begun on the eastern front where it ended in 1914, namely, with a German drive to dislodge the Russians from East Prussia and then envelop enemy positions in Poland in concert with Austro-Hungarian armies.[26] Not at all novel, this great pincer maneuver had been under discussion since pre–war days. The hero of Tannenberg, Paul von Hindenburg, believed that a truly massive offensive would obliterate the Russian army and end the European stalemate in Germany's favor. Falkenhayn doubted that much could be gained, especially after the autumn losses in East Prussia and Poland, but yielded somewhat to the near insubordination of the star of *Ober-Ost*, whose contacts with the kaiser rivaled Falkenhayn's. Five divisions from the western front, plus six newly recruited divisions, all of which OHL had preferred to use in the west, were sent east instead, permitting creation of a new Tenth Army to join Eighth, the victors of Tannenberg, and Ninth, the veterans of Lodz—altogether 28.5 regular and reserve divisions, plus contingents from the territorial guard (*Landwehr*), which had no artillery or machine guns and whose soldiers were older.

The brains of *Ober-Ost*, Erich Ludendorff, initiated the assault on January 31, 1915, with a feinting attack by the bulk of August von Mackensen's Ninth Army at Bolimov, west of Warsaw, minus one corps (20th), which had transferred to Eighth Army. After Ninth Army engaged three Russian armies (5th, 2nd, and 1st) in this way for ten days, 20th corps and other brigades that were stretched along "the long flank"[27] over Mlawa and Johannisburg to Russia's big fort at Osoweic

Trench Warfare: Russian Trenches Provide Little Protection From Artillery
Alfred Knox, *With the Russian Army 1914–1917* (London, 1921)

(southeast of Lyck) would lock the Russian Twelfth Army frontally. Simultaneously on February 9 the main effort by Eighth and Tenth Armies would eliminate the Russian Tenth around the Augustow Forest, and then swing around Osoweic. The fortress, and ideally all Russian armies between it and Warsaw, would be annihilated.

This bold operation achieved only limited success. Enjoying a large artillery advantage, the Germans nearly surrounded and annihilated the Russian Tenth before most of its elements escaped encirclement. Russian High Command (*Stavka*) managed to stabilize the front and halt the German advance by shifting Twelfth Army northward and counterattacking on February 22. Well sited amidst trees "on the only ridge of dry ground that crosses a forty-mile-long marsh,"[28] Osoweic had also resisted all attempts to take it. German divisions had advanced over one hundred kilometers and inflicted 200,000 casualties—altogether 2 million Russians had fallen on the eastern front since August 1914—but had failed to accomplish the overall operational goal of crushing Russian armies in northwestern Poland.

AOK's ineffectual chief, Franz Conrad von Hötzendorf, had unleashed his offensive on January 23, 1915. Massive conscription efforts had filled many of the gaps in the ranks with hundreds of thousands of new recruits. One force struck through the eastern Carpathians toward Cernowitz while the Austro-Hungarian Third and "South" (*Sud*) Armies, the latter reinforced by three German divisions, went through the central mountain passes to relieve Przemysl and retake Lemberg. The initial fighting seemed to favor Austro-Hungarian fortunes, for

A Critical Shortage: Russian Field Artillery
Harper's Pictorial Library

Cernowitz fell and sixty thousand Russians were captured. The principle attack to relieve the beleaguered fortress turned into another disaster, however, as Russian units poured deadly fire down from the passes onto the easily targeted attackers. Subzero temperatures took a horrendous toll too as thousands of men froze daily. Wolves added to the grisly carnage.

After two weeks Conrad called off the operation—but resumed it again on February 27, this time adding Second Army to his columns. Three armies moved up to the passes, but they suffered the same terrible fate during weeks of slaughter. On March 22, 1915, Przemysl, giving up all hope of being relieved, surrendered its 120,000 officers and men. A Russian attack through the mountains onto the Hungarian plain was halted only by the arrival of another German corps. Although Russia also suffered grievous losses during the winter campaigns, Conrad had lost another 600,000–800,000 soldiers through rifle and artillery fire, freezing, surrender, and desertion. Having itself lost 2 million men since August, the Imperial Austro-Hungarian Army was now broken and largely incapable of offensive or defensive action without significant German reinforcements—a "rotten and decayed"[29] force according to OHL's liaison with AOK.

This unpleasant but unshakeable reality compelled Falkenhayn to lean even closer to the operational preferences of the "Easterners," Hindenburg and Ludendorff, for without greater German efforts in the east Austria-Hungary would be overrun, and then the Cossacks would turn on Berlin. Under cover of the gas attack at Ypres in April 1915, therefore, he covertly transferred eight existing or newly formed divisions from the western front to the Carpathian Mountain sector of Galicia between Tarnow and the Lupka Pass, southeast of Gorlice on the way to Przemysl, occupied by a Russian Third Army attrited from the winter campaign.[30] These German transfers joined two Austrian divisions to form a new Eleventh Army under the command of a German, General Mackensen. There were other signs of the creeping German control of the eastern war effort, for Mackensen

The Civilians' War: Widow with Children Given Little Time to Evacuate
Alfred Knox, *With the Russian Army 1914–1917* (London, 1921)

would also control the Austro-Hungarian Fourth Army on his left flank, and eventually on his right the Third Army, designated to secure the Lupka Pass. In the center, Eleventh Army would lead the way over Gorlice.

Falkenhayn wanted minimally to prevent Austro-Hungarian collapse, reduce German requirements on the eastern front by blunting the offensive threat of the Russian army, and thus enhance his chances in the west. But the chief of OHL also harbored far-reaching strategic goals. He knew that British and French forces were gathering in the Aegean Sea for an assault on Gallipoli. On the outcome of this campaign hinged in all likelihood decisions made by Greece and Bulgaria either to remain neutral or declare war to settle old scores in the Balkans. In other words, an Anglo-French defeat in the Dardanelles, coupled with a quick, embarrassing victory over Russia in Galicia, could diminish the image of the Triple Entente, recruit new allies to the Central Powers, and lead directly to the crushing of Russia's Slavic ally Serbia. Falkenhayn had no illusions about Rumania and Italy—they were clearly leaning toward the Entente—but victories in Galicia, Serbia, and the Dardanelles might intimidate Bucharest and Rome into continuing their neutrality. Finally, and most important, the impact of an allied failure to open the straits to munitions-poor Russia, combined with heavy Russian casualties in Galicia, would possibly encourage the authoritarian tsarist government to sue for peace. Falkenhayn was convinced that a protracted war contradicted St. Petersburg's interests, for such attrition and misery had the potential to trigger revolution and destroy the monarchy. And if all of these strategic goals were met, how long could Britain and France fight on?

Operational plans called for a stunning artillery bombardment of Russian trench works and hill forts on the slopes of the Carpathians opposite Central

Power positions higher up the mountains. In some respects these defenses, which were impressive for the eastern front, resembled German lines in the west before their extension that summer—a single system of three trenches one hundred meters apart with barbed-wire entanglements in front and wooden roofs for cover. Russian combat engineers had placed machine guns and 76 cm field artillery in the hill forts for raking fire into the valleys descending toward these formidable field bastions.[31] In other ways, however, Russian positions lacked the depth of the German lines France and Britain were poised to attack, for the barbed wire was shallow and there were no deep dugouts under the trenches or machine gun pillboxes behind them. Third Army, furthermore, was comparatively deficient in artillery, especially at the point of Eleventh Army's attack, where Mackensen had more than a 3-to-1 advantage in field pieces and an overpowering 50-to-1 edge in heavier guns and trench mortars. Each of Eleventh Army's infantry divisions received backup from sixteen heavies, which, although low by western front standards, would more than suffice against the weaker Russian positions. To ensure surprise, troop transfers from the west had been conducted under the strictest secrecy. To draw off Russian reserves from Galicia in late April, OHL sent three infantry and three cavalry divisions of the newly formed Niemen Army into Lithuania to take Libau and perhaps threaten Riga.

"Army Group Mackensen" attacked with near complete surprise on May 2, 1915, one week before the allied assaults in Artois. The dazed and decimated Russian defenders were quickly overrun. Within days a huge hole had been torn in Third Army's line and the entire Austro-Hungarian army joined in the offensive. The allies crossed the San River on May 25. After regrouping and receiving a second wave of German divisions, they retook Przemysl on June 3 and Lemberg on June 22. The Russian Third Army lost 70,000 killed or wounded with 140,000 taken prisoner—84 percent of its strength—and fell back so fast that Fourth, Eighth, and Eleventh had to retreat too. Having taken back over two hundred kilometers of Galicia to the river Bug, Mackensen paused to regroup.

Although a brilliant tactical and operational success, the breakthrough at Gorlice/Tarnow achieved only a few of its strategic aims. Russia had lost hundreds of thousands of men but steadfastly refused to negotiate for peace, which it saw as a dishonorable betrayal of its western allies and in all likelihood a politically unacceptable loss of territory in Poland. As explained earlier, moreover, Italy had not been deterred by Mackensen's success from declaring war against Germany's ally. On the positive side, Rumania and Greece remained neutral for the time being, waiting with Bulgaria for news of the battle raging at Gallipoli.

With much still riding on the outcome of campaigns on the eastern front, the generals of *Ober-Ost* pressed OHL for reinforcements to wage a massive battle of envelopment over Kovno and Vilna, then swinging south to meet German and Austro-Hungarian armies striking north from Galicia. Their goal: to surround all nine Russian armies, kill or capture millions of the enemy, and force Nicholas II to surrender. Falkenhayn was not impressed, complaining that "the Russians can retreat into the vastness of their country, and we cannot go chasing them for ever

Fortress Warfare: Austrian 305 mm Howitzer and Crew
Harper's Pictorial Library

and ever."[32] He decided nevertheless to launch an offensive against the Polish salient but on a lesser scale than favored by Hindenburg and Ludendorff.

A reinforced Niemen Army would continue its penetration of Lithuania, and part of the Austro-Hungarian army continue its drive through Galicia to the Russian border, but the main pincer blows would fall north of Warsaw and south of Lublin-Kholm. Striking first was "Army Group Gallwitz," comprised of elements of Eighth Army and a new Twelfth Army formed from regular, reserve, and reconstituted *Landwehr* divisions that finally got a few light artillery batteries.[33] Gallwitz's divisions were backed up, however, by one thousand guns—Eleventh Army had seven hundred at Gorlice in May. To his south Gallwitz had support—to prevent Stavka from concentrating against him—from a similarly mixed Ninth Army and four *Landwehr* divisions of the "Woyrsch Corps." The fact that the northern pincer depended so heavily on territorial guards was another indication of the relatively limited nature of OHL's plans and its strategic dilemma of spreading efforts thin over eastern and western fronts. All Great War armies used territorials, of course, but not in the first wave of important offensive operations. Simultaneously out of Galicia four armies (1st, 4th, 11th, and Bug) would plunge over Lublin and Kholm to Brest-Litovsk. For this part of the operation there was yet another injection of German line divisions into the new "Bug [River] Army," which also absorbed the Austro-Hungarian Third Army. The goal of these pincer maneuvers was to trap and annihilate most of five Russian armies (12th, 1st, 2nd, 4th, and 3rd) between the rivers Vistula and Bug.

Adding to the rage at *Ober-Ost*, these operations were to proceed more in accordance with the tactical proposals of its rival, August von Mackensen. Rather

Fortress Warfare: German Soldiers March Russian POWs from Novogeorgievsk
Courtesy of the Library of Congress

than attempt grandiose Schlieffenesque envelopments, the victor of Galicia wanted to push straight ahead, pummeling Russian divisions with vastly superior artillery, forcing them back, and then pulling the guns up into position again and repeating the process. Breakthrough would be achieved somewhere, he assumed, leading to exactly the kind of "dam break" the British and French would attempt in the autumn.[34] The pinching direction of the attacks, which threatened to trap significant Russian forces in western Poland, was the only remaining hint of the great enfilading, annihilating schemes of Hindenburg, Ludendorff, and Conrad.

The kaiser agreed to Falkenhayn's scaled-back plan, which earned both of them the scathing criticism of postwar critics anxious to find culprits for Germany's loss of the war. Recent historical scholarship concludes that the emperor and OHL did not err, however, for the western front could not have held without adequate reserves; nor could the armies of the Central Powers have moved quickly enough over the poor roads and sparse rail system of Poland to prevent the Russians from falling back in reasonable order despite heavy casualties. Even if circumvented, moreover, the chain of fortresses in Poland would have created further delays and dissipation of German offensive punch. Indeed all of these factors had convinced Schlieffen twenty years earlier to invade France first, not Russian Poland.[35] All of these risks, of course, were also inherent in Falkenhayn's limited operation. Ludendorff maintained forcefully, in fact, that Falkenhayn would achieve no more than depress the Polish salient two hundred kilometers to the critical Osoweic-Bialystok-Brest-Litovsk railroad line, where the Russians would hold.

The campaign about to begin is best understood in RMA terms. Like all military establishments that considered their technological options in the rapidly evolving industrial revolution of the early twentieth century, many in the Russian army had recognized the crucial significance of state-of-the-art artillery. Indeed the Army Bills of 1910, 1912, and 1913 called by 1917 for 6,448 of the 76 mm field guns and 2,110 of the 122 mm and 152 mm howitzers. Compared with what Germany fielded in 1914, even on a per regular corps basis, these numbers would have pulled Russia closer in field guns—108 versus 144—and nearly even in light and heavy howitzers—36 versus 40. Knowing what was needed was one thing and producing it another, however, for only a fraction of these tubes were available when war broke out and Stavka fell further behind as German production soared in 1915. Complicating matters, more of the new guns were allocated to Polish fortresses than to divisions in the field.[36] From Dvinsk and Kovno in the northeast, over Grodno, Osoweic (northwest of Bialystok), Novogeorgievsk (northwest of Warsaw), and Warsaw itself, to the southeastern bastions of Ivanogorod and Brest-Litovsk, Russia possessed a shield of fortifications, many of them recently updated and bristling with hundreds of modern artillery pieces. Behind this barrier Stavka planned to mobilize and concentrate its forces for offensive operations. Alternatively, fortress zones blunted enemy offensives by barring river and rail lines with fortress guns ranging ten to fifteen kilometers and threatening the flanks of passing enemy armies with sorties by garrison units. This part of St. Petersburg's RMA had a problematic side to it, however, because its fortress renovations on the eve bolstered walls only to withstand Germany's heaviest mobile field gun, the 150 mm howitzer, not the "monster guns" of much higher caliber. "No one knew that there were such things," recalled one general, "until they were brought into use in Belgium."[37] Thus Stavka would have been better served with heavier field artillery to bolster defenses as Germany was doing in France. Without surrounding field armies fortresses cannot serve for long as roadblocks—and Russia's massive field army was about to be sent reeling backward.

The offensive started with the familiar "thunder, booming, slamming, and banging"[38] of Gallwitz's artillery on July 13, 1915, followed a few days later by the guns of Army Group Mackensen. Once again the underequipped Russian divisions could not resist the onslaught. Russian artillery shell output doubled that summer from 15,000 to 30,000 per day but remained far below requirements, and more importantly just a fifth of German and Austro-Hungarian production.[39] "The Germans plough up the battlefields with a hail of metal and level our trenches and fortifications, the fire often burying the defenders of the trenches in them," lamented one Russian corps commander. "The Germans expend metal, we expend life." Tsarist rifle production also fell far short of needs at the front such that most companies went into action half-armed. Infantrymen again received orders to pick up the rifles and ammunition of fallen comrades, but this proved nearly impossible when constantly retreating. "The further [back] we went the greater became the number of weaponless men,"[40] a Russian army commander remembered.

German armies pounded relentlessly forward, 8–10 kilometers a day in the north, 2–3 in the south against lines reinforced from the north in early July. By month's end OHL's minions had crossed the Narew River (Ostrolenka-Pulutsk), cut off the fortresses of Novogeorgievsk and Osoweic, approached the gates of Warsaw and Ivanogorod, and overrun Lublin and Kholm. At Stavka Grand Duke Nicholas ordered a systematic fighting withdrawal à la 1812, replete with the torching of fields; evacuation of expendable, unmodernized fortress towns, starting with Warsaw and Ivanogorod on August 5; and forcible removal of hapless Polish and Jewish civilians, who were not trusted to withhold their support for the Germans if left behind. The "Great Retreat" had begun.

But it was not a rout. The British attaché with the Russian army, Alfred Knox, worried about German artillery superiority and the morale of Russian infantrymen. Corps commanders reported that "superhuman efforts were required to keep the men in the trenches." Thus far, however, the officers were succeeding. Furthermore, Knox saw no danger of a German breakthrough, pointing to the slowness of Mackensen's advance and increasing exhaustion of his troops. "German prisoners complained that they were over-tired, and they certainly looked it."[41] Finally, all of Russia's most recently updated forts—Kovno, Grodno, Osoweic, Novogeorgievsk, and Brest-Litovsk—still blocked the path.

The German offensive pushed forward over the next ten days, approaching the line Osoweic-Bialystok-Brest-Litovsk. At this point two battles threatened to turn retreat into dam-break rout. On August 19 Novogeorgievsk fell after a weeklong bombardment by OHL's only large concentration of big guns: twenty 270 mm, 305 mm, and 420 mm howitzers. For a month one of Stavka's "modernized" bastions had diverted and then held up part of Gallwitz's group that could now move forward. The Great War was over for 30 generals and 90,000 prisoners. Around 900 guns had been destroyed and another 700 captured with hundreds of thousands of shells. This demoralizing defeat came one day after an even more crushing strategic blow at Kovno. Ludendorff had not given up his plans for breaking through there, taking two weeks to gather what reinforcements he could wrest from Falkenhayn, construct field railways for munitions depots, and amass shells for the heaviest guns he had, the 150 s. On August 6 the infantry attacked the massive fort, aided a few days later by the artillery. Finally on August 18 the garrison's survivors withdrew—one day *after* the commandant, who was later court-martialed—but left behind 1,300 cannon and a million artillery rounds.

Adding to the disaster, Kovno's fall jeopardized the main railroad supply line over Vilna to Grodno and Bialystok as well as the rear of four northern Russia armies, which in turn made the position of southern armies equally untenable. Now a panicky Stavka, its chief on the verge of a nervous breakdown, began to abandon fortresses it had lavished resources on before the war: Osoweic on August 22, Brest-Litovsk on August 26, and Grodno on September 2. The Germans took Vilna on September 18. The tsar's armies lost additional huge stores of rifles, rifle ammunition, modern artillery pieces, and shells as these forts surrendered. Making matters worse, because the bulk of the empire's sulfuric and nitric acid

The Soldiers' War: French Peasants and Medic Help a Wounded Compatriot
Harper's Pictorial Library

plants had been built in Poland, they also fell to the enemy, thereby compounding explosives shortages.

The offensive ended over three hundred kilometers east of Warsaw in late September. Russian casualties since May far exceeded a million, half of which were prisoners. A complete collapse was prevented by the Central Powers' lengthening supply lines over poor or nonexistent roads; the late summer rains, which turned roads into muddy quagmires; the consequent exhaustion of men and animals; and the attackers' own losses, which mounted to many scores of thousands for each army involved. The enervating effect of the fortress battles had also delayed the German advance. Russia's huge forts proved no match for the enemy's howitzers—Grand Duke Nicholas said Kovno should be renamed "Govno," Russian for crap[42]—but these siege battles lasted weeks. Moreover, by late September 1915 the Russians held a shorter, straighter, more easily defensible line stretching from Riga in the north to Czernowitz in the south. They even counterattacked in a few places, inflicting heavy casualties on Austro-Hungarian forces at Lutsk, for instance, and thus mitigating the disaster somewhat. As bad as Russian losses had been, in fact, AOK could take little consolation in a third of a million casualties of its own. Sensing that there was still life in his war effort, Nicholas II again refused to surrender.

By autumn 1915 the hopes of both warring camps for achieving the total victory that eluded them in 1914 had proven illusory. Germany's submarine campaign did not undermine the British war effort and had to be called off in September. Nor had the Central Powers achieved the grand strategic aims of their campaign on the eastern front. There was reason for Berlin and Vienna to believe, on the other hand, that they might be slowly gaining the advantage. Indeed the Entente, which now included Italy, had bloodied itself in Champagne and the

The Soldiers' War: Aussies in France View Graves of Comrades
Used with the permission of *The Trustees of the Imperial War Museum, London*. Photo Number: HU-63277B

Artois, along the Isonzo, and especially in Galicia and Poland. With no breakthrough yet at Gallipoli, furthermore, Turkish chances in the war, along with the prospects of Islamic Jihad, stayed alive and well, while the tsar's armies remained dangerously short of shells and munitions.

Many in and out of Russia were asking, in fact, if its military effort—and political system—could survive another year after such seemingly unbearable losses. Thus a general who had fought in Galicia, Alexei Brusilov, heard one of his men mutter that the establishment had "screwed it all up," landing the common soldier and man in the street with "cleaning up the mess." Another officer heard a sergeant blame the lack of shells, the retreat, and loss of all fortresses on inept and corrupt officials in the War Ministry. "A fish begins to stink from the head. What kind of a tsar would surround himself with thieves and chiselers?"[43] Ominous signs—ominous signs indeed.

SOLDIERS AND CIVILIANS AT WAR

Most historians today depart from the traditional practice of omitting casualty figures. What was once left out for respect of the dead and to avoid any indecent hint of criticizing or questioning the sacrifices they made is now included in order to illuminate the magnitude of the horror men faced. By citing numbers, in other words, historians begin the process of turning back toward describing what war was really like, and they do this despite the understandable loathing of the veterans themselves to remember or speak about traumatic experiences they have tried, usually unsuccessfully, to suppress. The problem historians encounter with casualty figures, however, especially the astronomical numbers of dead and wounded in twentieth-century wars, is that numbers have a numbing quality to them. Although shocking to read initially, they quickly lose descriptive effectiveness as minds fail to grasp horror in the abstract. In order to do historical justice to combat on the ground, therefore, it is necessary to go beyond the numbers to the gruesome eyewitness accounts, shaking off criticism that to go there is gratuitous. The Great War can only be fully understood if all of its aspects are exposed, dimensions of the front experience that not only affected soldiers' morale and eventually the outcome of the war but also home fronts and their critically important willingness to continue shouldering the war effort.[44]

All wars are horrible—tragedies for the dead, their relatives, and friends; hobbling, sometimes disfiguring injuries for others, turning wives, children, and parents into caregivers for life; and psychological minefields for veterans who may have escaped death and injury but not the terrible memories with which loved ones, too, are then forced to live. The Great War was especially hellacious, however, because it was the first to unleash the full mechanized fury of sophisticated industrial technology. The Napoleonic Wars and American Civil War had witnessed the deadly effect of large-caliber musket and rifle volleys, to be sure, and the Austro-Prussia War of 1866 saw rapid fire from breech-loading "needle-guns," but rate of fire leapt up with magazine rifles. British infantry used them with such frightening effectiveness at Mons on August 23, 1914, that German infantrymen thought they had attacked machine gun positions—every fourth man out of two full-strength corps fell. All infantrymen in the Great War soon learned the difference, however, between magazine rifles and "the devil's paint brush," as they dubbed the machine gun for its seemingly alien killing power. As the Germans swept into France near Guise a few days after Mons, for instance, a counterattacking French company stumbled up a dark road into a machine gun detachment that in seconds left 150 men piled hideously in a "human clump." At Loos a year later elements of two British divisions lost every second man to machine gun fire—so many fell—8,000 of 15,000—that German soldiers, sickened by the "corpse field of Loos,"[45] took pity and refused to fire on the retreating survivors. Artillery was not born in the Great War either—witness, for example, the butchering of Pickett's division by shrapnel at Gettysburg—but now these scatter-ball shells were more lethal and were fired more rapidly, "cutting down trees like wisps of straw," recalled Private Adolf Hitler, and slicing human bodies in half just as fast. Firing regular shells, lighter caliber field guns could send "tree trunks and branches flying in pieces through the air, throwing up showers of stone, earth, and sand, tearing up the heaviest trees by their roots and smothering everything in a horrible, greeny-yellow, stinking vapor."[46] Hitler survived the dreadful barrage but others, like many from the German 5th Corps in the Battle of the Frontiers who were caught in the flank by French 75s, did not. "The battlefield afterward was an unbelievable spectacle," remembered a shocked French officer. "Thousands of bodies were still standing, supported as if by a flying buttress made of bodies

Artillery Warfare: Destructive Effects of Shells and Poison Gas in No–Man's-Land (Flanders)
Courtesy of the Library of Congress

lying in rows on top of each other in an ascending arc from the horizontal to an angle of 60 degrees." The bigger guns were worse, blowing large chunks of fortress walls into the air "like toy balls," crushing defenders in forts under tons of concrete and pulverizing men in the field into unidentifiable remains. To have this happen to surrounding comrades could mangle the morale of survivors. "Blood is running everywhere," wrote the Austrian at Isonzo cited earlier. "All about are the dead—pieces of corpses lie in a circle." After one of the toughest soldiers in the war, German infantryman Ernst Jünger, saw 63 of 150 fellow troopers obliterated by a high explosive round, he ran from the scene, broke down, and wept uncontrollably.[47]

The panic-inducing effect of poison gas, one of the most inhumane novelties of the Great War, is evident from the vignette opening this chapter. Irene Rathbone, a British nurse serving in Belgium since the first days of the conflict, tended the wounded of Second Ypres in April 1915. "Our hospital soon became a shambles," she remembered, with victims of the Germans' ghastly invention lying about "fully sensible, choking, suffocating, dying in horrible agony." Neither nurses nor doctors could do anything to help. The gas victims were not the only nightmarish wards of this field hospital. "The operating theater became a slaughterhouse" of amputations, "ligatured blood vessels in important places," trephined skulls, and "huge abdominal wound cases"—they were "lifted off, a wet cloth mopped the blood onto the floor, and another was lifted on." Indeed one of the most effective methods of conveying to readers the depths of the human catastrophe of the Great War—although difficult sources to read—are the nurses' accounts. Another British volunteer, Vera Brittain, later wrote about her "baptism of blood and pus" in France as she tried to care for "men without faces, without eyes, without limbs, men almost disemboweled, men with hideous truncated stumps of bodies." A third British angel of mercy serving with the Russians in Poland during the Great Retreat of 1915, Florence Farmborough, never forgot the last minutes of one hapless subject of the tsar hit by German artillery. "I pushed the uniform back and saw a pulp, a mere mass of smashed body from the ribs downwards, the stomach and abdomen were completely crushed and his left leg was hanging to the pulped body by only a few shreds of flesh." An orthodox priest passed the bed, covered his eyes, and hurried away as Farmborough, realizing that nothing could be done for the wounded man, also turned to leave. "The soldier's dull eyes were still looking at me and his lips moved, but no words came."[48]

The Soldiers' War: Mutilated Veteran before Receiving Cosmetic Mask

Courtesy of the Library of Congress

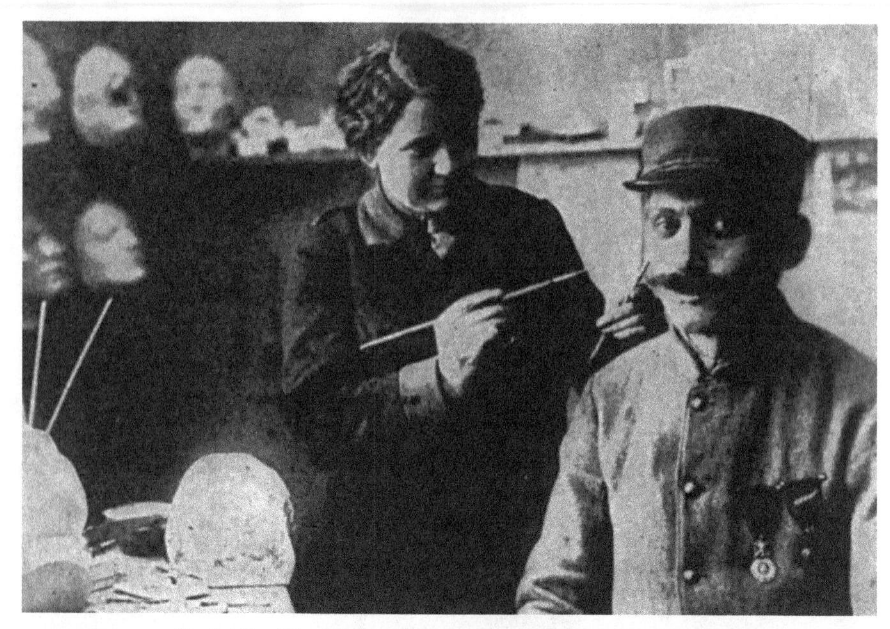

The Soldiers' War: Mutilated Veteran after Receiving Cosmetic Mask
Harper's Pictorial Library

Heart-wrenching experiences like these could mellow even the most adamant feminists like Rathbone, turning them away from the gender alienation of prewar suffrage struggles and sex wars toward gender reconciliation and sympathy for men's suffering. On the German side, similarly, one finds the testimony of Marie-Elisabeth Lüders, a civil administrator in occupied Belgium who also nursed behind the lines, which bears witness to the depth of feeling, the near guilt, in fact, that German women felt for their men:

> Even though we pondered our loss and suffering, work and pain, deprivation and worry, even though we had to read the long death lists that brutally ripped apart ties of love and friendship, even though we did without the most necessary staples of life, were afraid for our children, and concerned about material things, we always felt the immeasurable essential difference between two realities: our everyday life here, and the fate-bedecked, blood-soaked field there. This other reality, whose traces lay on the faces of so many wounded... was silent on their lips because the soul dared not put it into words, and we did not ask, for in our short time together with them, death was not to have the last word.[49]

With such dedication and affection shown to the wounded it is small wonder that male patients sometimes became endeared to their nurses. If Lüders and the half million European women who nursed men in the Great War felt guilt, however, it was sometimes because wounded soldiers made their caretakers feel that way. Many men went to war anticipating a great adventure, a quick and brutal reckoning followed by a triumphal return. After the grisly failure of the first offensives and the onset of trench warfare made a cruel mockery of such notions, combatants found themselves

Civilians Go to War: The Leeds Pals Battalion in 1914
Used with the permission of *The Trustees of the Imperial War Museum, London*. Photo Number: Q-111826

in a hellish world where one could get shot, bleed in pain, and be carted off to a field hospital. About 31 percent of European men who joined armies received wounds—more than 21 million males, with probably over half of them hit by artillery fire[50]—and for a time at least were helpless and obviously unable to conquer anything. A Red Cross poster, "The Greatest Mother in the World," featuring an oversized nurse cradling a doll-like, infantilized, emasculated casualty of war, illustrated well this relationship of inferiority. Because none of this humiliation and embarrassment could be hidden from the all-seeing nurses, some men directed their anger at the ones who saw. There was a certain twisted logic to hating one's caretaker, moreover, because this woman sometimes nursed a man right back to the front, another horrendous wound, and the likelihood of death. In the British and German armies, for instance, about two-thirds of all wounded soldiers returned to combat.[51]

The Great War generated a great deal of male hostility toward women. Men feared job displacement as the number of women in the labor force rose to meet wartime needs—from 24 to 38 percent in Britain, 32 to 40 percent in France, and 34 to 51 percent in Germany. Male politicians and voters also worried about a female political takeover if the more numerous women exploited the war politically to gain voting rights. As soldier-nurse relations demonstrate, however, male anger went far deeper to the perception of persecution by women—an emotion that found revealing expression in works of literature and art. Thus British poet D. H. Lawrence asked, "Why do the women follow us, satisfied/Feed on our wounds like bread, receive

Human Suffering and Religious Passion: Field Mass on the Russian Front
Harper's Pictorial Library

our blood/Like glittering seed upon them for fulfillment?" In *Shellhole with Corpses* German artist cum machine gunner Otto Dix depicted men who have sought refuge in mother earth and are hurled by explosions violently out of her womb. Not only are mothers powerless to protect their sons from the horror of war but also, as the soldier-producing side of humanity, they are responsible for it. One is reminded here of the "little mother" in Robert Graves's *Goodbye to All That,* who declared that mothers should gladly "pass on the human ammunition" for the cause. "We will emerge [from the war] stronger women to carry on the glorious work [their] memories have handed down to us." Another veteran of the fighting, German artist George Grosz, seemed to agree that women sacrificed men on the altar of war:

> Where have the nights gone? Where are the women? Where are the adventures? [We] have been mutilated, dispersed, duped, bewitched and turned into gray-uniformed butcher's boys!! What a finale to this hell, to this brutal murdering on all sides, to this witch's Sabbath, to this horrifying castration.

Grosz took a revenge of sorts with *When it Was All Over, They Played Cards*. Having mutilated a woman and stuffed her body parts into a crate, three men nonchalantly drink and deal. The same anesthetized indifference to death that sometimes came over soldiers in the trenches, lest they go insane, has been turned on women. Some men, in fact, did not just imagine doing this kind of violence. "Murder and brutal assault of women are of incessant occurrence," complained British suffragette Nina Boyle in 1916. "Men who have not gone to the trenches, and men who come back from them, vie with each other in this pleasing pastime."[52]

And back to the trenches they went, too, rejoining mates and comrades there who were doing their duty. Indeed, one of the mysteries to students of the Great War is this willingness of men to persevere in a conflict so full of horrors like those described earlier, for although the first signs of sagging morale appeared in certain Czech units in the Austro-Hungarian army and in places along the Russian line in 1915, generally the rank and file of most armies was not deserting or giving up easily. Moreover, a remarkably low percentage of wounded combatants experienced psychological breakdown or "shellshock"—in the British and German armies, only about 5 percent.[53] The reasons range from the kinds of things that have always motivated soldiers to much less obvious factors.[54] Reinforcing the need to defend God and country, kaiser or tsar, fatherland or motherland, was, for instance, the desire not to let down parents and hometown buddies and girlfriends—hence Grosz's "bewitched" lament—a motivation strengthened by the traditional belief that breaking down in combat reflected lack of character and moral fiber. One thinks here of the sacrosanct regimental banners that symbolized home behind which American Civil War soldiers rallied. In the Great War hometown pride factors found further reinforcement in the esprit de corps of regiments hailing exclusively from local regions in Scotland, Brandenburg, the Tyrol, or elsewhere. Whether or not one signed up or was recruited with "pals" back home, however, fellow soldiers usually bonded after months or years together in the same unit. Thus men also fought for comrades on the left and right, refused to desert them in combat, and swore to avenge their deaths in the next battle. Men could also develop special bonds with particularly charismatic junior officers, following them into the most dangerous battlefield situations. Throughout 1914, 1915, and beyond, furthermore, soldiers on all sides faced danger with the hope that this next battle or campaign would be the one that brought the war to a victorious end. Prayer reinforced hope, and when the brutality of combat undermined belief in the Prince of Peace, men could still entrust their fate to amulets and talismans or a belief in one's magical destiny to survive. After Hitler pulled through one scrape after another, for instance, his comrades began to say that the bullet hadn't been made with his name on it—and Hitler believed this.

"You see these crosses all over in France," wrote American Expeditionary Force member Joseph Dugan on this snapshot.
Private Collection

Not as well known or obvious are the negative/less noble inducements to do one's duty. As in past centuries, the ration of rum, schnapps, or vodka before going

The Soldiers' War: Soccer Match Behind the Front

Used with the permission of *The Trustees of the Imperial War Museum, London*. Photo Number: Q-26357

into combat screwed up a soldier's courage and by all accounts was an important factor in maintaining morale. Moreover, the alternatives to fighting, leaving aside being shamed before friends, family, mates, and popular officers, were not attractive. If a man cut and ran, he was subject to arrest by military police behind the lines. Court-martial, imprisonment, or execution followed. Surrendering was another option but a dangerous one. Enemy soldiers did not always immediately recognize willingness to yield and simply kept firing—the first to surrender often got killed. Finally, all soldiers knew, or thought they knew, of incidents where the other side shot rather than took prisoners. Unfortunately these kinds of atrocities did happen, beginning in August 1914 and continuing throughout the war, which created a negative incentive for men to fight.

In explaining why men persevered, however, it is important to add that they did not enter combat every day. Parts of the front remained inactive for months or years after 1914, and even the bloodiest battle areas were contested by different divisions as armies rotated units into the line and eventually out for refitting, replacements, rest and relaxation. Life behind the lines was no picnic either, but at least it was safer, warmer, drier, and quieter—all Great War soldiers complained of the nerve-fraying noise, not to mention the danger, of artillery bombardments. And occasionally, rather than ordering men into action again, officers announced furloughs. The much-anticipated home leave often frustrated and upset men in

Experience, Caution, and Humor Helped the Veterans: Tommie in a Tub
Used with the permission of *The Trustees of the Imperial War Museum, London*. Photo Number: Q-4626

Women in a Man's World: British First Aid Nurses in the Trenches
Harper's Pictorial Library

uniform who had neither the ability nor the inclination to explain that combat had changed from their father's or grandfather's day, that there was nothing glorious about it, and that victory might be long in coming or not come at all. But at least one was at home and not at the front.

The naiveté of civilians quickly changed, however, when War Office telegrams or posted death lists included the name of someone close and "brutally ripped apart ties of love and friendship," for family survivors typically became preoccupied with the details of a loved one's combat death, seeking out comrades or repeatedly writing the Red Cross until the whole terrible story was known. In late December 1915, for instance, Vera Brittain learned of the death of her fiancé, Roland, whom she had anticipated for Christmas leave. Instead she and relatives and friends spent days trying to piece together what happened until finally learning on January 2, 1916, that he had been shot while trying to repair the barbed wire in front of his trench.

> We had more details today—fuller, more personal, more interesting, and so much sadder. So the day opened once more—it has begun so all too often this week—with our sitting round the breakfast table scarcely touching our breakfast, but trying with eyes that tears had made to ache acutely, to see to read messages sent to us concerning him.[55]

In this way front and home front grew closer and closer together, especially as casualties mounted and more civilians got bad news.

NOTES

1. The best description of the attack is found in Lyn Macdonald, *1915: The Death of Innocence* (New York, 1993), 190–201. Also see John Keegan, *The First World War* (New York, 1999), 197–199; and Holger H. Herwig, *The First World War: Germany and Austria-Hungary 1914–1918* (New York, 1997), 169–171.
2. The French had used poison rifle bullets and hand grenades in the preceding months but not on the scale unleashed by Germany at Ypres. Germany had used xylyl bromide shells against the Russians at Bolimov, west of Warsaw, in February, but cold weather had negated the effects. See Herwig, *First World War,* 135, 169.
3. Cited in ibid., 170.
4. Cited in ibid., 170.
5. Cited in Macdonald, *1915,* 193.
6. Dennis Showalter, "'It All Goes Wrong': German, French, and British Approaches to Mastering the Western Front," in Pierre Purseigle, ed., *Warfare and Belligerence: Perspectives in First World War Studies* (Leiden, Holland, 2005), 41.
7. Keegan, *First World War,* 191–192.
8. George H. Cassar, *Kitchener's War: British Strategy from 1914 to 1916* (Washington, DC, 2003), 162–167; Herwig, *First World War,* 231; and Hew Strachan, *The First World War* (Oxford, 2001), 1:1037, 1048, 1100. Also see Robert K. Massie, *Castles of Steel: Britain, Germany, and the Winning of the Great War at Sea* (New York, 2003), 430–432. Daily German production of field gun and light (105 mm) howitzer shells stood at 65,000 in early 1915 and reached nearly 100,000 in late 1915. Austro-Hungarian production, at around 30,000–40,000 per day in 1915, doubled to 62,000 daily in 1916.

9. The most detailed description of the battle is Macdonald, *1915*, 75–143. Also see Keegan, *First World War*, 192–197.
10. Cited in Cassar, *Kitchener's War*, 165–166.
11. For the fighting in the Artois in May–June 1915, see Macdonald, *1915*, 295–310, 487–551; Keegan, *First World War*, 199–203; David Stevenson, "French Strategy on the Western Front 1914–1918," in Roger Chickering and Stig Förster, eds., *Great War, Total War: Combat and Mobilization on the Western Front 1914–1918* (Cambridge, UK, 2000), 304–307; and Robert A. Doughty, *Pyrrhic Victory: French Strategy and Operations in the Great War* (Cambridge, MA, 2005), 158–165. Stevenson places the number of heavies even higher at four hundred.
12. For good descriptions of the trenches, see Keegan, *First World War*, 175–186; and David Stevenson, *Cataclysm: The First World War as Political Tragedy* (New York, 2004) 146–149.
13. As OHL began to shift and transfer divisions between the eastern and western fronts, create new divisions, and reconstitute *Landwehr* units into numbered army divisions, French, Russian, and British intelligence provided valuable and extremely detailed and accurate insights. These were later compiled by the American Expeditionary Force (AEF) in *Histories of Two Hundred and Fifty-One Divisions of the German Army Which Participated in the War (1914–1918)* (Washington, DC, 1920). This source should be used together with the appropriate volumes of the fourteen-volume German army history issued by the *Reichsarchiv, Der Weltkrieg 1914–1918* (Berlin, 1925–1944).
14. Gerald D. Feldman, *Army Industry and Labor in Germany 1914–1918* (Princeton, NJ, 1966), 45–64; Strachan, *First World War*, 1:1037, 1055, 1067–1068.
15. See MacGregor Knox and Williamson Murray, "Thinking about Revolutions in Warfare," in their edited collection, *The Dynamics of Military Revolution 1300–2050* (Cambridge, UK, 2001), especially 11–14.
16. See Eric Dorn Brose, *The Kaiser's Army: The Politics of Military Technology in Germany during the Machine Age* (New York, 2001), 227–228.
17. For the autumn offensives in France, see Keegan, *First World War*, 200–203; Robert T. Foley, *German Strategy and the Path to Verdun: Erich von Falkenhayn and the Development of Attrition, 1870–1916* (Cambridge, UK, 2005), 168–180; and Doughty, *Pyrrhic Victory*, 187–202. Also for France in the RMA context, see Douglas Porch, "The French Army in the First World War," in Allan R. Millett and Williamson Murray, eds., *Military Effectiveness*, Vol. 1, *The First World War* (Boston, 1988), 200–225.
18. Citations in Doughty, *Pyrrhic Victory*, 189.
19. For an excellent discussion, see Tim Travers, *The Killing Ground: The British Army, the Western Front and the Emergence of Modern Warfare 1900–1918* (London, 1987), 16–19. The greatest detail on the battle is found in Macdonald, *1915*, 496–551.
20. Citations here in Keegan, *First World War*, 202; and Macdonald, *1915*, 548.
21. Keegan, *First World War*, 203.
22. "Thinking about Revolutions in Warfare," in Knox and Murray, *Dynamics of Military Revolution*, 13.
23. For the politics of Italian entry to the Great War, see Salvatore Saladino, *Italy from Unification to 1919: Growth and Decay of a Liberal Regime* (New York, 1970), 134–152; John Gooch, "Italy during the First World War," in Millett and Murray, *Military Effectiveness*, 1:157–165; and especially Klaus Epstein, *Matthias Erzberger and the Dilemma of German Democracy* (Princeton, NJ, 1959), 118–138.
24. For 1915 fighting on the Isonzo, see Keegan, *First World War*, 226–229; and Herwig, *First World War*, 151–154. For the Italian army in the RMA context, see Gooch, "Italy during the First World War," in Millett and Murray, *Military Effectiveness*, 1:165–184.
25. Cited in Herwig, *First World War*, 153.

26. For these campaigns, see Stone, *Eastern Front,* 107–127; Robert B. Asprey, *The German High Command at War: Hindenburg and Ludendorff Conduct World War I* (New York, 1991), 158–165; Herwig, *First World War,* 112–113, 129, 135–140; and Keegan, *First World War,* 170–174. Also see the AEF's *Histories of the Two Hundred and Fifty-One Divisions of the German Army.*
27. See Ludendorff's description of operational goals in *Ludendorff's Own Story August 1914-November 1918* (New York, 1919), 1:139–143.
28. For Osoweic's layout and the 1915 siege, see Robert R. McCormisck, *With the Russian Army* (New York, 1915), 219–247 (and 223 for the quote).
29. Cited in Herwig, *First World War,* 140.
30. For the fighting in Galicia and Poland from May to September 1915, a good discussion is Foley, *German Strategy and the Path to Verdun,* 127–155. From the indispensable memoirs see Erich von Falkenhayn, *General Headquarters and Its Critical Decisions 1914–1916* (London, 1919), 73–103; Ludendorff, *Ludendorff's Own Story,* 1:163–202; Alfred F. W. Knox, *With the Russian Army 1914–1917* (New York, 1971, originally published 1921), 280–323; and Alexei A. Brusilov, *A Soldier's Notebook 1914–1918* (Westport, CT, 1971, originally published 1930), 140–187. Also see Stone, *Eastern Front,* 165–191; Asprey, *German High Command,* 176–191; and Herwig, *First World War,* 140–149.
31. For a description of Russian defenses, see Bruce I. Gudmundsson, *Stormtroop Tactics: Innovation in the German Army, 1914–1918* (New York, 1989), 109–110.
32. Cited in Stone, *Eastern Front,* 176. The disagreement between *Ober-Ost* and OHL is mirrored nicely in Falkenhayn, *General Headquarters,* 112–131; and Ludendorff, *Ludendorff's Own Story,* 1:173–183.
33. For unit-by-unit comments on the summer 1915 campaigns of the 83rd through 89th divisions, all reconstituted *Landwehr,* and the 3rd, 4th, and 18th *Landwehr,* see AEF, *Histories of Two Hundred and Fifty-One Divisions,* 78–79, 99–100, 293–294, 550–570.
34. See Hew Strachan, *The First World War* (New York, 2003), 142.
35. See Foley, *German Strategy and the Path to Verdun,* 151–155, and for Schlieffen's thinking in the early 1890s, Brose, *Kaiser's Army,* 70–78.
36. For this paragraph, see David R. Jones, "Imperial Russia's Forces at War," in Millett and Murray, *Military Effectiveness,* 1:262–314; Strachan, *First World War,* 1:298–307, 1103–1104; and Brose, *Kaiser's Army,* 149–151, 228.
37. Brusilov, *Soldier's Notebook,* 168.
38. One German officer's description of the May 2 barrage, cited in Herwig, *First World War,* 142.
39. For production figures in the three nations, see Strachan, *First World War,* 1:1037, 1048, 1100.
40. Citations in Foley, *German Strategy,* 149; and Strachan, *First World War,* 146.
41. Knox, *With the Russian Army,* 301, 308.
42. Cited in Orlando Figes, *A People's Tragedy: The Russian Revolution 1891–1924* (New York, 1998), 267.
43. Citations in ibid., 268; and Allan K. Wildman, *The End of the Russian Imperial Army* (Princeton, NJ, 1980), 1:92.
44. See especially Stéphane Audoin-Rouzeau and Annette Becker, *1914–1918: Understanding the Great War,* trans. Catherine Temerson, (New York, 2002), 1–44.
45. Citations in Brose, *Kaiser's Amy,* 207, 201; and Keegan, *First World War,* 202.
46. For Hitler's letters of early 1915, see Werner Maser, ed., *Hitler's Letters and Notes* (New York, 1976), 76, 79.
47. Brose, *Kaiser's Army,* 196–197, 39; Herwig, *First World War,* 156; and Ernst Jünger, *The Storm of Steel: From the Diary of a German Storm-Troop Officer on the Western Front,* trans. Basil Creighton (London, 1929), 244.

48. Citations in Susan Kingsley Kent, *Making Peace: The Reconstruction of Gender in Interwar Britain* (Princeton, NJ, 1993), 61, 60; and Martin Gilbert, *The First World War: A Complete History* (New York, 1994), 154–155.
49. MarieElisabeth Lueders, *Das Unbekannte Heer: Frauen Kaempfen fuer Deutschland* (Berlin, 1936), 77–78, 6.
50. Alexander Watson, *Enduring the Great War: Combat, Morale and Collapse in the German and British Armies, 1914–1918* (Cambridge, UK, 2008), 15.
51. Ibid., 103.
52. For this paragraph (and citations), see Sandra M. Gilbert, "Soldier's Heart: Literary Men, Literary Women, and the Great War," in Margaret Randolph Higonnet et al., *Behind the Lines: Gender and the Two World Wars* (New Haven, CT, 1987), 199, 209; Maria Tatar, *Lustmord: Sexual Murder in Weimar Germany* (Princeton, NJ, 1995), 120; and Kent, *Making Peace*, 95, 101.
53. Watson, *Enduring the Great War*, 43.
54. For discussions of why men fought, see Niall Ferguson, *The Pity of War: Explaining World War I* (New York, 1999), 339–394; Audoin-Rouzeau and Becker, *Understanding the Great War*, 113–134; Stevenson, *Cataclysm*, 172–177; and most recently, Watson, *Enduring the Great War*, passim.
55. Vera Brittain, *Chronicle of Youth: Great War Diary 1913–1917*, ed. Alan Bishop (London, 2000), 302.

CHAPTER VI

The Wider War

1915–1916

On November 14, 1914, the Shaikh-ul-Islam, second in religious authority only to Sultan-Caliph Mohammed V, stood above the flag-draped Mecca Wall of the Grand Fatih Mosque of Mehmet the Conqueror, fifteenth-century Ottoman captor of Constantinople.[1] Flanked by leaders of the Young Turk Committee of Union and Progress attired in black coats and fezzes and white armbands, the dome and twin minarets of the wondrous mosque towering over them, the Golden Horn, Bosporus, and holy Mecca far away to the south, he called out for Muslims to wage holy war against the infidel enemies of Islam.

> Take them and kill them whenever you find them. He who kills even one unbeliever among those who rule over us, whether he does it secretly or openly, shall be rewarded by God. And let every Muslim, in whatever part of the world he may be, swear a solemn oath to kill at least three or four of the infidels who rule over him, for they are the enemies of God and of the faith. A Muslim who does this shall be saved from the terrors of the Day of Judgment.

This summons or *fatwa* was read in every mosque and published in every newspaper throughout the Ottoman Empire. Agents from Istanbul also smuggled it in leaflet form into Abyssinia, British and Italian Somaliland, the Sudan, Tripolitania, Egypt, the Caucasus, Persia, Afghanistan, India—into neighboring portions, in other words, of enemy empires—as well as other parts of the Muslim world.

Listening to the fiery, incendiary instructions of the *fatwa*, American ambassador in Constantinople Henry Morgenthau paid particular attention to one

Amphibious Warfare: Allied Battleships Bombarding the Gallipoli Shore

Used with the permission of *The Trustees of the Imperial War Museum, London*. Photo Number: Q-53526

frightening sentence: "Know ye that the blood of infidels in the Islamic lands may be shed with impunity—except those to whom the Muslim power has promised security and are allied with it." To Morgenthau this passage indicated clearly "that a German hand had exercised an editorial supervision." The American immediately rebuked his counterpart from Berlin, Conrad von Wangenheim, for his obvious part in inciting "a wildly fanatical people" to violence, confident as the German was that Jihad or no Jihad, "the mere threat of such an uprising would induce England to abandon Belgium and France to their fate."[2]

The failure of Turkish War Minister Enver Pasha's offensive into the Caucasus in late 1914 and Naval Minister Ahmed Djemal's similarly ill-fated attempt to seize the Suez Canal in early 1915 dampened the potential for such a massive insurgency. However, the wartime fortunes of the Ottoman Empire, and hence its prestige as protector of the faith, soon took major turns for the better. Indeed everywhere within the reach of its power in 1915 Turkey killed, captured, and devastated soldiers and civilians of Christian faiths, driving them mercilessly from the Ottoman heartland.

TURKEY'S HOLY WAR

Gallipoli: The Opening Rounds

In early January 1915 many different leaders of the Triple Entente, foremost among them British First Lord of the Admiralty Winston Churchill, saw enticing

Amphibious Warfare: Australians in Ships Boats at Gallipoli
Used with the permission of *The Trustees of the Imperial War Museum, London*. Photo Number: Q-58078

possibilities in running the Dardanelles and bombarding Constantinople with an Anglo-French battleship flotilla.[3] Russia hoped the action would take pressure off its armies in the Caucasus and open up a warm-water route through the Black Sea for export of Russian wheat to the West and import of munitions in such short supply at home. For their part, western civilian and military figures were excited about teaching the upstart Turks a lesson, knocking them out of the war; helping Russia; and then rallying the neutral Balkan states of Greece, Rumania, and Bulgaria to Serbia's side. This new Balkan League would help Russia push over the Austro-Hungarian house of cards and force Germany to surrender.

From the start the military discussion centered on the question of deploying only naval forces or rather simultaneously supporting the ships by landing troops on the Gallipoli Peninsula to attack forts on the northern side of the straits from the rear.[4] Churchill favored a "ships alone" approach, brushing aside the objections of Third Sea Lord Fredrick Tudor, who worried that Turkish mines and shore batteries would prove too formidable an obstacle. "You won't do it with ships alone," Tudor ventured, to which Churchill replied, "Oh yes we will."[5]

At first the first lord's optimism seemed warranted, for having failed to silence the guns of the outer forts guarding the entrance to the Dardanelles on February 19, an Anglo-French flotilla of four modern and twelve predreadnought battleships smashed most of these defenses six days later. Landing parties finished off the remaining outer forts in late February and early March before encountering stronger Turkish resistance and withdrawing.

However, moving farther into and through the straits where they narrowed and provided far less room to maneuver was another matter. After eight successive attempts to sweep the narrow waters of mines did not succeed due to fierce firing from both shores, Admiral John de Robeck succumbed to Churchill's bidding to

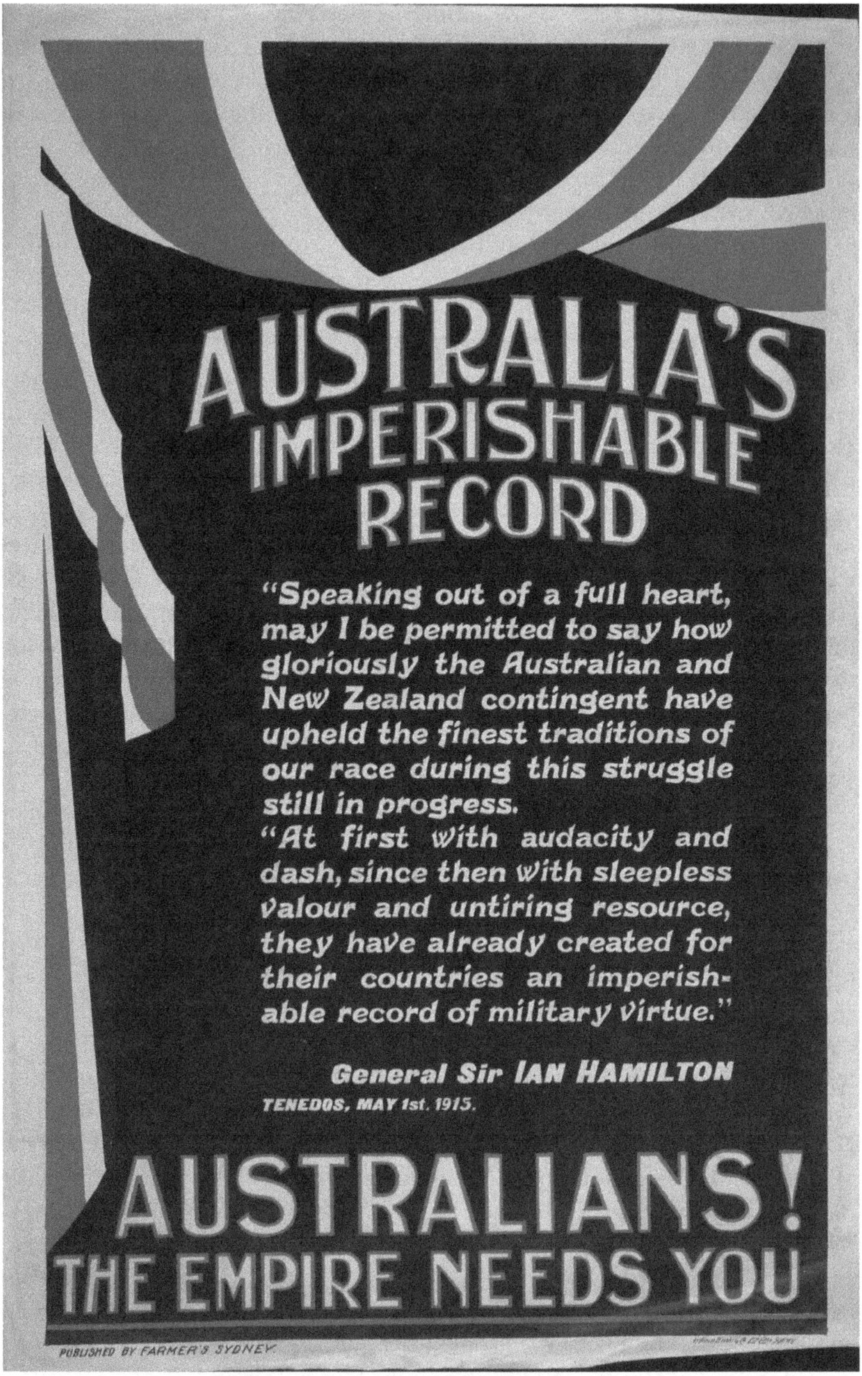

AUSTRALIA'S IMPERISHABLE RECORD

"Speaking out of a full heart, may I be permitted to say how gloriously the Australian and New Zealand contingent have upheld the finest traditions of our race during this struggle still in progress.

"At first with audacity and dash, since then with sleepless valour and untiring resource, they have already created for their countries an imperishable record of military virtue."

General Sir IAN HAMILTON

TENEDOS, MAY 1st. 1915.

AUSTRALIANS!

THE EMPIRE NEEDS YOU

PUBLISHED BY FARMER'S SYDNEY

Imperial Surplus: Sir Ian Hamilton Applauds Australia

Courtesy of the Library of Congress

send in the battleships. One of the admiral's officers thought the plan "madness," adding that "it is surely pressure from our cursed politicians which is making him even consider such a thing." Because seventy-five thousand troops were being assembled on the Aegean island of Lemnos to assist the navy, "why not wait for them?" All sixteen capital ships attacked, nevertheless, on March 18. In De Robeck's words, it was a "disaster":[6] three battleships hit mines and sunk, one beached, and two others were badly damaged.

The lesson and dilemma of the battle seemed clear: the navy could not destroy Turkish gun emplacements until the mines were swept, but it could not sweep the mines before silencing the guns. Secretary for War and leading figure on the war cabinet, Lord Horatio Herbert Kitchener, came gradually and rather reluctantly to the conclusion that it would be necessary, therefore, to use an army expeditionary force to secure the Dardanelles before capturing Constantinople, but an undaunted Churchill, spurred on by reports that German officers who had organized Turkish defenses were requesting more ammunition, urged his admiral to rush in a second time. Initially tempted, De Robeck eventually declined, giving rise to the view held by many later historians that the British had missed a golden opportunity to win a decisive victory and turn around a stalemated war. Still convinced he was right sixteen years later, Churchill recalls seeing "a vista of terrible consequences behind this infirm relaxation of purpose."[7] Recent research debunks the myth by showing that Turkish batteries were still stocked well enough that a second run would have been equally disastrous. "His attempt to place blame for the failure of the operation on others, while ducking his own culpability," writes his military biographer, Carlo D'Este, "must now be viewed as entirely self-serving."[8]

Now it would be the army's turn. Sir Ian Hamilton, commanding Anglo-British forces on Lemnos, wired Kitchener on March 19, 1915, advocating "a deliberate and progressive military operation carried out in force in order to make good the passage of the navy." His chief agreed: "Military operations must be carried through."[9] Before Hamilton was ready to attack, however, precious time would pass. Hamilton's problems stemmed from the patchwork nature of his command. From North Africa came a French colonial division; from Egypt two divisions of Australians and New Zealanders, the "Anzacs"; and from Britain the regular 29th Division. These units joined a division of royal marines already on the scene, but it took a solid month after the navy's defeat to assemble them on Lemnos, build up supplies, and acquire makeshift landing craft from all over the Middle East. The large-scale amphibious operation about to happen is one of the most significant chapters in the tragic history of the Great War's improvised, jerry-rigged revolution in military affairs (RMA).

Hamilton's delay gave defenders ample time to prepare. Turkish leader Enver Pasha put campaign planning in the able hands of a German general, Otto Liman von Sanders. "If the English will only leave me alone for eight days," he said toward the end of March. "The British gave me four full weeks,"[10] he later recalled. Sanders used his opportune reprieve wisely, digging trenches and fortifications along the coasts of the rugged Gallipoli peninsula and stringing barbed wire on the beaches and in nearby waters.

Imperial Surplus: Anzacs Embark for Gallipoli
Harper's Pictorial Library

However, this still left the operational puzzle—known to readers familiar with allied landings in Normandy twenty-nine years later—of where Hamilton's force would come ashore. When he assumed command of the Ottoman Fifth Army's eighty thousand Turkish and Arab conscripts, they were spread thinly along the shores of Gallipoli and southern banks of the Dardanelles. Sanders opted to concentrate his forces, keeping two of seven divisions on the Asiatic side, two a few miles inland from the western tip of the peninsula, and three at the eastern neck of Gallipoli near Bulair.

The latter decision seems to have been influenced by the interrogation of a Royal Navy lieutenant captured on April 17 who cleverly hinted at Bulair as the landing site to distract the Turks from the intended landings in the west.[11] Unaware of this incident, Hamilton would nevertheless contribute to Sanders's confusion by making a feint at Bulair on April 25 with twenty warships and his marines. A similar deception with the French colonials at Kum Kale on the Asiatic Dardanelles aimed to pull further troops away from the main thrusts at Cape Helles and farther north near Gaba Tepe at what would come to be known as "Anzac Cove." The goal of the first day's operation was to put thirty thousand men ashore, seize three high ridges several kilometers from the shore, and thereby threaten from the rear Turkish defenses stretching along the Dardanelles from the entrance all the way to the Chanak Narrows. The plan had potential, for Sanders left the coasts lightly defended by a few thousand men, opting to position the bulk of the 9th and 19th Divisions farther inland where they could react as British plans unfolded.

From the beginning, however, things went wrong for the allies. The naval bombardment did only moderate damage because in most cases the big ships anchored too far from shore for accurate spotting of shots. Without their own artillery on the beaches, moreover, allied units, particularly the Anzacs, took heavy losses from

Turkish shrapnel. Other advance elements got caught in barbed wire or trapped in wobbly lifeboats as machine gun fire raked the beaches. The British also paid dearly for ineptness, confusion, and poor communications. At Cape Helles, for instance, the first assault waves hitting beaches code-named Y and S—the far left and far right, respectively, of the five beaches attacked that day by the British 29th Division—encountered little or no opposition and could have cut off the Turks' rear but did not move inland. On S Beach the commander had only been ordered to seize a gun emplacement and failed to seize the initiative beyond his orders, while on Y Beach the order to encircle the enemy's beach defenses had not been clearly articulated.

Meanwhile, troops on V, W, and X Beaches in the center and center-left were pinned down. The Anzacs suffered a different kind of mishap. Due to either a strong current or perhaps the inexperience of the ship captains towing the first wave's assault boats, troops landed fifteen hundred meters north of the intended spot, finding themselves at the base of a hilly amphitheater. After brushing aside the lone platoon guarding the cove, the Anzacs rushed up the slopes but were soon lost and disoriented in a maze of gullies and ravines, many with no outlet. For reasons that remain difficult to explain, furthermore, the navy landed no artillery and interrupted troop disembarkments for four hours during the afternoon. By evening Turkish counterattacks led by Mustafa Kemal, the postwar leader of Turkey, threatened to push the Anzacs into the sea. Hamilton refused their urgent requests for disembarkation, ordering them instead to "dig, dig, dig, until you are safe."[12] Similar counterattacks at Cape Helles ended any possibility of the allies piercing Turkish lines. By nightfall all chance for a quick victory had been lost. Five thousand allied soldiers had been killed or wounded, twelve hundred on V Beach alone, where two battalions of infantrymen packed into the steamer *River Clyde* had been machine-gunned as they tried to exit a merchant ship not built for war and storm the shore.

Over the next two weeks Hamilton landed additional forces—the French colonials, the royal marines, and the regular 42nd Division and an Indian brigade brought from Egypt—and tried twice to dislodge the Turks to no avail. At Anzac Cove the Australians and New Zealanders remained clinging to the slopes they had reached the first day; at Cape Helles Hamilton secured the western tip of the peninsula but not the high ground of Achi Baba. The attacks failed because Sanders in the meantime had countered by rushing two divisions from Bulair, where they were no longer needed, and ferrying one of his divisions on the Asian side of the straits across to Gallipoli. He also received two divisions sent as reinforcements from Istanbul. Sensing his superiority, Sanders launched furious counterattacks, the biggest coming at Anzac Cove on May 18, but was unable to force the invaders off the peninsula. By late May each side had lost about twenty thousand men. By early summer these figures would triple. The stalemate and slaughter of the western front had replicated itself in Asia Minor.

THE GREEK AND ARMENIAN TRAGEDIES IN THE CONTEXT OF ATROCITIES AGAINST CIVILIANS IN THE GREAT WAR, 1914–1915

By summer 1915 the Great War had already become a humanitarian catastrophe. This went without saying for the roughly 5 million combatants who had died or

The Civilians' War: Austrian Army Atrocities in Serbia
Canfield, *World War*

been badly wounded. Early in the Great War, however, another monster reared its ugly head: soldiers killing civilians, often under orders to do so, often out of hatred for alleged ethnic and racial inferiors, always with little or no regard for the terrible plight of the victims.[13] One of the most infamous incidents of this sort occurred on May 7, 1915, when over twelve hundred passengers and crew on the *Lusitania* were killed by a German U-boat. Already in the war's first campaigns in East Prussia, Galicia, and Serbia, however, atrocities against civilians had sent panicked hordes of refugees in desperate flight. The Balkan fighting turned especially brutal, not only from the Austro-Hungarian shelling of Belgrade but also the actions of troops whose officers had told them they advanced into a country of assassins and fanatics that deserved no mercy. About four thousand civilians died as a result of such directives—many of the victims were horribly mutilated—triggered by largely unsubstantiated reports that villagers had fired on invading infantrymen.

German soldiers in Belgium were, in fact, fired on from windows and rooftops in many towns, but they struck back with a terrible vengeance, executing orders to gun down nearly 6,500 hostages in order to send a horrible message to their unseen enemies, the so-called *francs tireurs* (free shooters). Nor did civilians' woes end when the armies and the fighting moved farther west, for the Germans conscripted tens of thousands of civilians into labor battalions (e.g., for trenches) with the not infrequent result of death by exhaustion, hypothermia, malnutrition, or French shelling. German refusal to provision the 10 million people of occupied Belgium and France, blaming their fate with a certain twisted logic on the British blockade, also led to civilian deaths by starvation—and would have been much worse were it not for American Herbert Hoover's Commission for Relief in Belgium, which started to get food through in late 1914.[14] Finally, even in French-held land danger lurked for civilians as poison gas sometimes drifted with the wind into towns and villages.

The German/Austro-Hungarian summer offensive in Poland in 1915 led to even worse atrocities, in this case by Russian officers and rank and file against their own subjects. As the Russian armies reeled backward in what became known as "the Great Retreat," Russian High Command (*Stavka*) adopted a scorched earth policy that included uprooting Polish and Jewish inhabitants, considered disloyal

Past the Blockade and the U-Boats: Food to the Hapless Belgians
Harper's Pictorial Library

to the empire, and forcing them to evacuate homes and villages at gunpoint—whole cities like Warsaw, Brest-Litovsk, and Vilna were emptied, putting millions of refugees on the road back to Russia and a bleak, uncertain future.[15] How many were shot for resisting or died of disease, starvation, and exhaustion will never be known, but it must have been several hundred thousand. Of 600,000 Polish Jews uprooted, for instance, only two-thirds ever returned to their homes. "Starving and ragged masses are sowing panic everywhere," said one Russian minister. "Surely no country ever saved itself by its own destruction."[16]

This was the backdrop in Europe to the Great War's worst crime against civilians, which from 1914 to 1916 destroyed at least half of the estimated 1.8 to 2.1 million Armenians living in the Ottoman Empire. The Turks preceded this tragedy with another in 1914–1915, however, using similar premeditated brutality to kill or deport about a third of the 2.3 to 2.5 million Greeks of Asia Minor and Thrace. Whether these killings warrant the label of genocide remains the subject of heated controversy, both among politicians and historians, but the most recent historian of these murderous events, Taner Akcam, uses the 1948 United Nations' definition of genocide to argue convincingly for exactly this type of crime. He places the origins of the anti-Greek and anti-Armenian actions in the immediate prewar period, with wartime circumstances, especially the Turkish military disaster in the Caucasus in December–January 1914–1915 and the escalating battle for Gallipoli a few months later, as their precipitants.[17]

The First Balkan War of 1912–1913, leading to Turkey's defeat and accompanying withdrawal from most of the Balkan territory held by Constantinople for centuries, shocked and humiliated leaders of the ruling Young Turk Committee of Union and Progress (CUP). Making this outcome impossible to accept, over four hundred thousand Muslim civilians had fled these lands to escape the vengeance of Serbian, Greek, and Bulgarian soldiers, with perhaps fifty thousand refugees losing their lives in the process.[18] Enver Pasha, one of the Turkish generals

The Civilians' War: French School Children near German Lines with Gas Masks
Harper's Pictorial Library

in this campaign, mourned these killings but gained resolve from them. "Our anger is strengthening," he wrote home. "Revenge, revenge, revenge, there is no other word."[19] Simultaneously, the leadership of Turkey's Armenian population, which had been persecuted and maltreated for decades, began to exert international pressure on the Young Turks to change course. Constantinople's greatest enemies, Britain, France, and especially Russia, took up this cause, forcing Turkey, in its weakened state after the Balkan defeat, to pledge to introduce ameliorating reforms. For CUP leaders dreaming of restoring Ottoman power from Egypt to the gates of India, this Armenian "treason" was unforgivable.

The Greeks were the first to suffer. Months before war broke out in Europe deportation from Asia Minor to Aegean islands or the Ottoman interior began, with perhaps 100,000 uprooted and moved but not killed. When little criticism was heard from Europe and America, Constantinople escalated its campaign after entering the war in November 1914, dragooning both Greeks and Armenians into penal labor battalions to haul military supplies in all kinds of weather while being starved, whipped, and beaten, quite often to death. Simultaneously the Greek deportations accelerated and spread to Thrace, the hapless trodders treated no better than the forced laborers in the army. The whole forced migration seems to have been a conscious attempt to do to Greeks what they supposedly had done to Turks before the war, for when outrage was expressed from Greek circles the reply came back, "That's how it was done in Bulgaria and Greece—we learned about deportation from our neighbors." Allied attacks against the straits and Gallipoli in March and April 1915 exacerbated matters, for many Greek "traitors" lived in the general region of the battle. Liman von Sanders wired Constantinople that unless Greek civilians were removed, "he was unable to take responsibility for the security of the

The Civilians' War: Refugees on the Move in Poland
Courtesy of the Library of Congress

Ethnic Strife Writ Large: Slaughtered Armenians
Harper's Pictorial Library

REMEMBER SCARBOROUGH!

The Germans who brag of their "CULTURE" have shown what it is made of by murdering defenceless women and children at SCARBOROUGH.

But this only strengthens

GREAT BRITAIN'S

resolve to crush the

GERMAN BARBARIANS

ENLIST NOW!

British War Poster: Remember Scarborough

Courtesy of the Library of Congress

German War Poster: "What England Wants: Bomb the Germans Until They're Cured"

Courtesy of the Library of Congress

army." Could they not "throw these infidels into the sea?"[20] The best estimates place the death toll between 300,000 and 400,000 with another 350,000 deportees (i.e., not counting the prewar group) surviving the frightful deportation marches.

As bad as this was—a terrible payback for 1912–1913—the Armenian nightmare was even worse. They too died by the scores of thousands in labor battalions, and they too were marched out of their villages, but the Young Turks, incensed that Russian Armenians had contributed to Enver's defeat in the Caucasus, and panic-stricken when Franco-British ships tried to run the straits, issued orders in late March 1915 for the murder of deportees. Those Armenian men who had not already been forced into the penal battalions were led away from their homes and shot or knifed by gendarmes or soldiers. The women, children, and elderly started on their deportation treks but were met along the way by special death squads that the Young Turks had recruited from prisons. Constantinople even issued orders for the proper disposal of the bodies. Akcam does not know how many Armenians died, but he rests with the figure of 800,000—although some put it as high as 1.5 million, which jibes with other estimates of only a third of the prewar population surviving the Great War.

In almost every way one chooses to measure and assess what happened to the Greeks and the Armenians, the comparison with Nazi *Einsatzgruppen* in 1941 is a depressingly apt one. Highly significant to the broader history of man's inhumanity to man, the atrocities described in this passage are also important for understanding the narrower history of the Great War in its second year, for they fueled passions and galvanized home fronts—with the exception of Russia, which was well along the road to revolution. As Italy embarked on its blatant and highly controversial path of conquest, for example, nationalist prowar fanatics like Benito Mussolini used his widely read newspaper, *Il Popolo d'Italia*, to propagandize against the shooting of Belgian hostages and sinking of the *Lusitania* in order to pressure Rome into extending its state of war to Germany. His fellow traveler and mistress, Margherita Sarfatti, similarly lambasted Germany for executing Edith Cavell, a British nurse in Belgium. "History," she said in December 1915, "will never forgive the Hohenzollerns." Or imagine the unifying impact of the words of Arthur Winnington-Ingram, bishop of London, who evoked memories of the Belgian shootings, Armenian massacres, Serbian killings, and the *Lusitania* to urge his flock to crusade against the German coalition, in fact "to kill Germans lest the civilization of the world should itself be killed."

The Germans, of course, responded in kind by condemning Britain's hunger blockade and striking medals for the U-boat *Lusitania* heroes. And the nation's most prominent professors issued an "Appeal to the Civilized World" to remind people everywhere that "to the east of our country the earth is soaked with the blood of women and children slaughtered by the Russian hordes." Air attacks on German cities increased the clamor for revenge, especially when scores of children were killed in Freiburg and Karlsruhe.[21] In this way atrocities served the cause of persevering in a terrible conflagration.

One Less Ship to Help the Enemy: German "Commemorative" Postcard of the *Lusitania* (with Admiral Tirpitz in inset)
Harper's Pictorial Library

GALLIPOLI: ENDGAME

The alarming reports from Galicia about Russian setbacks in May and June 1915, compounded by subsequent bad news in July and August about the Great Retreat through Poland, strengthened arguments within the British Cabinet and War Council for reinforcing Ian Hamilton's Mediterranean Expeditionary Force (MEF).[22] At a meeting on June 7 Kitchener and Churchill, now demoted from the Admiralty, prevailed with their proposal to send extra divisions to Gallipoli to enable the MEF to break out of its beachheads. "If the army advanced just three or four miles up the peninsula," writes Alan Moorehead, "the fleet could steam through to the Sea of Marmora and all of the old objects could still be realized: the collapse of the Ottoman Empire, the support of Russia, the allegiance of the Balkans."[23] As they spoke another British expedition was moving north of Basra for a drive on Baghdad and achievement of many of the same objects. At an Anglo-French conference on July 6 Kitchener managed to convince a reluctant Joffre of the wisdom of conducting an active defense in France in order to send available resources to Hamilton and relieve pressure on Russia. By midsummer the MEF had expanded to fourteen divisions. Advance elements of these French, British, Indian, and Anzac units would attack on the night of August 6–7.

The operational plan did not seem illogical.[24] The main effort would be made at Anzac Cove with lead elements of four divisions going over the trench tops and forcing their way to the second highest ground in the region at Chunuk Bahr, or ideally all the way to the highest at nearby Sari Bahr. A minor feint in the east at Bulair, combined with a more serious diversionary assault at Cape Helles, where six allied divisions were dug in, would keep Liman von Sanders and his new commander of forces on the western tip of Gallipoli, Mustafa Kemal, off guard

Holy War: Turkish Reinforcements for Gallipoli
Harper's Pictorial Library

and guessing. To support the Anzac break out, two divisions would land north of Anzac Cove at Suvla Bay, with an additional two reserve divisions to follow up there. The rather obscure aim was to "secure" the bay as a port to support the Anzac breakout, but this also implied moving inland to the ridges at Kiretch Tepe. The apparently significant emphasis on Suvla Bay—Hamilton planned, after all,

Imperial War: Australians Charge at Gallipoli
Harper's Pictorial Library

to land as many divisions there as he committed to the Anzac breakout—would soon become a source of extreme controversy—among the participants when the attacks started to fail and among historians ever since.

The main problem with Hamilton's August offensive remained essentially the same as it been since April: Sanders and Kemal commanded the high ground with an equal number of divisions and their defensive superiority was not seriously challenged by naval gunfire. Nor were they fooled by the secondary assaults at Bulair and Cape Helles. At Anzac Cove, therefore, the gallant allied forces struggled up the slopes, managing to place some units on Chunuk Bahr, only to be pushed off by Kemal's counterattack on August 10. Hamilton's units at Suvla Bay could not offer much assistance, for the commander there, General Frederick Stopford, proceeded to secure the bay and a few nearby hills but did not press his attack inland. Hamilton, either because he remained oddly unfamiliar with his subordinates' intentions merely to secure the bay, or perhaps because he sensed an opportunity if the original plans were altered, intervened personally at Suvla late in the afternoon of August 8 and ordered Stopford to mount a major attack on Kiretch Tepe. An angry Hamilton, sacked two months later, would later claim that Stopford's men reached the summit a half hour after the Turks arrived on the morning of August 9, implying that valuable time had been squandered. Recent work by Tim Travers demonstrates convincingly, however, that the Turks had already moved two entire divisions into the region around Suvla Bay beginning late on August 7. Follow-up attacks at Anzac Cove and Suvla over the next days and weeks did not alter the unfixable situation.

British and French leaders now shifted their attention back to the western front. The quick-fix solution at the Dardanelles quickly lost political support after August. As it did, Joseph Joffre and John French played their trump cards in support of a massive attack against German lines. Hamilton was replaced in October, and his successor recommended evacuation, which Kitchener supported after personally inspecting the peninsula. "I had no idea of the difficulties you were up against," he told one British officer. "The country is much more difficult than I imagined and the Turkish positions are natural fortresses."[25] The shattered, disease-ridden MEF withdrew in late December and early January 1916. Allied casualties by then had risen to a quarter of a million. The Turks paid dearly for Gallipoli, losing at least a third of a million men, but the British had been forced to withdraw—a nightmarish admission of defeat by a western power unprecedented in the history of the modern Middle East.[26]

Far from winning the war on faraway fronts as Churchill had planned, the entire Balkan/Ottoman region now became a drain on allied force strength in the Great War. Paris and London felt the need, for example, to assemble an expeditionary force at Salonika that autumn to counter Bulgaria, which exploited the allies' debacle at Gallipoli by joining the Central Powers. Turkey moved from its exhilarating victory over Hamilton to a second triumph in the winter of 1915–1916, moreover, by pushing back and then surrounding a British expedition send to capture Baghdad. The impressive contribution of the Ottoman Empire to the war effort of the Central Powers—an often overlooked aspect of this escalating struggle—would force Great Britain, eager to protect its commercial and strategic interests in the area, to commit a million combat and support troops to the Middle East by war's end.

THE BALKANS

Ian Hamilton's hopes for reinforcements to undertake a third big push against the Turks had risen briefly in September 1915. That month the French government approved the proposal of General Maurice Sarrail to land six divisions on the Asiatic shore of the straits and drive to the Chanak Narrows in conjunction with Hamilton's divisions attacking on the European side. When word leaked out, however, that Bulgaria had signed a secret military convention with Germany and Austria-Hungary, Paris scrapped the plan and diverted the bulk of these troops to Salonika. They landed there, joined by the British 10th Division shifted from Gallipoli, on October 5.[27]

Bulgarian Prime Minister Vasil Radoslavov had long favored a declaration of belligerency.[28] German/Austro-Hungarian successes in France, the Isonzo, and Poland strengthened the impression gained from Hamilton's setbacks that now was the moment to side with an apparently unbeatable alliance. Throughout that summer, however, King Ferdinand vacillated. Of German descent paternally, he sympathized with the cause of the Teutonic empires, but maternally his bloodlines were French. Sentimentality aside, Ferdinand wanted to reacquire Macedonian territories snatched by Serbia and Greece during the Second Balkan War, lands that only the high-riding Central Powers could guarantee. On the other hand, the Bulgarian army had not fully recovered from the fighting of 1912–1913, and the prospect of another war's hardships angered most Bulgarian peasants. Their leader, Alexander Stambolisky, led a troublesome antiwar faction in parliament. But Entente defeats that summer, together with the enticement of territorial expansion, finally convinced the monarch to cast the die for war. Sofia signed the accord with Berlin and Vienna on September 6. As the army mobilized, police arrested Stambolisky.

Learning of these threatening developments, Serbia appealed to its ally of the Balkan Wars, Greece, to provide military assistance. This plea galvanized Greek Prime Minister Eleftherios Venizelos into action. Under the terms of the Serb-Greek alliance each side had to aid the other with 150,000 troops, a condition that Serbia, expecting imminent invasion, could not fulfill. Politically ambitious and carried away by the dream of a Greater Greece, Venizelos nevertheless pledged Greek help if Britain and France sent an army of this size to Salonika. The day the first two allied divisions arrived, however, King Constantine revoked the promise and dismissed Venizelos. That the Greek monarch, also of German descent, had married the sister of Kaiser William II certainly put him on a collision course with his prime minister, but even though the king, like Ferdinand, expected the Entente to lose, Constantine thought it made no sense to side with the Central Powers and subject his ports and coasts to the might of the British and French navies. Neutrality seemed the wiser course. Venizelos fled to Salonika, where the allies, pointing to the fact that the invitation to land troops had been made by the head of a legally constituted government, ignored Constantine's wishes and soon had four divisions in Salonika with four additional British divisions under way. Unfortunately for Serbia, no Greek divisions reinforced this so-called Army of the Orient.[29]

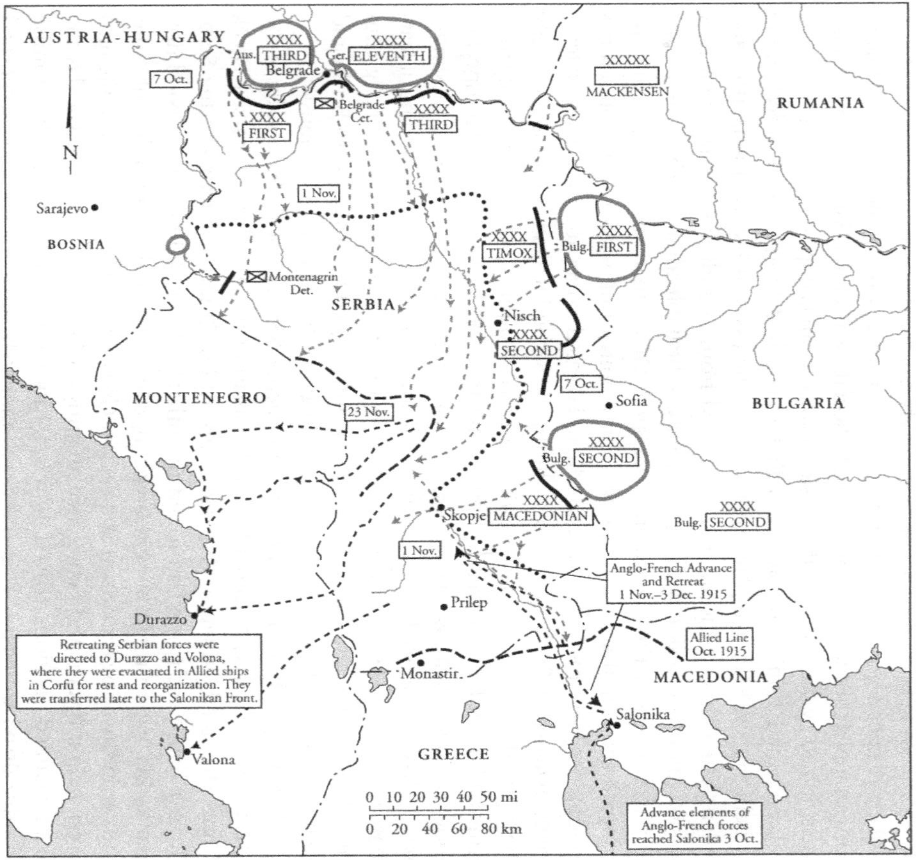

The Fall of Serbia in 1915

Maps Courtesy of the Department of History, United States Military Academy

Imperial Surplus: Men of the Indian Army in Mesopotamia
Harper's Pictorial Library

This force came too late to help Belgrade. On October 6, 1915, four divisions of the Third Austro-Hungarian Army and the crack German Eleventh Army crossed the border. The latter's ten divisions had trained south from Poland after the front stabilized there. Mackensen commanded the overall operation, yet another sign that Germany was rapidly gaining operational control of the war effort on the eastern front. The Serbian capital fell within days, forcing the Serbian First and Third Armies, greatly outnumbered and outgunned, to flee south. On October 11 Bulgaria attacked from the east with twelve divisions, overwhelming the Serbian Second and Timok Armies and pushing them west. The Serbs attempted to stand in historic Kosovo, site of an epic defeat at the hands of the Turks in 1389, still hoping for assistance from Salonika. Surrail had set out from Salonika with three divisions, in fact, but could not pierce Bulgarian defenses north of Lake Dorian, over 150 kilometers from Serb lines. The gallant but otherwise doomed defenders began a grueling, bloody retreat, therefore, across the mountains of Albania on November 25.

In January 1916 the Italian navy evacuated the by now half strength survivors to Corfu, where others would die of hunger. The allies reequipped what was left of the Serbian army, about 125,000 soldiers, and sent them to Salonika to fight another day. That day would not arrive until 1918, however, and in the meantime the allied debacles in Asia Minor, the Balkans, Poland, and France loomed much more significantly in contemporary impressions of Central Power ascendancy on land. So did the disaster that befell Britain in the Mesopotamian (Iraqi) provinces of the Ottoman Empire.

THE STRUGGLE FOR ISLAM: PERSIA, AFGHANISTAN, AND INDIA

On April 25, 1915—the same day as the Gallipoli landings—the Indian army's 6th Poona Division had moved north from Basra along the Tigris River.[30] Major General Charles Townsend was to push upriver, coordinating his operations with the 12th Indian Division advancing west from Ahwaz, center of the oil line in southwestern Persia that piped crucial supplies to the Royal Navy. Clearing southern Iraq and Persia of Turkish forces would also foil German/Turkish plans, uncovered by British intelligence, to send an expedition across Persia to Afghanistan in order to win Kabul for the holy war and thrust daggers at the heart of India. Townsend's fifteen thousand crack troops brushed aside everything the Turks put in the way, taking Qurna in late May and Amara in early June, capturing there the remnants of Turkish regiments retreating before the onslaught of 12th Division. He took Kut al Amara in September and then advanced as far as Ctesiphon, seventy kilometers south of Baghdad, by November 22.

There things began to go wrong. Unaware due to a reconnaissance mishap that Turkish General Nur-ud-Din had entrenched before the ancient Sassanid capital with eighteen thousand rifles backed by artillery equal to his, Townsend attacked anyway, losing over a third of his remaining soldiers. Western front and Gallipoli-like conditions had been replicated now in Mesopotamia. Blocked from taking Baghdad, the rash British commander withstood a few days of counterattacks and then fell back to Kut al Amara. Nur-ud-Din surrounded him there with superior forces in December. Another large detachment dug in east of the town on the northern bank of the Tigris at Sannaiyat to block an anticipated relief effort from an Indian army corps downriver at Qurna. Baghdad had been saved and the British dealt another humiliating blow.

This unfolding series of British setbacks emboldened the Germans in their intricate plot to unleash Jihad in Persia, Afghanistan, and India.[31] The Foreign Office assigned one key role to Prince Henry of Reuss, German ambassador to Persia. Having returned from Germany to his post in Teheran in April 1915, the prince would attempt to convince the young Ahmad Mirza Shah to respond to the sultan's summons by declaring war on the Entente. Although the shah's army was a negligible force, consisting mainly of a Russian-leaning Cossack brigade 8,000 strong, his well-armed brigade of 7,000 patriotic gendarmes, backed by extra thousands of fierce tribal warriors, could wreck havoc in the provinces, especially in the British-controlled south with its vital oil wells and pipeline to the Persian Gulf. Another critical assignment went to Wilhelm Wassmuss, German consul at Bushire on the Gulf (see map, pp. 98–99). From prewar days he possessed excellent contacts among the surrounding tribes that he would try to incite to rebel. The Germans also sent Captain Oskar von Niedermeyer through the Balkans and Turkey to Teheran with eighty hand-picked soldiers. Their mission was to travel into Afghanistan escorted by a large column of Turks and, once there, recruit Emir Habibullah to the Jihadist cause. If he could be persuaded to invade India with his 50,000 regulars and a horde of accompanying tribesmen, Muslim and Sikh

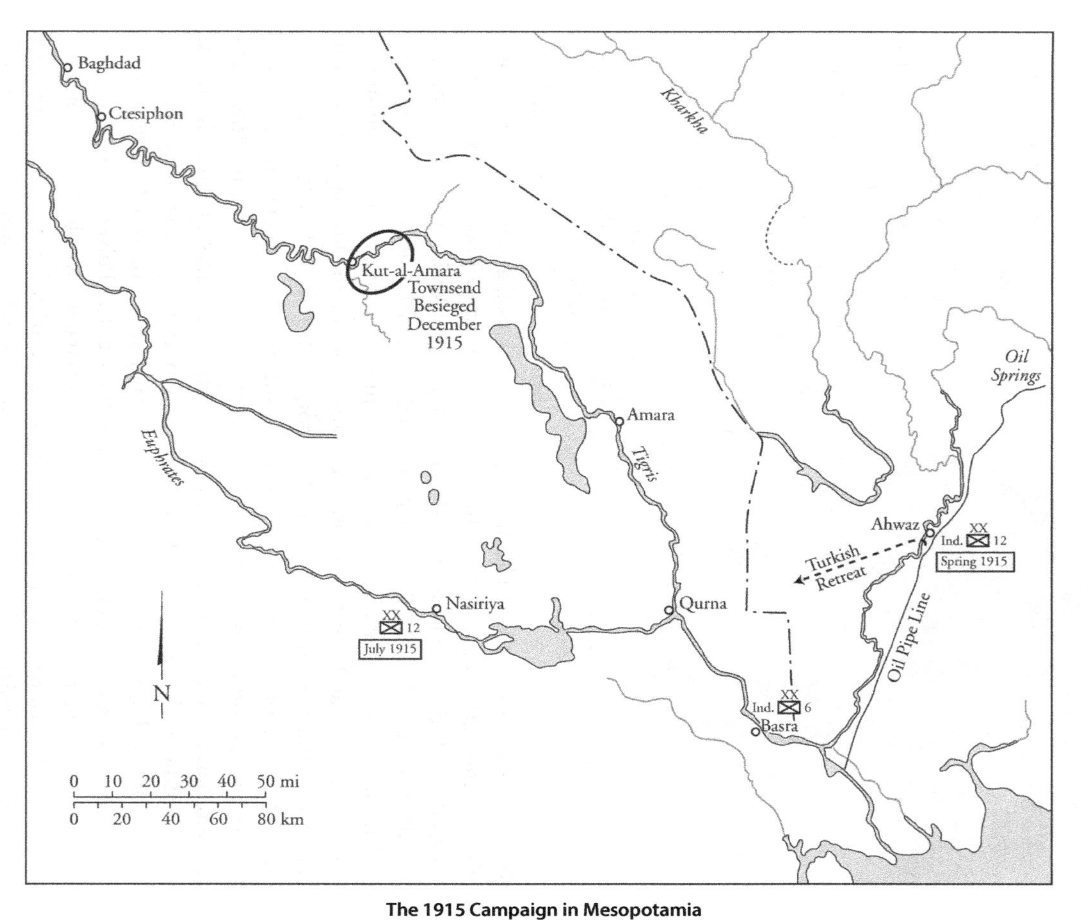

The 1915 Campaign in Mesopotamia

Maps Courtesy of the Department of History, United States Military Academy

Straddling the Fence: Emir Habibullah
Canfield, *World War*

dissidents in the lightly defended British crown colony—only a fourth of the Indian army was still there—would hopefully seize this opportunity to join Habibullah and overthrow their English overlords. The German Foreign Office and its overseas agents planned to aid the insurgents by smuggling arms and ammunition into India.

The Germans had good reason to be optimistic that their intrigues would succeed. In Persia the Tangistani tribe of the Bushire region, angry over Britain's termination of their lucrative arms smuggling into India, welcomed Wassmuss with open arms. In Fars province near Shiraz a coalition of tribes headed by the Kashgais capable of mobilizing eight thousand warriors longed for an opportunity to drive out the British. Their chieftain, Solat-u-Dola, was a leading figure in the nationalist movement. He and other "democrats" ensconced in the Majlis, Persia's now powerless parliament, resented the British and Russian deal that had divided Persia into foreign spheres of influence in 1907—the Russians controlled the north, including Teheran, the British the south. The gendarmerie was also imbued with nationalist anti-imperial politics.[32] It had been formed in 1911 shortly before the Russians snuffed out Majlis rule, and its educated Persian officer corps still saw their mission as spreading central democratic control in an independent nation. Reinforcing Persian officers' predilection to back Turkey, the enemy of Russia, was the training many of them had received in Turkish military academies. A cadre of Swedish officers in the gendarmerie strengthened anti-Entente sentiment, for they were Teutonic, German-trained, and convinced that the German army could defeat all comers. For all of these reasons, Persian patriots saw the Central Powers as natural allies in Persia's struggle for independence. The Majlis passed a whole series of protests in 1914–1915 against Britain and Russia, while compatriot nationalist journals urged "all true Persians" to free the land "from the infidel intruders." The gendarmerie stood ready to ally with Solat-u-Dola and proclaim war on the Entente.[33]

Niedermeyer's mission to Afghanistan also had promise. Because Britain had fought two wars with Habibullah's forebears in the nineteenth century, eventually imposing British-controlled "neutrality" on the Afghans, anti-British sentiment ran high among Muslim clergymen, the so-called mullahs, and among many in the emir's entourage. These included his brother, Nasrullah, his son, Amanullah,

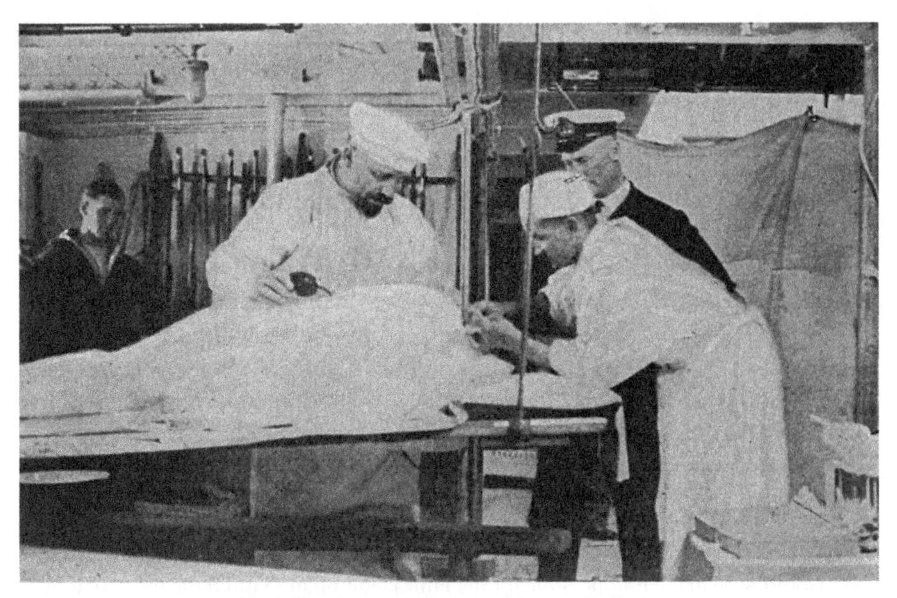

The Soldiers' War: British Hospital Boat on the Tigris
Harper's Pictorial Library

and his commander in chief, Nadir Khan. Habibullah was more circumspect but also chafed at the constraints placed upon his country's foreign policy.

In neighboring India, furthermore, officials who had not forgotten the violent Indian Mutiny of 1857 braced for the worst. In February 1915 they foiled an attempt by revolutionaries to foment an army insurrection inside the colony and that same month also suppressed an army mutiny in Singapore, but within a few months the tribes along the northwest frontier with Afghanistan created further trouble. Tens of thousands of Mohmand tribesmen rose up, while the nearby Afridi began to desert their army units—600 of 2,500 serving in the Indian army were gone by June. The British stationed three divisions and four additional brigades in this region—Indian army formations bolstered by an intermingling of the eight British regular battalions that remained behind to defend India—but native defections on this scale undermined the combat readiness of these units.[34]

> Among those who know, like myself [wrote the British Viceroy that September] there can be no doubt that the situation in India is slowly but surely deteriorating and, so long as the war lasts, is likely to continue to do so. The constant repetition of attacks on our frontier, the sulkiness of the [Muslims], the plots hatched outside with ramifications in India, and the cases of sedition in native regiments, all tend to show steady deterioration.[35]

Given the delicate conditions in Persia, Afghanistan, and India, therefore, Berlin's hopes for holy war do not seem to have been misplaced. "It is hard to conclude," writes Hew Strachan, "that Germany had been barking up the wrong tree."[36]

Accompanied by Werner Otto von Hentig, a career diplomat with prewar experience in the region, Niedermeyer's Afghan expedition left Isfahan in early July 1915. After a harrowing crossing of the Kavir Salt Desert, the German team evaded two cavalry detachments sent from India to intercept them and slipped across the border into Afghanistan in late August. The emir allowed them to proceed to Kabul but did not meet with Niedermeyer and Hentig until November—a bad sign.

The mission's chances had been undermined from the outset, in fact, by Enver Pasha's decision to withdraw the promised Turkish units from the expedition and deploy them instead on the Tigris to stop Townsend that summer and later to besiege him at Kut. Although thirteen thousand soldiers and support troops of India's 6th Division surrendered in April 1916 after an additional twenty-three thousand men had been lost trying to relieve him—one of the worst defeats in the history of the British army—Townsend's long stand still paid handsome dividends to the empire, as British General Sir Percy Sykes recalled:

> The arrival of even a single [Turkish] brigade with German officers in Afghanistan would have made it impossible for the Emir Habibullah to fulfill the treaty obligations [Britain had imposed on him]. Either he would have been deposed and murdered or else he would have been forced by a great wave of feeling to invade India. With our depleted garrisons, hampered by internal trouble in India, it is probable that the Turkish force, supported by the Afghan army and by thousands of brave tribesmen, would have involved us in disaster.[37]

Without the presence of this column to pressure or impress him, the emir felt it wise to dissimulate, professing that he would not shirk his duties as a Muslim leader and, ostensibly to prove it, calling a council of the chief mullahs to legitimate the holy war for Afghans, but on the other hand pointing out to his visitors that the Afghan army was not as well equipped and trained as the British, or also the Russian, and that he would need large numbers of foreign soldiers to accompany him as well as modern arms and substantial sums of money to finance operations after the British cut off his subsidy, as they were certain to do.

In January 1916 Habibullah finally signed an alliance with Germany that made joining the holy war dependent on such aid, but Niedermeyer and Hentig were not impressed. "One day the Emir says he is for us," wrote Niedermeyer, "and the next against us."[38] They had good reason to doubt the ruler's ultimate intentions, for the previous month he had secretly told an Indian emissary, "I am not a double-dealer—I intend to stand by the British if I possibly can."[39] Habibullah's statement belied his profession of innocence, however, for he was clearly playing a duplicitous game designed to buy time in order to determine which warring camp was more likely to win the war—which also explains his oft-stated wish that the Germans remain at court. Having finally realized that the emir would probably never act without news of an end to the stalemate in Europe, which was still not forthcoming, the German mission left Kabul for Persia in May 1916. In the meantime the British had uncovered and scotched another insurrectionary plot in India—a revolt scheduled for Christmas Day—and militarily contained the Mohmand uprising along the frontier.[40] Germany's once promising intrigues in this region had come to naught.

The same can be said for German designs in Persia. During the summer and fall of 1915 all had proceeded well enough. Wassmuss gathered Persian recruits, hundreds of German and Austrian POWs who had escaped from their Russian captors, and the Persian gendarmerie for a campaign of terror in southern and central Persia. They robbed British banks and consulates, kidnapped and murdered British and Russian officials, ambushed patrols, and forced Britain and Russia to divert troops to Persia. In Teheran, meanwhile, Prince Henry of Reuss gradually won over the eighteen-year old shah.

Without Turkish divisions in Persia, however, these efforts were destined to fail, for as the havoc mounted in 1915, fourteen thousand Russian troops closed in on the capital. In November Reuss managed to convince Ahmad to protest against the Russian advance by performing a *hejira*, a ceremonial exodus from Teheran to the holy city of Qum in emulation of a similar exodus made by the Great Mohammed.[41] This was to provide the spark for a nationalist, Jihadist revolt against the foreigners, but at the eleventh hour, after the shah had already ordered his carriage, a senior member of the royal family successfully pleaded with Ahmad not to act so rashly against the Russians as to perhaps bring down the Qajar Dynasty. Without the shah's lead, and with Russian units pushing gallant but overmatched gendarme units away from Teheran as far as Kermanshah and Isfahan, nationalist and tribal leaders decided to bide their time.

The moment had passed. Even the approach of eighteen thousand Turkish troops and extra thousands of gendarmes to the west of Teheran in the summer of 1916—after the evacuation of Gallipoli and fall of Kut had made such a penetration possible—did not move the tribes to revolt.[42] In any event, the Turks and their Persian levies were eventually halted by Russian forces in the Sultan Bulak Mountains near the capital. Ottoman units still held a line running from Kazvin in the north to Hamadan in the south, but the evacuation of Teheran, which at one point had seemed likely, did not occur.

Moreover, earlier that year the Russians had displayed impressive boldness in Turkish Armenia, capturing the seemingly impregnable mountain fortress at Erzurum (February), from there pushing south to take Bitlis (March), north to seize Trabizond (April), and farther west to secure Erzincan (July)—all this despite the reinforcement of eight Turkish divisions sent from now quiet Gallipoli. These actions seemed to confirm the wisdom of keeping tribal swords sheathed in Persia.[43]

An interesting epilogue occurred in December 1916. That month Habibullah dispatched an emissary, Sirdar Abdul Majid Khan, one of his regional governors, to Kermanshah for discussions with Turkish and German officials. Niedermeyer was present too. The emir's man reminded his interlocutors that Afghanistan represented the "big bomb" that would help the Central Powers win the war. If Berlin and Istanbul advanced over Isfahan and Yazd with a big army—Habibullah had put the number between 20,000 and 100,000—Kabul promised to join forces with them at Kerman, and from there the allies would surely pass from Persia through the "gate of India." The emir had chosen the moment for such pledges wisely, considering recent Turkish setbacks in Persia and Turkish Armenia and the ongoing stalemate in Europe. In other words, Habibullah continued to sit cleverly on the fence.[44]

THE STRUGGLE FOR ISLAM: THE ARABS UNDER TURKISH RULE

The Arabs of the Ottoman Empire became official participants in Turkey's holy war with the formal declaration of Jihad in November 1914. For Enver Pasha, Baron Wangenheim, and other proponents of this strategy the critical issue was not just whether others from Africa to India would rise but also whether or not the provincial Arabs of Iraq, Syria, Palestine, Jordan, and the Arabian Peninsula would remain loyal to the empire as it confronted the might of Britain, France, and Russia. As Bernard Lewis has shown in his many writings on the Middle East, the overwhelming majority of Arabs did, in fact, support the war effort.[45] One of the earliest signs of this occurred in February 1915 when fifty thousand Bedouin warriors rallied to Djemal Pasha's side as he marched on the Suez Canal. There is every indication, furthermore, that most of the Arab soldiers fighting at Gallipoli not only acquitted themselves very well against western troops who regarded themselves as superior to Muslims but, more important, that they saw their struggle as a necessary sacrifice for the Islamic faith.[46] In Iraq, too, the Turks' overwhelmingly Arab army stood its ground at Ctesiphon, Kut, and south of Kut to block a relief effort made by thirty thousand Anglo-Indian soldiers. British intelligence reported that the Shiite Arabs of southern Iraq also stood ready to lash out at the invaders. Reflecting these concerns in August 1915, Townsend knew that Britain could "take no risks of defeat in the East." He imagined a nightmare scenario of "retreat from Baghdad and the consequent instant rising of the Arabs of the whole country behind us, to say nothing of the certain rise, in that case, of the Persians, and probably the Afghans."[47] That the Iraqi revolt was postponed until 1920 (see chap. 12) is probably explained by the large and growing British troop strength in southern Iraq—eight months after Kut, in fact, four Anglo-Indian infantry divisions, backed by cavalry and tens of thousands of support troops, resumed the march on Baghdad (see chap. 9).

However, not all Arabs in the Ottoman Empire supported the holy war against Britain. Among the Arab urban elite of army officers and intellectuals—some living in Damascus and Beirut, some in exile in Cairo—dissatisfaction simmered over the centralizing, pro-Turkish, and therefore explicitly anti-Arab policies of Enver Pasha and other Young Turks.[48] The dissidents had founded two secret societies before the war, *al-Fatat* and *al-'Ahd*, to promote more opportunities for Arab speakers in high government office, or barring this, establish autonomy or perhaps even independence for Ottoman Arabs. After Turkey entered the war in November 1914 the Arab opposition considered two alternatives: bargaining with Constantinople for concessions or throwing in their lot with the allies fighting Turkey, especially Britain. The former option was preferred, for Turkey was a Muslim power, whereas Britain was Christian and notoriously prone to imperialize, not liberate. If the latter option had to be chosen, however, secret society leaders planned to foment revolution among the three Arab divisions that Djemal Pasha stationed around Damascus, but the wily Turkish commander sniffed out their plot in April 1915, executed some of the ringleaders, and dispersed the Arab divisions. In so doing, however, he almost guaranteed that the surviving Arab dissidents would now back Britain in the war.

Hussein ibn Ali, sherif and emir of Mecca, stood in self-serving contact with the secret societies of Damascus—because he had uncovered written evidence that the Turks planned to depose him after the war, opposition to Constantinople furthered his own interests. His son, Feisal, spoke with the Damascene plotters in May 1915, hearing from them about the arrests as well as their willingness to strike back, but only if Hussein initiated an Arab uprising supported by British troops, for the secret societies were now too weak to make the first move themselves. The societies also wanted London to agree to the founding of an independent Arab state encompassing all Arab-speaking parts of the Ottoman Empire—everything, in other words, from Syria and Palestine in the west, Iraq in the east, and Arabia in the south. Hussein communicated these wishes to British officials in Egypt in July 1915. His letter took the form of a treaty proposal between Britain and this yet-to-be-established Arab state—one to be headed by Hussein as caliph. It is important to note that "the security of this Arab independence" would be guaranteed by "both high contracting parties [offering] mutual assistance, to the best of their military and naval forces, to face any foreign power which may attack either party."[49]

The British were astounded. To be sure, Kitchener had sent sherif a message in late 1914 promising British support for an independent, Hussein-led caliphate *of Arabia*—other regions were not mentioned—but the legendary general was thinking more in terms of independence from Turkey: Arabia would be part of a wider British sphere of influence extending from Cape Town to Cairo to Calcutta. Moreover, he apparently envisioned nothing more than an Islamic pope, a religious leader who could bolster Britain's authority among its own Muslims after the war when the old "Great Game" rivalry with Russia in the Middle East and Central Asia might very well revive. Clearly, neither Kitchener nor his underlings in Egypt understood the nature of the caliphate, a position, like the Ottoman sultan's, that combined both religious and temporal power. They obviously had no appreciation for the grander visions that their promises spawned in Hussein. Initially, therefore, sherif received only a polite, noncommittal reply from the British high commissioner in Egypt, Sir Henry McMahon.

During the fall of 1915, however, General Ian Hamilton, British commander at the Dardanelles, learned from Muhammed Sharif al-Faruqi, a deserter at Gallipoli who belonged to one of the secret societies in Damascus, that an Arab uprising was planned. The mysterious Faruqi seems to have promised more than he knew the societies could deliver, but to British leaders deeply worried that their losses in Turkey could ignite a Jihad against the British Empire, such statements had to be taken seriously. For these reasons McMahon received instructions from London to respond cautiously but favorably to Sherif Hussein.

The Arab Revolt: The Hangman's Tree of Damascus
Courtesy of the Library of Congress

His letter of October 24, 1915, was a carefully hedged-about masterpiece. Hussein would have to abandon claims to coastal Syria and Lebanon. McMahon made it clear, moreover, that he could only make pledges "for those regions lying within those frontiers wherein Great Britain is free to act without detriment to the interest of her ally, France,"[50] which in all likelihood extended the region where Arab claims would have to be sacrificed to Palestine and inland Syria as well. Similarly, in Iraq "the Arabs will recognize that the established position and interest of Great Britain necessitate special administrative arrangements in order to secure [it] from foreign aggression." McMahon also cautioned that London could not promise anything that would prejudice "our existing treaties with Arab chiefs." Because one of these treaties was with Ibn Saud, who controlled eastern Arabia, this territory would presumably be excluded too. This left only the stretch from Jordan to Hussein's Hejaz, but even here the Arabs would receive "the advice and guidance of Great Britain" in establishing their government—which smacked of a protectorate, not a genuinely independent state. The Cairo-based founder of *al-'Ahd*, Aziz Ali al-Masri, saw through this immediately, warning the British that they could not achieve their aims in the Middle East "unless [they] were willing to leave its peoples free to exercise full and genuine independence."[51] Hussein must have known this too, but after a few futile attempts to exact more from the British he finally agreed in early 1916 to postpone negotiations over hotly disputed territories like Syria and Palestine until after the war. In the meantime he would play a double game, opening talks with the Turks while promising the British he would rise up when the time was ripe.

Hussein changed his mind in the spring of 1916, however, when he heard of further arrests, torture, and interrogation of secret society members who had likely exposed his contacts with the would-be rebels. Sherif had also learned that the Turks were sending a heavily armed mobile column of 3,500 men to reinforce the Hejaz's 11,000 garrison troops. If they were coming to seize him, then now the double game had to end. On June 5, therefore, he instructed his sons Ali and Feisal to raise the flag of revolt around the Turkish garrison at Medina, the southern terminus of the rail line from Damascus. A few days later the sheikh of a rebel tribe, the Harbs, attacked Jeddah, the port town of Mecca, while Hussein himself assaulted the holy city. Altogether 50,000 warriors had rallied to his call.[52]

The uprising registered successes at first. Mecca surrendered after a fierce four-day battle, as did Jeddah. The port's fall had been in doubt, however, as machine guns and artillery proved more than a match for 4,000 lightly armed tribesmen. Bombardment from two British cruisers and bombing runs from their seaplanes finally tipped the scales against Jeddah's 1,400 defenders. The northern ports of Rabegh and Yenbo as well as the inland town of Taif, east of Mecca, were also taken, but here too British sea power or, as at Taif, artillery detachments, had produced the victories, not thousands of desert warriors.

The underlying weakness of Hussein's forces became most evident at Medina. Feisal commanded thirty thousand men, but a third of them ran away during the first shelling from the fortress. Reinforced by the mobile column and a further eight battalions sent from Damascus, the garrison's commandant,

The Arab Revolt: Prince Feisal
Harper's Pictorial Library

Fakhri Pasha, lifted the siege in August 1916 and drove Feisal's dispirited compatriots back toward the coast and the protection of the British navy.

By now Hussein's rebel forces had dwindled to sixteen thousand men, and their military value, according to Britain's Arab Bureau in Cairo, was marginal: "That the Hejaz Bedouins are simply guerillas, and not of good quality at that, has been amply demonstrated, even in the early sieges; and it was never in doubt that they would not attack nor withstand Turkish regulars." Worse still, his promises, seconded by Faruqi, of as many as two hundred thousand Arab deserters from the Turkish Army had not materialized, while other Arab chieftains in the region, most notably his main rival, Ibn Saud, had not answered the call of revolt. Muslims in the Ottoman Empire, observed the British high commissioner in Egypt, "have hitherto regarded the Hejaz revolt, and our share in it, with suspicion or dislike."[53]

To be sure, the Arab revolt had paid some dividends to Britain, for the Turks were forced to commit forces in the Hejaz that could have bolstered defenses in Iraq, or strengthened the invasion of Persia in the summer of 1916, thereby also putting pressure on the fence-sitting Emir Habibullah. As explained later, Sherif Hussein's uprising also helped to undermine an anti-British insurgency in Somaliland. For the most part, however, Hussein's holy war had been a major disappointment to London. Something was needed to rejuvenate rebel fortunes, and it came that autumn in the person of T. E. Lawrence, the legendary "Lawrence of Arabia" (see chap. 9).

THE STRUGGLE FOR ISLAM: FROM TRIPOLITANIA TO THE HORN

The northeastern quadrant of Africa stretching from Italian Tripolitania over Egypt, the Sudan, Abyssinia (Ethiopia), and Somaliland was a source of growing concern for Britain by late 1915.[54] Although politically unstable, Abyssinia posed the greatest threat. No one in Europe had forgotten the Battle of Adowa, where nineteen years earlier one hundred thousand warriors armed with modern weapons decimated an entire Italian division and its native levies. The danger that Abyssinia would throw this kind of weight into the scales against Britain heightened as news filtered out of Addis Ababa that young emperor Lij Yasu sympathized with the Islamic faith and leaned toward the Turkish-German cause. British officials in the capital reported that the German minister there had promised the ambitious ruler vast territorial expansion into neighboring Sudan, Eritrea, Italian and British Somaliland, and British East Africa should Berlin and its allies win in Europe. Further complicating the regional situation, Yasu conspired with Muhammed Abdullah Hassan, dubbed by Britons the "Mad Mullah" for his long-standing Jihad against them in Somaliland, for a joint attack on Berbera to drive the infidels into the sea.

But this was not all. In Darfur, an autonomous region wedged between French Chad and the Anglo-Egyptian Sudan, Sultan Ali Dinar responded to Istanbul's call in 1915 with a raid through Chad to the border of British Nigeria. The incursion came at a terrible time for Britain and France, for they both faced native revolts and uprisings from Senegal to the Niger Delta triggered by wartime economic hardships, conscription into colonial military units, and dragooning into the hated porter battalions so essential for combat operations as the allied campaign in German Cameroon reached its climax. In early 1916 Ali Dinar turned his attention to making holy war in the Sudan. Just as lingering nightmares of the Indian Mutiny kept British officials in India on guard during this stage of the Great War, so too the frightening memory of the Sudanese uprising of 1883, a massive revolt that did not end until Kitchener's victory at Omdurman in 1898, worried vigilant British commanders in Khartoum and Cairo.

Making matters worse, Dinar had contacts with Ahmad al-Sharif, leader of the Arab tribes of eastern Tripolitania. Strict, devout followers of the fundamentalist Senussi sect, Ahmad's followers also took the Turks' holy war seriously. They planned to push the Italians into the Mediterranean and then invade Egypt while Dinar drove on Khartoum. After receiving money and arms from Turkey and Germany, the Senussi plundered more rifles, machine guns, artillery, and ammunition during a successful campaign against Italian forces in the summer of 1915. These victories emboldened Ahmad and his second in command, Jafar al-Askari, to lead two brigade-strength columns into western Egypt in November.

As it did in Persia, Afghanistan, and India, London drew once again on the strength of its empire to defuse these multifarious threats. Great Britain turned back the Senussi invasion in the course of 1916, for example, by deploying nearly forty thousand men, many of them in a newly formed British/Anzac Camel Corps reinforced with armored cars and airplanes. The defeat of the Senussi was an impressive accomplishment best measured, perhaps, by their continued vitality elsewhere. Indeed, deflected from Egypt, the movement that would eventually lay the foundation of modern-day Libya turned west and smashed the Italians at the Battle of Al-Karadabiyya, Rome's worst colonial setback since Adowa. Italy's presence remained limited to the coast around Tripoli.

Imperial Surplus: Sudanese Soldiers Defend the Empire
Harper's Pictorial Library

But Britain, having avoided this fate in Egypt, escaped from harm in other parts of the region too. In the normally rainless month of April 1916, for instance, an Anglo-Egyptian/Sudanese expedition of regiment strength under Sir Reginald Wingate left Khartoum with trucks to carry water. Airplanes provided extra punch. The bold move took Ali Dinar by surprise, chasing the Jihadist out

Imperial Surplus: South African Regiment Departs Cape Town for German East Africa
Harper's Pictorial Library

of his fortress capital of El Fasher. Later that year French units freed up from the Cameroon campaign helped the British crush Ali Dinar before he could do more damage.

In Abyssinia and British Somaliland, furthermore, Britain cleverly exploited native political divisions to foil enemy plans. Thus British and Italian ministers in Addis Ababa warned Coptic Christian nobles of the young emperor's pro-Islamic schemes. The ploy moved the anti-Muslim Coptics who already looked askance at Lij Yasu to overthrow him in September 1916. This coup ended the threat of Abyssinian expansion, including joint operations with the Mad Mullah in Somaliland. The British further undercut Hassan's position among Somali tribesmen by exploiting the traditional distrust that they felt for Abyssinia. Finally, Sherif Hussein's uprising against the Turks that summer, especially his capture of holy Mecca, convinced many Somali leaders that loyalty to Britain better coincided with loyalty to Islam.

THE CAMPAIGN IN GERMAN EAST AFRICA

By late 1915 the Germans had surrendered in Togoland and Southwest Africa. They had also lost most of Cameroon. Rather than shifting the West and South African forces used in these campaigns to Europe or the Middle East—options that were briefly considered—London shipped these reinforcements to East Africa instead for the conquest of Germany's only remaining colony. The decision paid immediate returns that winter, for when this news reached Paul von Lettow-Vorbeck, commander of the German East Africa Defense Force, the *Schütztruppe*, he cancelled plans to invade British East Africa and spread Berlin's holy war into the Sudan and neighboring regions—once again the resources of the British Empire had proven adequate to undermine the enemy's anti-imperial designs. Command of British operations in East Africa went initially to General Sir Horace Smith-Dorrien, a veteran of the fighting in France, but after he fell ill and had to return to England, the Committee for Imperial Defense (CID) agreed to the appointment of Jan Smuts, one of the leading lights in the cabinet of South African Prime Minister Louis Botha.[55]

Smuts took charge of an army that drew on the strength of the world's most powerful empire. To the two British battalions, one brigade of the native King's African Rifles, and three regiments of Indians already stationed in British East Africa, he brought two infantry brigades and one mounted brigade from South Africa backed by 70 field guns and 120 machine guns. CID also sent a white Rhodesian regiment, a fourth Indian regiment, a third British battalion from the Royal Fusiliers, and a squadron of the Royal Flying Corps. With the later addition of elements of the West Africa Defense Force and reinforcements from South Africa, Smuts had nearly sixty thousand men in the field supported by numerous cruisers and destroyers of the Royal Navy along the coast. His army was augmented by a Belgian expeditionary force of ten thousand men under General Charles Tombeur, who invaded German East Africa from the neighboring Belgian Congo in June 1916 (see map, p. 105).

Since the Battle of Tanga in November 1914 Lettow had quintupled the strength of the *Schütztruppe* to about fifteen thousand. Plundered British stocks at Tanga, 10 four-inch guns from the *Königsberg*, and the successful running of the Royal Navy blockade by two ships from Germany gave him adequate supplies of rifles, machine guns, artillery, and munitions. His units were also well trained, disciplined, and familiar with the terrain; he possessed excellent telegraph and railroad services as well as a highly organized system of native porters; and his medical corps was much better able to deal with malaria and pestilence than that of the invader. Furthermore, Lettow and his German field officers were tactically and operationally superior to the clever albeit amateurish Smuts and his collection of largely untested South African divisional commanders. Nevertheless, numbers alone dictated largely defensive operations for Lettow.

Smuts struck in a pincer move around the slopes of Mount Kilimanjaro in March 1916, taking the region but failing to trap the bulk of the *Schütztruppe* that Lettow had positioned there. Greatly hampered by Lettow's stout defense, occasional counterattacks, and the ravages of malaria and tsetse flies, Smuts's advance continued southward toward the Central Railway towns of Dodoma, Kilosa, and Morogoro, all falling that summer after extremely tough campaigning. Meanwhile, Tombeur moved in from the west, clearing Lake Victoria and the western end of the Central Railway and capturing Kigoma in July and Tabora in September. Lettow now retreated into the southeastern corner of the colony and eventually over the border into Portuguese Mozambique. The wily German had achieved his main aim, however, of drawing British and dominion forces into the region "in the greatest possible strength, and thus diverting them from other more important theaters of war."[56] By 1916–1917 the only likely alternative theater of action for these units was the Middle East. It is true, therefore, that by tying down scores of thousands of imperial troops Lettow had contributed to the ability of the Ottoman Empire to remain in the war until the final weeks of 1918.

However, the ultimate aim of Germany and Turkey spearheading a holy war that would so threaten the world's greatest empire that Britain would have to withdraw from France had not been achieved. Indeed Jihad had everywhere failed to realize the goals that Wangenheim and others had set for it as one threat after another had been beaten back. Moreover, the British were building up forces in Egypt and Iraq, the Arab revolt had begun in the Hejaz, and Lettow was on the run.

Indeed, although the Central Powers had won many spectacular victories in eastern and western Europe, the Balkans, Asia Minor, and Mesopotamia in 1915–1916, long-term prospects for their side winning the war began to worsen in 1916–1917 as Britain and its allies continued to benefit from unhindered access to overseas holdings and world markets, while Germany and its allies had none of these benefits in the zero-sum game of British blockade and oceanic power. Tipping points were near in the Great War as Germany came increasingly to the radical conclusion that it had to fight back with the only remaining weapon at its disposal that could hurt Britain—U-boats.

NOTES

1. For this scene, see Peter Hopkirk, *Like Hidden Fire: The Plot to Bring Down the British Empire* (New York, 1994), 54–65 (and photographs after p. 144). Also see Henry Morgenthau, *Secrets of the Bosporus* (New York, 1918); and Mohammad Gholi Majd, *Iraq in World War I: From Ottoman Rule to British Conquest* (Lanham, MD, 2006), 77–81.
2. Cited in Hopkirk, *Like Hidden Fire*, 60–61. For German influence in Istanbul on the eve of war and during the early stages, see Ulrich von Trumpener, *Germany and the Ottoman Empire 1914–1918* (Princeton, NJ, 1968), 21–61, 108–139.
3. For allied counsels, see Winston Churchill, *The World Crisis 1911–1918* (New York, 2005, originally published in 1931), 320–322, 355.
4. For the Gallipoli campaign, see Alan Moorehead, *Gallipoli* (New York, 1956); Michael Hickey, *Gallipoli* (London, 1995); Robert K. Massie, *Castles of Steel: Britain, Germany, and the Winning of the Great War at Sea* (New York, 2003), 426–502; and especially Tim Travers, *Gallipoli 1915* (Stroud, 2001). For relevant memoir literature, see Otto Liman von Sanders, *Five Years in Turkey*, trans. Carl Reichmann, (Annapolis, MD, 1927), 47–105; and Churchill, *World Crisis*, 347–534.
5. Cited in Travers, *Gallipoli 1915*, 21.
6. Citations in ibid., 26, 31.
7. Churchill, *World Crisis*, 404.
8. See Travers, *Gallipoli*, 31–32. Also see Paul G. Halpern, *A Naval History of World War I* (Annapolis, MD, 1994), 109–115, 491, n. 39. For the quote: Carlo D'Este, *Warlord: A Life of Winston Churchill at War, 1874–1945* (New York, 2008), 250.
9. Cited in ibid., 32.
10. Citations in Massie, *Castles of Steel*, 477; and Sanders, *Five Years in Turkey*, 58.
11. Travers, *Gallipoli 1915*, 38–44.
12. Cited in Moorehead, *Gallipoli*, 146.
13. For the following, see Stéphane Audoin-Rouzeau and Annette Becker, *14–18: Understanding the Great War*, trans. Catherine Temerson (New York, 2002), 45–90; John Horne and Alan Kramer, "War between Soldiers and Enemy Civilians, 1914–1915," in Roger Chickering and Stig Förster, eds., *Great War, Total War: Combat and Mobilization on the Western Front 1914–1918* (Cambridge, UK, 2000), 153–168; and Horne and Kramer, *German Atrocities 1914: A History of Denial* (London, 2001).
14. See Louis P. Lochner, *Herbert Hoover and Germany* (New York, 1960), 9–28.
15. See Peter Gatrell, *A Whole Empire Walking: Refugees in Russia during World War I* (Bloomington, IN, 1999).
16. Cited in Orlando Figes, *A People's Tragedy: The Russian Revolution 1891–1924* (New York, 1996), 268.
17. Taner Akcam, *A Shameful Act: The Armenian Genocide and the Question of Turkish Responsibility*, trans. Paul Bessemer (New York, 2006). The UN definition includes the partial or complete destruction of an ethnic/racial/religious group in peace or war, with destruction including both killing and exposing a group to grave danger and threatening its existence, as during a brutal deportation (Akcam, p. 9). There is also a good discussion of the Armenian genocide in Ulrich Trumpener, *Germany and the Ottoman Empire 1914–1918* (Princeton, NJ, 1968), 200–270. The work of then U.S. ambassador to Turkey, Henry Morgenthau, *The Murder of a Nation* (New York, 1915), also holds up well in light of Akcam's research. For a recent work that attempts to largely debunk the argument for genocide, see Guenther Lewy, *The Armenian Massacres in Ottoman Turkey: A Disputed Genocide* (Salt Lake City, UT, 2005).
18. One Turkish diplomat put the number at 350,000, but some hints from the Carnegie Endowment Inquiry of 1913 make the 50,000 figure—one-seventh—probable. Thus in one region alone Turks claimed around 3,500 died, whereas the investigation determined it to

be 700. See the Carnegie report, printed in *The Other Balkan Wars: A 1913 Carnegie Endowment Inquiry in Retrospect* (Washington, DC, 1993), 74; and Akcam, *Shameful Act,* 117.
19. Cited in Akcam, *Shameful Act,* 115.
20. Citations in ibid., 108, 105.
21. Citations in Philip V. Cannistraro and Brian R. Sullivan, *Il Duce's Other Woman* (New York, 1992), 138; and Audoin-Rouzeau and Becker, *Understanding the Great War,* 103, 151. For air attacks, see Roger Chickering, *The Great War and Urban Life in Germany: Freiburg 1914–1918* (Cambridge, UK, 2007), 99–111; and James J. Sheehan, *Where Have All the Soldiers Gone? The Transformation of Modern Europe* (Boston, 2008), 85.
22. See Cassar, *Kitchener's War,* 208–211.
23. Morehead, *Gallipoli,* 228.
24. For the August offensive at Gallipoli, see especially Travers, *Gallipoli 1915,* 114–162.
25. Cited in Cassar, *Kitchener's War,* 253.
26. For British fears that Gallipoli would have a "devastating effect on British prestige throughout the Muslim world," see ibid., 236, 251.
27. See ibid., 236–237.
28. For Balkan developments in 1915, see Barbara Jelavich, *History of the Balkans: Twentieth Century* (Cambridge, UK, 1983), 117–120; Keegan, *First World War,* 249–254; Misha Glenny, *The Balkans: Nationalism, War and the Great Powers, 1804–1999* (New York, 2000), 332–338, 349–350; and L. S. Stavrianos, *The Balkans since 1453* (New York, 2000), 557–564.
29. For Greek developments, the formation of the Army of the Orient, and its failure to rescue the Serbs in 1915, see Alan Palmer, *The Gardeners of Salonika* (London, 1965), 9–44.
30. For the Tigris campaign of 1915, see A. J. Barber, *The Neglected War: Mesopotamia 1914–1918* (London, 1967), 99–285; Paul K. Davis, *Ends and Means: The British Mesopotamian Campaign and Commission* (London, 1994); and more recently, Robert F. Jones, "Kut," in Robert Cowley, ed., *The Great War: Perspectives on the First World War* (New York, 2003), 197–216; and Majd, *Iraq in World War I,* 131–148, 179–220. Also see Sir Percy Sykes, *A History of Persia* (London, 1951), 2:440–442.
31. For this plot in general, see Hopkirk, *Like Hidden Fire.* Also see Hew Strachan, *The First World War* (Oxford, 2001), 1:770–791; and Anthony Wynn, *Persia in the Great Game: Sir Percy Sykes: Explorer, Consul, Soldier, Spy* (London, 2003), 248–271.
32. For the politics of the gendarmerie, see Stephanie Cronin, "Iranian Nationalism and the Government Gendarmerie," in Touraj Atabaki, ed., *Iran and the First World War: Battleground of the Great Powers* (London, 2006), 43–53.
33. For the citations, see Nasrollah Saifpour Fatemi, *Diplomatic History of Persia 1917–1923: Anglo-Russian Power Politics in Iran* (New York, 1952), 5. For the contacts between the gendarmerie and Solat, see Sykes, *History of Persia,* 2:471–472, 502–503.
34. See Strachan, *First World War,* 1:796–797, 807.
35. Cited in Cassar, *Kitchener's War,* 252.
36. Strachan, *First World War,* 1:813.
37. Sykes, *History of Persia,* 2:441.
38. Cited in Sir Percy Sykes, *A History of Afghanistan* (London, 1940), 2:257.
39. Cited in Hopkirk, *Like Hidden Fire,* 164.
40. Ibid., 179–194; Strachan, *First World War,* 1:807.
41. See Hopkirk, *Like Hidden Fire,* 174–176.
42. For the largely ineffective contribution of the Persian volunteers/gendarmes, see Otto Liman von Sanders, *Five Years in Turkey,* trans. Carl Reichmann, (Annapolis, MD, 1927), 134–137, 161–162; and Cronin, "Government Gendarmerie," in Atabaki, *Iran and the First World War,* 53–59.
43. Sykes, *History of Persia,* 2:451–452; and Stanford J. Shaw and Ezel Kural Shaw, *History of the Ottoman Empire and Modern Turkey* (Cambridge, UK, 1977), 2:322–323.

44. For the discussions, see Ludwig W. Adamec, *Afghanistan, 1900–1923: A Diplomatic History* (Berkeley, CA, 1967), 94, 103–104.
45. See, for instance, his *The Middle East: A Brief History of the Last 2,000 Years* (New York, 1995), 339.
46. Interesting in this regard is the opening part of Episode Three, "Total War," of the PBS documentary *The Great War and the Shaping of the Twentieth Century*. Also see the companion volume, Jay Winter and Blaine Baggett, *The Great War and the Shaping of the Twentieth Century* (New York, 1996), 107–117.
47. Cited in Jones, "Kut," in Cowley, ed., *Great War*, 204.
48. For this passage, see Cassar, *Kitchener's War*, 52–58, 146–154, 220–227; and Fromkin, *Peace to End all Peace*, 98–105, 173–187.
49. The letter is printed in Akram Fouad Khater, *Sources in the History of the Modern Middle East* (Boston, 2004), 128–129.
50. For the citations here, see ibid., 129–131.
51. Cited in Fromkin, *Peace to End All Peace*, 186.
52. For the first stage of the Arab revolt, see ibid., 218–228; and especially B. H. Liddell Hart, *Lawrence of Arabia* (New York, 1934), 58–92.
53. Citations in Fromkin, *Peace to End All Peace*, 223.
54. For this passage, see Harry A. Gailey, *History of Africa from 1800 to Present* (New York, 1972), 217–229; M. Crowder, "The First World War and Its Consequences," in A. Adu Boahen, ed., *General History of Africa* (London, 1981), 7:283–311; and Strachan, *First World War*, 1:744–749. For a recent discussion of the African campaigns, also see Edward Paice, *Tip and Run: The Untold Tragedy of the Great War in Africa* (London, 2007).
55. For the East African campaign in 1916, see Byron Farwell, *The Great War in Africa (1914–1918)* (New York, 1986), 250–319; and Strachan, *First World War*, 1:598–623.
56. Lettow is cited in Farwell, *Great War in Africa*, 261.

CHAPTER VII

Tipping Points in Europe

1916–1917

An overnight train flying the colors of Imperial Germany hissed to a stop in the station at Breslau. White clouds of steam from the engine hung almost motionless in the frigid morning air of early January 1917. Inside the center compartment Imperial Chancellor Theobald von Bethmann Hollweg put on a thick black overcoat and walked slowly to the door. His haggard, wrinkled face bore the strains of two and half years of Berlin's vicious wartime politicking.[1]

In recent months the capital city's political parties, bureaucratic factions, and high-level military cliques had been locked in one particularly venomous struggle: whether or not to wage unrestricted submarine warfare. Was radical use of the U-boats the quickest way to win a seemingly endless war, as the generals and admirals maintained? "Only people without a sense of reality and convinced enemies of the existing state order" could possibly argue against their use, said August von Mackensen, hero of Galicia and Poland. Or would unleashing them on the ships of neutral nations like the United States of America only increase the likelihood of defeat? Bethmann had entrained for Silesia to argue the latter position one last time, but his leverage was slipping, for a center-right majority of Germany's parliament, the Reichstag, swayed by the stark realities of Britain's tightening blockade, sympathized with the High Command.

Georg von Müller, chief of the kaiser's Privy Naval Cabinet, waited for the chancellor to step out of the train. He had bad news as they drove to the castle of the kaiser's good friend, Prince Hans von Pless. The previous evening William had abandoned his first minister, arguing now that U-boat warfare was a purely military affair that did not concern civilian officials. Müller too had switched sides. "For two years I have always been on the side of moderation, but now, in the altered circumstances," he told Bethmann, "I consider unrestricted [submarine] warfare to be necessary and that it has a reasonable chance of success." Agitated and depressed by these bad tidings, the chancellor kept his bleak thoughts to himself.

After a long drive, Pless's huge three-hundred-room estate, headquarters for German operations on the eastern front, loomed in the distance. As if taken from a Caspar David Friedrich painting, its frozen white walls were set against the backdrop of frost-covered parks, lawns, gardens, lakes, and giant leafless chestnut trees. Bethmann and Müller passed through the red damask reception hall with tall French windows on their way to the critical meeting with William, Generals Paul von Hindenburg and Erich Ludendorff, Chief of the Naval Staff Admiral Henning von Holtzendorff, and other military officials. The kaiser, nervous as was his nature in awkward situations, stood uncomfortably by a great chair as the lone civilian asked to the meeting entered the conference room. Bethmann made his case first as the others listened impatiently and disapprovingly. He told them, essentially, that unlimited submarine warfare would trigger American entry to the war and that adding the United States to Germany's already lengthy list of enemies would lead directly to a German defeat. William cut him off. Unlike 1915, he blurted, Germany now had enough submarines to finish off Britain. The kaiser was "not at all" interested in the mediation efforts of President Wilson, nor could America's reaction to its sunken ships be helped. "We shall move ahead." Holtzendorff strengthened the kaiser's resolve by downplaying the significance of Washington's likely declaration of belligerency. "I pledge on my word as a naval officer that no American will set foot on continental soil." Hindenburg seconded Holzendorff as Ludendorff sat by silently, nonchalantly waiting for the kaiser to give them the go-ahead. Germany's second-ranking soldier thought the Americans were "just bluffing." Even if they were not, it mattered

Verdun: Aerial View of Fort Douaumont

Harper's Pictorial Library

Verdun: General Pétain
Harper's Pictorial Library

little, for "a nation that has no military education whatsoever is not proficient at war." Bethmann knew that further argument was hopeless. "If the military authorities consider the U-boat war necessary, I am not in a position to oppose them." It was settled. The kaiser reached across the table and signed a document already prepared. Unrestricted submarine warfare would begin in three weeks: February 1, 1917.

Germany's chancellor remained behind, hunched in his chair as the others filed out. Entering the room and seeing this, an official of William's court asked innocently, "Have we lost a battle?" "No," said Bethmann, "but *Finis Germaniae.*"

GERMANY TAKES THE OFFENSIVE

The rash decision made at Castle Pless on January 9, 1917, resulted in large part from a series of military setbacks suffered by the Central Powers during the preceding year. Despite victories at Gallipoli and Kut, the Germans and Turks failed to unleash a serious Jihad or shake Britain's hold on northeastern Africa, critical portions of the Middle East and Central Asia, and India. As explained later, meanwhile, the fortunes of war had turned in Europe. Germany's attempt to break the French at Verdun in the late winter and spring of 1916 backfired miserably, while neither the submarines, putting to sea with some restrictions, nor the High Seas Fleet, were able to break the British blockade. Beginning in June and July, moreover, Russian and British offensives were contained only with great difficulty, and Italy had blunted an Austrian offensive designed to end Rome's war effort. Adding to Germany's worries, Rumania entered the enemy coalition in August. How had it come to this?

Falkenhayn's Plans for Verdun and Submarine Warfare

Of all of these failures and crises, none was more devastating militarily and politically than the Battle of Verdun. During the planning stage in late 1915 doubts about Germany's chances in a prolonged war had already crept into the thoughts of General Staff Chief Erich von Falkenhayn. "Time is against us,"[2] he told the kaiser. Despite terrible losses, France, Italy, and Russia would field significantly larger forces in the upcoming campaigns of 1916, especially the BEF, which was expected to double in size to 60–70 divisions as a result of the "new" or "Kitchener" divisions raised and trained since 1914. Because the Central Powers would soon be greatly outnumbered on every front it was important to knock one or two enemy countries out of the war and to do it quickly—but how could this be accomplished?

Falkenhayn discussed his plans with the kaiser, the generals, and the admirals in December 1915 and January 1916.[3] He ruled out a joint allied offensive against Italy, arguing that great victories there would not have a major impact on the outcome of the war in Europe. The general staff chief also rejected an option still favored by Hindenburg and Ludendorff of a drive on St. Petersburg or Moscow, operations that would disperse more than one hundred German divisions over the vast expanse of Russia without leading to decisive engagements as the tsar's armies repeated the strategy used against Napoleon and retreated ever farther into the empire's huge interior. The western front, on the other hand, offered promising opportunities for ending the stalemate and producing German victory in the war. In particular, Falkenhayn believed that an assault on the historic fortress zone of Verdun would provoke the archenemy to counterattack, thereby finishing the process (begun in 1914 and carried further in 1915) of making the French "bleed themselves white."[4] Fittingly enough, he code-named the operation *Gericht,* meaning court or judgment or sometimes a place of execution. The carnage wrought by German heavy artillery would be so devastating that within a week or two Britain would be compelled to attack on the Somme River or in Flanders to relieve pressure on Verdun. Once again, however, modern technology would tear huge holes in enemy lines and set the stage for a massive German counterattack. The campaigns in the British sector and around Verdun would restore movement to the western front by forcing the war-weary French back toward Paris, perhaps to the point of surrender, and driving the BEF into the sea. Although it may be true that Falkenhayn eschewed grandiose flanking maneuvers à la Schlieffen that made no more operational sense on the stalemated western front, it bears emphasizing that his hammer-blow strategy of "attrition" was designed to attrit only the enemy—and to attrit him quickly.[5]

Such a crushing of British forces in Europe would not necessarily defeat Germany's great island nemesis, however, for Great Britain could raise other

Verdun: French Defenders on Cote 304
Harper's Pictorial Library

armies at home as well as abroad in its extensive empire, easily arming and equipping them by drawing on world armaments and explosives markets. Germany had only two options for delivering a death blow to the mighty British. One possibility, supported by Germany's ambassador to Turkey, Conrad von Wangenheim, was to pour German troops into the Middle East; embolden Arab, Persian, and Afghan Jihadists; and then ultimately drive on Egypt and India. Falkenhayn opposed this "crusade à la Alexander the Great"[6] because he was not convinced that it would sufficiently weaken Britain and therefore did not promise war-ending decisiveness.

Rather, he gave the nod to another option—unrestricted submarine warfare. The chief informed the admirals at two meetings in late December and early January that he no longer shared the chancellor's concern for the reaction of neutral nations now that Bulgaria had joined the Central Powers. America would surely enter the fray, but this would matter little if German U-boats brought Britain to its knees in a matter of months. Could they? After the navy gave him assurances, Falkenhayn made up his mind to press the kaiser for a submarine decision. Reinforcing his resolve was the belief that an unlimited U-boat campaign might also contribute to Britain's willingness to wage a desperate offensive before its new divisions were ready—an operation, as explained earlier, that Falkenhayn welcomed.

Convincing William II, however, would not be easy. Largely excluded from army decisions by Falkenhayn, the kaiser had grown even more sensitive and proprietary about naval matters, the lone category of military decisions still controlled by the gloomy monarch. He looked askance, moreover, at the navy's arguments about the decisiveness of submarine warfare after decades of listening to the claims of Naval Secretary Alfred von Tirpitz regarding the decisiveness of battleships—arguments that seemed hollow as the behemoths of the High Seas Fleet remained idly anchored in harbor. Would the submarines accomplish little more than the "stupidity" of pushing Washington into the war?[7]

Accordingly it was not Tirpitz at first, but rather Henning von Holtzendorff who opened the campaign to recruit William. The new chief of the Naval Staff had assumed his duties in September 1915 as the one chosen by kaiser and chancellor to rein in radicals and insubordinates in the submarine corps, thereby maintaining Germany's delicate rapprochement with the United States. "Believe me, gentlemen," he had said at the time, "you will not scratch the whale's skin with your U-boat war." With prospects of success in an unrestricted U-boat war looking much better, however, Holtzendorff now changed sides.[8] For one thing, British shipyards were producing only a third of the merchant ship tonnage of late 1914 as warship production diverted labor, materials, and space. Making matters worse, the British navy had requisitioned hundreds of merchant vessels for transporting munitions, food, and other military supplies—about a fifth of the prewar merchant marine. Most important of all, Germany could put double the number of submarines to sea in the upcoming campaign—108 versus 52 in 1915. The new "fleet boat" and "UB-III" models were also bigger, faster, more heavily armed with torpedoes, and less vulnerable to attack because of their double hulls. Holtzendorff estimated that his submarine fleet could sink triple Britain's new ship construction and force an end to the war in six months. All enemy ships in the Western Approaches to the British Isles—and those on the high seas too, if armed—would be sunk without warning. The Naval Staff chief realized that these sinkings would inevitably extend to neutral vessels, but he assured his sovereign that America's entry would not save Britain in time. As a sop to diplomacy, he recommended that U-boats strictly avoid firing on luxury liners. Clearly swayed by such arguments, William began to waver in mid-January 1916. "Can I go against the counsel of my military advisers, and from humane considerations prolong the war at the cost of so many brave men who are defending the Fatherland?"[9]

Bethmann countered with his familiar objections at a meeting held at Castle Pless that same month. It was facile to underestimate Britain's resolve: even a greater number of sinkings and heightened social misery in the isles might not force the proud English to surrender. The possibility of meager benefits made the likely costs of unrestricted submarine warfare—provocation of America and subsequent military defeat—unbearable and unthinkable. As winter drew on toward spring, Tirpitz submitted his own memo, arguing that only "immediate and relentless recourse to the submarine weapon"—in other words, the unwarned torpedoing of neutral shipping, including luxury liners—would bring victory. William vacillated between these extreme positions but eventually leaned toward Falkenhayn and Holtzendorff. Tormented by the inevitable alienation of Washington, however, he feared for the outcome of the war: "One must never utter it nor shall I admit it to Falkenhayn, but this war will not end with a great victory."[10]

Germany's Battle Cry is
"Germany over All"
And her Navy drinks to
"The Day"
When she hopes to
Smash Britain's Fleet.

BRITAIN IS FIGHTING
Not Only for the
FREEDOM OF EUROPE
BUT TO DEFEND
YOUR MOTHERS,
WIVES & SISTERS
FROM THE HORRORS OF WAR.

We must crush this idea
Of "GERMANY OVER ALL".

The War at Sea: Winning or Losing the War in a Single Afternoon
Courtesy of the Library of Congress

The War at Sea: German Dreadnoughts Steam Into Harm's Way
Canfield, *World War*

He finally gave in and agreed to Holtzendorff's recommendations on March 13. The campaign would begin on April 1, 1916.

Tirpitz, furious over the remaining "restrictions" to submarine use, once again submitted his resignation. Tired of his naval secretary's stubbornness, William accepted it this time. Now Tirpitz, incensed at his sovereign's alleged weakness, conspired to have William step down for alleged health reasons. This conspiracy did not succeed, but it was a clear sign that Germany's legitimacy crisis had worsened, for not just the political left but also the right was ratcheting up its opposition to monarchical authority.

Verdun and the U-boats: Winter–Spring 1916

Three weeks earlier, on February 21, 1916, the German assault on Verdun commenced.[11] The task of breaking the French fell to Crown Prince William, commander of Fifth Army, and his chief of staff, Lieutenant General Constantin Schmidt von Knobelsdorf. Their plan, modified in significant ways by Falkenhayn himself, called for a nine-hour bombardment by over 1,400 tubes: 512 light field guns, 631 heavies ranging from six- to sixteen-inch calibers (150–420 cm), and 202 earthshaking trench mortars (*Minenwerfer*), all raining hundreds of thousands of shells on forward infantry positions, artillery batteries in the rear, and supply routes leading to Verdun. The scheme relied heavily on artillery lessons learned on the eastern front in 1915, namely, that accurate, concentrated fire could so obliterate defensive positions as to make the subsequent infantry assault succeed. It is noteworthy, however, that OHL clearly departed at Verdun from French artillery practice demonstrated only five months earlier in the Champagne offensive. The heavy gun support per assault division was significantly higher—92 versus 37—but Falkenhayn dispensed with a four–five day bombardment in favor of less than half a day, partly to surprise the shell-shocked defenders but also to conserve the shells that even Germany's mighty industrial establishment strained to produce in sufficient numbers for two big fronts under blockade conditions. To some extent, in other words, tactical innovation was the offspring of economic necessity.

The German chief assumed that nine oversized divisions, 140,000 men, could secure most of the fortress zone and advance easily to positions on the heights above the town of Verdun on the east bank of the Meuse, there to dig in and await French counterattacks. Knobelsdorf and his artillery experts had argued in December that the attack had to proceed on both banks if it were to succeed, for high ground on the western side offered an ideal opportunity for pouring flanking fire into German divisions as they moved south on the opposite bank. With the experience of the allies' near breakthroughs of September 1915 fresh in mind, however, Falkenhayn rejected this idea, for he feared it would deplete the western front of the men and material required to repel anticipated British attacks north of the Somme River. "I do not want to come to the same dangerous situation—I will not allow that to happen again."[12] This would prove to be a major mistake.

The original date of the attack—February 12—came and went as heavy wind and snow obscured the mandatory artillery observation. This intervention of nature may well have decided the outcome of the battle. The French had initially deployed only five divisions around Verdun and largely denuded the fortresses of heavy artillery, but the delay on the German side gave GQG enough time to detect the large concentration of men, guns, and supply depots north of Verdun. "In the woods ringing Verdun," writes one historian, "there was hardly room for a man to walk between the massed cannon and ammunition dumps."[13] Thus alerted, six more divisions accompanied by hundreds of additional light and heavy guns had been put in place when Knobelsdorf's bombardment began. Although at some points along the ten-kilometer attack front German cannon annihilated whole French divisions, literally tearing thousands of men to bits or burying them under tons of earth, at other parts of the line defenders were unharmed. French artillery fire from the west bank of the Meuse also played a critical role, inflicting heavy casualties on the German assault corps as early as the second day. Fearing a political crisis if Verdun fell, moreover, Paris insisted that GQG rush reinforcements. By February 26 a few extra divisions had come, and over the next week many more arrived—nearly two hundred thousand troops altogether. They marched along *La Voie Sacrée*, the Sacred Way, the lone road into Verdun undestroyed by German guns. Knobelsdorf retained a significant artillery advantage and had reserves of his own to call up, but against such defensive resolve the German advance slowed down, penetrating four to five kilometers in the first five days and capturing the massive citadel at Douaumont—a disastrous setback for France—then little more. The bulk of the east bank Meuse Heights remained in French hands by early March. Verdun itself lay more than six kilometers behind French lines, a disappointment compounded for Falkenhayn by the kaiser's weeks-long hesitation to declare intensified submarine warfare unless the town fell.

Something Wrong with Our Bloody Ships: Explosion of HMS *Queen Mary*

Used with the permission of *The Trustees of the Imperial War Museum, London.* Photo Number: SP-1708

On March 6 Knobelsdorf shifted his attacks to hills on the west bank of the Meuse in order to silence deadly fire from French artillery. All that month his divisions and batteries hammered away at their initial objectives, Le Mort Homme and Cote 304. A French soldier defending the first hill recalled firing for two straight hours, annihilating so many waves of attackers that German officers had to threaten their men in order to mount successive waves. "We were no longer men," remembered the *poilu*, "we were demons intoxicated by the powder." Not until late May 1916 did these hills fall, but some of the west bank area still remained in French hands.

In the meantime, assaults had resumed on the east bank as the Germans pushed beyond Fort Douaumont to Fort Vaux. Here, as on the other side of the river, the defenders yielded little ground. "At the present rate of progress," one of Knobelsdorf's commanders said sarcastically, "we will be in Verdun at the earliest in 1920."[14] As spring wore on the "Meuse Killing Mill" had claimed well over one hundred thousand casualties on each side of the lines. Falkenhayn's assumptions about bleeding the French white in a few weeks had proven badly illusory.

On April 1, meanwhile, German submarines began their new campaign against merchant ships trading mainly with Britain. That month they sank over 140,000 tons of shipping, very close to the goal that Holtzendorff believed would force Britain out of the war but far below Tirpitz's wild-eyed predictions of as much as a million tons per month. As recent research has shown, however, it is extremely doubtful that even this higher level of sinking would have starved

Britain into submission.[15] But none of the predictions would be put to the test, for once again the destruction of a passenger liner (with death to four Americans on board), France's *Sussex*, which the sub captain mistook for a troop ship, brought the predictable angry response from American President Woodrow Wilson: "If it is still the purpose of the Imperial government to prosecute relentless and indiscriminate warfare against vessels of commerce by the use of U-boats without regard to what the government of the United States must consider the sacred and indisputable rules of international law and universally recognized dictates of humanity, the [U.S.] is at last forced to the conclusion that there is but one recourse it can pursue: [the severing of] diplomatic relations with the German empire altogether."[16] On April 24, William yielded to the counsel of Bethmann over the strenuous objection of Falkenhayn, who insisted that unrestricted submarine warfare was indispensable to victory at Verdun, and ordered U-boat commanders to return to international "prize regulations." As they had in September 1915, German naval leaders refused to order their submarines to surface, warn, and inspect merchant ships before sinking them. Rather, they once again called off their U-boats from the waters around Britain. Only in the Mediterranean were German submarines able to put constant pressure on the British Empire. Operating out of the Austro-Hungarian naval base at Pola in the Adriatic Sea, a force of 39 U-boats began to wreak havoc on enemy shipping during the late summer of 1915 as the allies supplied Gallipoli and then later built up expeditionary forces in Salonika and Egypt. In eleven months U-boats sank 167 ships, nearly 500,000 tons. By March 1916 this menace grew serious enough for the British to reroute all supplies to Egypt around the Cape of Good Hope.[17] In the last analysis, however, these victories at sea were mere consolations, for they did little to interfere seriously with the British war effort.

Jutland

The decision to withdraw U-boats from the Western Approaches was made by Reinhard Scheer, commander in chief of the High Seas Fleet since January 1916. Eager for his battle wagons to make a contribution to the German war effort comparable to that of the army and the submarine corps, he had met with Admiral Holtzendorff as early as February to discuss significant but limited North Sea action—something short of engaging the entire Grand Fleet, a mistake that could only end in disaster. The kaiser reluctantly gave his consent. By May, with the assault bogged down around Verdun and the U-boats back in their bases, pressure inside the military establishment, and from the public, mounted on Scheer to commit the High Seas Fleet. "The unkindest cut of all," writes Holger Herwig, "was a popular slogan scrawled upon walls in Wilhelmshaven: 'Dear Fatherland, you may rest assured; the Fleet lies in the harbors—moored.'" Such displays of popular intolerance for naval inaction equated in the eyes of top naval leaders to charges of cowardice. "For this reason alone," confessed Scheer's second in command, Vice Admiral Franz von Hipper, "I wish that we may soon be able to do battle."[18]

Four days later, in the early morning hours of May 31, 1916, Hipper's Fifth Fleet Division slipped into the North Sea.[19] The imposing battle cruisers *Derfflinger, Seydlitz,* and *Lützow* constituted the van. Ninety minutes later the main body of the High Seas Fleet, First and Sixth Fleet Divisions, followed with Scheer aboard the modern dreadnought *Friedrich der Grosse.* Altogether sixteen dreadnoughts, five battle cruisers, six predreadnought battleships, eleven light cruisers, and scores of lighter vessels steamed through the darkness up the Danish coast toward the Jutland Bank.

Scheer planned to use Hipper's division as bait to lure the less threatening portion of the British navy, Admiral David Beatty's Battle Cruiser Squadron at Rosyth in the Firth of Forth, into the steel jaws of the whole German fleet. To avoid doing battle with the main body of Admiral John Jellicoe's Grand Fleet moored at Scapa Flow, he employed the ruse of sending the harbor call sign "DK" from an onshore wireless station as he put to sea. If the enemy could be deceived into thinking that Germany's biggest ships remained in port, then perhaps Scheer would not have to face Britain's superior numbers of dreadnoughts.

The British, however, achieved much greater deception. As in 1915 before the Battle of Dogger Bank, intelligence experts in Room 40 intercepted the German signal, "31 G.G. 2490." This seemed to indicate that Scheer was planning major operations for May 31. Thus alerted by Room 40, Beatty and Jellicoe raised steam and departed their moorings over three hours before Hipper. Unfortunately for Jellicoe, however, he did not know about Scheer's ruse, and, sensing little urgency therefore in what would apparently be an easy crushing of Hipper without Scheer, went into the North Sea at less than full speed. The one or two hours lost would play a critical role in the impending Battle of Jutland, the largest encounter between capital ships in the history of modern naval warfare, for Beatty would have to fight for over two hours without Jellicoe, and when reinforcements arrived it was almost nightfall.

The hard-charging Beatty could still have prevailed in this first stage of the battle, for he steamed in quest of "the next Trafalgar" with six fast battle cruisers and four of the newest, heavily armed dreadnoughts—far more firepower than Hipper with his three battle cruisers and two predreadnoughts. Because of a miscommunication with the dreadnought squadron, however, it fell sixteen thousand meters behind and far out of range when the first salvos were fired at shortly before four o'clock in the afternoon. Another disadvantageous factor on the British side soon assumed critical importance. After Dogger Bank the High Seas Fleet had installed fire doors between the main turrets and the magazines many decks below, but the Grand Fleet had not. Within forty-five minutes this technical flaw sent two British battle cruisers, *Indefatigable* and *Queen Mary,* to the bottom as German shells hit turrets, flashed fire to the magazines, and triggered massive explosions. Over two thousand sailors had perished. Beatty's flagship, *Lion,* avoided the same grisly fate by the narrowest of margins when a mortally wounded turret captain ordered the magazines flooded moments before they would have exploded. "There is something wrong with our bloody ships today,"[20] said a dumbfounded Beatty. Adding to his sense of peril, one of his officers reported sighting Scheer's divisions in the

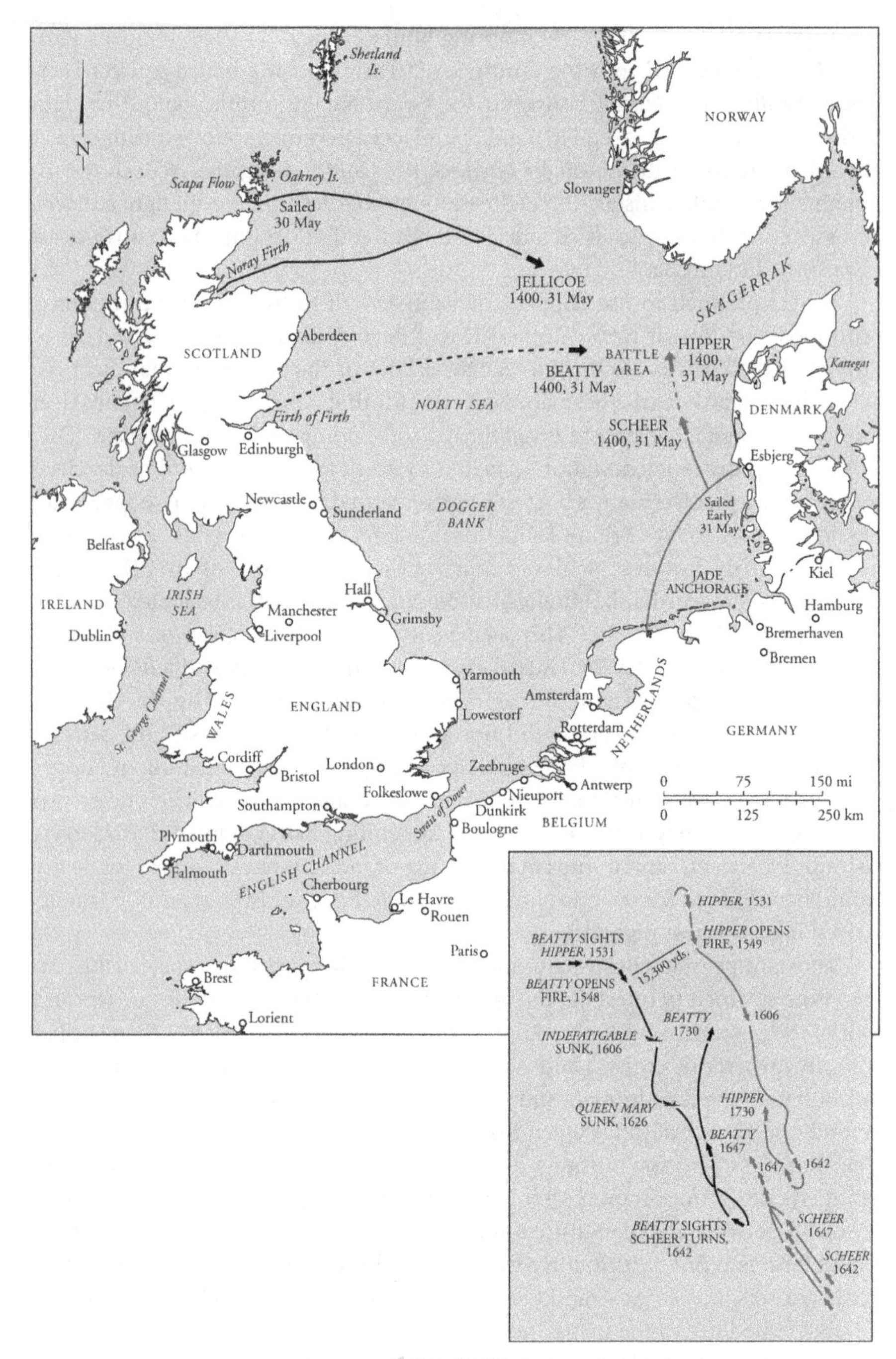

Battle of Jutland

Maps Courtesy of the Department of History, United States Military Academy

distance. So Beatty wheeled around, hoping that Hipper and Scheer would give chase and be drawn into Jellicoe's mighty flotilla bearing down from the north. For an hour Hipper and Beatty engaged in a running northward battle as Scheer strained to come within range. Staring into the misty, cloudy waters directly ahead, Hipper grew more and more apprehensive. "Something lurks in that soup," he warned his officers. "We would do well not to thrust into it too deeply."[21] Shortly before six o'clock his admonition proved shockingly, frighteningly correct as Jellicoe's twenty-four dreadnoughts came into view. Both fleets now pounded one another for a half hour, but the struggle was too lopsided for Scheer, who ordered the entire fleet to turn about and retreat. Shortly before seven o'clock he turned back toward Jellicoe—a baffling decision never adequately explained—but within a few minutes reversed course again, ordering his battle cruisers and destroyers to fight a heroic rear-guard action to cover the fleet's escape. As darkness fell at Jutland the two massive flotillas lost contact with one another. The next morning the High Seas Fleet limped back into port.

In the aftermath both sides claimed victory. In terms of major ships sunk the Battle of Jutland appeared to be a slight German victory: the British lost fourteen—three battle cruisers, three heavy cruisers, one light cruiser, and seven destroyers—while the Germans lost eleven—one battle cruiser, one predreadnought battleship, four light cruisers, and five destroyers; 6,094 British sailors died and 2,551 Germans. However, the fact that the High Seas Fleet remained bottled up in harbor for the duration of the war, and the blockade unbroken, points to a major setback for Germany and the Central Powers. If one considers the hypothetical alternative of Scheer's battle plan succeeding, moreover, German defeat and disappointment comes into proper perspective, for the near destruction or perhaps annihilation of Beatty's ten capital ships by the combined High Seas Fleet might have compelled the already cautious Jellicoe to call off offensive operations lest he suffer the same kind of defeat at the hands of the evidently qualitatively superior German navy. The blockade would at the very least have been less effective, not to mention the difficulties this would have created for maintaining large British forces on the continent. A tremendous opportunity had slipped away.

THE ALLIES TAKE PRESSURE OFF VERDUN

On June 1, 1916, as shocked sailors in port watched their battered surviving ships steam back into the Jade at Wilhelmshaven, Knobelsdorf renewed his attacks on the east bank at Verdun. The target, Fort Vaux, surrendered six days later. Now only one minor fort at Fleury and one major citadel, Fort Souville, stood between Fifth Army and control of the heights above Verdun and the Meuse River bridges—the original goal of the entire operation. The relentless German attacks elicited desperate pleas from GQG for a relief offensive elsewhere on the western front. If the BEF did not unleash its new divisions in the next five weeks, implored Joffre already in late May, "the French army would cease to exist." But one of his generals, Robert Nivelle, kept morale alive with perhaps the most famous statement of the war. "Comrades," he told the defenders of Verdun, "they will not pass!"[22]

Shadow Not Substance: Sir Douglas Haig Reviews His Troops
Harper's Pictorial Library

Thus far Falkenhayn's Verdun operation had almost achieved the desired tactical breakthrough that could lead to wider strategic victory on the western front. Together with Austro-Hungarian attacks in Italy, moreover, his offensive succeeded in partially disrupting allied planning. While OHL formulated Operation *Gericht* in early December 1915, Joffre had hosted a meeting of the allies in Chantilly to coordinate the campaigns of 1916. With Russian, Serbian, Italian, Belgian, British, and French representatives attending, the conferees designated Russia, Italy, and France as theaters where coordinated offensives, timed to be not more than ten days apart, could prevent Berlin and Vienna from shifting reserves between these threatened areas. If the allies "do everything they can to attrit the adversary" they would achieve "strategic rupture"[23] on at least one of his fronts and win the war. After February 1916, however, with the French committing ever greater resources to their desperate defense of Verdun, they successively scaled back grandiose plans for an Anglo-French offensive along the Somme River. Promised forty-five French divisions in March, BEF commander Sir Douglas Haig had less than a third of this at his disposal by June. The new British chief and the War Cabinet in London had intended for many months to make some sort of attack in this region, either as the primary thrust or as a diversionary assault to draw German reserves away from Haig's preferred targets in Flanders. Now both politicians and soldiers, reacting with alarm to their ally's pleas, accelerated battle plans lest Verdun's bleeding kill the French war effort.[24] This was exactly what Falkenhayn wanted.

The Brusilov Offensive and the Trentino

French calls for help had also sounded throughout the spring to the tsar and his generals on the eastern front. Almost none of them were eager to comply after a March assault designed to seize vital railheads in Lithuania failed miserably amidst terrible bungling and ineptitude. Massed artillery fired blindly to the west where Germans were thought to be, decimating a Russia division that had charged too early. Some units made progress into small salients, but enfilading artillery fire crushed them. Casualties totaled one hundred thousand.

Only one Russian general, Alexei Brusilov, commander of the southwestern sector of southern Poland and Galicia, recommended action to help the beleaguered French.[25] Although an officer of the cavalry, a military branch not normally known for promoting new ideas, Brusilov made a series of innovative proposals after the defeat in Lithuania. First, rather than punching through a narrow gap in opposing lines, he suggested striking five 30-kilometer-wide sectors along the entire 425-kilometer southwestern front, thereby dissipating enemy reserves and reinforcements. Second, he would dispense with the typical days-long preliminary bombardment. Aerial reconnaissance promised accurate pretargeting of opposing artillery batteries such that a shorter, hours-long barrage would both soften up defenders and preserve some element of surprise. Third, in the weeks before the offensive concealed trenches would be dug secretly up to a few hundred meters from German/Austro-Hungarian positions. Russian infantrymen would have less ground to cover and suffer fewer casualties. Fourth, Brusilov wanted to pack his reserves in protected dugouts near frontline troops in order to rapidly expedite breakthroughs. Tactically and operationally, his plan represented a significant advance for Russia's wartime revolution in military affairs (RMA). Not known for its progressivism, *Stavka* only grudgingly accepted this plan.

Five Russian armies—forty infantry and fifteen cavalry divisions, almost two-thirds of a million soldiers—went over the top on June 4, 1916. Brusilov supported them with 1,938 mostly small-caliber guns. In stark contrast to the much more heavily fortified and densely defended western front, where the emerging tactical orthodoxy leaned toward large concentrations of big cannon, each of Brusilov's attacking infantry divisions had only four heavies behind it. The economic side of Russia's RMA had progressed too, however, thanks largely to feverish efforts made throughout 1915 and early 1916 by industrialists and Duma parliamentarians to increase explosives output, which doubled; rifle production, which nearly doubled; and shell output, which more than tripled. All of this—and what was about to hit Central Power lines—shed a negative light on the faulty reckonings of Falkenhayn, who had assumed after German and Austro-Hungarian gains in 1915 that Russia would be incapable of further offensive operations. He had therefore shifted numerous German divisions to the west.

Silencing hundreds of enemy artillery batteries and achieving surprise as well, Brusilov's men pushed back four Austro-Hungarian armies and one Austro-German army, completely routing one of them. This latter success came in the north with the capture of Lutsk and the opening of a gaping, 90-kilometer-long, 50-kilometer-deep hole in the positions of the stricken Austro-Hungarian Fourth Army. Even greater success might have been achieved, ironically, if the ex-cavalryman had opted to amass horsemen in reserve to exploit breakthroughs, but he had not done so in order to preserve secrecy. Nevertheless, Falkenhayn had

Trench Warfare: British Artillery Crew with Gas Masks
Canfield, *World War*

to rush four of fourteen reserve divisions in France eastward, thereby jeopardizing his overall designs for the western front. Franz Conrad von Hötzendorf, the Austrian commander, similarly withdrew four divisions from the Italian front, where he had been attacking with some success since May and, for a time, preempting and frustrating Rome's plans to take pressure off Verdun.

Conrad's plan called for two armies, Eleventh with nine divisions and Third with five, to swarm out of South Tyrol into the Trentino, seizing Venice in six days, surrounding Italian forces along the Isonzo River, and knocking Italy out of the war. Ensconced in headquarters one thousand kilometers away in Austrian Silesia, he took neither the rugged mountainous terrain nor the still brutal weather of early spring into account. After climate-related delays of five weeks, his units attacked on May 15, overrunning portions of the badly outnumbered Italian First Army and pushing south twenty kilometers to Arsiera and Asiago.

The worried Italian commander in chief, Luigi Cadorna, began preparations for abandoning northern Italy. Snow, thaws, rain, and mud slowed the Austro-Hungarian advance after two weeks, however, allowing Cadorna time to assemble a new Fifth Army and counterattack on June 6. A week later Conrad began withdrawing divisions to Galicia, thus ending, at a cost of eighty thousand casualties, his "punitive expedition" against the "honorless"[26] Italians. On the other hand, Cadorna, his own plans disrupted by Conrad, could not mount the sixth offensive on the Isonzo River until early August.

In mid-June Brusilov paused to regroup and bring up supplies. The respite, and the arriving German and Austrian reinforcements, emboldened Hindenburg and Ludendorff to demand still more troops from the western front for a massive counterattack against the Russians. Falkenhayn rejected this counsel.[27] Rather, with welcome lulls on other fronts, he ordered a last push for the heights above

Verdun. Fleury fell quickly on June 21–22, prompting more French pleas for help. Fleury's fall set the stage for an attack on Fort Souville, which commenced on July 10. Initial gains were lost, however, when the French counterattacked four days later.

In the meantime Brusilov had renewed his attacks, advancing another sixty kilometers in Galicia and severely punishing the Austro-Hungarian Seventh Army, which, cut in two, fell back to the base of the Carpathian Mountains. Falkenhayn had to shift five divisions from the reserves of Hindenburg's northeastern front to Galicia. He was prevented from moving more men out of this sector when *Stavka* opened a clever second assault near the Pripet Marshes in early July. Falkenhayn lost the option of transferring additional forces from the western front, moreover, when the British and French finally unleashed an offensive astride the Somme River.

THE SOMME

Recent historians of this notorious battle continue to fault British chief Douglas Haig with overambitious goals and woefully faulty tactical and operational planning.[28] In a few days he wanted to rupture enemy defenses and then send horsemen thundering into the breach to rout Germans just as Napoleon had done. Unfortunately Haig faced what Winston Churchill later described as "the strongest and most perfectly defended position in the world."[29] The German Second Army had largely executed Falkenhayn's 1915 order for a kilometers-deep triple trench network—only the third line was still under construction. Additionally, their forward defenses boasted numerous fortified villages whose stone houses, woven into and around the trenches, concrete pillboxes, and barbed wire concealed hundreds of riflemen and machine gun crews. Breaking through would be extremely difficult, not to mention achieving the ambitious operational goal of rolling up German lines to Arras and Douai; overrunning rail lines; and forcing German armies to retreat, perhaps in conjunction with a second BEF offensive in Flanders. It may well be true, in fact, that the British chief's ultimate aim remained his *idée fixe* of a Flanders offensive after German reserves had been drawn away to the Somme and that by husbanding artillery resources for Flanders he denied Sir Henry Rawlinson, commander of the British Fourth Army on the Somme, the guns he needed to break through.[30] It also seems certain, however, that neither Haig nor his staff had a very deep understanding or appreciation for the artillery.[31]

Logically enough, Rawlinson worried that too much was being asked of his infantry. One of his corps commanders reviewing prebattle plans warned against "losing the substance by grasping at the shadow, a mistake that has been made too often in this war."[32] Indeed both the British and French had reached for grandiose operational and strategic "shadows" at Neuve Chapelle, Loos, Vimy Ridge, and Campagne in 1915 but lost sight of the "substance" in failing to solve tactical dilemmas. To its credit French High Command tried to adjust already in 1915 and then continued to do so in 1916. Thus the French Sixth Army, although only three frontline corps, went into the Somme with more than three times the highest allied density of heavy guns per frontline/first-wave division in 1915, which also more than tripled what the British took into the Somme—110 versus 33—and indeed was even higher than the Germans at Verdun—110 versus 92 (although the weight of shells still favored Verdun). Like Falkenhayn trying to improvise impenetrable defensive structures, Joffre also experimented in the race for a war-ending revolution in military affairs. Even though Rawlinson packed his divisions somewhat tighter—unit frontages of 2,000 versus roughly 3,000 meters for the French—Sixth Army still boasted twice the front-density of heavies, lighter-caliber cannon, and shells of all kinds, including the devastating high explosive rounds.

An artillery bombardment began on June 24 and lasted for a week. On the British side about 1,600 guns rained down 1.6 million shells on German deep dugouts along the curves of a 29-kilometer front. With French frontage included the line ran nearly 45 kilometers, the most ambitious "dam break" attack to date against Falkenhayn's killing zones. Although trenches were damaged at places, numerous artillery batteries destroyed, and thousands of soldiers killed, the British cannonade is generally considered to have been a failure. For one thing, less than 8 percent of the weight of shells fired was high-explosive, and even this, although much more effective on barbed wire, did less damage than British commanders anticipated on the trenches, "flinging upwards," writes John Keegan, "a visually impressive mass of surface material and an aurally terrifying shower of steel splinters but transmitting a proportionately quite trifling concussion downwards towards the hiding places of the German trench garrisons."[33] About two-thirds of the shells expended, moreover, came from light field guns firing shrapnel designed to spray lethally inside the trenches. This had little effect, however, for the defenders were thirty feet underground. Shrapnel also did limited damage to the barbed wire belts in front of the trenches—in fact at most places along the line shrapnel shelling merely heaved the wire up in the air, entangling it even more than before. Exacerbating matters, Haig insisted on a deep bombardment of German positions, thus dissipating the strength of his guns. French liaison officers were especially critical of this "dispersed and wasted"[34] gunfire. The tragic end result was that much of the German infantry, although dazed and weary after days of this kind of explosive mechanistic torture, survived to man the parapets and shoot their machine guns when the BEF attacked.

On July 1, 1916, fourteen British and five French divisions went forward north and south of the Somme. In the rear twelve allied infantry divisions plus a huge cavalry force stood ready to exploit the hoped-for breakthrough. The German Second Army defended its trench networks with six frontline divisions and five in reserve, plus abundant artillery. Because the French employed superior artillery and better technique and the defensive positions between Hardecourt and Dompierre were weaker, the first and second trench lines fell here (i.e., on the allied right). Benefiting from the French cannonade (and also encountering lighter resistance), the two southernmost British divisions (13th Corps) advancing left of the French made their day's objective of taking the first line.

To the north, however, British infantrymen paid a steep price for their artillery's failure. German machine gun crews opened a blistering fire—the guns shot so fast and so long that the water in water-cooling mechanisms boiled away.[35] One brigadier of British 8th Corps assaulting Serre proudly described the tactics of his doomed lead regiment without seeming to realize that such techniques had no place in 1916: "They advanced in line after line, dressed as if on parade, and not a man shirked going through the extremely heavy barrage, or facing the machine gun and rifle fire that finally wiped them out." Sadly, writes Tim Travers, the "late 19th-century ideal of war had bumped up against the new technology of war, but had not really engaged gears."[36] To be sure, the latest research shows that some of Britain's eighty lead battalions did not advance shoulder to shoulder but rather used flexible, logical tactics, rushing here, crouching there, others moving up slowly and safely in tighter formations behind gradually advancing "creeping" artillery barrages—one of the first instances of this. But it made little difference. Battalion after battalion got caught up in the barbed wire and mowed down. Other units raced for the few spots where the wire belts had been successfully breached. This created bottlenecks as troops packed tighter and tighter together into these gaps, which became a killing ground. The maxims cut down not only the first wave but also tightly packed second and third wave units waiting behind British lines for their turn to attack—about 18,000 British soldiers were killed or wounded like this before they could deploy. In most of this northern sector by day's end only one small portion of the German first line had been taken. About 20,000 British infantrymen lay dead and another 40,000 wounded. French losses totaled 7,000—about one-third the British casualty rate. The first day of the Somme was not a complete military failure, but it was a human catastrophe—the worst one-day losses in British history.

In subsequent days British commanders Haig and Rawlinson continued the attacks. By mid-July their battered regiments, finally using more heavies with high explosive rounds,[37] pressed to the German second line in the center of the battlefield, actually breaking through it at Mametz Wood. As the month wore on, Falkenhayn rushed division after division to the hard-pressed German Second Army—altogether fourteen came, some from neighboring armies, most from OHL's depleted western front reserve. He also transferred heavy artillery from Fifth Army at Verdun, which received orders to stop offensive action.

The Somme was now the main battle of attrition in the west, claiming two hundred thousand allied casualties by early August. The Germans had lost nearly as many, however, due to the punishing initial bombardment and Falkenhayn's insistence on repeated counterattacks to reclaim lost portions of the line. Nearly four hundred airplanes bombed and strafed German trenches, furthermore, bleeding the defenders "like lemons in a press."[38] Forced to abandon original plans for pushing the BEF into the sea—indeed Falkenhayn's entire operational scheme for the western front lay in tatters—the kaiser finally dismissed his General Staff chief in late August.

But the Battle of the Somme raged on. The most critical moment for OHL occurred in September when Haig, finally responding nicely to the RMA challenge,

Ready for the Spoils of War King Ferdinand of Rumania Reviews His Troops
Harper's Pictorial Library

employed a new weapon, the "tank," to spearhead a drive through the German third line of trenches between Flers and Les Boeufs. Altogether thirty-six of these 28-ton caterpillar-track vehicles, some armed with machine guns, some with cannon, rumbled into No Man's Land, terrifying infantrymen who initially found no way to stop the metallic monsters. Tank breakdowns and German artillery fire eventually halted this push, patched what was momentarily a dangerous breach in the third and last trench network, and restored the deadly stalemate on the Somme. When Haig called off his offensive later that autumn the allies had suffered a staggering 600,000 casualties, the Germans perhaps 500,000.

RUMANIA ENTERS THE WAR

By the time tanks made their frightening debut on the Somme in September 1916, Russia's great offensive in the east had come to a halt. Brusilov pressed forward with simultaneous attacks in Galicia and farther north in the Pripet Marshes that summer, forcing Falkenhayn, in one of his last decisions at OHL, to hurry more than fifteen divisions from west to east during a lull on the Somme in August. By now Brusilov had also lost the element of surprise and was experiencing difficulty bringing up supplies. Thus his casualties mounted. The Pripet campaign of General Alexei Evert was especially costly, for he abandoned Brusilov's more innovative tactics and sent wave after wave of doomed infantrymen into German rifle, machine gun, and heavy artillery fire. The Russian army had demonstrated that it was still quite capable of taking the offensive, but with a million men dead, wounded, or missing since June, and no breakthroughs in either north or south, *Stavka* had to suspend operations in this theater.

Rumania's declaration of war against the Central Powers on August 27 contributed to *Stavka's* decision by forcing it to extend the front southward from Galicia.

A series of faulty prewar assumptions would exacerbate Bucharest's ill-fated war effort. Ten days before entering the fray France and Britain promised Rumania Transylvania and neighboring portions of Hungary after an allied victory in the war. Because of this (as it turned out) disingenuous offer, Rumania committed three armies (First, Second, and Fourth) to an offensive in Transylvania—over three hundred thousand men, more than half of its 45-division army. Success depended on fulfilling two necessary preconditions: first, that the allied force building in Salonika would be able to tie down most of the Bulgarian army in the south, and second, that Evert's ongoing assault would prevent Austro-Hungarian and German reinforcements from rushing to Transylvania.[39]

Neither of these prerequisites was met. Well before the Rumanian offensive unfolded in late August a joint Bulgarian-German-Turkish strike force preempted the advance of Maurice Sarrail's Army of the Orient out of Thessaly by smashing the Serbian contingent at Florina and pushing far into Greece, thereby delaying the main offensive for almost a month. When this offensive finally got under way, moreover, it made only limited gains before bogging down. Although this multinational allied force boasted French, British, Italian, Serbian, and Russian contingents, mountainous terrain, Bulgarian trenches, and German reinforcements proved largely insurmountable—only the Serbian town of Monastir fell. This setback allowed another German/Bulgarian contingent, the so-called Danube Army led by an able German commander, August von Mackensen, to press into southeastern Rumania, reaching the outskirts of Constanza on the Black Sea by late September. Poorly equipped and trained, Rumania's seven divisions offered little assistance to the three Russian divisions that had been sent to bolster this front. The massive fortress of Turtukai surrendered just one day after learning of Mackensen's approach.

In Transylvania, meanwhile, the main body of the Rumanian army moved far into the region but then halted before limited resistance. OHL exploited this opportunity and the petering out of Brusilov's offensive by rapidly assembling a new Ninth Army under the recently demoted Falkenhayn—Rumania's declaration of war, in fact, had precipitated his fall. With two hundred thousand men, he launched a counterattack on September 18. Almost nothing, therefore, had gone as Bucharest planned.

As late summer drew on into the fall, Rumania paid the heaviest price for these miscalculations. Falkenhayn's Ninth Army pushed through the passes of the Transylvanian Alps onto the Wallachian plains and approached Bucharest from the west, while another contingent of Mackensen's Danube Army crossed the river at Sistova and pressed relentlessly toward the capital. With no relief coming from the allied Army of the Orient in the south—heavy autumn rains sapped most of the remaining momentum from this drive—Rumania counterattacked before Bucharest in late November, but to no avail. The city fell on December 6. Dobruja, the rich province between the Danube and Black Sea, had been completely overrun in the meantime. Having lost three hundred thousand men since the war began, the tattered remnants of Rumania's forces, mainly Fourth Army, withdrew into Moldavia to link up with Russian units.

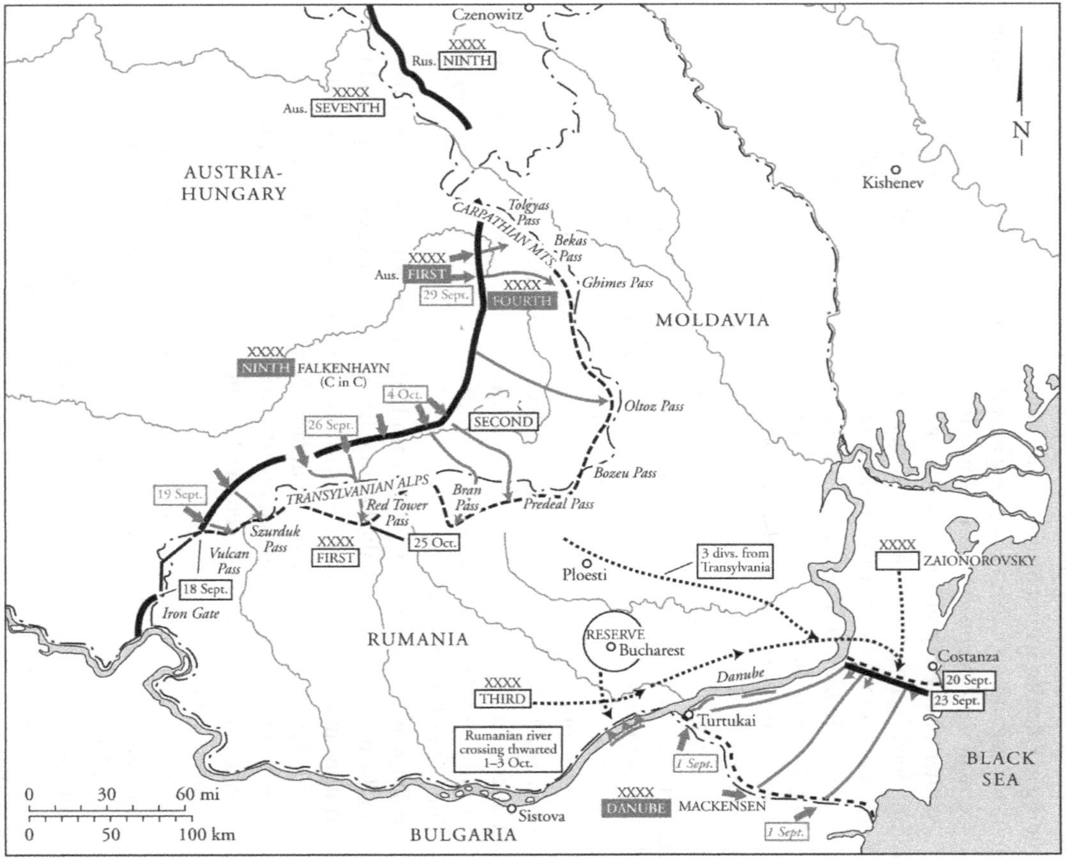

The Fall of Rumania in 1916

Maps Courtesy of the Department of History, United States Military Academy

The Central Powers now occupied the bulk of Rumania and stripped it of food, oil, and other resources, thus ameliorating somewhat the effects of the allied blockade. For Vienna and Berlin the Rumanian campaign was the lone bright spot, however, in what had been a disappointing year. There had been no smashing of the French and British, as Falkenhayn intended. Conrad had not knocked Italy out of the war. Russia, contrary to OHL's assumptions, had indeed mounted a major offensive. In fact, even the Central Power triumph over Rumania came at a price due to the fact that German and Austro-Hungarian divisions were now spread even thinner over the European theater of the Great War. Moreover, it was clear that no Jihad would flame up in the Middle East and Central Asia, at least punishing the British somewhere in the war. On the contrary, an Arab revolt against the Turks and a British offensive out of Egypt (see chap. 9) threatened to tip the balance further in Britain's favor. Finally, as explained presently, home fronts in Germany and Austria-Hungary were weakening. Berlin and Vienna found only a little consolation in the desperate hope that Entente home fronts would crack sooner.

VERDUN, GERMAN POLITICS, AND THE SUBMARINE DECISION

As the late summer and autumn campaigns of 1916 in Rumania, Galicia, Poland, and the Somme came to their ends, the killing at Verdun went grimly, relentlessly, murderously on. The French, having taken the offensive in July, pounded back at Fleury and Thiaumont, which changed hands repeatedly in August and September before the Germans finally withdrew. "By the end of the summer," observes Alistair Horne, "all that remained of Fleury (once a village of 500 people) was a white smear visible only from the air—the sole recognizable object found on its site a silver chalice from the church." Fort Douaumont was retaken on October 24, Fort Vaux on November 2, and other forts on December 15 that were only a few kilometers from the German jumping-off positions of February. After these latter actions both sides, exhausted by now, gave up the fight.

Although estimates of casualties vary widely, it seems fairly certain that total French losses approached half a million, German around four hundred thousand. "Who had 'won' the Battle of Verdun?" asks Horne. Pointing to the phraseology of official and unofficial histories on each side, he tips the scales convincingly toward France, whose writers described "the glory" of successfully defending home soil, whereas German authors emphasized "the tragedy"[40] of the battle.

For Germany, in fact, Verdun was equal parts military *and political* debacle. Although it was logical that Crown Prince William's Fifth Army command these operations—Verdun lay in his sector—Falkenhayn and other dedicated monarchists wanted the bleeding of the French to bolster crown authority. It was to be a great "newspaper victory," wrote Karl von Einem, commander of Third Army. When William failed to break through, however, common soldiers and civilians alike began to blame him for "the evil events of Verdun." It would have been better "for the monarchical principle,"[41] thought Einem, had Falkenhayn transferred

Called to Lead: Hindenburg and Ludendorff on the Way to Castle Pless in August 1916
Harper's Pictorial Library

the crown prince east where victories were being won. The prince's dissolute, womanizing behavior exacerbated the situation, for the rank and file learned of it and wrote nasty letters home about the intolerable contrast between his easy salacious life and the constant threats to theirs. Becoming more malicious with every retelling, these reports and rumors spread throughout the army until

Hindenburg, Falkenhayn's replacement, ordered all unit commanders to squelch the notion of Crown Prince William's guilt for the defeat at Verdun. Making matters worse, however, was the coincidence of these acidic complaints with the onset of serious grumbling over inadequate and decreasing food rations, whose aggregate caloric content fell by 20–25 percent during the war—numbers that were exacerbated in the harder-to-supply frontlines. Thus the British blockade began to sow distrust between German soldiers and their better-fed middle-level staff officers behind the front.[42]

Verdun also dragged Kaiser William into its delegitimizing quagmire. As the death toll of battle rose, he led the good life of multicourse meals, card games, and horse riding at Villa Bellaire, his opulent newly renovated estate near Sedan, or at the scores of royal palaces owned by the superrich Hohenzollern family in Germany. Servants in these mansions who faced all kinds of blockade-related hardships began to break their occupation's code of confidentiality in 1916 and gossip about the monarch's unacceptable lifestyle. As these stories mingled with letters from Verdun about the crown prince, artillery duels, and horrible carnage—even the unflappable Hindenburg admitted that Verdun was "a regular hell"—the kaiser's popularity among the people fell precipitously, particularly after summer did not bring victory at Verdun. Remembering earlier rosy predictions of victory, the popular mood soured. "We have fostered an evil optimism whose prophecies could never be fulfilled,"[43] wrote one journalist. As the summer and the battle wore on, William showed no more of a caring paternal side to his workers and soldiers. Accordingly, he lost still more respect and esteem.

Although the Social Democratic Party of Germany (SPD) and other reform-oriented parties felt these popular pressures and intensified pressure on Bethmann for legislative concessions, it was not the left but rather the political right that mounted the most serious assault on monarchical legitimacy. Right-radical nationalist organizations like the Pan German League and the German Defense League had long doubted the kaiser's ability to make the tough domestic and foreign policy decisions required of a leader in a struggle for both European and world power. His backing of Bethmann on submarine warfare and dismissal of Admiral Tirpitz, followed by the attrition of Verdun, however, galvanized the Pan Germans into a determined propaganda campaign against the throne. They flooded kiosks, cigar stores, barbershops, and corner pubs with thousands of pamphlets that scurrilously attacked William. The allegedly crazed, "half-English" monarch refused to unleash the zeppelins and submarines against England, it was said, because he had deposited a fortune in the Bank of England. German men died needlessly at Verdun, they charged, because of these pro-English sympathies. By August 1916 police had searched homes, seized papers, and made arrests, but the damage done was irreversible. Officials in the Reich Chancellery reported that rightist venom had weakened the people's will and "undermined state authority—above all crown authority—in a highly dangerous fashion."[44]

While the public image of the monarch continued to erode, the appointment of Hindenburg as chief of the General Staff and Ludendorff as second in command in late August 1916 further undermined William's authority behind the scenes. Of the two, Hindenburg was more reverent to his sovereign, but the larger-than-life popularity of the victor of Tannenberg offended the kaiser, which was the main reason the sensitive ruler held onto Falkenhayn, a personal favorite, long after Verdun had ruined the general's stature in the army and on the streets. Because Hindenburg had little patience for William's military amateurishness, however, he excluded him from army matters even more radically than Falkenhayn had done. Whereas Hindenburg was thus quite comfortable with the "silent dictatorship"[45] that now commenced, Ludendorff, the middle-class technocrat, held the unfortunate monarch in such barely concealed contempt that he sympathized with rightist schemes for eventually establishing full-fledged military rule. Despite William's awareness of his generals' low opinion of their sovereign, Hindenburg and Ludendorff remained virtually "untouchable" from above due to the widespread conviction in Germany that they would guide the war effort more competently than Falkenhayn, a feeling shared not only throughout the army but initially also by Bethmann and most of the Reichstag, even among the reformist parties and many of their lower-class constituents. It was a "good feeling" to know that the army had a firmer grip on the country, wrote General Einem, and that "no king or emperor can do anything about it."[46]

Although the ascent of Hindenburg and Ludendorff bolstered state authority in Germany despite the considerable controversy and dissension generated by their domestic policies (discussed later), the legitimacy of William II slipped further. For one thing, Hindenburg clearly overshadowed William II, much as Bismarck had done with William I, and such circumstances did nothing to boost the sovereign's image, either in the eyes of the people or the army. Much the same could be said of Ludendorff, certainly among upper- and middle-class nationalists but deep into the working class too. Against him, the "eminently competent, clever, and energetic one," recalled one officer, "there could be no protest." If anyone had tried to unseat him, "even if it were the Kaiser," he would have been "branded by the people as the instigator of defeat, then stoned—so deeply entrenched was the trust of the people and the troops in Ludendorff." The kaiser continued to be a public relations liability, moreover, by staying away from Germany and leading the good life with his entourage. Aware of the political problems this caused, and mindful of Russia's domestic crisis, a conference of military and civilian officials recommended in the spring of 1917 that the kaiser visit the bedsides of the wounded and homes of the poor and listen to the complaints of workers. But nothing changed, prompting one right-wing extremist to warn officials "how soldiers at the front and at home, in clinics and on leave, how people on the street talk about His Majesty when anything in the least sets them off."[47] The tactless, insensitive behavior of the crown prince made matters even worse, for throughout the winter of 1916–1917, while soldiers died and people struggled through subzero weather on low food and fuel rations, he constructed a conspicuously lavish new mansion outside Potsdam.

Nor did the widespread popular endorsement of the army's new leadership survive entirely unscathed. This was due mainly to OHL's reactionary, antilabor bent. Indeed Ludendorff and his chief aide, the dynamic radical nationalist Max Bauer, not only sympathized with Pan German criticism of the kaiser's weakness but also with that organization's long-standing anger over the nation's alleged drift to the political left under Bethmann's chancellorship. As professional warriors caught up in a worldwide power struggle, Ludendorff and Bauer believed fervently, in fact almost fanatically, that the needs of common men and women and the demands of their special interest trade unions and parties had to be ruthlessly subordinated to the needs and demands of the nation at war. Their reactionary mind-set included the one-sided notion that big business should receive everything it required, including higher prices and first claim to raw materials, in order to double and triple munitions and weapons production under the "Hindenburg Program" of September 1916, whose primary authors they were. Arguing that a laborer's work in the armaments industry was as crucial as a soldier's sacrifice at the front, on the other hand, Ludendorff and Bauer sought to militarize labor with the draconian Auxiliary Service Law they presented to the Reichstag in November 1916. Workers between the ages of seventeen and sixty would be conscripted for war service on the home front. To cut down on labor turnover as workers left one firm for higher wages in another, the freedom to change jobs would also be drastically curtailed. It was "high time" to silence the "screamers and agitators" and end the "screaming injustice" of labor looking out only for itself. "The entire German people should live only in the service of the Fatherland."[48]

Parliament accepted many of these measures but radically transformed the bill by giving trade unions the right to organize in war industries, legalizing collective bargaining and establishing labor-management committees to "co-determine" disputes over wages and work conditions. The High Command had no choice but to comply with the Reichstag majority in order to prevent a leftist backlash and accompanying strikes and disruption of armaments production but now began to blame the trade unions and their parliamentary supporters in the SPD, the leftist Progressive Party, and the moderate Center Party for selfishly undermining the war effort.

The so-called stab-in-the-back legend—the accusation that the home front had betrayed the battlefront—was born. Thus the anti-Semitic Bauer, incensed by what he saw as growing leftist pressure for democratization, complained bitterly that the longer the war lasted the more the government was being "terrorized by Jewish progressivism and international [i.e., Marxist] comrades." The military must seek a quick, victorious end to the war by all available means, including unrestricted submarine warfare, rather than permit the increasingly labor-oriented Reichstag to pull Germany into a democratic swamp as the war went on and on. "Of what purpose are all these sacrifices [at the front] in order finally to end up being smothered by Judaism and Proletarianism?"[49] Jews and socialists, ethnic enemies and advocates of a topsy-turvy social order, could be put in their place once Germany smashed its external enemies and these internal foes had no more wartime political leverage.

This angry political motivation fueling demands for unrestricted U-boat warfare added an extra sense of urgency—indeed a desperate, irrational urgency—to

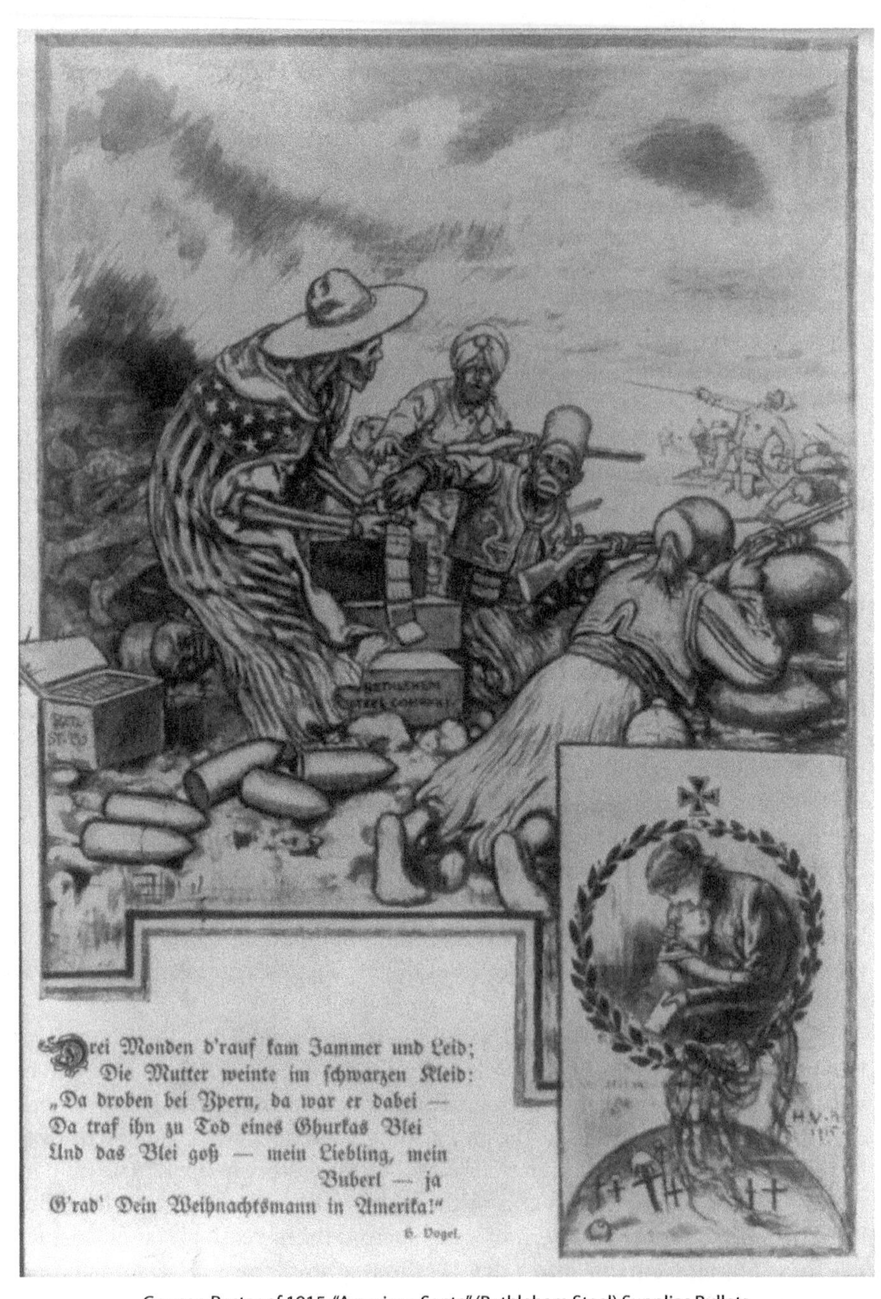

German Poster of 1915: "American Santa" (Bethlehem Steel) Supplies Bullets to British Imperial Troops at Ypres

Courtesy of the Library of Congress

all of the purely military arguments for unleashing the submarines. The German army had been stretched to its limits in 1916, fighting bloody campaigns in Rumania, Galicia, Poland, and France. The allegiance of Austria-Hungary, Bulgaria, and Turkey was certainly welcome, but the Central Powers faced a superior coalition that fielded many more divisions and held a distinct advantage in munitions production, a firepower superiority that grew most worrisome to the German High Command during the Battle of the Somme. The munitions problem alone, in fact, seemed to justify using submarines to undercut the British supply of shells. As Ludendorff put it when contemplating what 1917 might bring, the army "needed to be spared a second Battle of the Somme."[50] Because end-of-the-year peace initiatives by Bethmann and U.S. President Wilson had failed—feelers that the High Command did not want to succeed—the war would drag on into a fourth year, and perhaps ultimately a fifth, unless the U-boats produced a quick victory.

And without the subs, how long could Germany survive Britain's "hunger blockade"? As 1916 turned to 1917, caloric intake, which had already begun to fall in late 1914, slid to about a third of prewar consumption levels.[51] Money, connections, and the black market helped the lucky ones, but even the upper crust suffered. "We are all gaunt and bony now," said one noblewoman. "We have dark shadows around our eyes and our thoughts are chiefly taken up with wondering what our next meal will be."[52] Pork had almost disappeared from dinner tables and restaurants, where crow was now served; milk was reserved almost exclusively for young children; butter and sugar could be purchased in only very small quantities; eggs were rationed at two per person per month; and turnips and rutabagas had begun to replace potatoes. The rutabaga, next to the humiliation of eating animal fodder, was a particularly "loathsome guest": most people "found its texture stringy, its smell vile, its taste worse."[53] Inevitably as nutrition levels fell bodies succumbed to a variety of ailments like rickets, scurvy, dysentery, tuberculosis, and influenza. Estimates place the number of blockade-related deaths by war's end at 730,000, which makes popular outrage understandable. In working-class Hamburg authorities reported riots in the autumn of 1916 "by the poor classes, mainly women," who cried "down with the kaiser" and shouted for an end to the war. The rioters wanted to end the war, however, by winning it quickly with submarines against hated England and its food blockade, and they also spewed venom against America for trading with Germany's enemies.[54] Despite the widening rift between Germany's military and leftist elements over issues of labor and democratic reforms, therefore, the U-boat question cut across another plane and tended to unite more than it divided. It was clearly no simple matter.

The military, political, and social arguments for declaring unlimited submarine warfare seemed so compelling to Hindenburg, Ludendorff, Bauer, and Holtzendorff, nevertheless, that they closed their minds to all counterarguments. Did Germany possess enough submarines to end the British war effort in six months as the navy promised? Would the American army, navy, merchant marine, and tremendous industrial and financial capacity outweigh any harm done to Britain? "Your plan will lead to ruin," said one of Bethmann's ministers to Holtzendorff. "You are letting us drift to ruin," replied the admiral. "I don't give a damn about America,"[55] scoffed Ludendorff. As in 1914, Germany's leading warriors were prepared to roll the iron dice and gamble high stakes on victory.

HOME FRONT POLITICS IN AUSTRIA-HUNGARY, ITALY, AND RUSSIA

As witnessed by Germany's political dynamic, the war ratcheted up the emotions of people who lived through it, complicating feelings, stirring up violent thoughts and actions, and generating alarming levels of hate. The phenomenon so typical of 1914 and 1915 of just hating the enemy transformed itself in the course of 1915 and 1916 into a multifaceted damning of not only the enemy but also rulers and governments that sent hundreds of thousands of men to horrible deaths, or conversely, people who appeared to lack the patriotism, endurance, manliness, and racial purity necessary for a fight to the finish. Long and costly wars radicalize everything they touch, especially in countries that enter such conflicts with weighty political baggage.

This was certainly the case with Germany's long-standing monarchical ally, Austria-Hungary. To be sure, the Dual Monarchy's head of state avoided the kinds of personal scandals that surrounded the throne in Germany. Whereas scathing criticisms of those at the top undermined the legitimacy of the Hohenzollerns, Habsburg Kaiser Francis Joseph retained the respect of his people. Still widely revered in 1916 after sixty-two years on the throne as a competent, hardworking ruler and man of upstanding morals, the fragile octogenarian's good character served as at least one stabilizing force.

Francis Joseph's archconservatism, however, as manifested particularly in his retention of reactionary ministers, certainly undid much of what his personality accomplished for the survival of this unstable state. Rigid censorship and the unwillingness of Austrian Prime Minister Karl Stürgkh to convene parliament exacerbated the stress and misery associated with escalating casualties and worsening food shortages caused by the blockade. In the Hungarian half of the monarchy Prime Minister Istvan Tisza's refusal to grant universal manhood suffrage aggravated matters. "The Hungarian soldier in the trenches does not care about voting," mocked Tisza callously.

Indeed, without any political venting mechanisms in Austria and Hungary the war's mounting unpopularity threatened to topple the regime. Official prowar propaganda depicting a high degree of popular enthusiasm "has become a travesty of the innermost feelings of the people," declared a socialist newspaper, "and stands in sharpest opposition to secret general opinion."[56] Urban bread riots in 1916 led by angry women who protested against a seemingly uncaring establishment better reflected the harsh reality. So too did the restaurant murder that November of Stürgkh by a disaffected socialist who wanted to draw attention to the miserable plight of common people. An eyewitness that autumn noticed

> [queues] of poorly dressed women and children held in line by police waiting for milk, vessel in hand. Latecomers went home empty-handed, while lucky ones obtained only half as much as they expected.

Similar lines could be observed "in the morning hours in front of bakers' shops and stores where coffee, tea, and sugar are being sold." Indeed when it was reported that Stürgkh had lunched on mushroom soup, boiled beef with turnips, pudding, and wine the shooting of the already unpopular man "evoked little public sympathy."[57]

Furthermore, the high missing rate among soldiers of subject nationalities who clearly did not want to fight for a state that refused to grant them the same rights of autonomy given to Hungary in 1867 presaged the breakup of the empire desired by Czechoslovak and Yugoslav secessionists. Surrender and desertion, isolated phenomena in 1914, grew worse in 1915 and then became epidemic in 1916 and 1917. Fully 28 percent of all soldiers mobilized went missing in the Great War, the highest rate of any belligerent nation, higher even than Russia (22 percent), whose war effort was equally disastrous.

The kaiser sensed the bleak reality of things better than his top ministers. "The starving people can't stand much more," he said in July 1916. Francis Joseph doubted, in fact, whether his armies and subjects could endure another winter of war. "I mean to end the war next spring, whatever happens, for I can't let my realm go to hopeless ruin."[58] The passing of this lone stabilizing personage in November 1916 triggered an inevitable legitimacy crisis as a torrent of protests, partially stifled until that autumn, gushed forth about incompetent military leadership, the army's dictatorial rule, and the people's increasingly unbearable hardships. These outcries, accompanied by strikes and riots, peaked in March 1917 with the electrifying news of even worse troubles in Russia.

Wanting to avoid revolution, Kaiser Karl, great-nephew of the assassinated Francis Ferdinand, wisely decided to convene parliament in Vienna. Worried as his illustrious predecessor had been that Austria-Hungary would disintegrate if the war continued for much longer, the young emperor sent peace feelers to the French through his brother-in-law, Prince Sixte of Bourbon. By the time German Center Party parliamentarian Matthias Erzberger visited Vienna in late April 1917, however, Germany's unrestricted submarine campaign was in high gear, domestic unrest had subsided, and Charles had backed away from the notion of deserting Germany. But he warned Erzberger that the empire could not survive another winter of fighting. An early peace was imperative. For peace talks to get under way, furthermore, Germany must agree to scale back aggressive war aims.[59]

Across the Alps in the Entente camp, Italian politics also simmered close to the boiling point. This was not surprising, for the war had been controversial from the start.[60] Rome's declaration of war against Austria-Hungary in May 1915 was the product of an odd coalition of political forces. Interventionists of upper-class imperialist stripe eager to expand national territory into Dalmatia and Asia Minor found support for the war from antiannexationist democrats and radical leftists who saw the conflict mainly as a revolutionary crusade against authoritarian regimes in Berlin and Vienna—and in Rome too. But the far more numerous and well-organized Italian Socialist Party (PSI), grassroots Catholic organizations, and the Vatican itself had argued against war before Italy intervened and then gave at best only halfhearted backing to Cadorna's bloody offensives in the

Beyond the Isonzo: Italian Artillery Prepare to Dislodge the Austrians
Harper's Pictorial Library

north, and in some cases, especially in PSI ranks, spread antiwar propaganda among rural farmhands and blue-collar factory workers.

Wary of antiwar opponents in parliament and the press, and also not trusting maverick populist prowar radicals whose goals were far too far-reaching, Prime Minister Antonio Salandra and Foreign Minister Sidney Sonnino controlled the war behind closed doors and gave army commander in chief Cadorna mostly free rein throughout 1915 and early 1916. Rigid press censorship, stark curtailment of rights of assembly, drastic restrictions on labor mobility, and draconian army control of armaments works meant little difference in practice between democratic Italy and authoritarian Germany and Austria-Hungary.

No amount of policing and patriotic chest-thumping could prevent antiwar propaganda from slipping into the army, however, or transform some Italians, who complained that their country had not been attacked, into war enthusiasts. These circumstances often brought officers face to face with one of their worst nightmares—soldiers arguing in the ranks over the war itself. Thus after one of the most outspoken left-wing advocates of intervening in the war, Filippo Corridoni, was killed in action during Third Isonzo (November 1915), one grumbling private sought out Private Benito Mussolini, whose prowar views were also widely publicized, to relay the "good news" of Corridoni's death. The Austrians "did well, it pleases me. Damn them all, these interventionists."[61] Mussolini would have shot the man had a sergeant not appeared.

The threat of force had prevented chaos in the ranks, but unfortunately for the Italian officer corps the grumblers outnumbered the Corridonis and Mussolinis. More often than not in early 1916, in fact, only immediate threats like this, and the specter of battle police and court-martial, moved men on the brutal frozen Isonzo front to move out to attack. That two-thirds of all recruits hailed from the impoverished, semiliterate south of Italy reinforced the perceived need to impose the harshest form of discipline. Uprooted from locales that meant more to them than the concept of Italy, they had little or no understanding for why the war was being fought and consequently exhibited no patriotic enthusiasm. Over a third of a million Italian soldiers, about 6 percent of all men mobilized, were brought before military tribunals in the war with half found guilty. "It is vital to cut off the evil at its roots," said Cadorna, "and it is to be hoped that we have done so in time."[62]

During the winter of 1915–1916 Cadorna attempted two more times to smash through Austrian positions and two more times he failed. As casualties went up, war fervor, as one would expect, went down. Austria's invasion of the Trentino finally galvanized Salandra's enemies in parliament to vote him out of office in June 1916, but politics in Italy remained turbulent and tense. Paolo Boselli, a right-of-center moderate, put together a national government of sorts that attempted to bridge political fissure lines. In order to demonstrate the government's "purity of interventionist faith" to Italian nationalists and Triple Entente allies, he retained General Cadorna and Foreign Minister Sonnino. To further allay fears that Rome would sue for peace the new leadership declared war on Germany in August 1916. The cabinet's support for the war remained dubious, however, with many ministers having ties to those circles that had favored neutrality in 1915. Fairly typical was the slogan of the PSI, which supported but did not participate officially in the Boselli government: "Oppose the war, but do not sabotage it." Not surprisingly, relations between cabinet members and the hawkish Cadorna worsened as the latter became convinced that Rome pandered to defeatist "enemies within."[63]

Trying to Maintain Discipline: General Luigi Cadorna (center-front) Inspects His Troops
Harper's Pictorial Library

Indeed in July 1916 as the insensitive general lost 148,000 men in his counterattack, followed it with Sixth Isonzo in August, and then Seventh, Eighth, Ninth, Tenth, and Eleventh as 1916 stretched well into 1917, popular willingness to support the war sagged badly. In the autumn of 1916 the Catholic press and lay organizations called for peace talks, while Benedict XV expressed his sorrow for "a people madly oppressed by this regrettable war." In December 1916 the PSI introduced a peace resolution in parliament; by spring there were bread riots in Turin and Lombardy; in Milan the socialists threatened a general strike. Cadorna railed against these "assaults of cowardice and hesitation from the interior," then turned blue with rage when socialist pamphlets, proclaiming "next winter not another man in the trenches,"[64] turned up among his troops. But how long could the army hold together amidst so much war-weariness and longing for peace?

Russia had a veritable plague of home front woes. A backlog of unsolved political problems from before the war—peasant land hunger, urban labor misery, political suppression, and corruption in high places: the proverbial rotting fish "stinking from the head"—grew exponentially after 1914 as a result of the country's unimaginable suffering and sacrifice. Falkenhayn had misjudged the ability of the Russian army to attack in 1916, but there can be little doubt that the huge losses of that year's offensive brought the army dangerously close to this point and probably beyond it, making even defensive action a doubtful proposition. Survivors fortunate enough to have avoided the fate of those millions of comrades who had been killed or horribly wounded grumbled about low rations of bad food, icy trenches, the irregularity of leave, and the wretched welfare of their families. They scoffed at war profiteers, landlords, and shirkers who sat out the war and generals who urged their men forward by promising decisive victories that never occurred. Instead, inept leaders escaped death, so common in the ranks, as whole provinces like Poland with all its expensively stocked fortresses fell to the enemy. Officers close to the rank and file reported "an overwhelming desire for peace whatever the consequences." Alexei Brusilov, whose troops in Galicia had achieved the most success of any Russian army group, recalled receiving unsigned letters from soldiers warning him "that they did not want any more fighting, and that if peace was not concluded shortly, I should be killed."[65]

The overwhelming majority of people back home shared these pacifist sentiments. Indeed as early as 1915 angry subjects in St. Petersburg and many provincial cities had staged massive antiwar protests. Soldiers' wives and relatives mobbed draft offices and insisted that they spare husbands, brothers, and sons and call up the hated police instead. The disruptions accelerated in 1916 with an added layer of anger directed against Tsar Nicholas, who had taken personal command of the armies in 1915 at the behest of Tsarina Alexandra and her scandalous faith healer, Rasputin, unwisely ignoring ministerial advice that he would now be blamed personally for the ongoing slaughter. That somewhere between 3 and 6 million refugees were driven from their farms and homes in Poland as the Germans advanced, overtaxing the ability of the home front to feed and employ them, deepened Russia's home front crisis.

Workers had struck with renewed intensity in 1915 too, especially after police fired on textile operatives in Kostroma, killing and wounding scores of proletarians. Over 500,000 went on strike that year, followed by over 950,000 in 1916, and then two-thirds of a million in the first two months of 1917 alone—the highest level of labor unrest since the failed revolution of 1905–1906. By this time strikes were highly charged politically, agitators shouting "down with the monarchy" and "down with the war." Even Russia's enthusiastic "patriotic culture" retreated before the people's widespread revulsion against the seemingly endless bloodshed. The nationalistic wave of cartoons, posters, circus shows, cabaret acts, operettas, plays, and feature films that burst forth during the war's early campaigns became quite literally politically incorrect after the great retreat began. Popular culture turned to themes of hardship and suffering in 1916. The consensus among the most clear-thinking observers in positions of authority, in fact, was that revolution was rapidly approaching.[66]

As more and more Russian women experienced the ultimate hardship and donned the traditional black color of mourning, they and their families faced another bleak aspect of life on the home front—having enough to eat, especially in the cities. Grain, potato, and meat production declined by a third from 1914 to 1916 as war-induced labor shortages hampered operations on the big estates. Although this shortfall was largely mitigated by cutbacks in exports, food still grew scarce because peasants either hoarded grain or sold much of what they marketed to the army. A near breakdown in railroad transportation further aggravated the situation. Russia had relied on Western Europe for locomotives, cars, and spare parts before the war, but cut off from these imports after 1914, and lacking the machine tools (outside of the armament industry) to produce them, the number of engines and rolling stock plummeted as worn-out equipment could not be replaced. The decline in food sold to urban consumers, combined with transportation problems, created an emergency in cities and towns throughout European Russia. In St. Petersburg, for instance, where *minimally* 12,000 wagonloads of foodstuffs were required per month, less than 9,000 arrived in December 1916 and less than 7,000 in January 1917. Secret police reported early in the New Year that "children are starving in the most literal sense of the word." A revolution, "if it takes place, will be spontaneous," they concluded, "quite likely a hunger riot."[67] Adding to the people's misery, fuel for heating homes was also in short supply during one of the coldest winters on record. These were ominous signs—ominous signs indeed.

There were indications from Italy, but especially from Russia, therefore, that German and Austro-Hungarian hopes of the other side imploding first could come true.

NOTES

1. For the following, including citations, see Hugo von Reischach, *Under Three Emperors* (London, 1927), 260–261; Gordon A. Craig, *The Politics of the Prussian Army 1640–1945* (New York, 1956), 322, n. 1; Lamar Cecil, *Wilhelm II: Emperor and Exile, 1900–1941* (Chapel Hill, NC, 1996), 2:242–243; Holger H. Herwig, *The First World War: Germany and Austria-Hungary 1914–1918* (London, 1997), 312–317; and Robert K. Massie, *Castles of Steel: Britain, Germany, and the Winning if the Great War at Sea* (New York, 2003), 704–706.
2. Cited in Robert T. Foley, *German Strategy and the Path to Verdun: Erich von Falkenhayn and the Development of Attrition, 1870–1916* (Cambridge, UK, 2005), 182.
3. In his memoirs Falkenhayn published a "Christmas Memorandum" to the kaiser in which he surveyed the military situation in late 1915 and made arguments for how best to prosecute the war. In a fairly recent biography of Falkenhayn, Holger Afflerbach revived an old accusation from the 1920s that the memo was a fabrication (see his *Falkenhayn: Politisches Denken und Handeln im Kaiserreich* (Munich, Germany, 1994), 543–545). However, the most recent work by Robert Foley (see above, *German Strategy*, pp. 181–208) presents wartime evidence from other sources that verify much of what was in the memo. It seems reasonable to conclude, therefore, that the Christmas Memorandum, even if not actual, at the very least reflects the chief's genuine thoughts at the time. For a similar opinion, see Herwig, *First World War*, 180.
4. Cited in Foley, *German Strategy*, 189. Foley draw's on the diary entry of a general present at Falkenhayn's briefing of the kaiser on December 3, 1915. The plan to "bleed the French white" was one of the most unusual and controversial aspects of the Christmas Memorandum.
5. See Foley, *German Strategy*.
6. Cited in Herwig, *First World War*, 180.
7. See Cecil, *Wilhelm II*, 2:233–234.
8. For the Holtzendorff quote, see Holger H. Herwig, *'Luxury' Fleet: The Imperial German Navy 1888–1918* (London, 1991), 165. For the admiral's reasoning, see ibid., 218–219, 291. Also see Alfred von Tirpitz, *My Memoirs* (New York, 1919), 2:171–173.
9. Cited in Massie, *Castles of Steel*, 548.
10. Citations in Tirpitz, *My Memoirs*, 174; and Massie, *Castles of Steel*, 549.
11. For the early stage of the battle, see Alistair Horne, *The Price of Glory: Verdun 1916* (London, 1993), 41–124; Eric Dorn Brose, *The Kaiser's Army: The Politics of Military Technology in Germany during the Machine Age, 1870–1918* (New York, 2001), 228–229; and especially Foley, *German Strategy*, 193–227; and Robert A. Doughty, *Pyrrhic Victory: French Strategy and Operations in the Great War* (Cambridge, MA, 2005), 250–310.
12. Citations in Foley, *German Strategy*, 215, 195.

13. Horne, *Price of Glory*, 43.
14. Citations in Doughty, *Pyrrhic Victory*, 283; and Herwig, *First World War*, 194.
15. See Tirpitz, *My Memoirs*, 200; and Herwig, *'Luxury' Fleet*, 166.
16. Cited in Massie, *Castles of Steel*, 551.
17. See Herwig, *'Luxury' Fleet*, 172–173.
18. Citations in ibid., 177.
19. For the Battle of Jutland, see Richard Hough, *The Great War at Sea 1914–1918* (Oxford, 1983), 211–297; N. J. M. Campbell, *Jutland: An Analysis of the Fighting* (London, 1986); Paul G. Halpern, *A Naval History of World War I* (Annapolis, MD, 1994), 310–329; and Massie, *Castles of Steel*, 553–684.
20. Cited in Halpern, *Naval History*, 318.
21. Cited in Herwig, *'Luxury' Fleet*, 183.
22. Citations in Foley, *German Strategy*, 243; and Doughty, *Pyrrhic Victory*, 289.
23. For Chantilly (and the citations), see Doughty, *Pyrrhic Victory*, 251–252, and also 252–289. There is also good detail on allied plans in George H. Cassar, *Kitchener's War: British Strategy from 1914 to 1916* (Washington, DC, 2004), 264–274; and Robin Prior and Trevor Wilson, *The Somme* (New Haven, CT, 2005), 15–34.
24. See Denis Winter, *Haig's Command: A Reassessment* (Barnsley, UK, 2004), 45–67, originally published in 1991; and Prior and Wilson, *The Somme*, 28–31, 51.
25. For the offensive in Lithuania, subsequent Brusilov offensive (June–September 1916), and Russian economic mobilization, see Herwig, *First World War*, 208–219; Norman Stone, *The Eastern Front 1914–1917* (New York, 1975), 227–263; David R. Jones, "Imperial Russia's Forces at War," in Allan R. Millett and Williamson Murray, eds., *Military Effectiveness*, Vol. 1, *The First World War* (Boston, 1988), 306–308, 311–312; Hew Strachan, *The First World War* (Oxford, 2001), 1:1093–1104; and David Stevenson, *Cataclysm: The First World War as Political Tragedy* (New York, 2004), 159–160, 193–194.
26. For the citations and the campaign, see Herwig, *First World War*, 204–207.
27. See Foley, *German Strategy*, 242–251.
28. For the Battle of the Somme, see Cyril Falls' still useful *The Great War 1914–1918* (New York, 1959), 195–208; John Keegan, *The Face of Battle* (London, 1978), 167–236, and his *First World War*, 286–299; Winter, *Haig's Command*, 45–49, 58–67; Tim Travers, *The Killing Ground: The British Army, the Western Front and the Emergence of Modern Warfare 1900–1918* (London, 1987), 127–199; and more recently, Doughty, *Pyrrhic Victory*, 289–297; and especially Prior and Wilson, *The Somme*, 71–118.
29. Winston Churchill, *The World Crisis 1911–1918* (New York, 1931), 654.
30. This is the argument of Winter, *Haig's Command*, 45–67. Although the most recent study of the Somme, Prior and Wilson, *The Somme*, does not refer to Winter's work, the whole thrust of their analysis (see especially pp. 35–69) is consistent with his thesis. In particular, they note on p. 51 that penetrating to Douai was impossible without collapsing the entire German position in the north.
31. See Travers, *Killing Ground*, 135–139.
32. Cited in Prior and Wilson, *The Somme*, 41.
33. Cited in Keegan, *Face of Battle*, 194–195.
34. Cited in Doughty, *Pyrrhic Victory*, 294.
35. For this kind of Lyn Macdonald-style detail on the German side, see Jack Sheldon's well-researched *The German Army on the Somme 1914–1916* (Barnsley, UK, 2005), 142–143 (and for the whole battle, pp. 138–399).
36. Travers, *Killing Ground*, 145–146, and for the quote, 158.
37. See Paddy Griffith, *Battle Tactics of the Western Front: The British Army's Art of Attack 1916–1918* (New Haven, CT, 1994), 141.
38. Cited in Herwig, *First World War*, 203.

39. For Rumania's entry and military developments in the Balkans in 1916, see Alan Palmer, *The Gardeners of Salonika* (New York, 1965), 72–92; Barbara Jelavich, *History of the Balkans* (Cambridge, UK, 1983), 2:118–119; Herwig, *First World War*, 217–222; and Dennis E. Showalter, "Salonika," in Robert Cowley, ed., *The Great War: Perspectives on the First World War* (New York, 2003), 241–244.
40. Citations from Horne, *Price of Glory*, 301, 328.
41. Citations from Brose, *Kaiser's Army*, 230–231.
42. See Alexander Watson, *Enduring the Great War: Combat, Morale and Collapse in the German and British Armies, 1914–1918* (Cambridge, UK, 2008), 124–139.
43. Citations in ibid., 230, 233.
44. Cited in ibid., 234.
45. See the classic study by Martin Kitchen, *The Silent Dictatorship: The Politics of the German High Command under Hindenburg and Ludendorff, 1916–1918* (New York, 1976).
46. Citations in Brose, *Kaiser's Army*, 234.
47. Cited in ibid., 234.
48. Cited in Gerald D. Feldman, *Army Industry and Labor in Germany 1914–1918* (Princeton, NJ, 1966), 173.
49. Citations in ibid., 372, 491.
50. Cited in ibid., 271.
51. See Thierry Bonzon and Belinda Davis, "Feeding the Cities," in Jay Winter and Jean-Louis Robert, eds., *Capital Cities at War: Paris, London, Berlin 1914–1919* (Cambridge, UK, 1997), 310–317; and C. Paul Vincent, *The Politics of Hunger: The Allied Blockade of Germany 1915–1919* (Athens, GA, 1985), 127–146.
52. Evelyn Blücher, *An English Wife in Berlin* (New York, 1920), 158.
53. Roger Chickering, *The Great War and Urban Life in Germany: Freiburg, 1914–1918* (Cambridge, UK, 2007), 270.
54. For this important point, and the citation, see the memoirs of American ambassador James W. Gerard, *Face to Face with Kaiserism* (New York, 1918), 119–120.
55. Citations in Stevenson, *Cataclysm*, 214; and Herwig, *First World War*, 315.
56. Citations in Arthur J. May, *The Passing of the Hapsburg Monarchy, 1914–1918* (Philadelphia, 1966), 1:395, 308.
57. Citations in Herwig, *First World War*, 274; and Maureen Healy, *Vienna and the Fall of the Habsburg Empire: Total War and Everyday Life in World War I* (Cambridge, UK, 2004), 32.
58. Citations in May, *Passing of the Habsburg Monarchy*, 1:428, 2:638.
59. For Erzberger's visit, see Klaus Epstein, *Matthias Erzberger and the Dilemma of German Democracy* (Princeton, NJ, 1959), 172–174, 187.
60. For good discussions of wartime politics in Italy, see Salvatore Saladino, *Italy from Unification to 1919: Growth and Decay of a Liberal Regime* (New York, 1970), 150–161; John Gooch, "Italy during the First World War," in Millett and Murray, *Military Effectiveness*, 1:157–165; Denis Mack Smith, *Modern Italy: A Political History* (Ann Arbor, MI, 1997), 271–275; and Jonathan Dunnage, *Twentieth-Century Italy: A Social History* (London, 2002), 138–146.
61. For the Mussolini incident as well as morale problems on the Isonzo front, see Brian Sullivan's well-documented passage in Philip V. Cannistraro and Brian Sullivan, *Il Duce's Other Woman* (New York, 1993), 133–143.
62. See Dunnage, *Social History*, 44–45; and for the citation, Vanda Wilcox, "Discipline in the Italian Army 1915–1918," in Pierre Purseigle, ed., *Warfare and Belligerence: Perspectives in First World War Studies* (Leiden, Holland, 2005), 81.
63. Citations here and below in Saladino, *Italy from Unification*, 154–158; and Smith, *Modern Italy*, 274.

64. Cited in Rod Paschall, *The Defeat of Imperial Germany 1917–1918* (New York, 1994), 84.
65. Citations in Allan K. Wildman, *The End of the Russian Imperial Army: The Old Army and the Soldiers Revolt (March-April 1917)* (Princeton, NJ, 1980), 109; and Orlando Figes, *A People's Tragedy: The Russian Revolution 1891–1924* (New York, 1996), 268, 303.
66. See Stevenson, *Cataclysm*, 234–235, 236.
67. Cited in W. Bruce Lincoln, *Passage through Armageddon: The Russians in War and Revolution 1914–1918* (New York, 1986), 315.

CHAPTER VIII

War-Weariness and the Question of Peace in Europe

1917

Late on the night of December 30–31, 1916, Prince Felix Yusupov, scion of one of the richest families in Russia and husband of the tsar's niece, Grand Duchess Irina, directed his chauffeur-driven automobile into Gorokhovaya Street. It was shortly after midnight as he approached a locked gate protecting the apartment building of Gregory Rasputin, the bizarre faith healer who for years had held the unquestioning confidence of Tsarina Alexandra. Instead of entering the main entrance, Yusupov ignored the custodian and went directly to a back door. Groping up an unlit stairway with great difficulty, he found the apartment door and knocked.

Rasputin let in the young man, a trusted friend recently admitted to the inner circle of St. Petersburg's most controversial character. By the light of a bedroom candle Yusupov noticed the holy man's attire: "a silk shirt embroidered with cornflowers and girded with a thick crimson cord with two large tassels on the ends, wide black velveteen pants, and high boots—his fur coat and beaver cap were ready by the bed."[1] Normally dressed in much plainer garb, Rasputin, a weirdly albeit religiously zealous womanizer, obviously looked forward to a special night—Yusupov had promised a long-awaited chance to "meet" Irina. Together the two men descended the dark staircase and walked to the idling car. The driver sped off in the direction of the grand Yusupov palace on the Moika Canal.

A few minutes later they came to a stop inside the courtyard of the great house. Yusupov led his guest through a door and down a flight of stairs to a basement dining room. "Where be you, dear one?" said Rasputin in eager anticipation

The Tragic Romanovs: Tsar Nicholas II, Empress Alexandra, and the Royal Family
Canfield, *World War*

of his rendezvous. Then, noticing the sound of a gramophone playing "Yankee Doddle" and women's voices upstairs, he stopped on the steps and inquired more suspiciously, "What's going on there, a spree?" "No, my wife's got company. They'll be leaving soon. In the meantime, let's have some tea in the dining room."[2] They went down.

It was all a murderous ruse. Gathered in the Yusupov palace was a group of highly placed conspirators who believed that Rasputin had to be killed lest he undermine the monarchy and endanger a war effort he had consistently opposed since the July Crisis of 1914. The chauffeur was really a certain Dr. Lazavert, a physician from the hospital train of reactionary Duma member Vladimir Purishkevich. Together the two had laced the party room sweets and wine with potassium cyanide. They waited for the deed to be done in a back room up the stairs from the dining room. With them were Grand Duke Dmitry, son of the tsar's uncle, and Lieutenant Sukhotin, a young officer in the guards. The female voices came not from Irina, the lure, but rather the ballerina Vera Karalli, lover of Dmitry, and Marianna Derfelden, stepdaughter to Dmitry's father, Grand Duke Pavel. The two women hated the scandalous Rasputin as much as the other plotters.

The intrigue almost failed. Yusupov offered Rasputin the poison cakes, but the man who indulged in so many things refused them—he never ate sweets! The wine had no visible effect on the strange man either because, unknown to the conspirators, they had mixed too weak a solution of the poison. Yusupov ran upstairs to consult with his comrades, who quickly armed him with Dmitry's pistol and sent him back, where, seconds later, he shot the still unsuspecting Rasputin. He was left for dead as the murderers celebrated upstairs. But he regained consciousness and struggled out into the courtyard where Purishkevich, having been warned by a panicked Yusupov, shot twice at the bleeding, fleeing man

Making Short Work of Russia: Rasputin and Friends
Canfield, *World War*

but missed. Dmitry, an Olympic marksman, fired twice and hit his mark in the neck and head. The body was dragged back inside where Yusupov, clearly coming unraveled, pummeled the brightly dressed public enemy with a dumbbell handle. Later they stuffed their victim into a hole in the ice of a nearby river.

Rasputin's body washed up a few days later. An autopsy determined that he had drowned—the remarkable man had still been alive when they pushed him through the ice!

THE COLLAPSE OF RUSSIA

The murder of Rasputin was one more sign that the political dam was starting to break up in Russia, unleashing a revolutionary torrent that threatened to destroy everything in its way. Many soldiers were considering shooting their officers rather than continuing to follow orders. In the countryside those peasants who had not been mobilized for the army longed only for peace and a chance to acquire more land. In the cities workers struck with escalating frequency and intensity against their deteriorating standard of living, the tsar, the monarchy, and the war. Their sisters, wives, and mothers struggled in bread and food queues to bring home enough calories to delay the starvation process which began that arctic winter of 1916–1917. Nearly everything was going wrong—and Gregory Rasputin, as much as Nicholas and Alexandra, had become a symbol of the rotten political establishment that was blamed for things going wrong.

The Fall of the Romanovs

As his murder demonstrated, Rasputin got caught in the deadly current of Russia's wartime crisis. His odd, sometimes scandalous behavior certainly contributed, however, to the dam-break intensity of the flood that swept him and the monarchy away. Rasputin had made his way from the eastern reaches of the empire to St. Petersburg in 1903, shortly thereafter winning the trust of Alexandra due to his semihypnotic ability to ease the suffering of Alexei, the young hemophilic heir to the throne. Once the tsarina became convinced that God had sent a faith healer to ensure the posterity of the royal family, she refused to believe the shocking stories about him that soon began to circulate, namely, that he was a drunkard and lecherous womanizer.

Although she did not know it, the truth was, in fact, somewhat different. Edvard Radzinsky's new research shows that Rasputin's legendary excessive drinking was not so until a failed assassination attempt in 1914, followed by the carnage of war, unnerved him. As for lechery, he emerged from a strange sect, the *Khlysty*, who thought they could purge their bodies and souls of sin through orgylike lovemaking. Building on these early experiences, Rasputin believed his mission was to heal the spirits of women with troubled marriages through sexual intercourse with him, a holy man. By 1914 this zealous womanizer had built a worshipful following of scores of usually highly placed female devotees in the capital city. But Alexandra, whose marriage was rock solid, felt only spiritual devotion to "the friend" sent from heaven, while Rasputin, for his part, comported himself reverently at court and displayed a remarkable ability to sober up quickly when suddenly called to the palace after late-night revelries. Scandalous and irreverent rumors crisscrossed Russian society high and low, nevertheless, that the weird Siberian monk had seduced Alexandra too—and thus cuckolded the tsar. When Nicholas moved to the front in August 1915, leaving his wife and Rasputin, whose allegedly divine advice she fully trusted, virtually in charge of the country, hatred for the tsarina and her friend grew. Indeed the man in the street, the generals, and even close relatives of the royal couple seriously believed their German-born empress and her alleged lover were enemy spies.

This incendiary belief was stoked to higher and higher temperatures by the meddling of Alexandra and Rasputin in the most serious political and military affairs. Rasputin had unsuccessfully opposed Russia's declaration of war in 1914, fearing correctly that it would mean the destruction of the monarchy. "A threatening cloud hangs over Russia," he telegrammed Nicholas as mobilization began that July. "Misfortune, much woe, no ray of hope, a sea of tears immeasurable...an indescribable horror....Do not permit the mad to triumph and destroy themselves and the nation."[3] Grand Duke Nicholas, commander of the army, had wanted the healer arrested and tried for treason for trying to thwart Russia's ethnic mission, but the tsar refused. After the military debacle and great retreat of 1915 the grand duke pointed the finger of blame elsewhere and rashly accused Rasputin of hearing military secrets from the tsarina and passing them to German agents during drinking bouts and orgies. The intrigue against the trusted untouchable monk backfired, however, and for his pains the general was removed from command of the Russian armies—hence the tsar's decision to take personal charge. Possessing much more political leverage by 1916, the tsarina's friend advised her to urge the tsar to terminate Brusilov's offensive, which was done. How much longer Brusilov could have continued to sustain such high casualties is of course questionable, but the general blamed the meddlers and joined a plot to arrest Alexandra, depose the tsar, and give power to Grand Duke Nicholas. "If I must choose between the emperor and Russia," he wrote the grand duke, "then I march for Russia."[4]

Although these antiwar interventions were no doubt to Rasputin's credit—he was trying to save lives—his advice to Alexandra on ministerial appointments was inexcusably disastrous. Claiming to have received visions in the night from God, he set in motion a "ministerial leapfrog" that created chaos in the machinery of state and undermined Russia's military and civilian logistics just when the country's mobilization for the war began to improve. In the sixteen months between Nicholas's departure for the front and Rasputin's murder Russia had four prime ministers, five ministers of the interior, three foreign ministers, three war ministers, three ministers of transport, and four ministers of agriculture. In almost every case their only qualification for office was friendship with the holy man. "Is this folly or is this treason," asked an incredulous Paul Miliukov, a leading liberal in the Duma, in November 1916. His speech was followed in December by a stinging denunciation from fellow Duma member Vladimir Purishkevich. "It requires only the recommendation of Rasputin to raise the most abject citizen to high office," he shouted a few days before joining the murder plot. If the ministers were truly loyal, if the glory of Russia and the name of the tsar meant anything to them, they should throw themselves at the feet of their sovereign and "tell him that the multitude is threatening in its wrath, revolution threatens and an obscure [peasant] shall govern Russia no longer." And so, as we know from the opening scene, the conspirators carried out the grisly deed, killing, as Purishkevich said that night, "the most wicked enemy of the tsar and Russia, the one who is preventing us from fighting, who has saddled us with Germans in positions of authority, and who has taken the tsarina into his hands and through her has been making short work of Russia."[5]

Russian officialdom quickly identified the culprits but took only mild punitive action against members of the privileged elite who were widely perceived to be patriotic heroes: Yusupov was exiled to his estate, Dmitry to the Persian front, while Purishkevich slipped out of town on his hospital train. There had been much more afoot that December, however, than the removal of Rasputin. Radzinsky argues that for political reasons the plotters concocted the story that Purishkevich felled Rasputin—a story included in all accounts until now. "For in the event of a coup, Dmitry, a young military man, a favorite of the Guards, and an organizer of the deliverance from the Rasputin ignominy (but not the murderer himself) would be a realistic pretender to the throne—but as the peasant's murderer, he would have a much harder time becoming tsar."[6]

Indeed coups were in the making. The most serious, as noted previously, included Brusilov, his superior at *Stavka*, General Mikhail Alexeev, Prince Georgi

Old Wine in New Bottles: Kerensky's Divisions Prepare to Defend Democracy
Canfield, *World War*

Lvov of the Duma, and a vacillating Grand Duke Nicholas. Rasputin's murder was "without question a half measure," the grand duke confided to his diary, "since an end must without fail be put to both Alexandra and [Rasputin's handpicked prime minister] Protopopov." The former army chief had been "scared into taking action, and prodded, and pleaded with" to consider "murder plans" that were "still vague but logically necessary." With the departure of Purishkevich and the exile of Yusupov and Dmitry, however, "I see hardly any others capable of action." As 1916 yielded to 1917 he swung between the extremes of believing that he was "not of the breed of murderers" and the unnerving feeling that if he stayed in the capital he would actually "do such nonsense."[7] Shortly after New Year's Nicholas and Alexandra ended the grand duke's torment by exiling him to his country estate. And the horrible plot disintegrated.

It was already too late, however, to save the monarchy. On March 8 the revolution began spontaneously in St. Petersburg—as the police had predicted—with a protest by working-class women against worsening bread shortages.[8] Male workers in the massive Putilov armaments factory outside of the city quickly joined the irate women, causing near chaos in the streets over subsequent days as the commandant of the local garrison attempted to suppress the rioters. Government control evaporated when soldiers finally stopped shooting into the crowds, turned on their officers instead, and joined the mob. The reliability of the garrison had long been doubtful after wartime hardships and socialist propaganda, but over the last half year in particular the Rasputin scandal eroded soldiers' loyalty. They made "the most sordid insinuations" about his dirty relationship with the tsarina and grand duchesses and blamed the monk and Alexandra for the supposed "German stranglehold" on the state. "What's the use of [following orders] if the Germans have already taken over?"[9]

The police continued the struggle, however, killing hundreds and wounding thousands before Alexeev and the commanding generals, including the rebellious Brusilov, decided that the only chance of restoring order and waging a more successful war would be for Nicholas to abdicate. On their advice he did this, giving the throne to his younger brother Mikhail, who, having witnessed the street violence, had no stomach for rule and abdicated in his turn the next day. On March 16, 1917, over three hundred years of Romanov rule in Russia came to an abrupt but widely predicted end.

The Provisional Government, the Soviets, and the Kerensky Offensive

Into this sudden vacuum of power rushed two distinct, contrasting power blocs. The parties and underground movements representing the urban masses and peasants in the countryside—Marxist groups like the Mensheviks and Vladimir's Lenin's more radical Bolsheviks, non-Marxist worker parties like Alexander Kerensky's Trudoviks, and the peasant-oriented Socialist Revolutionaries (SRs)—built on the revolutionary traditions of 1905–1906 by founding "soviets," municipal and rural councils that set about the task of ruling Russia. Complicating such claims to legitimacy, however, leading Duma members like Georgi Lvov and Paul Miliukov formed a Provisional Government and called for elections to a constitutional assembly. The two bodies settled into an uneasy truce. Thus the Provisional Government accepted soviet decrees for radical reforms like the eight-hour workday and the election of soldiers' committees in the army to mediate disputes between officers and men, shield the ranks from abuses by officers, and authorize soldiers not to follow orders that contradicted soviet policies. Fearing an army backlash if simple workers and peasants actually tried to govern, however, the largest soviet in St. Petersburg quickly recognized the authority of the Provisional Government.

Of the two power blocs the soviets leaned most heavily toward peace. The St. Petersburg Soviet, epicenter of a movement that was rapidly spreading to other cities and into the rural hinterland, issued a manifesto on March 27 that urged the peoples of belligerent nations, especially the German proletariat, "to wage a decisive battle against the annexationist programs" of their governments in order to foster "international unity" and bring about an end to the war. Russian socialists would do their part, but if other nations ignored this example the Russian revolution would "not allow itself to be crushed by outside military force."[10]

Nine days later a controversy erupted when Miliukov, foreign minister of the Provisional Government, publicized his desire to liberate the Slavic peoples of Austria-Hungary, merge its Ukrainian provinces to Russia, and annex Constantinople and the straits. The furor this statement caused in the socialist press induced Miliukov to moderate his stance somewhat on April 9, asserting that the war aims of free Russia were "not domination over other peoples" or "the forcible annexation of their territory, but the establishment of a durable peace on the basis of national self-determination," an echo of American President Woodrow Wilson's war statement to Congress on April 2 (see later). Miliukov had no intention of signing a separate peace with Germany, however, a move that would dishonor Russia by violating its treaty pledge of 1915 to stand by Britain and France. Within a month street protests over Miliukov's objectionable views forced him to step down amidst a cabinet shake-up that brought six socialists into the Provisional Government.

Despite the obvious prowar preferences of Miliukov and other ministers including Lvov, soviet leanings in the other direction encouraged German chancellor Theobald von Bethmann Hollweg to attempt a peace initiative. He put out feelers in late March, commissioning one of the most talented and dynamic members of the Reichstag, Catholic Center Party leader Matthias Erzberger, to open negotiations in Stockholm with Joseph von Kolyschko, a former tsarist bureaucrat. Their two meetings (March 26 and April 20) resulted in a draft armistice agreement that aimed at winning over Alexander Kerensky, a leading non-Marxist member of the St. Petersburg Soviet as well as the Provisional Government, whom Kolyschko had probably contacted, at least indirectly, in the interim. With the major exception of Poland, which would not return to Russia, the borders of 1914 would be restored. Germany agreed, furthermore, "to sign an armistice with the other belligerent powers at any time for the purpose of negotiating a general peace settlement." This latter point was especially important to Russia, Erzberger reported to Bethmann, "for the sake of avoiding the odium of signing a separate peace" and "for securing the concurrence of the 'idealistic' Russian peace party centering around Kerensky."[11] The draft came to nothing, however, when German army command insisted on more territory and a skeptical but increasingly pliable Bethmann caved in. At some point Kerensky shelved the document too. Russian patriotism ran deep into the political left, which saw losing Poland as too high a price for peace.

Remarkably enough, most soviet leaders outside of Lenin's Bolsheviks that spring were coming around to the idea of not just defending the Russian revolution from reactionary Germany and Austria-Hungary—what they dubbed "revolutionary defencism"—but also attacking the armies of these authoritarian regimes as the best means of protecting what Russia had gained since the fall of the monarchy. As one soviet leader asked rhetorically, "Did we really overthrow Nicholas to bend our neck to Wilhelm?"[12] Many like Kerensky, who had become war minister after the cabinet changes in May, hoped that a successful offensive would also prod Russia's allies into peace talks. The St. Petersburg Soviet had seconded the initiative of the secretariat of the Second International, the prewar umbrella organization of worldwide socialism (see chap. 2), which had called for all comrades to come to Stockholm to work for peace. But would such a conference provide adequate pressure on France and Britain to moderate war aims like seizing the Rhineland or retaining conquered German colonies, demands that would keep Berlin away from the peace table? Suspecting, moreover, that America's declaration of war had minimized the importance of Russia to the democratic alliance, Kerensky wanted an offensive to honor wartime pledges; demonstrate Russian indispensability to the Entente; and enhance his diplomatic bargaining power, both with Britain and France as well as Germany, whose grasping militarism could only be curbed, as the failed Erzberger-Kolyschko negotiations showed, with a smashing Russian victory in the east. Following this rather convoluted reasoning, Kerensky and most of the Russian left came to advocate more war to end war.

It remained to be seen, however, just how effective Russia's newly "democratized" army would be. The most knowledgeable officers realized that the spontaneous revolution had been a product of hatred not just for the monarchy but also for the war. It was doubtful, they predicted, how long the average soldier would defend Russia, let alone attack on foreign soil. During an Easter break from fighting on the Galician front, for example, one Russian soldier proclaimed to a fraternizing German lieutenant that an offensive was out of the question. If one were ordered, "we'll throw the government out and bring in a new one that will quickly give the Russian people peace." During a three-week tour of numerous armies in May, however, Kerensky allowed the cheers of soldiers he visited to convince him that they were ready to attack to defend the revolution and bring about peace. His newly appointed army chief, Alexei Brusilov, witnessed the soldiers' true state of mind during his own tour. One group of Bolshevik sympathizers shouted him down near Dvinsk, their spokesman saying they all "had enough of fighting." If the general wanted to fight "then let him go and spill his own blood." As the troops cheered, this simple soldier read out a proclamation demanding immediate peace. Elsewhere Brusilov encountered an entire division that had expelled its officers, intending to go home to take land back from the nobles. "What will happen to Mother Russia," the general asked them, "if no one wants to defend it, and everyone like you only thinks of themselves?" The men were deaf to his pleas. During the impressive preliminary bombardment (June 29–30), in fact, there were dozens of mutinies and widespread desertions throughout the army. Kerensky, present to witness his new army, ran into thousands of men shouting "down with the war, down with everything."[13]

Kerensky's offensive in Galicia could not possibly succeed.[14] Things looked fine on Brusilov's operational charts. He had more infantry divisions than the year before—44 versus 40—and he chose to attack with a vastly greater artillery concentration along a front one-third as long. Indeed for the first time in three years Russian heavy artillery outnumbered enemy guns and each assault division had backing from fourteen heavies, over triple the previous year's concentration.[15] Against the main objective, Lemberg, his Eleventh and Seventh Armies hurled 31 oversized divisions against only 13 undersized divisions of the Austro-Hungarian Second Army and the mixed (Austrian/German/Turkish) South Army.

When "the Kerensky offensive" began on July 1 the Russians pushed enemy forces back several miles toward Lemberg, overrunning first and second lines and taking thousands of prisoners. Already in the first days, however, trouble signs appeared as some units refused to attack and reserves would not move forward to exploit gains. In some places, moreover, jubilant Russian infantrymen paraded through enemy trenches abandoned during the bombardment and simply marched back to their own lines—this was "revolutionary defencism" in practice. Heavy defensive fire exacerbated these problems, and soon the drive on Lemberg halted. Only in the south was momentum sustained. Jumping off on July 6, a third Russian army, the Eighth with thirteen divisions, caved in the front of the startled Austro-Hungarian Third and drove fifty kilometers in six days, moving halfway to the offensive's secondary objective, the oil fields at Debroczen.

But the end was near. A massive counterattack on July 19 spearheaded by eight German divisions hurried by rail from the western front routed the Russians all along the line, pushing them east of Tarnopol (July 26) and Cernowitz (August 3), over one hundred kilometers behind their initial lines. Kerensky's democratic army was no longer fighting but rather returning home, just as informed observers had predicted months earlier. Some officers who attempted to rally their men were shot. The only thing delaying this chaotic, headlong retreat, in fact, was the looting of shops for booze and the raping and murdering of hapless innocents. Finally in early August, Brusilov's replacement, Lavr Kornilov, managed with great difficulty to restore some measure of order to an army that had come close to disintegrating. It was not yet the end of the war on the eastern front, but it was the beginning of the end.

Perhaps now there would be peace, for the Russians, as will become clear, were not the only people in mid-1917 who had tired of the Great War.

GERMANY'S UNRESTRICTED SUBMARINE WARFARE, AMERICA'S ENTRY, AND THE REICHSTAG PEACE RESOLUTION

As winter turned to spring 1917 the German navy intensified the submarine warfare that many in the country had demanded as revenge for Britain's "hunger blockade."[16] The Germans had 105 operational U-boats when the unrestricted campaign began in February; this number rose to 129 in late May. Only half of these, however, were on patrol at any given moment: about 40 in the waters around Britain and Ireland and about 20 leaving Pola (on the Adriatic) for targets in the Mediterranean. Nevertheless, the sinking of merchant ships of all nations increased alarmingly, doubling to 234 in February, 281 in March, and 373 in April. German submarines destroyed 881,000 tons of shipping that month. The bulk of this sum, nearly 550,000 tons, was British—a shocking 400,000 tons went down in the "black fortnight" of April 17–30 alone. As thousands of sailors died each month, Britain's wheat stocks fell from twelve weeks to six, and its reserve of fuel oil, so vital to the Royal Navy itself, from six months to two. "It looks as though the Germans are winning the war," said U.S. Rear Admiral William Sims to the commander of the Grand Fleet, Admiral John Jellicoe, just before black fortnight. "They will win unless we can stop these losses—and stop them soon,"[17] replied Jellicoe.

The presence of Sims in London was one measure of the high price Germany paid for its early successes with unlimited submarine warfare, for, aware that

Growing Imbalance of Power: American Dreadnoughts Enhance the Grand Fleet
Canfield, *World War*

President Wilson would soon ask for a declaration of war against Germany, the Navy Department had ordered Sims across the Atlantic to see how America could help its allies. Declaring war had been difficult for a man who campaigned on the slogan "He kept us out of war." Despite lingering bad feelings over the *Lusitania*, in fact, the overwhelming majority of Americans had no desire to enter Europe's fray when they cast ballots in November 1916—even most German-Americans favored neutrality. This changed suddenly on March 1, 1917, when American newspapers published the infamous "Zimmermann Telegram."[18] In January German Foreign Minister Arthur Zimmermann, rightly assuming that American entry was all but inevitable with unrestricted U-Boat warfare set to begin, wired his nation's ambassador in Mexico City with unusual orders: he should offer Mexico an alliance with Germany against the United States. Victory would return the American states of Texas, New Mexico, and Arizona to Mexican sovereignty. The president of Mexico should also approach Japan about mediating peace with Germany and changing sides in the war. The rationale here: tie the United States down elsewhere than Europe by diverting it into a war with Mexico—the last thing, alas, that Mexico, alarmed by American intervention in the revolution there, wanted. The foolish blunder soon backfired when Britain's "Room 40" operators intercepted the message and leaked it to Wilson, who authorized newspaper publication. Coast-to-coast outrage was the immediate result, followed by swelling prowar sentiments in both houses of Congress, but Wilson, a genuine champion of peace, resisted taking action. On March 12, however, the first American ship was lost, and then on March 18 German U-boats sank three U.S. ships—one, the *Vigilancia*, with fifteen sailors killed.

Over the next few days the president grudgingly accepted the necessity of war. Strengthening his resolve was the knowledge that only belligerency would earn him a seat at the peace table—talks he hoped to use to promote peace and democracy in the postwar world. "It is," he told Congress April 2,

> a fearful thing to lead this great peaceful people into war, into the most terrible of all wars, civilization itself seeming to hang in the balance. But the right is more precious than peace, and we shall fight for the things which we have always carried nearest our hearts—for democracy, for the rights and liberties of small nations, for a universal dominion of right by such a concert of free peoples as shall bring peace and safety to all nations and make the world at last free.[19]

The Senate approved Wilson's request April 4, 1917, the House of Representatives April 6. America was at war with Germany.

As the United States began the slow and difficult process of raising and training a much larger army, Germany's U-boat gambit reached its climax. Sinkings fell from April's high of 881,000 tons to 596,000 in May but then rose again to nearly 687,000 in June. Thereafter, however, the situation gradually turned around. Tonnage lost descended to about 500,000 per month that summer, and further down to around 350,000 in September. Wheat stocks climbed back to thirteen weeks in August and continued to rise as Britain reached harvest time. This was crucial, for the submarine threat had brought more British land under the plough with the result that the island nation's agricultural output jumped 30 percent. Furthermore, American entry rapidly increased loan amounts to the allies for purchase of grain and foodstuffs. And, mercifully for Britain and France, the United States had ample supplies.

Once again Germany had gambled, and once again Germany had lost. What had gone wrong with unrestricted submarine warfare over the spring and summer?[20] The nearly 30 percent drop off in May resulted most probably from the exhaustion of German crews and machines—without many more U-boats, the torrid pace of April was simply impossible to sustain. Beginning on April 28, moreover, the Royal Navy organized its first convoy of merchant ships, and as the summer wore on, this became the norm. The most immediate advantage of convoys for the allies was to make it much more difficult for U-boats to find their prey. Indeed, scores of ships in convoy had as great a chance as a single ship of slipping through Germany's scattered submarine fleet, "and each time this happened," recalled Winston Churchill, "forty ships escaped instead of one." One submarine commander, Karl Doenitz, also of World War Two fame, agreed:

> The oceans at once became bare and empty. For long periods of time, the U-boats, operating individually, would see nothing at all; and then suddenly up would loom a huge concourse of ships, thirty or fifty or more of them, surrounded by a strong escort of warships of all types. The solitary U-boat, which most probably had sighted the convoy purely by chance, would then attack, thrusting again and

> again... until the physical exhaustion of the commander and crew called a halt. The lone U-boat might well sink one or two ships, or even several, but that was a poor percentage of the whole. The convoy would steam on... bringing a rich cargo of foodstuffs and raw materials safely to port.[21]

Of over 16,500 merchantmen protected in outbound and inbound convoys only 154 fell victim to U-boats.

America's declaration of war in early April had contributed greatly to the success of the convoy system, in fact, by boosting the number of escorting warships. The Royal Navy's 311 destroyers were either committed to battle fleets in home waters—the most modern 107 at Scapa Flow—or spread thinly around the world. Jellicoe, who appreciated the U-boat danger as much as anyone, nevertheless felt he could spare only 7 destroyers from Scapa Flow and 33 from other ports—72 were needed for escort duty. As early as May 4, however, 6 modern American destroyers arrived at Queenstown, Ireland, and 28 plied North Atlantic trade routes by late June. As destruction of U-boats by depth charge or surface action increased during the summer, submarine commanders shifted their attacks to coastal waters where convoys were easier to find, but now mines took a mounting toll. Germany lost only 15 subs from May to July, but 37 from August to December, or roughly as many as home shipyards could produce.

Meanwhile, as hundreds of cargo-carrying ships went down each month, the allies struggled to replace them—an eventuality not considered, surprisingly enough, by the generals and admirals at Castle Pless in January 1917. After American entry, for example, 50 German merchantmen interned in U.S. ports since 1914, totaling 130,000 tons, were seized and pressed into the allied cause. The same process of expropriation occurred throughout the hemisphere as most of Latin America followed the U.S. lead, declared war on Germany, and forced scores of German ships into wartime service. In Brazil alone, for example, 42 ships, about 100,000 tons, joined the effort. Britain accelerated construction of new steamers, furthermore, and also purchased neutral shipping wherever it could be found. According to an official account, the world's ports "were ransacked for tonnage."[22] By production and purchase Britain managed to replace a million tons of shipping, 25 percent of tonnage sunk in 1917. Finally, in a related development, the German admiralty had assumed that it could frighten neutral ships from the seas, thereby depriving Britain of even more imports. After the ferocity of Germany's U-boat warfare achieved this initial result, however, the Royal Navy threatened neutral captains in British ports with internment or seizure—600 neutral ships lay at anchor there. And soon German legations in Sweden, Norway, Denmark, Holland, Spain, and other neutral nations reported that British pressure had forced ships to sail for England. For all of these reasons unrestricted submarine warfare failed to bring Britain to its knees.

Center Party leader Matthias Erzberger returned from his visit to Vienna on April 24, 1917, worried about Germany's chances for victory if its strongest ally collapsed. He became increasingly interested, therefore, in promoting peace negotiations. The failure of his promising negotiations with Kolyschko shortly thereafter only heightened these worries, for now Vienna had to brace itself for the Kerensky offensive. Erzberger's troubled thoughts intensified as he learned from an impressively wide network of contacts in neutral nations that the U-boats, despite inflicting terrible losses, were not winning the war for Germany. The ease with which Britain prodded the neutrals into selling ships, and then coerced their merchant fleets back to sea despite heightened dangers, made a great impression on him. "I became completely convinced after my last trip to Sweden that the calculations of the Admiralty and other governmental bodies that showed that the unrestricted submarine campaign would bring peace by the end of July or the beginning of August were completely wrong."[23] These insights convinced him of the need to negotiate a peace treaty, and his determination grew after two meetings in June with Ludendorff's right-hand man, Max Bauer, who made anxious, deprecating remarks about the limited potential of submarines to undercut the allies' growing advantage in firepower. Although Bauer revealed no new strategy for achieving total victory, he still insisted that OHL was right to strive for annexations in the west (the Belgian coast, Liège, Luxembourg, and the iron ore mines of Lorraine) and the east (western Poland and the Baltic). The security of this Greater German Reich would be further enhanced by occupying the French fortress line and setting up German-dominated buffer states in Poland, Rumania, and the Ukraine. For his part, however, Erzberger left the meetings resolved to oppose most of these aggressive designs—goals that would surely scuttle any chance of peace.

Domestic politics also weighed heavily on his mind. Within the brief span of three weeks in March–April 1917 Germany found itself at war not just with West European democracies Britain, France, and Italy but also with the United States and newly democratic Russia. In early summer democratic Greece joined the fray (see chap. 10). For the Social Democratic Party (SPD), which had justified its support for the war as a defensive struggle against tsarist Russia, this sudden turn of events created extremely unfavorable political circumstances. Indeed, the very day America declared war the party's left wing broke away to form the Independent Social Democratic Party (USPD) in protest against authoritarianism at home, the army's annexationist goals, as well as the SPD's apparent backing for aggressive war aims. All of this occurred, furthermore, against the backdrop of escalating wildcat strikes. Fifteen thousand workers had struck in 1915, over 100,000 in 1916, and 665,000 in 1917 as casualties, hunger, cold, the behavior of William II and his son, and revolutionary events in Russia increasingly deflected popular anger against Britain toward Germany's own authoritarian, army-dominated regime. The array of democratic nations in the enemy camp, compounded by growing antiwar feeling in Germany, made it politically impossible for the SPD to offer parliamentary support for what it rightly perceived as a war of aggression. These circumstances reinforced Erzberger's conviction that the Reichstag must pass a bold peace resolution, for in addition to the troubling fact that Germany appeared unable to defeat a larger and much more formidable enemy coalition, there now arose the need to neutralize Pan German and OHL annexationists, unite leftist political forces during tough peace talks with the enemy, and keep the SPD behind the war effort until negotiators secured an acceptable treaty.

Erzberger fired his first salvo at the shortsightedness of the admirals before a Reichstag committee on July 4 and then let loose his full fury two days later, depicting in alarming detail the nearly hopeless military dilemma facing Germany and calling upon his colleagues to prepare a peace resolution. That same day SPD, Center Party, and Progressive Party representatives called for the rapid introduction of democratic voting procedures in Prussia, Germany's largest and most influential state, as well as the appointment of leading Reichstag members to the ministries of the Reich and Prussia. On July 19 these same parties voted "for a peace of understanding and the permanent reconciliation of peoples." The resolution went on to declare that "forced acquisitions and political, economic, and financial oppressions are irreconcilable with such a peace." Nations of the postwar world should oppose economic discrimination, maintain freedom of the seas, and foster organizations upholding international law. If Germany's enemies rejected this hand of peace, however, "the German nation will stand together as one man and steadfastly hold out and fight until its own and its allies' right to life and development is secured."[24]

The Peace Resolution passed 212 to 126. The Conservative Party and right-of-center National Liberal Party voted against, castigating it as defeatist, while the USPD rejected it as not categorically opposed to annexations. The drafters had word-crafted the document carefully, in fact, to give negotiators flexibility in arranging the establishment of "independent" nations like Lithuania or Poland, which would most likely become German- or Austrian-dominated buffer states, or bargain for certain territorial exchanges; hence also the reference to Germany's right to "development." The motion's ambiguity, however, would undermine its effectiveness.

The Reichstag Peace Resolution was the boldest challenge to military-monarchical authority in Germany since the constitutional crisis of the 1860s. The parliamentary majority strove to remove the emperor's imperious generals from control of the war effort, open peace talks, and simultaneously democratize Germany. The latter seemed somewhat closer to reality on July 9 when Bethmann won William's approval for moving quickly toward democratic voting in Prussia. But all came unraveled before the month was out. Long opposed to the chancellor because of his stance on unrestricted submarine warfare, willingness to pursue peace talks with Russia, and penchant for making concessions to the Reichstag, Hindenburg and Ludendorff threatened to resign on July 12 unless Bethmann were dismissed. The beleaguered first minister submitted his resignation on July 13 after learning that Erzberger and other party leaders behind the Peace Resolution also wanted him replaced. The majority preferred a successor unassociated with the regime's annexationist war aims and therefore better positioned to represent Germany in peace talks. William, dejected by the brusque, irreverent treatment meted out by OHL, let his chancellor of eight years go. "I have had to dismiss the very man who towers by heads over all the others," he lamented. "Now I can just abdicate."[25]

The Reichstag's ideal replacement did not emerge, however, because Hindenburg and Ludendorff once again exploited their tremendous leverage at court to secure the appointment of Georg Michaelis, a relative nonentity whom Hindenburg and Ludendorff considered a suppliant tool. The new man seized on the somewhat equivocal wording of the document, declaring to the deputies that he accepted the Peace Resolution "as I understand it," later gloating privately to the crown prince that "one can, after all, now make any peace that one likes under its terms."[26]

Michaelis actually proved more willing to compromise OHL's war aims than some accounts would have it.[27] In the west, for example, he felt it sufficient to retain only Liège, using the massive fortress complex as a lever to maintain far-reaching economic control of postwar Belgium. His willingness to reduce annexation demands did not result from Reichstag pressure, however, which he ignored, but was rather a response to changing international circumstances and his reading of German interests. The Austrians had been contacted that summer by French intermediaries who tried to lure Vienna out of the war with promises of territorial gains at Germany's expense. Michaelis believed concessions over Belgium might bring London to the table and split the Entente—turnabout was fair play.

Neither of these diplomatic intrigues bore fruit, but both Vienna and London had been tempted, and the longing for peace wafted perceptibly in the European air that summer: Pope Benedict XV issued a peace note just two weeks after the Reichstag; the French army, somewhat like the Russian, had mutinied in protest against further attacks; and the British got bogged down in the mud of Passchendaele. These events make it useful to speculate what could have been achieved if Germany's parliamentarians had insisted on replacing Bethmann with someone who agreed to follow the letter and the spirit of their motion. "Erzberger made the worst political mistake of his career," writes Erzberger's biographer, "when he joined hands with Bethmann's right-wing enemies without making sure in advance that a better man would get the chancellorship."[28] Ludendorff later admitted that OHL could not have resisted the Reichstag and its trade union backers if they had pressed the issue, but they did not, fearful of provoking a reactionary backlash, replete with seizure of trade union funds and arrest of strike leaders. Well into the ranks of the Center and Progressive Parties, furthermore, there lurked a nagging doubt about questioning the army, let alone challenging it in wartime.

And so throughout the critical summer months Michaelis, clearly not a man of peace, stayed at the helm. An opportunity to end the killing thus slipped away, for it is highly likely that with Reichstag leaders dictating a German willingness to join peace talks some sort of truce could have emerged from the deepening war-weariness of Europe. It might have been possible, for example, to thrash out an admittedly difficult agreement for a return to the status quo ante if all sides had come to the realization, as Russia had, that territorial gain stood in the path of peace. Woodrow Wilson would certainly have seen this as the moment to pressure Britain and France to moderate their war aims and make way for a peaceful, democratic world. That the postwar world would not stay peaceful or democratic for long—but probably would have if the Great War had ended in the summer of 1917—is one way to measure the significance of the opportunity that had slipped away.

Bolstering the Home Front: French Soldiers' Wives Queue for their Allowances
Harper's Pictorial Library

THE ENERVATION OF FRANCE, BRITAIN, AND ITALY

The relatively stable political situation in France, the oldest democracy among the Great Powers of Europe, stands in stark contrast to the troubled, scandal-ridden circumstances that prevailed in the authoritarian monarchies of Central and Eastern Europe or the turbulent young democracy in Italy.[29] As in all belligerent nations, the outbreak of war rallied the country and calmed prewar class and gender tensions. Representatives from the trade unions and women's suffrage groups participated in organizations to care for homeless refuges, widows, and others hurt by the German invasion. Strikes and suffrage marches were postponed while France weathered its time of crisis. "We will claim our rights when the triumph of right is assured,"[30] said one suffragette. This unity in society also carried over to the political arena where parliamentarians from all of the major parties, including the far-left French Socialist Party (SFIO) and (after October 1915) the Catholic right, joined the cabinet.

There were of course wartime tensions. Armaments workers pushed for an eight-hour day, women who entered the workforce in large numbers complained about male rudeness on the job, male laborers griped about women maybe taking their jobs, and city dwellers accused rural folk of having more to eat. The civilian leadership, particularly the more left-leaning parties, also chafed at the army's almost exclusive control of the war, especially after Verdun. But France was spared the controversial struggles of other countries for basic gains like the attainment of democracy. Frenchmen had possessed the vote since 1848 and parliamentary control of the state since 1871. Indeed the reforms that typically occur with democratic institutions helped France perpetuate its "sacred union" of 1914.

Trench Warfare: Reinforced Concrete Dugout Entrance on the Hindenburg Line
Canfield, *World War*

Thus women with husbands in uniform received generous allowances to replace lost wages. Legislators also shielded lower-class incomes by freezing rents. And in December 1916 the cabinet replaced Chief of Staff Joseph Joffre with Robert Nivelle, an innovative general with contacts on the left, and assumed supreme strategic control of the war.

But as people tried somehow to celebrate this third Christmas of the struggle, one issue—the war itself—was beginning to generate tensions and controversies similar to those that rocked other states. Indeed the Germans had killed over eight hundred thousand Frenchmen since 1914 and the nation was coming close to a collective psychological breaking point. The best-selling popularity of Henri Barbusse's *Le Feu* (Under Fire), a bleak picture of life and death in the trenches that called for French and German soldiers to unite, reflected this growing antiwar sentiment. So did the emergence of the "minoritarians," a minority faction in the trade unions and SFIO advocating a negotiated peace with no annexations or indemnities. These Young Turks nearly gained control of the SFIO in July 1916. During the late autumn counteroffensive at Verdun GQG also detected a drop in troop spirits that was blamed on Minoritarian propaganda. In early 1917, moreover, desertion rates increased significantly. One junior officer noted that many of his men "get drunk."

> Morale is low. They are fed up with the war. Certain corps court-martial some of the men for desertion, theft, insolence, etc. After condemnation they are transferred to another corps. My company is infested with them.[31]

Trench Warfare: Canadians Brave Shrapnel Fire (dark puffs) Going Over the Top at Vimy
Harper's Pictorial Library

Despite these alarm signals, however, the vast majority of soldiers seemed ready for one more offensive, especially after Nivelle promised a victorious end to the war. Nevertheless, as spring and the anticipated entry of the United States approached, Minister of War Paul Painlevé cast doubt on the general's plans, questioning the wisdom of risking another offensive. Why not just wait for American reinforcements? The cabinet granted the new man permission to attack only on the condition that he terminate operations after two days if he had not broken through.

Arras, Chemin des Dame, and the French Mutinies

The allies planned to smash in two phases through the northern and southern termini of Germany's "Siegfried Line," dubbed by British "Tommies" the "Hindenburg Line."[32] In late March–early April OHL had pulled twenty to forty kilometers out of the salient running between Arras and Chemin des Dames in order to increase the concentration of firepower and troops per mile. These newly prepared fortifications were even more formidable than the trench systems of 1915–1916. Once through at Arras, British forces would penetrate southeast over Cambrai to meet the French rushing north over the Chemin des Dame. The Hindenburg line would be surrounded or its defenders forced to retreat. But could the allies avoid the "mistake" of 1915–1916, namely, "to lose the [tactical] substance by grasping at the [strategic] shadow"?[33] And would the allies be able to conceal their preparations and gain the advantage of surprise?

Nearly twenty-nine hundred guns began to pound the Arras sector on April 4. Although still not up to French or German heavy gun levels, the barrage nonetheless had double the weight of the previous year's attempts along the Somme with more high explosive shells to destroy barbed wire, plus the added advantage of being shorter than German defenders anticipated. When the advance elements of eighteen divisions, including four Canadian and two Australian divisions, attacked along a fairly broad 25-kilometer front on April 9, therefore, they surprised and overwhelmed Sixth Army's seven forward divisions and pushed 3–5 kilometers forward. On the left the Canadians captured Vimy Ridge, so hotly contested in 1915, and entered Canadian military lore. German reserve divisions were too far back to counterattack and counter battery fire had neutralized defensive artillery.

To Free French Soil: General Robert Nivelle
Canfield, *World War*

As had happened many times before, however, the British did not press their advantage, giving Sixth Army reserves time to move up and dig in. The Battle of Arras now turned into an all-to-familiar stalemate, one that forty attacking tanks that mostly became easy targets for German gunners or mired in mud could not break. Both sides took over one hundred thousand casualties by battle's end in May, but the British had not penetrated to the unentrenched rear of the Hindenburg Line.

Nor had the French. Nivelle entered the battle overconfident from the success of artillery tactics used in the final stages of Verdun, where so-called creeping barrages shifted forward every few minutes to stay ahead of the advancing troops, which had worked against weary German defenders only too eager to retreat to more easily defended positions. There were other reasons the Frenchman believed he had finally made enough adjustments to Europe's military revolution to affect a revolution in military affairs that would win the war. He ordered a massive and

To Free French Soil: French Tanks Move to the Front
Courtesy of the Library of Congress

intense two-week bombardment featuring 2,300 heavy guns and mortars—77 heavy guns/mortars per first-wave infantry division, the greatest allied average yet for a full-scale offensive. Joffre's successor planned to send thirty divisions of Fifth and Sixth Armies behind a creeping barrage up and over the ridge, followed shortly by Tenth Army's ten divisions, all to achieve a first-day advance of 8–9 kilometers that would rupture enemy lines. Attacking along the lengthiest front to date on the western front—over 60 kilometers, plus subsidiary assaults further east beyond Rheims—Nivelle anticipated a huge "dam break."

From the heights, however, German Seventh and First Army observers had seen Nivelle's preparations. During a routine raid on April 4, moreover, the French battle plan had been seized from captured officers. Accordingly, the Germans left the first line on the hill undefended and concealed about four thousand machine gun nests in ravines and cave openings farther up. Their main strength, twelve divisions in front with a stronger force behind, was kept over the crest of the ridge and largely out of artillery range. For two months prior to the battle, furthermore, German rear artillery emplacements more than quintupled.

Compounding Nivelle's problems, April 16 was cold and rainy, turning the artillery-pummeled slope into an impossibly slippery mess. As his men groped their way, falling farther and farther behind a creeping barrage that moved relentlessly forward, they caught machine gun fire in their flanks and rear as German

To Free French Soil: French Infantry before Zero Hour
Courtesy of the Library of Congress,

crews allowed attackers to pass before firing. Nivelle's 128 tanks had no more success than the British farther north, breaking down quickly, "ditching" in the mud, or succumbing to German artillery fire.

After five days French troops had managed to secure some of the Chemin des Dames road that crossed the crest of the ridge—roughly five hundred meters from their original lines—but at a cost of 130,000 casualties. An angry French President Raymond Poincaré struggled with Nivelle for days, finally managing on April 23 to stop further massive attacks. A minor push by Sixth Army netted another kilometer or so on the German right flank. When it all ended on May 9 over 185,000 French soldiers had been killed or wounded. Disgraced, Nivelle was replaced by Henri Phillippe Pétain, the hero of Verdun. The Germans had lost 165,000 soldiers.

The French army, in the meantime, began to unravel from acts of "collective indiscipline,"[34] as Pétain described them to American General John J. Pershing. Already on Day 2 of the offensive 17 soldiers of one regiment left their post and went to the rear, and then in May 30,000 infantrymen abandoned the Chemin des Dames line. A junior officer recorded the scene at one train station receiving men who had been rotated out of the line:

> As soon as the train enters with what you would say a horde of savages, all the doors open on both sides and men flood out on the platforms. Shouts, insults, and

Over There: General Pershing Disembarks at Boulogne, June 13, 1917
John J. Pershing, *My Experiences in the World War* (New York, 1931)

> threats fly in all directions: death to the shirkers at home, murderers and pigs that they are; long live the revolution, down with the war, it's peace that we want, etc.[35]

The troubles spread to 68 of 112 divisions of the French army in June, each reporting one to five mutinous incidents but no killings of officers. The rank and file demanded an end to further attacks, better pay and living conditions, and more furloughs. They also expressed concern for the welfare of mothers, wives, and sisters, some of whom were themselves on strike for higher wages and improved working conditions. Many on the front and home front cried out for peace and condemned the war—one division almost marched on Paris before officers brought the men to their senses. The demonstration effect of the revolution in Russia certainly exacerbated relations in and out of the ranks.

But the French strain of rebelliousness was not as virulent as the Russian—they had overthrown their government, the French had not. Historians generally agree, in fact, that what seized France was "defencism" not defeatism. For the time being at least few had stomach left for going over the top, but no one wanted the Germans to win the war—the men were ready to hold the line. Pétain gradually managed to restore order with the proverbial carrot and the stick: he ended big offensives, deployed fewer units in perilous frontline trenches, granted more leave, and improved food rations; over three thousand soldiers were court-marshaled, on the other hand, and hundreds sentenced to death with forty-nine actually tied to execution posts and shot. Strikers in Paris and other towns got wage and working hour concessions too.

Over There: Advance Elements of the First Army Division at Boulogne, June 26, 1917
Harper's Pictorial Library

Nevertheless, how long could France stay in this war? "We are not here to lie to ourselves," said one young socialist to the lengthy, heavy applause of the Chamber of Deputies. "There is in France a weariness of war and a pressure for peace." Minister of War Painlevé felt the same pressure. Thus in late June he balked at the idea of meeting German intermediaries in Switzerland to discuss possible territorial exchanges accompanying peace talks, partly out of fear that if Germany made generous offers, particularly over Alsace and Lorraine, and publicized this, then the French people would accept these terms and end the war. "There is a limit to what flesh and blood can stand," an old friend told Pershing in Paris, "and the French have just about reached this limit."[36]

The U.S. declaration of war undoubtedly helped France overcome such pressures and persevere. Convoys protected by American destroyers brought food; generous loans permitted greater purchases of grain, explosives, and other war-related items; and the arrival of the first "doughboys" boosted French morale. Pershing's motorcade through the streets of Paris on June 14, for example, was mobbed by joyous crowds that pressed forward to get a glimpse of America's leading soldier. "Though I live a thousand years," said his chief of staff, "I shall never forget that crowded hour."[37] The scene was repeated on June 28 when a regiment of the 1st Division paraded through the city. The diplomatic situation had also changed, for once Wilson was at war he flatly rejected the notion of a compromise peace and communicated this stance to his allies as well as the pope. The president refused visas to American socialists wanting to attend the Second International's peace initiative in Stockholm, furthermore, and France and Britain followed his lead to the ire of their Labour and Socialist Parties. Only the defeat of authoritarian Germany could prepare the ground for the idealistic world order the American chief envisioned.

Trench Warfare: French Sappers Tunneling Under German Lines

Harper's Pictorial Library

There can also be little doubt, on the *hypothetical* other hand, that the success of the Reichstag's peace initiative that summer would have brought on the hour for peace that Wilson awaited. Fifteen months later he insisted on negotiating cease-fire terms with a German government representative of the people, not the militarists, but representative government was exactly what the Reichstag strove to attain in 1917—and it was blocked by Michaelis and OHL. Certainly Wilson would have used his considerable leverage to hammer out peace terms with Reichstag leaders. Thus his closest political adviser, Colonel Edward House, told British radicals who opposed more killing for territorial gains that "when the time comes, you] will find him on the right side." In April, similarly, House had told visiting Foreign Minister Arthur Balfour that the annexationist goals of Britain, France, and Italy were "all bad" and "a breeding ground for future war." In his reply to the pope, moreover, Wilson castigated the plans of all belligerents for "punitive damages, the dismemberment of empires, and the establishment of exclusive economic leagues."[38] If the Reichstag had pressed its political advantage and prevailed, Wilson's influence with Britain and France would have parlayed Western Europe's widespread war-weariness into a war-ending peace conference, particularly with leftists in both countries pressing for peace. This was what the Reichstag majority wanted; after the disastrous Kerensky offensive, Russia desperately needed it too. Without the lynchpin democratization of Germany, however, the war dragged on. Millions of soldiers paid dearly, in other words, for the shortcomings of the German opposition and the iron determination of an unfettered OHL.

British Democracy and the Yearning for Peace

Britain, Europe's second-oldest democracy among the Great Powers, also avoided the radicalizing, delegitimizing effects that war brought to Germany, Austria-Hungary, and Russia.[39] Like French trade unionists, the British, who had threatened a general strike before the war, called a labor truce and flocked to the colors. The women, too, rechanneled the heat of their gender war against the enemy. Thus Britain's radical suffragette, Christabel Pankhurst, initially described the war as "God's revenge upon those who held women in subjection," but by 1915 she stood squarely behind men "who at the risk of death are resisting the leader of the Anti-Suffragettes—William II."[40] The seemingly intractable Irish problem had also receded. Most Irish Catholic nationalists preferred independence from Britain but were prepared to accept home rule on their island, which meant joining Canada, South Africa, Australia, and New Zealand as self-governing dominions of the British Empire. In Northern Ireland, however, their Protestant, pro-British opponents preferred direct rule from London rather than become part of an unsympathetic Catholic dominion. Disagreements over Irish Home Rule brought Ireland to the brink of civil war in July 1914, but in August Catholic nationalists and Protestant "unionists" enlisted in great numbers and redirected their angry energy against Germany.

Parliamentary life also stayed relatively tranquil. The government of Liberal Party leader Herbert Asquith ruled alone until May 1915. At that time the debacle at Gallipoli and another war-related controversy, an alleged shell shortage in the BEF, induced him to add Conservatives to the cabinet, grant one ministry, the Admiralty of discredited Winston Churchill, to Conservative Arthur Balfour, and establish a new Ministry of Munitions under the Liberal's rising star, David Lloyd George. The disappointment after Kut and the Somme brought Lloyd George to Downing Street in December 1916, but the transition went fairly smoothly when he prudently opened the cabinet to more Conservatives as well as Labour Party leader Arthur Henderson.

And again like France, the timely functioning of British democracy preserved a good measure of domestic peace. Political leaders calmed striking workers, who had defied union leaders and struck in large numbers in 1915, by granting wage concessions and rent controls. Asquith also promised Irish MP leader John Redmond that home rule would be implemented after the war. "We have won at last a free constitution,"[41] Redmond declared. Parliament granted the suffrage, furthermore, to women thirty and older. To be sure, there were strike problems again in 1916, and Irish militants, worried by the popularity of Redmond's prowar stance, led an abortive coup in Dublin in March 1916. Significant German support did not materialize, however, because the army was still heavily engaged at Verdun and the navy balked at risking an amphibious landing. The uprising was easily put down, but the execution of many of the ringleaders made martyrs out of them, soured Irish Catholic support for the war, and greatly hampered military recruiting. With the exception of Ireland, however, Britain's home front remained an asset, not a liability, to the war effort.

Unlike France, Britain did not have enemy armies on its soil to rally the nation and perpetuate prowar sentiment. But German atrocities in 1914–1916—the shooting of Belgian hostages, the naval bombardment of Scarborough, the use of poison gas at Ypres, the *Lusitania* killings, the execution of Edith Cavell, a nurse who had helped allied POWs escape from captivity in Belgium, and the execution of Charles Fryatt, a captured merchant sea captain who had attempted to ram a U-boat—kept prowar anti-German feelings at a high pitch. Only a tiny minority disagreed. Thus pacifist zealots like Helena Swanwick refused to abandon the antiwar preference of the pre-1914 women's movement. She led a small faction of like-minded suffragettes to a poorly attended international peace conference at The Hague in 1915, where resolutions were passed advocating, among other things, a peacekeeping "league of nations," but the majority of women's activists in Britain denounced them as "wild women of theory" and "poisonous pacifists." The Independent Labour Party (ILP), a socialist offshoot of the parent party, pursued similar goals and criticized Britain's imperialist war aims. ILP speakers made little headway, however, in the year of the *Lusitania*. "We were called white-livered curs, bloody pro-Germans, friends of the Kaiser, and traitors to our country,"[42] remembered one agitator. Another Labour faction, the Union of Democratic Control (UDC), called for more democratic control of foreign policy, but despite the defection to the UDC of prewar Labour leader Ramsay MacDonald, its initial membership drive netted only five thousand.

As in so many other belligerent countries, however, Britain's national temperament changed noticeably in 1916. The withdrawal from Gallipoli, the surrender of Townsend in Iraq, and the glaringly costly failure on the Somme ended the easy, unquestioning acceptance of rah-rah patriotism. The official war film, *Battle of the Somme*, contributed to this more somber attitude. Viewers—probably several million—were in many cases horrified by newsreel footage of British soldiers getting killed on the first bloody day. Like the protagonist of H. G. Wells's 1916 best-selling novel, *Mr. Britling Sees it Through*, many had learned that war "has lost its soul, it has become mere incoherent fighting and destruction, a demonstration in vast and tragic forms of the stupidity and ineffectiveness of our species." Another sign of this spreading sense of "tragic disillusionment in a civilized mind," as Wells put it, was the publication of an anonymous article, "Reflections of a Soldier," in an influential liberal journal. The author, R. H. Tawney, castigated the flag-wavers and chest-thumpers who were ignorant of the soldier's "sensation of taking a profitless part in a game played by monkeys and organized by lunatics." The man in the trenches could not hate Germans. "Do you not see that we regard these men who have sat opposite us in mud as victims of the same catastrophe as ourselves, as our comrades in misery?"[43]

Small wonder the desire to seek a diplomatic end to the war grew as this ill-fated year wore on. Thus agitators of the ILP, who noticed that "war-weariness was setting in and [that] it was much easier to make anti-war speeches,"[44] condemned the coming of conscription in May 1916 and called for a negotiated peace. Similar sentiments for cease-fire and treaty talks spread far into the back benches of the Liberal Party and into the Labour Party too: its MPs backed the new government but only by a vote of seventeen to twelve. Reflecting the same antiwar skepticism, UDC membership swelled past half a million. There can be no doubt, therefore, that the ascendancy of Lloyd George and his all-party cabinet was not just a response to hawks demanding more effective leadership than Asquith had provided. Government members hoped the majority in Britain would persevere, but they found little solace in this hope. In demanding a fight to the finish they were clearly reacting to growing antiwar fever and asking Britons to stiffen backbones, find extra reserves of strength, and deliver knockout blows to a determined enemy.

Germany's determination soon became alarmingly evident. Unrestricted submarine warfare, an attempt to impose a reverse blockade on the British and sap their willingness to persevere, was not without effect. Supplies of wheat, meat, sugar, and tea grew short. The government responded by placing restrictions on brewing and reducing flour in bread. Now white bread yielded to "war bread." Despite these measures, prices soared: a four-pound loaf cost nearly four times more than 1914. These circumstances, in turn, exacerbated Britain's labor problems. Skilled adult male workers, already resentful of less-skilled women and youths who had entered the factories and earned high piece-rate wages on new, more productive machines, responded to the call of radical shop foremen, defied trade union leaders, and struck—two hundred thousand in March and May 1917. News of the Russian Revolution added impetus to this strike wave as both skilled and unskilled laborers "expressed distrust in, and total indifference to, any

Trench Warfare: British Tanks at Cambrai with Fascines
Used with the permission of *The Trustees of the Imperial War Museum, London*. Photo Number: Q-46932

promise the government may make,"[45] according to one investigating commission. As it had earlier in the war, Britain's democracy proved responsive, abandoning unpopular plans to further "dilute" skilled with unskilled labor, jettisoning the so-called leaving certificate system that restricted the movement of workers to higher-paying jobs, and introducing bread subsidies.

An uneasy calm returned to factories and workshops, but one issue—the war—grew more contentious. Britain's most popular novelist, H. G. Wells, advocated a negotiated settlement; Siegfried Sassoon, a widely read poet and decorated veteran of the Somme and Arras, denounced the war as imperialist; and that summer a Labour Party conference voted three-to-one to accept Russia's invitation to the socialist peace conference in Stockholm.

If antiwar sentiment was deepening, however, peace remained politically infeasible, for Michaelis, after briefly tempting Lloyd George with a deal over Belgium, backed away from further disingenuous feelers, and America's resolve to bring down German authoritarianism bolstered the British government. Lloyd George joined Washington and Paris in denying Labourites their visas. The Stockholm conference never met.

Messines Ridge, Passchendaele, and Cambrai

After the demoralizing Battles of Arras and Chemin des Dame, Sir Douglas Haig pressed a somewhat skeptical Lloyd George and the War Cabinet for an offensive in Flanders.[46] It was well known at GHQ that the prime minister looked askance at costly repetitions of previous western failures, in particular another blunder on the Somme, and that he regarded Italy, Greece, or the Middle East as theaters that could produce more decisive battles. Lloyd George did not possess the military expertise to counter the objections of professional soldiers, however, and appears to have been tempted by the idea of taking Flanders, a traditional British war aim. He found it difficult, furthermore, to discount Haig's carefully selected strategic arguments. Because Russia's sputtering war machine could not long resist the Central Powers, time was short before they shifted massive reinforcements to other fronts. With the resiliency of the Italian and French armies also in question—weak points the enemy was likely to exploit—Britain had to deliver punishing blows in its sector while opportunities presented themselves, for enemy victories elsewhere, coupled with pacifist demands at home, could lead to a peace conference before the end of 1917. "The pressure of war is becoming very acutely felt on the allied side," noted one of Haig's staffers that spring. If "the desire for peace" led to negotiations "before the war is fought to a military decision," then Britain's last operational plans "must bear in mind the desirability of depriving Germany of her assets in bargaining."[47] In other words, pushing the Germans out of occupied Belgium would strengthen Britain's hand at the peace table. And ideally, success in Flanders could render the enemy's position on the western front so precarious as to break "the fetters of trench warfare." The ever upbeat Haig took this for granted, promising his political chief "great results this year," nothing less than "to smash up the whole of the German army."[48]

He wanted first to seize Messines Ridge and then rapidly move up stronger forces to capture the rest of the Messines-Passchendaele ridge line east of Ypres—tactically crucial high ground that enemy forces had occupied since 1914—and drive northeast toward the coast. The landing of a marine division on Belgian beaches during this final push would threaten the German rear and speed victory. At critical meetings with the politicians in June, the height of the U-boat danger, First Sea Lord John Jellicoe's emphatic backing for the Flanders campaign helped Haig avoid rejection—but not yet win approval—for the wider push beyond Ypres. The navy chief stressed the urgency of taking German submarine bases in Belgium.

The Battle of Messines Ridge began in the pre-dawn hours of June 7 with a series of massive explosions under German trenches. British engineers and miners had labored for a year eighty feet under enemy dugouts to put a million pounds of explosives in twenty-four tunnels. The terrifying blasts, heard as far away as southern England, buried ten thousand German soldiers. A well-coordinated creeping barrage by more than two thousand guns multiplied the carnage as the German Fourth Army suffered an additional fifteen thousand casualties. By nightfall Haig's Second Army commander, Sir Herbert Plumer, had secured much of the eastern slope of the ridge along a thirteen-kilometer front.

For two years the tactical initiatives and innovations of trench warfare had favored the Germans, but now the British had achieved a major tactical victory that placed the enemy's defenses along the Belgian border in jeopardy. In consolidating positions on the ridge line, however, Plumer suffered losses equal to what he had

Ready for the Breakthrough: British Cavalryman and Horse with Gas Masks
Canfield, *World War*

inflicted as German guns pummeled his men trying to entrench—an alarming sign of things to come. Moreover, both Plumer and Fifth Army commander at Ypres Sir Hubert Gough resisted Haig's entreaties to push up the slopes of the next ridge to overrun Group Wytschaete: he had no time to shift artillery, said Plumer; it would create a vulnerable salient, said Gough. Their overcautiousness, and Haig's puzzling, "bewildering"[49] acquiescence in it, looms tragic in retrospect.

Seventeen frontline divisions under Gough finally renewed the assault on German trench networks on July 31, 1917—the British Second and Fifth Armies, and on their left, the French First Army, composed of troops unaffected by the spring mutinies. Ten days earlier Lloyd George had finally approved the broader "breakthrough"[50] campaign—five days *after* the preparatory bombardment had begun—with the proviso that London would reconsider its option of shifting divisions to Mediterranean theaters if Haig did not succeed. Almost from the beginning it appeared that he would not. The obsolete long barrage, necessitated by the inability of British artillery spotters to observe German batteries behind high ground, confirmed what German officers could see from their ridges after the fall of Messines, namely, that the British were coming again.

This gave Fourth Army's new defensive expert, Colonel Fritz von Lossberg, ample time to prepare an even stouter "defense in depth" than that used at Chemin des Dame. Forward trenches were left largely undefended, except for storm trooper squads heavily armed with mortars, machine guns, grenade launchers, and the "hideous" flamethrowers. These small ten-man teams were trained to infiltrate, outflank, and punish advancing enemy infantry. More powerful, artillery-backed counterattack forces would move up next but also before the British could entrench. The artillery would employ the relatively new technique of predicted fire, whereby gunners aimed at carefully reconnoitered map coordinates rather than first "registering" (i.e., firing ranging shots), which warned defenders of an impending barrage. The German High Command planned to use similar tactics a few weeks later at Riga (see later) but as a purely offensive (as opposed to counteroffensive) technique. Thus Passchendaele and Riga were critical experiments in perfecting the devastating storm troop tactics of March 1918.[51]

Most of the German first line fell quickly to Gough, not surprisingly, but as the innovative tactical edge swung back to the defenders, further gains proved nearly impossible, especially against Group Wytschaete on Gheluvelt Plateau, which Second Army failed to secure. Complicating matters, an almost constant rain turned the battlefield into an impassable morass as attempts continued throughout August. "Thunderstorms, welcome rain, our most effective ally,"[52] said one German general. Fifty-two tanks proved too few; too prone to breakdown and ditching; and too easy targets, furthermore, to make a difference. Haig called a halt on August 25, having gained only one–four kilometers. He had lost another sixty-eight thousand men. Despite this, surprisingly enough, Haig won political approval in September to continue the battle. It seems that with peace talks still a possibility Lloyd George remained tempted enough by potential conquests in Flanders to accept GHQ's depictions of a German army on the verge of retreat. It is also true that he was too distracted by the U-boats, zeppelin attacks on London, and the impending invasion of Palestine to seriously scrutinize further operations. In particular the zeppelin attacks, which would indeed kill or injure 4,821 civilians, "seemed to occupy an inordinate amount of [the War Cabinet's] attention"[53] in comparison to the real bloodbath in Flanders.

Still fearful of setbacks, however, Haig turned to Plumer, who believed he had a tactical riposte to German defense in depth. Rather than risk another battle of attrition, he proposed a series of short, one-thousand-meter hops accompanied by brutal creeping barrages using more high explosive shells that would paralyze survivors, enabling British infantry to dig in before the enemy mounted its countermeasures. Aided by drier weather in late September and early October, Plumer made three "bite and hold" attacks, advancing British lines four kilometers against Group Ypres farther north on the Gheluvelt Plateau. His third assault was especially effective, for Lossberg had abandoned defense in depth and moved divisions up. Tens of thousands of infantrymen were pulverized by British artillery as a result.

Dominion forces proceeded over subsequent weeks to take most of the German high ground, including Passchendaele village on November 6, eight kilometers from the original British line. The return of rainy weather and attrition tactics had made Flanders a bloody, corpse-filled quagmire in the meantime, however, and a few days later Haig called off the controversial campaign. He had failed to penetrate eight kilometers beyond Passchendaele to Roulers, the point, when reached, that the marines were supposed to land.

Some charge that Lloyd George contributed to this end by withholding reinforcements and thus scuttling Haig's battle plan.[54] Although it is true that the prime minister and other cabinet members finally lost patience with costly offensives, deciding to adopt defensive strategies and save British lives in 1918 for a victorious final push with the Americans in 1919, London, in fact, had not left GHQ in the lurch. Despite absorbing over 750,000 casualties in 1917, at least 250,000 of these at Passchendaele alone,[55] BEF strength at the end of the year was only approximately 60,000 less than in early 1917. To be sure, Haig wanted more troops, especially frontline soldiers, but clearly he had still received massive reinforcements. Mixed with the cabinet's loss of faith in Haig's generalship, moreover, were other weighty considerations: men were needed at home for the navy, shipbuilding and aircraft production, agriculture and forestry, not to mention home defense against possible insurrection—or even invasion if Russian and Italian collapses made the Central Powers too strong on the western front. Defense also seemed wiser than offense because the BEF was physically and mentally spent after its terrible losses. "The British Army lost its spirit of optimism [in 1917]," observed war correspondent Philip Gibbs, "and there was a sense of deadly depression among the many officers and men with whom I came in touch." Only the ample supplies of food and ammunition, coupled with knowledge that the Germans had also suffered badly, kept the hope of ultimate victory alive.[56]

Indeed Ludendorff had lost about 250,000 men himself in halting an "almost irresistible"[57] offensive. He had rotated 51 exhausted divisions out of Flanders and 67 rested divisions in but had faced 57 allied divisions that were nearly twice as large as his undersized units—an alarming disadvantage. As a world power, furthermore, Britain could draw on fighting resources from around the globe to aid its effort in Europe, just as it had done in 1915–1916 to ward off the threat of Jihad. By 1917, for instance, Haig's ranks included ten Canadian and ANZAC

Trench Warfare: Ditched British Tank at Cambrai
Canfield, *World War*

(Australian and New Zealand Army Corps) infantry divisions, plus one South African brigade and two Indian cavalry divisions—he could even afford to shift Indian infantry divisions to Egypt. The Briton complained about a replacement shortage, but the German, aware that his uniformed manpower had peaked in mid-1917 and then begun a slight descent, could only see such "shortages" as a luxury. The British had complained about shell and explosives shortages too earlier in the war, but they had a decided four-to-one edge in 1917 according to Ludendorff's top aide, Max Bauer. Passchendaele had shown, moreover, that the allies were perfecting their tactics by trial and error. And, as Ludendorff recalled, there was more:

> The troops had borne the continuous defensive with uncommon difficulty. Skulkers were already numerous. They reappeared as soon as the battle was over, and it had become quite common for divisions which came out of action with desperately low effectives to be considerably stronger after only a few days. Against the power of hostile weapons the troops no longer displayed their old stubbornness in defense.[58]

Thus it seemed only a matter of time to Ludendorff before the enemy broke through the Hindenburg Line. Therefore only an offensive in 1918 would improve the sagging morale of troops who, punished constantly in their trenches, were beginning to surrender in larger numbers.

Haig, too, believed that he had to attack, produce victory from difficult circumstances, and restore his men's spirits, but unlike Ludendorff, whose standing in Berlin remained high, the British general needed a military success to buttress his sagging position in London. Thus shortly after Passchendaele he issued orders for an innovative assault on more weakly defended Cambrai.

Tank enthusiasts at GHQ like Brigadier General H. J. Elles longed to disprove detractors who scorned the steel elephants as big slow-moving targets that easily ditched, broke down, stuck in mud, or incapacitated crews with heat and exhaust fumes.[59] Elles insisted that tanks could break through before breaking down if deployed in mass formations over drier, flatter ground, especially with close airplane and infantry support as well as predicted artillery fire to have an element of surprise. If the tanks could overrun all three trench systems in a day—all that could be expected—massed cavalry and infantry reserves could exploit the breach, swinging north and south to roll up German positions. The objective, a characteristically optimistic Haig agreed, "was no less than the destruction of the German army in the west."[60]

Would the new tank tactics produce the elusive revolution in military affairs? Shortly before dawn on November 20, 1917, Third Army's unregistered artillery fire lit up the dark skies around Cambrai and 216 tanks rumbled forward with 54 trailing as reinforcements—army commander Sir Julian Byng kept back another 54 tanks in general reserve. It was by far the largest armored attack to date. Soon three hundred planes flew overhead, bombing and strafing the startled three divisions of German Second Army. Six infantry divisions moved out too, most employing tactics recommended by Elles's staff: trotting single file behind the tanks for cover, a cleared path through the barbed wire, and a way over the trenches. Indeed the tanks carried thick ten-foot-long bundles of wood ("fascines") to drop in the trenches as makeshift bridges. By noon the British left and right flanks had advanced four–six kilometers to Bourlow Wood and Crevecoeur, taking thousands of prisoners and seizing a hundred guns. In the center, however, Major General G. M. Harper ordered his infantry division to trail far behind to avoid the artillery shelling that previous battles had shown tanks attracted. Consequently, German infantrymen were able to run forward and immobilize many tanks by placing grenades under the treads. Attrition and artillery fire took others and the attack petered out near the village of Flesquières. Although the British advanced over subsequent days, the chance of a large-scale breakthrough had already been lost, for Ludendorff immediately rushed division after division to Cambrai and then successfully counterattacked on November 30, once again using storm trooper tactics. The tanks had ceased to be a factor long before this: 71 had broken down, 43 had ditched, and 65 had fallen to enemy action. The tank corps was right, however, in attributing this defeat to Harper's faulty tactics as well as Byng's unwillingness to use *more* tanks—of 476 tanks amassed at Cambrai he deployed only 324 in the front lines or in reserve.

And it would not get better, for the balance of BEF opinion after Cambrai favored not the tank enthusiasts but rather a dominant faction of "traditionalists" still very skeptical of tanks but also fundamentally averse to an overemphasis on mechanical warfare as opposed to human endeavor. The tankers considered it "a monstrous state of affairs."[61] With one major exception in August 1918, however, the Battle of Amiens, the British did not again deploy tanks in mass formations.

Caporetto: Infamy and Redemption on the Italian Front

Haig's exhausted halt at Passchendaele, followed by the disappointing Battle of Cambrai, coincided with other signs that Central Power fortunes in Europe were beginning to improve. As explained later, Germany exploited the disintegration of the Russian army to roll up the Baltic coast to Riga and then a few months after the collapse of Russian democracy in November 1917 impose draconian peace terms on a weak Communist government. Rumanian opposition also came to an end, and Italy very narrowly avoided the same fate when German and Austro-Hungarian armies flung themselves across the Isonzo River into the dramatic Battle of Caporetto.[62]

In two years of campaigning Italian commander Luigi Cadorna had managed to push his armies up from the Isonzo River into rugged terrain. Gorizia, the western edge of the Bainsizza, and the high ground past Caporetto had fallen but at a terribly high cost. Eleventh Isonzo in August–September 1917 was the worst yet, bleeding the army of 182,000 dead, wounded, and missing. Discipline under the iron hand of Cadorna and the military police had not broken, but after more than half a million killed in action since 1915 "the sense of 'one's number being up' may have been collective."[63] The battle was accompanied by strikes on the home front and radical appeals to solidarity with Lenin and the Bolsheviks. Pope Benedict XV spoke for the vast majority of Italians that summer when he implored the warring nations to end "the useless carnage." Popular tribune Giovanni Giolitti seconded the pontiff, and even former prime minister Antonio Salandra, the man most responsible for maneuvering Italy into the war, felt that the time had come for secret peace talks with Germany and Austria-Hungary. Outside the Reichstag, unfortunately, no one in Berlin was listening, and this prowar stance made it extremely difficult for Kaiser Karl in Vienna to follow his instincts. Although Karl knew his realm would fall to "ruin" before an annexationist "German peace"[64] were won, William II, buoyed by OHL, would not hear of it, blurting that he would rather cut ties with Vienna than sacrifice Liège.

With no peace in sight, the soldiers of the Dual Monarchy did not like their chances on the only active front they faced—the Isonzo. Reduced to their last mountain defenses, and fearing an Italian breakthrough and capture of Trieste, Cadorna's main operational goal, the Austrians appealed to Berlin. Pressed by Kaiser William himself, Ludendorff had to comply. He shifted seven divisions from quiet sectors in France for temporary deployment on the Isonzo. Joining seven Austro-Hungarian divisions in a new Fourteenth Army, they assaulted the Italian Second Army near Caporetto on October 24, 1917. Simultaneously, ten divisions of Second Army attacked the elite Italian Third on the coast of the Gulf of Venice.

The poorly led, demoralized Italian Second Army crumbled before the Central Power onslaught. After a short but very effective artillery bombardment, well-trained German and Austrian mountain battalions moved out, stealthily using trees, reverse slopes, and ravines to circle around pockets of defenders, cut off lines of retreat, and compel surrender. At first platoons and companies waved

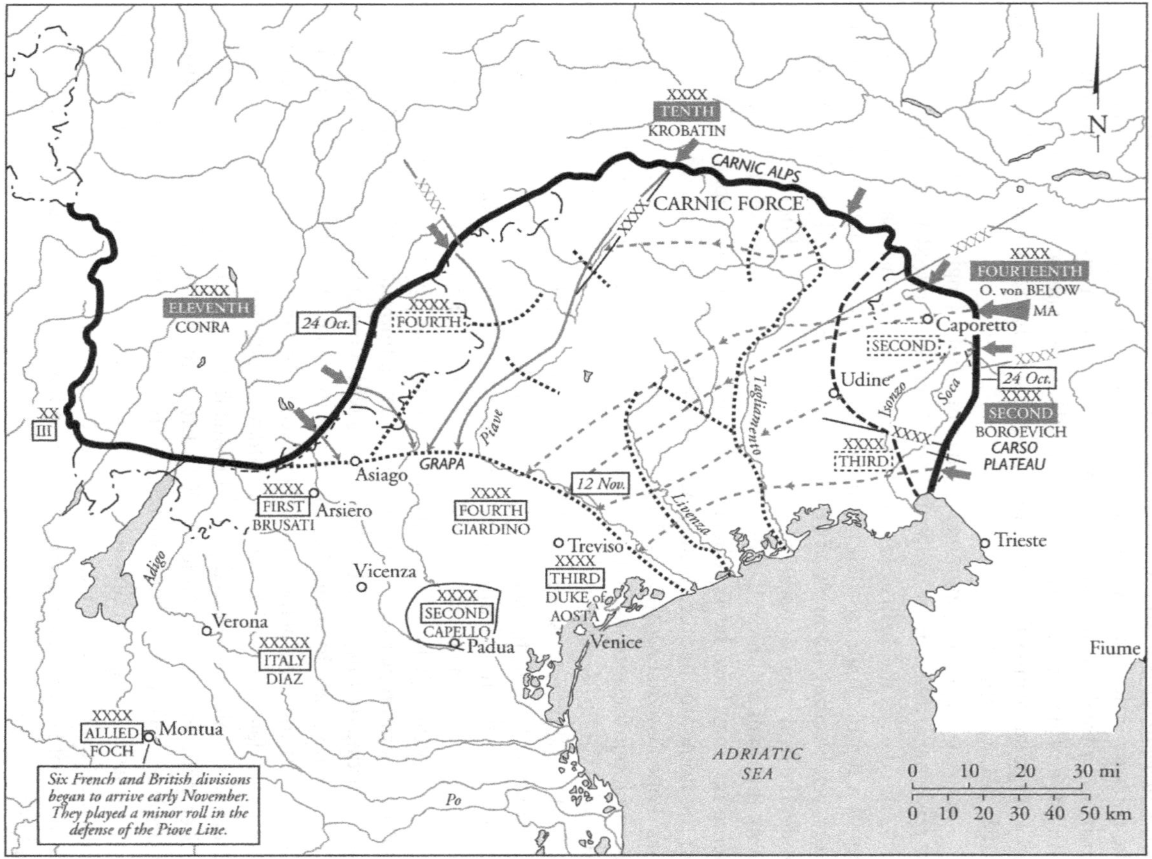

Battle of Caporetto in 1917

Maps Courtesy of the Department of History, United States Military Academy

the white flag, but then as infiltration tactics became more menacing, whole regiments put up their hands. One German captain in the Württemberg Mountain Battalion, Erwin Rommel, the later "Desert Fox" of World War II, took sixteen hundred prisoners on the morning of October 26, then encountered another regiment whose men shoved their officers aside, rushed the startled German, and hoisted him on their shoulders, exclaiming "Long live Germany."[65]

By October 28 the remnants of Second Army were streaming back 80 kilometers to the Tagliamento River, where Cadorna hoped to make a stand. Most of this large force had been killed, wounded, or captured, however, which forced another withdrawal of Third and a rump Second to the Piave River another 60–70 kilometers to the rear. There, with First and Fourth Armies, which had abandoned the entire Tyrolean front, the Italians managed to hold in mid-November. Their defense of Monte Grappa anchoring the center was critical to this stand, for its fall would have exposed the rear flank of the Piave defenders and forced a further 120-kilometer retreat to the Po River.

It would be difficult to exaggerate the extent of the disaster. The Italian army lost 10,000 killed, 30,000 wounded, 293,000 taken prisoner, and another 400,000 to desertion—733,000 men, over a third of the entire army. During the chaotic retreat 5,000 cannon and mortars—half of the army's tubes—3,000 machine guns, vast stores of munitions and equipment, and almost the entire province north of Venice were abandoned. Not since the German campaigns in France and Poland in 1914 and 1915 had armies made such long, rapid advances. Only the invaders' lengthening supply lines, and Central Power inability to divert more divisions from other fronts to Italy, prevented an even greater, war-ending rout.

Indeed Caporetto had been a crisis. Two generals and one politician committed suicide. Cadorna was sacked and Prime Minister Paulo Boselli ousted. King Victor Emmanuel considered abdication. Britain and France rushed six divisions to Italy in November to avert the loss of a valuable ally. Allied heavy artillery played a critical role at Monte Grappa. On the other hand, the army had rallied before allied reinforcements arrived. Resistance had stiffened considerably between the Tagliamento and the Piave as both soldiers and civilians responded to the need to defend Italian soil. Even the socialists spoke of resisting to the end. And Boselli was replaced by Vittorio Orlando, a former advocate of neutrality who now stepped forward to salvage what was left of the war effort. "For the first time in history," writes Denis Mack Smith, "the Italian people stood together almost as one."[66] The infamy of Caporetto had generated a national redemption of sorts, but the army and the people were exhausted.

BOLSHEVISM AND THE END OF THE RUSSIAN WAR EFFORT

Nowhere did the passing of peace opportunities have more far-reaching political and military consequences than in Russia.[67] Kerensky's July offensive had been motivated by the desperate hope that success would strengthen Russia's voice in Entente circles, moderate allied war aims, and facilitate general peace talks. Miserable battlefield failure had the opposite effect, reducing British and French respect for Russia's position to near zero as they looked to themselves and the Americans to produce victory. Accordingly, many in the Provisional Government lost interest in their own peace initiatives. Thus Foreign Minister Tereshchenko abandoned the foundering Stockholm conference and promised once again not to sign a separate peace. Some optimists in the cabinet hoped that an interallied strategy conference scheduled for November would enable Russia to press its allies to accept peace based largely on the status quo ante. In the meantime, despite mounting signs of hatred for the war, Kerensky believed he had no alternative but to continue it.

The new commander of Russian forces, Lavr Kornilov, certainly agreed, but he believed in winning the war, and to do this, destroying the growing power of the soviets of workers, peasants, and soldiers, especially the increasingly radical St. Petersburg Soviet. Kornilov, the brawny but not very brainy son of a Cossack, had restored some order to the ranks of the 6 million men who remained under arms—2 million had deserted—but he wanted to restore the kind of discipline necessary for victory by reimposing the army's death penalty. Russia's fledgling democracy was falling apart, however, as witnessed in late August when Kerensky convened a conference of all parties to rally the nation around his leadership but failed to achieve unity among the country's polarized factions. With no apparent hope for effective parliamentary rule, and with the allegedly "weak and womanly"[68] Kerensky vacillating on the death penalty issue, the general was tempted to embolden his political chief by marching on the capital. Rightist business, noble, and military circles were urging Kornilov, in fact, to seize power and save Russia. While Kornilov pondered his options, the German army suddenly ended the relative quiet on the eastern front by seizing Riga in a daring and innovative attack. Opposing lines ran along the lower Dvina River, except for the Riga area where Russia still commanded the western bank and southern shore of the Gulf of Riga. Reinforced by Ludendorff, General Oskar von Hutier's Eighth Army sent a powerful strike force across the Dvina on September 1. A short, unregistered artillery bombardment preceded the river crossing by storm troop squads heavily armed with machine guns, mortars, and flamethrowers; supported by strafing airplanes; and advancing behind a creeping barrage. Follow-up battalions mopped up remaining pockets of resistance.[69] The Russian Twelfth Army fought hard enough for most defenders to escape—proof that the army had not yet fully disintegrated—but the city fell on September 3.

The military reasons for eliminating this bridgehead mattered less to Ludendorff, however, than the political rationale. Germany had long known of the real potential of the Bolsheviks to disrupt and undermine the Russian war effort. Their leader, Vladimir Ilyich Lenin, regarded the fall of the monarchy and establishment of democratic institutions as mere prelude to his party's seizure of power, an act that could very well trigger civil war given the Bolsheviks' refusal to cooperate with less radical parties. For this reason Berlin had allowed Lenin to leave Switzerland, cross German territory, and return to Russia in April. The Bolshevik rank and file rose up against the Provisional Government in July amidst the controversy of the summer offensive, but the ill-planned Putsch failed miserably and many party leaders, including Lenin, went into hiding. Bolshevik fortunes revived in August and September, however, as escalating strikes, food riots, land seizures, and antiwar emotions drew the urban masses to Lenin and his insistent demand for "peace, land, and bread." By taking Riga and opening the road to St. Petersburg, the "heart and brain of the revolution,"[70] Ludendorff gambled that politically unstable Russia might sink into war-ending revolutionary or counter-revolutionary violence.[71]

Three days after the fall of Riga, Kerensky's deputy war minister, Boris Savinkov, ordered Kornilov to move a cavalry corps into the capital. He anticipated a Bolshevik demonstration and perhaps another coup attempt. The general had already decided to do this, for Riga had alarmed him: only by restoring the authority of the officer corps could Russia defeat Germany, and this required imposition of the death penalty and martial law. Kornilov wanted to include Kerensky in the cabinet, perhaps even as prime minister, and he believed (through contact with an unreliable intermediary) that Kerensky had agreed. Thus Kornilov's decision to comply with Savinkov's request was probably not the "mutiny" of legend. The beleaguered Kerensky either had not agreed initially or else changed his mind, unwilling to accept a political demotion and no doubt fearing arrest and the firing squad. On September 9 he dismissed the surprised general and mobilized the workers of St. Petersburg against alleged counterrevolution. Armed socialists from various parties, including thousands of Bolshevik "Red Guards," met Kornilov's advance units and easily convinced them not to proceed. The "mutiny" was over, but so was Kerensky's last chance of survival. Not only had he put weapons into the hands of his most determined opponents, he had also angered the officer corps by arresting their popular commander. The generals and their compatriots on the right would not help Kerensky when the left made its move.

Indeed the so-called Kornilov Affair had immediate political repercussions. Having already won majorities in the soviets of five big towns in August, including Samara and Tsaritsyn, the Bolsheviks now won control of Saratov, Moscow, and on September 12, St. Petersburg itself as soviet deputies left other socialist parties to join Lenin and brace the revolution against counterrevolution. His dynamic comrade, Leon Trotsky, became chairman of the St. Petersburg Soviet on October 8. From his exile in Helsinki, meanwhile, Lenin kept constant pressure on Bolshevik leaders, taunting and haranguing them mercilessly to rise up against the Provisional Government. Fearing a repeat of the near disaster of July, however, they resisted his increasingly insulting prodding. On October 12, for instance, he castigated all cautious Bolsheviks as "miserable traitors to the proletarian cause." To wait any longer was "utter idiocy, sheer treachery."[72]

Days later Ludendorff again sought to manipulate Russia's political drama. He planned an amphibious assault on Baltic islands at the mouth of the Gulf of Finland. "The blow," he recalled, "was aimed at St. Petersburg, and . . . was bound to make a profound impression there." He was right, for since early September rumors had spread, becoming more frantic with each retelling, that the German army was nearing the capital. Then came alarming news that a German navy flotilla had steamed into the Gulf of Riga, taking Oesel on October 16, Moon on October 18, and Dagoe on October 20. "How far these... attacks accelerated matters in Russia I do not know," wrote Ludendorff, but this Baltic expedition did, in fact, "make a profound impression"[73] in St. Petersburg.

There, as autumn expired, political pundits roundly assumed that Kerensky planned to send the city's radicalized garrison to a faraway front, abandon the defenseless city for Moscow, and allow "the advancing Germans" to decapitate the soviet head of the dual-headed revolution. In rightist circles "it was a dinner-party commonplace," writes Orlando Figes, "that only the Kaiser could restore order."[74] To defend the revolution from the Germans as well as from counterrevolution at home Trotsky organized the Military Revolutionary Committee (MRC) of the St. Petersburg Soviet on October 22. One day later Lenin, having returned from Finland, finally convinced Bolshevik colleagues to seize power, but no date was chosen—the cautious ones, mindful of July's failed coup, still had influence. While the Bolsheviks vacillated, an overconfident Kerensky looked forward to the imminent test of strength: "I would be prepared to offer prayers to produce this uprising," he said. "I have greater forces than necessary—[the Bolsheviks] will be utterly crushed."[75] To induce this trial-by-combat on November 2, he ordered the bulk of the St. Petersburg garrison to the front—similar orders had precipitated the Bolsheviks' July putsch. Now Trotsky's MRC swung into action, easily won over the soldiers of the garrison to Bolshevism, and then on November 5 pulled off a similar coup at the Peter and Paul Fortress, where one hundred thousand rifles fell into party hands. When the MRC finally moved against the Winter Palace housing the Provisional Government on November 7, 1917, Kerensky had only a few soldiers to fight back. Shocked by this, he fled to the front to rally the army, but the generals ignored him—only a few hundred cavalrymen followed him back to the city. Russia's seventy-four year Communist reign had begun.

One of Lenin's first acts on November 8 was to draft a "decree on peace" for the Bolshevik-dominated All-Russian Congress of Soviets that had convened in St. Petersburg the day before and in whose name the MRC had seized power. The ever pragmatic Lenin realized that his regime must end the war before another faction in Russia expropriated his own antiwar slogans to seize power. The decree called on all belligerents to make peace, but when the western allies refused he settled for an armistice with Imperial Germany. The cease-fire took effect on December 15, 1917.

Now the Russian army did indeed melt away as soldiers left their units for home, land, bread, and peace. Six days earlier those Rumanian forces who had escaped in 1916 to Russian Moldavia surrendered to pursuing German armies. The Central Powers had no one left to fight in the east. Since late November 1917, in fact, Ludendorff had begun a massive transfer of divisions to the western front for a final reckoning with the British, the French, and the newly arriving Americans. The logjam stalemate of the Great War was about to break.

NOTES

1. For Yusupov's description of events, and this opening scene in general, see Edvard Radzinsky, *The Rasputin File*, trans. Judson Rosengrant (New York, 2000), 464. Based on a wealth of new sources, Radzinsky's remarkable work revises older misleading interpretations of Rasputin and his murder.
2. Citations in ibid., 465.
3. Cited in Radzinsky, *Rasputin File*, 262.
4. Cited in Orlando Figes, *A People's Tragedy: The Russian Revolution 1891–1924* (New York, 1996), 289.
5. Citations in ibid., 287; Robert K. Massie, *Nicholas and Alexandra* (New York, 1967), 367; and Radzinsky, *Rasputin File*, 472.
6. Radzinsky, *Rasputin File*, 483.
7. Citations in ibid., 488.
8. For the March Revolution, see the still useful Michael T. Florinsky, *Russia: A History and An Interpretation* (New York, 1970), 2:1374–1405; W. Bruce Lincoln, *Armageddon: The Russians in War and Revolution* (New York, 1986), 315–345; Edward Acton, *Rethinking the Russian Revolution* (London, 1990), 107–128; and Figes, *People's Tragedy*, 307–353.
9. For the Rasputin scandal and the army, see Allan K. Wildman, *The End of the Russian Imperial Army* (Princeton, NJ, 1980, 1987), 1:110–113.
10. Citations here and below in Florinsky, *Russia*, 2:1397–1399.
11. Cited in Klaus Epstein, *Matthias Erzberger and the Dilemma of German Democracy* (Princeton, NJ, 1959), 171.
12. Cited in Wildman, *End of the Russian Imperial Army*, 2:16.
13. Cited in Alfred W. F. Knox, *With the Russian Army 1914–1917* (New York, 1921), 2:638. For earlier citations, see Figes, *People's Tragedy*, 415–418. For the classic analysis of the deteriorated state of the Russian army, see Wildman, *End of the Russian Imperial Army*, 1:275–290, 332–372, and 2:3–111.
14. For good descriptions of the offensive and its aftermath, see Lincoln, *Armageddon*, 404–414; and Wildman, *End of the Russian Imperial Army*, 2:89–147.
15. See Knox, *With the Russian Army*, 2:641.
16. For U-boat warfare in 1917, see Holger H. Herwig, *'Luxury' Fleet: The Imperial German Navy 1888–1918* (London, 1980), 220–229; Richard Hough, *The Great War at Sea 1914–1918* (Oxford, 1983), 301–314; Paul G. Halpern, *A Naval History of World War I* (Annapolis, MD, 1994), 335–380; and Robert K. Massie, *Castles of Steel: Britain, Germany, and the Winning of he Great War at Sea* (New York, 2003), 715–738.
17. William S. Sims, *The Victory at Sea* (New York, 1920), 9.
18. The most recent discussion is David Paull Nickles, *Under the Wire: How the Telegraph Changed Diplomacy* (Cambridge, MA, 2003), 137–160. The standard account remains Barbara W. Tuchman, *The Zimmermann Telegram* (New York, 1958).
19. Cited in John Morton Blum, *Woodrow Wilson and the Politics of Morality* (Boston, 1956), 130.
20. For the best discussions of this question, see David Stevenson, *Cataclysm: The First World War as Political Tragedy* (New York, 2004), 263–266; John Keegan, *The First World War* (New York, 1999), 350–355; and especially Massie, *Castles of Steel*, 715–738.
21. Karl Doenitz, Memoirs: *Ten Years and Twenty Days* (Annapolis, MD, 1959), 89.
22. Cited in ibid., 717.
23. Cited in Epstein, *Matthias Erzberger*, 186.
24. Cited in ibid., 202–203.
25. Cited in Lamar Cecil, *Wilhelm II: Emperor and Exile, 1900–1941* (Chapel Hill, NC, 1996), 250.

26. Cited in Epstein, *Matthias Erzberger,* 206.
27. For the best corrective, see David Stevenson, *Cataclysm: The First World War as Political Tragedy* (New York, 2004), 289–292.
28. Epstein, *Matthias Erzberger,* 209.
29. For wartime politics in France, see James F. McMillan, *Twentieth-Century France: Politics and Society 1898–1991* (New York, 1992), 65–76; and *Stevenson, Cataclysm,* 215–219.
30. Cited in Steven C. Hause and Anne R. Kenney, *Women's Suffrage and Social Politics in the French Third Republic* (Princeton, NJ, 1984), 191.
31. The diary of Henri Desagneaux is excerpted in Marilyn Shevin-Coetzee and Frans Coetzee, eds., *World War I and European Society: Sourcebook* (Lexington, MA, 1995), 252.
32. For good discussions of allied plans, the military outcome, and political aftermath, see Rod Paschall, *The Defeat of Imperial Germany 1917–1918* (New York, 1994), 29–54; John Keegan, *The First World War*(New York, 1999), 322–332; Stevenson, *Cataclysm,* 139–143, 268–302; and Robert A. Doughty, *Pyrrhic Victory: French Strategy and Operations in the Great War* (Cambridge, MA, 2005), 344–354.
33. One of the BEF's skeptical corps commanders before the Battle of the Somme, cited in Robin Prior and Trevor Wilson, *The Somme* (New Haven, CT, 2005), 41.
34. Cited in Donald Smythe, *Pershing: General of the Armies* (Bloomington, IN, 1986), 21–22.
35. The diary of Henri Desagneaux is excerpted in Coetzee and Coetzee, *World War I and European Society,* 253.
36. For Painlevé, see Stevenson, *Cataclysm,* 292. For the citations, see John J. Pershing, *My Experiences in the World War* (New York, 1931), 78.
37. James G. Harbord, *The American Army in France 1917–1919* (Boston, 1936), 79–80.
38. Citations in Stevenson, *Cataclysm,* 298.
39. For wartime politics, see Trevor Wilson, *The Myriad Faces of War: Britain and the Great War, 1914–1918* (Cambridge, UK, 1986); John Turner, *British Politics and the Great War: Coalition and Conflict, 1915–1918* (London, 1992); and Stevenson, *Cataclysm,* 219–225, 286–287, 291–292.
40. Cited in Sandra M. Gilbert, "Soldier's Heart: Literary Men, Literary Women, and the Great War," in Margaret Randolph Higonnet et al., *Behind the Lines: Gender and the Two World Wars* (New Haven, CT, 1987), 197.
41. Cited in D. George Boyce, *Ireland 1828–1923: From Ascendancy to Democracy* (Oxford, 1992), 88.
42. Citations in Susan Kingsley Kent, *Making Peace: The Reconstruction of Gender in Interwar Britain* (Princeton, NJ, 1993), 77. The remembrance of Scottish ILP leader James Maxton is excerpted in Coetzee and Coetzee, *World War I and European Society,* 260.
43. Tawney's article is excerpted in Coetzee and Coetzee, *World War I and European Society,* 257–258. Also see Alfred F. Havighurst, *Twentieth-Century Britain* (New York, 1962), 138, 139.
44. Maxton's remembrance is excerpted in Coetzee and Coetzee, *World War I and European Society,* 262.
45. The commission report is excerpted in ibid., 276.
46. For good accounts of the Battles of Messines Ridge, Passchendaele, and Cambrai, see Keegan, *First World War,* 355–371; Peter Simkins, Geoffrey Jukes, and Michael Hickey, *The First World War: The War to End All Wars* (Oxford, 2003), 126–139; but especially Paschall, *Defeat of Imperial Germany,* 55–80, 103–127; Tim Travers, *How the War Was Won: Command and Technology in the British Army on the Western Front, 1917–1918* (London, 1992), 11–31; Denis Winter, *Haig's Command: A Reassessment* (Barnsley, UK, 2004), 68–113, originally published in 1991; and Robin Prior and Trevor Wilson, *Passchendaele: The Untold Story* (New Haven, CT, 1996), 55–200.

47. Cited in Winter, *Haig's Command*, 103–104.
48. Citations in Cyril Falls, *The Great War 1914–1918* (New York, 1961), 298; Keegan, *First World War*, 358; and Holger H. Herwig, *The First World War: Germany and Austria-Hungary 1914–1918* (London, 1997), 331.
49. Prior and Wilson, *Passchendaele*, 64.
50. That breakthrough was indeed the goal, as in earlier offensives, see Tim Travers, *The Killing Ground: The British Army, the Western Front, and the Emergence of Modern Warfare 1900–1918* (London, 1987), 205–219.
51. For the evolution of new tactics on the German side, see Timothy T. Lupfer, *The Dynamics of Doctrine: The Changes in German Tactical Doctrine during the First World War* (Ft. Leavenworth, KS, 1981); Bruce I. Gudmundsson, *Stormtroop Tactics: Innovation in the German Army, 1914–1918* (New York, 1989), as well as his "'These Hideous Weapons,'" in Robert Cowley, ed., *The Great War: Perspectives on the First World War* (New York, 2003), 307–319; Stevenson, *Cataclysm*, 306–308; and specifically for predicted fire, Jonathan B. A. Bailey, "The First World War and the Birth of Modern Warfare," in Macgregor Knox and Williamson Murray, eds., *The Dynamics of Military Revolution 300–2050* (Cambridge, UK, 2001), 132–153.
52. Cited in Falls, *Great War*, 302.
53. Prior and Wilson, *Passchendaele*, 144 (and their discussion of the cabinet's almost inexplicable lack of attention to the ongoing tragedy in Flanders, pp. 143–155).
54. The accusation began with Haig himself but is often accepted by historians (e.g., Paschall, *Defeat of Imperial Germany*, 63, 77–78). The best discussions are Travers, *How the War Was Won*, 36; and Stevenson, *Cataclysm*, 330–331. Also see Winter, *Haig's Command*, 174–175.
55. For higher, 500,000 casualty estimates for Passchendaele, see Winter, *Haig's Command*, 110–113. For lower, 240,000–275,000 numbers, see Paschall, *Defeat of Imperial Germany*, 79; Travers, *How the War Was Won*, 17; and Prior and Wilson, *Passchendaele*, 195. All of these sources also include estimates for German losses of 200,000–250,000.
56. Citation in Simkins et al., *War to End All Wars*, 137. Also see Alexander Watson, *Enduring the Great War: Combat, Morale and Collapse in the German and British Armies, 1914–1918* (Cambridge, UK, 2008), 154–155, 179.
57. Cited in Paschall, *Defeat of Imperial Germany*, 79.
58. Erich von Ludendorff, *Ludendorff's Own Story: August 1914-November 1918* (New York, 1919), 2:164.
59. For the tank's limitations in 1917–1918, see Paddy Griffith, *Battle Tactics of the Western Front: The British Army's Art of Attack 1916–1918* (New Haven, CT, 1994), 162–169; and especially Martin Blumenson, ed., *The Patton Papers 1885–1940* (Boston, 1972), 1:458 ff., 2:523 ff.
60. Paschall, *Defeat of Imperial Germany*, 106.
61. Cited in Travers, *How the War Was Won*, 48, and for the months-long debate in the BEF, 32–49.
62. For this passage, see Salvatore Saladino, *Italy from Unification to 1919: Growth and Decay of a Liberal Regime* (New York, 1970), 158–163; Denis Mack Smith, *Modern Italy: A Political History* (Ann Arbor, MI, 1997), 273–276; Herwig, *First World War*, 336–346; and Keegan, *First World War*, 343–350.
63. Keegan, *First World War*, 346.
64. Citations in Saladino, *Italy from Unification to 1919*, 158; and Herwig, *First World War*, 336. Also see Philip V. Cannistraro and Brian R. Sullivan, *Il Duce's Other Woman* (New York, 1993), 157–158.
65. Cited in Keegan, *First World War*, 349.
66. Smith, *Modern Italy*, 275.

67. For the political situation in Russia from July to December 1917, see the still very useful Adam B. Ulam, *The Bolsheviks: The Intellectual, Personal and Political History of the Triumph of Communism in Russia* (New York, 1965), 343–410; and more recently, Acton, *Rethinking the Russian Revolution*, 107–185; Figes, *People's Tragedy*, 419–551; and Stevenson, *Cataclysm*, 287–289, 306–307, 311–324.
68. Kornilov's opinion of Kerensky is cited in Figes, *People's Tragedy*, 446.
69. For Riga, see Robert B. Asprey, *The German High Command at War: Hindenburg and Ludendorff Conduct World War* I (New York, 1991), 338; and Stevenson, *Cataclysm*, 306–308.
70. Florinsky, *Russia*, 2:1440.
71. Stevenson, *Cataclysm*, 312.
72. Cited in Figes, *People's Tragedy*, 470.
73. Ludendorff, *Ludendorff's Own Story*, 2:122, 124.
74. Figes, *People's Tragedy*, 422.
75. Cited in ibid., 480.

CHAPTER IX

War, Politics, and Diplomacy in the Middle East and Russia

1916–1918

On Friday, December 7, 1917, Turkish-German defenses on the Jaffa Road finally broke down. British General Edmund Allenby's forces pressed ever closer to Jerusalem, forcing the defenders to evacuate hurriedly, hauling dead and wounded with them in oxcarts. The screams and groans of the soldiers, their blood dripping on the road, appalled and frightened local residents.[1]

On December 8 violent rains fell from the heavens. It was as if angry fatherly tears were trying to cleanse the carnage that divine creation had deteriorated to in the twentieth century. The British advance came to a muddy halt. That night the skies cleared over a silent Holy City dimly lit by myriad stars. Only a few isolated cannon shots and an occasional dog's bark interrupted this requiem on the tragedy of human combat.

Fittingly, Sunday, December 9, turned sunny and astoundingly beauty. As the morning brightened and warmed, Hussein Salim al-Husseini, mayor of Jerusalem, mounted his horse and set out to present the Turkish writ of surrender to the city's new rulers. At first al-Husseini encountered two British enlistees foraging for breakfast. The khaki-clad soldiers ignored his request and went about their more important business. Two artillery officers and a lone lieutenant colonel also declined to play the historic role, until finally a brigadier general accepted the writ and the Arab's makeshift white flag in Allenby's name.

The conqueror made his triumphal entry to Jerusalem on December 11. Allenby dehorsed at the Jaffa Gate and proceeded on foot, accompanied by representatives from France, Italy, and the United States. He passed by the elders of Jerusalem's Christian, Jewish, and Muslim communities and then read a declaration, carefully word-crafted in London, that pledged Britain to protect and preserve all of the city's holy sites. It was more than a symbolic occasion—it was indeed historic—for no Christians had ruled the Holy City in over seven hundred years.

It was difficult to know at the time, however, whether the capture of Jerusalem would have more than symbolic significance for the outcome of the Great War. In truth, 1917 had been a disappointing year for the allies. British and French offensives on the western front had failed like all the others, and at great cost. The Americans seemed to be a year away from making an impact on the continent. U-boats had taken a frightful toll. Italy had nearly collapsed, while Russia and Rumania had stopped fighting and begun to negotiate their exits from the war—surrenders that certainly overshadowed al-Husseini's. Wresting control of Jerusalem from the Turks was a victory amidst many more important-seeming setbacks, but it was a victory with a sensational side, one that could inspire the peoples of the hard-pressed Entente to persevere and prevail. With these thoughts in mind, British Prime Minister David Lloyd George allowed the bells of Westminster Cathedral to peal out the good news of Jerusalem's fall. They had not rung in three years.

THE MARCH ACROSS THE SINAI

By the waning months of 1916 Great Britain had parried every blow Jihadist enemies had thrown at the world's most powerful empire. The overrunning of German East Africa prevented its valiant commander, Paul von Lettow-Vorbeck, from joining forces with Emperor Lij Yasu of Abyssinia and Muhammed Abdullah Hassan, the "Mad Mullah" of Somalia, co-conspirators whose dreams of pushing Britain out of the region failed. In the Sudan Sultan Ali Dinar had been chased from his stronghold in Darfur, while the Senussi forces of Ahmad al-Sharif had retreated from the deserts of western Egypt. Farther east, moreover, Turkish-German efforts to prod Persia and Afghanistan into a holy war that would sweep all before it into India had not yet succeeded.

These successes allowed Britain and its ally Russia to pursue the war more aggressively against the core regions of the Ottoman Empire and its forward salient in Persia. If victory came quickly, perhaps ten–twenty divisions could be freed for fighting in European theaters of action in the summer of 1917, placing critical pressure on Central Power forces spread ever more thinly over many fronts. Alternatively, a slower grinding down of the Turks meant a relative easing of pressure on Germany and Austria-Hungary. As Ludendorff recalled, "The stiffer the Turks' defense in Palestine and Mesopotamia, and the larger the force absorbed in the English effort to achieve their object, the more our burden in the west would be lightened."[2] But an eventual British victory in the Middle East, however long it took, would at least buttress Britain's empire in the postwar world. Such a drawn-out defeat of Turkey would be especially significant if the Great War ended in a cold war-style cease-fire, eventually necessitating another war against a German coalition shorn of one valuable ally.[3] After the withdrawal from Gallipoli, the surrender at Kut, and the Ottoman drive on Teheran in mid-1916, however, victory of any sort seemed very distant. The way back began in the Sinai.

The bulk of empire forces withdrawn from Gallipoli, many of them wounded and demoralized, streamed back to their original staging area in Egypt. A sense of urgency reigned in Cairo and London, where worries proliferated that Turkish leader Enver Pasha, exhilarated by remarkable Muslim victories over the British, would attack the Suez Canal to prove Islamic supremacy over infidels.[4] Advisers to Sir Archibald Murray, commander of the Egyptian Expeditionary Force (EEF), pointed to Pasha's twenty, now idle divisions at Gallipoli and raised the specter of a quarter of a million Turks storming across the Sinai to cut Britain's lifeline to India. But Murray's superior in London, Sir William Robertson, the chief of the Imperial General Staff (CIGS), soon imposed his own better sense of reality on these exaggerated fears. A "westerner" who agreed with Sir Douglas Haig that the defeat of Germany required victories in France, Robertson discounted the Turkish threat to Egypt and began to transfer Murray's troops to the western front. Nine divisions had arrived by June for the buildup to the Battle of the Somme, while another was sent to Iraq for the relief of Townsend at Kut. Robertson prevailed so easily over politicians skeptical about Haig's chances in France because when appointed in late 1915 he had largely wrested control of troop strengths and field operations from civilian politicians weakened by Gallipoli, which was seen in military circles as the blunder of civilians, in particular, of Winston Churchill.

Left with four infantry and two cavalry divisions, Murray opted to protect the canal by pushing his defensive line ten kilometers east into the Sinai.[5] During the spring of 1916, as laborers bridged the canal, built railway extensions and metal roadways, and entrenched and wired the new position, he revised his plans. Now Murray would push across the desert to a line running inland from el-Arish. He assumed correctly that any Turkish offensive must cross here. In the scorching heat of summer his army snailed into the Sinai, constructing a railroad, a water pipeline, storage tanks, and a roadway built by pegging wire netting into the sand. Murray's engineers performed a great feat, one made absolutely necessary by the scarcity of summer well water to sustain his men and horses, but progress was excruciatingly slow. The creation of what one veteran described as a "movable reservoir"[6] holding five hundred thousand gallons, barely two days supply for the EEF, provided the army only a modicum of flexibility in venturing away from the rail and pipeline. A Turkish force of sixteen thousand, reinforced with German artillery and machine gun crews and commanded by a German colonel, Baron Kress von Kressenstein, caused further delays with a daring attack on the British railhead in early August. The Turks were beaten and lost half of their men, but it took Murray until late December to expel enemy forces from the eastern desert and occupy the el-Arish line. Consequently, he could offer no flanking support to Sherif Hussein's revolt in the Hejaz, which had broken out that summer and then quickly languished.

At this point home front politics influenced Murray's operational planning. As his divisions entrenched for their forward defense of Suez, David Lloyd George replaced Asquith. The new prime minister had long doubted the westerners' military wisdom, looking to the Middle East for a quick knockout blow against Germany's formidable Ottoman ally. The strategic alternative in Salonika had lost much of its attractiveness after the halting performance of French General Maurice Sarrail's allied army in Bulgarian-occupied Serbia that autumn (see chap. 7) and the difficulty of continuing to supply it through U-boat-infested Mediterranean waters.

Although somewhat humbled himself after the Somme, the CIGS opposed Downing Street's desired move on Palestine. In meetings lasting into January 1917, Robertson reminded his political chiefs of the critical importance of the western front and the inadvisability of diverting troops from it, especially after commitments had been made to France for a springtime offensive. He also spoke of the seas, where British shipping was already overstretched to support other theaters and where "we may presumably expect an even more ruthless German submarine campaign in the spring." Besides, concluded the CIGS, Murray's railroad and pipeline were still sixty kilometers short of the Palestinian border and would not reach Gaza-Beersheba until winter's well-water advantages had passed. A campaign for the conquest of Palestine was not feasible, therefore, until the autumn of 1917. Robertson's recommendations resulted in compromise: Murray "was informed that his primary mission for the present would be the defense of Egypt" but that "he was, by aggressive action, to hold as many enemy troops on his front as possible." It was in character for Robertson, however, that he not only refused to give this "sideshow"[7] expedition reinforcements but also transferred another infantry division to France.

The change to more offensive operations reflected an important shift in London's Middle East policy. Under the influence of Field Marshall Horatio Herbert Kitchener and his subordinates in Egypt and the Sudan, the previous government of Herbert Asquith had made an ambiguous pledge to Sherif Hussein in October 1915 that Britain would create some kind of Arab state in formerly Ottoman-controlled areas. The British carefully worded their promises, stating clearly that coastal Syria, Lebanon, and Iraq would be excluded, vaguely hinting that inland Syria, Palestine, and eastern Arabia, the territory of Ibn Saud, might be excluded too. In secret follow-up talks in January 1916, moreover, British negotiator Sir Mark Sykes agreed with his French counterpart, Francois Picot, that an entire swath of the Ottoman Empire from coastal Syria and Lebanon inland over Damascus and Mosul to the Iraqi-Persian frontier would be directly or indirectly controlled by Paris. The British would receive the Palestinian ports of Acre and Haifa as well as a narrow strip of land for a railroad to British Iraq stretching from Basra to Baghdad. The bulk of Palestine would fall under international control to placate the religious concerns of Protestants, Catholics, Orthodox Christians, and Muslims. Lloyd George entered office, however, inclined to rescind the Sykes/Picot agreement and exclude France from the Middle East, especially from Palestine, which should be Britain's by right of conquest. It made no sense to conquer the Holy Land, he said, only "to hew it in pieces before the Lord" with a portion going to "agnostic atheistic France." With Hussein's revolt against the Turks already under way, British-Arab dealings were a different and more delicate matter, but the prime minister was not particularly sympathetic to their territorial aspirations either. Thus he instructed Sykes, newly appointed political liaison to the EEF, not to make pledges to the Arabs "and particularly none in regard to Palestine."[8]

As General Murray finalized his operational plans that winter, therefore, Palestine had taken on new significance for London. Robertson belittled the idea of taking Palestine, calling it a private obsession of Lloyd George, but in reality enthusiasm for conquering the Holy Land extended far into the British establishment. The vast majority of British politicians and diplomats were Christians, after all, and most of them attached religious importance to the removal of Jerusalem, Bethlehem, and other biblical sites from Muslims. Many of the advisers and confidants around Lloyd George also stressed the strategic importance of Palestine for the empire, men whose enthusiastic views were no longer scotched by the skeptical, domineering Kitchener, who had scoffed that Palestine did not even possess a good port but died at sea earlier in 1916. With British forces again inching closer to Baghdad (see later), similar success by Murray would not only push the buffer zone for Egypt and the Suez Canal well beyond the Sinai but also, far grander, extend the Cape Town-to-Cairo axis across the Middle East to the Persian Gulf and India. "The fight with Turkey had a special importance all its own," recalled the prime minister. "The Turkish Empire lay right across the track by land or water to our great possessions in the east—India, Burma, Malaya, Borneo, Hong Kong, and the dominions of Australia and New Zealand." Or as one newspaper close to the prime minister phrased it, "the whole future of the British empire as a sea empire" hinged on the conquest of Palestine and the establishment there of a British-controlled buffer state "inhabited by an intensely patriotic race."[9]

The writer, journalist Herbert Sidebotham, referred not to the British race but rather to the Jewish race. Indeed his newspaper, like Lloyd George and much of his political entourage, was pro-Zionist—and so historians must dig even deeper to explain the politics behind the Palestinian campaigns of 1917. Founded by Hungarian Jew Theodore Herzl in 1896, the Zionist movement sought to realize the centuries-old Jewish dream of reestablishing the ancient homeland in Palestine. By 1914 some eighty-five thousand European Jews, most from Russia and Eastern Europe, had come back to the old capital city of Jerusalem, to towns like Jaffa, Tel Aviv, and Haifa, and to farms and communes purchased surreptitiously from Arab landowners. The newcomers were proud, assertive, and determined not just to settle but rather eventually to build another Jewish state encompassing the territory of what is today Israel as well as much of present-day Lebanon and Jordan. Not surprisingly, the ambitious Zionist movement had already sparked Jewish-Arab tensions before the war, prompting spokesmen like Chain Weizmann in Britain and David Ben-Gurion in Palestine to favor a British protectorate of some sort in Palestine as an indirect means to Jewish statehood. Lloyd George favored this approach and was unconcerned about the difficulties this might create with Sherif Hussein's Arabs. "Palestine did not seem to give them much anxiety," he wrote later about wartime communications with the Hejaz. "We could not get in touch with the Palestinian Arabs," he continued indifferently, "as they were fighting against us [on the Turkish side]." Sykes, too, worried more about guarding Palestinian Jews against Armenian-style persecution at the hands of Djemal Pasha, Turkish satrap in Damascus, adding dismissively, "The Arabs can be managed." Foreign Secretary Arthur Balfour, another pro-Zionist, also favored a Jewish state. "Zionism," he said, "is rooted in age-old traditions, present needs, and future hopes of far profounder import than the desires and prejudices of the seven hundred thousand Arabs who now inhabit that ancient land."[10] Furthermore, as explained later, motivations on the British side were very complex, involving the deep-seated prejudicial belief in the influence of international Jewry and the strategic-political wisdom of not alienating allegedly powerful Jews during a hard-fought world war.

Thus very much politically was at stake in the field. Remaining at his headquarters in Cairo, Murray put Palestinian operations in the hands of Lieutenant General Sir Charles Dobell.[11] With three infantry divisions and a powerful column of nine thousand ANZAC and British cavalry, he marched on Gaza City. With water supply undoubtedly the most critical factor, Dobell had to strike quickly to secure the town's wells: any delay meant retreating to his railroad and pipeline. Plans looked promising, however, for the Turks held Gaza with only seven battalions and five batteries, three of them Austrian-German. Dobell ordered his cavalry to move east around Gaza, cutting off reinforcements that Kress von Kressenstein already had under way. With their overwhelming numbers, the infantry would overrun the town from the south.

All went well initially on March 26, 1917. Dobell's assault made slow progress against Turkish trenches, cactus hedge rows, and the thick fog enveloping them, but his cavalry penetrated around and into Gaza, then began watering horses. A brilliant victory eluded Dobell, however, when, mistakenly assuming that the enemy was poised to outflank the infantry, he ordered the cavalry to pull out, when in fact Kressenstein's two divisions were a day away. His right flank actually threatened now, Dobell fell back into the desert.

It had been a stinging defeat: 523 killed; 412 missing; 2,932 wounded; and Kressenstein given ample time to extend his trench line and reinforce it. Misinformed, or perhaps merely attempting to put a positive spin on his defeat, Murray sent an egregiously misleading telegram to London that led the CIGS and others to believe a victory had been won. "The operation was most successful," he wrote, "and owing to the fog and waterless nature of the country round Gaza just fell short of a complete disaster to the enemy."[12] Murray received orders to push on and take Jerusalem.

Dobell's second attempt on April 17 was not as promising as the first, for the defenders had now dug redoubts for miles southeast along the Gaza-Beersheba road to prevent Dobell's cavalry outflanking the town. The British pressed their attack for four days before retreating again, this time at a cost of 509 killed; 1,576 missing; and 4,339 wounded. Murray sacked the commander of his spent EEF, but in June London sent a new man to Cairo, General Edmund "The Bull" Allenby, who began the slow work of rebuilding the EEF and translating his reputation into reality.

TURKISH DEFEATS IN MESOPOTAMIA AND PERSIA

Baghdad or Bust: Sir Frederick Stanley Maude
Harper's Pictorial Library

The debacle at Kut left British strategists divided over the empire's next move in Mesopotamia (see map, p. 181). Should the army make a renewed push on Baghdad during the summer of 1916? Remain on the defensive in the vicinity of Kut? Or fall back to defend Amara, halfway back down the Tigris to Basra, thereby greatly alleviating what had become a logistical nightmare along overstretched, inadequate lines of supply? Preoccupied with the grave situation in France, Robertson favored the latter option, which meant freeing up a division for the Somme while also fulfilling the original mission of the Mesopotamian Expeditionary Force (MEF), namely, protection of oil flows out of Persia. The Turkish march on Teheran that summer (see chap. 6), however, argued for digging in near Kut lest a British retreat down the Tigris fan the flames of Jihad throughout the region.[13] The new commander, Sir Stanley Maude, received orders in late September 1916 "to improve the river and railway communications" and maintain "as forward a position as the state of communications will allow . . . without incurring heavy losses."[14]

Already at work to improve logistics, Maude accelerated the Herculean material transformation under way behind his forward lines.[15] The engineering corps dredged channels to the port of Basra, marked them with buoys, and provided lighting for round-the-clock activity. The harbor received modern wharves, offloading equipment, and access roads and light railways. Provisions from sea were augmented by a vast network of local suppliers. Maude also recruited, paid, and supervised Arab and Kurdish laborers who built hospitals and medical supply depots. Workers laid down railroad tracks from Basra to Nasiriya on the Euphrates, where Maude stationed one infantry division, and to Amara. These lines were supplemented by roads for motor transport and fuel depots and repair shops. A light railway and the Tigris supplied his main body of four Anglo-Indian infantry divisions and two cavalry brigades upriver from Amara. His army made this possible by expanding the number of boats. "We could see the results of the work of General Maude," observed an American accompanying the army.

> We could see the tremendous reinforcements getting into positions to be used. We could see the piles of supplies, the railways, the transport facilities, a hundred boats where there had been a dozen, a hundred automobiles where there had been none. We could see all manner of machines and factories, ready to repair equipment and guns, to make ice and furnish electric current. We could see splendidly equipped hospitals where there had been a system that absolutely broke down under the strain of the first campaign. But most important of all, we could see a good spirit in the place of the dejected attitude that followed the failure to relieve Townsend.[16]

All of these efforts were necessary if Maude were to reverse his predecessor's defeat. It all seemed possible, for the new man commanded altogether 166,000 soldiers in Iraq—a fact that made him chafe under the cautious advice of Robertson.

General Charles Monro, Ian Hamilton's replacement at Gallipoli, proved an invaluable ally to Maude. Under way in October 1916 to India, Monro consulted with Maude, who "poured out his woes to his important visitor."[17] Impressed, Munro urged Robertson to sanction an advance toward Kut, threaten Turkish positions on the Tigris and Euphrates, and enhance British prestige with and control over Arab tribesmen.[18] Robertson approved, thus tacitly encouraging Maude to reinterpret his earlier order to maintain his "forward position" to mean taking revenge for Townsend by retaking Kut.

Khalil Pasha, commander of the Turkish Sixth Army headquartered in Baghdad, deployed a division at Nasiriya and four in 18th Corps around Kut in the capable hands of General Kiazim Kara Bekr, who had only a third the infantry strength of Maude's, around 10,000–15,000 rifles, but had prepared seemingly impregnable defenses. One division entrenched south of the Tigris along the Shatt-al-Hai to Kata Haji Fahan, another north of the river on the Kudhairi Bend at Kut, and the other two solidly entrenched for thousands of meters along the river between Kut and Sannaiyat. "The Turks had spared no labor in building their trenches," noted one observer. "Everything was there, concealed machine-gun pits, elaborate parapets, barbed-wire entanglements, military pits, land mines."[19] Sannaiyat anchored these defenses, blocking passage between the river and a marsh with six lines of trenches. Although it is true, therefore, that Khalil let Britain's embarrassment at First Kut fill his head with irrational dreams of conquest, the bastion that Kara Bekr had erected around Kut made it reasonable for Khalil to assume that Maude would not get through, thus freeing up soldiers for other ventures. Therefore he sent a corps into Persia in the summer of 1916 spearheaded by crack troops flush from victory at Gallipoli.

But as he watched Maude's preparations upriver from Amara an even more ambitious operation began to form in the mind of this latter day Saladin: Khalil became preoccupied with cutting the British off by sweeping out of western Persia to the Tigris north of Amara. Details remain sketchy, but he probably intended to shift backup divisions from the Baghdad-Mosul region into Persia to replace the elite 18,000-strong 13th Corps deep in Persia, which would head south over the Karkha River and the border to Amara. There were two serious problems with this

Revenge for Townsend: British Cavalry Enter Baghdad After the Fall of Kut, March 1917
Canfield, *World War*

plan. First, Maude had well over 100,000 troops elsewhere in Mesopotamia. They were not all combat troops, but nonetheless the trapper, Khalil, would likely be trapped himself. Second, because of these daring plans Kara Bekr's vainglorious superior denied reinforcements to Kut despite warnings that four weak divisions, regardless of formidable defenses, could not hold.

Maude began the campaign on December 13, 1916, with a brilliant end run. While feigning an attack at Sannaiyat he sent cavalry and infantry over the Shatt-al-Hai at Besouia, threatening the flank of the Turks on the west bank of the Hai. Probing with infantry and cavalry brigades upriver at Skumran a week later, however, Maude's men, who probably could have forced a crossing, pulled back after taking heavy fire. The Briton had wanted to cut the Turks' supply line and win the battle quickly but had apparently not adequately communicated this desire to his corps commander, N. A. Marshall, who insisted to Maude the next day, "You didn't really mean them to cross." "Of course I did,"[20] said the general, fixing the man with an icy stare. Rain delayed further efforts until after the New Year.

Maude now bore down for a long slog. Concentrating on Turkish positions south of the Tigris, his sappers advanced Anglo-Indian trenches to only a few hundred meters from Turkish lines along the upper Hai and Kudhairi Bend. On January 9, 1917, British and Indian brigades went over the top at Kudhairi Bend. After twenty days of artillery bombardment, aerial strafing, bayonet charges, and furious Turkish counterattacks with terrible casualties on both sides, the surviving defenders slipped across the river. The same process of weeks-long attrition cleared the Hai salient, and thus everything south of the Tigris, by February 16. Next day Maude threw an entire division at Sannaiyat but was mauled.

Second Battle of Kut 1916–1917

Maps Courtesy of the Department of History, United States Military Academy

On February 23 he tried a cleverer approach, making another assault on Sannaiyat as cover for a three-pronged amphibious operation against Skumran Peninsula, which succeeded. With a division across by nightfall and a second set to cross next day, Kara Bekr realized that Kut and Sannaiyat were untenable and retreated with the bloodied remnants of his corps toward Baghdad—he had lost over five thousand men. Maude had lost easily twice this many, but he had been able to replace them. Kut was British again—that was the main thing. The most important victory of 1917 in Mesopotamia had been won.

Indeed Kut ended a fourteen-month stalemate on the Tigris that the British followed with one rapid-moving success after another. Aided by constant shelling from five gunboats of the Royal Navy, Maude pursued Kara Bekr relentlessly up the river, not allowing the Turk to prepare even temporary defenses until he had fallen back nearly 150 kilometers to Baghdad. Khalil decided to retreat farther, however, and British columns entered the ancient city triumphantly on March 11. The decision of Sixth Army's commander made operational sense, for two weeks earlier, finally abandoning plans for trapping Maude, he had ordered Ali Isham Bey's 13th Corps to pull out of Persia and back into Iraq. Ali was still in western Persia over 250 kilometers from Baghdad, however, as Maude approached the city.

Now Khalil sought to concentrate his two corps and fight the British with somewhat more even odds. The conqueror of Baghdad prevented this in late March–early April 1917 by sending half his force northeast to the Persian border to engage and hold Ali, while remaining units met the Turkish 18th Corps farther up the Tigris. The latter Battle of the Marl Plain drove the Turks farther upriver and thus away from 13th Corps. The final battles of the campaign occurred in late April south of Samara. The wily Ali came very close to reuniting Sixth Army there, but Maude succeeded in defeating the two Turkish forces in detail and then entered the town.

These victories left Britain in possession of the bulk of what constitutes present-day Iraq, having penetrated 650 kilometers inland from the Persian Gulf (see map, p. 98). After the fall of Kut, moreover, those few thousand Arab fighters who had joined Kara Bekr turned on him, and for the time being the Turkish-German Jihad remained stymied—not only in Iraq but also in Persia and Afghanistan. British conquests had been costly—eighteen thousand casualties, with twice as many diseased and in hospital—but the mission was not yet accomplished, for despite suffering even higher losses than the British, Sixth Army had survived the campaign and Khalil was determined at the very least to surrender no more ground. His Tigris Corps fell back from Samara to Tikrit and entrenched, while the division that had guarded Nasiriya retreated up the Euphrates and dug in at Ramadi (northwest of Baghdad).

Ali, meanwhile, rejoined his rearguard in the Jebel Hamrin Mountains hard on the Persian border, where he hoped to exploit the disintegrating condition of Russian General Baratov's army corps, which stretched from Kermanshah to Isfahan. The Cossack had pursued Ali out of Persia in February, but news of the tsar's abdication and the antiwar stance of the soviets made further offensive operations

Waiting for Tracks and *Yildirim*: Berlin-Baghdad Railroad Station at Mosul
Courtesy of the Library of Congress

against the Turks ill advised, if not impossible. "The troops who had fought so stubbornly for more than two years became demoralized and lost to military honor and discipline," noted the commander of the South Persian Rifles, Sir Percy Sykes, in June 1917. "The old Russian Army is dead, quite dead," observed another British officer on the spot that spring. "Our efforts to resuscitate it stand useless."[21]

The same circumstances had convinced Enver Pasha, in fact, that he could do much more than merely hold the line in Iraq. With a nod of approval from Hindenburg and Ludendorff, he withdrew tens of thousands of soldiers who had faced the Russians in Eastern Europe and Turkish Armenia and then began to assemble them in Aleppo, where the railroad, once completed, could rush them to Mosul. On paper the *Yildirim* or "Thunderbolt" Army comprised fourteen Turkish divisions and a brigade of handpicked German veterans bolstered by artillery and machine gun contingents.[22] Enver placed some of his best officers in this imposing strike force, including one of the heroes of Gallipoli, Mustafa Kemal. Overall command went to Erich von Falkenhayn, who redoubled efforts to complete the Aleppo-Mosul railway by the end of the year and pounce on the British at Ramadi. It was neither coincidence nor surprise, therefore, that Maude moved a division to Ramadi and that London condoned the formation of two new divisions to bolster the empire's new Mesopotamian outpost. The hopes of the politicians for quick victory in the Middle East had once again proved elusive.

THE ARAB REVOLT

In the last days of June 1917 General Edmund Allenby took up his new duties in Cairo as commander of the EEF. Before the new man departed England Lloyd George urged him to capture Jerusalem by Christmas. Such victories would build

The Arab Revolt: Lawrence of Arabia
Canfield, *World War*

on recent success in Iraq, foil Turkish plans to regain the upper hand in the Middle East, and by thus "knocking down the props" convince Constantinople to sue for peace. The prime minister and his ministerial colleagues also had their eyes on the home front: "Cannot you give us Jerusalem as a Christmas box for the people, so as to cheer them up?"[23] Robertson recalled. Allenby was given reason to believe that he would receive the additional divisions and artillery needed for the job. While submitting his formal request for reinforcements in the second week of July, the general received an unknown British visitor dressed in Arab garb. It was Thomas Edward Lawrence, who added to the growing optimism in Cairo by conveying excitingly good news about Sherif Hussein's desert revolt.

T. E. Lawrence was one of the most remarkable personalities of the Great War. Educated in history and archaeology at Oxford, he had deepened an impressive Middle Eastern expertise with prewar digs and travels on the upper Euphrates, in Syria and Jordan, and across the Sinai to Aqaba and beyond, along the way picking up decent conversational Arabic, contacts with Arab nationalists, and a genuine sympathy for the cause of Arab independence from Turkey. His training and experience made it logical for the army to appoint Lawrence to the Geographical Section of the General Staff in London after war broke out, and from there, once his strengths were realized, to general staff work in Cairo. The highly intelligent—albeit arrogant—twenty-six-year-old did map work and prepared reports on the Turkish army, quickly alienating superiors "who could not tolerate Lawrence's 'cheek' or his superior knowledge." He repaid their obvious dislike by "correcting their prose, on paper, and their ignorance, over the telephone," and then submitting a scathing indictment of the entire Mesopotamian debacle that the men around EEF Chief Murray found "revolting."[24] For all of his Napoleonic mannerisms, however, the fact remains, as his biographer sees it, that Lawrence shared much of Napoleon's military brilliance, in particular the rare ability to look beyond orthodoxy and formulate new ways of waging war. It was thus fortunate for Britain's war in the desert that shortly before being banished from Cairo an appointment was arranged for him in the new Egypt-based Arab Bureau created by Sir Mark Sykes in early 1916 to influence and implement British policy on the Middle East.[25] From this new posting Lawrence used the first opportunity that presented itself to view Hussein's faltering revolt firsthand.

He landed on the Arabian coast in mid-October 1916, inspecting Arab encampments near Mecca, Rabegh, and Yenbo headed, respectively, by the sherif's sons, Abdullah, Ali, and Feisal, who commanded altogether sixteen thousand men. The three warrior princes' numbers had shrunk since early summer, however, as over thirteen thousand Turkish regulars based in the Medina area pushed the rebels back to the sea. Lawrence was impressed with the political savvy, charisma, and daring of Feisal, who possessed "far more personal magnetism and life than his brothers," and, although "rash when he acts on impulse [he has] enough strength to reflect, and then [is] exact in judgment." The visitor discounted Arab chances in pitched, showdown battles with the Turks, preferring to see the rebellion spread out guerilla-style. "A difference in character between the Turkish and Arab armies is that the more you distribute the former the weaker they become, and the more you distribute the latter the stronger they become."[26] Otherwise, Lawrence split sharply with reigning views in British army circles. Noticing, for example, how suspicious the men around Feisal were about the British commitment to Arab unity and independence, his posttravel report rejected sending one of Murray's brigades to the Hejaz lest this actually weaken the revolt by seeming to confirm "Britain's established reputation for swallowing up the territories she came to protect."[27] These reinforcements were unnecessary, moreover, for as soon as the Arabs were given machine guns and modern artillery they could defend the hilly country around their camps for the time being and then later shift to asymmetric offensive tactics. The wisdom of sending arms rang truer in December when Turkish units came close to taking Yenbo from the brave but poorly equipped followers of Feisal. Lawrence's recommendations came as a welcome pleasant surprise to the top brass in Cairo and London—obviously neither Murray, let alone the parsimonious Robertson, wanted to divert British regulars to Arabia. On the strength of the impression he had made Lawrence was sent back to the desert as British military adviser and liaison to Arab forces. British guns, gunboats, supplies, and money would now bolster his keen, militarily insightful advice regarding how best to fight the Turks.

The legendary status that "Lawrence of Arabia" acquired after the war, coupled with the paucity of Arab sources, makes it difficult to weigh the exact contribution he made in comparison with others to the victories that lay ahead. Thus Lieutenant Colonel C. E. Wilson was on the ground there too, playing an important advisory role to Hussein's sons and keeping the often exasperatingly difficult sherif in line with Britain's operational recommendations. Of the princes, furthermore, Feisal was an exceptionally quick study. Already in the early autumn of 1916, for instance, he realized the need for major tactical and operational adjustments such as better equipment, putting an end to pipe-dream plans for attacking Turkish strongholds like Medina, rather striking far up the coast at Wejh to threaten the enemy's lines of communications along the Hejaz Railway, and in general trying to disperse Turkish forces.[28] There can be no doubt, however, that Lawrence, with natural soldierly instincts reinforced by a wide-ranging study of military history, became the key ingredient of success.

In late December 1916, for example, with Feisal hesitating to move after the near disaster at Yenbo, the Briton emboldened him with a clever plan. The southernmost Arab army of Abdullah had advanced from Mecca toward Medina the previous month with four thousand men and lofty dreams, apparently, of sacking the fortress, but Lawrence argued that he should instead be used for diversionary action to free Feisal for the attack on Wejh. Feisal agreed, selecting a new target for Abdullah, the Wadi Ais Valley, some one hundred kilometers north of Medina, there not only to disrupt supplies to the town but also to threaten the rear of Turkish units moving on Rabegh and force them to turn around. With British gunboats offering further protection to Rabegh, Feisal and his army, which had swollen to well over ten thousand, mainly as a result of Feisal's personal appeals to local tribes, could slip far north to take Wejh.[29] The plan went into motion

The Arab Revolt: Mighty Auda
Canfield, *World War*

a few days later, and by the end of January 1917 they had registered a nearly bloodless victory.

With one stroke the Arabs reversed their fortunes, for they had forced the Turks to halt conventional offensive operations, fall back to Medina, and spread much of their strength along the Hejaz Railway to guard supply lines. And because of these altered circumstances Djemal Pasha, Turkish satrap in Damascus, may have ordered his Medina force to make preparations for evacuation of the Hejaz—British intelligence had intercepted one of his dispatches. The evacuation never took place, but the possibility of Turkish regiments speeding north so alarmed Cairo on the eve of Dobell's first assault on Gaza in March 1917 that Feisal received an urgent appeal to assault Medina or cut off the departing enemy units at a station up the line. By early April Colonel Wilson and other British officers on the scene were coordinating plans for a major attack at Medain Saleh on the Hejaz Railroad almost due east of Wejh.[30]

By this time, however, Lawrence had devised a bold and—if it worked—brilliant alternative. To all who would listen that spring he argued for a long arcing maneuver from Wejh, northeast over the railway line and vast intimidating desert stretches to present-day southern Jordan and the land of the Howeitat tribe, and from there, with a force comprised mainly of these fierce warriors, back west-south-west to Aqaba.[31] An object of conquest long coveted by the British navy as well as Feisal, the Red Sea fortress would be captured in this scheme from the relatively undefended inland rear, a weakness Lawrence had noticed during his prewar visit to the region. This prize also had operational significance for Murray and later Allenby because its fall would provide a base for Arab forces to move north to guard the EEF's flank in the Sinai.

Although filled with myriad risks, not least from the pitiless terrain his 750-kilometer expedition had to travel, the campaign seemed much more feasible after the fall of Wejh. Two additional local tribes joined the revolt in late January 1917, and gifts began to arrive at Feisal's camp from the Howeitat too, followed in February by the appearance of their legendary warlord, Auda, who immediately warmed to the prospect of the glory—and British gold—that would come with Aqaba's fall. His participation was the lynchpin of the entire operation: Auda had the gravitas in the north to recruit among the Howeitat; convince other tribes nearer Aqaba to come on board; and make the necessary arguments to Nuri Shaalan, emir of the South-Jordanian Ruwalla, an even more powerful chieftain who not only controlled the wells the expedition needed before heading back across the desert but could also threaten Auda's rear unless neutrality were granted.

In March and April 1917 Lawrence began to formulate a parallel operation that, like the fall of Aqaba, would weaken the Turks at Gaza and in Palestine. Rather than besiege Medain Saleh, whose besiegers would be vulnerable to conventional counterstrikes, he wanted to initiate asymmetric warfare all along the railroad, striking stations; ambushing isolated detachments; and forcing the Turk into futile retaliatory efforts but not forcing him out of Arabia to the Sinai or Palestine, where his Hejaz divisions would bolster Turkish defenses. "Our ideal was to keep his railway just working, but only just, with the maximum of loss and discomfort"[32]—to force the enemy, in other words, to engage in a costly counterinsurgency campaign, which, noted Lawrence in one of his most famous phrases, "is messy and slow, like eating soup with a knife."[33] Meanwhile the growing Arab revolt could economize its forces for use elsewhere, spreading from Aqaba across Palestine and Syria to Damascus.

Lawrence, Auda, and a small troop of camel riders set out from Wejh on their now legendary, Hollywood-movie-inspiring mission in early June 1917. They had Feisal's blessing, and his emissary accompanied them, but to a British command that had other plans in mind what followed came as a fait accompli.[34] The company experienced a number of harrowing incidents. On the way to Nuri Shalaan, the worst desert stretch, El Houl ("The Desolate"), nearly claimed them as victims. After all went well with Auda's dealings, the recruitment of 500 Howeitat tribesmen, and crossing the desert again the element of surprise was lost when Lawrence and Auda stumbled upon a Turkish force while still eighty kilometers behind Aqaba and had to fight their way over a series of outer forts to the sea. However, aided by local tribes—the expedition's strength had risen to more than 700—and the fact that Aqaba's trenches and gun emplacements faced the sea, the attackers took their prize on July 6, 1917. They had lost only a few men but killed 600 Turks and took 600 prisoners. This was the good news that Lawrence brought to Allenby a few days later, having hurriedly crossed the Sinai.

In the meantime, earlier plans to seize Medain Saleh had evaporated: the Turks prevented any large concentration of Arabs along the rail line that spring by filling in all of the wells between major stations. After Aqaba fell, therefore, Lawrence prevailed easily with his strategy of pinning down Turkish units that could tip the balance in Palestine and making them "eat soup with a knife" in the Hejaz. Indeed this worked even better than he had anticipated, for, alarmed, Djemal Pasha and Falkenhayn dispatched six thousand infantry and a cavalry regiment from Palestine and Syria to Ma'an, on the railroad northeast of Aqaba, with orders to retake the port. Feisal and Lawrence countered by shifting the

Lifeline to the Hejaz: Railroad Station at Ma'an
Courtesy of the Library of Congress

bulk of the prince's growing army to Aqaba as reinforcement for Auda's veteran warriors and then using their forces to bait Turkish companies into ambushes and undertake repeated demolition raids against the railroad around Ma'an. British airplanes further punished the new arrivals, killing scores, wounding hundreds, and destroying depots. Consequently, the Turks never retook Aqaba. Using similar tactics, the Arabs harassed the enemy at various points along the line between Ma'an and Medina that summer.

Jerusalem by Christmas: Sir Edmund Allenby
Canfield, *World War*

Lawrence and his favorite Hashemite prince could now turn their gaze to the north. With Aqaba as their forward base, barely two hundred kilometers south of the Gaza-Beersheba line, they represented extra security for Allenby's right wing as he prepared to take this position. The Arabs had other things to offer. In his meeting with the general on July 9, Lawrence stressed Feisal's good relations with Arab tribes east of the Jordan River and the vital contribution their uprising would make to the conquest of Jerusalem and Damascus. The visitor's performance waxed dramatic, replete with historical allusions to the prowess of Arab fighting men from the time of Saladin the Great. Allenby was intrigued but "hardly prepared for anything so odd as myself—a little bare-footed silk-shirted man offering to hobble the enemy by his preaching if given stores and arms and a fund of two hundred gold sovereigns to convince and control his converts." "Well, I will do for you what I can,"[35] said Allenby, and the session ended.

THE INVASION OF PALESTINE AND WEAKENING OF TURKEY

What Lawrence had to say was especially welcome in Cairo, for as the two spoke Allenby was already assembling forces and planning operations for the upcoming offensive. Lloyd George had been true to his word: two infantry and one cavalry division came to the EEF from Macedonia, while two additional infantry divisions were formed from British and Indian units already in Egypt. With a total of ten divisions—seven infantry and three cavalry, a truly imperial force of nearly 100,000 Anzacs, Indians, and English—Allenby discarded Murray's strategy of taking Gaza by frontal assault. False dispatches referring to another such attack were indeed allowed to fall into Turkish hands through an elaborate ruse, but Beersheba and its 5,000 defenders would be the main target with only a feint at Gaza. Isolated from other units, this town and its crucial wells formed sort of a forward outpost several kilometers from the main defensive positions (circa 30,000 men) running between Gaza and Tell esh Sheria. From Beersheba, perhaps with supporting attacks at Gaza too, the EEF could overwhelm this main line in Phase 2 of the campaign.

In order to keep the Turks off guard, Allenby thought in terms of employing the Arabs, and duly the remarkable Lawrence was flown back from Aqaba to consult. He was tempted to help Allenby with an uprising recently promised by a sheikh commanding 12,000 tribesmen in the region of Deraa, east of the Jordan River and junction of the Haifa-Jerusalem/Damascus-Medina rail line—and therefore absolutely critical to supplying the 50,000–70,000 soldiers that Colonel Kress von Kressenstein had at his disposal west of the Jordan.[36] But, after returning to Aqaba to speak with Feisal, it was decided not to gamble with this revolt. The two worried that if Allenby failed and Feisal could not move his forces quickly enough to Deraa, the Turks would massacre these "great untouched reserves of Arab fighting men, educated and armed by Feisal from Aqaba."[37]

However, the capture of Aqaba, combined with Allenby's impressive buildup later that summer, had already paid the British handsome dividends, for Constantinople had been forced to rush a strong detachment to Ma'an and then in September 1917 abandon Operation Thunderbolt, the reconquest of Baghdad, and divert the *Yildirim* army to Palestine. Its paper strength in Aleppo of fourteen Turkish divisions had shrunk to seven in actuality, but three heavily armed German battalions formed a solid core.[38] Unfortunately for the Turks, *Yildirim*'s confusion of purpose—"order, counter-order, disorder" goes the old military saying—caused delays, and only one division was near Jerusalem when Allenby finally attacked Beersheba on October 31. Nevertheless, the decision to put off an uprising in Deraa seems very wise in retrospect.

The one-day Battle of Beersheba was textbook brilliant.[39] Allenby sent the advance elements of four infantry divisions forward at daybreak into artillery and machine gun fire to cut wire and overwhelm the Turkish trench line. As they progressed slowly toward the town the spearhead of two cavalry divisions, which he had moved stealthily under cover of the previous night, fell upon the defender's left rear flank where aerial reconnaissance had revealed that the defenses there had no wire or anticavalry ditches. An entire brigade of Australian horsemen thundered into the position and beyond, creating havoc, taking fourteen hundred prisoners and turning the battle into a rout. Completely fooled by Allenby's ruse, which was made even more credible by a bombardment of Gaza the same day, Kressenstein had kept his strongest units in the main line and consequently could not make a timely counterattack.

Creating even greater disruption to the entire defensive line, Allenby had sent a small company of eighty heavily armed camelmen around Beersheba to raise up Bedouin tribesmen, which failed, but the riders continued on their mission, reaching the road to Hebron north of Beersheba just as the town fell. Kressenstein and his subordinates, fearing in the "fog of war" that a larger, enfilading force threatened to surround them, shifted two reserve divisions from Gaza and Tell esh Sheria to join the only available *Yildirim* division at Hebron. In the first days of November, as his Beersheba force moved toward Tell esh Sheria, the EEF continued to bombard Gaza. The attackers' already superior artillery was aided by fire from ten warships in the Mediterranean. When the two wings of the EEF simultaneously attacked Gaza and Tell esh Sheria on November 6, they prevailed rather easily against defenses with no reserves. Kressenstein's Eighth Army fled in near disorder to positions shielding Junction Station while other units defended Hebron.

As Allenby's historic campaign proceeded, history of a different sort issued forth from London.[40] On November 9, 1917, a letter from Foreign Minister Arthur Balfour to Lord Edward Rothschild, scion of Britain's leading Jewish family and a prominent Zionist, appeared in *The Jewish Chronicle*: "His Majesty's Government view with favor the establishment in Palestine of a national home for the Jewish people, and will use their best endeavors to facilitate the achievement of this object."[41] After the war controversy swirled around the so-called Balfour Declaration as Britain attempted to deal with the seemingly contradictory promises and pledges it had made to the Arabs, the Jews, and the French, but at the time this cabinet-backed statement of sympathy for Zionist goals emanated from worries over the outcome of the war, and particularly, the role that international Jewry could play in securing victory. As the muddy attrition of Passchendaele drew to a costly close, British leaders looked anxiously at America, whose tremendous energies seemed so unexpectedly and disappointingly slow to mobilize, and Russia, where democracy did not appear strong enough to withstand Bolshevism's appeal for "peace, land, and bread." In order to keep the weight of Russia on Britain's side, and add more from America, British officials like Balfour, sympathetic to Zionism but wildly exaggerating the alleged ability of Jews to pull puppet strings on the world stage, compounded an already complex motivation behind the Palestinian military campaign by issuing this statement of support for Zionist goals. Three months before approving this declaration the cabinet had also voted to establish a Jewish Legion in Palestine to help Allenby reverse Murray's failures at Gaza. It was not present that autumn, in fact, but Lloyd George still waxed sanguine as the EEF made ready: "The Jews might be able to render us more assistance than

Defending Islam: Djemal Pasha and Kress von Kressenstein Review Turkish Troops in Jerusalem
Courtesy of the Library of Congress

the Arabs."[42] To such a prejudicial and unrealistic assessment was added another, namely, that Germany, where newspapers reported—incorrectly as it turned out—the government ready to make its own pro-Zionist declaration, might outbid the British and earn the supposedly considerable benefits of world Jewry for itself.[43]

On November 13, meanwhile, Allenby took Junction Station and two days later Ramleh on the Jaffa Road. Falkenhayn, now commanding the campaign, threw brigades of his slowly arriving *Yildirim* army into a series of counterattacks, but gradually Allenby gained the advantage as his army concentrated before Jerusalem. Hebron and Bethlehem fell next, and on December 7 the Jaffa Road was cleared of defenders. Allenby made his triumphal entry four days later, returning to Christian hands the city Saladin the Great had taken so long ago. Just as in Iraq, the cost of six weeks' combat had been mutually high: British losses totaled 18,000 and Turkish-German 25,000. Rights of conquest paid for so dearly by the British would not be sacrificed or compromised lightly.

As the church bells rang out in London Britain's prospects in the Middle East seemed bright. Maude, the captor of Baghdad, had died of cholera in November, but his army, freed from worries about powerful Turkish reinforcements, had continued its advance with the return of cooler weather, overrunning Ramadi in September, chasing Ali Isham Bey out of the Jebel Hamrin Mountains in October, and seizing Tikrit in November.[44] Shortly after Allenby's victory at Jerusalem, moreover, Falkenhayn concentrated most of *Yildirim* army in a bid to retake the city but failed. With his sights now on the next rich prize, Damascus, Allenby convinced Lawrence and Feisal to transfer the "Arab Northern Army" from Aqaba to the country east of the Dead Sea, there to disrupt transport and grain shipments to the Turks. Finally, to make doubly sure that Falkenhayn's defenses did

End of an Epoch: Allenby Reclaims Jerusalem for Christendom
Harper's Pictorial Library

not hold Robertson shifted two divisions from Mesopotamia, where troop needs had diminished.

Like the Turks' defensive lines in Arabia, Palestine, and Iraq, the Ottoman home front also showed signs of crumbling.[45] This was perhaps inevitable given the regime's propensity for treating much of its internal opposition as a racial contagion or ethnic infection to be cauterized and cleansed from the body politic. The Armenians and Greeks became the twentieth century's first victims of genocide in 1914–1916, but other groups suffered too. Until 1917 the Turks inflicted "scarcely tolerable misery" on Arabs and Kurds in the bulk of Iraq. When Maude entered Baghdad, "food in some quarters was deficient to the point of starvation, economic life was dead, the public services had ceased to exist, and a cowed population looked forward to the rumored blessings of British rule."[46] Djemal Pasha treated his subjects even more brutally. After executing suspected Arab nationalists in 1915 and 1916 the Tyrant of Damascus "resettled" five thousand families of Syrian Arab notables to Anatolia. Worse happened to the Arabs and Jews of Palestine as fighting intensified in 1917. The Turks forcibly evacuated the entire populations of Gaza, Tel Aviv, and Jaffa, leaving over eighty thousand people to their fate with what belongings and food they carried with them. Thousands died and many more suffered terribly from malnutrition, their plight exacerbated by the allied blockade of the entire Mediterranean coastline.

The widespread misery among civilians extended to the Turkish people too. Indeed the allied blockade, the disruption to agriculture caused by the Russian incursion to Eastern Anatolia/Turkish Armenia in 1916, and the accompanying outbreak of typhus, all compounded by drought conditions, spread discontent into the towns and cities of Turkey proper. Istanbul responded with appeals to patriotism and religion, and when this failed to revive morale, with tight censorship and police suppression. As in prewar Russia, the army, not the police, represented a more important pillar of state authority, but the rank and file of many divisions had begun to desert or surrender in greater numbers in 1917, while the loyalty of the officer corps appeared doubtful. Insiders worried that the transfer of units from Europe through the capital to form the *Yildirim* army could lead to a coup. All across the Ottoman Empire people questioned why their leaders had initiated such a long, disastrous war. The yearning for peace deepened after two revolutions in Russia demonstrated that cease-fires and negotiated exits to the war were possible.

BERLIN, VIENNA, AND BREST-LITOVSK: THE CENTRAL POWERS ON THE BLACK SEA

Things looked good that Christmas from the British purview, but experts knew then, as we do now, that Middle Eastern sands can shift quickly. As 1918 dawned, in fact, there were worrisome indications that British footing in the region was becoming less secure. Fighting in Turkish Armenia had almost ceased months before the Bolshevik armistice as the Russian army lost its appetite for combat. After the cease-fire of December 1917 enemy soldiers who had pierced deeply into Turkish territory in 1916 began to go home, leaving Enver Pasha with tempting options. Reinforcements could be sent by the shortest routes to fight the British in Palestine and Persia—this is what Berlin and OHL urged—or enter the vacuum the Russians had created, taking back Erzurum and then moving even farther eastward to Baku on the Caspian Sea, and from there finally into northern Persia to gather even more Turkic-speaking peoples into a regenerated Ottoman Empire. The secession of Georgia, Armenia, and Azerbaijan from Russia in December to form a weak Tran-Caucasian Republic, followed by accusations from Istanbul of mistreatment of Turkish nationals and Turkic Azerbaijanis there, signaled to observers in London the likely beginning of a Turkish offensive, which began, in fact, in February. This alone was ample reason to send a team of specialists under General Lionel Dunsterville into the Caucasus to embolden the young republic to train and defend itself lest its collapse endanger lands to the south as far as India.[47]

The Foreign and Indian Offices had additional worries, however, for when Germany tired of negotiating with the Bolsheviks in February 1918, broke the armistice, and began a rapid advance all along the eastern front, including seizing most of the Ukraine, alarming scenarios were spun of German divisions resuming their southward advance or a German mission like Dunsterville's appearing in Tashkent to liberate and reoutfit the reportedly 100,000-plus German and Austrian POWs still held there by the disintegrating Russian regime. The longstanding British nightmare of a formidable enemy coalition at the gates of India could come true.

Leon Trotsky's monocled spectacles perched nicely on the bridge of his nose. Keen, intimidatingly intellectual eyes peered out of the Bolshevik's trademark glasses. Through an icy smudged train window he stared, half-incredulously, half-assuredly, and fully torn by contradictory emotions, at the moonscaped ruin that was Brest-Litovsk in early January 1918. Tsarist troops had razed the Polish town to the ground during their scorched-earth retreat of 1915. Sadly but surely, the bleak panorama surrounding the wagon as it came to a screechy halt confirmed for Trotsky the wisdom of words he had spoken to comrades just three weeks earlier. With this brutal, destructive war "man, king of nature, has descended into the trench-cave, and there, peeping out through narrow holes, as from a prison cell, he is lurking for his fellow man, his future prey—so low has mankind fallen."[48] Only the old citadel of Brest-Litovsk remained intact. The German High Command had chosen the fortress as its eastern front headquarters, and here, in this grim architectural symbol of German military might Trotsky intended to negotiate a war-ending treaty for his young Communist state. Because tsarist Russia's western allies had ignored Bolshevik feelers for a general peace conference, the treaty, disappointingly, would only be a separate one between Germany and Russia.

As he left his compartment to be received by officers and diplomats from all of the Central Powers, Trotsky had other reasons to both hope and worry. All along the route from St. Petersburg he had observed Russian trenches almost completely abandoned by their defenders. The army had rapidly disintegrated after the Bolsheviks' calls for peace, but what options did that leave the country's new leaders? Weeks earlier Trotsky had feared for the outcome if the German army broke the cease-fire and attacked: "I do not know whether—with this disrupted economy and universal chaos entailed by war and internal convulsions—whether we could go on fighting." And then, viewing Russia's phantom army from the train, he "grew ever more and more depressed," according to a German officer accompanying him. Bolshevik circles eagerly anticipated a rising of workers in other capitals, especially Berlin and Vienna, to drag down the awesome imperial eagles threatening Russia, but thus far only a "dead silence" reigned there, leaving

Trotsky's head full of gloomy scenarios of Bolshevik martyrdom and defeat for the common man.

> One is oppressed by a feeling of shame for man, his flesh, his spirit, his blood, when one [sees how people]...kill each other like miserable slaves under the whip of the ruling classes. Should the war have this outcome only that people return to their managers, to pick the miserable crumbs thrown down from the tables of the properties classes, should this war finish with the triumph of imperialism, then mankind would prove itself unworthy of its own sufferings and of its own prodigious mental efforts....Sooner or later the popular masses of all countries will come to us and stretch out a helpful hand, but even if the enemies of the people were to conquer us and we were to perish, our memory would still pass from generation to generation and awaken posterity to a new struggle.[49]

As he stepped off the train, Trotsky shrugged off these nagging forebodings and resolved to do everything humanly possible to ensure that they would never come to pass.

"It would have been much easier," said Trotsky in December 1917, "if the peoples of Europe had risen with us," if Russia faced negotiations with "German Independent Social Democrats Karl Liebknecht, Klara Zetkin, and Rosa Luxemburg," as opposed to the German and Austro-Hungarian High Commands. "This," however, "has not happened."[50]

To be sure, politics in Germany had intensified that year, moving from crisis to crisis as the political extremes squared off against one another.[51] In July a Reichstag majority challenged the generals' control of the war by calling for a compromise peace, but Hindenburg, Ludendorff, and the reactionary replacement for ousted Chancellor Bethmann Hollweg, Georg Michaelis, largely ignored the so-called Peace Resolution and prosecuted the war full throttle. In order to whip up popular enthusiasm for their policy of a crushing victory, extensive annexations, and rejection of the left's democratization efforts, they encouraged the formation of a new single-issue political organization, the Party of the Fatherland, in September 1917—money from military budgets also lined its coffers. The peace parties and their trade union backers immediately answered in kind with their own proreform propaganda weapon, the People's League for Freedom and Fatherland. Germany's political polarization worsened during the autumn as both sides exchanged ugly accusations and insisted that only one program benefited the nation.

Further controversy swirled around the highly contentious issue of replacing the antiquated plutocratic voting laws in Prussia, the empire's most powerful state, with the Reichstag's more democratic suffrage, thus terminating control of the diet by conservative propertied elements. Leftist pressure felled Michaelis in late October after the High Command, fearing strikes in armaments factories at the height of the Battle of Passchendaele, did nothing to save him. The new chancellor, aging Center Party leader Georg Hertling, prepared a democratic suffrage bill for the diet in November, and both the Majority and Independent SPD readied protest marches if reactionary deputies did not accept it. Escalating political

German Poster of 1918: "Bolshevism Means War, Unemployment, and Hunger"
Courtesy of the Library of Congress

tensions, strike threats, and potential street demonstrations did not, however, a revolution make. The armaments workers of Berlin were the best paid in Germany, and their employers scoured the black market for food to keep the men hard at work. These were not the Russian-style conditions required for an insurrection against the army and its tight grip of martial law.

Conditions in the big cities of Austria were worse. The allied blockade hurt the Dual Monarchy more than its northern ally, for there was no "windpipe" like neutral Holland or Denmark or German-conquered lands like Belgium or Rumania to provide the steady trickle of food shipments that made their way into Germany. Thus Germans complained rightly that they had less than a pound of potato to eat daily per person, but for their ally potato consumption was only a fifth of that: a mere mouthful of two and a half ounces. Worse still, the Hungarian breadbasket of the empire proved far too stingily nationalistic to supply the Austrian half of the state on a regular basis. Consequently, when the government announced on January 13, 1918, that flour rations were cut to below six ounces a day, enough for only a few slices of bread, strikes broke out in Vienna and spread throughout Austria—six hundred thousand had walked off the job by January 16. The police could do nothing to restore order as the strikes rapidly politicized into a determined push not just for more food but also an end to martial law. Moreover, with all eyes on continuing negotiations at Brest-Litovsk that the Bolsheviks had done their best to publicize and propagandize, many strikers demanded an end to the war against Russia. "Whoever does not want to close his eyes must see that this monarchy is lurching on the edge of the abyss,"[52] reported the German ambassador. Only after the bread decree was revoked, more food and electoral reforms promised, and seven army divisions dispatched to arrest strike leaders and patrol cities and towns did the strike wave subside.

The Austrian disorder spread almost immediately to Germany. Much of the workforce in the large munitions and metallurgical plants of the capital and other industrial cities had slipped out of the control of the Majority SPD and its associated trade unions into the hands of radical shop foremen who headed a network of factory committees established by the Reichstag's Auxiliary Service Bill of December 1916 to regulate work conditions. Leaning more toward the Independent SPD, and probably toward its revolutionary "Spartacus" wing, the shop stewards were emboldened by the Austrian troubles to hit the streets for more food at cheaper prices, electoral reforms in Prussia, termination of army control of factories, and an end to the war, starting with peace in the east. By late January upwards of half a million workers had struck in Berlin, with roughly the same number walking off the job elsewhere in Germany. The Austrian ambassador warned Vienna that "class warfare"[53] had broken out, but, as noted earlier, the German working class was not yet ripe for revolution. Indeed it was the army that proved more willing to use force, manning striking factories with soldiers, shutting down left-wing newspapers, and arresting tens of thousands of ringleaders and shipping them off to battlefields in France.

Meanwhile, even before the first disorders in Austria, Trotsky had taken over the Russian peace delegation at Brest-Litovsk and begun his remarkable political and intellectual battle with the civilian and military leadership of the Central European empires.[54] For ten days he attempted to distribute revolutionary leaflets to enemy soldiers and shift the talks to Stockholm, and when these efforts failed, to embarrass Germany and Austria-Hungary by making a mockery of their claim to have fostered national self-determination in Poland and the Baltic. "In the conventional language which we use in such cases this is described, not as self-determination of peoples, but by quite a different expression—annexation." When the spokesman for the German army, General Max Hoffmann, scoffed at Trotsky's masquerading as "a victorious invader" rather than acting more appropriately as a prostrated enemy, and then further protested the Bolsheviks' unacceptable "interference in the affairs of the occupied areas," the soldier's much more brilliant adversary had only to rest his case and smile wryly.

Trotsky asked for a pause in the negotiations on January 18 to consult with party leaders in St. Petersburg. The worsening troubles in Austria strengthened his belief in a "permanent revolution" that would spread to Vienna, Berlin, and beyond, and hence, too, his determination to obstruct the talks and refuse to sign an annexationist treaty. The western strikes also affected the belligerent mood of the Bolshevik majority—Lenin and the men around him being the major exceptions. If the moment were not quite ripe for a revolutionary war it soon would be, so there could be no talk of a shameful surrender to the imperialists—in Trotsky's famous phrase: "neither war," for the moment, "nor peace."[55]

When negotiations began again at Brest-Litovsk on January 30, however, the news from Austria, and soon that from Germany too, had turned bleak. With the strikes broken, the ringleaders arrested, and hopes for permanent revolution temporarily dashed, the Russian Revolution stood alone in a dangerous world. Trotsky managed to string out the wrangling until February 10, but when Hoffmann presented a large map displaying the huge territories Germany proposed to annex, the Soviet leader seized the last word. With the British taking African colonies, Baghdad, and Jerusalem and the Germans occupying Belgium, Poland, and the Baltic there could be no more pretense to a war of defense; rather this was a power struggle "for the partitioning of the world."

> We do not want to take part any longer in this purely imperialist war, in which the claims of the possessing classes are openly paid for in human blood.... We are withdrawing from the war.... We are issuing an order for the full demobilization of our army.... At the same time... we refuse to endorse terms which German and Austro-Hungarian imperialism is writing with the sword on the flesh of living nations. We cannot put the signature of the Russian revolution under a peace treaty which brings oppression, woe, and misfortune to millions of human beings.

In reply to this amazing statement Hoffmann was nearly speechless: "Unheard of,"[56] he exclaimed. Trotsky hurried back to St. Petersburg, where, on February 17, 1918, the revolutionary hawks heard the rest of Germany's reply—fifty divisions had attacked that day, their spearheads advancing rapidly against almost nonexistent resistance. "Neither peace nor war" had proven a sham.

In the north an army group of sixteen divisions overran the Baltic, taking the port of Reval on February 25 and Narva, less than 150 kilometers from St. Petersburg, a day later. A somewhat smaller contingent pushed due east, seizing first Dvinsk, then Minsk, and finally on February 27 Mogilev, the former tsarist military headquarters. Half of Germany's available divisions were formed into

Central Powers Advance into Russia in 1918/Treaty of Brest-Litovsk Demarcation Line

Maps Courtesy of the Department of History, United States Military Academy

a powerful southern group and dispatched into the Ukraine, where Kiev, only recently retaken by the Bolsheviks, fell into German hands on March 2. "This is the most comic war I have ever experienced," jotted Hoffmann in his diary.

> It is waged almost exclusively with trains and cars. One puts on the train a handful of infantrymen with machine guns and one gun, and one rushes to the next railway station. One seizes that station, arrests the Bolsheviks, entrains another detachment and travels farther.[57]

In two weeks Hoffmann's forces had captured 63,000 prisoners, 2,600 artillery pieces, and 5,000 machine guns. In St. Petersburg Lenin issued orders to move the capital to Moscow and pleaded with his belligerent compatriots to sign a treaty with a dangerous foe "armed to its teeth"[58] before there was no more revolution to defend. Remarkably, the prospect of ending the war this ignominiously was so detested that Lenin's resolution carried the day in party counsels by only one vote—Trotsky had swallowed his pride and backed the leader lest Lenin's threat of resignation split the movement and trigger intraparty warfare.

So harsh and onerous was the Treaty of Brest-Litovsk, signed by the Soviet delegation on March 3, 1918, that it took another bitter debate and very close vote before the "Communists," as the party now named itself, accepted it three days later.[59] Lenin's henchmen had to accept German policing of Baltic lands, some combination of German and Austro-Hungarian control of Poland, the independence of Finland and the Ukraine, and abandonment of all claims to White Russia and the Caucasus. Over a million Austro-Hungarian and tens of thousands of German POWs would be repatriated. A supplementary treaty charged Moscow 6 billion marks in reparations.

German aspirations soared, however, to higher, significantly more grandiose heights. Thus the kaiser wanted to eradicate communism: "The Bolsheviks are tigers," he said, "round them up and shoot them." For this purpose Hoffmann wanted to march on Moscow, and Ludendorff too was tempted by "Operation Capstone." Probably with an eye on his forthcoming offensive in the west, however, he overruled Hoffmann in favor of a less ambitious venture, ordering instead planning for a drive over St. Petersburg to Murmansk to smash Communist rule and secure the region from troops that the western allies had landed there. Nothing came of this operation either, but clearly OHL was merely biding its time, eagerly awaiting the first good opportunity to crush Bolshevism.[60]

Indeed the earlier extension of German power eastward had carried with it an anti-Bolshevik agenda. In the fall and winter of 1917–1918, for instance, Ludendorff and his underlings tried to midwife two embryonic grand duchies in northern Lithuania and the Baltic (Grodno to Riga), which behind the façade of personal ruling union with the House of Hohenzollern would provide the army with manpower, garrisons, raw materials, food, and strategic positioning for future warfare on the eastern front. And in Finland, which broke away from Russia in December 1917, the two sides actually came to blows when a division-strength German expeditionary force landed at Helsinki to aid Finnish nationalists in defeating leftist opponents and pushing their Soviet backers out of the newly established nation. Later in 1918 the Finns chose Friedrich Karl of Hesse, the kaiser's brother-in-law, as their king and agreed to provide the Reich with army and navy bases, not to sign any anti-German alliances, or to raise tariffs against German imports.[61]

The Teutonic agenda waxed even more pronounced in those vast, one thousand square miles of grain-rich southern Russia that fell to Germany after Brest-Litovsk. Hoffmann's divisions chased the Reds out of Kiev in March 1918, and after the Ukrainian parliament proved recalcitrant, established a protectorate under pro-German puppet Pavel Skoropadsky. During the spring Germany's massive, twenty-five-division army group fanned out in all directions from the capital, moving into Odessa—which was soon allotted to Vienna—overrunning the Crimea, and occupying the valuable coal basin of the River Don. In May, furthermore, Berlin induced the breakup of the extremely unstable Trans-Caucasian Republic by extending German commercial and military dominance into a willing, albeit helpless Georgia. With Tiflis under their control Reich officials expected the whole Caucasus to fall "automatically"[62] into their lap.

Much has also been made of Ludendorff allegedly succumbing "to the kind of megalomania that was to affect Adolf Hitler in the Second World War."[63] Although it is true that he strove to resettle the million-odd Germans from the Volga River region to the Ukraine, there to live and work "side by side with our soldiers"[64]—an idea not unlike Nazi "blood and soil" schemes—Ludendorff remained far too preoccupied with western operational preparations in early 1918 to give much thought to "building a bridge to Central Asia in order to threaten the British position in India."[65] As the western offensives progressed in March and April, furthermore, OHL shifted eight more divisions to France, further undercutting any chance of an imminent "Crusade à la Alexander."[66]

Others, however, actively worked toward this end. In Constantinople General Hans von Seeckt, appointed OHL liaison to Enver Pasha in January 1918, backed the Turk's plan to capture the Caucasus and eventually advance south to the Indian Ocean, all the while struggling with Ludendorff, revealingly enough, who adamantly opposed the scheme lest Baku oil fall into Turkish not German hands.[67] Only later, two months into his western offensive, did Ludendorff warm even a little to the Indian expedition, writing Seeckt in May 1918 that the prospect of Britain surviving, even if France fell, made it necessary "to prepare ourselves" for striking at "their most sensitive spot." Seeckt continued to support Constantinople, arguing that Turkish control of the Caucasus was the operational sine qua non for what all sides wanted strategically, namely, weakening or dislodging the British in Iraq, penetrating into Persia, and opening the gate to India.[68]

Small wonder, therefore, that the British trickled available troops into the southern Caucasus in a desperate attempt to ward off these nightmarish prospects. Sir Percy Sykes, a British colonel present in Persia, recalled that the situation facing the British Empire "was serious." Emir Habibulla Khan, "in face of the strongest pressure, moral and religious, had maintained the neutrality of

Afghanistan," but now "it seemed at least possible that enemy divisions might actually arrive on the frontiers of Afghanistan and overwhelm our ally."[69] British intelligence in Persia exacerbated anxieties, for nationalistic elements in Teheran allied with restive, well-armed tribal leaders appeared on the brink of moving against the hated British. These circles were especially emboldened to act by the virtual disappearance of Russia's military presence from their country. Against these ominous threats the British had only those units that Baghdad could send to reinforce Persia. There had been seven infantry divisions on or near the fighting fronts of Mesopotamia during the autumn campaign of 1917, but then London shifted two to Palestine for an anticipated push on Damascus.[70]

As news flashed to the Middle East and Central Asia of a massive and apparently very successful German offensive on the western front in late March 1918, therefore, the sands of the whole region, and perhaps of the world war itself, seemed ready to shift.

NOTES

1. For this scene, see Tom Segev, *One Palestine, Complete: Jews and Arabs under the British Mandate,* trans. Haim Watzman, (New York, 2000), 30–32, 50–56.
2. Erich von Ludendorff, *Ludendorff's Own Story: August 1914-November 1918* (New York, 1919), 1:302.
3. For stalemate worries in British leadership circles in 1916, see Denis Winter, *Haig's Command: A Reassessment* (Barnsley, UK, 2004), originally published in 1991, 72–73.
4. For the politics behind British military operations in the Sinai and Palestine, see David Fromkin, *A Peace to End All Peace: The Fall of the Ottoman Empire and the Creation of the Modern Middle East* (New York, 1989), 253–301; Benny Morris, *Righteous Victims: History of the Zionist-Arab Conflict 1881–2001* (New York, 2001), 67–73; and more recently, Segev, *One Palestine, Complete,* 33–43.
5. The best descriptions of the Sinai and Palestinian campaigns of 1916/early 1917 remain those of Cyril Falls, *The Great War 1914–1918* (New York, 1961), 241–244, 323–324; and idem., *Armageddon, 1918: The Final Palestinian Campaign of World War I* (Philadelphia, 2003), 3–11.
6. Falls, *Armageddon,* 6.
7. Citations in William Robertson, *Soldiers and Statesmen: 1914–1918* (New York, 1926), 2:166, 167; and Fromkin, *Peace to End All Peace,* 282.
8. Citations in Fromkin, *Peace to End All Peace,* 268, 270, 287.
9. Citations in ibid., 270–271, 282.
10. Citations in ibid., 297, 286; and Morris, *Righteous Victims,* 75–76.
11. For the first and second battles of Gaza, see Falls, *The Great War,* 323–324; and *Armageddon,* 9–11.
12. Cited in Falls, *Armageddon,* 10. Also see Robertson, *Soldiers and Statesmen,* 2:169, 171–172.
13. Robertson, *Soldiers and Statesmen,* 2:69. For the second Iraqi campaign, see A. J. Barber, *The Neglected War: Mesopotamia 1914–1918* (London, 1967), 304–384; and Mohammad Gholi Majd, *Iraq in World War I: From Ottoman Rule to British Conquest* (Lanham, MD, 2006), 275–331. Also see the excellent eyewitness accounts of Arthur Tillotson Clark, *To Baghdad with the British* (New York, 1918), 109–204; and George Buchanan, *The Tragedy of Mesopotamia* (Edinburgh, Scotland, 1938), 146–173.

14. Cited in Robertson, *Soldiers and Statesmen,* 2:73.
15. See good descriptions of these efforts in Stephen Hemsley Longrigg, *Iraq, 1900 to 1950: A Political, Social, and Economic History* (London, 1956), 88–89; and at greater length in Buchanan, *Tragedy of Mesopotamia,* 95–145.
16. Clark, *To Baghdad,* 131.
17. Falls, *Great War,* 251.
18. Robertson, *Soldiers and Statesmen,* 2:74.
19. Clark, *To Baghdad,* 136.
20. Cited in Barker, *Neglected War,* 328.
21. Situations in Sir Percy Sykes, *A History of Persia* (London, 1951), 2:486; and Barker, *Neglected War,* 416.
22. For the intended size of *Yildirim* army, see Barker, *Neglected War,* 413–415, 421; and Stanford J. Shaw and Ezel Kural Shaw, *History of the Ottoman Empire and Modern Turkey* (Cambridge, UK, 1977), 2:323.
23. Citations in Robertson, *Soldiers and Statesmen,* 2:178, 186.
24. Citations in B. H. Liddell Hart, *Lawrence of Arabia* (New York, 1989), 75, 74, originally published as *Colonel Lawrence: The Man behind the Legend* (New York, 1935). Lawrence's full-length memoirs, originally written in 1919, appeared in a private publication in 1926 and were eventually published as *Seven Pillars of Wisdom: A Triumph* (Garden City, NY, 1935). An abridged version appeared years earlier as *Revolt in the Desert* (New York, 1927). Although *Seven Pillars* is a classic that Great War experts need on their shelves, the shorter *Revolt in the Desert,* surely more reasonable for students, is cited here. For his wartime dispatches from Arabia, see Malcolm Brown, ed., *T. E. Lawrence in War and Peace: An Anthology of the Military Writings of Lawrence of Arabia* (London, 2005). Also see Malcolm Brown, *T. E. Lawrence* (New York, 2003).
25. See Fromkin, *Peace to End All Peace,* 168–172.
26. The citations here are taken from notes that Lawrence made in Arabia and used for his posttravel report after returning to Egypt in November. See Brown, *T. E. Lawrence in War and Peace,* 80, 77.
27. Hart, *Lawrence of Arabia,* 84.
28. See Lawrence's notes, printed in Brown, *T. E. Lawrence in War and Peace,* 68–69; and Lawrence, *Revolt in the Desert,* 22–23.
29. For the origins of the plan, see Lawrence, *Revolt in the Desert,* 41; and Lawrence's postraid notes of February 6, 1917, printed in Brown, *T. E. Lawrence in War and Peace,* 91–92.
30. Hart, *Lawrence of Arabia,* 106–107, 116–117, 122, 142.
31. See ibid., 42–43, 114–115, 118–119, 150–151.
32. Lawrence, *Revolt in the Desert,* 66.
33. Cited in Hart, *Lawrence of Arabia,* 135.
34. For the details, see Lawrence, *Revolt in the Desert,* 77–116.
35. Ibid., 122.
36. For the total, see Robertson, *Soldiers and Statesmen,* 178, 183.
37. Lawrence, *Revolt in the Desert,* 153.
38. For the timing of the diversion of the *Yildirim* army to Palestine, see Frank G. Weber, *Eagles on the Crescent: Germany, Austria, and the Diplomacy of the Turkish Alliance* (Ithaca, NY, 1970), 239–240. For its actual strength, see Otto Liman von Sanders, *Five Years in Turkey,* trans. Carl Reichmann, (Annapolis, MD, 1927), 173–180; and Hart, *Lawrence of Arabia,* 190.
39. For brief descriptions of this battle and subsequent engagements, see Falls, *Armageddon,* 11–15; Martin Gilbert, *The First World War: A Complete History* (New York, 1994), 370–372; and especially Hart, *Lawrence of Arabia,* 188–197.

40. For the background to the Balfour Declaration, see Morris, *Righteous Victims,* 73–75; Segev, *One Palestine Complete,* 33–50; and especially Fromkin, *Peace to End All Peace,* 263–297.
41. Cited in Fromkin, *Peace to End All Peace,* 297.
42. Cited in ibid., 278.
43. Segev, *One Palestine Complete,* 38.
44. For Iraq, see Barker, *Neglected War,* 434–457; and Mohammad Gholi Majd, *Iraq in World War I: From Ottoman Rule to British Conquest* (Lanham, MD, 2006), 333–350.
45. See Segev, *One Palestine Complete,* 19–22; Fromkin, *Peace to End All Peace,* 308–309; Shaw and Shaw, *History of the Ottoman Empire,* 2:324; Hasan Kayali, *Arabs and Young Turks: Ottomanism, Arabism, and Islamism in the Ottoman Empire, 1908–1918* (Berkeley, CA, 1997), 192–200; and Weber, *Eagles on the Crescent,* 230.
46. Longrigg, *Iraq,* 84–86, and for the quote, 92–94.
47. See Barker, *Neglected War,* 447–449.
48. Cited in Isaac Deutscher, *The Prophet Armed: Trotsky 1879–1921* (New York, 1965), 357.
49. Ibid., 360, 357–358.
50. Ibid., 358.
51. See Gerald D. Feldman, *Army, Industry, and Labor in Germany, 1914–1918* (Princeton, NJ, 1966), 425–458; Eric Dorn Brose, *Christian Labor and the Politics of Frustration in Imperial Germany* (Washington, DC, 1985), 356–360; and Roger Chickering, *Imperial Germany and the Great War, 1914–1918* (Cambridge, UK, 1998), 156–167.
52. Cited in Holger H. Herwig, *The First World War: Germany and Austria-Hungary 1914–1918* (London, 1997), 362.
53. Cited in ibid., 379.
54. See Deutscher, *Prophet Armed,* 361–404; and Adam B. Ulam, *The Bolsheviks: The Intellectual, Personal and Political History of Communism in Russia* (New York, 1971), 388–414.
55. All citations here from Deutscher, *Prophet Armed,* 369–370, 382.
56. Citations in ibid., 380–381.
57. Cited in ibid., 383.
58. Cited in Ulam, *Bolsheviks,* 409.
59. For the treaty as well as its aftermath in the East, see Herwig, *First World War,* 381–387; Cyril Falls, *The Great War 1914–1918* (New York, 1961), 186–189; and Robert B. Asprey, *The German High Command at War: Hindenburg and Ludendorff Conduct World War I* (New York, 1991), 355–371.
60. Ludendorff asserts this repeatedly in his memoirs (Erich von Ludendorff, *Ludendorff's Own Story: August 1914-November 1918,* New York, 1919), 2:182–191, 258–266, 296–301). For earlier citations, see Asprey, *German High Command,* 360; and Vejas Gabriel Liulevicius, *War Land on the Eastern Front: Culture, National Identity, and German Occupation in World War I* (Cambridge, UK, 2000), 210.
61. See Matti Klinge, *The Baltic World* (Helsinki, Finland, 1994), 137–139; and Liulevicius, *War Land on the Eastern Front,* 196–210.
62. Cited in Ulrich Trumpener, *Germany and the Ottoman Empire 1914–1918* (Princeton, NJ, 1968), 182.
63. Gordon A. Craig, *Germany 1866–1945* (New York, 1978), 392.
64. *Ludendorff's Own Story,* 2:304.
65. Craig, *Germany,* 392.
66. For this transfer, see David Stevenson, *Cataclysm: The First World War as Political Tragedy* (New York, 2004), 339.
67. Trumpener, *Germany and the Ottoman Empire,* 178–189; and Walter Goerlitz, *History of the German General Staff,* translated by Walter Millis, (New York, 1953), 192.

68. Ludendorff's letter to Seeckt is cited in Hew Strachan, *The First World War* (New York, 2003), 298–299. Strachan exaggerates, however, in lambasting Ludendorff for "engaging in Napoleonic fantasies." For Seeckt's replies regarding Enver's Middle Eastern/Central Asia goals, see Trumpener, *Germany and the Ottoman Empire,* 179. That there were indeed Turkish aims on Iraq by moving into northern Persia from Baku, see Otto Liman von Sanders, *Five Years in Turkey,* trans. Carl von Reichmann, (Annapolis, MD, 1927), 244, 268–269.
69. Sykes, *History of Persia,* 2:487–488.
70. Ibid., 452–504; Barker, *Neglected War,* 440; and Majd, *Iraq in World War I,* 342–343.

CHAPTER X

The Last Furious Year of the Great War

1917–1918

One hundred and twenty-eight kilometers northeast of Paris, the forest of Crepy-Fourdrain concealed sinister secrets. Deep inside the primeval woods man had cleared away trees for an ugly concrete command post. Its stark, cold walls, dripping with dew from an early-morning fog, contrasted garishly to the greenery and chirping of springtime. Uniformed men entered and walked to a map table and then peered outside at their colossal cannon. Clinking and clanking as it cranked to higher degrees of elevation, a monstrous metallic tube rose out of the misty forest floor. Over one hundred feet long and weighing two hundred tons, the creature waited for sustenance. Cranes hoisted a brass-tipped projectile into its mouth. "Toi toi, toi—do your job, Jeanette," said one artilleryman affectionately as the shell went in.

Inside the bunker a phone rang. It was OHL ordering the giant to fire on Paris far away to the southwest. The order to shoot passed down the line. Thirty heavy artillery batteries stood ready to fire simultaneously to provide a camouflage of sorts to prevent counterbattery fire. At 7:09 a.m. on March 23, 1918, the salvo went skyward with a hideous roar. One shell left the others far below, rocketing into the icy stratosphere at two thousand meters per second. A few minutes later it reappeared in the skies above Paris and took only a few seconds to plummet into the City of Light.

The gargantuan "Paris cannon" shot 367 shells at the French capital that spring and summer, most exploding murderously in the inner city.[1] Hundreds were killed and wounded, the worst incident coming on Good Friday, March 29,

The Civilians' War: Hospital Ward Hit by the Paris Cannon
Canfield, *World War*

when a direct hit on the Church of Saint-Gervais killed 88 worshippers and injured 68. Its mission was to break enemy morale as German shock divisions crashed into the British Fifth Army on the old Somme battlefield. Monstrous Jeanette would do her part to force western enemies to their knees just weeks after Germany's Carthaginian Peace had been imposed on the east.

GERMANY THROWS THE IRON DICE

General Philippe Pétain, commander of French forces in the field, grew more pessimistic about further allied offensives during the autumn of 1917. He informed BEF chief Douglas Haig that Russia's likely surrender and Germany's probable transfer of fifty divisions westward necessitated shifting to defensive operations. He also cautioned disbelieving politicians in Paris against further attacks and received firm support from his political boss, Premier Georges Clemenceau. Upon entering office in November "The Tiger of France" called for "war, nothing but war"; however, the new man quickly faced the facts and swung behind Pétain: "I support him entirely."[2] Haig and Chief of the Imperial General Staff (CIGS) William Robertson scoffed at French war-weariness, but they had no political backing. David Lloyd George and Foreign Minister Arthur Balfour had tired of failed offensives, preferring to defend in 1918 until American reinforcements justified a war-ending offensive in 1919.[3] Assessing his battle losses in the context of Bolshevik calls for peace, Haig finally yielded in early December and ordered the BEF to prepare defenses.

There would be a three-line trench system patterned after the Germans. Battalions would be raised to full strength by consolidating existing units (i.e., reducing their number) and divisions reorganized with nine instead of the twelve

Lifelines: Irish-American Joseph Dugan and American Railroad Personnel on Tracks Behind the Western Front
Private Collection

battalions. And in January 1918 the man who had complained about inadequate reinforcements now told an anxious and skeptical War Cabinet that fifty-eight mostly understrength British and Commonwealth divisions (bolstered somewhat by fourteen Belgian and Portuguese[4]) sufficed to contain Germany's growing strength in his sector, despite having recently extended it by fifty-four kilometers to relieve French units on the Oise River. "Robertson called Haig a fool,"[5] recorded one participant at the meeting.

Had Robertson exaggerated? Did Haig know something London did not? No fool, in fact, the BEF commander had predicted a number of things correctly, including the approximately two hundred divisions available to Germany in the west, the tactics they would employ, the timing of the offensive, and its multiple sites: an initial strike between Arras and the Oise, followed by a second around Ypres, with others simultaneously or later in French sectors.

He deployed his armies accordingly.[6] The Belgian army and Britain's Second, First (including the Portuguese), and Third Armies defended from the Channel to below Bapaume (145 kilometers). From there beyond the Oise (54 kilometers), the stretch recently taken over from GQG, Haig placed Fifth Army. He laid greater emphasis on the sea-to-Bapaume front—four armies with 60 divisions (counting reserves) versus Fifth Army's 14 divisions—but this made military sense, for a short 35–80 kilometers behind three of the four northern armies lay the lifeline ports of Dunkirk, Calais, and Boulogne, while Sir Julian Byng's Third, anchoring the center-right with 16 divisions, was only 85–95 kilometers from the coast. Hubert Gough's Fifth Army, like much of Third still battered in body and spirit from Passchendaele, was obviously weaker, a fact made more troubling by the undeveloped trench network bequeathed by the departing, offensive-minded French. However, Haig and Gough knew that Fifth Army had about

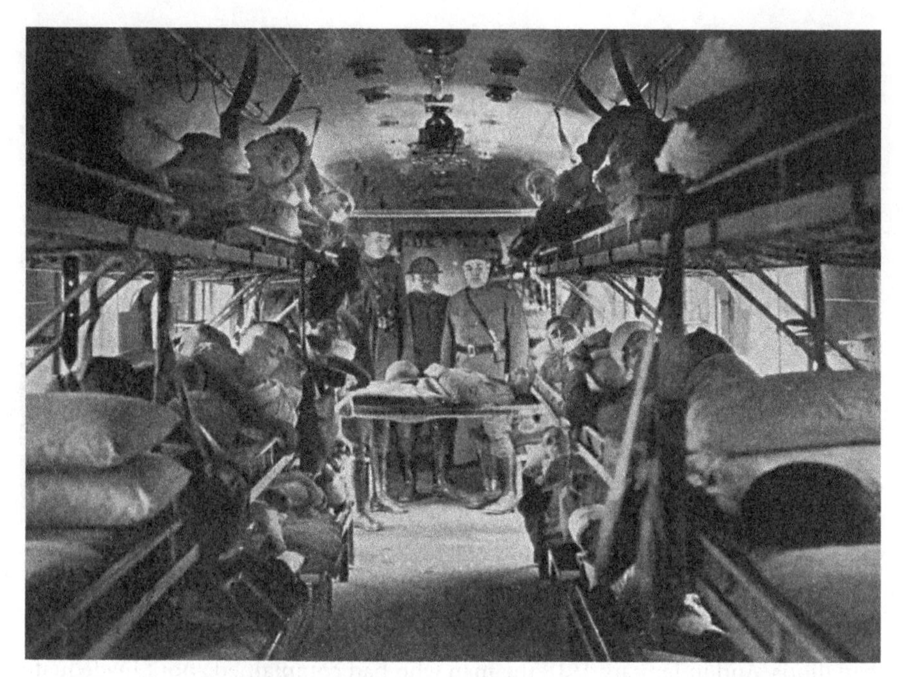

Moving the Mountain to Mohammed: American Hospital Train with Casualties

Harper's Pictorial Library

150 kilometers of rear ground to the Channel: they planned to fall back 30 kilometers if necessary to easily defensible positions along the Somme River and Canal du Nord, 50–70 kilometers from the critical rail junction at Amiens, which itself lay 50–60 kilometers from the coast. Haig could also count on help here from the French. Behind 63 frontline divisions stretching from the Oise to Switzerland Pétain placed 37 divisions in GQG reserve. Many of these reserves bordered on Gough, whom the French agreed to support with at least 6 divisions.

Allied thinking rested on several critical assumptions formed from intelligence reports, analysis of past enemy offensives, and knowledge of their own experience attacking trenches. As Haig and Pétain watched German strength increase from around 150 divisions in November to 194 divisions in March—not an overwhelming lead over the allies' 174—both believed OHL would disperse its reinforcements and assault simultaneously or in rapid succession in various sectors: Verdun, Champagne, the Somme, and Ypres. Despite the swelling number of enemy divisions, in other words, they assumed that attack force *at any one point* would still correspond to the 1917 scale of 15–40 divisions. Furthermore, Haig thought attacks would gradually mount in intensity in his sector in March (Somme) and April (Ypres) before a bigger push in May, probably again at Ypres. "The Germans must be expected to follow sound principles," he instructed army commanders in February. "They will try to wear us down before the main attack."[7] Assuming that he would have adequate time and opportunity to shift reserves and supplies between his armies according to needs, therefore, the Briton used available labor resources in early 1918 to expand existing rail lines behind the front. His own slow progress at Passchendaele—eight kilometers in three months—not only strengthened his confidence that there would be sufficient time to react but also his belief that Ludendorff would be making a rash "gambler's throw" if he attacked. Haig feared "that the enemy would find our front so very strong that he will hesitate to commit his army to the attack with the almost certainty of losing very heavily."[8]

Operation *St. Michael*

The Germans manipulated allied expectations with systematic deception and disinformation. They marched troops back and forth behind the entire front, sent out raiding parties all along the line, bombarded a variety of sectors in the weeks before their attack, and planted false orders. An observation balloon was set loose, for instance, with phantom plans for an assault in Champagne, which fooled Pétain. The real target was carefully concealed with nighttime troop movements, camouflaged supply depots, and dispersed airfields. In the weeks before March 21, 1918, Ludendorff amassed 75 divisions—far more than the allies thought possible. Formed into Seventeenth, Second, and Eighteenth Armies, they stretched for seventy kilometers opposite Haig's Third and Fifth Armies. OHL picked the very best divisions and the youngest, fittest soldiers for this operation, moreover, and systematically trained first-wave units in storm troop tactics. This significant force advantage was magnified by German artillery superiority: 6,600 light and heavy guns versus barely 2,600, plus a lopsided six-to-one superiority in trench mortars. OHL supported each of its 32 first-wave divisions with 118 heavies (including heavy trench mortars). Not even the French on the Somme (110), the Germans at Verdun (92), or Nivelle on Chemin des Dames (77) had packed more steel per unit. With only 30 artillery-poor divisions to defend before reinforcements could arrive, Haig's armies were in great peril made greater by the 1,070 airplanes that OHL massed behind the lines, nearly half of its active planes in the west.

Historians usually criticize Ludendorff for focusing on tactics and deemphasizing or even ignoring operational and strategic objectives.[9] One should not completely discount such criticism, but the goals of "Operation *St. Michael*" were initially very clear. In the first waves came storm troopers heavily armed with machine guns, light mortars, poison-gas-grenade-launchers, and the "hideous"[10] flamethrowers, followed by specially trained and even more formidable attack divisions, both waves fighting their way with air support quickly through 15–20 kilometers of British lines. Storm troopers had orders to take as many British positions as possible but go around the most persistent pockets of resistance, leaving them for the stronger attack divisions and strafing airplanes to destroy. In subsequent days, with second-wave backup divisions pouring into the breach, Seventeenth and Second Armies would sweep northwest behind Arras to threaten the rear of Haig's northern armies and push them toward the sea. Eighteenth Army would secure the southern flank from French reinforcements. A second campaign strike north of Ypres, "Operation *George*," might also be necessary, especially if Haig weakened northern positions by rushing aid to Gough and Byng. Crushing the British and separating them from the French would demoralize both war-weary nations—with help from the Paris cannon—before America could make a difference, perhaps forcing another Brest-Litovsk or at least giving Berlin tremendous leverage during negotiations. All of this followed the long-standing General Staff credo that "strategic victory follows tactical success," a wise approach on the tactically stalemated western front. A more germane criticism of the overworked, temperamental Ludendorff should focus, therefore, on whether he possessed the poise and coolness by 1918 to stick to his own simple operational strategy. That he did not seems almost certainly reflected in an oft-quoted reply to a general who inquired about operational objectives. Ludendorff cut him short: "We chop a hole and the rest will take care of itself."[11] Would operational goals be forgotten in the stress and confusion of tactical struggle?

A massive, unregistered "hurricane" bombardment began before dawn on the 21st and for five hours alternately targeted all defensive zones with regular, high-explosive, poison-gas, and tear-gas rounds.[12] Concentrated here, German artillery fired two-thirds as many shells as the BEF in a week before the Battle of the Somme. Of the 17,000 defenders killed or wounded this day most fell during this unimaginably horrendous firing, a toll made worse because Gough and Byng, but especially Gough, placed too many men in forward areas. Experienced defenders, the Germans had learned to move soldiers back, but the BEF, more accustomed to attacking, had not. Many who survived the bombardment were dazed, furthermore, and thus largely unable to defend themselves when the enemy's creeping barrage passed and the storm troopers appeared out of the early-morning fog. "Nobody could stand more than three hours of sustained shelling before they started feeling sleepy and numb," said one soldier. "It's a bit like being under an anesthetic; you can't put up a lot of resistance."[13] Consequently, the Germans captured 21,000 Tommies. The firing also destroyed hundreds of guns and machine guns as well as communications between forward zones and the rearward artillery, thereby preventing regimental and brigade commanders from calling in precise support. Compounding these problems, the BEF's top-heavy command structure failed to respond quickly to the day's challenges. As the Germans had learned, effective defense-in-depth required decentralization with rapid local initiatives by battalion and regimental commanders. By day's end Ludendorff's armies had overrun most of the first line and some of the middle and rear zones as well, but the onrushing units had not "chopped a hole." Despite losing 17–18 percent of their overall combatant strength—with much higher casualties in frontline divisions—Third and Fifth Armies had fought back tenaciously, actually inflicting a greater number of casualties—39,000—on the Germans.[14]

Over the next five days to March 26, however, the British had to fall back before superior numbers as their own reserves proved inadequate to stem the tide. Fifth Army abandoned its defensive zones and withdrew to the Somme and Canal du Nord, Gough's prebattle last-stand position, but then yielded that line too. Third Army's defense had been more successful, but as Fifth's battered brigades scurried backward, Byng had to retreat too lest he lose contact with Gough's left wing, which did, in fact, happen. Gaps also opened between the British and

Air Auxiliaries: German Biplanes at the Ready
Harper's Pictorial Library

French across the Oise, sending Haig into near panic as he ordered trenches dug to protect the Channel ports, shifted six divisions from his northern armies, including three from the front line, and implored Pétain to rush twenty divisions. "Haig is cowed," noticed the new CIGS Sir Henry Wilson on March 25. "He said that unless the whole of the French Army came up, we were beaten and it would be better to make peace on any terms we could."[15]

Already by this time, however, Operation *St. Michael* had begun to lose momentum. Most historians fault Ludendorff's generalship and there is truth to the charge. Pleased with Eighteenth Army's progress and displeased with Seventeenth and Second, for example, he poured six fresh divisions into the south after the 21st and none to the north, seeming to forget the original operational goal of rolling northwest in preparation for Operation *George*. On March 23, moreover, Ludendorff issued new orders for a three-pronged advance, his armies to attack, respectively, northwest behind Arras (Seventeenth), west to Amiens (Second), and southwest toward Montdidier-Noyon (Eighteenth), but then five days later he used uncommitted divisions for Operation *Mars*, a frontal attack on heavily defended Arras. After *Mars* failed badly, he finally concentrated his attack on the most important prize, Amiens and its vital rail junction, which no doubt would have fallen if a united effort had been made earlier. As it was, the drive halted eight kilometers away. The moment of victory may have been sacrificed by this dissipation of strength in an apparently frantic search for a hole to punch.

As the Germans advanced seventy kilometers—unheard of success in the west—other factors contributed to ultimate failure. Supply grew worse with insufficient numbers of trucks and horses to keep pace with the troops, who began to run short of food and ammunition after two or three days of tough combat. The badly chewed-up ground of the 1916 battlefield west of the Somme exacerbated these supply difficulties. Similar problems impeded the shifting of reserves, which had to move along north-south railroads behind the Hindenburg Line and then trudge west into the moonscape created by old and new battles.

Furthermore, that constant, aggravating nemesis, the ever worsening British blockade, greatly compounded Ludendorff's logistical nightmare by weakening his forces from the outset. Trucks lacking rubber tires made do with iron wheels that ruined roads and easily bogged down. Not only were there fewer horses after years of war had killed so many, they were also underfed, underweight, and unable to endure long hauls of heavy cannon and supplies, especially over the old craters and dilapidated trenches between the Somme and Amiens. Although they ate better than their relatives at home, soldiers, too, were undernourished, so much so, in fact, that the discovery of well-stocked British supply depots (that instantly put the lie to army propaganda about U-boats starving the enemy) had a demoralizing effect. And when, after three or four days, German infantrymen realized that the British front had bowed and bent but not broken, discipline crumbled in many units as tired and hungry men forgot about the need for speedy advance and sacrifice and fell to gorging and drinking what the Tommies had left behind. Summing up the long list of German problems, John Keegan concludes that "[battlefield] desolation and the temptation to loot may have been enemies as deadly to the Germans as the resistance of the enemy itself."[16]

Blockade-induced enervation was one indication of the poor odds facing OHL in the last stage of this war, but there were other signs that Germany was outmatched. The High Command had already removed divisions from other fronts—about forty-five—and called up the last available levy of youth for *St. Michael*. Although a million men remained in the east, the best divisions as

Storm Troop Tactics: Flamethrower Team Advances on an Allied Trench
Canfield, *World War*

well as younger soldiers from remaining units had gone west. Making German prospects even bleaker, Ludendorff had lost 240,000 of his best soldiers between March 21 and April 4, necessitating further transfers of lesser-quality battalions from Russia, but his elite storm troopers could never really be replaced.

Allied prospects, on the contrary, were much brighter. To be sure, Haig had lost 178,000 and greatly thinned out his northern armies, but he had held. Pétain contributed to victory, moreover, with reinforcements that began to arrive north of the Oise on March 23. The French would lose 77,000 men by battle's end, at which point an impressive fifteen divisions stood beside the British with eight more under way. Meanwhile in London, the War Cabinet had canceled furloughs for 88,000 BEF veterans, who headed back to the fray. Britain also called up 50,000 men from home reserves, the rifle strength of five extra divisions. The equivalent of five more were at sea from Sir Edmund Allenby's Egyptian Expeditionary Force in Palestine and battalions equaling another division from Salonika. Undoubtedly most troubling for OHL, the Yanks were coming—over 400,000 stood on French soil in late April with more than 100,000 pouring in every month. They were not fully trained and obviously untested but still aided the allies by taking over parts of French lines as Pétain came to Haig's rescue. Finally, organizational changes augured well for the allies as French General Ferdinand Foch ascended to the post of supreme allied commander with the charge of overseeing military operations of all armies in France, including the rapidly expanding American Expeditionary Force (AEF) of General John Pershing.

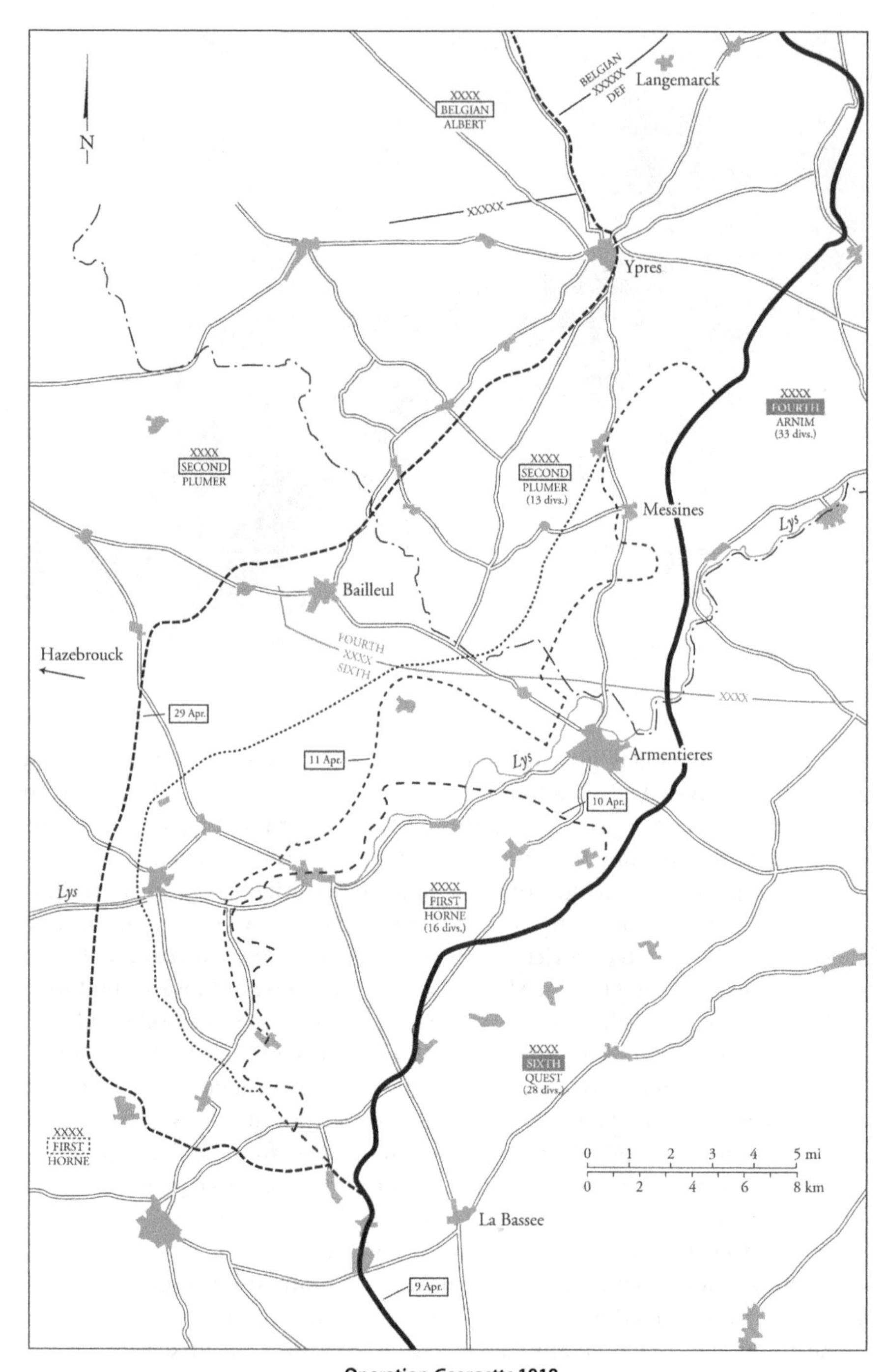

Operation *Georgette* 1918

Maps Courtesy of the Department of History, United States Military Academy

The Allies Coordinate: Marshall Foch to the Fore
Harper's Pictorial Library

Operation *Georgette*

Although distracted from campaign goals during *St. Michael*, Ludendorff had not fully lost sight of his broader operational strategy. Even before April 4 he began to move heavy artillery north for an attack that had figured prominently in planning discussions. OHL preferred to hit Haig where his back was closest to the sea, in fact, but needed to wait for the end of Flanders's winter rains and floods. On the drier, harder ground of spring, Operation *George* originally called for a massive offensive blow between La Bassée and Ypres, but after the attrition of *St. Michael* OHL scaled back operations to a thirty-kilometer stretch south of the town and diminutively redesignated the operation *Georgette.*[17] By 1917 standards, nevertheless, the assault was still immense. Backed once again by superior numbers of guns, two armies (Sixth and Fourth), altogether 61 divisions on a comparatively narrow front, were to smash through the British First and Second Armies, overrun the railroad junction at Hazebrouck, press allied forces to the sea, and sever their connection to the south. *Georgette* would be supported by only a fourth as many specialized attack divisions as *St. Michael*—12 versus 47—and the enemy entrenchments were far better than those Fifth Army inherited from the French. On the other hand, most of First and Second Armies' regular divisions had been transferred to the Somme during *St. Michael*. Haig replaced some (but not all) of them with battered units from Third and Fifth Armies: where 44 allied divisions stood guard from the Channel to Arras in March only 34 remained. Worse still, along Sixth Army's attack front British First Army commander Henry Horne had only 1 fresh division, 2 demoralized Portuguese divisions, and 5 British divisions mostly worn out from the earlier battle.

Ludendorff had chosen the point of attack well. On April 9, 1918, Sixth Army unleashed its hurricane bombardment and then attacked with the vanguard of

German Poster of 1918: "The Big Battle in France"

Courtesy of the Library of Congress

28 divisions. On his far right opposite La Bassée, Horne's rested division butchered the attackers. Next in line where the spearhead of the assault hit, however, a Portuguese division Horne had pulled back but not yet replaced and beside it two exhausted Scottish brigades fell back in disarray as the Germans advanced six kilometers, a third of the distance to Hazebrouck. Fourth Army joined the offensive on the following morning, amassing lead elements of its 33 divisions north of Armentières against Herbert Plumer's Second Army with 13 divisions. By April 12 Messines had fallen in the north, while in the south Sixth Army had pushed to within eight kilometers of the crucial rail lines.

Once again near panic, Haig rushed divisions from Byng's adjacent Third Army and pleaded with Foch for reinforcements. "If the necessary measures are not taken," he implored, "the British army will be sacrificed, and sacrificed in vain." Anticipating another German offensive between Arras and the Somme, however, Foch would do no more than shift a handful of reserve divisions closer to Flanders. Recent research confirms the contemporary British suspicion that Foch, worshipping the offensive much more than a pessimistic, cautious Pétain, carefully husbanded resources throughout the early spring for a big counterattack and the day of liberation.[18] Desperate, Haig issued a dramatic order of the day to his troops:

> There is no other course open to us but fight it out! Every position must be held to the last man: there must be no retirement. With our backs to the wall, and believing in the justice of our cause, each one of us must fight on to the end. The safety of our homes and the freedom of mankind alike depend on the conduct of each one of us at this critical moment.[19]

British resistance, which had not flagged even before Third Army help arrived, stiffened over the next four days as the Germans ground more slowly but ever closer to Hazebrouck. Upset with the slowing pace, Ludendorff shifted his efforts on April 16 to the Belgian front around Langemarck, but Fourth Army failed to crack the brave, well-fortified defenders. This abortive assault finally moved Foch, however, to send eight infantry divisions with supporting cavalry into Flanders—four were already in position on Mount Kemmel (northeast of Bailleul) by April 18. Showing the same impatience with German failure to punch holes, Ludendorff ordered another attack on Amiens, where, presumably, the allies had drawn away too much of their strength to meet the emergency in Flanders. Once again, however, defenses proved too strong. A final attack pushed the French off Mount Kemmel on April 25, but to the southwest Hazebrouck still held. Its northern armies spent, OHL called off the operation four days later.

St. Michael and *Georgette* had failed for many of the same reasons. Like its predecessor, the latter suffered from Ludendorff's impetuous quest for soft spots in allied lines, whereas a more consistent and concerted effort might have seized rear zone railroads. April's fighting also demonstrated once again the underlying weaknesses of the German army after four years of war. Gaunt horses struggled and strained to keep forward units supplied with ammunition and artillery support, preventing Sixth Army in particular from pressing its early advantage. Logistical breakdowns undermined *Georgette* even more than *St. Michael*, in fact, for the weaker "trench" divisions that Ludendorff had been forced to use in greater numbers had fewer horses than the elite units. The backup divisions had not learned storm troop tactics, furthermore, which meant they usually attacked in the massed waves preferred by older officers and paid dearly against well-entrenched defenders. OHL suffered almost 260,000 casualties while inflicting less than 150,000. Worst of all, indiscipline increased with more uncontrolled eating, drinking, and looting in captured British depots and whole units disobeying orders, dire factors that Ludendorff singled out in his memoirs.[20] Clearly, troubles on the home front had begun to affect the fighting front too, although fatigue and hunger probably weighed more heavily.

Accumulating German problems "provided food for thought"[21] to the increasingly frustrated Ludendorff. Would he ever break through? Emphasis had been put on tactical success leading to strategic gains. When asked in February about the implications of tactical failure, he knew only one thing to say: "In that case Germany must go under."[22] Now two operations had failed and Ludendorff was forced to improvise a third in order to avoid the unacceptable fate of losing the war. Prior to March 21 the French had assembled huge reserves and then moved whole armies north to the Somme and later into Flanders to rescue a nearly totally exhausted BEF. In late April 1918, therefore, OHL saw forcing the French to defend Paris as the only way to eliminate their ability to save the BEF when Ludendorff attacked it for a third time.

Operation *Blücher*

Designed as a highly complex feint, OHL's next offensive targeted the Chemin des Dames. Since Nivelle's debacle in 1917 German units had withdrawn from the crest of the ridge and allied divisions had moved up to the Ailette River south of Laon: 4 French on the left, 3 British on the right, with 9 in reserve (including two British). Ludendorff and his generals used the month after *Georgette* to assemble over four thousand guns and two armies (Seventh and First) whose 41 divisions would take ten or twelve days to penetrate over the Ailette, Chemin des Dames, and Aisne to the Vesle River, sufficient time to shock French leaders into concentrating available reserves before Paris. Eighteenth Army, the big gainer of *St. Michael*, would provide support on the right flank, and then after ten days launch its own major assault along the Oise to whipsaw the allies south of Noyon.[23] Once Seventh Army reached the Vesle, however, lead elements had orders to entrench and shield a prearranged transfer of artillery trains and reinforcements to Flanders for Ludendorff's coup de grace against Haig.

Early on May 27 the "hellish orchestra"[24] of the now perfected German hurricane bombardment broke unexpectedly on allied lines. Shifting between forward and rear zones for nearly three hours, it left few regiments willing or able to fight. Once again Ludendorff had chosen his target well, for French commanders had shunned defense in depth, following Foch's unwise directive of May 5 not to sacrifice an inch of French soil. All five British divisions, moreover, had been moved from the Somme and Flanders to this allegedly quiet sector for rest and refitting. By midmorning the entire Chemin des Dames had been overrun, and by nightfall Seventh Army's lead corps touched the Vesle. Over the next two days the entire river line was secured. On the German right Soissons fell, on the left First Army stood before Rheims, and in the center vanguards crossed the Ourcq River and were driving on the Marne, having raced thirty-eight kilometers from their jump-off positions. Not even Eighteenth Army had penetrated so far and so fast in the first days of *St. Michael*. OHL ordered the campaign to continue.

Going Over There: Joseph Dugan (left) Heads East

Private Collection

The unexpectedly quick success of *Blücher* had automatically changed operational plans. Although Ludendorff is roundly criticized by historians for doing so, he seems to have had little choice, in the first few days at least, but to press his attack forward, for by May 29 when the entire Vesle lay in German hands the French had only begun to shift their reserves. To be sure, Pétain immediately sent twenty of the divisions that he controlled, but Foch initially refused to budge reserves from the Somme and Flanders for what he saw correctly as a feint. Only on May 29–30, with the spearhead of Seventh Army preparing to cross the Marne a panicky eighty kilometers from Paris, did he order French units south and encourage Haig to follow suit. As these forces began to assemble ahead of the German advance on May 31–June 1 the moment for *Blücher* to end had probably come, but Ludendorff opted instead to keep pushing—he ordered northern armies, in fact, to send reinforcements south.

Perhaps he correctly divined the fright surging through allied counsels. On June 5 the War Cabinet discussed withdrawing the BEF from Europe and decided to draw up contingency plans for a Dunkirk-style evacuation. Defense of Britain and threatened imperial outposts loomed as a higher priority. At Compiègne, simultaneously, GQG considered a massive retreat from northern and eastern France for a last-resort battle around Paris.[25] Neither move was made as reports filtered back of stiffening resistance, but the mere discussion of these drastic options showed the depth of despair induced by *Blücher*. Panic had also raised its ugly head. Instinctively assessing the huge scale of losses on their side—a shocking sixty-five thousand prisoners had been taken, more than the dead or wounded—demoralized French infantrymen turned wearily to American units marching to

Over There: Dugan's Military ID in France
Private Collection

the front, saying the war was over. British Tommies talked about making for Switzerland. An exodus of over a million refugees began from Paris, moreover, and in the Chamber of Deputies angry parliamentarians shouted down Clemenceau, literally chasing him from the room. After returning, his only means of evoking more positive, hopeful emotions was to remind colleagues, "The Americans are coming."[26] Seen in the context of such waning Anglo-French willpower, Ludendorff's gamble on victory does not seem quite as rash.

On the eve of *Blücher*, Oskar von Hutier, the victor of Riga and now commander of Eighteenth Army, worried about the outcome. "If the pending operation does not have truly decisive success," he wrote, "then we are stuck."[27] Two operations had already bogged down, leaving deep salients that were vulnerable to flanking attacks, harassed constantly by enemy air patrols, and hard to supply. Now Ludendorff's decision to press on got him stuck again and for all of the same reasons: horse-drawn supplies could not easily reach front lines; the artillery fell behind; and tired, hungry, flu-weakened, demoralized infantrymen ignored military police and pillaged captured food and wine. Steadily increasing enemy reinforcements also slowed the German advance. As casualties passed one hundred thousand on June 6, OHL called off *Blücher* but was by now so deeply committed between the Vesle and Marne that further shoring-up operations were required before either advancing on Paris or attacking again in Flanders.

And as summer neared one more factor troubled German generals—the Yanks were indeed coming. Although it is an exaggeration to claim that "the Americans saved the allies,"[28] they had definitely begun to provide significant support on the ground. With defensive lines bowed precariously from Soissons to Rheims, three strong U.S. divisions (with total rifle strength of nearly 40,000) took up position between Chateau Thierry and Rheims. Although many more French and British units finally brought *Blücher* to a standstill, these American divisions by themselves represented replacement of about a third of total Anglo-French losses in the campaign. In a celebrated, albeit very costly engagement at Belleau Wood near the Marne on June 6, moreover, a marine corps brigade actually counterattacked and slowly gained ground. "The spectacle of this magnificent youth from across the sea... had an immense effect," noted one French officer, for the newly arrived ally "offered a striking contrast with our regiments in soiled uniforms, worn by the years of war, with our emaciated soldiers and their somber eyes who were nothing more than bundles of nerves held together by an heroic, sacrificial will."[29] Counting large numbers of support troops, the AEF had swelled by this point to 650,000 and by mid-July passed a million, strengthening already existing, already deepening suspicions among common German soldiers that the war was no longer winnable. After *St. Michael* Ludendorff ultimately moved half a million men out of Russia—half of his forces there—but with odds nonetheless lengthening these reinforcements did not alter pessimistic perceptions in German ranks.

AMERICA, WILSON, AND THE INFLUENZA

A half year earlier it had been the allies expressing their pessimism and anxiety. By New Year's Day 1918 only four American divisions had disembarked in France, and although on paper each of the AEF's eight brigades roughly equaled (in combat troops) an undersized British or French division, only one of the American divisions was full strength and none had finished training. An angry, disappointed British journalist blurted to one of Pershing's aides that in the eight months that had taken Russia out of the war, brought the French army close to collapse, and led the British into the horrors of Passchendaele "you haven't really fired a damned shot!" The French, too, had lost the morale boost of seeing the first Yankee "doughboys" enter the country in June 1917. Clemenceau quipped privately that Pershing's "chief occupation seems to be having dinner in Paris." Publicly his government announced that the American army would not be trained and ready until 1919, a statement that produced a "deplorable" effect in French ranks. "It is true that we have the Americans," wrote one soldier, "but they have seen the war only in the movies, and it will be two years before they are ready." American officers confirmed this, observing that "a strong feeling of 'oh what's the use?' is spreading throughout France." Pershing felt the pressure on him mounting: "Look at what is expected of us and what we have to start with—no army ready and no ships to bring over an army if we had one!" In Washington President Wilson also strained under the weight of criticism from "preparedness" groups that blamed him for neglecting military matters throughout his first term, from pacifists who felt he had abandoned them, from suffragettes protesting their exclusion from federal voting, and from consumers angry over rising food prices. The chief executive repaired to his yacht "to get away from the madness (it is scarcely less) of Washington," he wrote his daughter. "I do not see how any but a well man could safely be trusted to decide anything in the present circumstances."[30]

As exasperating as American mobilization was for the president, for Pershing as well as for democratic allies who repeatedly demanded "men, men, and more men" the United States had not been idle since April 1917. Amidst considerable controversy in a nation no more disposed to conscription than Britain had been in 1914–1915, the Wilson administration shepherded a bill through Congress in May, euphemistically labeled "selective service," while also calling for volunteers. By autumn the better part of 1.7 million draftees and volunteers had assembled in thirty-six newly constructed army cantonments, each to produce a division of 30,000 infantrymen and support troops. The army aimed to have 20 frontline and 10 replacement divisions ready in 1918, a meteoric rise from the prewar regular army of 133,000 and National Guardsmen totaling 185,000.

Training, equipping, and transporting the AEF "over there" turned into a transatlantic squabble, however, of major proportions. Because boot camps in the United States could not adequately prepare soldiers for a war drill sergeants had not experienced, Pershing eventually agreed to have many of his divisions complete training in England and France. The number of confiscated, purchased, chartered, or newly built troop transports rose by war's end to 1,700, many of these escorted in convoys by the navy's 51 newly commissioned destroyers, but these impressive feats took well over a year to achieve and never fully met AEF needs. Complicated arrangements had to be negotiated, therefore, with the British amidst the great U-boat crisis of 1917. American armaments and munitions works already at capacity supplying the Entente, furthermore, could neither expand their plants nor negotiate syndication agreements quickly, especially with antitrust sentiment strong among congressional progressives. Consequently, most doughboy units shipped with great difficulty to Europe required allied artillery and airplanes. Thus Pershing had only four divisions ready when OHL overran the Chemin des Dames.

The greatest quarrel in the allied camp, however, swirled around the issue of how to use the American army. As the allied body count rose in 1917, both France and Britain argued that the United States should feed its strong, one-thousand-man battalions into Anglo-French divisions. Leaving support troops and equipment behind would also decrease burdens on British shipping. From the standpoint of London and Paris the logic of these requests strengthened after Caporetto, the Russian collapse, and Haig's decision to reduce British divisions to nine battalions—Canadian and ANZAC units remained at twelve. But Wilson objected to the notion of using American men essentially as replacements. Rather, he wanted a freestanding American army in France—and Pershing was so ordered—to magnify his leverage in arranging an armistice and shaping the peace.[31]

Indeed the president already had his eye on the postwar period. In arguably the most important speech of his political career, Wilson came before Congress on January 8, 1918, to outline a crusading fourteen-point plan. In Europe this included restoration of Belgian independence; withdrawal of the Germans from

France and return of Alsace and Lorraine; creation of a genuinely independent Poland; evacuation of Russia by German armies; the fullest possible autonomy for the various peoples of Austria-Hungary; restoration of Rumanian, Serbian, and Montenegrin independence; and adjustment of Italian borders along ethnic lines. Turkey proper would remain independent, but Constantinople had to open the Dardanelles and guarantee safety, security, and autonomy for its non-Turkish nationalities, especially the Armenians. Wilson would insist on freedom of the seas; free trade; an end to secret diplomacy; a reduction of armaments; a "free, open-minded, and absolutely impartial adjustment" to all colonial claims; and most remarkable of all, an association or league of nations "under specific covenant for the purpose of affording mutual guarantees of political independence and territorial integrity to great and small states alike."[32] Obviously the military rulers of Germany would not agree to this peace plan—one had only to look at Brest-Litovsk—hence their defeat was imperative, but Wilson's vision of a new world order would also be difficult if not impossible for Britain and France to accept. An American army making an indispensable contribution to victory became the lynchpin, therefore, for realization of the Fourteen Points.

Pershing shared Wilson's commitment to the AEF's role in securing U.S. war aims. He planned to build up his own army in Lorraine, strike the German rear at Metz, and force OHL to pull out of France and sue for peace. But Pershing also had military reasons for this ambitious American campaign. The British and French had failed to dent German defenses over three campaign seasons, sacrificing a generation of young men in their abortive offensives, thus he had seemingly good reason to free America's youth from foreign generals. Moreover, although the South Africans, Canadians, Australians, New Zealanders, and Indians were accustomed to dominion or "commonwealth" requirements, Pershing knew all too well that the American public and its citizen soldiers, having long ago fought successfully for independence from Britain, would not tolerate subordinating themselves to British officers—after Gallipoli even the Australians bristled at this, after the Somme and Passchendaele the Canadians too. Throughout the crises of March and April, therefore, the American refused to integrate his units into the other armies except on a temporary training basis. Operation *Blücher* actually strengthened his position in early June, for in its despairing mood GQG argued that a 100-division AEF—dwarfing either the French or British armies—had become the sine qua non for ultimate victory in 1919. Pershing endorsed the idea, and after assessing available resources the War Department agreed to jettison its 30-division plan of 1917 for an 80-division AEF. Pershing put a few divisions under French command on the Marne in the June emergency, while others went to the British sector, but kept building up the AEF in Lorraine.

As spring turned to summer, oddly enough, the American army achieved through other means what it could not yet accomplish on European battlefields. Recent research demonstrates that the first comparatively nonlethal wave of the great influenza pandemic of 1918–1919 began not in China, South Africa, Spain, or France, as variously claimed in the literature, but rather in rural Haskell

Going Over There: American Nurses Disembark in Britain
Canfield, *World War*

County, Kansas.[33] From the countryside in late February the flu spread quickly to nearby Camp Funston, infecting 1,100 of 56,000 soldiers. Over the next month it rampaged through two-thirds of the army's new cantonments; scores of adjacent towns and cities; hundreds of troopships; and via these transports to Brest, France. Adjacent French army units reported their first cases on April 10, the British armies in Flanders a few days later, and soon German soldiers who came into contact with the enemy during Operation *Georgette* also contracted the flu. Although scores of thousands of allied soldiers throughout France got so sick they required hospitalization—over 36,000 in the British First Army alone—the blockade-weakened Germans by all accounts suffered much more. By early summer 1918, in fact, influenza was decimating OHL's western armies, removing twice as many soldiers from German lines as from British. Roughly 400,000 soldiers—every seventh man in Germany's 2.8 million-man force on the western front—lay in bed or hospital. In harder-to-supply front line divisions in the thick of exhausting combat, every third man suffered from the flu.[34]

THE SWING FROM GERMAN OFFENSIVE TO ALLIED COUNTEROFFENSIVE

Like his first two offensives, Ludendorff's third left a deep sixty-kilometer salient threatened on its flanks and perilously difficult to supply. Only one railroad through Soissons serviced the area and it was vulnerable to allied artillery and airplanes. OHL deemed it imperative, therefore, for Hutier's Eighteenth Army to proceed with Operation *Gneisenau* along the Oise between Montdidier and Noyon with support from Seventh Army attacking west of Soissons. Converging

American Poster of 1917: "Democracy's Vanguard"
Courtesy of the Library of Congress

on the rail center at Compiègne, German forces could secure their supply line, disrupt allied supply, and bolster the Marne salient. Seventh and First Armies would later sweep around Rheims to solidify the eastern edge (Operation *Marneschütze-Reims*). Only then could Ludendorff proceed with Operation *Hagen* in Flanders, followed, it was hoped, by peace on German terms.[35]

Hutier attacked with twenty-two alarmingly understrength divisions along a 30-kilometer front on June 9, 1918. Partly because the allies had detected his slow preparations, however, two days' fighting brought only a 9–10 kilometer gain and twenty-five thousand casualties. Seventh Army had even less success, running—as had Eighteenth—into allied reserves trucked, trained, and force-marched to the sound of the guns. Clearly the German army had come dangerously close to the end of its offensive momentum and fighting effectiveness as evidenced by the familiar storm warning signals of earlier attacks (i.e., faltering logistics, looting and skulking, insubordination, and the flu). The very timing of *Gneisenau*, in fact, coming ultimately two weeks after *Blücher*, also reflected OHL's rapidly waning punching power, for Ludendorff had wanted *Blücher* and *Gneisenau* to overlap, but was prevented by ammunition shortages compounded by supply bottlenecks. We can easily appreciate how devastating *Blücher* would have been had Eighteenth Army captured Compiègne and opened a road to Paris while Seventh and First pushed across the Marne, the geographic symbol of French victory in 1914.

Five weeks passed before OHL opened its fifth offensive around Rheims. Artillery shells had to be produced and transported from defense plants. Semimutinous soldiers who painted pro-Bolshevik signs on troop trains and yelled "strike breakers" at new arrivals from the eastern front, former Russian POW camps, and restive factories back home had to be disciplined and the deleterious effects of their propaganda eliminated or reduced through indoctrination. Men in sick bay or recovering from minor wounds had to get back on their feet. New storm trooper squads had to be trained. By mid-July Ludendorff had readied three armies (Seventh, First, and Third) and fifty-two divisions—most of them only partially rebuilt, retrained, and replenished—for Operation *Marneschütze-Reims*, an overambitious pincer maneuver around Rheims. Alerted to the July 15 date of the assault by reconnaissance and information from German deserters, however, the allies had thirty-four divisions in line and many more in reserve, all backed by strong, well-supplied artillery and superior air squadrons. OHL appeared destined to fail again after a short advance. Indeed, having established only a six-kilometer bulge below the Marne by July 17, Ludendorff began to shift divisions for Operation *Hagen*.

On the next day, however, Foch unleashed his counterstroke. He had assembled sixteen divisions in Tenth Army under the cover of the dense Villers-Cotterets Forest. The smaller Sixth Army would provide support on the right. Both armies had U.S. support. Shortly before dawn the attack began with no preliminary bombardment. Instead the infantry exploded out of the forest behind a creeping barrage and 301 tanks—almost as many as Cambrai—into the vulnerable western flank of the German salient above the Marne.[36] Tenth Army pierced eight kilometers through the shocked defenders to Tigny, cutting the road to Chateau-Thierry and threatening the entire salient. The attack surprised Ludendorff too: he acted like "a beetle on its back," writes Correlli Barnett, "waving and wriggling furiously to no effect."[37] Eventually facing up to an uncomfortable reality, OHL ordered its armies back on the defensive.[38] There would be no attack in Flanders.

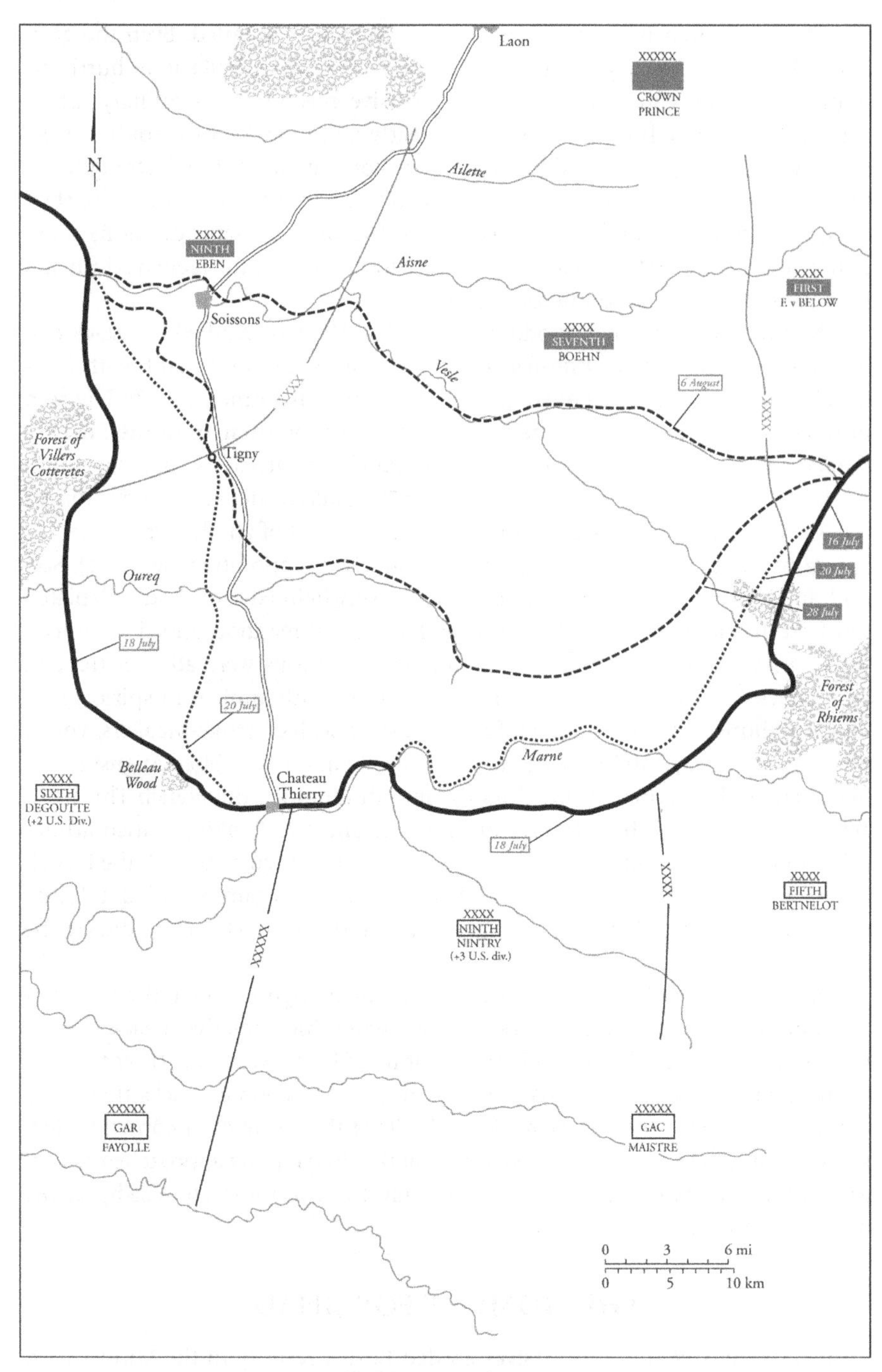

Allied Counterstrokes, 1918

Maps Courtesy of the Department of History, United States Military Academy

The great offensive gamble on the western front had failed. Even the great Ludendorff with his frightening storm troop tactics and hellacious hurricane bombardments could not complete the elusive revolution in military affairs sought by all generals of the Great War. Nearly a million German soldiers were dead, wounded, or missing. Allied losses were comparable, but their strength was growing, not diminishing. They had absorbed Germany's hardest blows and then counterattacked. From July 18 to August 3 Ludendorff's depleted divisions abandoned the Marne and pulled all the way back to the Vesle as the French Ninth and Fifth Armies joined the counteroffensive.

Nor was Foch finished. Prodding a skeptical Haig, he readied an attack east of Amiens.[39] The hesitant Briton's Fourth Army took the north flank with fourteen British, Canadian, and Australian divisions, with the American 33rd Division in reserve—together an awesome demonstration of the strength of the English-speaking peoples—while the French First Army's ten divisions took the south flank. The allies had 1,900 airplanes and over 700 tanks of all kinds—they pointed the way toward the revolution in military affairs (RMA) of another great war.

Although the new technologies proved largely disappointing (see later), Second and Eighteenth Armies' outnumbered, overwhelmed, and badly depleted fourteen divisions reeled backward. They had only three thousand rifles apiece, while the Canadian, Australian, and American divisions were all overstrength. As reserves rushed into the gaps left by divisions nearly broken in spirit, many retreaters hurled insults at the reinforcements: "Blacklegs, strike-breakers, you're prolonging the war!" In his memoirs, Ludendorff famously dubbed August 8 "the black day of the German army."[40] As the month unfolded the French Third and Tenth Armies joined the offensive on the Oise and two flanking British armies (First and Third) extended the assault to Cambrai. On August 20, with the French advancing rapidly south of the Oise, Ludendorff once again recorded a "black day."[41] By September 2, 1918, OHL had lost almost every inch gained during the spring.

Already in mid-August, moreover, the German High Command and Kaiser William had recognized the necessity of attempting tentative peace feelers. Because they deemed the "suitable time" for these initiatives to be "after the next German success in the west"—a reference to planned counterattacks that never occurred—the peace probes were shelved.[42] That they were even contemplated, however, indicated a growing conviction that the time rapidly approached to bargain, while Germany was still strong enough, for a peace treaty worthy of the nation's sacrifices.

THE MOMENT FOR JIHAD

Germany's massive spring offensives eroded British security in the Middle East, creating another propitious moment for Muslim holy war. Already in early 1918 London had transferred two of its seven frontline divisions in Mesopotamia to Palestine. Expanding Allenby's EEF to nine infantry divisions would threaten Damascus, which after Baghdad and Jerusalem would be the third ancient Ottoman city to fall into British possession. After Operation *St. Michael* the War Cabinet awoke from such dreams with a start, however, canceling major offensive operations throughout the Middle East and shipping sixty thousand men—two British divisions and British battalions equaling three more, the bulk of the EEF—to France.[43] Allenby kept the two veteran Indian divisions from Iraq and received about twenty-five raw Indian battalions to replace his losses, but at the cost of downgrading his army and weakening already depleted defenses in India.

It was only slight consolation to British officialdom, therefore, when reports trickled back from Tashkent that released German and Austrian POWs were fewer in number (40,000 not 140,000) and more important, not forming into an army as had been feared in late 1917. Rather, Ludendorff used those relatively few POWs who had not already escaped or deserted to strengthen his hand in France.[44] That Turkish leader Enver Pasha ordered most of his crack Anatolian divisions (plus reinforcements from Palestine) to move on Baku, furthermore, as opposed to striking directly and immediately against vulnerable British positions in Palestine and Persia also caused only slight relief in London. Although far away, the Turkish "Army of Islam" gathered daily more support from tens of thousands of armed Muslim Azerbaijanis in the Caucasus. Its vector of advance could still lead over Teheran and Kabul to Delhi and Calcutta (see map, pp. 98–99).

Wrangle as they did over short-term objectives, in fact, Berlin and Constantinople agreed that ultimately they had to exploit the "sensitive spots" of the British Empire. As OHL readied its Chemin des Dames offensive in May the spearhead of Enver's 60,000-strong expeditionary force of six to nine divisions had advanced four hundred kilometers over Erzurum and the pre-1914 border. Nor had he completely ignored Persia. Into the vacuum left by homeward-bound Russian soldiers the Turk moved a small army of two weak divisions around Lake Urumia to seize defenseless Tabriz, which fell in April. From there a long line of battalions spread south almost to Kermanshah.[45] OHL and Otto Liman von Sanders, newly appointed German commander of Turkish-German forces in Palestine, questioned the wisdom of invading the Caucasus as a roundabout avenue to Persia and Iraq and ultimately to India as opposed to directly reinforcing Iraq and/or Palestine, but clearly Berlin and Constantinople were basically on the same strategic page.

The most immediately threatened soft spot, Persia, caused extra anxiety in London. Most Russian forces that had prevented Shah Ahmad from joining Constantinople's holy war in 1915–1916 trudged north after Brest-Litovsk, abandoning the virtual protectorate Russia had maintained since 1911. Only a smallish regiment of 1,200 men under General Bicherakov remained south of Kazvin. Russian officers still commanded the 8,000-strong Cossack division, but as they too trickled away it began to fall under the sway of Persians like future Iranian strongman Reza Pahlavi. This transition would not augur well for the weakling shah but seemed destined at the time to spark some sort of Persian revival. This dramatic reversal of fortunes emboldened nationalists in Teheran led by Minister of the Interior Mukbar-u-Saltana not only to reject a British ultimatum in March but also to foment anti-British revolts by unruly tribes sometimes pursuing their own agendas.

Waiting for the Army of Islam: Dunsterforce and Armenian Volunteers in Baku
Used with the permission of *The Trustees of the Imperial War Museum, London*. Photo Number: Q-24869

This certainly applied to Kuchik Khan and three thousand warriors of his "Union of Islam" in the region between Tabriz and Enzeli. Armed and encouraged by both the Turks and Germans, this renegade chief despised politicians in Teheran and waited for an opportunity to make Jihad against the British and seize power. In March he took over the British consulate in Resht and would have begun his uprising if Bicherakov had not force-marched into Kazvin and blocked the route to Teheran. Against Kuchik Khan and Enver's Turks in Tabriz, unfortunately, the British had only Bicherakov—and he was eager to leave the country.

In southern Persia the more powerful Solat-u-Dola, chief of the Kashgais, also bided his time before unleashing a religious-patriotic rebellion in southwest Fars province. Against him Britain had only a few regiments remaining in the originally 8,000-strong South Persian Rifles (SPR), organized and trained by Sir Percy Sykes in 1916–1917, which were buttressed by 2,400 Anglo-Indian troops around Shiraz.[46] The loyalty and fighting quality of the Persian regiments was low, however, such that when Saltana denounced the SPR in April as a foreign insult to Persian independence and the mullahs of Fars picked up the chant, imploring their followers to "put the traitors to death," two-thirds of the force promptly deserted. Sykes had unwittingly caused himself extra problems in 1916 by taking over the anti-British Persian Gendarmerie, incorporating it into the SPR and attempting to neutralize them with regular pay, but the move only exacerbated discipline problems. Far from enhancing the security of South Persia, the unit "finally became a danger to the safety of the British," recalled Sykes. "The officers slept in the crater of a volcano."[47]

Assuming that Sykes could respond to any emergency with the troops at his disposal, nevertheless, the War Cabinet instructed its commander in Baghdad, Sir William Marshall, to send a task force into northwestern Persia to reinforce

Lionel Dunsterville. The major-general and a team of specialists had attempted to rally peoples of the Caucasus against an anticipated Turkish-German invasion in February 1918 but were forced to turn back by pro-Bolshevik soldiers in Enzeli. Dunsterville used Hamadan as a base during the spring, recruiting a few local platoons of Persians and Kurds and waiting anxiously for the promised reinforcements from Baghdad. In June the first wave arrived—a British battalion, an Indian company, a company of lancers, and an artillery battery—and sped to Kazvin to join Bicherakov. Together they proceeded to Enzeli. Under way Kuchik Khan attempted to bar their path. His warriors proved no match, however, for professional soldiers firing shrapnel. After the Russians finally left Persia in July the angry chieftain attacked again, suffered heavy losses, and then melted away into the rugged hills. Having grown by early August 1918 to nearly a brigade, "Dunsterforce" sent six companies ahead to Baku to organize anti-Turkish forces against the Army of Islam, which had advanced another four hundred kilometers to the outskirts of this critical oil center.

Meanwhile, Solat had begun his Jihad. A proclamation of May 22 condemned the SPR and called on the Kashgais and their confederates, the Kaserunis, "to take action for the defense of Islam."[48] He then positioned 3,000 Kaseruni and allied tribesmen around an SPR outpost at Khaneh Zinian, a day's march from the British cantonment at Shiraz. Solat planned to lure a British relief column to this outpost, falling on it with his main force of 4,800 proud, allegedly invincible Kashgais armed with German Mauser rifles. Sykes's officers sniffed out the trap, however, and marched 1,600 troopers to Solat's hill camp south of Khaneh Zinian. The ensuing battle on May 25 showed that even an elite tribal army like the Kashgai confederation armed with machine guns and cannon could not defeat Bengal Lancers, Burma Mounted Rifles, and Indian infantrymen, many of them veterans of prewar campaigns in India and backed by superior artillery and machine guns.

Solat lost six hundred men, but the holy war actually gained momentum that day when the SPR garrison at Khaneh Zinian mutinied; killed its British officers; and opened the gates to the Kaserunis, who seized sixty thousand rounds of ammunition. The British column had to pull back to Shiraz, which was soon besieged and badly outnumbered, for in order to protect the entire region Sykes had sent detachments to Bushire and Bandar Abbas, north to Abadeh, and east to Kerman province. For anxious days in June 1918 the fall of Shiraz seemed likely.

It would have been "a second Kut,"[49] Sykes wrote later, with far-reaching consequences not only in Persia but more important, in Afghanistan, and therefore quite possibly in India too. Indeed Emir Habibullah had lost considerable popularity by eschewing holy war in 1915–1916. Political pressures and the threat of assassination increased that spring as Russia dropped out of the regional power equation, the Germans and Turks made huge advances, and the Persians began to rise. What faithful Muslim would continue to ignore the call of the faith to wage Jihad? Only the undecided verdict in France and the lingering possibility of British victory supported Habibullah's logic of remaining neutral and using this wartime loyalty to bargain for postwar Afghan independence. A British collapse in

Persia precipitated by the uprising in Fars and Turkish resurgence to the northwest would probably have changed the equation—at least so thought jittery political leaders in London, who now urged Calcutta to scrap decades-old British Afghan policy and offer the emir an offensive military alliance.[50] Any new ally made strategic sense with those around Lloyd George envisioning in dark, despairing shades a Great Britain shorn of its Russian, Italian, and French allies; the BEF evacuated; and "Germany left in control not only of Europe and most of Asia but of the whole world."[51]

With much at stake in Central Asia, therefore, Sykes's commanders risked an attack before food and water ran out and sympathetic Shirazi townsmen joined the uprising. On June 16 detachments struck out in three directions and inflicted light casualties on the surprised warriors but then retreated in hopes that the enemy would seek revenge. The ploy worked, British riflemen and gunners punishing Solat with another 500–600 casualties. In subsequent days the morale of the Kashgais and Kaserunis declined, defections occurred, and the siege was lifted. Solat retired to the southwest in July, made an unsuccessful stand, and fled. Still defiant, he raised another 1,500 men before losing his final battle a few months later and going into hiding for good.

In the meantime (mid-August 1918) Dunsterville had arrived by sea in Baku with 1,200 men to bolster the city's defenses.[52] Enver's advance guard enveloped the outer trench networks and began a bombardment that daily intensified. Local defenders—10,000 untrained Russian and Armenian volunteers hoping to prevent the region's domination by Turks and Turkic-speaking Azerbaijanis—provided the British scant aid. Correctly assessing the hopelessness of the situation on September 14, the British expedition withdrew. It returned to Enzeli, there to rejoin the rest of Dunsterforce and additional regiments that Marshall had received orders to send from Iraq. In its panicky mood of June 1918, in fact, London had instructed him to direct his "main attention" to Persia and the Caspian. "His Majesty's government attaches more importance to success in that sphere than you appear to appreciate."[53] These forces of perhaps altogether a division (plus local levies) thinly manned a line running three hundred kilometers south from Enzeli. They braced themselves for the threatened offensive from Baku and Tabriz readied by Enver with his apparent aim of breaking Britain's hold on the wider region, including Iraq, and realizing his Pan Turkic dreams.

PALESTINE

After a few minor engagements in the spring and summer of 1918 army positions stabilized north of Jerusalem.[54] Turko-German defenses snaked almost eighty kilometers from the sea north of Jaffa to the east bank of the Jordan River near Jericho. Three army groups totaling 12.5 divisions entrenched along this line under German general Otto Liman von Sanders, the veteran commander of Gallipoli who had replaced Erich von Falkenhayn in February. Included in the mix Sanders now had six well-armed German battalions at his disposal, three as part of a Turkish-German "Asia Corps" on his center-right, three merged with Turkish units to form a "Composite Division" anchoring the far left on the Jordan where he anticipated Allenby's main thrust.

Although the EEF could muster only 7.5 largely Indian infantry divisions, two French regiments (colonial troops and Armenian volunteers), Feisal's Arabs, and a newly formed battalion-strength "Jewish Legion," Sanders pondered his chances in near despair. The part of his memoirs describing the situation in September 1918 amount to a savage indictment, in fact, of Constantinople. At full strength like British units, Turkish divisions should have contained about ninety thousand rifles, but his divisions were smallish regiments with 1,100 to 2,200 men, giving him overall strength of only about 20,000 combat infantry.[55] In February Enver had promised Sanders "unreserved support," including the necessary "troops and everything I should ask for," but fewer than 10,000 replacements went south from April to August, and desertions caused by hunger, poor cladding, heat, and disease were of like magnitude. Worse still, Enver dispatched only four of *Yildirim* Army's seven divisions to Palestine while three went to the Caucasian/Persian front. Sanders railed against this decision. With Enver's divisions at full strength or even greater, some of them at 9,000 men, its officers well clad and well paid, his objectives, to the extent they could be discerned, seemed wildly overambitious. To the caustic German Enver was guilty of strategic ineptitude. "Through the advance [of 13th Corps] into Persia [in 1916–1917], against which I urgently warned, the Turks have lost Baghdad," complained Sanders, "through the initiation of the *Yildirim* enterprise against Baghdad the Turks have lost Jerusalem, and now through the bottomless advance into Trans-Caucasia they are going to lose all of Arabia, Palestine, and Syria."[56] To objective observers it appeared that Enver had come close to writing off Turkey's Arab provinces, banking on the economically more lucrative, ethically purer gains to be made in Central Asia.[57]

Indeed Sanders had good reason to be worried. Allenby had almost a 3-to-1 edge in infantry, 4-to-1 in cavalry, a similar advantage in artillery at the impact point, naval support offshore, overwhelming air superiority, plus a small but menacing Arab army of twelve hundred east of the Jordan. The EEF also had ample stores of ammunition, food, and water because engineers had extended the Sinai rail line from Gaza to Jaffa. Poor intelligence worsened the odds for Sanders's armies as Royal Air Force (RAF) planes nearly swept the skies clean of Turkish and German fliers. What they observed, furthermore, proved highly damaging, for Allenby executed a series of effective ruses, marching the same soldiers back and forth and dragging mule sleds near the Jordan to kick up the dust of an evidently larger force, stationing fifteen thousand canvas dummy horses in this region, and spreading disinformation through his Arab allies that he targeted Amman in Jordan.

Meanwhile, using his planes to limit enemy reconnaissance and making troop movements at night, he amassed the bulk of the EEF opposite Sanders's right flank near the sea: five infantry divisions, three cavalry divisions, over half his artillery, and half of his air squadrons. Allenby's operational plan was very similar to Norman Schwarzkopf's ingenious assault in the Gulf War of 1991: he ordered the infantry to open a door on the left for the cavalry, which would sweep north along the coast, the lead division passing through the Lajjun Defile at Megiddo onto the Plain of Esdraelon and then pushing over El Affule to Beisan on the Jordan, almost one hundred kilometers behind Turkish lines. The enemy would either be surrounded or forced into immediate headlong retreat.

Allenby heightened the element of surprise and further diverted attention from the coastal point of attack by assaulting Nablus with two infantry divisions on September 18, ten hours before the real zero hour. The same purposes were served by probing attacks across the Jordan by the ANZAC mounted division and a few supporting infantry units—the only real troops stationed in the area. A few days earlier, moreover, Lawrence's Arabs made successive strikes against the railroad around Deraa, the eastern hub of Sanders's rear transport lines. The demolition raids not only succeeded in disrupting his supply at the worst possible moment but also in drawing to the defense of Deraa a German reserve battalion garrisoning El Affule.[58]

The ensuing Battle of Megiddo was the most devastating and comprehensive combined arms engagement of the Great War. Allenby's artillery, supported by two ships offshore, suddenly opened fire early on September 19, 1918, pounding Turkish trenches for a few minutes only, then shifting to rear areas as the massed infantry swarmed into the enemy's first line. By day's end five divisions overran first and second trench lines, reached the artillery line, and pressed farther. The door had been opened for the cavalry after only two to three hours, however, and by midmorning three mounted columns penetrated rapidly to the north, passing through defenseless Megiddo shortly after midnight. At first light the air squadrons had also taken off, covering the cavalry and raiding enemy transportation and communication lines. In the center of Sanders's line the German-bolstered Asia Corps and divisions to their left blocking Allenby's diversionary attack held throughout much of the day but to no avail, for with his right wing smashed Sanders had to order a general withdrawal.

On September 20 the lead cavalry division took El Affule and Beisan, forcing the retreating Turks and Germans to scramble eastward to reach fords across the Jordan, stung mercilessly along the way by swarms of allied planes that "had a paralyzing effect" on fleeing columns. "What little remained of the artillery, the autos and other vehicles blocked the road in many places with their demolished vehicles and dead horses and men,"[59] wrote Sanders of the decimation of two of his three battered armies (Eighth and Seventh). He had wanted them to pull back to the Sea of Galilee, but instead they were largely destroyed or captured before crossing the river.

By September 25 the EEF held Acre on the coast, Nazareth inland, and Samakh on the southern shore of Galilee. Simultaneously, Fourth Army's two divisions defended the approach to Amman and another corps garrisoned Ma'an on the northern fringe of the Hejaz. As all of these forces attempted to escape and help Sanders make a stand north of Galilee they too were mostly killed or captured by pursuing British cavalry and the mobile Arab contingent, Amman having also fallen on September 25.[60]

Only a fraction of Sanders's twenty thousand combat infantrymen had survived to slow the British advance. Thus Allenby's vanguard, preceded a few hours earlier by Lawrence's Arabs, entered Damascus on October 1, 1918—a romp of 175 kilometers in less than two weeks. The German commander's dire prediction had come true: the Ottoman Empire had lost Arabia, Palestine, and Syria in a disastrous final campaign. Combined with further bad news from the Balkans, Constantinople began to look desperately for a way out of the war.

MACEDONIA

On September 14, 1918, French general Franchet d'Esperey, longtime veteran of the western front, let loose his Army of the Orient on Bulgarian mountain defenses at Dobro Polje (see map, p. 79).[61] For weeks allied engineers had used tractors and winches by night to move hundreds of guns into camouflaged artillery perches above the enemy. D'Esperey's hurricane bombardment broke with "immense force" against the Bulgarians' natural stone fortifications, hammering and shaking crags and peaks with a deafening ferocity magnified many times over by horrible mountain acoustics. "Trees come crashing down, branches and stones fall like hail, and the positions are drowned in smoke and debris."[62] Breakthrough came in a few days, followed within ten days by a Bulgarian breakdown, both military and political, that reverberated not just in Sofia but also in Constantinople, Vienna, and Berlin. Highly significant, Bulgaria's fall precipitated the collapse of the Central Powers. It makes sense, therefore, to backtrack with a series of digressions that explain the background of this critical campaign.

Against Bulgarians of inferior strength D'Esperey had 28 divisions: 1 Italian, 8 French and French colonial, 4 British, 6 Serbian—the gallant survivors of their country's overrunning in 1915—and 9 Greek, altogether an impressive multinational force whose presence within striking distance of Sofia or even Vienna underscored the worsening power predicament of the Central Powers. Greece had entered the Great War in July 1917, making the Army of the Orient a much more formidable force. Until then King Constantine, Kaiser William's brother-in-law, had resisted German pressure, arguing logically that eventual Central Power victory would not prevent Anglo-French ships and armies from crushing him in the interim. Simultaneously, however, he rejected the pro-Entente position of his ambitious, hawkish prime minister, Eleutherios Venizelos, who strove to ride allied victory to significant territorial gains for Greece. When the king refused, the premier resigned, fled to the allied base at Salonika, and fomented intrigues against his sovereign, who gave back more than he got, assassinating Venizelos' followers and influencing the patriarch in Athens to excommunicate the rebel politician.

Finally in April 1917, with American sensibilities no longer a concern after Wilson declared war, Britain and France removed all false pretense to respect Greek neutrality and issued Constantine an ultimatum: either he abdicated in twenty-four hours or they would shell Athens. The humiliated monarch stepped aside for his son, Alexander, who ended the blood feud with Venizelos and appointed him prime minister again. Greek belligerency did not lead immediately to renewed fighting against Bulgarian and German forces in occupied southern Serbia, however, for malaria ravaged the camp at Salonika throughout 1917. Furthermore, after *St. Michael* twenty thousand men went to the western front and more were ready to ship out until OHL's offensives ended.

D'Esperey began to prepare his attack in August. The plan he adopted came in part, fittingly enough, from Serbian generals who thirsted to liberate their homeland. The Serbs, buttressed by three French and two Greek divisions, targeted the Dobro Polje sector held by elements of the Bulgarian Eleventh Army and a single German battalion. The left flank of the Serbian advance would be shielded by a five-division Franco-Greco-Italian army with a strong contingent of cavalry. To prevent the Bulgarians from reinforcing this sector the British, bolstered by six Greek divisions, would sweep around Lake Doiran, holding the Bulgarian First and Second Armies and their lone German battalions in place while the last two French divisions moved west of Monastir—these attacks to come a few days later, respectively, on September 18 and September 21.

Aided by the weight of 20 heavy and 500 light artillery pieces, the Serbs, French, and Greeks broke through Bulgarian lines and repulsed repeated counterattacks, advancing thirty kilometers in three days. The smaller flanking group on their left also made good progress, pushing close to Prilep and opening a door for the cavalry. Hurrying to the front, Crown Prince Boris found Eleventh Army in headlong retreat, some of the men refusing to fight. "Condition of the army here more grave than I would have thought," he wired King Ferdinand. "There are signs of Bolsheviks."[63]

Indeed the condition of the Bulgarian army was grave in 1918. It had endured almost constant warfare since the First Balkan War of 1912, and then over one hundred thousand soldiers had died in the Great War. The harvest of 1917 was poor, that of 1918 poorer still, as the shortage of labor and fertilizer drove down yields, causing hunger pangs at home and also in the ranks. "The troops live from day to day," complained the commander in chief, General Nikola Jekov, eating little but bad bread and paltry vegetables "from their own kitchen gardens they keep behind the front line." Making matters worse, many soldiers had no shoes, socks, or underwear. None had seen a new uniform since 1915. "Empty stomachs, naked bodies, worries about families back home, and the suspicion that our allies will not earnestly back our national aspirations—all this makes the troops apathetic."[64]

Sofia's allies contributed in major ways, in fact, to the grumbling and increasingly left-wing politicizing in the army. Some of this controversy centered on Dobrudja, the rich Rumanian province between the Danube and Black Sea. Bulgarian soldiers had fought with German to take this land in late 1916 and had good reason to demand its cession to Bulgaria, especially because Sofia received assurances in 1915 of territorial gain beyond Macedonia should Rumania join the Entente. After Germany forced peace on Rumania in December 1917, however, it imposed the harsh Treaty of Bucharest, sister to Brest-Litovsk, in May 1918. Dobrudja was to be governed by all four Central Powers, but then powerful

Germany began to encroach on this land, especially the Danube delta.[65] "It is the first [postwar] treaty concerning Bulgaria, and it has already [sheared] its national aspirations," bemoaned Jekov to King Ferdinand in June. "It made of Bulgaria, in the words of the soldiers, [a sheep without wool] that nobody can fleece."[66]

While the allies gathered a large army in Macedonia, moreover, the Bulgarians believed with a good measure of justification that Austria-Hungary and Germany had deserted them, leaving their worn-down soldiers at the not-so-tender mercy of d'Esperey's burgeoning Army of the Orient. Hoping to capitalize on Ludendorff's spring offensives, for instance, Austro-Hungarian commander in chief Franz Conrad von Hötzendorf denuded other fronts, including Macedonia, to amass thirty divisions in northern Italy for another ill-advised mountain campaign. The short disastrous Battle of the Piave River in June 1918 cost him 140,000 casualties.[67] Simultaneously, OHL had shifted its last remaining German division in Macedonia to France. Thus when d'Esperey probed Bulgarian forward defenses that June and decimated a regiment, Ferdinand lambasted his representative at OHL for "rhapsodizing about German victories" when, "thanks to the criminal, heartless, and extremely selfish orders of Ludendorff," the Bulgarians had suffered losses they could not afford. "May yesterday's defeat and the massacre of an entire Bulgarian regiment fall like a curse over those who, despite my furious protests, so mercilessly withdrew their troops and exposed the Bulgarian soldier, against all treaties and laws of interallied solidarity, to evident slaughter!"[68] The Treaty of Bucharest and German/Austro-Hungarian troop withdrawals kept anti-German sentiment high in Bulgarian ranks, both factors exacerbated by the awkward fact that Jekov remained subordinate to theater commander Friedrich Scholtz, a German general.

On September 18 the British and Greeks opened their attack around Lake Doiran but could not punch through. Success here prompted Jekov to urge Scholtz to send German divisions to bolster Eleventh Army—Boris made the same appeal—while counterattacking with First and Second against Orient's base at Salonika. D'Esperey would be stranded north of Dobro Polje or forced to retreat. But Scholz had no German or Austrian reinforcements to offer. He also rejected Jekov's aggressive operation against Salonika on logistical grounds, ordering instead a withdrawal of First Army through the Kosturino Pass to join Eleventh Army for a counterattack in the center. The move proved disastrous on September 21 when allied planes hit Bulgarian columns in the narrow defile, inflicting on them the same hell the Turks had suffered near the Jordan a day earlier. Soldiers of First Army deserted en masse, further disheartened by what struck them as the foolish order to pull out of their seemingly impregnable positions.

By this time the Army of the Orient had all of its divisions in action, for on September 21 the French attacked between Monastir and Lake Ohrid, caving in the defenses of Eleventh Army's right wing. In the center French cavalry took Prilep on September 23 and Skopje six days later. The Serbian army group, joined by the British and Greeks, swept over the Vardar River and pressed toward the Bulgarian border by September 29, over 125 kilometers from their starting positions. Fearing that the Army of the Orient could roll unopposed over Serbia and Austria-Hungary into Germany itself, meanwhile, OHL finally issued orders to divert six German and Austro-Hungarian divisions under way from Russia to France and form them into a new army group at Nisch in central Serbia. Ludendorff also transferred the German Alpine Corps out of France. "The Western Front thus lost six or seven divisions,"[69] he lamented, which it could ill afford amidst successive allied offensives ineluctably pressing the enervated Germans back home.

Long before this army could assemble in Nisch Bulgaria's collapse ran its course. Already on September 26 representatives of the Bulgarian government arrived in Salonika to ask d'Esperey for an armistice, which they grudgingly signed three days later after the fall of Skopje demonstrated that no hope of victory remained. Bulgaria would evacuate occupied foreign lands, demobilize and disarm all but a few divisions, expel German and Austro-Hungarian troops and nationals, and permit the allies to temporarily occupy strategic points within the country. D'Esperey issued the cease-fire order late in the evening of September 29. Within days, Ferdinand, his country defeated and whole regiments in open rebellion, abdicated and Boris became king.

The victorious Frenchman now boasted that he could "cross Hungary and Austria with 200,000 men, mass in Bohemia covered by the Czechs, and march immediately on Dresden."[70] His center army groups did indeed race as far as Belgrade in late October, pushing OHL's reinforcements before him, but d'Esperey's Army of the Orient began to fragment before the city's liberation. Weeks earlier, in fact, allied leaders in Paris ordered Sir George Milne, commander of the British group, to march on Constantinople with a multinational force in support of Allenby's EEF, which had advanced past Damascus to threaten Turkey.

Turkey's ongoing implosion, coupled with the bad news from Bulgaria, compelled Ludendorff to face facts that so rudely faced him. On the evening of September 28 he entered Hindenburg's room at OHL to outline the imperative nature of cease-fire talks. "The position can grow only worse, on account of the Balkan position, even if we hold our own in the west," he said. Ludendorff advised making contact with Woodrow Wilson, whose Fourteen Points suddenly looked very attractive compared with the vindictiveness one could expect from France and Britain. The field marshal agreed, for in recent days the ability of the Germans to "hold our own in the west" had suddenly grown more doubtful.

THE WESTERN FRONT: ENDGAME AND ARMISTICE

As September dawned, with Allenby's offensive in Palestine and d'Esperey's push into Serbia weeks away and these fronts still seemingly solid, the situation on the western front also looked tenable to German High Command. OHL's armies had retreated out of the Marne and Amiens salients in July and August, but the Hindenburg Line and other deep, imposing trench defenses inspired a modicum of confidence that the allies, whose summer campaigns had run their course, would not pass. During the lull, moreover, reinforcement divisions were under way from the east; tens of thousands of the patched-up walking wounded were returning to their regiments; scores of thousands of additional replacements were being found in home garrisons and rear-echelon units; and most important of all, the next levy of hundreds of thousands of eighteen-year-olds neared the end of training. "Too bad about the young blood,"[71] said General Hutier, but if it made the difference between defeat and an acceptable armistice, then so be it.

While the British and French rested, refitted, and reinforced their spent divisions, the AEF finally entered the fray. Could the largely inexperienced Americans make enough of an impact to end the war in 1918? Only one man on either side answered affirmatively: Pershing, who believed fervently that America's born country riflemen; America's unblemished character; and the AEF's big divisions, so able to absorb punishment, would soon bring an end to the world's worst conflagration.[72] Throughout August the Yankee commander assembled fifteen of the nineteen battle-ready American divisions in France—four of nine that had bled for the allies stayed in British and French lines—for his pet project: an attack over the St. Mihiel salient to seize Metz, sever key railroads to the German rear in France, and force Hannibal to return home to defend Carthage.

Better acquainted with the near impossible challenges of capturing Metz's huge fort system, Foch vetoed the plan. Let the AEF pound out the St. Mihiel salient but then strike north under French command into the Meuse-Argonne to the Mézières rail center with indispensable lifelines coming from Trier and Metz and passing to Lille. The enemy would have to withdraw from the western front without the transport to evacuate huge depots of arms, ammunition, and supplies.[73] Unwilling to defy the allied supreme commander, Pershing agreed but insisted on maintaining an autonomous AEF. In a short battle at St. Mihiel on September 12–13, a Franco-American task force of 13 divisions took the salient. Over subsequent weeks the quiet so welcome to OHL returned to the western front as Pershing moved into position for Foch's preferred Meuse-Argonne offensive.

This operation began with the crash of artillery on September 26. Pershing committed nine divisions along a thirty-five-kilometer front, the Meuse River on the right, the heights of the Argonne Forest ahead on the left. The French Fourth Army with fourteen smaller divisions joined the assault on AEF's left flank. Pershing wanted to overrun all three trench systems (sixteen kilometers) on Day 1, but his forces got pinned down after minor gains, caught in the cross fire of carefully positioned machine gun nests and punishing artillery fire from the Argonne hills and east bank of the Meuse. The French experienced similar problems. Casualties mounted alarmingly over the following days, exacerbated by confusion at headquarters, congestion on inadequate supply roads, and the rampage of a much more lethal influenza. It took Pershing three weeks to reach his first day's objective, but Ludendorff had to rush successive reinforcements lest he lose Mézières and with it the war.

Foch obviously placed great importance on this offensive, but it constituted only one act of a brutal multipart play. Indeed on September 27 two British armies went over the top at Cambrai, followed on September 28 by an attack of Belgian, British, and French armies north of Ypres. From September 26 to 28, furthermore, British artillery pounded the Hindenburg Line around St. Quentin in preparation for an infantry assault on September 29. In none of these attacks did the allies

Trying to Stop the Tanks: German Antitank Barrier in 1918.
Courtesy of the Library of Congress

repeat the massed tank/airplane experiment of Amiens, preferring to relegate both technologies to a lesser auxiliary role. Indeed the tactics and coordination of combined arms had not been perfected—far too many tanks and planes had been lost in just a few days at Amiens. But all of this reinforced the predilections of tradition-minded officers around Haig who were not comfortable with mechanized warfare in the first place.[74] Nonetheless, the Germans still fell back from all of these threatened points of the line as hundreds of thousands of tired, hungry, demoralized soldiers, often encouraged by their junior officers, surrendered en masse. Some of the harm done by those who surrendered was compensated for, however, by other infantrymen as well as elite machine gunners and artillerymen who refused to give up, such that the retreat unfolded gradually and grudgingly, earning the respect of allied high command. The German army was Janus-faced in 1918: one side more so over the brink of collapse than actually on strike; the other on guard.[75]

Perhaps OHL could have held its own in the west well into 1919, but already by the evening of September 28 the dire news from Macedonia and the dispatch of western-bound reserves to that front, compounded by further bad tidings from Palestine, all of this mixed with the punishment of Foch's well-orchestrated strikes, forced Ludendorff and Hindenburg to initiate—this time in earnest—armistice talks with Woodrow Wilson. On October 3, 1918, with the kaiser unhappily on board, OHL told Reichstag politicians in Berlin that "as a result of the collapse of the Macedonian front, and of the weakening of our reserves in the west which this [Bulgarian collapse] has necessitated, and in view of the impossibility of making good the very heavy [western] losses of the last few days, there appears to be no possibility to the best of human judgment of winning peace from our enemies by force of arms."[76] The approach was made to Wilson the following day.

The remaining Central Powers had already been informed of Germany's intentions and urged to follow suit. They hardly needed prodding. In response to the complete disintegration of the Bulgarian army and the potential threat to the Austrian heartland, Emperor Karl made two appeals to Washington for an armistice—the first already on September 16, the second on October 4.[77] In addition to the military threat to his empire, Karl feared internal disintegration as Czechoslovak, Polish, and "Jugoslav" (Serb, Croat, and Slovene) separatists exploited antiwar sentiments to establish independent states. To prevent this he issued a manifesto on October 16 proclaiming autonomy for all ethnic groups in the Austrian half of the Dual Monarchy—to no avail, for Wilson's formal reply of October 19 demanded full independence for the Czechoslovakian and Jugoslav peoples, while the secessionists simply ignored Karl's decree and completed spadework on their new states. By the time Austria-Hungary's armistice with Italy took effect on November 4, 1918, Austria-Hungary had already splintered into separate Austrian, Hungarian, Czechoslovakian, and Yugoslavian entities. The Poles had also seceded to join a Polish state just coming into being. Thus Austria-Hungary became the second great European monarchy destroyed by the Great War.

Events in the Ottoman Empire took a somewhat different course. On October 1 with Constantinople even more vulnerable than Vienna, Minister of the Interior Mehmed Talaat Bey convened ministerial colleagues to second Germany's call for an armistice. As one of the controlling triumvirate of War Minister Enver and former Damascene strongman Djemal Pasha, Talaat had witnessed Bulgaria's collapse on a return trip from consultations in Berlin. Cease-fire talks now, he said, offered Turkey the best chance of a lenient settlement. Enver and Djemal vehemently disagreed, arguing that an offensive in Persia would save the war effort. The other ministers backed Talaat, however, and that day ordered the withdrawal of the Army of Islam from Transcaucasia. As the threat to British possessions in Asia disappeared, London ordered Marshall to take Mosul and complete the conquest of Mesopotamia. Like overstretched Germany and Austria-Hungary in the Ukraine and Italy—armies that were far away from where they were really needed that September—Enver's eastern expedition had proved disastrous for the empire. Simultaneously, Turkish leaders expressed readiness to negotiate with the American president for a cessation of hostilities and then initiate peace talks based on his Fourteen Points.[78]

The Turkish note to Wilson came to nothing because Washington, not at war with Constantinople, delayed its response in order to consult with London. In the meantime, a cabinet reshuffling on October 14 brought to power former commander of the Ottoman Second Army Ahmet Izzet Pasha. Talaat, Enver, and Djemal had also slunk out of the country. The Turks finally agreed to armistice talks with the British on the Aegean island of Lemnos and surrendered on October 30, 1918. They had to demobilize the bulk of the army; open the straits; surrender numerous garrisons, including forts guarding the Bosporus and the Dardanelles; and permit the allies to occupy other strategic points. Constantinople would also grant "autonomy to territories under [Turkish] sovereignty [presently] occupied by the allies."[79] On November 12, 1918, a British squadron led by HMS *Agamemnon* steamed into the straits past the site of ancient Troy.

On November 11 Germany also signed an armistice. It had been a long five weeks in coming. Two days before it did, a third great European monarchy was removed from the scene, the culmination of a dramatic series of diplomatic, political, military, and revolutionary developments. In late September, Ludendorff and Hindenburg reacted to military setbacks in Palestine and Macedonia and renewed pressures on the western front by prodding German politicians into approaching Wilson for a cease-fire, but neither saw truce talks as an admission

The End Is Near: Germans Surrender En Masse

Used with the permission of *The Trustees of the Imperial War Museum, London*. Photo Number: Q-9353

of German defeat, much less of their own failure, rather as a respite to build up army reserves, replenish supplies, block the allies in Macedonia, and shore up wobbling Turkey. The lull would either facilitate a peace favorable to Germany or a continuation of hostilities.

Ludendorff clearly hated to make these peace overtures. Ranting against his political enemies, the increasingly unstable generalissimo displayed to embarrassed subordinates his psychological inability to take blame. He viewed himself as strong while others were despicably weak, especially Reichstag parties and allied trade unions that allegedly thought only of selfish class politics and treasonously refused to support the life-and-death struggle of frontline soldiers whose spirit and discipline the left had also riddled, he charged, with socialism, pacifism, feminism, and defeatism. Ludendorff flew into a rage when reports came from Berlin that Philipp Scheidemann of the Social Democrats and Matthias Erzberger of the Center Party demanded democratization of the monarchy to better position Germany for armistice talks with democratic America. So if Woodrow Wilson wanted to negotiate an armistice with German democrats, "those circles which we mainly have to thank that things have come to this," blurted Ludendorff, then why not promote a few of them to high-profile positions and let them "clean up the mess for which they are responsible."[80] Accordingly, the kaiser appointed chancellor a well-known liberal and opponent of unrestricted submarine warfare, his cousin Prince Max of Baden.

Sent through neutral Switzerland, Max's note to Wilson arrived on October 6. In a pair of exchanges over the next two days the American chief executive sought and received assurances that Germany welcomed a peace based on the Fourteen Points, including the evacuation of all conquered territories, and that the prince, not the kaiser and his martinets at OHL, truly represented the German people. On October 14, however, with congressional elections only weeks away and Republicans accusing the president and his party of being soft on Germany, Wilson's tone and message became more "frank and direct," as he put it, rejecting Max's proposal for a mixed commission to discuss how Berlin would evacuate foreign lands it still held—a task that would be left to allied commanders—demanding an end to "illegal and inhumane" U-boat warfare, condemning the "wanton destruction" of Flanders and France, insisting that any armistice would provide "absolutely satisfactory safeguards and guarantees of the maintenance of the present military supremacy"[81] of the allies in the field, and requesting convincing proof that Max's government spoke only for the people.

While the new chancellor called off the subs and informed Washington about ongoing democratic constitutional reforms, the German old order wiggled and squirmed. William reacted furiously to Wilson, lambasting the latest note as "a piece of unmitigated frivolous insolence." Moreover, Hindenburg and Ludendorff began to doubt their armistice strategy. Even though three hundred thousand German prisoners had been taken since the "black day" in August, the army still yielded ground slowly, falling back from one fortified line to the next. "Wherever you hit them they hit back hard and inflict heavy casualties," admitted Haig. OHL conducted its retreat "in perfect order and with the greatest skill." Fronts in western Belgium and northeastern France could be "regarded as being secure," insisted Hindenburg on October 18. German High Command, which had already concentrated seven divisions in Serbia, felt confident enough in early October, in fact, to send four divisions from the Crimea and Caucasus to keep Turkey in the war.[82] Therefore, when Wilson fired a fourth salvo on October 23, demanding "unrestricted power" to make it "impossible" for Germany to renew hostilities, stating further that he would not negotiate with the kaiser but only with the "veritable representatives of the German people," the military duo brandished their loyalty to the kaiser and proclaimed it as their soldierly duty "to resist [the allies] to the utmost of our capabilities."[83] So much for an armistice, which Ludendorff now claimed he had never believed to be such a pressing matter.

This, however, was too much for Max, and especially for Scheidemann and Erzberger, who demanded Ludendorff's dismissal. William kept the aristocratic Hindenburg and let go the bourgeois Ludendorff, whom he had never liked anyway. The kaiser then renounced most of his considerable constitutional powers and placed decision making in the hands of ministers picked from Reichstag parties and responsible not to him but to parliament. Germany had become a democratic monarchy. Wilson now turned to the extremely difficult business of securing allied approval of an armistice based on the Fourteen Points. His personal adviser, Colonel Edward House, arrived in Paris on October 26 for this purpose.

Three days later events took a radical turn in Germany. The navy, now under new Chief of Staff Reinhard Scheer, had bristled at Max's submarine recall and swung behind Ludendorff. Scheer and his fleet commander Franz von Hipper therefore put in motion a bold plan of attack against the Grand Fleet. By provocative raids against the Thames estuary and coast of Belgium (recently abandoned by the army) they hoped to draw the superior Anglo-American fleet across minefields and submarine traps toward the coast of Holland. Lying in wait for the survivors would be twenty-three battleships and battle cruisers of the High Seas Fleet. What Scheer and Hipper viewed as a battle to retrieve German honor and perhaps also strengthen Berlin's hand at the peace table, however, was seen as folly by the common men of the fleet. When the battlewagons assembled outside Wilhelmshaven on October 29, the sailors mutinied, forcing Hipper to postpone and then cancel his sortie.

Worse still for the monarchy, the mutiny occurred amidst escalating antiwar and antiestablishment emotions fueled to red heat by disappointing news from fronts in Bulgaria, Turkey, and France. With many blaming the kaiser for prolonging the war, the naval revolt widened into political rebellion as sailors and workers in other ports seized ships and city halls. In early November "workers' and soldiers' councils" openly emulating the Bolsheviks cropped up in Cologne, Hanover, Stuttgart, Munich, and finally Berlin. Fearing that Germany's parliamentary monarchy would be overturned by a Russian-style Communist coup unless the magnet for popular anger—William II and his royal house—were removed, Scheidemann proclaimed a republic on November 9.

The kaiser accepted Scheidemann's fait accompli after most generals at OHL stated baldly that their soldiers would not follow him into Germany "to reconquer the home front."[84] He went into exile, joining as ex-monarchs Ferdinand of Bulgaria and Karl of Austria-Hungary. Months earlier Nicholas II and his immediate family had been shot by the Bolsheviks. It was the end of an era.

One last act of the Great War remained to be played out. On November 8 Erzberger and his cease-fire delegation motored to GQG in Compiègne.[85] Foch received them coldly and then, as rain and leaves fell outside, doused what remained of German hopes for leniency. Over the next three days Erzberger managed to negotiate only a few ameliorations for his stricken country. Much of the High Seas Fleet, including sixteen capital ships and all of the U-boats, would be interned. The army would abandon Belgium, France, and Alsace, annul the Treaties of Brest-Litovsk and Bucharest, and evacuate all eastern territories when the allies thought the moment "suitable" given the apparently growing danger of Bolshevik power. As it pulled out of conquered lands OHL would leave behind tens of thousands of cannon, trench mortars, machine guns, airplanes, locomotives, railway cars, and trucks. The blockade would continue until completion of a formal peace treaty. Furthermore, the allies would indefinitely occupy the Rhineland and east bank of the river. Although appalled by the severity of these terms, Erzberger had no choice but to sign.

ARMISTICE DAY

An American field hospital near Belgium bustled with activity as the hours drew on toward noon. Outside the hastily constructed structures of corrugated iron the day had remained cold and gray. Mist and drizzle exacerbated the dreariness of late autumn 1918 as if to accentuate, fittingly or unfittingly, the inevitability of more fighting in 1919. Inside, the inescapable stench of wounds clung to the young women of the Red Cross nursing corps. The sickly sweet odor filled up their nostrils when they walked into the countryside for fresh air, harassed them during rare opportunities to bathe, almost knocked them over when ambulance doors opened, attached itself to blankets, and sneaked into beds at day's end.

Since America joined the war in 1917 her female volunteers had witnessed all of the behind-the-lines horrors seen earlier by nurses of the European powers.[85] Were these the same men who had marched through the streets in 1914 so full of life and youthful vigor? No, machine guns and heavy artillery, the ghastly maiming machines of modern war, had changed all that. The worst casualties for the nurses to cope with were the defaced ones, their lips and jaws blown away, feeding tubes inserted where mouths had been, wads of gauze stuffed in nose holes bigger than silver dollars.

The survivors would somehow have to adjust to civilian life. As for the nurses, they learned to cope by growing immune and thick-skinned during the working day—even to the point of taking tea amidst piles of amputated body parts—then releasing the horrors with nightmares about the poor suffering men. Soon the caretakers would have to make the same transition to civilian life. The postwar world would bear little resemblance, however, to that imperfect peacetime world of 1914, now remembered wistfully as the end of a golden era.

At eleven o'clock on this eleventh day of November 1918, the guns fell strangely silent. Usually a dull thunder of artillery fire sounded at a distance. It had become as normal to the nurses and patients as the fetid odor and the maddening, emasculating pain. Now there was just an unnerving stillness: no explosive booms, no birds chirping, not even a cow mooing. Word spread that this silence meant the long-awaited cease-fire—an end, perhaps, to four and a half years of war. But nobody in the hospital rejoiced. If the Great War were really over, there was time to celebrate after tending to today's horrible casualties.

NOTES

1. See Heinz Eisgruber, *So Schossen Wir nach Paris* (Berlin, 1934), 50, 65–77, 156; and Robert L. O'Connell, "Die Pariskanone," in Robert Cowley, ed., *The Great War: Perspectives on the First World War* (New York, 2003), 404–409.
2. Robert A. Doughty, *Pyrrhic Victory: French Strategy and Operations in the Great War* (Cambridge, MA, 2005), 393–410, and for the citations, 402, 404.
3. Denis Winter, *Haig's Command: A Reassessment* (Barnsley, UK, 2004), originally published in 1991, 174–175.
4. After Germany declared war on Portugal in March 1916 for seizing German ships in port, Lisbon sent a small expeditionary force to join the BEF.
5. Winter, *Haig's Command*, 175.
6. For Haig's preparations, allied expectations in early 1918, and German operational planning, see Correlli Barnett, *The Sword-Bearers: Supreme Command in the First World War* (New York, 1964), 269–305; Robert A. Asprey, *The German High Command at War: Hindenburg and Ludendorff Conduct World War I* (New York, 1991), 363–378; Lyn MacDonald, *To the Last Man: Spring 1918* (New York, 1998), 1–71; and especially Winter, *Haig's Command*, 171–183; and Doughty, *Pyrrhic Victory*, 410–430.
7. Cited in Winter, *Haig's Command*, 182.
8. Cited in Asprey, *German High Command at War*, 376, 378.
9. See, for instance, Barnett, *Swordbearers*, 281–293; Asprey, *German High Command*, 363–371; Holger H. Herwig, *The First World War: Germany and Austria-Hungary 1914–1918* (London, 1997) 393–400; and most recently, Hew Strachan, *The First World War* (New York, 2004), 292–295. On the other hand, Rod Paschall, *The Defeat of Imperial Germany 1917–1918* (New York, 1994), 128–135, and John Keegan, *The First World War* (New York, 1999), 392–395, largely avoid criticizing Ludendorff.
10. See Bruce I. Gudmundsson, "'These Hideous Weapons,'" in Robert Cowley, ed., *The Great War: Perspectives on the First World War* (New York, 2003), 307–319; and for the new tactics, Gudmundsson's *Stormtroop Tactics: Innovation in the German Army 1914–1918* (New York, 1989), 155–168.
11. Citations from ibid., 367.
12. Good accounts of this operation are MacDonald, *To the Last Man*, 73 ff.; and Tim Travers, *How the War Was Won: Command and Technology in the British Army on the Western Front, 1917–1918* (London, 1992), 50–91. Also see Barnett, *Swordbearers*, 306–330; Paschall, *Defeat of Imperial Germany*, 128–146; Keegan, *First World War*, 392–405; Stevenson, *Cataclysm*, 332–336; and the excellent summary of this and the other German offensives of 1918 in Martin Kitchen, *The German Offensives of 1918* (Stroud, UK, 2001).
13. Cited in Keegan, *First World War*, 398.
14. Many accounts exaggerate the extent of German success in the early going. Welcome correctives are MacDonald, *To the Last Man*, 75–144; and Alexander Watson, *Enduring the Great War: Combat, Morale, and Collapse in the German and British Armies, 1914–1918* (Cambridge, UK, 2008), 172–183.
15. Cited in Winter, *Haig's Command*, 173.
16. Keegan, *First World War*, 404. For a recent account of sagging German morale in 1918, see Watson, *Enduring the Great War*, 184–231.

17. For good accounts of *Georgette*, see Cyril Falls, *The Great War 1914–1918* (New York, 1961), 337–341; Paschall, *Defeat of Imperial Germany*, 146–150; Asprey, *German High Command*, 391–399; and Travers, *How the War Was Won*, 91–100.
18. Doughty, *Pyrrhic Victory*, 407–411, 440–442, and for the Haig citation, 443.
19. Cited in Asprey, *German High Command*, 395.
20. Ludendorff, *Ludendorff's Own Story*, 2:245.
21. Ibid., 2:245.
22. Cited in Asprey, *German High Command*, 367.
23. For Operation *Blücher*, see Falls, *First World War*, 342–346; Barnett, *Swordbearers*, 331–335; Paschall, *Defeat of Imperial Germany*, 150–156; Stevenson, *Cataclysm*, 339–341; and especially Asprey, *German High Command*, 411–424; Travers, *How the War Was Won*, 100–109; and Doughty, *Pyrrhic Victory*, 446–456. For Noyon (*Gneisenau*), see Doughty, *Pyrrhic Victory*, 456, and Ludendorff, *Ludendorff's Own Story*, 2:250–251.
24. Falls, *Great War*, 343.
25. Winter, *Haig's Command*, 193; and Doughty, *Pyrrhic Victory*, 453.
26. See Gregor Dallas, *At the Heart of a Tiger: Clemenceau and His World 1831–1929* (New York, 1993), 534–538; and Travers, *How the War Was Won*, 104.
27. Cited in Herwig, *First World War*, 415.
28. See John Mosier, *The Myth of the Great War: A New Military History of World War I—How the Germans Won the Battles and How the Americans Saved the Allies* (New York, 2001).
29. Cited in Doughty, *Pyrrhic Victory*, 454–455.
30. The classic study of the U.S. home front remains David M. Kennedy, *Over Here: The First World War and American Society* (New York, 1980). For American mobilization and strategic thinking, see Timothy K. Nenninger, "American Military Effectiveness in the First World War," in Allan R. Millett and Williamson Murray, eds., *Military Effectiveness*, Vol. 1, *The First World War* (Boston, 1988), 116–134; and Allan R. Millett and Peter Maslowski, *For the Common Defense: A Military History of the United States* (New York, 1984), 328–349. Thomas Fleming's *The Illusion of Victory: America in World War I* (New York, 2003) is a readable popular account but too opinionated. For the citations see Doughty, *Pyrrhic Victory*, 404; and Fleming, *Illusion of Victory*, 129, 158, 184, 186.
31. For the connection, see Nenninger, "American Military Effectiveness," in Millett and Murray, *Military Effectiveness*, 1:126; and Millett and Maslowski, *Common Defense*, 330–333, 345.
32. The Fourteen Points, and excerpts from the speech, are printed in Julius W. Pratt, *America and World Leadership 1900–1921* (New York, 1970), 220–224.
33. See John M. Barry, *The Great Influenza: The Epic Story of the Deadliest Plague in History* (New York, 2004), 169–175.
34. For the German numbers, see Herwig, *First World War*, 417; and Watson, *Enduring the Great War*, 187.
35. For the course of these operations, see Paschall, *Defeat of Imperial Germany*, 157–162; Asprey, *German High Command*, 427–443; Herwig, *First World War*, 415–419; and Doughty, *Pyrrhic Victory*, 456–475.
36. See Doughty, *Pyrrhic Victory*, 469–475.
37. *Swordbearers*, 342.
38. Winter, *Haig's Command*, 196–197, argues on the basis of a French intelligence report that OHL decided in late July to adopt a defensive posture, yielding ground if need be for the rest of the year but avoiding at all costs loss of the critical rail line between Lille and Metz. If this report was accurate, such an extensive retreat was certainly seen as an extreme worst-case scenario. Ludendorff refers only to his anticipation of further allied offensives and that "we [would] be able to defeat the imminent attacks and to deliver counterstrokes, though on a smaller scale than heretofore" (*Ludendorff's Own Story*, 2:324).

39. That it was Foch's show in July and August, see Winter, *Haig's Command*, 191–210; and more recently, Doughty, *Pyrrhic Victory*, 466–481. Also see Ludendorff, *Ludendorff's Own Story*, 2:326–359; Falls, *Great War*, 372–380; Barnett, *Swordbearers*, 349–356; Travers, *How the War Was Won*, 116–130; Asprey, *German High Command*, 445–455; and Stevenson, *Cataclysm*, 347–348.
40. *Ludendorff's Own Story*, 2:331, 326.
41. Ibid., 2:344.
42. The account of German chancellor Georg Hertling is cited in Asprey, *German High Command*, 452. Also see Winter, *Haig's Command*, 212–213.
43. Falls, *Great War*, 394.
44. For the real situation in Tashkent in 1918, see Peter Hopkirk, *Setting the East Ablaze: Lenin's Dream of an Empire in Asia* (London, 1984), 7–35.
45. For this paragraph and the following, see Ludendorff, *Ludendorff's Own Story*, 2:255–263, 299–303; Otto Liman von Sanders, *Five Years in Turkey*, trans. Carl Reichmann, (Annapolis, MD, 1927), 196, 244, 256–257, 268–269; Sir Percy Sykes, *A History of Persia* (London, 1951), 2:469–515; A. J. Barker, *The Neglected War: Mesopotamia 1914–1918* (London, 1967), 447–453; Ulrich Trumpener, *Germany and the Ottoman Empire 1914–1918* (Princeton, NJ, 1968), 166–199; and Peter Hopkirk, *Like Hidden Fire: The Plot to Bring Down the British Empire* (New York, 1994), 263–351.

Actual Turkish divisional strength in the east is difficult to determine. T. E. Lawrence's intelligence report of November 26, 1916, placed 18 Turkish divisions in eastern Anatolia and a reserve of 6 in Syria (printed in Brown, ed., *T. E. Lawrence*, p. 85). Longtime German commander in Turkey, Liman von Sanders (*Five Years in Turkey*, pp. 154, 180), listed only 13 facing the Russians by early 1917 and 12 that summer—and no doubt far fewer by early 1918. But according to Hopkirk (*Like Hidden Fire*, pp. 290–291, 302, 333), Enver withdrew units from the forces arrayed against the EEF, probably from *Yildirim* in Aleppo, for his ambitious eastern expedition. Indeed only 4 of 7 *Yildirim* divisions fought in Palestine (Sanders, *Five Years*, pp. 180, 256, 271). Probably 6–9 Turkish divisions of varying strengths were sent into the Caucasus—hence Hopkirk's figure of sixty thousand troops—and another 2 into northern Persia (Sykes).
46. For recent discussions of the SPR, see Anthony Wynn, *Persia in the Great Game: Sir Percy Sykes: Explorer, Consul, Soldier, Spy* (London, 2003), 259–312; and Stephanie Cronin, "Iranian Nationalism and the Government Gendarmerie," in Touraj Atabaki, ed., *Iran and the First World War: Battleground of the Great Powers* (London, 2006), 59.
47. Citations in Sykes, *History of Persia*, 2:502, 503.
48. Cited in ibid., 2:502.
49. Ibid., 2:517.
50. For the political pressure applied in June 1918, see Ludwig W. Adamec, *Afghanistan, 1900–1923: A Diplomatic History* (Berkeley, CA, 1967), 105–106.
51. Lord Milner's advice to the prime minister on June 11, 1918, cited in Winter, *Haig's Command*, 193.
52. For the battle of Baku and its aftermath, see Sanders, *Five Years in Turkey*, 244, 256, 268–269; Sykes, *History of Persia*, 2: 493–495; Barker, *Neglected War*, 450–453; Trumpener, *Germany and the Ottoman Empire*, 187–199; and Hopkirk, *Like Hidden Fire*, 331–351.
53. Cited in Mohammad Gholi Majd, *Iraq in World War I: From Ottoman Rule to British Conquest* (Lanham, MD, 2006), 3342–343.
54. For the following, see Sanders, *Five Years in Turkey*, 268–320; T. E. Lawrence, *Revolt in the Desert* (New York, 1927), 263–323; B. H. Liddell Hart, *Lawrence of Arabia* (New York, 1935), 248–304; Cyril Falls, *Armageddon, 1918: The Final Palestinian Campaign of World War I* (Philadelphia, 1964), 19–155, as well *Great War*, 394–402; and Martin Watts, *The Jewish Legion and the First World War* (New York, 2004).

55. Sanders writes (*Five Years in Turkey*, p. 270) that his divisions averaged 1,300 rifles, giving him perhaps 17,000. Allenby estimated 23,000, and Cyril Falls believes the total could have risen as high as 25,000 (*Armageddon*, p. 23; *Great War*, p. 395).
56. Sanders, *Five Years in Turkey*, 196, 243–244.
57. Falls charges this (*Armageddon*, p. 26), and Sanders too (*Five Years in Turkey*, pp. 256–257, 268–269).
58. For the Arab expedition against Deraa, also see Lawrence's dispatch of October 22, 1918, printed in Malcolm Brown, ed., *T. E. Lawrence in War and Peace* (London, 2005), 167–170.
59. *Five Years in Turkey*, 291.
60. The Jewish Legion fought in the campaign for Amman. Although it did not perform well, this had less to do with their inexperience and lack of drive, as Falls would have it, but with the unit's disease-decimated ranks. See Falls, *Armageddon*, 46; and Watts, *Jewish Legion*, 187–188.
61. For the final Balkan campaign and political developments discussed below, see Ludendorff, *Ludendorff's Own Story*, 2:365–371; Stephane Groueff, *Crown of Thorns: The Reign of King Boris III of Bulgaria 1918–1943* (Lanham, MD, 1987), 1–14, 34–48; Misha Glenny, *The Balkans: Nationalism, War and the Great Powers, 1804–1999* (New York, 1999), 346–361; L. S. Stavrianos, *The Balkans since 1453* (New York, 2000), 566–570; and Dennis E. Showalter, "Salonika," in Robert Cowley, ed., *The Great War: Perspectives on the First World War* (New York, 2003), 235–253. The most detailed account, however, is Alan Palmer, *The Gardeners of Salonika* (New York, 1965), 181–239.
62. One German officer's recollection, cited in Glenny, *The Balkans*, 353.
63. Cited in Groueff, *Crown of Thorns*, 10.
64. Cited in ibid., 3–4.
65. See Frank G. Weber, *Eagles on the Crescent: Germany, Austria, and the Diplomacy of the Turkish Alliance* (Ithaca, NY, 1970), 243.
66. Cited in Groueff, *Crown of Thorns*, 5.
67. See Herwig, *First World War*, 368–371.
68. Cited in Groueff, *Crown of Thorns*, 3.
69. Ludendorff, *Ludendorff's Own Story*, 2:371.
70. Cited in Palmer, *Gardeners of Salonika*, 229.
71. Cited in Herwig, *First World War*, 422.
72. For Pershing and the AEF, see Nenninger, "American Military Effectiveness," in Millett and Murray, *Military Effectiveness*, 1:134–153; and Paschall, *Defeat of Imperial Germany*, 163–192.
73. Doughty, *Pyrrhic Victory*, 482–483. For a recent detailed account of the impending AEF action, see Edward G. Lengel, *To Conquer Hell: The Meuse-Argonne, 1918* (New York, 2008).
74. See Travers, *How the War Was Won*, 127–130, and for the "traditionalists," 32–49.
75. See Roger Chickering, *Imperial Germany and the Great War, 1914–1918* (Cambridge, UK, 1998), 183–187; Winter, *Haig's Command*, 211–222; and especially Watson, *Enduring the Great War*, 184–231.
76. *Ludendorff's Own Story*, 2:376, 386.
77. See Herwig's fine discussion of "finis austriae," *First World War*, 433–440.
78. Trumpener, *Germany and the Ottoman Empire*, 196–197, 352–365; Barker, *Neglected War*, 454–457; and David Fromkin, *A Peace to End All Peace: The Fall of the Ottoman Empire and the Creation of the Modern Middle East* (New York, 1989), 363–372.
79. Cited in Trumpener, *Germany and the Ottoman Empire*, 357.
80. Cited in Herwig, *First World War*, 425. For parliamentary pressures in Berlin, see Klaus Epstein, *Matthias Erzberger and the Dilemma of German Democracy* (Princeton, NJ, 1959), 257–259.

81. Citations in Herwig, *First World War,* 426.
82. For these reinforcements, see Trumpener, *Germany and the Ottoman Empire,* 355.
83. Above citations in Herwig, *First World War,* 428, 427; and Fleming, *Illusion of Victory,* 299. Also see Winter, *Haig's Command,* 211–216.
84. Cited in Herwig, *First World War,* 445.
85. For a detailed account, see Epstein, *Matthias Erzberger,* 274–281.
86. See the memoir sketch of American nurse Laura Smith, printed in Peter Jennings and Todd Brewster, *The Century* (New York, 1998), 86, and especially the graphic descriptions in Susan Kingsley Kent, *Making Peace: The Reconstruction of Gender in Interwar Britain* (Princeton, NJ, 1993), 51–73.

PART THREE

SLOWLY OUT OF THE ABYSS 1918–1926

CHAPTER XI

The Violent Aftermath of the Great War in Europe

1918–1926

The ornate Victorian apartment at 78 Rue de L'Université lay silent as the early-morning hours of October 30 drew on toward morning. For much of the night diligent staffers of Colonel Edward M. House, special envoy in Paris to American President Woodrow Wilson, had put the latest dispatches in code for Washington. Around three o'clock a motorcycle courier ended the nocturnal stillness by starting his engine and speeding away. The noisy invasion yanked the president's closest adviser and confidant out of a fitful sleep full of insurmountable nighttime worries. Unfavorable developments loomed gnawingly large as he thought about the past day. Was he in over his head negotiating allied approval of Wilson's controversial new world order?[1]

Germany had agreed to stop fighting in return for a treaty based on the president's Fourteen Points, but none of America's allies had come on board. During a private luncheon in the exquisite sitting room of the apartment British Prime Minister David Lloyd George paid lip service to the "free, open-minded, and absolutely impartial adjustment of all colonial claims," even to the anti-imperial idea that colonial powers should not own their newly conquered territories but rather act "as trustee for the natives and for the interests of the society of nations," but in reality he just wanted the victors to "freely take what they desire." London angled for outright British protectorates in Iraq and Palestine, a French sphere of influence in Syria, and an "autonomous" Arabia, which probably meant another British protectorate. If the treaty denied German Southwest Africa to South Africa and prevented Australia and New Zealand from acquiring German New Guinea,

What the French Wanted Wilson to See: The Ruins of Rheims
Courtesy of the Library of Congress

the Solomons, and Western Samoa he said Britain might face a "revolution" in its dominions. Lloyd George was more skeptical about freedom of the seas, which he "could not agree to,"[2] and worse for House, Wilson's hobbyhorse League of Nations found only conditional support.

Things had gone from bad to worse during an afternoon session with Lloyd George, Georges Clemenceau of France, and Italian Foreign Minister Sidney Sonnino. Lloyd George defended the absolute necessity of maritime blockades like the one that had enervated Germany. Wilson's entire postwar vision seemed jeopardized by this issue, in fact, for Lloyd George suggested that the allies "make it clear to the German government that we are not going in on the 14 Points of peace." Clemenceau complained that he had not been consulted about them, which was seconded by Lloyd George, prompting the Frenchman to insist that they be discussed now. Almost immediately, however, the point-by-point discussion hit the freedom-of-the-seas minefield as the Briton scoffed at the notion of leaving oceanic security to a yet-to-be-established intergovernmental body. "If naval power is to be handed over to the League of Nations and Great Britain were fighting for her life, no League of Nations would prevent her from defending herself." House fought back, threatening that economic giant America would build the biggest navy in the world to protect its shipping, even against Great Britain. This made little impression, so he hinted that Washington would sign a separate peace with Germany if the allies rejected the Fourteen Points. "We would be sorry," countered Lloyd George, "but we could not give up the blockade." Britain would "fight on." "Yes," added Clemenceau, "war would not be war if there was freedom of the seas."[3] Sorely overmatched, House adjourned the discussion for the next day.

Staring into the darkness of his room that night, the Texan's anxiety mounted as he pondered the upcoming meeting. Thus far Britain was the greatest obstacle to Wilson's agenda, but France was certain to contradict the lenient spirit of the Fourteen Points by demanding harsh punishment of Germany, which went directly against Wilson's most recent instructions. House had been told to hold out for armistice terms "as moderate and reasonable as possible" because yielding too much to allied vindictiveness "will make a genuine peace settlement exceedingly difficult if not impossible."[4] Everything would have been easier in 1917, with peace so near, but the allies now had the upper hand.

Finally it occurred to House what he must do—make more threats. He could say that Wilson would put allied reservations before Congress and let it decide whether "fighting on" under these conditions justified further U.S. casualties. And did the allies really want to so badly crucify Germany as to produce "a state of Bolshevism"? As Russia sank deeper into violence in 1918, frightening reports were already coming west that seemed to speak to the true nature of communism. The German ambassador had been gunned down in Moscow, and then Tsar Nicholas executed, prompting Wilson to lament that "a great menace to the world has taken shape." Could the allies afford to overlook the potential of this "menace" spreading to Germany, not to mention "the consequent communist danger to England, France, and Italy"?[5]

Alternately using threats and finesse over the next three days, the president's envoy won allied acceptance of the Fourteen Points as the terms of peace with Germany—subject, however, to a series of controversial qualifications. Britain only agreed to discuss freedom of the seas later. Lloyd George also added a point of his own, namely, "that compensation will be made by Germany for all damage done to the civilian population of the allies and their property by the forces of Germany by land, by sea, and from the air."

This was not enough for Clemenceau, however, who got House to agree to potentially much more—that the allies reserved the right to make "all future claims or demands," thereby opening the possibility of a general indemnity or reparation like those imposed on vanquished nations in centuries past, or more recently at Brest-Litovsk, a treaty House knew full well his president considered "palpably fraudulent."[6] When the Frenchman went even further to insist on an allied occupation of Germany's Rhenish provinces, House played his Bolshevik card, but Clemenceau was not moved. Lloyd George, who was in fact deeply concerned about a red tide sweeping west, thought seizing the Rhineland excessive, but House, eager for closure on the remaining Fourteen Points, abandoned him. Thus the Rhineland would be indefinitely occupied. The American envoy also avoided further discussion of colonial issues, which seemed to imply tacit American acceptance of Lloyd George's imperial leanings.

House cabled Wilson on November 5, 1918, that "we have won a great diplomatic victory."[7] Had he saved the Fourteen Points, however, or mortgaged them?

CIVIL WAR BREAKS OUT IN RUSSIA 1918–1919

Colonel House's days in Paris showed that crafting a durable peace would be very difficult. All of the domestic and international pressures building before 1914 and continuing to escalate throughout the worst war in history would not dissipate, evaporate, or disappear with the mere signing of armistices and treaties. It defied common sense to think so, although the task would probably have been manageable had peace come a year earlier before the crushing of Germany and overthrow of Russian democracy. Like structural instability along the fault line of a recent earthquake that causes severe aftershocks, Europe's fractured state would shake the continent and the world for many years and kill many millions more. Very much a part of the tragedy of the Great War, this persistent violence forms an important part of our story.

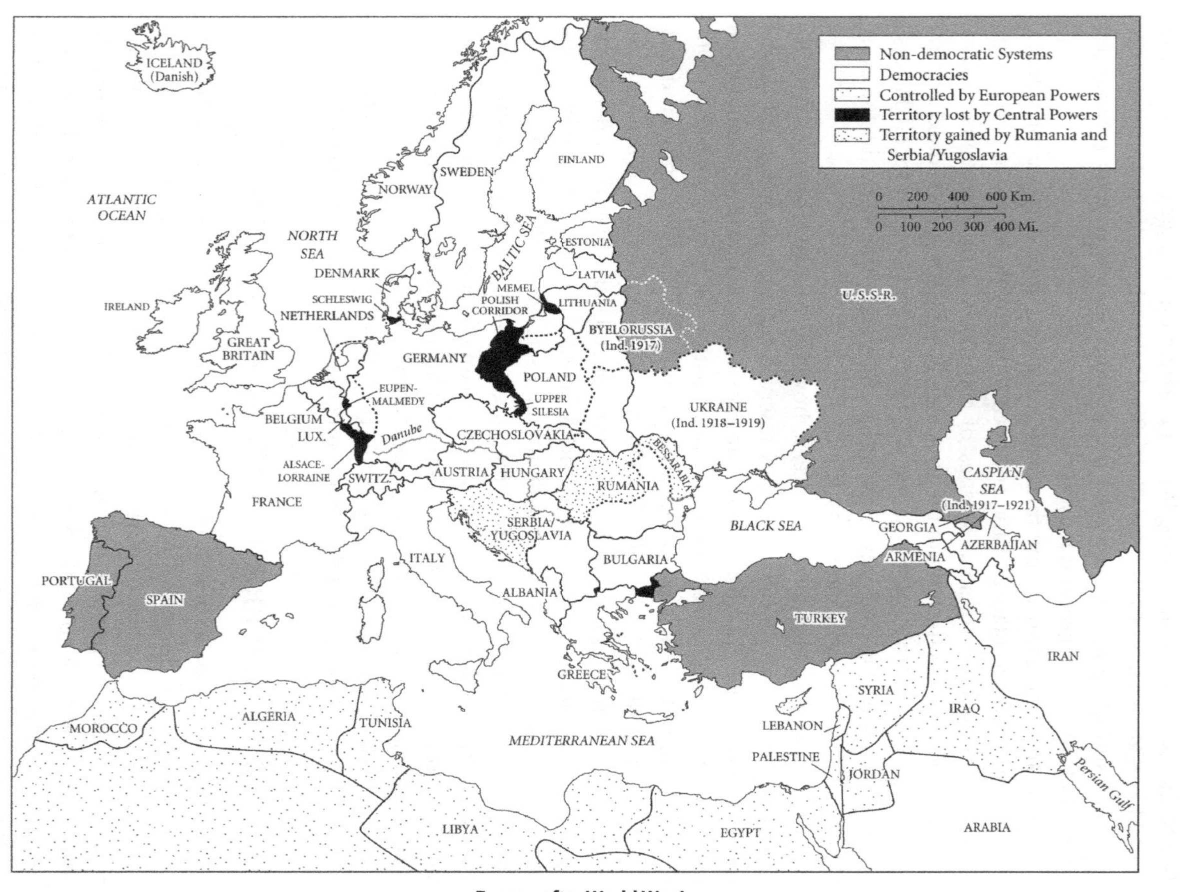

Europe after World War I

Arguably the worst aftershock of World War One occurred in Russia. While Mr. House negotiated the armistice, in fact, the east was falling apart in civil war. Historians are loath to dub anything inevitable, for inevitability implies little or no place for human agency, but the likelihood that the Bolshevik seizure of power—itself one of the most significant long-term products of the war—would deteriorate into fratricidal violence was probably as close to the inevitable as one finds in history. It began with reactionary forces from the old imperial army that began to assemble "White Guard Volunteers" in December 1917 to fight the first detachments of the new and still very rudimentary "Red Army" in the northern Caucasus.[8] Their leader was the successor to Lavr Kornilov, General Anton Denikin.

Simultaneously, relations between the Bolsheviks and non-Marxist Socialist Revolutionaries ineluctably reached the breaking point. After national elections gave 58 percent to the peasant-oriented Socialist Revolutionaries (SRs), the Bolsheviks shut down the Constitutional Assembly in January 1918, thereby virtually guaranteeing interparty violence. By spring, SR assassins and agents of Cheka, the Bolsheviks' ruthless police squad, were hunting one another down, and by summer the Red Army and an SR army in the Ural Mountain region battled back and forth before Lenin's soldiers finally prevailed. "The meaning of civil war is: kill that you may not be killed,"[9] exclaimed one top Bolshevik. By the time Lenin himself took an SR bullet in August 1918, the Cheka was already unleashing its "Red Terror," executing thousands of SRs and other perceived enemies of the revolution throughout Bolshevik-controlled Russia.

There was also a threat to Bolshevik rule throughout those provinces of the former empire lost to Russia during the winter of 1917–1918, although here dangers remained more potential than real. The German army occupied the vast expanses from the Black Sea to the Baltic, and newly independent Finland was largely a German proxy too, but however much an anti-Communist crusade tempted Berlin such plans remained mere contingencies while the great battles of 1918 raged on the western front. After the armistice of November and the German withdrawal, more genuinely independent states emerged in Finland, the Baltic, Poland, the Ukraine, and the Caucasus, all looking askance at Moscow but none planning any immediate hostilities.

Britain, France, and the United States, on the other hand, had already turned openly hostile. Incensed at Lenin for signing a separate peace with Germany, wary of his anticapitalist and antiwestern rhetoric, and repelled by what the American ambassador to Russia described as the "inhuman brutishness" of the regime, the western allies landed troops in Murmansk, Archangel, Vladivostok, and on the Black Sea. More important, they pledged anti-Bolshevik financial and military aid that began to arrive in significant quantities after the Germans surrendered. Although it was not official policy in any allied capital, combat against the Reds actually broke out in March 1918 when British units landed in Murmansk and moved on to Archangel, fighting and winning minor skirmishes against the Bolsheviks and proclaiming the mission, said the British general on the ground, of restoring to Russia "liberties and institutions of true popular government."[10] American units joined the British in Archangel in September.

This allied incursion might have become more of a threat if there had been anti-Bolshevik counterrevolutionaries in the region to support, but Moscow had already crushed the SRs, especially at Yaroslav (see map, pp. 98–99), and no White Guard force had yet appeared in the north. Moreover, the man who would eventually raise such forces in the Baltic, Nikolai Yudenich, spent most of 1918 in underground hiding in St. Petersburg. Thus the Bolsheviks could afford to leave insignificant screening forces all along the western and northern frontiers, devoting their main efforts to the Caucasus and the Urals.

To defend their revolution Lenin and his comrades adopted a series of emergency measures. The state commandeered thousands of factories in a desperate and unsuccessful bid to produce as many armaments as White forces, whose own meager output of guns the western allies augmented with ever increasing supplies—foreign shipments over Vladivostok and the Black Sea in the first half of 1919 alone quadrupled the entire Soviet production for that year, and this did not count large deliveries to Archangel. Communist survival would depend more on the wholesale emptying of what remained in tsarist arsenals than on domestic production of arms. Moscow also sent armed detachments into the countryside to compel hostile peasants to give up their crops, but this policy too fell short of expectations. To be sure, much grain was seized, but the Red "food brigades" also triggered hundreds of uprisings throughout the summer and fall of 1918 by angry peasant bands armed with pitchforks—and guns, for many of them had been drafted into the Red Army only to desert, carrying arms and ammunition home to protect their recently acquired land.

Leon Trotsky's reorganization of the Red Army in the summer of 1918 enjoyed somewhat more success. He dragooned thousands of former tsarist officers to lead scores of new divisions that filled up with hundreds of thousands of conscripts. Although this draft was slightly reminiscent of France's *levée en masse* of 1792, peasants, not surprisingly, proved harder to force into the ranks than pro-Bolshevik urban workers. Desertion also remained a huge problem caused in no small measure by continuing difficulties with procuring adequate armaments and rations for the men. On the other hand, both leadership and discipline improved as Trotsky built up to a strength of almost eight hundred thousand by late 1918. Although spread out over many fronts, the Red Army managed to defend the revolution in the east and south, while in the southwest an army group pushed over the Brest-Litovsk demarcation line toward Kiev. Not long after the Germans withdrew, the Ukrainian capital fell on February 5, 1919.

By this time, however, Red fortunes of war had worsened as the threat from the east returned. In November 1918 Admiral Alexander Kolchak, former tsarist commander of the Black Sea Fleet, proclaimed an anti-Bolshevik crusade. He began to raise an army from among workers already disenchanted with Moscow's brave new world, the many Russian peasant pioneers who had sought independence and prosperity in Siberia before 1914, as well as the Ural Cossacks. Basing his government and army in Omsk, Kolchak routed the Red Army at Perm in the Urals on Christmas Eve and then advanced with one hundred thousand troops west of the Urals. Jumping off in early March 1919, three White columns struck, quickly moving to within a few days' march of the Volga.

Other negative reports streamed into Moscow. Polish leader Joseph Pilsudski did not wait long to expand his young state, marching into Vilna and setting sights on Minsk as Kolchak neared the Volga. Denikin gathered strength in the south, moreover, as allied supplies accumulated after the New Year. The troops of the hated "imperialists" came too: 70,000 Anglo-French in the Black Sea region; 83,000 Anglo-Canadian-American and Japanese in the Far East; and 31,000 Anglo-Americans plus additional thousands of White conscripts in Murmansk/Archangel. Enemy flotillas also blockaded the Gulf of Helsinki and sunk Red ships when they ventured to sea.

With the prospects of revolutionary survival darkening, Lenin began to think slyly in terms of another Brest-Litovsk. Early that winter Moscow called for a cease-fire in the civil war and an end to allied intervention and assistance to the Whites in return for a general "understanding" that would allow the Bolsheviks "to develop their social program peacefully." They offered "all possible concessions,"[11] including financial indemnities and cession of territory already in White hands. Largely on the prodding of Lloyd George and Wilson, allied leaders in Paris issued an invitation in late January for warring factions in Russia to attend peace talks on Turkey's Prinkipo Islands. With Kolchak advancing rapidly in mid-March 1919, Lenin, backed by a unanimous vote of the Central Committee of the Communist Party, repeated Moscow's willingness to make a deal.

THE POLITICS OF PEACEMAKING IN PARIS: GERMANY AND RUSSIA

The representatives of twenty-nine victorious countries began their deliberations in Paris in mid-January 1919. "We are the league of the people," proclaimed Clemenceau; "we are the state,"[12] said Wilson, pompously echoing the seventeenth-century Sun King. In reality, however, the executive heads of Britain, France, Italy, the United States, and Japan met with their foreign ministers in a so-called Council of Ten to decide things privately. The work list was daunting: drafting a charter for the League of Nations; balancing imperial interests with national and racial aspirations of the peoples of Asia, Africa, the Middle East, the Balkans, and Eastern Europe; dealing with civil war in Russia; and of course imposing treaties on Turkey, Bulgaria, Austria, Hungary, and Germany. The only real accomplishment of January and February was near agreement on the League charter. Other issues were either bumped to commissions or else deadlocked in the Council of Ten.

The conference's two most contentious issues—Germany and Russia—converged in acrimonious council discussions involving mainly Britain, France, and the United States. Regarding Russia, Lloyd George and Wilson disparaged military solutions that would cost too many lives, bankrupt home governments, and lead to political instability as pro-Bolshevik labor elements protested intervention. However disturbing the Red Terror, warned Lloyd George, a large-scale anti-Communist crusade was "the surest road to Bolshevism in Britain." Aid to the Whites was one thing but combat with the Red Army another, added Wilson, who instructed House to "make plain that we are not at war with Russia."[13] Both men also hoped that if communism survived, the return of normal times would make it less violent. Thus they pushed for the Prinkipo Island talks, prevailing over the objections of Sonnino and Clemenceau.

The Frenchman had refused to invite Bolsheviks to Paris and looked askance at Prinkipo. "Beaten,"[14] blurted Clemenceau after failing to lance the truce parlays. Together with Marshal Foch, however, he killed the peace initiative by urging White leaders who needed little encouragement to refuse to negotiate. France could not forgive the Communists their betrayal of the allies at Brest-Litovsk, repudiation of Russian debts to French investors, and the Red Terror, especially the execution of Nicolas and other Romanovs. Reports already circulated that Nicholas's entire immediate family as well as his brother and sister-in-law had also perished. Indeed with Prinkipo pigeonholed in February, Foch began to promote grandiose plans for sending 50,000 Polish soldiers who had fought in France augmented by Czechoslovak and Rumanian units and Greco-French divisions from the Army of the Orient to bolster the 60,000 French troops already at Odessa, all this to ensure the success of the counterrevolution in Russia.[15] Strengthening French resolve to continue the war in the east was the fact that many in official circles, including Clemenceau himself, saw Lenin as a pawn of the Germans, having received free transport over Germany and money from Berlin to overthrow Kerensky. France wanted to apply the same remedy to alleged "German proxies" that they had already used successfully on the western front.

To guarantee the fruits of its great victory in the field—and clear the way for an eastern campaign—Paris sought quick agreement to overtly punitive treaty terms against Germany. Recent historians have qualified the traditional view of vindictive France by demonstrating that Paris did not stand alone on many of the harsher aspects of the German peace. Thus Lloyd George, Wilson, and Italian Prime Minister Vittorio Orlando also wanted Berlin to lose its colonies, sacrifice Alsace-Lorraine and other western borderlands, and be prevented from uniting with millions of ethnic Germans in Austria and the Bohemian Sudetenland. They agreed, moreover, on all but eliminating the German army and navy, bringing German military and political leaders to trial, including the kaiser if he could be extradited from Holland, and compelling Germany to pay some form of reparation. After these historical revisions, however, the impression still lingers of France as the lone advocate of extreme punishment, for it found none of the aforementioned sufficient or adequate to guard against being overrun a third time. To provide an added measure of security, therefore, Paris bargained for French-occupied satellite states in the Rhineland and the Saar; a bolstering of France's new ally Poland with a large chunk of eastern Germany; and an enervating, bleeding reparations bill. France requested an astronomical $220 billion—more than eighteen times Germany's prewar national income. Britain also insisted on a harsh reckoning, initially seeking $120 billion to cover the cost of sunken luxury liners, thousands of merchant ships, and extensive destruction caused during costal raids and zeppelin attacks over London. The Americans considered $22 billion enough to pay for the "restoration" of Belgium and northern France mentioned in the Fourteen Points and the "compensation" for damage to allied civilians agreed to by House in the prearmistice negotiations. One expert estimated these damages at about $15 billion.[16]

As winter came to a close, developments in Central Europe worked against the French agenda. Although Kolchak was advancing, sporadic reports about his progress were overshadowed by alarming news from Germany and Hungary. Bolshevik-style revolutionaries calling themselves "Spartacists" rose up in Berlin and the Ruhr. Hastily organized "free corps" of Germany's provisional democratic government smashed the rebels, but in Munich leftists founded two "Soviet" republics in rapid succession early that spring. In Budapest, meanwhile, Communists around Bela Kun seized power and called to Moscow for help. To advocates of foreign intervention against Lenin's regime these events strengthened the case for eradicating the communist cancer at its source, but the means to this end shriveled with every passing week. British inability and American unwillingness to fund him undercut Foch, who ran out of other options with the French financially strapped too; the Poles, Czechoslovaks, and Rumanians committed to other actions; and Army of the Orient commander Franchet D' Esperey complaining that his men had no stomach for fighting in Russia. After troop morale sank in Odessa that mission was withdrawn, moreover, leaving the Whites to fend alone against the Red Army with only rear-guard allied support in Archangel and Vladivostok. The Whites' only consolation was the somewhat surprising reluctance of Wilson and Lloyd George to respond to Moscow's most recent peace feeler. Both men had grown distrustful of Lenin's sincerity given his repeated calls for world revolution. Lloyd George had also come under intense right-wing pressure not to recognize the Bolshevik regime.

What was to be done? The British prime minister thought he knew the answer. In one of the most famous documents of the Paris settlement, the so-called Fontainebleau Memorandum of March 25, 1919, Lloyd George implored Clemenceau to moderate his treaty demands on Germany lest revolution and war plunge the continent once again into the abyss. He worried most about the blatant injustice of placing under Polish rule 2 million Germans who would be misruled, revolt, and beg Berlin for assistance, which would trigger a German-Polish conflagration and perhaps another European war. By severing western provinces from Germany, furthermore, France would implant irredentist urges across the Rhine that were as unlikely to dissipate as France's desire for revenge after losing Alsace and Lorraine in 1871, especially with unreasonably high reparations added to the explosive mix. "Whatever happens we are going to impose a hard peace on Germany," he reassured his French counterpart, but piling on a thick layer of injustice guaranteed trouble. In Lloyd George's nightmare scenario an extremely unfair treaty would facilitate the Spartacists' revolutionary agenda as they promised "to save Germany from . . . indebtedness to the allies and indebtedness to their own richer classes." And if the Spartacists took over, he continued,

> It is inevitable that [Germany] should throw in her lot with the Russian Bolshevists. Once that happens all Eastern Europe will be swept into the orbit of the Bolshevik revolution and within a year we may witness the spectacle of nearly 300 million people organized into a vast Red Army under German instructors and German generals equipped with German cannon and German machine guns and prepared for a renewal of the attack on Western Europe. This is a prospect which no one can face with equanimity.

French Poster of 1919: Kicking the Germans Back Over the Rhine
Courtesy of the Library of Congress

That Bela Kun had already seized power in Hungary confirmed the wisdom of these dire predictions for Lloyd George, for this rising combined the two-edged attractiveness of social justice at home with nationalist ire that Hungarians were being "handed over"[17] to the control of Rumanians and other foreign peoples.

In his equally famous reply two days later, Clemenceau was polite and diplomatic—but essentially unmoved. The Spartacist threat he waved off as exaggeration by the current government in Berlin designed to weaken a treaty that had to be harsh in order "to spare the world from German aggression for a long time." Clearly the French premier was less worried about the Red Army, which White forces might still defeat, than the German army. Given the militarist "German spirit," which will "not change so quickly" regardless of what political party was in power, Foch was right to want French troops on the Rhine and a strong Polish bulwark in the east. After Lloyd George's mocked the marshal as "a child on political questions," Clemenceau reminded him that military men had saved the West in its great crisis. "Let's not make the error of not taking their advice at a moment like this" lest when the "day of danger and of trial" came again "they would say to us: 'It is not our fault if you did not listen to us.' "

Over the next month the allies finally agreed on a German treaty, later named after the famous Palace of Versailles, where it was signed. The terms presented to Germany in early May contained all of the stiff provisions that were not at dispute: war crimes trials, the loss of all colonies, the return of Alsace-Lorraine, minor territorial cessions to Belgium and Denmark, and virtual disarmament to a lightly armed 100,000-man army and a navy of six antiquated battleships. On the main contentious issues the conference's three chief democratic leaders also managed to bridge their differences. Democratic leaders usually do this, but Wilson's severe bout with influenza in April seems to have broken his remaining resolve to do political battle with Clemenceau and probably added an extra irrational measure of confidence in the League of Nations as a panacea for treaty imperfections. In bending a little himself to Clemenceau, furthermore, Lloyd George probably recalled the Frenchman's generosity in supporting British claims to oil-rich Mosul in northern Iraq.[18]

All things considered, the compromise leaned toward French demands. Germany had to accept primary responsibility for the outbreak of war—the so-called war guilt clause—and as the liable party pay an as-yet-unspecified amount of reparations. The last discussions of this indemnity pointed, however, to a substantially lower bill between the final American ($25–$35 billion), French ($31–$47 billion), and British ($55 billion) figures—the victors would finally agree on $33 billion in 1921, still almost three times Germany's national income in 1913 and more than double the upper-bound estimate for civilian damages, largely because the cost of pensions to war widows had been included in the bill. In the east Lloyd George managed to whittle away at Poland's gains with plebiscites that returned parts of East Prussia and Silesia to Germany, but the bulk of the so-called Polish Corridor running to the Baltic Sea remained. Warsaw did not receive Danzig, however, which rather became a free city administered by the League. In the west, France won ownership of the Saar mines, but this region fell similarly under League administration with a plebiscite after fifteen years to determine its ultimate fate—it voted to return to Germany in 1934. Finally, France abandoned its claim to a Rhenish buffer state in return for an Anglo-American pledge of military assistance; occupation of the Rhineland phased out over fifteen years; German demilitarization of the province (including the eastern riverbank); and the right to keep troops indefinitely in the Rhineland should Germany fail to meet other treaty obligations, especially disarmament and reparations. The relieved victors and crestfallen vanquished penned the Treaty of Versailles on June 28, 1919, five years to the day since the assassination at Sarajevo.

The Germans reacted with disbelief and incredulity to a treaty that they considered, virtually unanimously, a dishonorable act of betrayal by the allies. Worried specialists in the German Foreign Office who kept a close watch in 1919 on allied negotiations in Paris were not surprised to see how far the final treaty had drifted from the Fourteen Points, but to the public at large, even better-informed democratic politicians in Berlin, the publication of the terms in May came as the proverbial cold-water shower. Knowledgeable foreign observers commented on how tenaciously Germans had clung to their hope for a positive outcome. After the surrender they became "subconsciously optimistic" that somehow Woodrow Wilson "would arrange a compromise peace satisfactory to Germany." "When they see the terms in cold print," said one pundit, "there will be intense bitterness, hate, and desperation." And there was. "You Americans go back home and bury yourselves with your Wilson," blurted one leading Social Democrat in a typical response. Much of German anger centered on the nation's eastern borders, where the allies made exceptions to the principle of national self-determination by placing millions of Germans under Polish and Czechoslovakian rule and

German Poster of 1919: "What We Are to Lose: Land, Population, Coal and Iron, Farm Land, Colonies"
Courtesy of the Library of Congress

denying Austria its petition to unite with Germany. Losing all its colonies, 13 percent of its European territory, and paying hefty reparations was also hard to square with Wilson's peace points, not to mention his frequent speechifying about "no annexations, no contributions, no punitive damages." That Germans were unrealistic to expect a lenient peace after so many allied losses and naïve not to anticipate changes to what Wilson wanted is not the point—they saw it differently, and this became the political reality in their young democracy.

Nor did they lack empathizers in allied ranks, especially in the American delegation, where twelve resigned rather than accept their president's compromises, but among the British too. Chief of the Imperial General Staff Henry Wilson thought that Germany's reading of the Fourteen Points "is much more coherent than ours," while Deputy Prime Minister Bonar Law found the German objections "in many particulars very difficult to answer."[19] In 1919 the brilliant young economist John Maynard Keynes also published *The Economic Consequences of the Peace,* a blistering criticism of the handiwork of allied leaders.

But many Germans—alas, far too many—reserved a significant portion of their anger for the democratic coalition in Berlin. Although Foch was prepared to hurl forty-two divisions into an unstoppable offensive if governing politicians did not sign the treaty, millions of shocked, incredulous voters ignored this reality and began to pay more serious attention to rightist demagogues. Having called acceptance of the November armistice "criminal," Pan Germans and other militant antidemocrats like Adolf Hitler and his Nazi movement now skewered those who had signed the treaty as "traitors." The venerable Hindenburg lent credence to these accusations in November 1919 by testifying before parliament that the army had lost because it had been "knifed from behind"[20] by leftists on the home front. Free Corps fighters idle after finally "cleansing" Munich of its Soviet Republic in May, meanwhile, turned on democratic politicians at the local, regional, and national level, eventually assassinating hundreds of them, including Matthias Erzberger, the driving force behind the Peace Resolution of 1917. For a few days in March 1920 the Free Corps even seized control of government in Berlin before a general strike by trade unions paralyzed and chased out the Putschists. National elections in June registered a stinging defeat, however, for the Social Democrats, the Center, and the German Democratic Party. This so-called Weimar Coalition lost nearly 10 million votes from its early 1919 total and slipped from 76.2 to 49.8 percent of the electorate. Ominously, the republic's chief democratic parties no longer commanded a parliamentary majority. Reparation payments soon added an extra measure of economic and political volatility.

Thus the Weimar Republic, born of war and revolution, grew up amidst treaty-related violence and instability. However, we should not press the case against Versailles too far. How truly unstable, for instance, was this young democracy? It certainly did well by comparison in the 1920s with the new states and fledgling democracies of Central, Eastern, and Southern Europe, where five of fourteen had fallen by middecade (Poland, Hungary, Bulgaria, Albania, and Italy) and most of the others teetered near the edge of collapse—only Czechoslovakia was clearly more stable than Germany. And there were good reasons this was so, for the recent trend of violence in German politics mixed with an older tradition, not present in these other states, of parliamentary elections and political party give-and-take stretching far back into the 1800s. To be sure, most of this experience came from opposition to authoritarianism as opposed to actually ruling, an experience that also included a lot of bickering and feuding among opposition groups. The final war year witnessed a transition to greater communication and cooperation between the parties, however, and also one of their own, Centrist Georg Hertling, serving as chancellor. After 1920 this deeper parliamentary tradition facilitated a succession of admittedly short-lived center-left and center-right minority governments but on two occasions a left-center-right "Grand Coalition" that included the German Peoples' Party and its leader Gustav Stresemann, one of the outstanding statesmen of the Weimar Republic. It is facile, therefore, to assert that the Treaty of Versailles, as problematic, controversial, and divisive as it was, doomed German democracy to failure and boosted Hitler into the saddle. We must look elsewhere in a subsequent decade for more direct causes. It is even less convincing to argue that the Great War and Versailles spawned "war without end"—in other words, that it made World War Two all but inevitable.[21]

THE BOLSHEVIKS SURVIVE, 1919–1920

By early spring 1919 Kolchak's three army groups had advanced so far along a broad front toward the Volga that Lenin warned colleagues of "an extreme danger to the Soviet Republic."[22] Moscow rushed units east from other fronts accompanied by tens of thousands of party member volunteers, loyal factory workers, and Communist youth group enthusiasts to bolster the retreating Red Army. Lenin also called off the hated food brigades in an effort to recruit peasant soldiers, a new policy that began to show some signs of success. In late April, with the allies in Paris ready to recognize the seemingly victorious White commander as "supreme ruler" of Russia, the Reds unleashed a furious counterattack that sent White forces quickly scrambling. A despondent Kolchak admitted to his diary that "our offensive has played itself out," and worse, that it had "become necessary to ask if we shall be able to hold the Urals."[23]

Had the Whites fought their way to the Volga and secured a wide defensive line their growing weaknesses would not have been so exposed, their army less vulnerable, and the outcome probably different, but the usual early spring rains slowed their offensive. Indeed without the protection of the river a series of emerging problems on the White side assumed magnified significance. Wanting to exploit the rout of a Red Army group at Perm in December, Kolchak had attacked as soon as he felt he could—March 4—but before five divisions training at Omsk were ready. He also hoped to produce impressive victories rapidly to win more support from Paris. When Trotsky hit back, therefore, the Whites found themselves spread too thin with no reserves. Exacerbating matters, allied supplies moved too slowly, or sometimes not at all, along the Trans-Siberian Railway from faraway Vladivostok. Most of Kolchak's generals were too inexperienced for army group command, moreover, and they fought without the large numbers of Cossack cavalry, artillery, machine guns, and even tanks that supported Denikin. As the retreat accelerated peasants leery that Kolchak's conservative backers would reinstitute serfdom began to harry his columns. The attrition of the March–April advance, followed by defeats, desertions, and defections of entire units in May and June, reduced White numbers from 110,000 in the front lines to a mere 15,000, not enough to make a stand in the mountains against pursuing Reds easily ten times their rifle strength with an added advantage in cannon and machine guns. As the retreating army withered away, emboldened peasant bands struck more frequently. Their uprisings, marked with red dots by White staffers, made their maps look like cases of "advanced spotted fever,"[24] according to one senior officer.

Twice in the summer of 1919 Kolchak's armies attempted to reverse the tide, most notably at Chelyabinsk, but to no avail as the Red Army marched relentlessly east. When Omsk and its garrison of thirty thousand recruits fell in November, the offensive having covered 1,300 kilometers in less than seven months, the civil war in the east was all but over. Kolchak did not survive it. The once powerful counterrevolutionary leader fell into Bolshevik hands at Irkutsk, 2,000 kilometers east of Omsk, on January 21, 1920—so quickly had the Reds advanced. Cheka operatives shot him two weeks later.

As the Red Army readied its counterattack into the Urals, long-awaited good news finally streamed into Moscow from the southern front. Lenin and Trotsky built up forces there to nearly one hundred thousand frontline troops (altogether a quarter of a million soldiers), who raced by April 1919 from Kiev to the Rumanian border, Odessa, and the Crimea and pressed Denikin back down the Don River. These successes allowed transfer of units to the Volga to defeat Kolchak, whose demise, Trotsky assumed, would cause White implosion in the south. "The collapse of the Kolchakites will lead at once and inexorably to the complete collapse of Denikin's volunteers—'volunteers' driven with a lash."[25] The withdrawal of France's sixty thousand soldiers from Odessa amidst disorder as panic-stricken upper-class Russians pleaded to be taken on board lent credence to Trotsky's optimistic scenario.

But he had underestimated the threat. After spring rains literally bogged down Red attacks in April and May, Denikin's three army groups struck back, capturing Ekaterinoslav, Kharkov, and Belgorod in the northwest and Tsaritsyn, the "Red Verdun," in the east by early July. Fighting with only half as many soldiers, the Whites had expanded their zone into the western Ukraine and up the Don. The reasons for this remarkable success centered on man, beast, and machine. Denikin had more veteran officers with greater discipline, esprit, and ideological fervor than Red counterparts who rarely fought with the zeal trumpeted in later Soviet propaganda films. Although it would be a mistake to describe the brutish White rank and file in the same way, their victories, producing ample opportunity to loot and pillage, kept spirits high. The Red Army also refused at first to employ cavalry units, an army branch that they denigrated as a relic of the discredited bourgeoisie. But White Guard and Cossack horsemen played an important part, harrying the enemy rear, disrupting supply and communication, and dragging along their own cannon and machine guns for frontal assaults somewhat like Allenby's mounted divisions in Palestine and Syria. Finally, Denikin's divisions went into battle with a discernible two-to-one advantage in artillery, an edge in machine guns, and a few score tanks that produced the same frightening effects on demoralized Red infantrymen as they had on the enervated Germans. White forces in the south built up to 100,000 frontline and 50,000 second-line troops after their late spring victories, enabling them to swing over to the offensive and occupy Kiev on August 31, 1919. "What is going on?"[26] asked an angry Lenin.

The advance on Kiev initiated an ambitious operation formulated by Denikin in early July. With the Ukrainian capital and Dnieper River anchoring their western flank, three White army groups would descend on Moscow: the left, comprising the main Volunteer Army, over Tula; the center, boasting the Don Cossacks, over Riazan; and the cavalry-strong right rolling up the Volga to Saratov and then swinging far to the northeast around Nizhni-Novgorod. Jumping off in early September, the Whites took Voronezh, Chernigov, and finally Orel on October 14. Only the right wing, spent after beating back six weeks of Red counterattacks, failed to move forward, but Denikin smelled victory. "Do not worry," he told a friend, "I will drink tea in your house in Moscow."[27]

With Denikin's leading divisions only three hundred kilometers from Moscow, St. Petersburg, the cradle of the Bolshevik Revolution, actually came under siege. Throughout 1919 General Nikolai Yudenich build up the third White army from a base in northern Estonia and attacked even though his army barely numbered Twenty thousand. Positive news from the south spurred him on. After three weeks of battlefield successes Yudenich's forces reached the heights above St. Petersburg on October 20, confidently expecting to storm and capture the city the following day. The Reds sallied forth from the old imperial capital a few days after Yudenich reached it, however, driving him all the way back to Estonia by mid-November. He fled the former Russian province under British protection in January 1920.

Simultaneously, Trotsky's minions counterattacked in the south, winning a critical battle at Voronezh on October 24. The very Communists who shunned cavalry had trained a crack mounted corps and penetrated deeply enough behind White lines to threaten the rear of forward units at Orel. Now the long White front imploded. Denikin's forces did not stop falling, in fact, until they hit bottom on the Kuban River, south of Rostov, in February 1920. Denikin joined Yudenich in exile two months later. With Kolchak and his hopes of victory dead too, only mopping-up operations remained for the victorious Reds, who demonstrated the type of grit and perseverance that would maintain them in power for seven more decades.

Red Army size had a lot to do with its success. Trotsky's forces sextupled in 1919, peaking at 5 million men overall with perhaps a million frontline soldiers. Moreover, the spring and summer victories over Kolchak enabled the Bolsheviks both to reinforce St. Petersburg and concentrate against Denikin. For all its qualitative edge and (in the south) technological superiority, therefore, the White military "was like the mythical warrior struggling with the hundred-headed hydra," as one Cossack leader put it. "He cuts off one head, and two heads grow to replace it."[28] The French withdrawal from Russia in April 1919, followed by British and American pullouts later that year, exacerbated numbers liabilities for the Whites—disadvantages that arms shipments from the West could not overcome.

Political albatrosses hung heavier around White necks than around Red, furthermore, in the final stage of the civil war. Whereas Lenin and the Central Committee eventually realized the counterproductive nature of their grain-requisitioning efforts, the Whites, who imposed draconian marshal law wherever they went, never shook off the damaging stigma of authoritarianism and the suspicion that accompanied it of wanting to reinstitute long-abolished feudal institutions. Kolchak paid dearly for this, but Denikin undoubtedly more so. Indeed as he advanced the southern Ukraine fell almost completely under the control of a peasant rebel firebrand, Nestor Makhno, whose seemingly omnipresent guerilla raiders forced Denikin to commit ten thousand reserves to restore supply lines and communication with depots around the Black Sea—troops that were not available to halt Red counterattacks that autumn.

Rigid adherence to Russian ethnic agendas also undermined the White cause. Thus Denikin refused to support Cossack longings for independence, which explains why they went their own way at first. He also turned away Ukrainian nationalists willing to help. Ethnic chauvinism squandered even greater opportunities in the northwest, where Finnish leader Carl Mannerheim offered his 100,000-man army to the anti-Bolshevik crusade in return for White recognition of Finland's independence. Around Archangel a White army of 50,000 (admittedly less than eager) militiamen had slowly emerged in 1919 under the command of Evgenyi Miller, who pleaded with Kolchak to send emissaries to Helsinki. Yudenich also grudgingly asked to recognize Finland. Both Miller and Yudenich yielded to "supreme ruler" Kolchak, however, who vetoed these plans so as not to break up Mother Russia. Consequently

Mannerheim did not intervene, thereby preventing large numbers of Finns flanked by Yudenich and Miller driving on the heart of Red Russia just as Denikin neared Tula and its huge armaments works. Finally, opportunities were also squandered in Poland. Pilsudski turned a deaf ear to urgent French requests that he attack Russia "because he knew that Denikin's or Yudenich's victory would mean an end to Poland's independence." If Pilsudski and Mannerheim had not "hung fire"[29] the history of twentieth-century Russia might well be written differently today.

The Russian civil war was the hallmark event of the violent aftermath of the Great War. Many Americans felt understandably duped by Wilson's rhetoric about fighting "the war to end all wars." Was the Great War really over? Were wars really over? Certainly not in Russia, where the civil war and soon-to-erupt war with Poland left 2 million people dead by gunshot: soldiers, victims of political executions and ethnic/religious pogroms, and other innocent civilians who simply got in the way of the ruthless soldiers who for two years trampled through Russia's vast spaces. The horrific human tragedy of the civil war did not end with the shootings, however, for all of the apocalyptic horsemen rode through Russia. Many more people died of typhus, typhoid, cholera, influenza, syphilis, famine, and infanticide, in fact, than on the battlefields, execution posts, and bloody streets or country lanes. A recent historian estimates the death toll during this modern time of troubles at 10 million.

The terrible losses that Russians suffered during the Great War, followed with no respite by the cataclysmic horrors they experienced in the civil war, marked a major caesura in their history. It was not just that tsarism had fallen and communism had survived but also the ways that people—party officials, workers and peasants, parents and children—changed. Soviet doctors and psychiatrists in the 1920s worried that mass slaughter, death, and widespread instances of cannibalism had shaken families and communities, the mainstays of every society, and induced a kind of collective mental illness. In subsequent decades historians concurred that war and civil war had brutalized the surviving population and coarsened public life to the point where even worse atrocities—the denunciations, large-scale deportations, and mass executions under Soviet dictator Joseph Stalin in the 1930s—became all but inevitable. More recent studies adopt a softer determinism, arguing that few people could have lived through the 1914–1920 nightmares without changing in some way but that most common folk remade their lives and groped back to normalcy as best they could.[30] Although most people succeeded in this endeavor, the past nevertheless bequeathed a heavy burden, for survivors were psychically weaker, emotionally less resilient, less prone to resist wrongdoing, and more inclined to bury heads in the sand the next time tough times came along. From the Kremlin leadership down to the zealous party rank and file, moreover, cruder Bolsheviks like Stalin himself waited for the moment to demonstrate how well they had learned the civil war's brutal "kill-or-be-killed" lessons about dealing with opponents. It would be a tragic mixture of popular passivity and official aggression amidst partly genuine, partly state-manipulated mass hysteria.

THE LEAGUE OF NATIONS, POSTWAR WARS, AND THE COLLAPSE OF DEMOCRACY'S FIRST TIER, 1919–1921

The spread of democracy factored largely into Woodrow Wilson's conception of a new order in the world. He trusted the sagacity of people to choose good leaders and representatives. He trusted the pacifistic tendencies of democratic governments, especially in their dealings with other democracies. And he distrusted the dark militaristic designs that too often emerged from the halls of authoritarian power. The League of Nations would be the first pillar supporting the noble edifice of worldwide peace and democracy the second. It was with profound satisfaction, therefore, that Wilson surveyed the political scene in Europe as allied delegates met in January 1919 to hammer out League statutes. Throughout the eastern half of the continent, where semiabsolute monarchs once reigned with only slight or moderate checks from parliamentary institutions, new democratic states like Finland; Poland; Czechoslovakia; the Kingdom of the Serbs, Croats, and Slovenes (later renamed Yugoslavia); and recently democratized, former enemy states like Germany, Austria, and Hungary, had surfaced. Indeed almost all of Europe east of the Soviet Union—all but Portugal and Spain—was democratic. Democracy, writes one historian, had become "the alpha and omega of political wisdom."[31]

The committee responsible for writing the League's charter completed its work on February 13, 1919.[32] With a few important exceptions, the peace conference approved this document in April, paving the way for nation-by-nation ratification over subsequent months. Respect for the territorial integrity of all states, mandatory arbitration of all disputes—a concept that made scant progress before 1914—and condemnation of and sanctions against aggressor nations were the central ideas behind the League. When disputes occurred the organization's executive council or a new Permanent Court of International Justice, the so-called World Court, would render an arbitral decision. During and immediately after this process neither nation could legally take up arms, a nine-month "cooling off period" that Wilson confidently predicted would settle most questions. "If the Central Powers had dared to discuss the whole purposes of this war for a single fortnight it never would have happened, and if, as should be, they were forced to discuss it for a year, war would never have been conceivable." He scoffed at the notion that rogue nations could successfully defy a world now awakened by the tragedy of the Great War to the unacceptability of territorial aggression. Those that ignored the outcome of arbitration and attacked anyway would "go down in disgrace"[33] as trade embargoes, financial sanctions, and international ostracism were imposed and then military action if need be. The latter possibility caused considerable debate on the committee draft as the French pushed for a League with its own standing army, but Wilson and Lloyd George prevailed with their idea of the executive council calling ad hoc style on member nations to supply necessary forces. Significantly enough, the League reserved the right to prevent war in these ways even when neither party to a dispute belonged to the new intergovernmental body. When the League finally opened its doors in January 1920, however, forty-eight countries—over three-quarters of the nations in the world at that time—had affixed signatures. Thus the League "Covenant" swept away the centuries-old legal order that had sanctioned the norm of "might is right," defended violence between states as natural and necessary, and recognized no outlaw behavior in seizing and taking title to enemy territory without provocation or preemptive justification. The ramifications of the Great War in the realm of international *statutory* law were immediate and lasting.[34]

But League statutes could not change norms. Indeed although some Europeans had experienced heartfelt conversions to the rising pacifistic movement, others had not.[35] For Italian nationalists, for instance, the nation's half-million war dead in the blood-soaked northeast quadrant legitimized a commensurate territorial expansion into the Tyrol, the Trentino, Istria, Dalmatia, and other holdings around the Adriatic littoral, especially because the Entente had promised much of this when Italy entered the war. Shortly after the armistice Italian troops swarmed into these lands and then in April 1919 also took the Istrian port city of Fiume, which had *not* been mentioned in 1915. Yugoslavia protested that the Adriatic seizures, carved from its Slovenian, Croatian, and Bosnian provinces, violated principles of national self-determination. With the League not yet ready to open, adjudication fell to the western powers not party to the dispute. In the end Italy pulled back from the Bosnian coast and parts of Dalmatia, but for months no amount of diplomatic pressure could budge them from Istria and the northeastern Adriatic, including Fiume. When Rome finally bent to demands that it leave this city in September 1919, poet-warrior Gabriel D'Annunzio and a regiment of Great War veterans and volunteers simply took it over. Rome would eventually get back Fiume, but this port, surrounding Istria, and neighboring islands were all lost to Belgrade, which had good reason to doubt the shelf life of Wilson's new world order.

Not that Yugoslavia held the new ideas in such high regard either, at least when it came to carving out territory for itself from the defunct Austro-Hungarian Empire. Having liberated Belgrade in late October 1918, the Serbian army pushed north into Voivodina and the Banat; southwest into Bosnia; and northwest over Slavonia, Croatia, and Slovenia. Yugoslavia clearly had ethnic rights on its side, but this still amounted to a huge landgrab and fait accompli to the allies in Paris. France welcomed the expansion of its wartime Balkan ally, however, and cried crocodile tears over Belgrade gorging itself at the expense of Vienna and Budapest.

The French also applauded that winter and spring as Czechoslovakia sent troops 50 kilometers into prewar Hungary along a 500-kilometer front and Rumania overran all of Transylvania, not stopping until they reached the Tisza River east of Budapest. Allied sanctioning of almost all of these seizures by what France dubbed its "Little Entente" of Yugoslavia, Czechoslovakia, and Rumania triggered the fall of Hungary's young democracy at the hands of left-wing superpatriot Bela Kun in March 1919. The largely casualty-free actions of previous months now turned bloody, however, as Kun raised a sizeable army and moved against the Czechs and Rumanians. His forces experienced initial success before succumbing in August 1919 to the superior Rumanians, who occupied and ransacked Budapest before departing to their new border farther east. In the final treaty settlement the old Kingdom of Hungary lost 229,000 of its 325,000 square kilometers. About 30 percent of the Hungarian populace lived under surrounding foreign rule, creating a perceived injustice similar to the ethnic grievances that contributed so explosively to the Balkan powder keg before 1914.

Throughout Eastern Europe, in fact, ethnic minorities lived under alien rule. Seeing how nearly impossible it would be to implement pure national self-determination in regions so ethnically intermingled and troubled, Wilson and the allies insisted that the new East European democracies offer constitutional guarantees of fair treatment to their minorities. The League of Nations would monitor minority relations. Even before it inaugurated operations in Geneva, however, troubling signs came from America that put the League's ability to protect national minorities in doubt. Indeed the U.S. Senate, wary of getting dragged by the new organization into unwanted foreign obligations, or worse, that it would attempt to block enforcement of America's century-old Monroe Doctrine, rejected League membership in November 1919. "It is not possible to speak of the League of Nations unless great and powerful America becomes a member," wrote a Swiss newspaper. Small nations unable to provide their own national security worried that without Washington a genuine *collective* security system would be impossible. In March 1920, however, the Senate voted against the League a second time. Thus the United States joined nonmember pariahs Germany, which had not been invited because of its militaristic past, and Russia, whose Communist regime preached world revolution behind the vanguard Red Army. These prominent gaps in League ranks worried General Secretary Sir Eric Drummond. How could the League maintain world peace if powers like Russia and America, or perhaps a revived, revanchist Germany, went their own way? "So long as great and powerful states remain outside, the League cannot, of course, be altogether what you and your colleagues at Paris intended to create," he wrote Wilson. Washington's defection, in particular, "left the League maimed at its inception."[36]

Already in its first months of international crisis management, unfortunately, the League faced a major challenge, for in April 1920 Poland attacked the Soviet Union.[37] Like nineteenth-century patriots in Greece, Serbia, and Rumania and their early twentieth-century counterparts in Croatia, Slovenia, and Czechoslovakia, Joseph Pilsudski of Poland had dreamed not only of restoring his people's state but also of reviving its great "historic" dimensions. Indeed Poland had once expanded its heartland into the Baltic, White Russia, and the Ukraine. Pilsudski envisioned a federation of these peoples under Polish tutelage, which seemed modern, progressive, and unobjectionable to him, but the problem with these kinds of visions in 1919 was that they would be realized by force of arms, not Wilsonian negotiation, arbitration, and treaty-writing. Polish divisions marched into Vilna in April 1919, Minsk in August, and then took Kiev from the Bolsheviks in early May 1920.

The formidable Red Cavalry Corps, however, soon struck back. Its 12,000 sabers and accompanying armored trains, horse artillery, and fast-moving machine gun wagons offered contemporaries a glimpse of Blitzkrieg. Supported by 50,000 infantry, the spearhead retook Kiev and shuffed the startled Poles back across their border. To the north, simultaneously, an even stronger army with 120,000 frontline infantry and its own mobile cavalry corps attacked westward toward Minsk. The Poles retreated in disorder here too. By August 1920 the first army group closed in on Lvov (Lublin) and the second on Warsaw itself. Bolshevik dreams of spreading the world Communist revolution—and western fears that Moscow could succeed—intensified.

In Geneva Drummond worried that Lenin would ignore League attempts to arbitrate, causing more damage and embarrassment to an organization already lamed at birth. Instead he allowed his countrymen in the British Foreign Office to propose peace talks. Bolshevik Foreign Commissar Georgi Chicherin not only shunned the offer, however, he also unleashed a scathing attack on the League, which was his way of warning it not to interfere. Although ostracized and kept totally uninformed about the League Covenant, Moscow had learned from press sources "that according to Article 17 non-members in case of conflict with members of the so-called League [like Poland] can be invited to submit to its decision as if they were members."

> The Soviet government [however,] . . . absolutely rejects the pretensions of any foreign groups of powers claiming to assume the role of supreme masters of the fate of other nations. It absolutely rejects therefore every inmixation of this association in the cause of peace between Russia and Poland.[38]

Now London, Paris, Geneva, and a threatened Berlin watched anxiously to see if Warsaw could play by the old rules and save itself.

Leaving fifteen divisions and thousands of citizen volunteers to defend the capital, Pilsudski committed his five remaining divisions to a daring counterattack on August 16. He struck southeast of Warsaw into a largely unmanned gap between the two Soviet armies. The coup worked brilliantly as the Poles easily broke through and turned north behind enemy lines. When the Warsaw units joined the operation a few days later, Soviet surprise turned to panic as their forces were routed with heavy losses. Now it was their turn to rush headlong backwards. Both exhausted belligerents agreed to a cease-fire in November 1920 but not until Poland had pushed its eastern border 400–500 kilometers east of Warsaw to the region around (but not including) Minsk. Seven months of war over territories already scarred by the Great War and Russian civil war had cost minimally another one hundred thousand lives.

Proponents of the new world order could at least point to the fact that Poland's young democracy had repelled the onslaught of a brutal regime and thus preserved the chance to deepen democratic culture, cultivate rule of law, and become a more responsible member of the League. But the same could not be said, unfortunately, for five new republics and potential democracies that succumbed to the red tide as it swept to civil war victory. Moscow reconquered White Russia in late 1918; Azerbaijan, the Ukraine, and Armenia in 1920; and Georgia in early 1921. The turbulence of the Great War had felled monarchies and spawned new states, but the conflict's disruptive influences cut in many directions, felling fledgling nations too.

This troubling antidemocratic trend was also evident in Eastern and Southern Europe. Hungary's democracy yielded to authoritarianism in 1919, while Italy, Bulgaria, and Albania suffered similar fates, respectively, in 1922, 1923, and 1924. Poland's turn came in 1926 when military hero Pilsudski, tired of the "sterile, jabbering howling thing" called democracy, sent parliament's "band of thieves"[39] packing. Lithuanian soldiers followed his lead that same year. The failure of eleven democratic states in less than a decade—twelve when adding the fall of Russia's Provisional Government in 1917—raised eyebrows among Wilsonian devotees of peace, for if it were true that democracies never wage war against one another, but authoritarian states tend to behave oppositely, creating now an explosive mix of armed dictators and vigilant democrats with fingers on triggers, what pacifist could find solace in the overthrow of so many parliamentary regimes by military or fascist juntas?[40]

THE RESOLUTION OF THE GREAT WAR IN EUROPE 1923–1926

Although the fall of democracy's first tier unsettled pacifists everywhere, at least peace had finally come to Europe. The turbulence and death of the Russian civil war and Russo-Polish War had subsided, as had the chaos and fighting that followed the disintegration of the Austro-Hungarian Empire. In Western Europe, the killing had stopped years earlier with Armistice Day. Trouble brewed, however, on either side of the Rhine.

Most Germans felt betrayed that the Treaty of Versailles had departed so blatantly from the Fourteen Points, especially on the issue of reparations. After an allied commission agreed on a total of $33 billion in 1921, Berlin went through a painful—and to France angering—process of foot-dragging: initially protesting, then requesting a moratorium, next announcing its intention to fulfill the allegedly impossible reparation terms, and finally denouncing reparations again in a controversial statement with the Soviet Union at Rapallo in April 1922. Lloyd George's nightmare specter of Russia's masses linking up with Germany's science and technology in an apparent alliance—indeed, secret German-Soviet military cooperation began soon after Rapallo—left Great War victors, especially France, nervous and edgy.

Thus when Germany fell further and further behind in reparations payments in the months after Rapallo, Paris answered with force. Two French divisions accompanied by Belgian and Italian technical units occupied the vital industrial region of the Ruhr Valley in January 1923 and began exacting reparations in kind. No longer a military threat, Berlin ordered passive civilian resistance, but tensions were high. Violence broke out on both sides, in fact, as the French fired on striking workers, killing twelve, and the people struck back by attacking French sentries and committing deadly acts of sabotage. As winter turned to spring, France sent in more troops. Sir Eric Drummond, general secretary of the League of Nations, watched the debacle in helpless frustration and dismay, for all three occupying powers had seats on the League Council and refused under any conditions to discuss the crisis.

Solutions to European peace would have to originate outside Geneva. This began to happen in late 1923 as a worried American business community and the sympathetic administration of President Warren G. Harding surveyed the shambles of Europe's economy. Germany was unwilling (and probably unable) to make reparation payments to Britain, France, Italy, and other victors; Britain, France, and Italy were unable to repay war debts to the United States without reparations; and an upward-spiraling inflation and international tensions over the Ruhr invasion threatened to ruin interdependent transatlantic finances. Therefore an allied commission of banking experts chaired by Chicagoan Charles Dawes began to discuss solutions in January 1924 that won European-wide approval by August. The so-called Dawes Plan granted Germany a two-year reparations moratorium with reduced payments for another two years but made in German marks rather than hard-to-obtain gold or foreign currencies, as Versailles had stipulated. A private American loan to Germany would facilitate repayment and revitalize domestic investment, while a similar loan to France would be made as soon as it evacuated the Ruhr, smoothed over relations with Germany, and agreed to arbitrate any future reparations dispute. The coincidence of economic self-interest and the democratic culture of negotiation and compromise worked to facilitate diplomatic understanding.

In October 1925 five of Europe's democratic states built on the pacific momentum of the Dawes Plan with a series of remarkable agreements in the Swiss resort town of Locarno. France, Belgium, and Germany recognized the permanence of their respective borders, publicly renounced the use of military force against one another, and agreed to submit all future disputes to international arbitration supervised by the League. Germany remained adamantly opposed to the way borders had been redrawn in the east but nevertheless signed arbitration treaties with Czechoslovakia and Poland, thereby tacitly renouncing the use of force against its eastern neighbors. Finally, the Locarno deliberations paved the way for German entry to the League with a permanent seat on its executive council.

On September 8, 1926, German delegates entered the assembly hall of the League in Geneva, where German chancellor Gustav Stresemann asserted proudly that his nation and its former enemies were now gathering in "permanent and peaceful cooperation."[41] The world was not a perfect place in 1926—witness the fall that year of democratic regimes in Poland and Lithuania; the nationalist opposition looking over Stresemann's shoulder in Germany; the presence of Benito Mussolini's inherently militaristic Fascist regime in Italy; the suspicious, anticapitalist policy of the Soviet Union; and irate antiwestern movements in Japan—but in 1926 optimism was paramount, and with good reason, for the dust of the Great War had finally settled.

NOTES

1. Charles Seymour, *The Intimate Papers of Colonel House* (Boston, 1928), 4:118–200; and Inga Floto, *Colonel House in Paris: A Study of American Policy at the Paris Peace Conference 1919* (Copenhagen, Denmark, 1973), 25–60.

2. Citations in Seymour, *Intimate Papers,* 4:195, 161; and Floto, *Colonel House in Paris,* 59.
3. Cited in Seymour, *Intimate Papers,* 4:162–166.
4. Cited in Floto, *Colonel House in Paris,* 42.
5. Citations in Robert K. Massie, *Nicholas and Alexandra* (New York, 1967), 520; and Seymour, *Intimate Papers,* 4:118–119.
6. Citations in Floto, *Colonel House in Paris,* 55; and Seymour, *Intimate Papers,* 4:185, 170–171, 196.
7. Cited in Seymour, *Intimate Papers,* 4:188.
8. For the Russian civil war to early 1919, see Adam B. Ulam, *The Bolsheviks: The Intellectual and Political History of the Triumph of Communism in Russia* (New York, 1965), 414–446; Evan Mawdsley, *The Russian Civil War* (Boston, 1987), 3–193; W. Bruce Lincoln, *Red Victory: A History of the Russian Civil War* (New York, 1989), 25–193; Orlando Figes, *A People's Tragedy: The Russian Revolution 1891–1924* (New York, 1996), 555–654; and Robert L. Willett, *Russian Sideshow: America's Undeclared War 1918–1920* (Washington, DC, 2003), xix–xxxiii, 3–176.
9. Cited in Lincoln, *Red Victory,* 146.
10. Citations in Lincoln, *Red Victory,* 163, 183.
11. Citations in Mawdsley, *Russian Civil War,* 127–128, but also see Floto, *Colonel House in Paris,* 115, 185; and Margaret Macmillan, *Peacemakers: The Paris Peace Conference and Its Attempt to End War* (London, 2001), 71–88.
12. For recent discussions of the Paris negotiations discussed below, see Macmillan, *Peacemakers,* 61–88, 167–214; and David Stevenson, *Cataclysm: The First World War as Political Tragedy* (New York, 2004) 409–430. For citations, see Macmillan, *Peacemakers,* 65.
13. Citations in Mawdsley, *Russian Civil War,* 130; and Seymour, *Intimate Papers,* 4:348.
14. Cited in Macmillan, *Peacemakers,* 82.
15. For Foch's designs, see Floto, *Colonel House in Paris,* 115–119.
16. Macmillan, *Peacemakers,* 195; and John Maynard Keynes's 1920 estimate in William R. Keylor, *The Legacy of the Great War: Peacemaking, 1919* (Boston, 1998), 128–129.
17. The Fontainebleau memorandum is reprinted in Arthur S. Link, ed., *The Papers of Woodrow Wilson* (Princeton, NJ, 1987), 56:259–265, and Clemenceau's reply in Link, ed., *The Deliberations of the Council of Four (March 24-June 29, 1919): Notes of the Official Interpreter* (Princeton, NJ, 1992), 1:31–38. Both documents can also be found in Keylor, *Legacy of the Great War,* 32–46.
18. For these points, see John M. Barry, *The Great Influenza: The Epic Story of the Deadliest Plague in History* (New York, 2004), 382–388; and David Fromkin, *A Peace to End All Peace: The Fall of the Ottoman Empire and the Creation of the Modern Middle East* (New York, 1989), 375.
19. Citations in Macmillan, *Peacemakers,* 197, 471, 476, 478–479.
20. Cited in Erich Eyck, *A History of the Weimar Republic,* trans. Harlon P. Hanson and Robert G. L. Waite, (New York, 1970), 1:138. For good accounts (along with Eyck's two volumes) of the postwar period, and Weimar in general, see Klaus Epstein, *Matthias Erzberger and the Dilemma of German Democracy* (Princeton, NJ, 1959), 284–398; Detlev J. K. Peukert, *The Weimar Republic: The Crisis of Classical Modernity,* trans. Richard Deveson (New York, 1989); and Richard Bessel, *Germany after the First World War* (Oxford, 1993).
21. For this line of reasoning see above all Jay Winter and Blaine Baggett, *The Great War and the Shaping of the Twentieth Century* (New York, 1996).
22. Cited in Lincoln, *Red Victory,* 251, and for the last stages of the civil war, 197–328. Also see Mawdsley, *Russian Civil War,* 132–229; and Figes, *People's Tragedy,* 653–682.
23. Cited in Lincoln, *Red Victory,* 261.
24. Cited in Mawdsley, *Russian Civil War,* 150.
25. Cited in ibid., 169.

26. Cited in Lincoln, *Red Victory*, 223.
27. Cited in ibid., 225.
28. Cited in Mawdsley, *Russian Civil War*, 164.
29. Isaac Deutscher, *The Prophet Armed: Trotsky 1879–1921* (New York, 1965), 458.
30. See Catherine Merridale, *Night of Stone: Death and Memory in Twentieth-Century Russia* (Oxford, 2000), 111–112, 160.
31. V. Stanley Vardys, cited in Ivan T. Berend, *Decades of Crisis: Central and Eastern Europe before World War Two* (Los Angeles, 1998), 162. For the rise of democracy after the Great War and problems associated with this, see Eric Dorn Brose, *A History of Europe in the Twentieth Century* (New York, 2005), 148–166.
32. The League Covenant is printed in numerous sources. See George Scott, *The Rise and Fall of the League of Nations* (New York, 1973), 407–418; and Gary B. Ostrower, *The League of Nations: From 1919 to 1929* (Garden City Park, New York, 1996), 19–25.
33. Citations in John Morton Blum, *Woodrow Wilson and the Politics of Morality* (Boston, 1956), 159, 169.
34. For this point, see Sharon Korman, *The Right of Conquest: The Acquisition of Territory by Force in International Law and Practice* (Oxford, 1996), 180–192; and Ward Thomas, *The Ethics of Destruction: Norms and Force in International Relations* (Ithaca, NY, 2001), 1–45.
35. For the following passage, see Macmillan, *Peacemakers*, 119–145, 240–253, 265–280, 288–314; Philip Longworth, *The Making of Eastern Europe* (New York, 1994), 65–94; and Paul Lendavi, *The Hungarians: A Thousand Years of Victory in Defeat* (Princeton, NJ, 1999), 356–388.
36. Citations in Elmer Bendiner, *A Time for Angels: The Tragicomic History of the League of Nations* (New York, 1975), 164; and James Barros, *Office Without Power: Secretary-General Sir Eric Drummond 1919–1933* (Oxford, 1979), 29–30.
37. For the Russo-Polish War, see Mawdsley, *Russian Civil War*, 250–261; and Lincoln, *Red Victory*, 392–421.
38. Cited in Scott, *Rise and Fall of the League of Nations*, 58.
39. Cited in Waclaw Jedrzejewicz, *Pilsudski: A Life for Poland* (New York, 1982), 185.
40. See Spencer R. Weart, *Never at War: Why Democracies Will Not Fight One Another* (New Haven, CT, 1998).
41. Cited in Ostrower, *League of Nations*, 70.

CHAPTER XII

The Problematic Legacy of the Great War in the Wider World

1918–1926

Early in the morning of September 30, 1918, Lawrence and his entourage left Deraa for Damascus. All around them an Arab army dispatched the miserable remnants of the harried Turkish Fourth Army. The blue-mist-colored Rolls Royce finally halted for the night in the hills outside the ancient city. Liman von Sanders's columns had hurriedly evacuated that day, leaving only demolition crews behind to destroy ammunition supplies. Although tired, Feisal's advance guard got no sleep from the endless succession of explosions. "Damascus is burning," Lawrence said sadly. "At each such roar the earth seemed to shake; we would lift our eyes to the north and see the pale sky prick out suddenly in sheaves of yellow points as the shells, thrown to terrific heights from each bursting magazine, in their turn burst like clustered rockets."[1]

The next morning "Urens" and his Arab compatriots were happy to see that Damascus was mostly unscathed. "The silent gardens stood blurred green with river mist, in whose setting shimmered the city, beautiful as ever, like a pearl in the morning sun." Presently they were motoring again, down a steep-banked road, through the gates, and into the government district by the river. Their way was packed with hundreds of people by the roadside, at windows, and on rooftops and balconies, cheering at the dawning moment of Arab liberation and independence.

At the Town Hall, however, the specter of Arab factiousness raised its ugly head to mock the notion of independence. Feisal had chosen the man to head his political organizing committee in Damascus wisely: Shukri el Ayubi, beloved by Damascenes as a martyr to Djemal's wartime cruelty. But a faction of Algerians exiled a generation earlier for resisting the French stepped forward to form the government. Conveniently forgetting their support for the Turks, they proclaimed Sherif Hussein "King of the Arabs." When Lawrence backed Shukri, the Algerian leader, white with rage, pulled a dagger and was only cowed when mighty Auda of the Howeitat pulled his. The great warrior had made many enemies, among them Sultan el Atrash, chief of the Lebanese Druse, who struck Auda, which immediately touched off a brawl. It took Lawrence and four men to separate the thrashing pair, remove Auda to an adjacent room, and a further hour to calm him to the point of agreeing to delay his revenge for three days. "We must prove the old days over," said the courageous Briton, who put his full authority behind Shukri until Feisal could make his triumphal entry on October 3rd.

With Arab unity patched together for now, he set off in the blue Rolls with Shukri, who was descended from Saladin the Great and whose appearance in the streets "was itself a banner of revolution for the citizens." The crowds had swelled to ten times the thousands that greeted them on the way in, the whole city "mad with joy."

> The men tossed up their tarbushes to cheer, the women tore off their veils, and householders threw flowers, hangings, and carpets into the road before us: their wives leaned through the lattices, screaming with laughter, and splashed us with bath-dippers of scent.

Lawrence understood the delirium well, for he knew what a free Damascus meant to the Arabs. Prior to the coming of the Mameluke Sultans and the Ottoman Turks this city had been Saladin's capital and, before that, seat of the Omayyad caliphs of the Prophet's day. The power of Islam extended from Damascus to make enemies tremble as far away as Spain and southern France. What had been could be again.

A "PEACE TO END ALL PEACE": THE MIDDLE EAST AND CENTRAL ASIA, 1919–1922

The Great War had one of its most profound and long-lasting impacts on the territories of the Ottoman Empire and those other lands from Egypt to Afghanistan and northern India that Istanbul had hoped to bring under its Turkic wing. It was not the Turkish but rather the British agenda, however, that appeared destined for implementation as the victors gathered in Paris. Britain had over a million troops on the ground in the Middle East proper. Cairo, Jerusalem, Damascus, and Baghdad flew the Union Jack; French leader Georges Clemenceau was willing to cut deals over Syria and Iraq; and Britain's Arab ally, the House of Hashem of Sherif Hussein and his sons, waxed proud of its wartime exploits, feeling confident that political rewards would follow. Indeed London, in its panicky mood of June 1918, had gone well beyond the hedged-about pledges of 1915 to offer the Arabs "complete and sovereign independence" in return for aid against the Turks. In early October, moreover, the British recognized the Arabs as co-belligerents, an honor that carried with it the implicit right to a voice in the peace talks. And then in a joint statement with the French government on November 7, 1918, London promised "the complete and definite freedom of the peoples so long oppressed by the Turks, and the establishment of national governments and administrations deriving their authority from the initiative and free choice of the native population."[2] Hussein's son Feisal accepted British rule in Palestine, furthermore, and even the eventuality of a British-fostered and British-administered Jewish homeland there. In short, there was little or no indication in early 1919 that peacetime in the Middle East would be the troubled "peace to end all peace"[3] that came. Only on the periphery in Egypt and across the Afghan-Indian border did storm clouds gather.

The Egyptian Riots

Through four years of war and Turko-German Jihad the British rear areas in Egypt stayed relatively calm. There may have existed what one British officer identified as a "bitter if silent hatred"[4] of the British wartime protectorate, but neither the approach of a Turkish-Bedouin army to the Suez Canal in early 1915, the Senussi invasion from Tripolitania (Libya) in early 1916, nor a web of enemy agents throughout the land seriously destabilized the Egyptian home front. In weighing their options, of course, Egyptian patriots had no reason to desire a return to the Turkish yoke or submit to Libyan fundamentalists when independence was the goal and the British had said repeatedly over the years that this would eventually happen. Just two months after the armistice, therefore, one of Egypt's leading nationalists, Saad Zaghlul, began to whip up mass support for "complete autonomy" to be negotiated by a delegation sent to Paris headed by him. Were not the Egyptians "an ancient and capable race with a glorious past—far more capable of conducting a well-ordered government than the Arabs, Syrians, and [Iraqis], to whom self-government had so recently been promised?"[5] he asked rhetorically.

The British High Commissioner in Cairo, Sir Reginald Wingate, resisted Zaghlul's demands, first privately in November 1918, then more publicly in January by forbidding the aging leader to give speeches and finally by arresting and deporting him on March 9, 1919. The following day demonstrations and strikes shook the cities and towns, spreading rapidly into the normally passive countryside. On March 18 eight military personnel were murdered on a train, prompting nervous British officialdom to have nightmares about violence rising to the scale of the Indian Mutiny of 1857. From Aswan to Cairo Britain had "no means of regaining control,"[6] cabled a panicky Wingate.

General Edmund Allenby was summoned a week later with the portfolio of Special High Commissioner. The pragmatic soldier studied the situation for a time, and then, contrary to London wisdom, wisely released Zaghlul from custody on April 7. The rioting ratcheted downward over the spring and summer of 1919 as Allenby, and later the Colonial Office in London, began negotiations with Zaghlul and his Wafd Party in order to achieve some kind of compromise. Britain could not afford to abandon this country and its invaluable canal. Nor could it afford a full-scale rebellion, on the other hand, lest it be forced somehow to learn, as Lawrence of Arabia had put it, "to eat soup with a knife."

Amritsar and the Third Afghan War

The unwelcome prospect of a raging insurgency also worried British leaders in India. London had avoided the scary scenario of wartime implosion in its huge subcontinental colony by intimidating and buying off the clever Emir Habibullah of Afghanistan and sniffing out and stifling insurrection plots before they happened. In August 1917, furthermore, Britain announced that after hostilities it would strive for "the increasing association of Indians in every branch of the administration and the gradual development of self-governing institutions with a view to the progressive realization of responsible government in India as an integral part of the British Empire."[7] Britain had promised India, in other words, that it would be placed on the path of autonomy and self-government traveled for decades before the war by the white dominions of Canada, Australia, New Zealand, and South Africa.

Because the details of the so-called Montagu-Chelmsford Reforms were not worked out by Parliament until late 1919, however, and not scheduled to take effect until 1920–1921, the moderating effects of these changes could not counterbalance the radicalizing impact of another, extremely ill-advised policy, the so-called Rowlatt Acts of early 1919, which continued the wartime practice into peacetime of imprisoning suspected subversives without trial. As February gave way to March, violent protests spread through the land, uniting Muslim, Hindu, and Sikh against British rule. With control slipping away, especially in the northern Punjab province, army authorities proclaimed martial law, banned further rallies, and then on April 13, 1919, fired on defiant demonstrators at Amritsar. "The panic stricken multitude broke at once," observed a British journalist, but the soldiers "kept up a merciless fusillade on that seething mass of humanity, caught like rats in a trap."[8] Over five hundred people were killed or wounded. The inhumane brutality of this incident lengthened the list of Great War atrocities against civilians and reflected the sad state to which humanity had sunk, numbed as so much of it was to bloodshed. That the commanding officer, General Reginald Dyer, believed that he had no other way to restore order also reflected the near inevitability that India would someday become free—it did in 1947. One recent, rather shameless apologia for Dyer, however, gets at least a few things correct: the demonstration was political, not a religious festival as sometimes portrayed; the ringleaders knew of the ban on meetings; and the violence did, in fact, subside as Indians resigned themselves for the time being to autonomy under the new constitution.[9]

Amritsar factors into post-Great War world history in another significant way, for this massacre probably triggered the Third Afghan War.[10] Pressure for action against British India had been mounting in the mountainous kingdom after Habibullah finally fell victim to assassins on February 20, 1919. Although the plot remains obscure, both schools of thought on its origins see the regicide as an act of revenge by the Afghan war party against the emir's unpopular policy of neutrality during a conflict fought by the Christian West against Istanbul, seat of the Islamic caliphate. Turkey's defeat and occupation by allied forces, coupled with the loss of holy Mecca and Medina to Hussein's pro-British Arab clan, deepened the sense of humiliation among Muslims in Afghanistan and across the Indian border (i.e., in present-day Pakistan). Habibullah's son, Amanullah, championed these feelings, but despite obvious bad blood for England the new emir initiated peaceful relations with Britain's Indian viceroy. In a statement of March 3, 1919, for instance, he broke new diplomatic ground by boldly referring to Afghanistan as a "free and independent" country but also expressing his willingness to sign treaties of friendship and trade. So was he, as the British later charged, already secretly plotting to invade India?

On the contrary, the Egyptian riots and concomitant disturbances in India, climaxing with the terrible shootings at Amritsar, seem more likely to have rushed him into an attack that would have fared much better had it occurred at the height of the protests, that is, before the British cracked down. At any rate, in late April Amanullah ordered three regular army strike forces to the border, altogether about twenty thousand infantrymen with accompanying cavalry and artillery. Afghan tribesmen near the staging areas of Kandahar, Khost, and Khyber swelled the ranks of the emir's holy warriors by many thousands. Tribesmen across the border were also encouraged to join the Jihad. "I ask you if you are prepared for holy war. If so, gird up your lions! The time has come!"[11]

Other indications of overhasty preparations occurred on May 3, 1919. That day the vanguard of the first strike force at the Khyber Pass blocked a British column from proceeding and justified their action by presenting Amanullah's Holy War Proclamation (Jihad Firman). Unfortunately, this alerted Britain to Afghan intentions before the main groups were prepared to attack or Indian rebels in nearby Peshawar ready to rise up. Hastily planned and disadvantageously timed—as noted, the Rowlatt Acts riots had been crushed weeks earlier—Amanullah's invasion was also, not surprisingly, badly executed, with the first engagements around the Khyber Pass occurring in early May, the next incursion from Khost not until two weeks later, and the last from Kandahar never really getting under way.

The Indian army could have been caught at a very weak moment. Many divisions had returned from the Great War, but much of the Indian rank and file was being demobilized and many British officers and soldiers were on the way home. With time to react, however, Britain managed to disband politically unreliable units like the 700-strong Khyber Rifles; recall veteran personnel; and concentrate four infantry divisions (of twelve battalions each), three independent brigades, and numerous cavalry, artillery, machine gun, and airplane units on or near the northwest frontier. Although the Afghan drive from Khost caused considerable alarm, with many garrisons abandoned or besieged after heavy losses, by June the threat had been contained and the Afghans retreated to their own territory. Leaving well enough alone, the British did not pursue. The two sides negotiated a treaty in August 1919.

The Third Afghan War illuminated one of the most important results of the Great War, namely, that the old one-sided game of European imperialism had entered a new stage. Despite failing to achieve its main aim of pushing the British out of the adjacent Muslim provinces of India, Afghanistan could nevertheless claim victory in the war, for it finally broke free of decades of control by Britain and embarked on an independent course, which, although often a turbulent one, has remained independent to this day. Before 1914 only Japan had struggled out of the shackles of western domination. Afghanistan became the second as Europe, weakened by its long fratricidal conflict, began to loosen its grip on the world. Other peoples in the Middle East and Central Asia would attempt to follow Kabul's lead, and some—but not all—would succeed.

Compromised Independence for the Arabs

A perceptive newspaper reader who had kept a close eye on events in the two years since the armistice of November 1918 could not have been sanguine about the prospects for peace, order, and a new nonbelligerent way of doing things in the world. From the northeastern Adriatic; across the Hungarian plains and the borderlands of Poland, the Baltic, and White Russia; through to the Urals and Western Siberia; south into the Ukraine and the Caucasus; then farther on to the Afghan-Indian frontier, armies had trampled the guilty and the innocent, adding millions of lives to the Great War's death toll. During the summer and fall of 1920 the comparatively tranquil Middle East had also deteriorated into violence. The allies did not draft a treaty with the Ottoman Empire in 1919. They were far too preoccupied haggling over the German treaty and monitoring disturbing events in Russia to place Middle Eastern issues higher up on their agenda. The international legal question of how the victors would divide their colonial conquests caused further delays. Wilson and House made it clear in October 1918 that they favored a kind of "trusteeship" for the inhabitants of former German and Turkish holdings in the Pacific, Africa, and the Middle East, which would be administered by their conquerors in "the interests of the society of nations." Native populations could not be abused. Their interests must have "equal weight"[12] with those of the governors. All of this implied an internationally supervised process of colonial rulers preparing their wards for self-governance and eventual independence. Wilson accepted a compromise of this sort proposed by South African leader Jan Smuts in early 1919 whereby the League would monitor three categories of colonial "mandates" with the most-favored "A" peoples of the Middle East slated for reasonably fast tracks to independence. Great Britain and France were obvious choices for Middle Eastern mandates, but Wilson wanted the United States to participate in this noble mission as well. The whole issue hung undecidedly in the air, however, as the Senate rejected League membership once in November 1919, a second and final time in March, and then consistently scotched the idea of American mandates in May 1920.[13]

In the meantime, developments in the region took their own, initially very promising course. Drawn less to the lofty principles of Wilsonianism that colored his government's declaration of November 1918 than the camaraderie bonding men in arms, Allenby supported the Arab municipal government that Lawrence and Feisal set up in Damascus at the end of the military campaign. Not only this, the general also awarded the Arabs governing authority in the entire area from Aleppo over Damascus and Amman to Aqaba, where it joined Hussein's Hejaz with its southern terminus at Mecca—altogether a territorial belt 1,800 kilometers long and variously 200–400 kilometers wide.[14]

In the late fall and winter of 1918–1919 Lawrence and Feisal presented their demands and positions in London and Paris: power-sharing with the French in coastal Syria and Lebanon; Feisal as king of inland Syria and present-day Jordan; and British control of Palestine west of the Jordan River, including Jewish settlement and autonomy there. The British would control Iraq too, but with nominal Arab monarchies under Hussein's sons Zeid in the north (Kurdistan/Mosul) and Abdullah in the south (Baghdad/Basra). The two wartime comrades were mum about what role, if any, Hussein himself would play, but "the old man of Mecca," as Lawrence called him, wanted to be "King of the Arabs," uniting the four fiefdoms of the House of Hashem.[15]

Soon enough, trouble arose. When the question of League mandates came up at Paris in February 1919, for example, Feisal stressed the Arab desire for "self-determination," while Woodrow Wilson clung rigidly to the new compromise worked out with Smuts, asking the prince whether the Arabs wanted to be under the mandate of one of the "advanced nations" or part of many mandates. In what was an extremely awkward moment, Feisal must have wondered whether the president understood his own liberationist terminology. Somewhat more to his credit, Wilson suggested in March that the powers send a fact-finding commission to determine what the Arabs really wanted, but like so many commissions this one played no role except to cause further delays.

Ibn Saud, ruler of Eastern Arabia, had much less respect for the dynastic aspirations of the House of Hashem. On May 25, 1919, Hussein sent Abdullah and 5,000 well-equipped soldiers to teach lessons in respect to his rival. A Saudi advance guard of 1,100 traditionally armed tribesmen attacked the camp at night, however, mercilessly massacring all but the prince and his entourage, who managed to slip away before suffering the same grisly fate. This carnage-laden debacle did not augur well for the embryonic Hashemite Empire. Shrewd observers could not fail to notice, furthermore, that Sherifan regulars died alone that night with no British support.

British retrenchment had started to cause ominous problems, in fact, for the Hashemites. In short, Britain could no longer afford the political and financial costs of maintaining large military missions in foreign lands. Consequently, it took all troops out of Russia and most of them from the Middle East. With British strength descending from a million to a third of that, London announced in September 1919 that it would remove its garrisons from Syria too, making it necessary for Feisal to deal with the unsympathetic French. Throughout the year Clemenceau had put off grasping colonial lobbyists who recalled French participation in the alleged glories of the Crusades; pointed to the Sykes-Picot

Fie on League Mandates: Arab Demonstration in Damascus, March 8, 1920
Courtesy of the Library of Congress

agreement of 1916; and accordingly demanded a "Greater Syria" including Jerusalem, Damascus, and Mosul. Instead he let the British keep Mosul and struck a deal with Feisal to set up an Arab Syrian state pledged to accept French advisers and guarantee French interests. Later the League of Nations would sanction the arrangement as a French "A" mandate. Clemenceau fell from power in January 1920, however, leaving imperialists in Paris and Feisal's followers in Damascus both chomping at the bit of this compromise.

In Iraq problems also simmered close to the surface. In 1917 the British army proclaimed its mission as one of liberation, not occupation, but the latter seemed truer than the former three years later. Basra, Baghdad, and Mosul, three administrative districts of the Ottoman Empire with little in common, became the political responsibility of the British India Office and a civilizing tradition of noblesse oblige that rejected the idea of Hashemite kingdoms, even nominal ones, proposed by Lawrence and Feisal. This latter plan, too, faced the challenge of uniting Kurdish and Persian minorities, feuding Shia and Sunni Muslims, displaced Ottoman bureaucrats and soldiers, and independent-minded tribal clans under a government of British-protected Sunni Arab nationalists, but it stood a better chance than a British military occupation that flew in the face of London's alleged commitment to national self-determination. Already before New Year 1920 disgruntled Iraqis murdered four British officials. "It's like a nightmare," worried Middle East specialist Gertrude Bell, "in which you foresee all the horrible things which are going to happen and can't stretch out your hand to prevent them."[16]

As spring drew on to summer 1920, radicalized politics, insurgencies, counterinsurgencies, and wars, all so familiar to modern eyes, descended chaotically on the Middle East. In Damascus Feisal struggled to erect his new state, setting

Enemy at the Gates: Anti-Lebanon Mountains near Damascus
Courtesy of the Library of Congress

up public services, training the first units of a regular army, and holding elections for a congress designed to legitimize his work with an appropriate response to Wilson's fact-finding commission. Nationalist factions less realistic and accommodating than he gained control of the podium, however; spat on the notion of League mandates; and passed resolutions for Iraqi and Syrian independence, including Arab secession from British Palestine and opposition to Zionism. When the prince warned them of collision courses with France or England, the radicals shouted that they were "ready to declare war on *both* France and England."[17]

The Hotspurs got their wish that summer. French general Henri Gouraud left Beirut with an expeditionary force of nine thousand men, marched through the Bequaa Valley, and entered the Anti-Lebanon Mountains on the way to Damascus. Debouching out of the Maysalun Pass on July 23, 1920, he found his route blocked by Syrian war minister Yusuf-al-Azmah, two companies of untested regulars, and a few thousand lightly armed citizen volunteers. Feisal had counseled against resistance given the unreadiness of the army, but his prudent advice landed once again on stone-deaf ears. Gouraud sent one of his two Sengalese brigades forward behind a screen of tanks and airplanes that easily broke through the Syrians, killing four hundred of the brave hearts and wounding many more. The capital fell three days later and Feisal was sent packing into exile.

The arrogant Gouraud, who presently felt the need to hurl insults at the tomb of Saladin the Great, might have met a more cunning and deadly enemy above him in the pass had Lawrence been present with Arab veterans long since back in faraway homes and villages. As it was, the bloody one-day battle and war crushed the losers, delayed Syrian/Lebanese independence three decades, and added

Palestine for the Arabs: Anti-Jewish Demonstration in Jerusalem, April 2, 1920
Courtesy of the Library of Congress

tarnish to the record of postwar democracy. Certainly the White House could feel only disappointing sadness for the fate of worldwide democracy, even if Wilson himself had not trusted in the readiness of Feisal's people to govern themselves. Indeed had not France, the country of established government by the people, smashed the aspirations for popular rule, however rash and unlikely, of the Syrian Arabs? This standard of behavior had always been, and would remain for decades, the great contradiction and inconsistency—the great double standard—of European imperialism.

This was how Lawrence saw it in early August as he struggled to understand the escalation of violence in neighboring Iraq. "It would show a lack of humor if we reproved [the French] for a battle near Damascus and the blotting out of the Syrian essay in self-government," he wrote in *The Times*, "while we were fighting battles near Baghdad and trying to render the Mesopotamians incapable of self-government by smashing every head that raised itself among them."[18] Two months earlier Britain's announcement of intent to accept a League mandate for Iraq had triggered a revolt that quickly spread. Tribesmen, ethnic minorities, and patriotic veterans of three years of military operations ambushed British columns, seized garrisons, cut telegraph wires, blew up trains, and executed prisoners. The occupiers lashed back, hanging rebel leaders who tried to form a provisional government and systematically shelling and strafing scores of villages that formed the scattered centers of the insurgency. By early 1921 Britain had more than 100,000 soldiers in Iraq who accomplished their draconian mission of reimposing order—at a cost, however, of nearly 2,000 casualties. Lawrence put the horrific figure of dead Iraqis at 10,000.

Watching from London as the Middle East boiled over, Colonial Secretary Winston Churchill knew that a long-term political solution must take the place of his nation's costly short-term military strategy. An intensive conference in Cairo worked out the details of a regional solution in March 1921. "All authorities have reached agreement on all the points, both political and military,"[19] Churchill wired London after the last of almost fifty sessions in four days. Jordan was separated from British-controlled Palestine at the river to become an almost entirely independent monarchy under Abdullah, whose younger brother would be king of Iraq in its present-day boundaries. Feisal's authority was circumscribed by a continued British military presence, however, given Britain's economic and strategic interests in this oil-rich land.

Meanwhile, Allenby pressured Zaghlul's nationalists for similar pro-British arrangements in the land of the vital Suez Canal. He applied the traditional carrot and the stick, splitting the Wafd Party with concessions to the moderates and police suppression of diehards who, like Zaghlul himself, wanted Egypt to be free of foreign rule. The so-called Declaration of Independence of February 28, 1922, established a third Arab constitutional monarchy under Ahmed Fu 'ad, the former sultan in Egypt. Under this compromise British troops remained and British citizens continued to enjoy extraterritorial legal rights.[20]

The Third Afghan War, the Syrian-Iraqi troubles, and the Cairo declarations of 1921 and 1922 put much of the modern stamp on the Middle East and Central Asia—an independent Afghanistan; separate Arab-populated states in Egypt, Jordan, Syria/Lebanon, and Iraq that joined the ranks of independent nations after World War Two; and a separate Palestine struggling unsuccessfully under British rule, as it would under Israeli after 1948, to reconcile the conflicting claims and aspirations of Jews and Palestinian Arabs.

Iran became independent too after Reza Pahlavi seized power in February 1921, immediately afterward abrogating all of Britain's economic privileges. The shrewd commander of the Persian Cossack Brigade assumed correctly that London would not punish him after it had demonstrated two years earlier how unprepared it was to reestablish controls in Afghanistan.

Ibn Saud also studied British retrenchment and demobilization in the Middle East, expanding his power base throughout Arabia during the early 1920s without significant interference from the West. In the process his 150,000 Wahabi tribesmen overran the entire Hejaz, claimed the holy cities for the House of Saud, and chased the unenviable Sherif Hussein into exile. This latest military campaign to bloody the postwar world resulted in today's Saudi Arabia, the third state in the region to acquire full independence as a result of the Great War.[21]

Turks, Armenians, and Greeks

After numerous delays, the victors finally imposed a settlement on Ottoman Sultan Mehmed VI in early August 1920.[22] The Treaty of Serves sanctioned the "mandated" takeover by France and Britain of much of the Arab Middle East; gave autonomy to the Kurds and independence to the Armenians, the two abused minorities of Eastern Anatolia; placed the straits under international control; and ceded Thrace, Turkey's Aegean Islands, as well as Smyrna and its hinterland to

Greece. This Hellenic foothold on the coast of Asia Minor was not to become permanent until a plebiscite was held, but Greek occupation of Smyrna fifteen months earlier and subsequent military buildup there exposed their intention to hold on to it and push inland when ready. Finally, Sevres sanctioned Turkish and British legal proceedings under way against much of Turkey's wartime leadership for mistreatment of POWs and the killing of Armenians and Greeks.

Sevres was a devastating and highly resented blow to the once mighty Ottoman Empire, but already for over a year protests triggered by the Greek landings in Asia Minor and the first trials and executions of former Young Turks had been mounting. This trouble turned to open resistance in late 1919 after Turkish patriots got wind of the allied treaty agenda. At first their anger manifested itself politically with defiant nationalistic resolutions in Istanbul. After New Year 1920, however, a bold new leader, veteran general Mustafa Kemal, began to reorganize the army and prepare to renew hostilities. Younger captains and colonels rallied to his standard, seized surrendered weapons from poorly guarded allied depots, and distributed them to hard-core rank-and-file types who yearned for a return to the violence and camaraderie of wartime, especially with a good cause to uphold.

First Kemal sent elements of his remodeled army south. Already with an impressive thirty thousand men in arms on February 28, 1920, he crushed the French at Marash in Southern Anatolia. That spring successive hammer blows inflicted more heavy losses on Gouraud's outnumbered Army of the Levant and pushed it across the border into Syria. The turn of the Armenians came next. Instead of recognizing the independence of Eastern Anatolia as mandated by Sevres, Kemal's rejuvenated forces used it as a staging area for an invasion of the neighboring Democratic Republic of Armenia. From September to November 1920 a Turkish corps of fifteen thousand took Sarikamish, Kars, Alexandropol, and Erivan while the Red Army moved in from the east, snuffing out the last hope of this hapless people.

Indeed the experience of the Great War and its violent aftermath was especially galling to the Armenians. After at least a million countrymen perished in the wartime atrocities and Enver Pasha's Army of Islam overran the newly independent Caucasus in 1918, peace and independence had returned. Along with this came the promise of self-determination proclaimed by Wilson and the expectation, in fact, that America would hold its hand over the troubled area by accepting a League mandate that would actually amount to something more than cloaked colonialism. But the U.S. Senate, the Turks, and the Soviets swept all of this away during a terrible six months of 1920. The promise of justice from war crimes trials also dissipated that year as Kemal's aggressive nationalist backlash induced first the impotent government of the sultan and then the British in their turn to cancel further trials and release scores of indicted Young Turks.[23] The only real justice to come to the Armenians they took themselves by hunting down and assassinating Djemal and Talaat Pasha, two members of the wartime triumvirate, and others in 1921 and 1922.

These two years also witnessed vigilante justice between Greeks and Turks but on a horrifically larger scale. By the summer of 1921 a Greek army totaling two hundred thousand (i.e., eight–nine combat divisions) had extended its zone of control up the river valleys from Smyrna to the fringes of the Anatolian plateau. That July they launched a major offensive that pushed the outnumbered Turks into the flatland and then, after regrouping for a second assault in August, across the heavily fortified Sakarya River near Ankara. The Greeks accomplished this feat but only after unsustainable losses compounded by a lengthy supply line—they had advanced three hundred kilometers from the coast. Now the weary invaders fell back into the plateau, pursued by Kemal's vengeful legions, for the Greek soldiers had ravaged the land and its Turkish inhabitants during the 1920 and 1921 campaigns.

In August 1922 the Turks shuffed the Greeks off the flatland and back down the valleys to Smyrna and its Greek-inhabited environs, where terrible retribution took place. The Greek-Turkish War killed about 50,000 soldiers but left higher civilian casualties in its wake—perhaps 200,000 victims of ethnic cleansing on both sides. When it was over Kemal's nationalist movement had defeated the enemy, successfully defied the Treaty of Sevres, which was renegotiated in Turkey's favor the following year at Lausanne, and forced an orderly deportation of 1.5 million Greeks from Asia Minor. Only now did relative calm descend on the Middle East.

Thus Mustafa Kemal, not his onetime nemesis and Young Turk rival Enver Pasha, became the "Father of the Turks," the forger of modern Turkey, and the one who avoided the funeral that European powers had long desired for Turkey, the alleged "Sick Old Man of Europe." As for Enver, the former war minister and power boss fled to Berlin, from there to Moscow, and ultimately to Bukhara in Russian Turkestan. He had not abandoned his dream of a Turkish imperium, which he hoped to build upon the foundation of warlike Turkic-speaking peoples in the region. Units of the Red Army killed him leading a hopeless cavalry charge in August 1922.[24]

AFTER THE GREAT WAR IN THE WIDER WORLD

The war that erupted in 1914 resulted from a European power struggle that had been escalating on the continent for decades. After Great Britain committed to France and Russia in August, however, and Turkey to Germany in November, a conflict whose operations would otherwise have been thrashed out in Europe with limited colonial campaigns in Africa between Germany on the one side and France and Belgium on the other became a terrible worldwide war, its tentacles spreading rapidly into the Middle East; Central Asia; the Pacific, where Japan's entry intensified the fighting; and Africa, where British belligerency guaranteed a much bloodier conflagration throughout the dark continent. Turkey's declaration of war was a major coup for Germany, one that certainly enhanced Berlin's chances in a genuine global struggle, but there can be no doubt that the world war that came in 1914 was one for which Germany was sorely and irresponsibly unprepared. Its ships were quickly sunk throughout the seven seas, its island holdings in the Pacific seized by Australia, New Zealand, and Japan, and the core of its overseas empire in Africa—huge land masses many times the size of the fatherland—captured.

Africa

France, Britain, South Africa, and their victimized ally Belgium expected massive territorial returns from their wartime efforts in Africa. German Togoland had fallen to British and French forces in 1914; Southwest Africa to the new South African army in 1915; Cameroon to an Anglo-French expedition in early 1916; and East Africa, defended by Paul von Lettow-Vorbeck's valiant fighters, finally overrun by Anglo-Indian, South African, and Belgian units by the end of 1917.

Woodrow Wilson and Jan Smuts worked out the legal details of transferring these conquests to the victors soon after the peace conference began in Paris. Next to the "A" League mandates of former Ottoman holdings in the Middle East, only two of which (Jordan and Iraq) came even remotely close to the eventual independence promised under this arrangement, Wilson and Smuts placed the "B" and "C" mandates of what had been German Africa. The "C" category they reserved for peoples so unready for self-determination that they would likely remain indefinitely dependent on the mandatory power. In Africa this status applied only to Southwest Africa and its overlord, South Africa. "B" mandates fell vaguely between the statuses of the other two. These were Togoland and Cameroon, both divided between France and Britain, and East Africa, now called Tanganyika, divided between Britain and Belgium.

Smuts described the reality of Pretoria's Southwest Africa mandate as "annexation in all but name," a frank appraisal that seemed apt for the other African mandates too. In faraway Geneva League officials established a supervisory commission to ensure humane rule in all mandates, but it had no right to demand access to a mandated territory during investigations of abuses, having to rely solely on information supplied by the mandatory power itself. "This was equivalent to doing cancer studies," writes one historian, "by relying exclusively on data supplied by the tobacco companies."[25] The Mandatory Commission also had no power to enforce its edicts in the unlikely event that it found anything amiss. In short, the situation in Africa after the Great War became exactly what Colonel House in October 1918 had feared it might become—a revival of old-school colonialism "in all but name."

The victors had good reason to appreciate the power-political worth of the spoils they had won. Indeed Britain, France, and Belgium had benefited significantly from their colonial manpower, an asset that would be augmented by the new acquisitions.[26] Through voluntary enlistment as well as conscription, France raised at least 483,000 soldiers from Algeria, Senegal-Niger, Madagascar, and other African colonies, although some push the figure as high as 600,000. French *askari* served in the Middle East, the Balkans, and the western front in great numbers—135,000 in the latter theater—but were used primarily to keep order, suppress revolts, and overrun German colonies in Africa. When Africans fighting in British and Belgian ranks are added, the total hovers just short of a million, roughly equivalent to the 1,000,038 Canadians, Anzacs, and white South Africans who shipped overseas from 1914 to 1918 or the 827,000 frontline soldiers and 446,000 noncombatants recruited into the Indian army. The contributions of allied colonials to winning the Great War—the "imperial surplus" that Germany could not match—has been emphasized repeatedly in this study.

However, ten times as many Africans as Indians were dragooned into the dreaded carrier corps or porter battalions—at least a million—and as many died in these columns as in combat—at least one hundred thousand. One expert writes of the "reeking mud and blinding dust" through which the black porters struggled. "The saga is remembered in African folklore, and should be noted by a world grown callous by so many instances of humble people being plunged by national rivalries into even greater depths of woe."[27]

Given the degree of exploitation and suffering in a war caused by (and fought exclusively for the purposes of) alien Europeans, it begs explanation why one finds so few traces in Sub-Sahara Africa of the postwar revolt against European rule so apparent in the Middle East and Central Asia.[28] To be sure, disorders swept the Belgian Congo in 1920 and 1921 under the leadership of millenarian anticolonial rebel Simon Kimbangu. Simultaneously in neighboring British Rhodesia, Nyasaland, and Tanganyika, the "African Watchtower" movement of Tomo Nyirenda, who called himself "the son of God," challenged authorities and propagated the same message of "Africa for the Africans." Kimbanguism slowly died out with the prophet's arrest and imprisonment in September 1921, however, and African Watchtower fell apart a few years later after the capture and execution of Nyirenda. Both failed revolts confirmed the lesson of John Chilembwe's abortive 1915 rising in Nyasaland, namely, that the Europeans were still too strong to be overthrown, which helps to explain why others wisely opted not to risk it. Returning allied *askari* who had seen the potency of modern weapons were among the prudent, choosing to oppose their own chiefs for joining in what has been labeled "the new slave trade"[29] of the porter battalions rather than rise up against the European powers. The explanation for black Africa's comparative passivity also extends to tribal/ethnic rivalries that dissipated anticolonial energies—witness the zeal of many Nigerians to participate in the conquest of German Cameroon—and clever imperial policies like the establishment of representative institutions by the French, and later the British too, throughout West Africa.

We find closer parallels to the anti-imperial disruptions of the Middle East in the northern parts of Africa. These peoples were Muslim too, and they struggled against European infidels with the same ethnoreligious intensity. Indeed the Mahdists of the Sudan, the Senussi of Libya, and the Rif of Morocco had fought against the foreigners on their soil before the Great War began. Now this ill-fated fight continued, emboldened and intensified by the belief that wartime losses had weakened Europe, given added justification and legitimation by the Wilsonian rhetoric of self-determination that buzzed around the world.

Abdullah al-Sihayni picked up the cudgel of the Mahdi and Ali Dinar in Darfur in September 1921, sending five thousand warriors against the British. Sihayni was captured and hung in October, but his small army of followers was not subdued until May 1922. By this time the Senussi had enjoyed virtual independence from Italy for five years. The rise to power of Benito Mussolini and the Fascists quickly undid this, however, for they reconquered western Libya (Tripolitania) in the winter of 1922–1923 and then more gradually tightened the noose around Senussi strongholds in the eastern provinces (Cyrenaica), throwing some eighty thousand unfortunates into deadly concentration camps.

Like the Senussi, the Rif of Morocco appeared initially to have succeeded in their dream of expelling the infidels. For six days in July 1921 Abdel Karim and an army of 10,000 cut off and butchered a larger Spanish column at Anwal in the Atlas Mountains. Spain's "Adowa" cost it 15,000 dead and many thousands wounded or captured—the worst defeat inflicted on the Europeans in the history of imperialism on the entire continent of Africa. Karim crushed the Spanish almost as badly at Shafshawin in November 1924. Having built up his forces to an impressive 60,000, he pushed into French Morocco in April 1925, calculating that French weariness with war since 1918, and Muslim disaffection behind French lines, would enable his freedom fighters to sweep all before them. But he miscalculated. France and Spain joined forces, mobilized 280,000 troops in their adjacent colonies, compelled Karim's surrender, and sent him into exile.

THE BRITISH DOMINIONS, THE FAR EAST, AND THE UNITED STATES, 1919–1922

Just as it significantly impacted Central Asia, India, the Middle East, and Africa, the Great War also affected the British dominions. The long four-year struggle did not so much create new relationships in the empire, however, as much as greatly accelerate trends long under way.[30] For many decades before 1914, Canada, Australia, and New Zealand had enjoyed self-governing autonomy in their domestic affairs while willingly submitting to London in matters of foreign policy and defense. The Union of South Africa adhered to these impressive traditions when it came into being in 1910. Given the strong cultural and historical bonds to the mother country, making common military cause came naturally. The first imperial military cooperation occurred during the Boer War (1899–1902) as more than eighty thousand Canadians, Anzacs, and white South Africans took their places in line. Moreover, when Britain removed ships from the Far East after signing an alliance with Japan in 1902—a move that unnerved Australia and New Zealand lest Japanese friendship prove false in the long run—both countries clamored to fill the perceived naval vacuum. Queensland contributed subsidies for a battle cruiser, HMS. *New Zealand,* to bolster Pacific and Indian Ocean defenses, and Cape Town followed suit after the union went into effect. Sydney actually launched a ten-ship navy in 1913 around the flagship battle cruiser *Australia.* Canada appropriated funds for construction of its own ships too, but the vessels were not yet afloat before the war. Both of these dominion fleets were to fall under the operational command of the British Admiralty. When Britain's declaration of war met universal enthusiastic approval and support in the dominions, therefore, it represented an unsurprising culmination of developments anchored in the prewar period.

The wartime years of hardship, sacrifice, maiming, and death placed all belligerent regimes under political pressure to alter or reform the status quo, and this unavoidable dynamic affected Britain's imperial relations too. In India, whose men served in massive numbers, native politicians insisted on progress to full dominion status. Britain nudged its most important colony slightly in this direction but did not avoid postwar violence. As explained later, the same imperatives were at work in Ireland, where events took an even bloodier turn. For the four already autonomous dominions, wartime exigencies and pressures moved these lands further along the path to parity with the motherland. At the outset British generals adopted the pattern of the Indian army, naturally assuming command of all Canadian and Anzac divisions and corps. By war's end in France, however, success in combat, coupled with complaints about British military conservatism, promoted to these commands officers of the "British Commonwealth," the term that came increasingly into vogue after 1914. Similarly, in the early years dominion politicians felt shut out of wartime decision making in London and railed against being treated as "toy automata,"[31] but with the advent of Lloyd George in late 1916 they received much better treatment. He convened a special "imperial war conference" to discuss military developments and co-opted dominion and Indian leaders into cabinet-level deliberations. Although it is true that most politicians, whether British or dominion, never really penetrated the innermost decision-making circle around Lloyd George, imperial relations had nevertheless evolved. Whereas the initial reality was that Britain waged war "assisted by her empire," observes one historian, the new reality became the British Empire fighting a war "orchestrated by Britain much more as a *primus inter pares*."[32]

The measure of dominion equality with Britain—and virtual sovereignty—came at Paris in 1919. The prime ministers of Canada, South Africa, Australia, and New Zealand rotated as delegates of the five-seat British Empire Delegation, while all of the dominions also sent their own delegations to the peace conference. Canada and Australia even signed the Treaty of Versailles for themselves. This new Commonwealth status received confirmation the following year when the four dominions joined the League of Nations separately and received, as separate nations, the spoils they had fought for, namely, "C" League mandates for South Africa in South West Africa, Australia in New Guinea and the Solomons, and New Zealand in Western Samoa. Although it would take a few more years to define the relationship among Britain, Canada, South Africa, Australia, and New Zealand, the statement word-crafted in 1926 already fit the reality of 1920 with the sole exception of Ireland: "They are autonomous communities within the British empire, equal in status, in no way subordinate one to another in any aspect of their domestic or external affairs, though united by a common bond to the crown, and freely associated as members of the British Commonwealth of Nations."[33]

Ireland halfheartedly joined the Commonwealth in 1922 but not until passing through a tortuous three-year gauntlet of postwar struggle.[34] Political temperatures had risen steadily on the troubled island since the aftermath of the ill-fated Dublin Castle uprising of April 1916, for the British executed fourteen of the ringleaders who became martyrs to their cause. The popularity of breaking all ties with England spread as battlefield losses mounted during the last two years of the war, propelling the proindependence "Sinn Fein" party to an overwhelming majority of votes in the Catholic south during House of Commons balloting in December 1918. Sinn Fein leaders Eamon de Valera and Michael Collins threw down the gauntlet in January by proclaiming Irish independence and unleashing their Irish Republican Army (IRA) against British officials and the police.

With violence increasing throughout 1919 and 1920, the British struck back by recruiting demobilized veterans of the Great War for auxiliary police squads. Twisted ones who remained eager, like their counterparts in Russia, Germany, and Italy, for more combat, they were called the "Black and Tans" because of their black police hats and belts and surplus khaki army uniforms. The political gang warfare worsened now as raids, ambushes, hostage killings, revenge shootings, and sectarian mob violence killed more than a thousand. A truce in July 1921 finally led to negotiations and political compromise at the end of that year. The south, to be known as the Irish Free State, received Commonwealth status, customarily recognizing the British monarch as head of state and allowing Britain to retain naval bases in Irish ports. The largely Protestant north won the right to retain union with Britain, which it has to this day. The Irish Free State yielded to a fully independent Republic of Ireland after 1945.

The *Nation*, a prestigious American journal, ran a series of articles in the spring of 1921 that identified Ireland's troubles as the number-one barrier to improved Anglo-American relations. Indeed since the Dublin Castle executions Irish-American voters clustered along the politically important East Coast had railed against British and Black and Tan cruelties, defended the IRA's fight for freedom, and warned England of the consequences, some even talking about going to war.

Irish-American threats evoked cries of "sheer folly"[35] from moderates on both sides of the Atlantic who wanted the two great democracies to stand united, but the Irish problem was compounded by other hot-button issues in the United States. Freedom of the seas, a traditional concern of Americans that had flared up anew with Great War submarine atrocities, continued to fuel passions after 1918 when Britain asserted its intention to defend the Isles in any way it deemed necessary, including the right to ignore freedom-of-the-seas arguments emanating from Washington. As 1919 turned to 1920 both the Royal Navy and U.S. Navy Department pressed their governments for huge battle line increases. One American admiral actually published an article describing a naval war scenario with Britain.

Complicating the situation even more, especially from Washington's purview, was the specter of rising Japanese power in the Pacific.[36] Since the wartime crisis over Tokyo's "21 demands" on China, Japan had enhanced its position by imposing the right to move troops freely across the former Asian giant—ostensibly to guard against Soviet expansion in the Far East—bargained successfully for allied recognition of its seizure of German holdings in the Shantung Peninsula;

landed seventy-five thousand soldiers in Siberia—also to counter the threat of communism—and received the German Mariana, Caroline, Marshall, and Gilbert Islands, vast maritime conquests it had already held for six years, as "C" mandates of the League of Nations. To protect its new acquisitions, not surprisingly, Japan was also expanding and modernizing its fleet. Already in 1919 the U.S. Joint Army-Navy Board perceived all of this as such an unavoidable threat to America's position in the Pacific, especially the Philippines, that it began to draw up "War Plan *Orange*." Although it took several years to evolve, this innovative operational scheme realized the near impossibility of defending the Western Pacific, calling instead for the battleship fleet and the Marine Corps to steam west from Hawaii, methodically seize a chain of Japan's mandated islands with a succession of punishing naval bombardments and amphibious landings, engage and defeat the Japanese navy in a mighty clash at sea, and then liberate the Philippines.

American planners also cast an anxious eye at Britain during the early stage of War Plan *Orange* deliberations, for London had signed a military alliance with Tokyo in 1902 and this pact remained in effect. Would not a Japanese-American collision commit Britain to the side of "Enemy *Orange*"? Even more worrisome, would not the accession of Japan, Britain, and Britain's Pacific dominions Australia, New Zealand, and Canada to the League of Nations make likely some sort of punitive League war against outlier nonmember America? Britain's brow furrowed at these possibilities too. Already in July 1919 Sir Maurice Hankey of the Imperial War Cabinet looked askance at the ire of Irish-Americans, the warship-building agenda of the U.S. Navy, Pacific Ocean tensions, and the lame-duck status of Woodrow Wilson, warning against what might happen "if a truculent, overbearing and anti-British president should secure election."[37] The inauguration in March 1921 of Warren G. Harding, a Republican whose party had ridden pro-Irish, anti-Wilson, anti-League, anti-Japanese immigration sentiments to victory, seemed to fit Hankey's bill.

From today's vantage point such fears may appear exaggerated, but we would do well to remember the threatening climate of 1919–1921, with so much war raging in Eastern Europe and Russia, Central Asia and the Middle East, and some parts of Africa that the western front armistice of 1918 had become a teasing memory. No doubt with this reality in mind, Harding reached beyond platitudes in his inaugural address to pledge his willingness to negotiate with "nations great and small" to achieve disarmament and promote any other ideas that would "lessen the probability of war."[38] At the Imperial Conference of June 1921 in London, moreover, the prime minister of Canada spoke out against the Anglo-Japanese alliance and conveyed his fullest sympathy with Washington's alarm over belligerent Pacific Ocean scenarios. Realizing that the civil war in Ireland had gone too far—and also that the necessary rapprochement with the United States was impossible without peace in Ireland—Lloyd George offered IRA leaders a truce that same month. Aware of the British agenda, and hoping to preempt it, Harding invited Japan, China, Britain, France, Italy, Holland, Belgium, and Portugal to a conference set to open in the autumn. Representatives from Australia, New

Zealand, Canada, and India were content to participate as part of a British imperial delegation.

Organized and chaired by a champion of peace, Secretary of State Charles Evans Hughes, what came to be known as the Washington Naval Conference (November 1921–February 1922) was arguably the most impressive diplomatic achievement of the young twentieth century. The Hague Peace Conferences of 1899 and 1907 were more unique and unprecedented but accomplished little, whereas the Paris treaties of 1919–1920, the Cairo Declarations of 1921–1922, and the Treaty of Lausanne with Turkey in 1923 all accomplished much for a world trying to return to stability but resulted from the violence and bloodletting that preceded them. The Washington treaties, on the other hand, removed potential causes of war in advance of shots fired by returning the United States and Britain to a friendly footing and, more impressively, defusing the racially tinged power standoff between America and Japan. One need not look too far in explaining the success of the conference. The economic interests of all participants pointed unmistakably toward fiscal retrenchment and the attendant limitation of military expenditures. Furthermore, every nation at the table was either a democracy or, like Japan, a parliamentary state sufficiently accustomed in its home dealings to compromise and the rule of law that diplomatic understandings with other democratic or semidemocratic states flowed naturally from its domestic political culture. The hawks were put back on their perches as moderation prevailed.

In the initial agreement of early December 1921 the United States, Japan, Britain, and France pledged to respect (i.e., not to attack) each others' "insular possessions and insular dominions"[39] in the Pacific region. Any controversy over these territorial rights not settled through bilateral diplomacy—for instance between the United States and Japan—would be relegated to a joint conference of the four nations for potential "consideration and adjustment." This so-called Four-Power Treaty also pledged signatories "to communicate with one another fully" if one were threatened by aggression from "any other power"—a transparent reference to the Soviet Union. Replacing the Anglo-Japanese alliance of 1902, the Four-Power Treaty had created a kind of "Pacific Concert" like the old nineteenth-century Concert of Europe.

Shortly before New Year's came a Five-Power Treaty between the aforementioned four and Italy. The naval agreement that lent the conference its name in history found the world's big naval powers setting ratios and limits to this power. The battleships and battle cruisers of the United States and Britain were set equally at a total tonnage of 500,000, or 18–20 vessels, with no heavier than 16-inch guns. Japan followed with 300,000 tons—10 battlewagons—trailed by France and Italy with 175,000 tons. Each navy could convert two of its capital ships to aircraft carriers. After a "building holiday" of ten years, newly constructed ships could replace old and obsolescent ones as they were retired but not in excess of the tonnage limits of 1922. Hughes wanted to establish additional limits on heavy and light cruisers, destroyers, and submarines but had to settle for an arrangement on heavy cruisers whereby signatories could "balance" or flesh out their fleets with these vessels as dictated by budgets and naval doctrine, but the new cruisers could not exceed 10,000 tons and 8-inch guns. Finally, in return for limiting its fleet Japan enhanced its security with a treaty ban on new island fortifications in the Western Pacific, including Hong Kong (British); Taiwan and the Ryukyu Islands (Japanese); and Wake, Guam, and the Philippines (American). The treaty had fifteen-year tenure to December 31, 1936.

In rapid succession in late January and early February 1922 three final treaties were penned in Washington. First, Japan agreed to pull its troops out of Siberia. Next, Hughes and British delegation head Arthur Balfour brokered a compromise between Japan and China over Shantung whereby Tokyo finally relinquished title to the former German colony but retained military control of the Tsingtao-Tsinan Railway for fifteen years. Finally, all participants signed the Nine-Power-Open-Door Treaty, agreeing (1) to respect China's neutrality in any conflict Peking did not wish to join; (2) honoring its "sovereignty, independence, [and] territorial and administrative integrity" in areas not already conceded by earlier treaties to foreign powers; (3) permitting "equal opportunity for the commerce and industry of all nations in China"; (4) agreeing not to make any "treaty, agreement, arrangement, or understanding infringing the above principles"; and (5) consenting to "consult fully" if any problems arose.

For the moment, Peking appreciated the main concession it received, namely, international guarantees against Japanese encroachment. China signed, but excluded itself in the text of the treaty from the Open Door policy, continued to lobby against its lack of freedom in determining tariff levels, and made known its disdain for all of the "unequal treaties" that kept parts of the country under foreign military rule. Later in the decade under the leadership of Chiang Kai-shek China would take by force what she had not been given. His "Great Northern Expedition" began in August 1926, painfully accomplishing for his country what the Afghans, Persians, Saudis, and Turks had already done for theirs.

By the time Chiang was trying to unite China the aftershocks of the Great War had passed in most parts of the world as "postwar" wars and diplomacy produced relative tranquility. Kemalist Turkey had defeated the Greeks, backed down the British, and won a significant measure of independence in the Treaty of Lausanne. Afghanistan, Persia, and Saudi Arabia had also carved out independent niches for themselves, while Arab insurgencies and protests had either failed completely, as in French Syria, or won autonomy, as in Egypt, Jordan, and Iraq after Britain's Cairo declarations. The Montagu-Chelmsford reforms took a similar approach, granting autonomy to India and inducing the same kind of uneasy calm. Equilibrium of sorts had also come to the Far East after the successes of the Washington Conference. Outside Europe, Abdel Karim's war of independence in Morocco was still a blemish on a world returning to peace, but his exile in May 1926 ended the fighting there, too.

NOTES

1. For the citation and what follows, see T. E. Lawrence, *Seven Pillars of Wisdom: A Triumph* (New York, 1962), first published in 1935, 664–674.

2. Cited in B. H. Liddell Hart, *Lawrence of Arabia* (New York, 1935), 310.
3. The classic formulation of David Fromkin, *A Peace to End All Peace: The Fall of the Ottoman Empire and the Creation of the Modern Middle East* (New York, 1989), for the postwar, 383–567. Also see Margaret Macmillan, *Peacemakers: The Paris Peace Conference of 1919 and Its Attempt to End War* (London, 2001), 357–466.
4. P. G. Elgood, *Egypt and the Army* (Heliopolis, 1928), 1.
5. Cited in Macmillan, *Peacemakers*, 412.
6. Cited in Fromkin, *Peace to End All Peace*, 419.
7. Cited in Ainslie T. Embree, *India's Search for National Identity* (New York, 1980). 68. For India, also see W. David McIntyre, *The Commonwealth of Nations: Origins and Impact, 1869–1971* (Minneapolis, 1977), 209–219.
8. Cited in Embree, *India's Search*, 75.
9. See Andrew W. Roberts, *A History of the English-Speaking Peoples since 1900* (New York, 2007), 148–153.
10. For the following, see Ludwig W. Adamec, *Afghanistan, 1900–1923: A Diplomatic History* (Berkeley, CA, 1967), 108–123; T. A. Heathcote, *The Afghan Wars: 1839–1919* (London, 1980), 172–182; and Fromkin, *Peace to End All Peace*, 421–423. For the most detail but also an obvious pro-British bias, see the Government of India's *The Third Afghan War, 1919: Official Account* (Calcutta, 1926).
11. Cited in Adamec, *Afghanistan*, 112.
12. Citations in Charles Seymour, *The Intimate Papers of Colonel House* (Boston, 1928), 194–195.
13. For the issue of mandates, see Gary B. Ostrower, The League of Nations: From 1919 to 1929 (Garden City Park, NY, 1996), 79–80; Fromkin, *Peace to End All Peace*, 398–399; and Macmillan, *Peacemakers*, 107–113, 455.
14. See the accounts by T. E. Lawrence, *Revolt in the Desert* (New York, 1927), 319–328, and *Seven Pillars of Wisdom*, 682–683; and Hart, *Lawrence of Arabia*, 310.
15. For this and the following discussion of Syria and Iraq, see the documentation on Lawrence's discussions with British leaders in late 1918, printed in Malcolm Brown, ed., *T. E. Lawrence in War & Peace: An Anthology of the Military Writings of Lawrence of Arabia* (London, 2005), 211–215; Hart, *Lawrence of Arabia*, 307–322; Fromkin, *Peace to End All Peace*, 383–411, 424–426, 435–440, 449–454; and Macmillan, *Peacemakers*, 399–420.
16. Cited in Macmillan, *Peacemakers*, 411.
17. Cited in Fromkin, *Peace to End All Peace*, 437.
18. His article is printed in Brown, *T. E. Lawrence in War & Peace*, 243.
19. For the citation and the Cairo Conference, see Fromkin, *Peace to End All Peace*, 502–506.
20. See H. A. Ibrahim, "Politics and Nationalism in North-East Africa, 1919–1935," in A. Adu Boahen, ed., *General History of Africa* (London, 1985), 7:581–587.
21. Ibid., 425–426, 455–462, 510, 513–514.
22. For this passage, see ibid., 406–408, 427–434, 540–557; and Macmillan, *Peacemakers*, 377–391, 438–466.
23. For the sad chapter of the trials, see Gary Jonathan Bass, *Stay the Hand of Vengeance: The Politics of War Crimes Tribunals* (Princeton, NJ, 2002), 106–146; and Taner Akcam, *A Shameful Act: The Armenian Genocide and the Question of Turkish Responsibility* (New York, 2006), 205–376.
24. See Peter Hopkirk, *Setting the East Ablaze: Lenin's Dream of an Empire in Asia* (London, 1984), 152–171; and Fromkin, *Peace to End All Peace*, 480–490.
25. See the discussion in Ostrower, *League of Nations*, 79–81, and for the citation, 81, 80.
26. For the figures in this paragraph, see M. Crowder, "The First World War and Its Consequences," in Boahen, *General History of Africa*, 7:292–295; Melvin E. Page, "Black Men in a

White Man's War," in Melvin E. Page, ed., *Africa and the First World War* (New York, 1987), 14; Robert Holland, "The British Empire and the Great War, 1914–1918," in Judith M. Brown and Wm. Roger Louis, eds., *The Oxford History of the British Empire* (Oxford, 1999), 4:117; and Hew Strachan, *The First World War* (New York, 2003), 81.

27. Geoffrey Hodges, "Military Labour in East Africa and Its Impact on Kenya," in Page, *Africa and the First World War,* 148.

28. For the remainder of this subchapter, see Holland, "British Empire and the Great War," in Brown and Louis, *Oxford History of the British Empire,* 4:121; James K. Matthews, "Reluctant Allies: Nigerian Responses to Military Recruitment 1914–1918," in Page, *Africa and the First World War,* 111; and the various articles in Boahen, *General History of Africa,* 7, by (with pages in parentheses) A. Laroui (98–99, 106–107), H. A. Ibrahim (589–593), J. Berque (603–612), A. Adu Boahen (635–636, 642–647), E. S. Atieno-Odhiambo (654–655), and A. D. Davidson, A. Isaacman, and R. Pélissier (691–693).

29. J. Osuntokun, "West African Armed Revolts during the Great War," *Tarikh* 5 (1977) 3: 6–17.

30. See Percival Griffiths, *Empire into Commonwealth* (London, 1969), 244–253; McIntyre, *Commonwealth of Nations,* 3–193; and Holland, "British Empire and the Great War," in Brown and Louis, *Oxford History of the British Empire,* 4:114–137.

31. Cited in Holland, "British Empire and the Great War," in Brown and Louis, *Oxford History of the British Empire,* 4:132.

32. Ibid., 4:125.

33. Cited in McIntyre, *Commonwealth of Nations,* 189.

34. For good accounts of the civil war in Ireland and its origins, see D. George Boyce, *Ireland 1828–1923: From Ascendancy to Democracy* (Oxford, 1992), 94–108; and Donald McCartney, "From Parnell to Pearse: 1891–1921," in T. W. Moody and F. X. Martin, eds., *The Course of Irish History* (Lanham, MD, 2001), 245–259.

35. For the citation, and the discussion here, see Anne Orde, *The Eclipse of Great Britain: The United States and British Imperial Decline, 1895–1956* (New York, 1996), 70–77.

36. For this paragraph, see Louis Morton, "War Plan *Orange*: Evolution of a Strategy," *World Politics* 11 (1959): 221–250; Paul H. Clyde and Burton F. Beers, *The Far East: A History of the Western Impact and the Eastern Response (1830–1965)* (Englewood Cliffs, NJ, 1966), 274–283; Allan R. Millett and Peter Maslowski, *For the Common Defense: A Military History of the United States of America* (New York, 1984), 361–376; and Macmillan, *Peacemakers,* 331–353.

37. Cited in Orde, *Eclipse of Great Britain,* 74.

38. For the citation, and a discussion of the U.S. elections of November 1920, see Thomas Fleming, *The Illusion of Victory: America in World War I* (New York, 2003), 461–473. For the following, see Raymond J. Sontag, *A Broken World: 1919–1939* (New York, 1972), 95–97; McIntyre, *Commonwealth of Nations,* 185, 199–200; and Orde, *Eclipse of Great Britain,* 74–76.

39. For citations and the discussion here, see Clyde and Beers, *Far East,* 281–287. Also see Franz H. Michael and George E. Taylor, *The Far East in the Modern World* (New York, 1964), 716–722; and Millett and Maslowski, *For the Common Defense,* 363–365.

CHAPTER XIII

Epilogue: Bereavement, Economic Collapse, and the Climate for War

In a self-portrait of 1910 Kaethe Kollwitz peers wearily forward, sad eyes shaded from the harsh glare of the future by a consoling motherly hand. Germany's preeminent female sculptress and artist always seemed to know. She was vacationing in Königsberg with husband Karl and sons Hans and Peter when the Great War broke out. People gave hurrahs outside her hotel. Peter cheered too. But Kollwitz sat helplessly on the bed and wept incessantly. Peter would die in Belgium barely three months later.

Kollwitz's prewar works had featured the poor people she found so beautiful. After 1918 antiwar themes predominated. Her seven-print woodcut of 1922–1923, *War*, typified the messages conveyed by this mother-heart of the world. The second in the series, entitled "The Volunteers," shows five young men following the bony-faced drummer, Death. The two trailing youths shout patriotic slogans, but in front of them a volunteer, who has been shot, jerks a tortured face toward the sky. Ahead of him a fourth young man, face upturned, is unconscious, while the last, closest to the drummer, stares with glassy eyes skyward, presumably already dead. The third woodcut, "The Parents," depicts a mother and father totally enveloped by grief.[1]

In October 1925 Kollwitz began work on her famous sculpture *The Mourning Parents* and in June 1926 took Karl to Belgium to visit Peter's graveyard, where the work of art would be placed. By this time other grieving parents like Kaethe and Karl Kollwitz had turned the same emotional corner. As 1926 expired and the end of a decade approached that had begun so mired in troubles, there was finally

Kaethe Kollwitz, Self-Portrait with Hand on Forehead 1910

Swarthmore College Peace Collection/© 2004 Artists Rights Society [ARS], New York/VG Bild-Kunst, Bonn

apparent closure on the Great War. Consequently, people sought closure on personal grief and mourning. They cleared battlefields of the last remains and skeletons; built cemeteries for the fallen; communed with the dead in séances when no remains permitted the closure of a funeral; constructed elaborate memorials and tombs for unknown soldiers; and gathered there on Armistice and Memorial Days to honor sacrifices made for a better, saner world.[2]

Dispassionate observation of international relations in the late 1920s seemed to justify some measure of hopefulness that this world was within reach. To be sure, for all of the popular enthusiasm generated by the Locarno treaties, Europe's leading statesmen had no illusions about the limitations of these agreements. There was still no solid guarantee of peace when extreme German nationalists, Italian Fascists, and Russian Communists, all of whom worshipped some form of violence, scoffed at pacifism. The champions of peace also knew that the disarmament efforts begun in Geneva by the League of Nations in 1926—a task "seriously undertaken for the first time in human history"[3]—would make only minimal progress until some workable form of international "collective" security was created superior to the ancient means of national security. In the absence of the former, said the French repeatedly, no nation could responsibly dispense with the latter. This awareness explains the feverish work in Geneva to improve collective security.

The 1927 League session passed a resolution condemning war and calling for peaceful settlement of all disputes. That year the Assembly also established an Arbitration and Security Committee that produced a set of nine "Model Treaties" approved in 1928. One subset of treaty drafts was designed for small groups of nations wanting to emulate Locarno by signing arbitration and mutual military assistance pacts. The other drafts were universal calls for pacific settlement of all conflicts, whether by compulsory arbitration, judicial action, or conciliation. The latter model treaties went beyond the Covenant itself to renounce war as a means of national policy and clear the way, if need be, for collective punishment of aggressors.

The Kellogg-Briand Pact of 1928 reinforced these efforts and enhanced the chance of converting them into international reality. Initiated by French Foreign Minister Aristide Briand and U.S. Secretary of State Frank Kellogg and signed by fifty-five nations, the pact, like the League's 1927 resolution, outlawed wars of aggression. Although hedged about by declarations that nations still possessed the right to defend themselves—indeed to decide unilaterally when recourse to defensive warfare was necessary—the pact greatly reinforced the pacifist spirit and spreading antiwar legal norm as well as the League's own simultaneous efforts to give all of this more concrete statutory substance.

The election of Herbert Hoover in November 1928 lent further momentum to the cause of peace, for the new American president announced that he supported disarmament. Specifically, the United States would support army and navy reductions already agreed to secretly by France and Britain in an attempt to build on the Washington naval limits of 1922. Hoover's statement paved the way for Great Power negotiations in London during the fall of 1929.

As the 1920s drew to a close another happening reinforced the contemporary impression of the dawning of a more pacific era. When the Tenth Assembly of the League of Nations opened in September 1929 Aristide Briand asked the nations of Europe to form a closer federal union. At a private gathering of all continental delegations Europe's most tenaciously realistic champion of peace requested each country to give serious consideration to his idea and that he be charged with the task of drawing up a plan over the next year. The delegations agreed but respectfully and prudently made no commitments—with one notable exception. German Foreign Minister Gustav Stresemann welcomed this promising idea, alluding to the nineteenth-century customs union that had preceded the political unification of Germany.

A world peacekeeping organization, binding international arbitration agreements, Great Power guarantees to punish aggressors, multilateral pacts renouncing wars of aggression, unprecedented Great Power willingness to discuss arms reductions, and a United States of Europe: were these not the outlines of a new pacific world order? To optimists it seemed that only time was required for these seeds to bear fruit. They had learned from 1914, understood the world's problems, knew how to solve them—and were finding those solutions.

There was one main set of problems emanating from the Great War that world leaders did not understand, however, and for which no solutions were found.

These problems were economic. The New York stock market crashed on October 24, 1929, and by mid-1930 a new term—the Great Depression—was used throughout the world. Although clearly the crash triggered this depression, most historians point to the Great War as the underlying cause of this economic disaster.[4] The last delayed explosion of that conflict, in fact, was economic, touched off by the slumping American economy. The war had left European economies enervated and weak. Like tables teetering ominously on three legs, they could not absorb the concussion from New York. Contemporaries knew that there were problems and weaknesses, holding conferences to discuss ways to return to economic normalcy, but the situation was far too complex to understand fully, even for experts like John Maynard Keynes.

Britain illustrates the point. While British industrialists neglected foreign customers to produce for the war and investors liquidated overseas investments to finance it, American, Japanese, and Commonwealth firms stole British markets and undercut London's role as world banker. The legacy of war amounted to reduced earnings from overseas investments, stagnant exports, and high unemployment—8 percent on the eve of the crash. Rigid insistence on returning to the gold standard in 1926 and pegging the pound to its prewar rate of exchange with the dollar did further damage. It was a matter of honor and pride for British bankers to repay Britain's war debt to the United States with pounds that had not depreciated in value—hence the importance of the prewar exchange rate—but the harsh reality was that the pound had indeed depreciated and that by pegging it at the old rate Britain's currency was overvalued, which made British goods too expensive for many foreign buyers. Nor did the gold standard work the way it had before 1914 (see chap. 1). Because Britain could no longer balance imports from Europe with exports to Asia, the Commonwealth, and North and South America—too many markets had been lost there because of the war—the pound could not play its lynchpin prewar role as a reserve currency and gold surrogate, which meant that gold, not pounds, flowed out of Britain and other countries during times of trade deficit, thereby creating an added measure of financial instability in the world. The old international economy was gone with the war.

The war hurt Germany even more. The loss of colonies and European provinces combined with the punitive aspects of the Treaty of Versailles to keep production low and unemployment high well into the 1920s. The Dawes Plan and American credit created only an artificial recovery. Already in late 1928, in fact, short-term loans from the United States began to be recalled so that banks could speculate in stocks. Without this credit Germany could not simultaneously pay reparations and fuel expansion. Consequently, unemployment rose to 9 percent in the summer of 1929, months before the events on Wall Street.

The fall of the great Austro-Hungarian and Russian Empires also caused severe economic repercussions and disruptions. Where a pair of huge free-trade blocs existed before 1914 now stood nine struggling states. Poland was plagued by three different railroad systems, each with a different gauge and signaling system.

Czechoslovakia's rails ran north from Vienna and Budapest, whereas its commercial axis ran east to west. Suppliers of industrial raw materials often found their customers across a new border behind a new protective tariff wall, for the fledgling states of Eastern Europe wanted to develop their own industries for national security reasons, regardless of the economic inefficiencies. Reflecting the overall dilemma of the region, trade along the Danube River, which flowed through six states, sank in the1920s to 17 percent of prewar levels. These new trade barriers exacerbated the export woes of Germany, France, Britain, and other nations that had sent goods to Eastern Europe—total West European exports, figured as a percentage of overall production, slipped to 60 percent of the prewar level in 1920 and never climbed above 80 percent before 1929.

Perhaps the greatest disequilibrium created by the war occurred in agriculture. Farmers in Argentina, Australia, Canada, and the United States expanded food production to meet the voracious demand of the Great War but did not curtail output after 1918. Thus wheat acreage in these countries rose from 87.5 million in 1914 to 117.4 million in the mid-1920s. By this time, however, Europe's tens of millions of acres of ruined farmland had been restored and Russian production soared after the civil war. Stockpiles rose by 75 percent and prices cascaded by 30 percent from 1924 to 1929. Farmers' purchasing power dropped proportionately with particularly drastic consequences in countries where much of the population depended on agriculture: 36 percent worked the land in France; 44 percent in Italy; 53 percent in Hungary; 58–66 percent in Estonia, Latvia, Poland, and Greece; and 71–80 percent in Finland, Lithuania, Rumania, Bulgaria, and Yugoslavia. Throughout Eastern Europe by the late 1920s, in fact, the ability to import manufactured goods declined as a result of the worsening agricultural crisis created by the Great War.

In so many ways, therefore, war-weakened Europe was not prepared to absorb the shock waves of the crash and subsequent U.S. recession, which knocked the third leg out from under the European economy. Unlike the prewar period when so much of world finance had been controlled in London, moreover, no one hegemonic banking center existed either to prevent the crash or to coordinate international recovery efforts when it hit. European manufacturers panicked and covered declining sales by reducing inventories, curtailing production, reducing wages, and laying off workers. Unemployment climbed to 11 percent in Britain and 22 percent in Germany during 1930. Workers receiving meager unemployment payments could afford few purchases. Hence factories had to cut production again and lay off more workers, which worsened the downward spiral of purchasing power and production.

Farmers tried to compensate for falling prices by expanding acreage, but this had disastrous results. As food stockpiles continued to rise, overall agricultural prices nose-dived 44 percent from October 1929 to December 1930, then fell another 40 percent in 1931–1932. As European farmers reduced purchases of industrial goods, especially farming nations in Eastern Europe, manufacturing output fell rapidly from 1929 to 1932: a 16 percent drop in Britain, 28 percent in France, 31 percent in Belgium, 36 percent in Czechoslovakia, and 47 percent in Germany. Unemployment rates in 1932 ranged from 17 percent in Britain to nearly 40 percent in Germany. It was the worst socioeconomic catastrophe in modern times.

The continental climate changed from optimism and hope to pessimism and despair. As spirits sagged it grew harder to refute fascist and Nazi demagogues who had never stopped preaching that war was the natural order of things. This is not to say that the Great Depression made another war inevitable, for there were still men and women of peace who resisted the deepening mood of resignation. In many concrete ways, however, economic collapse accelerated violent, disruptive forces that made pacifists' work increasingly difficult.

For one thing, the Great Depression distracted nations from the promising peace efforts of the 1920s. To the frustration of the champions of peace, national leaders spent less time in Geneva, removed from peace work by the pressing need to solve problems at home. The economic theory of that day, however, prescribed no correct solutions for politicians to find. Operating on the assumption that a recession would cure itself by low prices and interest rates eventually stimulating spending and investment, most governments cut spending and shrank money supplies—policies that only worsened economies too shaken to respond to normal stimuli. When the standard solutions failed, leaders redoubled domestic efforts and postponed or canceled peacekeeping work. Not until March 1930 did Britain, the United States, and Japan agree on further naval reductions, but France and Italy had backed out. Another nine months expired before the League had finished an agenda for its disarmament conference and a further fourteen months before it convened. In the meantime Briand's notions of European union had been permanently shelved.

And when the Disarmament Conference finally began in February 1932 there was much more bad will in the world. For two years nation after nation had tried to shut out foreign goods with higher tariffs and currency devaluations, triggering a wave of retaliation as others raised tariffs and devalued currencies, which only worsened a depression caused in large part by weak exports. Consequently, the value of world trade spiraled further downward. Selfish economic nationalism undermined the chances of peace in other ways. France hosted 2 million foreign workers before the depression struck, the bulk hailing from Italy, Poland, and Spain, but then laid off or deported half of them, generating considerable bitterness. The United States, Britain, and other countries created more bad blood by tightening immigration policies.

Chances for implementing peaceful alternatives to war grew slimmer after Japanese army radicals drew their own conclusions from the Great Depression. Pointing to the alleged fallacy of trading for raw materials vital to national security in a world of slumping trade, they defied democratic rulers in Tokyo and seized Manchuria from China in the autumn of 1931. Within a few years the military had supplanted the democratic leadership altogether. Exuding a spirit of belligerent autarky, the radicals transformed the stolen province into a military-industrial complex. The seizure of Manchuria was but a twisted logical extension of the tactics of tariffs, currency devaluations, deportations, and immigration quotas—zero-sum policies that boosted the home country by taking from others. An act of aggression was worse, of course, but the world did nothing to punish Japan because the United States and Great Britain had no desire to exacerbate the depression by imposing economic sanctions or spark another world war by sending troops, and without British willingness to fight, the League of Nations itself remained paralyzed. "War is re-enthroned," warned one British newspaper, "a straight road back to 1914 lies open."[5]

As the Japanese example demonstrates, the most menacing and frightening development for those who desired peace was the havoc the Depression wreaked on democracy. Parliamentary rule by the people, already eroding quickly in the 1920s, lost more ground as people questioned the worth of democratic governments that could not solve the depression. The suffering of the 1930s felled six more European democracies—Germany (1933), Austria (1933), Estonia (1934), Latvia (1934), Greece (1935), and Rumania (1938). If it is true that established democracies never wage war against one another, then it was certainly tragic that democracies fell to dictatorships advocating violence, not peace.

Of all these nondemocratic regimes, that of Adolf Hitler and his jackbooted followers was clearly the worst, for it exuded hate, worshipped violence, and wanted another war. The conflict they provoked, moreover, would be waged after careful study of the military lessons of the Great War and the technology that had evolved from it. There would be hurricane bombardments and storm troop tactics but also better models of tanks, frightening dive-bombers, and airborne infantry paratroopers, in short, *Blitzkrieg*, the terrifying German answer to the elusive revolution in military affairs.[6]

In sum, the Great Depression sidetracked national leaders from the work of peace in Geneva, whipped up ill will between nations, prompted the first act of aggression in Manchuria, brought militarist regimes to power in Japan and Germany, and in all of these ways "re-enthroned" the climate for war. The Great War-induced Great Depression hurt the chances for peace in other ways too. Hitler cleverly dissimulated his desire for revenge, repeatedly professing his desire for peace to leaders in Britain, France, and America, who for years remained too preoccupied with improvised economic recovery efforts to pay heed to those who warned against trusting the Nazis and ignoring a gathering storm. Furthermore, for peoples who had only recently closed the mourning process on one horrendous war, it was far too tempting to believe Hitler than risk more bloodletting. These appeasing sentiments ran especially deep in the hearts and minds of Britons, but the necessary realism, pragmatism, and resolve was also lacking in France, with its escapist "Maginot-Line-Mentality," as well as in America, with its self-serving isolationism. We have encountered a somewhat similar *High Noon* process in Russia, whose people so badly depleted its reserve of morale courage during six years of brutal war and even bloodier civil war that resisting Stalinist evil, or at least resisting the evil of false denunciation, had grown too difficult. By the time Hitler was finally warned in 1939 it was too late to halt his mad headlong dash back into the abyss. Japanese militarists had preceded him two years earlier with their invasion of China.

In 1940, years after the high hopes of the 1920s had morphed for pacifists into cynical remorse, Kaethe Kollwitz finished a bronze relief known as *The Lament*. The woman's countenance bears a resemblance to its creator. Now the eyes cannot look forward. They are closed and protective hands cover half the face. A close friend had died, and the world was at war again, but Kollwitz always seemed to know: it would get worse before it would get better.

She spent the final nine months of her life in the resort town of Moritzburg. Husband Karl had passed away and a grandson had perished at the front. Her Berlin home had gone up in flames during an air raid. "In days to come people will hardly understand this age," she wrote. Aside from rare visits by her surviving son Hans, Kollwitz had only two consolations. One was to look skyward, immersing herself in the clouds as they blew by. She had always imagined Peter looking skyward in his last moment, and now he was there. The other was the firm conviction that her troubled epoch would someday seem incomprehensible to future generations that had finally constructed an unshakeable edifice of peace and social justice. "I am dying in this faith," she said in the autumn of 1944. "People will have to work hard for that new state of things, but they will achieve it."[7]

Kaethe Kollwitz died in April 1945 a few weeks before V-E Day. "The war accompanies me to the end," she wrote Hans. Over sixty years later it is probably still too early to celebrate the completion of the unshakeable edifice she believed in. What the European Union has already achieved is perhaps enough, however, to soften her mournful countenance.[8]

NOTES

1. See Hans Kollwitz, ed., *The Diary and Letters of Kaethe Kollwitz,* trans. Richard and Clara Winston (Evanston, IL, 1988), 183, 198, 196; and Robert Cowley, "The Mourning Parents," in Robert Cowley, ed., *The Great War: Perspectives on the First World War* (New York, 2003), 471–488.

2. See above all Jay Winter, *Sites of Memory, Sites of Mourning: The Great War in European Cultural History* (Cambridge, UK, 1995).

3. F. P. Walters, *A History of the League of Nations* (London, 1952), 1:365.

4. For a variety of arguments about the origins of the Great Depression, see W. Arthur Lewis, *Economic Survey: 1919–1939* (London, 1966); Charles P. Kindleberger, *The World in Depression, 1929–1939* (Berkeley, CA, 1986); Gerold Ambrosius and William H. Hubbard, *A Social and Economic History of Twentieth-Century Europe* (Cambridge, MA, 1989); Gilbert Ziebura, *World Economy and World Politics, 1924–1931: From Reconstruction to Collapse* (Oxford, 1990); Barry Eichengreen, *Golden Fetters: The Gold Standard and the Great Depression, 1919–1939* (New York, 1996); and Charles H. Feinstein et al., *The European Economy Between the Wars* (Oxford, 1997).

5. Cited in Charles Loch Mowat, *Britain Between the Wars 1918–1940* (Chicago, 1955), 420.

6. See Williamson Murray, "May 1940: Contingency and Fragility of the German RMA," in MacGregor Knox and Williamson Murray, eds., *The Dynamics of Military Revolution 1300–2050* (Cambridge, UK, 2001), 154–174.
7. Kollwitz, *Diary and Letters,* 196, 198.
8. For Europe's troubled path to peace and democracy, see Eric Dorn Brose, *A History of Europe in the Twentieth Century* (New York, 2005); and James J. Sheehan, *Where Have All the Soldiers Gone? The Transformation of Modern Europe* (Boston, 2008).

INDEX

Printed in the USA/Agawam, MA
April 3, 2019